Cyclops

Cyclops

The Myth and its Cultural History

MERCEDES AGUIRRE AND RICHARD BUXTON

OXFORD
UNIVERSITY PRESS

OXFORD
UNIVERSITY PRESS

Great Clarendon Street, Oxford, OX2 6DP,
United Kingdom

Oxford University Press is a department of the University of Oxford.
It furthers the University's objective of excellence in research, scholarship,
and education by publishing worldwide. Oxford is a registered trade mark of
Oxford University Press in the UK and in certain other countries

First Edition published in 2020

Impression: 1

Published in the United States of America by Oxford University Press
198 Madison Avenue, New York, NY 10016, United States of America

British Library Cataloguing in Publication Data
Data available

Library of Congress Control Number: 2020930614

ISBN 978–0–19–871377–7

Printed and bound by
Bell & Bain Ltd., Glasgow

Preface

Tucked away in a pleasantly shady corner of the Jardin du Luxembourg in Paris, just across the road from the Café Le Rostand, the Fontaine Médicis features a grotto containing a group of figures sculpted in the 1860s by Auguste Ottin. Polyphemus, huge and Michelangelesque in bronze, with a cloak of bull's hide slung around his shoulders, kneels on a crag above a cave, and looks down. Below him he spies the nymph he adores, Galatea, near naked and swooning in the arms of a beautiful youth. The white marble in which the pair are carved is the only chaste thing about them; all the rest is passion. Oblivious of everything but each other, they little realize that their happy present will have no future, for Polyphemus' wrath will destroy their idyll, even though Acis, the beautiful young man in question, is destined for everlasting, watery renewal in the form of a river.

The seed from which the present book grew was sown a decade ago during a visit that the authors made to this Parisian grotto. As we looked at Ottin's sculptural group, we wondered whether anyone had yet made a detailed study of the development of Cyclopean myths from antiquity until today. In due course we discovered that, to the best of our knowledge, no such study existed, or at least nothing that dealt with the material in the way we thought illuminating. What follows is a gesture towards filling that gap. We are under no illusions about the difficulty of the task, especially in relation to post-classical receptions of these myths. In that area we are almost always out of our comfort zone, so our debt to our predecessors is especially heavy. In spite of the challenges, however, we thought it better to try than not to.

In principle, the work has been divided: Aguirre has focused on ancient and modern art, gardens, and grottoes, Buxton on most of the rest, especially the literary texts, both ancient and modern. But every word written by the one has been revised by the other, so that responsibility for the outcome is shared. Moreover, the whole project has proceeded as a dialogue, so that at this stage it would be impossible, as well as pointless, to try to disentangle who thought of what first.

Preliminary versions of our ideas have been presented to audiences in Bristol, Cambridge, Colchester, Delphi, Edinburgh, Leiden, Łodz, London, Madrid, and Oxford; we are grateful to all who gave us the benefit of their comments on those occasions. Two other settings, each in its own way an ideal environment for research and reflection, have helped us to develop our ideas: the Fondation Hardt near Geneva, where we spent several delightfully productive weeks, and Clare Hall, Cambridge, where we had the honour to be elected to six-month Visiting Fellowships. The colleagues whom we met in both institutions showed marvellous patience in putting up with our relentless chatter about one-eyed (or two-eyed, or three-eyed) ogres.

In spite of the radical changes in research methods implied by the resources of the internet, it is still true that, especially for those studying topics in the humanities, to work in a library stocked with physical books remains a fundamental method of investigation. We therefore express our gratitude to the unfailingly courteous and efficient staff of, in the UK, the University Libraries of Bristol and Cambridge, and, in Spain, the libraries of the Universidad Complutense and the Deutsches Archäologisches Institut in Madrid.

In order to bring our arguments more vividly home to the reader, we wished to include a substantial number of illustrations. But images, and especially the permissions to reproduce them, do not come cheap. We were therefore extremely lucky to receive financial help towards covering these costs from Asteria: Asociación Internacional de Mitocrítica.

Finally, it is our pleasure to single out and warmly thank some individuals. Michael Wright gave us valuable insights into the practices of blacksmiths and other metalworkers. Michael Trapp pointed us towards the importance of Salomon and Isaac de Caus, while Ellen O'Gorman expertly interpreted for us the music that Salomon attributed to Polyphemus, and even sent us a recording of her own sprightly performance of it on the recorder. Ian Jenkins put at our disposal his unrivalled knowledge of Sir William Hamilton. We had valuable advice from Pantelis Michelakis and Luis Unceta about the relationship between classical antiquity and cinema. On certain linguistic matters our patient mentors were James Claxton and Torsten Meissner. Others whose expertise we shamelessly exploited were Domenico Accorinti, Adriano Aymonino, Alberto Bernabé, Jan Bremmer, Judith Bryce, John Carey, Paul Cartledge, Stephen Clark, Cristina Delgado Linacero, Filip Doroszewski, Ana González-Rivas, Tonio Hölscher, Pascale Linant de Bellefonds, Michael Liversidge, Geoffrey Lloyd, José Manuel Losada, Gina Muskett, Derek Offord, Susanna Phillippo, Jonathan Prag, Michael Reeve, Rush Rehm, Brendan Smith, Michael Squire, Susan Stephens, and Luigi Venezia. We absolve all of them from any responsibility for the use to which we have put their guidance. We also record our gratitude to Charlotte Loveridge and Georgie Leighton of Oxford University Press, both for their faith in our project and for their near-saintly patience in waiting for it to be completed; likewise to Hilary Walford, for her keen-eyed excellence in the art of copy-editing, and to Erica Martin and Rosanna van den Bogaerde, for their exemplary skill in picture research. On a different note, the artist Gema Navarro Goig generously presented us with a magnificent woodcut of the Cyclops that she had created for us. We are profoundly in her debt.

M.A.
R.G.A.B.

Madrid and Clevedon

Contents

List of Figures

Further details of items marked '*Cat.*' can be found in the Catalogue on pp. 377–382.

Abbreviations

Cat.	References are to the *Catalogue of Artistic Representations Cited*, which can be found at the end of the book
Fig.	References are to the *List of Figures*, which can be found at the beginning of the book
AJP	*American Journal of Philology*
BICS	*Bulletin of the Institute of Classical Studies*
CP	*Classical Philology*
CQ	*Classical Quarterly*
CVA	*Corpus Vasorum Antiquorum*
FGrH	F. Jacoby (ed.), *Fragmente der griechischen Historiker* (Berlin, 1923–)
G&R	*Greece and Rome*
GHI	P. J. Rhodes and R. Osborne (eds), *Greek Historical Inscriptions 404–323* BC (Oxford, 2003)
GRBS	*Greek, Roman, and Byzantine Studies*
JHS	*Journal of Hellenic Studies*
JWCI	*Journal of the Warburg and Courtauld Institutes*
KRS	G. S. Kirk, J. E. Raven, and M. Schofield (eds), *The Presocratic Philosophers*, 2nd edn (Cambridge, 1983)
LIMC	*Lexicon Iconographicum Mythologiae Classicae* (Zurich and Düsseldorf, 1981–2009)
Migne, *PL*	J.-P. Migne, *Patrologiae cursus completus. Series Latina* (Paris, 1844–64)
PCG	R. Kassel and C. Austin (eds), *Poetae Comici Graeci* (Berlin, 1983–)
RA	*Revue archéologique*
RE	G. Wissowa et al. (eds), *Paulys Real-Encyclopädie der classischen Altertumswissenschaft* (Stuttgart, 1894–1980)
RM	*Mitteilungen des Deutschen Archäologischen Instituts: Römische Abteilung*
Roscher	W. H. Roscher (ed.), *Ausführliches Lexikon der griechischen und römischen Mythologie* (Leipzig, 1884–1937)
TAPA	*Transactions and Proceedings of the American Philological Association*
ThesCRA	*Thesaurus Cultus et Rituum Antiquorum* (Los Angeles, 2004–14)
TrGF	B. Snell, R. Kannicht, and S. Radt (eds), *Tragicorum Graecorum Fragmenta* (Göttingen, 1971–2004)
WI	*Word and Image*
ZPE	*Zeitschrift für Papyrologie und Epigraphik*

Authors and works of Greek and Roman literature are usually abbreviated according to the practice of the *Oxford Classical Dictionary*, 4th edn (Oxford, 2012).

Names, Dates, Translations, References

As every Hellenist or Latinist knows, achieving consistency in the rendering of ancient Greek and Roman proper names is fiendishly difficult. In a book such as this one, where the same mythological characters recur in a sequence of disparate cultural guises—Greek, Roman, post-classical—the task becomes virtually impossible. 'Odysseus' is the most glaring example. Were we only to describe him in a Greek context, his name might remain unchanged in that form. But what of his Roman alter ego 'Ulixes', and his descendant 'Ulysses'? We soon abandoned the idea of giving him a single name throughout, hoping that our readers will be in no doubt whom we are referring to. With two of our other major characters, our approach has been different. We decided to identify each of them by a single name, preferring the Latinate to the Hellenic form even when the context is unambiguously Greek: so 'Polyphemus' not 'Polyphemos', 'Galatea' not 'Galateia', *passim*. With characters who appear less often we usually follow a similar strategy. For instance, for 'Telemos' (as in Homer) to morph suddenly into 'Telemus' (as in Ovid) seems to us to create a pedantic impression that serves little purpose; so he is 'Telemus' throughout. Similarly Latinate is our predominant use of the name 'Cyclops', though we occasionally opt for 'Kuklops' when etymological issues arise. If the overall 'feel' of the names comes across as more Latinate than Hellenic, this is due not to personal inclination but to a sense that clarity is best served thereby. However, the reader should not expect perfect consistency. We are obstinate enough to leave the names of Greek islands (for instance) in their original Hellenic clothing: so Seriphos, not Seriphus. We also decided to retain a Greek flavour for two mighty cosmic powers indelibly stamped by Hesiod's foundational *Theogony*: Ouranos and Gaia. Moreover, a few characters mentioned exclusively or almost exclusively by authors writing in Greek will also keep their Hellenic form; examples are some of the lesser-known Cyclopes mentioned by Nonnus. Reader, forgive us our caprice.

In the course of the book, works are referenced by author's name and date of publication. If two or more authors share a surname, their initials too are referenced. In one case, where the initials as well as the name are identical, the authors are distinguished by forename.

Where there is any risk of ambiguity about a date, we add the designation BCE (= BC) or CE (= AD). Where there is no such risk, as with most of the dates in Chapters 10 and 11, we give the numerals only. In the case of authors and their literary works, our usual practice is to provide dates when the writer is first mentioned. Dates of artists and their works can be found in the text or in the Catalogue, or both.

As for translations from ancient or other languages, when we have borrowed from existing printed versions, we have done our best to acknowledge the fact. In other cases, translations should in principle be taken to be our own.

From time to time, during extended discussions of this or that text, we cite lines simply by number, rather than specifying the work each time; so, for example, (123) rather than (Eur. *Cyc.* 123). Analogously, in our frequent discussions of passages from *Odyssey* book 9 we usually give line numbers only without specifying the book, whereas for passages from elsewhere in the poem we specify the book as well as the line. We trust that our readers will go along with this procedure, which is designed in the interests of economy, without (we hope) sacrificing clarity.

PART I
THE CYCLOPES IN ANTIQUITY
Themes And Variations

1
A Story

Once upon a time, in a far-off land, there lived an ogre. His lair was a cave by the sea. In addition to his enormous size, two other things made him monstrous: he had a single eye; and he ate people.

One day a group of wanderers, led by a resourceful and wily hero, chanced upon the ogre's cave. They were sailing homewards after an expedition to fight a great war, but a storm had driven their ships off course. When they arrived at the ogre's cave, there was no one in; for the ogre was a herdsman, and was away tending his flocks. The hero and his men entered the cave, helped themselves to some of the cheeses they found there, and waited for the cave's owner to come back. At last he arrived, driving in some of his animals for milking; then he blocked the cave entrance with a huge boulder to keep out the rams and the he-goats. When everything was in order in the cave, he kindled a fire. Then he spied the hero and his men. In answer to the ogre's unfriendly questioning, the hero explained where he and his men had come from, and how they now hoped to receive hospitality. The ogre responded by devouring two of the hero's men, after which he promptly fell asleep. It would have been possible to kill the ogre there and then—possible, but pointless, since with the ogre dead there was no way to remove the boulder. Brute force was of no use: what was needed was a trick.

When the ogre awoke next morning, he milked his flocks, breakfasted on two more of the intruders, and drove his flocks outside; then he put the boulder back in position and strode away. Imprisoned in the cave along with his remaining crewmen, the hero now devised a plan, which involved sharpening a wooden stake and hardening it in the fire. Back came the ogre with his flocks—this time he drove the males as well as the females into the cave—and two more men became his evening meal. Now was the moment for the trick. On his earlier travels the hero had been presented with some delectable and potent wine as a guest-gift. He now offered this to the ogre, who gleefully accepted it and drank deeply and repeatedly. The ogre then asked the hero his name. 'Nobody,' came the cunning reply. 'Well,' said the ogre, in a mood of apparent benevolence, 'now let me offer you *a guest-gift. My gift will be that I shall eat Nobody last of all.' With that, he lay down in a drunken coma.*

This was the opportunity the hero and his men had been waiting for. They reheated the sharpened stake and thrust it into the ogre's eye. In agony he cried out to his fellow ogres to come to his aid. 'Who is harming you?', they called to him. 'Nobody,' he groaned from inside the cave. 'In that case, some sickness must have

Cyclops: The Myth and its Cultural History. Mercedes Aguirre and Richard Buxton, Oxford University Press (2020).

DOI: 10.1093/oso/9780198713777.001.0001

come upon you; all you can do is to pray to your father' (the god of the sea); and they went away and left him alone.

The blinded ogre removed the boulder to let his flocks out, since, in spite of his pain, he still attended to his responsibilities as a herdsman. In case his assailants were riding on top of the sheep as a means of escape, the ogre felt along the animals' backs. But the crafty hero and his men had tied themselves underneath the animals' bellies, enabling them to make their getaway. Unable to resist taunting his outsmarted foe, the hero boastfully revealed his real name. The ogre tried to land one final, crushing blow by hurling huge crags at his enemies; but he missed. He could do no more than pray to his divine father to bring harm and misfortune on the puny little man who had robbed him of his eyesight.

One of the commonest types of myth worldwide is that which depicts a hero in combat against a formidable adversary, so as to highlight the hero's physical strength, agility, or cunning. Sometimes the adversary is human, usually in the context of war or some other type of aggressive confrontation, such as those that pitted Achilles against Hector, Aeneas against Turnus, Cú Chulainn against Ferdiad, or Robin Hood against the Sheriff of Nottingham. Alternatively, the adversary may be a fearsome animal, such as the Calydonian boar hunted by Meleager, or the bull, lion, and black camel stallion successively overcome by Kan Turali, young hero of the Oghuz Turks.[1] But in countless other cases the hero's opponent is a creature that threatens the differentiae that separate one species from another. Such scary 'monsters', which populate the mythologies of every culture, constitute the adversaries par excellence for heroes: the lion-headed, goat-bodied, snake-tailed Chimera for Bellerophon, or, for the Japanese warrior Minamoto no Yorimasa, the spectacular hybrid creature known as a *nue*, with, in one variant, the face of a monkey, the legs of a tiger, the body of a raccoon dog, and the tail of a snake.[2]

Among such boundary-crossers there are some that, while exhibiting most of the characteristics of human beings, also possess a certain peculiarity, whether anatomical or behavioural, that sets them apart. One such creature is the man-eating giant often designated as an 'ogre(ss)' (sometimes 'hogre(ss)'), a word cited by the *Oxford English Dictionary* as first used by Charles Perrault in his 1697 collection of fairy tales, and plausibly related to an Italian dialectal form **ogro*/**orgo* = Italian *orco*, meaning 'demon' or 'monster'.[3] Examples range from the blind, bestial *Orco* in canto 17 of Ariosto's *Orlando furioso*, to the orcs popularized by Tolkien in *Lord of the Rings*. In the story we summarized at the outset of this chapter, the hero's gigantic, anthropophagous antagonist can perfectly be

[1] In G. Lewis (1974: 117–32).

[2] One variant: the medieval *Heike monogatari*, on which see Oyler (2008).

[3] Perrault (1697).

described as an 'ogre'. This story was endlessly retold and depicted by the ancient Greeks and Romans, and was later adapted by tale-tellers and artists in numerous other cultures. For the Greeks, the name of the hero of the story was 'Odysseus', for the Romans, 'Ulixes', corresponding to an earlier, alternative Greek spelling in which lambda replaces delta in the hero's name—for example, 'Olyteus'.[4] From 'Ulixes' derives the English 'Ulysses', alongside similar derivatives in other modern languages (Spanish 'Ulises', French 'Ulysse', Italian 'Ulisse', Russian 'Uliss (Улисс)', Chinese 'Yóu lì xī sī (尤利西斯)', etc.). The hero's gigantic, monocular, ogrish adversary belonged to the race of the Cyclopes; he was known to the Greeks as 'Polyphemos', and to the Romans as 'Polyphemus'.

Accounts of the Polyphemus-and-Odysseus encounter go back at least as far as the Homeric *Odyssey* (perhaps 8th cent. BCE), although, as comparative folklorists especially have argued, aspects of the narrative may draw on considerably older tale types. In Graeco-Roman antiquity the Homeric version undoubtedly held a special authority, but many other stories about Polyphemus were told too, sometimes amplifying the Odyssean version, sometimes modifying it with new details and emphases. One apparently new, post-Homeric development was Polyphemus' erotic passion for the sea nymph Galatea. Most myth-tellers, though not all, depicted this attachment as lopsided and unrequited: the ogre was extra-keen, but the nymph was having none of it. From Ovid (43 BCE–17 CE) onwards another element was added, in the person of Galatea's handsome young lover Acis, doomed to be obliterated by Polyphemus in a jealous frenzy.

Nor was this the end of the multiplicity. As well as the Odyssean pastoral ogres, two other types of Cyclopes were familiar to the myth-tellers. These were, first, the mighty metalworkers who forged the gods' thunderbolts and were often said to toil as the assistants of Hephaestus/Vulcan, and, secondly, the master builders, credited with the construction of colossal ('Cyclopean') stone walls for such cities as Tiryns and Mycenae. What the three homonymous groups may have had in common will concern us later.

Cyclopean myths belonged to the intricate web of narratives ('Graeco-Roman mythology') from which post-classical cultures have drawn imaginative, emotional, and intellectual stimulus, in a process that seems inexhaustible, or, at any rate, shows no signs of being exhausted. Inevitably, different aspects of Cyclopean mythology have gained or lost prominence owing to changing historical, social, and literary or artistic developments, for reasons that are seldom random and often revealing. Reworkings of the Odysseus-and-Polyphemus encounter still continue today, particularly in literature, theatre, and cinema; by contrast, the Polyphemus/Galatea/Acis love triangle has become less prominent, as have the

[4] Lambda not delta: see Brommer (1982–3; 1983: 18) on the numerous (twelve!) different ways of spelling the name in inscriptions on Greek vases. Burgess (2001: 111) argues that the early artists who used the lambda form of the hero's name were unlikely to have been taking the *Odyssey* as their model.

Cyclopes' roles as metalworkers and builders. One noteworthy aspect of many modern and contemporary retellings is that the Cyclops' single eye has become his dominant—in some cases, virtually his only—characteristic.

The purpose of our book is to investigate the shifting developments of this story. In doing so we adopt three interrelated perspectives.

The first stresses context. The meanings of any cultural item—such as an object, image, or tale—are inevitably moulded, initially by the context of production, and subsequently by the changing contexts of reception. Thus the generic presuppositions underlying Euripidean satyr play and Theocritean pastoral are not those that shape Homeric and Virgilian epic; the cultural framework of Handelian Baroque contrasts starkly with the Romantic agenda espoused by Victor Hugo, not to speak of the modernist aesthetic evoked by Joyce's *Ulysses*; the visual assumptions implicit in Pompeian wall painting have little in common with the symbolist *imaginaire* of Odilon Redon, or with the artistic–technological environment that generated the robot-like constructions of Eduardo Paolozzi. The Cyclopes who inhabit each of these contexts draw meaning from those contexts; our analysis will stress this embeddedness.

Our second perspective relates to themes. The whole of the section of the book devoted to classical antiquity (Part I) is organized thematically, to emphasize connections and continuities that have not, we believe, been sufficiently highlighted before. Our intention is to build up a composite, multilayered picture. This entails returning repeatedly to the same texts and images in order to analyse them under different thematic headings. A consequence of this method is that our readers need to persevere to the end of Part I before they can be sure they have heard our last word on any particular text or image. We recognize that this demands patience, but we hope that such patience will be rewarded if we are able to offer a convincingly 'thick' description of the relevant features of the myths.

Our third perspective concerns representativeness. We have not aimed for exhaustiveness, nor would such an objective have been realistic or palatable. Instead we have chosen examples to illustrate what seem to us to be significant trends. To the reader who protests at the omission of her or his favourite Cyclops, we can only offer the hope that the Cyclopes who *are* present have earned the right to be so.

In his account of the representation of monstrosity in Western art, Gilbert Lascault warned that an excessively rational ('Cartesian') approach to the classification of monsters might result in the loss of a sense of astonishment and scandal on the part of the viewer.[5] That is one risk: loss of impact due to over-intellectualized analysis. There is another risk: monotony. Constant exposure to images and ideas

[5] Lascault (1973: 181–3).

of monstrosity may deaden one's response; monsters may cease to threaten, and may instead become merely tedious. All we can say is that we have done our best to be aware of these twin risks, and to avoid them so far as we could. When all is said and done, few constellations of myths are so appealing and engrossing as that which we have set ourselves the task of interpreting.

2
Seven Ways to Approach a Cyclops

No one seeking to explore a group of Greek myths can do so in a mental vacuum. Well over two-and-a-half millennia separate us from the earliest recorded Greek narratives of gods and heroes, and throughout the intervening period attempts have been made, at first within Greek culture and eventually far beyond it, to get to grips with their meaning. Often such explorations have been implicit, through literary and artistic adaptations of the tales to new cultural contexts; this process of renewal shows no sign of decline. Complementary to these adaptations have been repeated, explicit efforts on the part of scholars and speculative thinkers, both ancient and modern, to investigate this body of material. As with the reimaginings, the scholarly analyses continue to proliferate.

Myths about the Cyclopes are no exception to these general developments. During and since classical antiquity, stories about these extraordinary figures have been retold countless times; the history of these retellings will unfold in the pages that follow. But there has also been a flood of academic analysis. Before we offer our own tributary, we shall describe some recent and contemporary trends—the 'Seven Ways' of our chapter title. We do not pretend that these 'ways' cover every approach that has been adopted towards the Cyclopes, but they do seem to us to embrace the bulk of them. Of course, many scholars interweave several of the 'ways'. Precisely for this reason, it seems useful to do some preliminary disentangling.

Folktales

If any single approach to the myths of the Cyclopes has predominated in recent scholarship, it is the attempt to understand the Homeric Polyphemus episode by comparing it with folktales that it seems to resemble (variously designated as *comparanda*, 'parallels', or 'analogues'). But that predominance has not passed unchallenged, nor is there agreement, even among scholars who adopt a folktale-oriented perspective, about how those folktales relate to the Homeric version.

The founding father of the folktale approach is usually acknowledged to have been the Prussian diplomat H. F. von Diez, who in 1815 published an account of a

Cyclops: The Myth and its Cultural History. Mercedes Aguirre and Richard Buxton, Oxford University Press (2020).

DOI: 10.1093/oso/9780198713777.001.0001

manuscript housed in the Royal Library of Dresden.[1] Under the title of *The Book of Dede Korkut*, the manuscript records stories of the Turkish tribe of the Oghuz.[2] Among the events narrated is an encounter between the Oghuz hero Basat and a cave-dwelling ogre called Tepegöz ('Head Eye', 'Top Eye'), distinguished by a single eye on the top of his head.[3] Basat blinds him with a red-hot spit, then escapes from the cave by slaughtering a sheep and donning its skin.[4] In Von Diez's view, the story of Basat and Tepegöz was the model for the Homeric version. His study inaugurated a long line of comparative investigations exploiting a growing corpus of folktale material, drawn especially from Europe, the Middle East, and North Africa. Wilhelm Grimm discussed ten tales, and his list was extended by others, but a step change occurred with the compilation and analysis of 221 tales by the Finnish folklorist Oskar Hackman.[5] Since Hackman, others have added more tales to his dossier, though no subsequent treatment has replaced his account, published as long ago as 1904.[6]

What, then, is the corpus of folktales to which the Homeric version is usually compared? The technical answer is: that classified as AT 1137 ('The Ogre Blinded (Polyphemus)') in the tale-type index developed by the Finnish folklorist Antti Aarne, and revised by the American scholar Stith Thompson.[7] An extended summary of this tale type is given by the doyen of contemporary folklorists working on classical antiquity, William Hansen, who adds some of the main variants in parentheses:

> Alone (or with a number of companions) a man comes to the dwelling of an ogre, usually a giant. The ogre keeps him (them) in his lair (and eats some of the men). In self-defence the hero, sometimes pretending to be able to cure the ogre's faulty eyesight, destroys the ogre's eyes (his only eye, his one good eye) by means of a spit (boiling liquid, etc.).

[1] On von Diez, see Bremmer (2002: 136). [2] See G. Lewis (1974).

[3] S. West (2013: 203).

[4] Cf. Glenn (1971: 137–8); O. Spies (1981); Meeker (1992); Conrad (1999).

[5] Grimm (1857). Extended by others: especially Nyrop (1880–2). Hackman (1904).

[6] Later additions: Germain (1954); Naumann (1979); see also Burkert (1979: 156 n. 13). For a possible Mesopotamian antecedent, see Knox (1979).

[7] Aarne and Thompson (1961). More recently still, the tale in question is designated as ATU 1137, according to the further revision of Aarne–Thompson in Uther (2011). On the Aarne–Thompson classificatory system, see Dundes (1997). For stinging criticism of the lack of knowledge of folkloristics on the part of classicists, see Dundes (1986: esp. 262–3). As W. F. Hansen (2002: 30 n. 109) points out, the Aarne and Thompson tale-type index must be distinguished from Thompson's *Motif-Index of Folk-Literature* (1955–8): whereas *The Types of the Folktale* 'classifies whole tales from a limited geographical area and a limited range of time, [the *Motif-Index*] classifies the small narrative ideas that in combination make up whole stories, and includes material from all folk-narrative genres from all parts of the world and from all periods of history, whether it is attested in oral tradition or not'. For the motifs ('small narrative ideas') that make up the stories, see also d'Huy (2015: 49–50).

> Subsequently the hero covers himself (and his companions) with a sheepskin (sheepskins), joins the ogre's sheep, and crawls out of the lair (or they cling or tie themselves to live sheep).
>
> Having escaped from the ogre's dwelling, the hero sometimes mocks the ogre, provoking him to retaliate in some fashion, such as by casting something harmful at the hero or by tossing to the hero a magic ring (or other magic object) that, when the hero puts it on his finger, repeatedly yells 'Here I am', thereby guiding the blinded ogre to him; since the ring cannot be removed, the man is obliged to cut (bite) off his finger, after which he escapes, sometimes taking with him the ogre's sheep.[8]

An alternative and briefer summary is offered by Graham Anderson, another scholar working at the interface of classics and folklore:

1. A man encounters a cannibal giant in a confined space.
2. He uses what is available to blind the giant.
3. He escapes his confinement by means of a trick with an animal.
4. The giant nearly traps him by a counter-trick.[9]

Any summary is bound to be reductivist, and these, that of Anderson in particular, inevitably bleach out some of the specificity of the data. For instance, Anderson's phrase 'what is available to blind the giant' covers, among other instruments, boiling oil, boiling water, molten lead, roasted fat, a red-hot spit, a firebrand, a sharpened stick, burning coal, a heated knife—and a shot from a pistol. Nevertheless, both summaries highlight some common features of the *comparanda*.[10]

But what exactly is to be done with such summaries? More precisely: how do the *comparanda* relate to the version told in the *Odyssey*? There is no consensus.[11] The fault line is: does the Homeric narrative draw on one or more pre-existing tales that the later folktale tradition also independently draws on, or does the whole later tradition derive ultimately from the *Odyssey*?

[8] W. F. Hansen (2002: 289).

[9] Anderson (2000: 124). Yet another summary is given by Burgess (2001: 96–7).

[10] Louden (2011: 184) gives his own, quite different summary, this time of characteristics shared by the Homeric Polyphemus episode and the slaying of Humbaba in the *Epic of Gilgamesh*. But the comparison is at times rather forced ('The monster's face is distinguished by some unusual physical feature…The hero despoils the monster of the item with which he is most closely identified (flocks, cedars). The hero's defeat of the monster brings him fame…').

[11] Some examples: Van Gennep (1908); Frazer (1921: ii, app. XIII at 404–55, a summary of thirty-six tales); A. B. Cook (1925: pt 2, pp. 988–1003); Germain (1954), focusing on Berber tales, and arguing for a North African origin for the tale type; R. Carpenter (1958); Glenn (1971), comparing Homer with the folktales in respect of twenty-five motifs; Röhrich (1976), principally on the medieval tradition; Naumann (1979), on *comparanda* in Old Norse sagas; Anderson (2000: 123–31); Bremmer (2002); W. F. Hansen (2002: 289–301); S. West (2013).

The former view had already been advocated by Wilhelm Grimm, for whom, in keeping with the *Zeitgeist*, discovery of the 'original' form of the Homeric tale lay at the heart of his enquiry. He published his account in 1857, a time of burgeoning interest by European intellectuals in the recovery of 'popular' culture.[12] For Grimm and those who have followed his lead, the folktale *comparanda*, just like the Homeric version, are expressions of an oral tradition, and overlaps between them are due to the fact that each is an adaptation of an 'international' tale or tales.[13] Furthermore—the crucial move—it is assumed that such (an) international tale(s) pre-dated, and constituted the background for, the Homeric episode.

Within this interpretative framework, probably the most influential contribution remains that of the Hellenist Sir Denys Page.[14] Page noticed a number of differences between the narrative in *Odyssey* book 9 and the assumed folktale background, and explained them in terms of the poetic purposes of the Homeric narrator. For example, unlike the *comparanda*, the *Odyssey* portrays the ogre eating his victims raw, not cooked. In Page's opinion this represents a choice by the poet of the *Odyssey* to make the ogre less barbaric (a dubious observation, to say the least).[15] Again, Page notes the divergence, at the end of the episode, between the Homeric version, in which the hero's final moment of danger comes when he shouts out to the ogre his real name (no longer 'Nobody', but 'Odysseus'), and the widespread folktale motif according to which the hero has to rid himself of an irremovable, magic, self-locating ('Here I am') ring that the ogre throws to him. For Page, the absence of the magic-ring motif from the *Odyssey* chimes in with the general 'suppression of the supernatural' in Homeric epic, in favour of a more 'realistic' portrayal of human behaviour—an argument that, even though it has apparently become a self-evident truth in Homeric scholarship, seems to us to be questionable, given the constant interventions by divinities in both epics, not to mention the 'supernatural' events that recur throughout the *Odyssey*.[16] Be that as it may, the important point for us here is not the detail of Page's arguments but the three assumptions they rest on: that Homer was constructing his Polyphemus episode against the background of international folktales; that those folktales can, with a decent degree of probability, be reconstructed by means of *comparanda*; and that the Homeric divergences from these can be explained in terms of Homeric poetics.

[12] Grimm on 'origins': see Calame (1995: 140). Hackman (1904: 6) followed Grimm in targeting the '*Grundform des Märchens*'. On European interest in popular culture, Burke (2009) is fundamental.

[13] See e.g. Glenn (1971: 136); W. F. Hansen (2002: 16).

[14] Page (1955: 1–20).

[15] See Schein (1970: 74–5), against Page (1955: 11).

[16] Auffarth (1991: 314) is one of many who assume that the omission of the magic-ring motif from the *Odyssey* is due to the poem's alleged minimization of magic. Burgess (2001: 169), citing with approval J. Griffin (1977: 40–1), finds more 'supernatural content' in the poems of the Epic Cycle than in Homer. By contrast, S. West (2013: 205) rightly acknowledges 'the prominence of magic and the supernatural in the *Odyssey*'.

In making these assumptions, Page has been followed by the majority of scholars.[17] Nevertheless, none of the alleged folktale parallels can be *demonstrated* to be earlier than the *Odyssey*, the vast majority of them having been recorded during the nineteenth century at the apogee of folklore investigation. True, a few of the tales can be shown to go back at least several centuries earlier than that, notably the episode from *The Book of Dede Korkut* (perhaps *c.*1400 CE), one of the stories in the *Dolopathos* (a collection put together by a French Cistercian monk *c.*1190 CE), and a tale from the Third Voyage of Sindbâd the Sailor recorded in *The Thousand and One Nights* (perhaps 9th cent. CE).[18] But to assume that these and the other texts preserve stories told millennia earlier requires a considerable leap of faith.[19]

It is a leap that not everyone has been willing to take. According to the dissenters, the stories that comprise the assumed folktale background are, in spite of many obvious discrepancies, ultimately derived from Homer.[20] In the words of Jan Bremmer: 'it is hardly to be doubted that directly or indirectly... all [the folklore versions] ultimately derive from Homer.'[21] Of course, such a view has to explain several points at which the Homeric narrative diverges from many or most of the *comparanda*. For instance, in the *Odyssey* there is no magic ring; the hero gives his name as 'Nobody' rather than 'Myself'; the ogre eats his victims raw not cooked. Bremmer's response is uncompromising: 'All these differences can easily be explained as variations by an artist who knows how to make a familiar story interesting to his audience.'[22] He might have added the argument advanced by Michael Reeve, an expert in the stemmatology of manuscript traditions, a field that could offer a serviceable analogy to the development of oral traditions. In Reeve's opinion it is perfectly possible that the folktale versions could indeed ultimately go back to the *Odyssey*, via an intermediate, innovative, variant version into which the ring motif was introduced and from which the 'Nobody' motif was absent.[23]

Which side of the fault line should we jump? Until securely datable, pre-Homeric *comparanda* are found—and such a discovery is by no means impossible—we think it not unreasonable to reserve judgement about whether or not an 'international tale' such as that summarized by Anderson and Hansen did

[17] e.g. Glenn (1971); Newton (1983: 138 n. 5); Auffarth (1991); Anderson (2000); W. F. Hansen (2002). Burgess (2001: 94–114) gives a nuanced account that highlights the divergences between the early artistic and the Homeric treatments (e.g. the artistic portrayals of what looks more like a gigantic metal spit rather than a wooden stake), and also stresses the difficulty of reconstructing the pre-Homeric version(s) of the tale on the basis of the *comparanda*.

[18] See Bremmer (2002: 137); W. F. Hansen (2002: 289–90). For uncertainties about the dating of the *Dolopathos*, see Gilleland (1981: pp. vii, with xx, n. 1).

[19] Among those who dispute the stability of oral folktale traditions over a long period of time is Fehling (1977: 89–97); the opposite view is taken by Holbek (1987: 250–7).

[20] Some dissenters: Mundy (1956); Fehling (1977); J. N. O'Sullivan (1987); cf. Meuli (1976: 639–40).

[21] Bremmer (2002: 138).

[22] Bremmer (2002: 138).

[23] Reeve (2011: 49).

actually constitute the background to the Homeric episode, and, if it did, what form it might have taken. As Jonathan Burgess puts it: 'one must not equate the modern folktales with the presumed Homeric source.'[24] The problem of chronology is not the only reason to be cautious. For one thing, the Grimm/Hackman/Page case assumes a strong distinction between myth and folktale, yet it is hard to justify imposing this distinction on ancient Greece (the distinction is certainly 'etic' rather than 'emic', though of course this in itself is not a decisive objection). Over this terminological question, though, we should not lose sleep, since nothing much hangs on whether we classify the Polyphemus episode, or its alleged parallels, as a myth, a folktale, or just a story.[25] But there is a more serious reason to be cautious. The limits of the dossier compiled by Hackman, and amplified later, are in the end arbitrary, since the question of precisely which 'background tales' are relevant is an open one.[26] For instance, if the presence of *both* anthropophagy *and* blinding are taken to be necessary to the tale type, then many of the items in Hackman's corpus have to be excluded.[27] Alternatively, if the 'essence' of the tale is held to consist of the outwitting of an ogre by a weaker opponent, then additional fairytale parallels, such as Puss-in-Boots, Jack, and Hansel and Gretel, come into play.[28] It follows that any stemma claiming to set out genealogical relationships between the items of the 'Polyphemus dossier' must be no less arbitrary. The same qualification must apply to the characteristically bold hypothesis proposed by Walter Burkert, who highlighted certain aspects of the Polyphemus episode that relate to animals, and conceived the fundamental role of the ogre to be that of a 'Master of Animals'. For Burkert, the assumed tale-telling background went back further than anything envisaged by Page, into the Palaeolithic Age: 'Man eats animals, and consumes them, disturbing the balance of life; to make up for this, myth introduces an agent who preserves the flocks and eats men.' For Burkert, the detail about the hardening of the wooden stake in the fire is also significant: 'during the entire early Paleolithic period, this was the only effective weapon for hunting.' This is why Burkert stresses the detail of *putting on sheepskins*, found in the folktale 'parallels' but not in Homer: 'to gain the edible animals, man has to assimilate himself to them.'[29] For Burkert, as for Grimm/Hackman/Page, reconstructing the genealogy of the tale-telling background is

[24] Burgess (2001: 110).

[25] Fuzziness of distinction: see Edmunds (1990: 240), with ref. to Kirk (1974: 30–7). (Interestingly, the passage has been removed in the 2014 edition of Edmunds's book.) Mondi (1983: 22 n. 18) admits the flimsiness of the myth/folktale distinction, but argues that it works in the present case. He uses it (1983: 22–3) to make a point about the complex genesis of the *Odyssey* narrative, which in his opinion involved an amalgamation of the ogre of not-specifically-Greek folktale with the storm demon Cyclopes of Greek myth. More on folktale/myth: Peradotto (1990).

[26] As has been vigorously argued by Calame (1977; 1995: 139–73); echoed by d'Huy (2015: 48).

[27] Pointed out by Calame (1977: 64).

[28] Warner (1998: 316–17).

[29] Burkert (1979: 33–4).

crucial. Nevertheless, that hypothetical background can be no more than, to borrow Plato's phrase, an *eikōs muthos*—a likely story.[30]

But let us be clear: none of these uncertainties about dating and genealogy undermines the truth that there are numerous overlaps between the Homeric Polyphemus narrative and many European, Middle Eastern, North African, and other tales. In other words, the issues raised in the *Odyssey* narrative are far from being unique to Archaic Greece. *Whatever* the 'original' dating of the tales in the folktale dossier, the existence of dozens of narratives from elsewhere that overlap with the Homeric Polyphemus episode—even if some, many, most, or, just conceivably, *all* of those narratives postdate the *Odyssey*—confirms the fact that the concerns explored in that episode are echoed by the imaginations of numerous other historically, geographically, and culturally diverse peoples.

Location

A second major focus of modern discussion of the Cyclopes concerns their putative location. This question usually arises as part of wider speculations about Odysseus' wanderings after he had left Troy. The quest for the supposed real-world equivalents of the hero's ports of call has induced many to put to sea, literally as well as metaphorically. The home of the Cyclopes has been variously identified. Majority opinion favours somewhere in the western Mediterranean, but there the agreement stops. The Flemish cartographer Abraham Ortelius (1527–98) located them on the east coast of Sicily. The fascinatingly idiosyncratic Victorian author Samuel Butler (1835–1902) also went for Sicily, but western rather than eastern, specifically the foothills of Mount Erice above Trapani; in his view the whole poem was written by a young Sicilian woman who set all the action in her native island.[31] Trapani was also the choice of yachtsman and writer Ernle Bradford (1922–86).[32] Victor Bérard (1864–1931), politician, diplomat, and Odysseus-tracker par excellence, argued for Posillipo near Naples.[33] Others have looked further south or west. In 1968 Armin and Hans-Helmut Wolf reviewed dozens of earlier theories before settling on their own, according to which the

[30] The same would seem to be true of a recent attempt to use phylogenetic software in order to generate branching diagrams or 'trees' depicting the lineage of the Polyphemus tale and its antecedents (d'Huy 2015). But we freely admit that we are not competent to evaluate the particular software employed in d'Huy's investigation.

[31] Butler (1922). See Raby (1991: 246); Lo Schiavo (2003); Paradis (2007).

[32] Bradford (1963).

[33] Bérard (1924: ii. 31). More generally: Bérard (1902–3: ii. 114–79; 1927–9).

Cyclopes lived in Tunisia.[34] Mauricio Obregón (1921–98), Colombian sailor and aviator, opted for Mallorca.[35]

But the really bold theorists have ventured even further afield. Jonas Ramus (1649–1718), Norwegian priest and historian, put the Cyclopes at Cape Finisterre in Galicia, a wild and stormy spot ideally suited to their temperament.[36] Even more imaginative was Anton Krichenbauer's interpretation (1877) of the *Odyssey* as an account of a circumnavigation of Africa; *his* Cyclopes lived on the coast of Somalia.[37] The Chicago attorney Henriette Mertz (1898–1982) wrote a book situating Odysseus' wanderings in the Atlantic and Caribbean; he got back home thanks to the Gulf Stream.[38] Felice Vinci (1946–) thought the key to Homer lay in Scandinavia: the Cyclopes lived in Tosenfjorden on the central-northern Norwegian coast.[39] Physicist Enrico Mattievich (1938–) was convinced their home was in South America.[40]

Some of these writers show intimate knowledge of the topography they describe; a few are formidably expert, thanks to first-hand navigational experience of the currents and winds prevailing in the Mediterranean or beyond it; many clearly feel a sincere passion for Homer that has sometimes lain dormant for decades, yearning to find its outlet in print. *Primus inter pares* among the adventurers must be Tim Severin, whose other quests include those in pursuit of Marco Polo, St Brendan, Sindbâd, Jason, Genghis Khan, Moby Dick, and Robinson Crusoe. His sea search for Odysseus led him to the painstakingly argued conclusion that the Cyclopes lived on the coast of the south-west corner of Crete.[41] Such practical skills and imaginative aspirations deserve genuine respect. Nor should the fact that many of the authors are 'amateurs' make the slightest difference—Schliemann was an 'amateur', yet he made the world sit up and take notice. Nevertheless, as each successive theory claims to have outsmarted all its predecessors and to have uncovered *the truth* about Odysseus' wanderings, the impression grows ever stronger that there is something hollow about the whole business. This is the 'Quest for Atlantis' genre—or the Golden Fleece, or Camelot, or Noah's Ark, or the Grail. Such uncoverings of 'the reality behind the myth' are, of course, hugely popular. Television producers cannot get enough of them, especially if the Quester can be presented as a hands-on, free-spirited adventurer—quite unlike those fuddy-duddy 'armchair' classicists.[42]

[34] The second edition of their book (= Wolf and Wolf 1983) was deliciously reviewed by P. V. Jones (1985).

[35] Obregón (1971: 70–82). [36] Ramus (1716).

[37] Krichenbauer (1877: 48–52). Also according to Krichenbauer (1877: 16–19), Odysseus' voyage included a visit to the Cimmerians at the South [*sic*] Pole.

[38] Mertz (1964). [39] Vinci (2006: 53). [40] Mattievich (2010).

[41] Severin (1987: 84–107).

[42] In fact, many contemporary classical scholars spend a lot of time on site, including on deck; and no classicist that we know writes or types in an armchair—the posture is all wrong.

But the Quest for Atlantis is not the only way of going about things. There is an alternative strategy for thinking about myths, a strategy that recognizes that *a mythical tradition becomes a mythical tradition only when decoupled from its hypothetical origin*, wherever that origin may be held to reside. In the words of Walter Burkert, 'it is not the "creation", not the "origin" of myth which constitutes the basic fact, but the transmission and preservation'—a comment that deserves to be printed in capital letters at the head of every internet website about Greek or any other mythology, as an intellectual health warning.[43] To spell out the implications of Burkert's words: the tale *is* the tale, and not some pale reflection of a hypothetical 'reality' that allegedly shores up fantasy with the prop of actual truth.

If it is accepted that myths need to be decoupled from their alleged real-world origins in this way, what does this imply for an enquiry into the Cyclopes' location? There is no straightforward answer. One implication might be that the *whole* narrative of Odysseus' voyage, from Troy to Ithaca, should be exempt from the search for a kernel of historical reality; some scholars have indeed taken this line.[44] Others, however, highlight the terrible storm off Cape Malea (*Od.* 9.80–1) as a defining moment of dislocation and disjunction, when Odysseus leaves the 'real' world behind and enters Wonderland—the space of the Lotus-Eaters, the enchantress Circe, and the Cyclopes—where normal geographical rules cease to operate.[45] And yet, as Alain Ballabriga has pointedly asked, 'why should the Greeks...not have sailed on a sea which was *both* "known" *and also* a place of enchantment?'[46] In other words, since 'supernatural' events occur from one end of Odysseus' voyage to the other, is it not misleading to split the hero's wanderings neatly into two, the 'real' and the 'imaginary'?

Yet another modern take on Odysseus' wanderings concerns their motivation. Many scholars have seen his journeyings as a reflection of a colonial enterprise.[47] Others are more cautious. As Irad Malkin has observed: 'Nothing that Odysseus does in the *Odyssey* even remotely resembles the foundation of a colony.' That leads to the conclusion that the hero's wanderings belong to a '*proto*-colonial' context, on the grounds that, whereas a colonist sails out and settles, a 'proto-colonist' sails out, reconnoitres, *and then sails home again*—which is exactly what Odysseus does.[48] What is certain is that the last word on Odysseus' wanderings has not been said; we return to the topic in more detail in Chapter 3.

[43] Burkert (1979: 2). [44] e.g. Niese (1882: 250).

[45] Contrast between 'real' and 'imaginary' worlds: Germain (1954: 511–82); Stanford (1965: on *Od.* 9.80–1); Vidal-Naquet (1981: 83). See also Most (1989: 22) for a distinction between, on the one hand, 'the fabulous episodes' and, on the other hand, the 'realities', respectively military and domestic, of Troy and Ithaca.

[46] Ballabriga (1998: 8); emphasis added, our translation.

[47] e.g. Dougherty (2001: 134): 'the Cyclopes' episode opens within a clear colonial context'; Konstan (1990: 222 n. 34): 'In the *Odyssey,* Odysseus has rather the mentality of a colonizer...'.

[48] Malkin (1998: 21). Malkin's book is extensively reviewed by Calame (2002).

Anthropology

A third vantage point from which to view the Cyclopes involves examining their way of living. An anthropological perspective (taking 'anthropology' to mean 'the comparative study of human cultures') has been adopted towards Cyclopean myths less often than either of the approaches previously considered. Nevertheless, anthropological modes of thought have shed more light on those myths than has the approach via location, and have even, it might be argued, done at least as much to deepen and broaden our understanding as the approach via folktale. But an anthropological perspective does have two things in common with the approaches via folktale and location. Like them, it has principally targeted the pastoral ogres, while sidelining the metalworkers and the builders.[49] Again like them, it has devoted most attention to the *Homeric* Cyclopes, because of the extensive and intriguingly complex evidence embedded in the narrative.

Anthropological interpretations of the Cyclopes may be separated into several strands. First, a number of culturally diverse peoples appearing in the *Odyssey* have been analysed ethnographically (taking *that* term to mean 'by means of a detailed description of a people's distinctive customs and habits'). The poem offers a spectrum of contrasting cultural systems against which to situate the Cyclopes: for example, those exemplified by the Phaeacians, the Lotus-Eaters, and the Laestrygonians; those found on the islands inhabited by Aeolus, Calypso, and Circe; and those characteristic of communities closer to 'home', such as Pylos, Sparta, and Ithaca.[50] All these cultural systems, it has been suggested, 'function as paradigms of social and natural order'.[51] Secondly, the culture of the Odyssean Cyclopes has been compared with their representation elsewhere in Greek texts and images, for instance in Euripides' satyr play *Cyclops* (*c.*408 BCE).[52] Thirdly, characteristic features of the Cyclopes' way of life—such as diet, herding, and (lack of) hospitality—have been explored in the light of other representations of these same features elsewhere in Greek thought and behaviour.[53] Finally, aspects of Cyclopean culture have been set into the context of wider anthropological debates, such as that about cannibalism.[54]

Most anthropologically influenced studies of the Cyclopes interweave some or all of these interpretative strands. For instance, one perspective on the lifestyle of the Cyclopes in the *Odyssey* has highlighted the contrast between the agricultural and the pastoral, a recurring polarity in Greek thought.[55] Discussion of Cyclopean

[49] Principally, but not exclusively: see Bremmer (2002: 139–40) on social implications of the handiwork of the smiths and the master builders.

[50] Vidal-Naquet (1981).

[51] The phrase is that of Austin (1975: 132). Phaeacian society as opposed to Cyclopean: Mondi (1983: 24–8); Dougherty (2001: 122–42).

[52] See Seaford (1984: 51–9); Konstan (1990); Dougherty (1999).

[53] B. D. Shaw (1982–3).

[54] See p. 18.

[55] B. D. Shaw (1982–3); Ballabriga (1998: 85–90).

pastoralism has led to studies extending to the whole of Greek antiquity, investigating the figure of the herdsman and the nature of pastoral poetry, since pastoral is one of the key genres in which Polyphemus has featured during and since antiquity.[56] Another distinctive trait of the Homeric Polyphemus is his diet, in respect of beverages (milk but also, exceptionally, wine) and food, since in many narratives and images of his encounter with Odysseus he is represented as eating people.[57] Whether or not this should be called 'cannibalism' depends on whether, in any given version, the consumed human victim is categorized as 'the same' as a Cyclops;[58] the safer term is therefore 'anthropophagy', which designates the food consumed as human, but implies nothing about the species of the consumer. In any event, whether cannibalistic or anthropophagous, the Cyclopes' alimentary preferences are certainly relevant to the cross-cultural discussion of cannibalism stirred up by William Arens's provocatively iconoclastic book.[59] In relation to the diet of Polyphemus in particular, interest has focused on the raw/cooked polarity (and sometimes, more problematically, on nature/culture), since in some post-Homeric versions, notably that of Euripides, as well as in a few remarkable visual images, the ogre cooks his victims.[60] Another cultural solecism relating to diet, this time already evident from the Homeric narrative, is that Polyphemus does not sacrifice before eating, a failure that has been argued to be one of the markers of his non-civilized state.[61]

It hardly needs pointing out—though it is worth doing so anyway—that neither Homer nor any other ancient teller of myths about the Cyclopes was a professional ethnographer or anthropologist. Not only did these jobs not exist in antiquity, but such descriptive accounts of Cyclopean culture as we do find are invariably subordinated to the broader purposes of the tale-tellers. However, one distinctive strategy of Greek and Roman myth narration is to investigate the world of human conduct by exploring different types of extreme case: 'Just suppose…' 'What would it be like if…' Although many such explorations concern individuals ('Just suppose there was a man who unwittingly killed his father and married his mother'), others relate to groups ('Just suppose there existed a race of warrior women who had no use for men except, once in a blue moon, for procreation'). Stories about the Cyclopes span both categories. Polyphemus is very much an individual, but the Cyclopes are a group—arguably, three groups—whom

[56] Herding: Berman (2005); Gutzwiller (2006). Pastoral poetry: Gutzwiller (1991); Cusset (2004: 55–6).

[57] Milk: Graf (1980); B. D. Shaw (1982–3). Wine: Mondi (1983: 27 n. 35); Konstan (1990: 223–5); Auffarth (1991: 302–3, 316–18); Hartog (2001: 112–13).

[58] Superb discussion in Konstan (1990: 210–12).

[59] Arens (1979). Subsequently, e.g. Forsyth (1985); Barker, Hulme, and Iversen (1998); Goldman (1999); Vento Canosa (2005); Pancorbo (2008); Van Duzer (2012: 428–9). Cannibalism in fairy tales: Warner (1998: *passim*).

[60] Raw/cooked: S. D'Onofrio (2003: 136). Diet of Cyclops: Longo (1987). Nature/culture: Kirk (1970: 162–71); Calame (1976); S. D'Onofrio (2003: 133).

[61] Vidal-Naquet (1981: 86).

myth-tellers describe in fascinatingly complex and sometimes contradictory ways.[62] Anthropological insights help us to unravel those complexities and contradictions.

Art and Text

Especially since the 1990s, the relationship between art and text in classical antiquity has been vigorously and sometimes acrimoniously debated.[63] Given that the subjects depicted and narrated are so often mythological, the terms 'myth' and 'story' have been added to 'art' and 'text' to comprise a quartet whose interrelationships have been variously unpacked. Although the debate enjoys the luxury of being able to draw on the indispensable repertoire-cum-analysis of classical mythological images contained in the *Lexicon Iconographicum Mythologiae Classicae* (*LIMC*), the ready availability of such data has done little to settle the arguments.

The nub of the problem is this: to what extent do artistic images of mythical subjects depend on—or even act as illustrations for—verbal versions of the 'same' subjects? 'Verbal', not 'textual': for the debate becomes more complex with the realization that verbal narrative can be transmitted through oral performance as well as through the circulation of written texts. Nor need the opposition between oral and written be a matter of either/or: the work of Ruth Finnegan has conclusively shown, especially but by no means exclusively in relation to African storytelling, how oral and written traditions can interpenetrate.[64] Against such an intricate verbal background, 'placing' artistic representations becomes that much more complicated.

In relation to Graeco-Roman antiquity, scholars have adopted a variety of positions.[65] At one end of the spectrum are those whose instinct is to hunt for a text lurking behind every image; favourite targets for this style of interpretation have been art objects allegedly drawing on Homer or the Attic dramatists.[66] At the other end are the out-and-out sceptics, for whom ancient artistic traditions and verbal narratives are virtually always separate and self-standing; according to this view, 'the painter and the poet were and are independent types of creative artists,

[62] 'Arguably, three groups': see pp. 28–32 on homonyms.

[63] See e.g. the introduction to Goldhill and Osborne (1994), in which the editors fulminate against the approach followed by T. H. Carpenter (1991), only to be, in their turn, comprehensively beaten up in the review of their book by Jenkins (1995). For Rome, see Elsner (1996).

[64] e.g. Finnegan (1988, 1992, 2007).

[65] See references in Small (2003: 177 n. 7). For vase-painting and literature, see Moret (1984: i. 153–62); Schefold (1984); Stewart (1987: 31, with 40 with n. 9); Metzger (1988); Taplin (1993).

[66] Homer: Brommer (1983: p. ix): 'All later artistic representations [*sc.* of the deeds and sufferings of Odysseus] depend directly or indirectly on the Homeric epics...' (our translation). Attic drama: Séchan (1926); Webster (1967).

with different sources, different interests, different techniques'.[67] Somewhere in the middle are those who maintain that verbal narratives, whether oral or written, *might sometimes* feed into artistic representations, but that such texts were only one of several different potential sources for artists.[68] According to yet another gambit, what artists were typically doing was depicting not texts but *stories*, which verbal narrators and visual artists handled in their own ways.[69] A development of the latter approach stresses the importance of historical and generic discrimination. That which applies to Archaic Greece need not apply to the Hellenistic period, when written texts became more readily available, nor *a fortiori* to the Roman period; that which applies to the relationship between Homeric epic and visual art need not apply to pictorial representations of stories dramatized in tragic and comic drama.[70]

Studies of two chronologically differentiated groups of images of the Cyclopes exemplify these arguments.

Concerning Greek art of the Archaic period, discussion has focused on the degree of overlap between the *Odyssey* narrative (together with possible folktale parallels to it) and analogous images on certain seventh-century BCE vases, three Greek (*Cat. 1* (Fig. 2.1), *2*, and *3* (Figs 3.3 and 3.4)) and one Etruscan (*Cat. 5* (Fig. 4.7)).[71] Prominent in the debate have been Anthony Snodgrass, Irad Malkin, and Jonathan Burgess, all of whom exploit data previously collated by Odette Touchefeu-Meynier and Frank Brommer.[72] Snodgrass finds no evidence for direct Homeric influence on the Greek vases, although he believes the case to be stronger for the Etruscan vase.[73] Burgess, after triangulating the relationships between Homer, folktale, and art, goes further, concluding that 'the influence of the Homeric poems [*sc.* on art] was minimal throughout the Archaic Age'.[74] Malkin, by contrast, finds it implausible that a contemporary—that is, seventh-century BCE—viewer of the vases would not have recognized a specific allusion to the Polyphemus of the *Odyssey*, instead of just a generic, folktale-derived, one-eyed ogre.[75] Three factors conspire to complicate any definitive adjudication between such views: the relative paucity of Archaic artworks depicting Polyphemus (let alone many other characters from the *Odyssey* who are even less frequently depicted); the comparatively small quantity of relevant texts from early Greek epic other than the *Iliad* and *Odyssey*; and the impossibility of dating the folktale 'parallels' securely.

[67] Snodgrass (1979: 128). Similarly 'anti-philological': Moret (1975, 1984), with reference to the myths of the Sack of Troy and Oedipus. 'Anti-philological': the wording is that of Taplin (1993: 21).

[68] e.g. Giuliani (2013). [69] So Hedreen (1996).

[70] This perception is one of the many strengths of the fine book by Small (2003).

[71] On the general debate about Homer and art, see Lowenstam (1992, 1997).

[72] Malkin (1998); Snodgrass (1998); Burgess (2001); see also Touchefeu-Meynier (1968) (though that book contains numerous inaccuracies—see the review by Raab 1972); Brommer (1983). Marvellous illustrations of Odysseus/Polyphemus in Andreae (1999).

[73] Snodgrass (1998: 100). [74] Burgess (2001: 127). [75] Malkin (1998: 41).

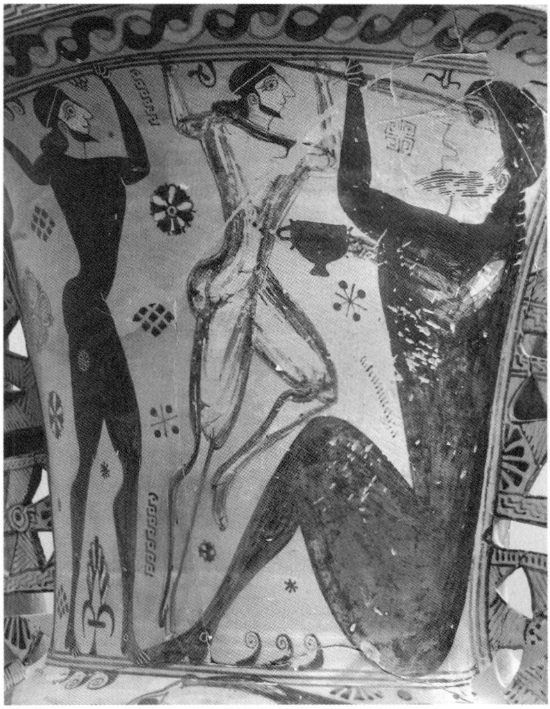

Fig. 2.1. The blinding. Proto-Attic amphora from Eleusis, *c.*670 BCE.

There may, however, be a way of having one's cake and eating it. On the one hand, there is much to be said for the general position taken as long ago as 1882 by the great Hellenist Jane Harrison. Still as fresh as ever, her argument stresses that artists working with themes *also* found in Homer were, at any rate before the Graeco-Roman period, anything but mere illustrators-of-a-text; rather, the usual situation was that 'both Homer and the artist drew their inspiration from one common source, local and national tradition'.[76] On the other hand, there is no reason to rule out the possibility that *in specific cases* close convergences between visual images and a certain text—as it might be, the *Odyssey*—*might* be explicable by mutual influence, in one direction or the other.

The second exemplary context of debate is Roman (most often, Campanian) wall painting; and it concerns not Odysseus but Galatea. Two studies in particular have attempted to demonstrate the complex interdependence between art and

[76] Harrison (1882: p. ix). Among the many wonderful things in this book is Harrison's stress (p. xiii) on the importance of seeing original art objects, as opposed to their copies or photographs. If only this were taken to heart by the administrators of contemporary museums, from whom all too often (*expertis crede*) the answer to the question 'May I see the object?' is 'No, but it's available online'.

text, by focusing on the notion of looking. In a subtle essay that takes as its starting point Poussin's *Landscape with Polyphemus* (*Cat. 108* (Fig. 10.29)), Eleanor Winsor Leach listens in to what she calls the 'oblique dialogue between literature and the visual arts'.[77] Key figures for Leach are Theocritus (early 3rd cent. BCE) and Philostratus (2nd–3rd cent. CE), whose exploration of vision, landscape, and song she analyses in relation to the exploitation of analogous themes in Campanian and subsequently Renaissance art. More recently, Michael Squire has also investigated the symbiosis of art and literature, developing an intricate, twin-pronged approach that aspires to go beyond the oversimple perception that 'text and art developed in different ways'. For Squire, the act of viewing images of Polyphemus in Campanian painting 'was itself informed by a literary tradition which images helped to shape and mould: the same issues, concerns and questions framed responses to these paintings as those that influenced the literary development of the myth (and vice versa)'.[78] Along the way, Squire argues for some allusive overlaps, in both text and art, between the sad state of the lovelorn Polyphemus and his 'Homeric' plight as victim of Odysseus.[79] As sometimes happens with highly sophisticated interpretations of visual art, one may wonder how many viewers in antiquity would have found this extraordinary subtlety of response meaningful or even intelligible. One may also speculate, more generally, that future generations of classical art historians may be less inclined than the present one to invoke 'the gaze' as an interpretative panacea. Nevertheless, *as regards the specific topic under investigation*, the mythology of the Cyclopes is indeed incontrovertibly connected with the motif of the eye, which lends that much more plausibility to an interpretation of *these* stories that privileges 'looking'.

The Eye

The general theme of the eye and its symbolism has been analysed from various angles, even if in most such studies, whether cross-cultural or anchored to classical antiquity, the Cyclopes tend to play a limited role.[80] However, a number of scholars have not only paid special attention to Cyclopean monocularity, but also identified in that trait what they see as *the source* of the myth. Two convictions link the advocates of this approach: that a feature of the real world, typically a rare or anomalous feature, explains the myth's origin; and that such a feature belongs to the field of investigation of one of the natural sciences.

[77] Leach (1992: 66). [78] Squire (2009: 305). [79] Squire (2009: 322–9).

[80] Cross-cultural: Deonna (1965); Potts (1982). Classical antiquity: Malten (1961); Steinhart (1995); Rizzini (1998).

One of the founding fathers of palaeobiology was Othenio Lothar Franz Anton Louis Abel (1875–1946), an Austrian whose career included professorships at the Universities of Vienna (where he became Rector) and Göttingen. His research earned him prestigious international accolades, including the Bigsby Gold Medal (Geological Society of London) and the Daniel Giraud Elliot Medal (US National Academy of Sciences). His political affiliations are less glittering, although there is some doubt about the extent of his Nazi sympathies.[81] The reason why Abel comes into our story is that in 1914 he published a book arguing that many mythical monsters, including the Cyclopes, originated in discoveries of vertebrate fossils by ancient humans.[82] According to this view, the Cyclops myth could be traced back to observations made in antiquity of the skull of the prehistoric dwarf elephant, notable for the large hole in the middle of its forehead. Although this hole was in fact the nasal cavity, its form lent itself, so Abel maintained, to be interpreted as a single, central eye socket (Fig. 2.2).

Abel derived the notion of the Cyclops from an animal antecedent. But others long before him had already linked the Cyclops with the discovery of *human* bones. A memorable passage in Giovanni Boccaccio's *Genealogy of the Pagan Gods* (4.68) graphically describes the chance discovery, by peasants in his own time, of a colossal grotto at the foot of a mountain above Trapani in the far west of Sicily. What they came across was an immense, seated figure, his left hand resting on a huge staff. Both staff and figure crumbled into dust at a touch, though a few, more substantial items remained intact, including three enormous teeth, part of the skull, and a leg bone; extrapolation from these finds led to a rough calculation of the figure's height at around 300 feet. Boccaccio refers to several possible identifications of the giant, such as Hercules' pugilistic adversary King Eryx, or another mythical boxer, Entellus, described in Virgil's *Aeneid* (late 1st cent. BCE). But an alternative suggestion was the Cyclops Polyphemus (Boccaccio quotes Virgil's description of his towering bulk).[83] Boccaccio's claims were revisited three centuries later by the astonishingly gifted Jesuit polymath Athanasius Kircher, who compared the alleged Boccaccian Polyphemus to other legendary giants such as Goliath, and concluded that the Cyclops of Trapani stood no more than a paltry thirty feet tall.[84]

The hypothesis that the myth of a one-eyed ogre originates with ancient finds of fossil bones continues to be advocated. The most popular form of the theory reverts to that put forward by Abel, bolstered by recent discoveries—for instance, on Crete—of the fossil remains of prehistoric cousins of the modern elephant. Adrienne Mayor, a classical folklorist with a deep interest in natural history, is not uncritical of Abel, but she too has argued that finds of such bones in antiquity

[81] Deichmann (1996: 71, with 388 n. 19). [82] Abel (1914).
[83] Solomon (2011–17: i. 606–7), on *Genealogy* 4.68.11.
[84] Kircher (1664: ii, VIII.2.4 at pp. 56–60); see Debus (2010: 13).

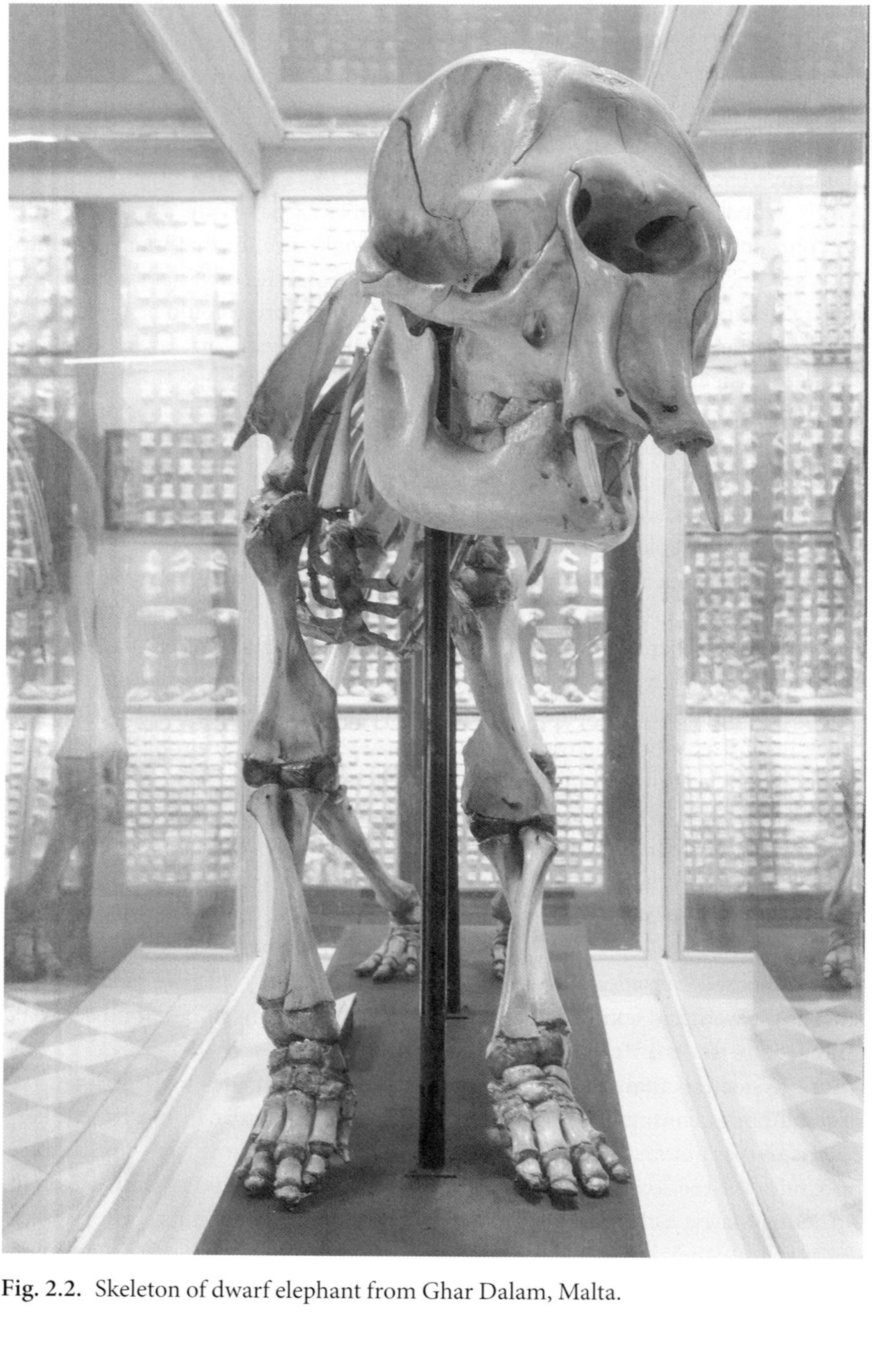

Fig. 2.2. Skeleton of dwarf elephant from Ghar Dalam, Malta.

might have shaped the way in which ancient myth-tellers envisaged the Cyclopes, as well as other mythical creatures such as griffins.[85] Her approach, which has been widely diffused in scientific and geographical periodicals, is praised by no less an authority than Sir John Boardman as 'thorough and inspiring'.[86]

The second natural-scientific perspective is geological. Various aspects of volcanic activity have been taken to be the source for the Cyclops' eye. Noting that many ancient writers, from at least the fifth century BCE onwards, located the Cyclopes near Mount Etna, the Icelandic volcanologist Haraldur Sigurdsson detected the clue to the ogres' physiognomy in the tremendous visual impact made by that volcano by night: 'The legendary association of the Cyclopes with the Etna volcano probably stems from the glow in the night sky over the summit crater, visible far away as a red "eye" reflected from the clouds back to Earth when the volcano is active.'[87] But an eruptive glow is not the only feature of volcanoes to have been invoked: there are also the craters. Victor Bérard, who, as we saw earlier, located the Cyclopes near Naples, linked them with the landscape of Campania: 'The country of the "Round Eyes" is the volcanic land whose active and extinct craters border the north of the gulf of Naples from Baiae to Vesuvius.'[88] As well as glows and craters, there are also the lakes and pools bubbling with water and mud that may proliferate near active volcanoes. These too have been connected with the Cyclopean eye.[89]

One other take on the eye-as-volcano may be mentioned. For the Parisian philosopher and traductologist Jean-René Ladmiral, the Cyclops is a cross between a volcano and an 'archaic figuration of femininity'. On this view, the myth derives from a literally explosive combination of volcanoes, women, and sex: 'His single, central eye is like a woman's sex, destined to be penetrated by the phallic stake which Ulysses drives into it... If the Cyclops is a volcano, that is one more reason for interpreting it as a metaphor for female sexuality, which is in many respects (one will readily agree) "volcanic"'.[90] Volcanoes and women, Ladmiral suggests, have in common 'periodic phases of emission separated by gaps'; moreover, a volcano has a crater that enables contact with 'the entrails of the Earth', and the same goes for a woman's sex. Peculiar and frankly sexist though Ladmiral's approach may seem—isn't male ejaculation more 'volcanic' than the female period?—it has strong echoes in some later visual representations, especially by the Surrealists and their artistic successors.

The third scientific discipline to be invoked to solve the riddle of the Cyclops' eye is medicine. There exists in humans an extremely rare anatomical abnormality whose relevance to the Cyclops myth is signalled in the very name of the

[85] Mayor (2011: 6–8, 35–6, 284–5 nn. 5–7).
[86] Boardman (2002: 33).
[87] Sigurdsson (1999: 16).
[88] Bérard (1924: 31, n. on *Od.* 9.106–16); our translation; cf. Dion (1969: 7).
[89] Lessing (1966: fig. 56) (caption: 'Volcanic spring in the land of the one-eyed giants'). See p. 27.
[90] Ladmiral (2003: 310); our translation.

condition: cyclopia, a defect resulting from holoprosencephaly, a failure of the embryonic forebrain properly to subdivide. The condition manifests itself as a drastic departure from normal facial characteristics: there is only one, centrally placed eye, situated where the root of the nose would usually be; the nose is either wholly absent or appears as a proboscis above the eye.[91] Affected infants rarely survive, so it is extremely unlikely that observation of an adult patient could have played any part in the development of the myth. Moreover, whereas the mythical Cyclops is usually thought of as having his single eye *above* the nose, the single eye of cyclopic infants always lies below, or in place of, the nose.[92] Nevertheless, the argument has been advanced that 'observation of cyclopic infants and perhaps cyclopic animals may have left vivid impressions that underwent mythical transformation'.[93]

A key figure in the development of this approach is Willem Vrolik (1801–63), a Dutch anatomist and pathologist who specialized in 'teratology' (from Greek *teras*, 'monster', 'prodigy', 'portent'), the study of abnormal living forms. Vrolik's teratological collection is housed in a museum in Amsterdam, on public view to all who have a taste for seeing it.[94] The most notable of Vrolik's publications was devoted to the illustration of normal and abnormal development in humans and animals.[95] Among the individuals depicted, both human and mammalian, were several suffering from the condition that Vrolik named cyclopia, following the precedent of studies by Isidore Geoffroy Saint-Hilaire.[96] While it is clear that the modern, medical *naming* of cyclopia can unquestionably be attributed to perceived similarities between the facial characteristics of patients and those of the mythical Cyclops, the possibility of an inverse relationship—that the idea of the mythical Cyclops was *generated* by observed cases of medical anomaly—is susceptible of serious doubt. Nevertheless, at least in the view of some, medical cyclopia remains in the frame as one of the supposed 'origins' of the myth.

Each of the scientific explanations—palaeobiological, volcanological, medical—claims to have identified the real-world origin of the single Cyclopic eye. And each explanation has about it an air of plausibility: the palaeobiological and the medical, because of the undeniable analogy with the Cyclops' traditional physiognomy; the volcanological, because the Cyclopes of mythology were often associated with Mount Etna. But three comments need to be made.

First, it is hard to see how any of these explanations could ever be falsified, let alone verified. What is missing in each case is a robust chain of argument, a

[91] Apple and Rabb (1991: 15–17). [92] Leroi (2003: 71).

[93] M. M. Cohen (2010: 8), cf. M. M. Cohen and Sulik (1992) and Stahl and Tourame (2010). More sceptical about the derivation of the mythical Cyclops from observed medical cases are Kalantzis, Tsiamis, and Poulakou-Rebelakou (2013).

[94] Leroi (2003: 65–8); other references to Vrolik are listed in Leroi's index. [95] Vrolik (1849).

[96] Saint-Hilaire (1837: ii. 271–302).

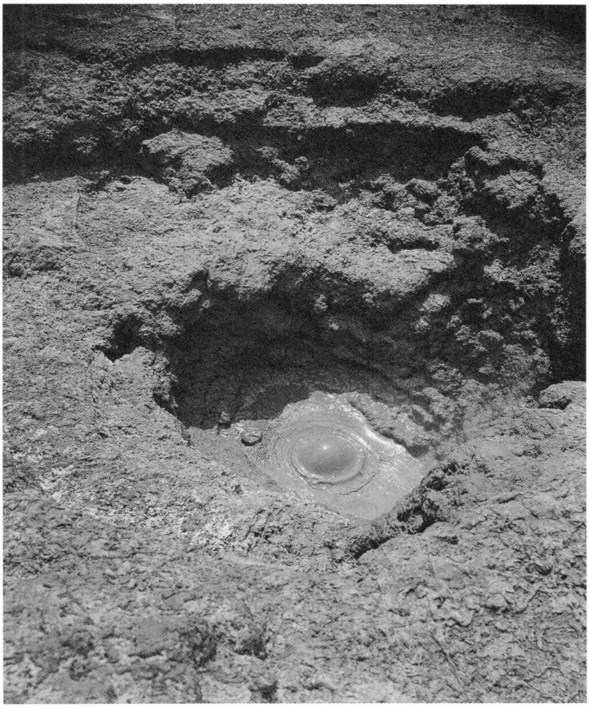

Fig. 2.3. Bubbling 'eye' of volcanic mud from the crater of Solfatara at Pozzuoli, near Naples.

demonstrable sequence of circumstances, that might link the supposed origin with the myth.

Secondly, it is quite unclear by what criterion any one of the proposed explanations could be preferred to any of the others; this is something about which the proponents tend to be strangely silent. As it happens, one of the authors of the present book *does* have a sneaking preference—for the bubble of volcanic mud. But the motivation for this preference is purely sentimental. A photo of such a muddy bubble appears in the beautiful book given to Buxton by his friends on his twenty-first birthday: Erich Lessing's *The Voyages of Ulysses* (Fig. 2.3).[97] However, sentiment is not much of a criterion for preferring the volcanic-mud explanation to the others (although it is probably as good a criterion as any).

Thirdly, none of the science-driven, origin-oriented explanations weakens in any way the validity of the fundamental point made by Walter Burkert, that what makes a myth a myth is not its putative and usually long-forgotten 'origin', but the fact of its transmission. In Burkert's words: 'Reality does not automatically yield a

[97] Lessing (1966: fig. 56).

tale... The form of the tale is not produced by reality, but by language' (including, we might add, the 'language' of the visual arts). Burkert goes on, unanswerably: 'All interpretations on these [*sc.* origin-targeting] lines must use Procrustean methods to make the tale isomorphic with the purported reality, must cut off excesses attributed to uncontrolled "fantasy", and thus really kill the tale, and the myth.'[98]

Taking these considerations into account, from now on—and we apologize for disappointing some of our readers—this book will pay virtually no further attention to any science-based theory claiming to have isolated 'the origin' of the Cyclops' single eye.

Homonyms

Ever since classical antiquity, the Cyclopes' identity—single or multiple—has been considered to be a puzzle.[99] The fact that some ancient sources credit them with one set of parents, some with another, and the further fact that some ancient sources represent them as mortal, some as immortal—these discrepant attributes could without much difficulty be regarded as belonging to the 'same' mythological figures, given the extraordinarily wide tolerance of variation that characterizes Greek mythology as a whole. After all, different versions are reported of the parentage of Aphrodite, Helen, Heracles, and Theseus, among countless others; as for characters who are variously recorded as divine or mortal, Asclepius, again Helen, and again Heracles, are high-profile examples. Nevertheless, the divergence between the areas of practical expertise of the pastoral ogres, the metalworkers, and the builders has been thought to stretch such tolerance of variation to, or beyond, its limit.

Various gambits have been developed to address the problem. One consists of sidestepping the issue altogether, by assuming that the Cyclopes are independent groups who just happen to share the same name. Another involves searching for a common factor that underlies two or all three of the groups, though there has been no agreement about what that factor might be. The puzzle presents itself most acutely to writers of entries for dictionaries, encyclopaedias, and lexica, genres in which classification and subdivision are fundamental. Entries on 'Cyclopes' range from the flyweight to the superheavyweight. At the lighter end of the scale are encyclopaedia thumbnails that list the Cyclopes' disparate characteristics side by side, with no attempt to reconcile them.[100] Among the

[98] Burkert (1979: 3–4). [99] Antiquity: see Fowler (2013: 53–6).

[100] e.g. Van Aken (1965); Aghion, Barbillon, and Lissarrague (1996); March (1998). Price and Kearns (2003) distinguish the Homeric from the Hesiodic Cyclopes, and conflate the builders with the latter, qua craftsmen; the same approach is adopted by R. A. S. Seaford in Hornblower, Spawforth, and Eidinow (2012), and by H. von Geisau in *Der Kleine Pauly* (= von Geisau 1969).

middleweights are longer accounts that register the discrepancies and begin to address them, either by noting that *in antiquity* different types could be distinguished, or by sketching possible historical changes in conceptions of the Cyclopes, or by frankly admitting that we just do not know why the same name was applied to disparate groups.[101] At the other extreme are the entries on 'Kyklopen' in two bookshelf-bending monuments of late-nineteenth- and early twentieth-century Germanic scholarship: Roscher's *Ausführliches Lexikon der griechischen und römischen Mythologie*, and Pauly-Wissowa's *Realencyclopädie der Classischen Altertumswissenschaft*, which subsequently gave birth to a robust baby (*Der Kleine Pauly*), and was succeeded by an even beefier nephew (*Der Neue Pauly*, translated as *Brill's New Pauly*).[102]

The entry in *Brill's New Pauly* operates with a three-way division between the master builders, the pastoral congeners of Polyphemus, and the lightning-forging sons of Ouranos, later regarded as Hephaestus' assistants; this amounts to an endorsement of an emic classification already made in antiquity.[103] But bolder, etic claims are made both in Roscher's *Lexikon* and in the (*Grosse*) *Pauly*. The Roscher article, written by the editor himself, also uses a tripartite division, but the first part is split: (1a) *daimones* of the thunderstorm and (1b) volcanic *daimones*, these concepts being fully in the spirit of the nineteenth-century Germanic passion for *Naturreligion*;[104] (2) Homeric Cyclopes; (3) mythical masons.[105] (*Daimones* is our back-translation into Greek of the German *Dämonen*, denoting divine powers usually thought of as possessing lesser authority than other and greater gods such as the Olympians.) Roscher canvasses a number of possible relationships, either of overlap or of descent, between the various types of Cyclopes, for example: that the Homeric ogres might be a blend of the thunderstorm-*daimones* with north-European forest-spirits of the sort championed by Wilhelm Mannhardt;[106] or that both the Homeric and the Hesiodic conceptions of the Cyclopes might have derived from the master builders (as G. F. Schoemann had argued in an excellent but long-forgotten essay).[107] As for

[101] Grimal (1985); Falcón Martínez, Fernández Galiano, and López Melero (1980). Kakridis (1986–7: ii. 342), in a careful discussion, notes the ancient discrimination between three types, and cites Wilamowitz-Moellendorff's possible answer (1931–2: i. 277–8) to the conundrum: the giant, artisan Cyclopes (an amalgam of the builders and the smiths) were transposed in Ionian epic to a far-off coast in their role as man-eaters.

[102] See Bibliography under Roscher, Wissowa et al., *Der Kleine Pauly*, and *Brill's New Pauly*.

[103] Confusingly, though, the entry (= Walde 2003) begins by stating that 'C[yclopes] is the term used to describe about 18 groups or individual figures in Greek myth who differ not just in their descent and location but also in their outward form and characteristics'. The number '18' can *only* refer to *individual* Cyclopes mentioned here and there in our sources; there is no question of such a large and differentiated multiplicity of *groups*.

[104] See Konaris (2016).

[105] Roscher (1884–1937: ii.1, cols 1676–90).

[106] Roscher (1884–1937: ii.1, col. 1686), referring to Mannhardt (1905: 103–12).

[107] Schoemann (1859). Few have agreed with Schoemann about the primacy of the master builders. For example, Bremmer (1984: 13) asserts without argument that the idea of the Cyclopes as builders does not belong to their 'original character'.

the *Grosse Pauly* entry, this was written by the Norwegian historian of religion Samson Eitrem, who, like Roscher, was always ready to chance his arm.[108] For Eitrem the key was fire: all the apparently diverse Cyclopean types 'probably' derived ultimately from *Feuerdämonen* (*daimones* of fire), 'who may sometimes help men and gods, and sometimes harm them'.[109] Eitrem's interest in 'daimonic' powers of nature is—again as with Roscher—clearly a product of its time; but the role of fire in Cyclopic myths is one that, as we shall see later, should on no account be underestimated.[110]

Turning from lexica to more discursive essays, we begin with two contrasting figures who have significantly influenced public perception of classical scholarship. Jane Harrison eloquently detected a Cyclopean unity, in terms that neither Roscher nor Eitrem would have found strange:

> It is not hard to see that at the root of all these three Cyclops conceptions lies the one thought, diverse though its forms may be, of mighty nature-forces, existing before man and, in the earlier stages of his civilisation, beyond his power to control... These wild nature-forces... were in themselves, so to speak, neutral; they might be tamed to the service of the gods and of men; then we have Cyclopes forging thunderbolts and uprearing masonry; they might expend themselves in lawless violence; then we have the giant-robber of many lands.[111]

Much more individual was the interpretation proposed by the poet and novelist Robert Graves, for whom, in discussing classical myths, going beyond the evidence was a goal to be aimed at rather than a trap to be avoided. Graves believed that the key to Cyclopean mythology lay in the combination of two ideas: the Cyclopes as bronze-smiths, and the image of concentric circles. A smith 'would guide himself with such circles, described by compass around the centre of the flat disk on which he was working'. Moreover, the Cyclopes were 'likely to have been tattooed with concentric rings on the forehead, in honour of the sun, the source of their furnace fires'. The Cyclopes' monocularity could also be explained in the same context, since 'smiths often shade one eye with a patch against flying sparks'.[112] It is a sobering experience to surf the dozens of websites that repeat these conjectures without attributing them ('many scholars believe...'), and without signalling their status as pure speculation. In particular, the notion that blacksmiths wore a single eyepatch has evidently become an accepted truth simply through repetition (like the delicious fantasy, also incessantly recycled with every appearance of seriousness, that pirates sported the same eyewear to accustom themselves to seeing in the dark). That does not mean—it goes without saying—that such ideas may not recur, with perfect appropriateness, in *imaginative*

[108] *RE* xi, cols 2328–47. [109] *RE* xi, col. 2340; our translation. [110] See pp. 227–30.
[111] Harrison (1882: 28–9). [112] Graves (1960: i. 32–3); see also Pharand (2007: 60).

reworkings of Cyclopean mythology, as with the eyepatch worn by the racially bigoted Polyphemus-equivalent played by John Goodman in *O Brother, Where Art Thou?*[113]

Few critics writing about the different kinds of Cyclopes have done so with such devil-may-care nonchalance as Graves. The approach of the Hungarian–Italian historian of religion Angelo Brelich was altogether less whacky. For Brelich, the unifying idea is craftsmanship, most clearly represented in the Cyclopean activities of wall-building and forging weapons.[114] But how to shelter the Cyclopes of the *Odyssey* under the same conceptual umbrella? Brelich's answer is agile, and essentially synchronic. Instead of talking of hypothetical historical developments from one Cyclopean type to another, he points out an analogy with another group of mythical craftsmen, the mischievous and helpful/harmful Telchines, whose capacity for disregarding the gods recalls that same quality as ascribed to the Odyssean Cyclopes.[115] Both groups share the potentially risky quality of 'going beyond', a theme central to Brelich's analysis of Greek heroes and their behaviour.

Three more discussions of Cyclopean homonymy may be mentioned, each sketching a different 'likely story' by means of a different diachronic trajectory. In an often cited paper, Robert Mondi suggested that Polyphemus and the other Cyclopes must have had separate origins. The story of a one-eyed ogre emerged, Mondi argued, from a folktale background extending far beyond Greece, whereas myths about the other Cyclopes were rooted in a more localized Greek tradition concerning, at first, divine powers of thunder and lightning, and then later a group of Hephaestus' assistants who forged weapons.[116] In Mondi's view, these two originally separate traditions were amalgamated by Homer, though not without contradictions. Mondi extended his diachronic account to take in the versions recounted by later myth-tellers, in which the pastoral ogres become 'entirely distinct' from the forging metalworkers, a view that, as we shall see, completely overlooks some fascinating overlaps in the evolving tradition.[117]

Writing two decades later than Mondi, Jan Bremmer echoed him in tracing a diachronic change in the perception of the non-Odyssean Cyclopes, first as the formidable weapon-makers of the gods, and then as assistants of Hephaestus. Like many other interpreters of Cyclopean myths, Bremmer found close similarities between the builders and the metalworkers *qua* artisans. Also like many others, he found the Homeric Cyclopes to be a different kettle of fish from their homonyms in Hesiod and elsewhere. What distinguishes Bremmer's approach (in addition to a characteristic emphasis on initiatory motifs) is his use of the notion

[113] See p. 364. [114] Brelich (1958: 325–51 *passim*).

[115] Callim. *Aet.* fr. 75, 65, cf. *Od.* 9. 275–8; see Brelich (1958: 335 with n. 47). On the Telchines, see Fowler (2013: 45–9).

[116] Mondi (1983). [117] Mondi (1983: 37).

of social marginality in an attempt to reconcile all three Cyclopean types: 'Homer has transformed the one marginal activity, that of smiths, into another one, better suited to the narrative, that of herdsmen...'.[118] One way in which the study of ancient religion has changed direction since the later nineteeth century is perfectly illustrated by the contrast between the nature-oriented approach, as adopted by Roscher and Eitrem, and the social–structural model of religious thought and practice implied by Bremmer's concept of the margin (and its implied complement and polar opposite, the centre).

It remains to notice the treatment of the Cyclopes by Robert Fowler in his magnificent commentary on the early Greek mythographers. Fowler sets the Cyclopes alongside other groups of minor deities—Cabiri, Dactyli, Telchines, Couretes, and Corybantes—all of whom, he argues, share a family resemblance, the characteristics of which include possession of 'magical' powers, a propensity for malicious envy, and craftsmanship, especially the craft of the blacksmith; Fowler also notes the tendency for the attributes of one of these groups to be assimilated to those of another ('syncretism'). As Fowler admits, this way of seeing the Cyclopes works best for the types who are most evidently skilled artisans—namely, the builders and the weapons-makers; in contrast, 'the real puzzle is the Odyssean lot'.[119] Fowler addresses the puzzle by constructing his own 'likely story'. According to this, the name 'Kyklopes', applied to the craftsmanly types, could be a Greek calque on a foreign word; once this hypothetical calquing had occurred, the name would have suggested *in Greek* the idea of being one-eyed (or rather, round-eyed). And *that* could have led to an assimilation with 'the one-eyed ogre of folktale'.[120] But why are the Odyssean ogres shepherds and not smiths? For Fowler as for Bremmer, this is the trickiest part of the problem. In Fowler's view, 'the free invention of an epic poet' takes the place of Bremmerian marginality as the missing piece of the jigsaw, although Fowler, this time following Bremmer, believes that there is also a case for the presence of a residual ritual schema common to *all* the Cyclopean types, according to which the Cyclops would be a 'master of initiation'.

The question of the Cyclopes' singularity or multiplicity is far from being sheer mythographical pedantry. While some questions about the Cyclopes—their 'real' location or their 'real' origin, for example—are much *less* interesting than they are usually held to be, the question 'Were there one, two, or three types of Cyclopes?' is much *more* interesting than is normally thought. In fact the whole question of mythical homonyms is under-researched. As we shall see later, thinking about the homonymy of the Cyclopes offers one way into that more general problem.[121]

118 Bremmer (2002: 142).

119 Fowler (2013: 55).

120 For much more on the etymology of 'Cyclops', see pp. 195–7.

121 See pp. 224–30.

Reception

We know of no comprehensive account of the reception of Cyclopean myths—in other words, the ways in which those myths have been subsequently 'used'. However, aspects of the data have been well catalogued, and there are also valuable guides to some of the territory.[122]

On the reception of Cyclopean myths within antiquity, important work has been done on a number of major authors.[123] Numerous studies have explored the interface between Euripides' *Cyclops* and its Homeric model.[124] There have also been broader accounts of the reworking of the character of Polyphemus in Greek drama, especially comedy.[125] Plato's allusion to the Homeric Cyclopes in his *Laws* (mid-4th cent. BCE) has attracted less attention, though there is a welcome recent exception.[126] Given the current literary-critical interest in intertextuality, it is no surprise that scholars have exhaustively investigated how Virgil and Ovid have engaged with their poetic predecessors, especially Homer, Hesiod (perhaps *c.*700 BCE), and Theocritus.[127] Theocritus' own weavings in-and-out of Homer have not been forgotten, nor have those of Lucian (2nd cent. CE).[128] Another type of reception involves the interrelationship between visual and verbal media. We have already noticed scholarly interest in the possible reciprocal influence between the *Odyssey* and contemporary and/or later artists.[129] Another focus has been the work of Philostratus the Elder, probable author of the text we know as *Imagines*. His evocation of a painting, real or imagined, depicting Polyphemus and Galatea is rich in allusions both to earlier literary tradition and to earlier paintings (again, real or imagined), as has been tellingly demonstrated.[130]

Beyond antiquity, a framework for thinking about the Polyphemus–Odysseus interaction has been provided by a number of wide-ranging, reception-oriented studies of Odysseus/Ulysses. Scholars writing in Italian have been prominent, especially the literary critic Piero Boitani.[131] However, more than half a century

[122] Catalogue: Reid (1993: s.v. 'Cyclopes' (i. 317–18), 'Galatea' (i. 444–52), and 'Odysseus: Polyphemus' (ii. 732–4)). Guides: Hall (2008: 89–100); Moog-Grünewald (2010: s.v. 'Galatea and Polyphemus' (290–4, by G. M. Müller)). A collection of Cyclops-related essays in Dutch, published as an issue of the journal *Hermeneus* for 1984, includes relevant material, but is necessarily sporadic. We cite individual contributions from it along the way.

[123] Note already the impressive study by Holland (1884).

[124] e.g. Seaford (1984); Perotti (2005); Hunter (2009: 53–77); all refer to earlier discussions.

[125] e.g. Mastromarco (1998); Venezia (2007).

[126] Prauscello (2017).

[127] Virgil: e.g. Glenn (1972) and Leroux (2004: 67–72), as well as discussions in the standard commentaries. Ovid: e.g. A. H. F. Griffin (1983); Farrell (1992); Hopman (2012), as well as the relevant parts of Bömer (1969–86).

[128] Theocritus: e.g. Fantuzzi (1996); Hunter (1999) on *Idylls* 6 and 11; Mori (2017). Lucian: Perotti (2005).

[129] See pp. 20–1.

[130] Kostopoulou (2009); Squire (2009: 340–56).

[131] Boitani (1994); Boitani and Ambrosini (1998); Nicosia (2003). Non-Italian scholarship: Matzig (1949); Fowler (2004: 272–375 *passim*); Burgess (2015: 133–67). Note also Montiglio (2011), though this confines itself to Odysseus in antiquity.

after its first publication, W. B. Stanford's rich and insightful book *The Ulysses Theme* remains the brand leader. Near the beginning Stanford makes two deceptively simple but crucial points. The first concerns an aspect of how we might want to think about reception: 'One cannot equate any particular author's knowledge of a myth with the total bulk of information available'—in other words, the particular mental horizon and assumptions of a given author (or, we may add, artist) need not coincide with the broader cultural world in which that author (or artist) lived. Stanford's second insight concerns the disjunction between scholarly and imaginative uses of myths: 'one cannot assume that an author's method of gathering and arranging his material is the same as a scholar's. Accident, ignorance, misunderstanding, or carelessness—fatal faults in a work of scholarship—may lead a creative author to valid new conceptions of the traditional myths.'[132] These observations seem too obvious to need stating; yet they are all too easy to overlook. And they are every bit as pertinent to Cyclopean myths as they are to any other aspect of the reception of antiquity.

Interest in postclassical adaptations of the Polyphemus–Odysseus encounter has centred on a number of specific areas. Renaissance painting is one such.[133] Another, especially among anglophone critics, has been the shift in perceptions of Polyphemus in relation to colonialism: narrow-minded bigot, or victim of colonialist exploitation?[134] A third focus has been the 'Cyclops episode' in James Joyce's *Ulysses*, where the Jewish Ulysses-figure Leopold Bloom gets into an argument with the one-eyed, anti-Semitic 'Citizen' in Barney Kiernan's pub.[135]

But there is far more to the reception of the Cyclopes than the Odysseus encounter. One 'race' that intrigued the medieval imagination consists of people with a single eye, an image that has been examined in relation to broader studies of the 'Wild Man'.[136] As for Polyphemus' relationship with Galatea, dozens of Renaissance pastoral poets gave their own versions of his love triangle; much of this poetry was composed in Italian or Spanish, and critics writing in those languages have taken centre stage in interpreting these texts in the light of earlier traditions.[137] The figure of Acis has never caught the limelight, but Galatea has

[132] Stanford (1968: 3). Incidentally, we cannot resist mentioning the foreword by Charles Boer to the 1992 reprint of Stanford's book. Boer's *idée fixe* is that Stanford was a British gentleman ('Stanford's most typical British anachronism'; 'the move of the British classicist' etc. (p. xi)). In fact—as Boer acknowledges!—the Belfast-born Stanford, son of a Church of Ireland clergyman, spent forty years of his career at Trinity College, Dublin, and was for more than two decades a member of the Irish Senate. In addition to being 'British', Stanford's other major deficiency, in Boer's view, was that he failed to approach his subject matter via Jungian psychology (the centre of Boer's own intellectual interests). True this may be, but it is not a hanging offence.

[133] Lorandi (1996); Mangiafesta (1997).

[134] See Rankine (2006: 121–51); Hall (2008: 89–100); McConnell (2013).

[135] e.g. Schneidau (1978–9); Scott (1995); Norris (2006). More generally on Joyce and Homer: Zajko (2004); Flack (2015: 95–123). See pp. 352–4.

[136] Bernheimer (1952) is still valuable. See also Friedman (2000); Bildhauer and Mills (2003); Bartlett (2008); Steel (2012); Strickland (2012); Piñol Lloret (2015). See pp. 235–43, 266–8.

[137] e.g. Acquaro Graziosi (1984); Sbacchi (2002); Ponce Cárdenas (2009, 2010); also Lehrer (1989).

received more attention, as in a brief but pioneering study by Heinrich Dörrie.[138] More elusive still has been any analysis of the modern reception of the Cyclopes as metalworkers or builders; an article by Thierry Dufrêne is the more valuable for being exceptional.[139] The topic that has caught virtually all the attention has been the (single) eye; some studies of this motif have included discussion of the Cyclopes.[140] But scholarship on *any* aspect of the Cyclopes in modern and contemporary art is thin on the ground.[141] Much of the analysis, such as it is, is buried in exhibition catalogues, which rarely have the space to situate a work against the *longue durée* of the mythical–artistic tradition.

Given the state of play as we have outlined it, there is, we feel, scope for a more sustained account of the post-classical reception of Cyclopean myths. For this, we refer the reader to Part II of this book.

So much for our Seven Ways. In setting them out, we have aimed to give some idea of the foundations on which we build. We have already hinted at some issues on which we agree with or differ from other scholars. Even when we diverge from them, we hasten to add that without them it would have been literally impossible to write this book.

[138] Dörrie (1968); see also Czapla (2006), and the article by Manuel Baumbach in Grafton, Most, and Settis (2010: 380–1), especially on the Galatea named by Rousseau as Pygmalion's wife. It is this 'other' Galatea, formerly a statue, who now attracts the lion's share of critical and popular interest.

[139] Dufrêne (2004).

[140] Schmidt-Burkhardt (1992) is outstanding.

[141] One of the authors of this book has endeavoured to fill the gap with a series of articles: Aguirre Castro (2013, 2016a, b, 2017).

3
Landscape

Where did the Cyclopes live, and where did they work? The answers are surprisingly complex. Some of the complexities derive from the fact that the Cyclopes are linked with distinct types of work—building, metalworking, herding—each of which relates differently to the natural setting. Then there are divergences between genres: epic, satyr play, pastoral, vase painting, and wall painting each has its own characteristic ways of evoking landscape; moreover, needless to say, individual narratives also exploit particular nuances. Next, various topographical features appear in myths of the Cyclopes, including cave, sea, seashore, mountain, volcano, island, pastureland, and city, the last mentioned being enclosed by that indispensable boundary, a wall; the interplay between all these features complicates the overall picture. Finally, there are significant diachronic shifts, involving especially the various geographical locations in which chronologically disparate sources place the pastoral ogres. In this chapter we shall try to tease out these intricacies, and to investigate how they impact on wider issues about Cyclopean mythology.

Masons from Elsewhere

> Who will give me my bow, my arrows, and my club? I shall go to Mycenae; I must grasp crowbars and forks, so as to shatter again with a tool of curved iron those foundations built by the Cyclopes, squared with a red marker and mason's picks.

The speaker of these lines from Euripides' tragedy *The Madness of Heracles* (942–6) is a 'Messenger'—that is to say, a character in a tragedy who brings news, often catastrophic, from offstage. In this case, the report is of an outburst by the temporarily deranged Heracles, who threatened, in technical language worthy of a builder's manual, to demolish the walls that encircled the power base of his arch-persecutor Eurystheus. But what concerns us here is not demolition but construction. A city, to be truly a city, needs walls, and those of Mycenae had been built, so the story went, by the Cyclopes, thanks to their capacity to harness brute strength

Cyclops: The Myth and its Cultural History. Mercedes Aguirre and Richard Buxton, Oxford University Press (2020).

DOI: 10.1093/oso/9780198713777.001.0001

to the techniques of culture. In the words of a scholiast commenting on Euripides' *Orestes*, they were *aristoi technitai*, 'supreme craftsmen'.[1]

That Mycenae's huge walls were the work of gigantic, primordial hands was assumed throughout antiquity. The traveller and geographer Pausanias (2nd cent. CE) had seen the evidence with his own eyes: 'There still remain, however, parts of the city wall [of Mycenae], including the gate, upon which stand lions. These works, too, are said to have been made by the Cyclopes, who constructed for Proetus the wall at Tiryns' (2.16.5).[2] A little later in his description of the Argolid, Pausanias added some craftsmanly detail to his allusion to the walls of Tiryns, just down the road from Mycenae (2.25.8):

> The wall [of Tiryns], which is the only part of the ruins still remaining, is a work of the Cyclopes made of unwrought stones, each stone being so big that a pair of mules could not move the smallest from its place to the slightest degree. Long ago small stones were so inserted that each of them binds the larger blocks firmly together.

These passages from Euripides and Pausanias are typical of many others going back to Pindar (*fl.* early 5th cent. BCE); there was general agreement that the Cyclopes' building activities centred on the Argolid, especially Mycenae and Tiryns, and that their forte was the construction of city walls out of massive blocks of stone.[3] It has even been suggested that the very name of the Cyclopes could be traced back to the circular wall or *kuklos* constructed around a city.[4]

The Cyclopes' masonic skills were not confined to walls. They were also linked with the building of a funerary mound, altars (according to one source, they built the primordial altar on which the Olympians swore an oath before their cosmic battle with the Titans), and a head of Medusa that Pausanias saw in Argos.[5] Such objects formed part of the socio-religious as well as the material fabric of culture;

[1] Schol. Eur. *Or.* 965.

[2] Proetus was a mythical ruler of Tiryns; see pp. 38–9.

[3] Pind. frs 70a6, 169a7 Maehler; Bacchyl. 11.77–81; *TrGF Adesp.* F269b (from Hsch. s.v. '*Kuklōpōn hedos*'); Soph. fr. 227 Radt: wall (*teichos*) as wheel (*trochos*) (cf. Rautenbach 1984: 46); Eur. *HF* 15, *El.* 1158, *Tro.* 1088, *IT* 845, *IA* 1501; Hellan. fr. 88 Fowler; Pherec. Atheniensis fr. 12 Fowler; Strabo 8.6.11; Apollod. *Bibl.* 2.2.1; Paus. 7.25.6; Sen. *HF* 996–8; Stat. *Theb.* 4.150–1; Nonnus, *Dion.* 41.268–9. See Fowler (2013: 36, 53 n. 206). Pliny the Elder (*HN* 7.56), citing Aristotle, describes the Cyclopes as the first builders of 'towers'. Paus. 1.42.1–2 refers to gods called 'Prodomeis' ('Builders before'), to whom sacrifice was made by King Alcathous before he began to build the wall of the citadel of Megara. Should these Prodomeis be identified with the Cyclopes?

[4] See Schoemann (1859: 12), preferring the form *Κύκλοψ* to *Κύκλωψ*. *Kuklos* as city wall: Hdt. 1.98; Thuc. 2.13 etc.; Dem. 18.300. For names, see pp. 195–7.

[5] Funerary mound: Antipater of Sidon in *Anth. Pal.* 7.748. Altars: Eur. *IA* 152. Primordial altar: Eratosth. [*Cat.*] 39, on which see Pàmias (2004) and Pàmias and Geus (2007); also Bremmer (2002: 140). Eratosthenes adds enigmatically that the Cyclopes 'made a cover over the flame to ensure that they [who?] should not see the power of the thunderbolt'. As Hard (2015: 193) comments, the relationship between the thunderbolt and the altar is unclear; Pàmias (2004) had made the same point ad loc. Head of Medusa: Paus. 2.20.7.

and all were made of stone. The same material features in a quite different piece of Cyclopean construction. The geographer Strabo (1st cent BCE–1st cent. CE) mentions 'caverns and the labyrinths built in them' near Nauplia (once more, in the Argolid), caves that are, Strabo says, known as 'Cyclopean'; a little later, he refers to the same constructions inside the caves as 'works' (*erga*).[6] This enigmatic detail suggests that the Cyclopes could also be associated with a type of stone-working closer to nature than to culture—remodelling the natural landscape *in situ*, as opposed to reshaping and meticulously repositioning detached blocks of it.[7]

How did the locations linked with the Cyclopes relate to their building activities? We need to distinguish the places where they carried out their work from the areas where they allegedly originated. Their preferred construction site was the Argolid; presumably the myth-tellers who related this were reflecting a perception that the use of massive stone blocks typified some of the 'ancient' features of the built environment in this region, features still imposingly visible today. Such a perception would not be unfamiliar to tale-tellers about other builder-giants, such as the Jentilak of Basque mythology, legendary builders of cromlechs and dolmens, or Cormoran, who made St Michael's Mount in Cornwall.[8] In the preface to his *Danish History*, the medieval historian Saxo Grammaticus argued that giants were *bound* to have once existed in Denmark: how else could one account for the huge boulders found near ancient burial mounds and caves?[9]

The places of origin ascribed to the mason-Cyclopes are less readily explained than the sites where they worked. One such origin is Lycia, the region of southern Turkey that, in antiquity, experienced a variety of political relationships with the Hellenic and Roman worlds, ranging from enmity to independence to incorporation. To the Graeco-Roman myth-tellers, Lycia was of no more than occasional interest, though it did figure in a sequence of myths linking it with the Argolid. The best-known incident involves the adulterous passion of Stheneboea, the Lycian-born wife of King Proetus of Tiryns, for the young hero Bellerophon (an echo of the Hippolytus–Phaedra–Theseus or 'Potiphar's wife' syndrome). But an episode earlier in the same story is of more relevance to us. According to the mythographer Apollodorus (perhaps second century CE), Acrisius and his twin brother Proetus quarrelled over the sovereignty of Argos. Proetus was expelled and went to Lycia, where he married the king's daughter Stheneboea. The Lycian king (Iobates or Amphianax), now Proetus' kinsman by marriage, led an army of his countrymen to the Argolid and restored Proetus to power; Proetus thus

[6] Strabo 8.6.2, 11.

[7] See also Verg. *Aen.* 8.418–19, about the hollowing-out of a cavern by means of the Cyclopes' metalworking skills—a crossover between the *métiers* of masons and smiths.

[8] Basque giants: see Barandiarán (1960: 72).

[9] In H. E. Davidson (1979–80: i. 9, with ii. 24 n. 38).

became ruler of Tiryns, 'which the Cyclopes had fortified for him'.[10] What *could* be inferred from this, although it is not explicitly stated, is that the Cyclopes too came from Lycia. However, in another passage, this time from Strabo, the association between the Cyclopes and Lycia is unequivocal: 'Now it seems that Tiryns was used as a base of operations by Proetus, and was walled by him through the aid of the Cyclopes, who were seven in number, and were called "Bellyhands" because they got their food from their handicraft, and they came having been sent for from Lycia' (8.6.11).[11] Why the link with Lycia? Might the idea have been prompted by the extraordinary sight of hundreds of tombs cut out of cliffs in various parts of that region? Surely only mighty, primordial hands could have effected such works, so who better to invite to the Argolid than those who had already shown their skill and strength elsewhere? And had not Lycia once been known as Gigantia, and its inhabitants as Giants?[12]

Lycia was not the only 'outside' location said to have been the origin of the masonic Cyclopes. In a passage from the mythographer Pherecydes of Athens (*fl.* 465 BCE), Perseus, his mother Danae, his bride Andromeda, and the Cyclopes are said to have sailed from the western Cycladic island of Seriphos to Argos; there, Perseus intended to confront his grandfather Acrisius, who had formerly cast out Danae and himself (then a baby) in order to preserve his own power.[13] But when Perseus arrived in Argos, Acrisius had already made himself scarce and gone up north to Thessaly. Perseus went in pursuit, leaving Danae, Andromeda, and the Cyclopes in Argos. There can be little doubt why Perseus brought the Cyclopes with him from Seriphos to Argos: to do some construction work in the place where he intended to rule. What the Cyclopes had been doing in Seriphos in the first place is unclear, although the association between Seriphos and stoniness goes well beyond Cyclopean building: it was the famously 'rocky' island where Perseus turned the population to stone by showing them the head of the Gorgon.[14]

One more place of origin ascribed to the Cyclopes is worth mentioning. In Euripides' *Orestes* the chorus of Argive women at one point (965) describe their homeland as 'Cyclopean', invoking the familiar story that the masonic Cyclopes had built its walls.[15] An ancient commentator on this line reports that the Cyclopes were a Thracian people, who took their name from a King Cyclops;

[10] Apollod. *Bibl.* 2.2.1.

[11] Trans. H. L. Jones, adapted. For a possible 'monstrous' [*teratologei*] reading of the concept of Bellyhands—that their hands grew directly and literally from their stomachs—see Eustathius' commentary on *Il.* 2.559. Alternatively, for Bellyhands as meaning, metaphorically, 'living from their hands', see the entries s.v. '*gasterocheires*' in Hesych. and *Etym. Magn.*

[12] Hesych. and *Etym. Magn.* s.v. 'Gigantia'.

[13] Fr. 12 Fowler. On Pherecydes in general, see Fowler (2013: 706–27).

[14] Strabo 10.15.10; cf. Apollod. *Bibl.* 2.45, where it is just Perseus' persecutor Polydectes and his friends who undergo petrifaction.

[15] See M. L. West (1987: ad loc.).

from Thrace they had been forcibly driven out in various directions.[16] The logic is not hard to discern. In mythology Thrace was consistently imagined as wild. It was the home of rampaging Ares; of impious Lycurgus, foe of Dionysus; of the maenads who tore off Orpheus' head; of cruel Diomedes, owner of man-eating mares; of the brutal rapist Tereus. One place of origin for the Giants, those 'impious and lawless' opponents of the Olympians, was Pallene in Thrace.[17] So, although the Cyclopes were cast, from Hesiod onwards, as *helpers* of the Olympians, that obscure detail about the Cyclopes' Thracian origin hints at the potential danger lurking in a group of beings whose awesome strength needed to be treated with kid gloves.[18]

In the end, though, what matters more about the masonic Cyclopes than where they originate is what they do when they arrive. They may have supra-normal abilities, but in the end they are 'Bellyhands', at the beck and call of their employer, and able to earn enough to eat only thanks to the labours of their hands.[19] Moreover—most crucially of all, from the perspective of location—the masonic Cyclopes are *itinerant*. That enigmatic little detail about the presence of the Cyclopes on Seriphos makes the point perfectly: they travel hither and thither, wherever they are needed.

From Tartarus to Etna

Hesiod's *Theogony* is stronger on imaginative power and symbolic impact than on elaborate description, whether of people or of places. Virtually the only location whose characteristics the poet describes extensively is Tartarus, yet even here the portrayal has nothing about it that could conceivably be called realistic. Instead we find a cluster of interlocking images and impressions: darkness, near-infinite depth, decay, mist, dankness, imprisonment by means of bronze doors, and a chasm so vast as to make the gods themselves shudder.[20] As for Earth (Gaia), Heaven (Ouranos), Chasm (Chaos), and Olympus, these are not so much visually individualized parts of the landscape as highly charged spatial symbols.

[16] Schol. Eur. *Or.* 965. One of the places they had been driven to was 'Kouretis', which *might* be Euboea, though the Couretes were also linked with Acarnania, Aetolia, and Crete, among other places (Strabo 10.2.4; 10.3.1–2, 6–8, 11–12, 19; see Blakely (2006: 18–19, with 237 n. 30); Fowler (2013: 35, 49–53)). At any rate, it was on Euboea that the Cyclopes were said to have made the first weapons (schol. *Il.* 10.439, citing Istros); see Schoemann (1859: 6 n. 11).

[17] Strabo 7. frs 25, 27.

[18] We might think of the giants Fasolt and Fafner, builders of Valhalla in Wagner's *Das Rheingold*; as Wotan discovered, they were seriously dangerous if their will was crossed.

[19] Dickens understood the matter perfectly when writing of the workers (the 'Hands') in his fictional, industrial hell, Coketown: 'a race who would have found more favour with some people, if Providence had seen fit to make them only hands, or, like the lower creatures of the seashore, only hands and stomachs…' (*Hard Times*, ch. 10).

[20] On the complexities of Hesiodic and other portrayals of Tartarus, see Ballabriga (1986: 257–90).

Such is the poetic world within which the Cyclopes make what may be (depending on the relative dating of Hesiod's *Theogony* and the *Odyssey*) their debut in the Greek *imaginaire* (*Theog.* 139–46):

> And again, [Gaia] bore the Cyclopes, overbearing in spirit, Brontes, and Steropes and strong-hearted Arges, who gave Zeus the thunder and made the thunderbolt: in all else they were like the gods, but one eye only was set in the middle of their foreheads. And they were surnamed Cyclopes (Circle-eyed) because one round eye was set in their foreheads. Strength and might and craft were in their works.

Like all the other children of Gaia and Ouranos, they were loathed by their father, who 'concealed them in a hiding place of Gaia/Earth' as soon as they were born, along with the Titans and the awesome trio of Hundred-Handers—anyone, in fact, who could threaten the permanence of Ouranos' power (154–9).[21] In due time Zeus would release the Cyclopes and the Hundred-Handers from their incarceration; in gratitude the Cyclopes conferred on their benefactor the gifts of thunder, lightning, and—the ultimate weapon—the thunderbolt (501–6; 624–6).[22] There is, however, a problem. When Cronos castrates his heavenly father and so breaks his monopoly on power, the logic of that act is that *all* of Cronos' siblings should consequently be released. Why is it, then, that only the Titans are set free, whereas the Cyclopes and Hundred-Handers remain locked up?

Perhaps Hesiod's text has been inaccurately transmitted; perhaps his narrative is just awkward at this point.[23] Either way, a smoother version was provided centuries later by the more lucid though duller Apollodorus. According to his account, the Cyclopes were the second batch of children of Ouranos and Gaia, the first being the Hundred-Handers (*Bibl.* 1.1.1–2). As in Hesiod, the Cyclopes are three in number; again as in Hesiod, they are named Brontes, Steropes, and Arges, embodiments of thunder, lightning, and thunderbolt. Modifying Hesiod's subterranean geography, Apollodorus goes on to relate Ouranos' imprisonment of the Cyclopes 'in Tartarus in Hades', along with all the rest of the brood of Ouranos and Gaia. But then came Cronos' castration of Ouranos, which led to the release of *all* the prisoners, the Cyclopes included (1.1.4). Apollodorus now includes a detail that restores a credible logic to the episode: Cronos *again* locked up the former detainees—that is to say, the Cyclopes and the Hundred-Handers

[21] As M. L. West (1966) argues on *Theog.* 158, *keuthmōn* ('hiding place') is ambiguous, referring both to Gaia's womb and to the landscape.

[22] Compare the role of the gods' blacksmith Tvaṣṭṛ in making the thunderbolt with which the storm god Indra slew the Dragon (*Rigveda* 1.32.2). For other *comparanda* from, for example, Canaanite and Norse mythology, see Eliade (1971: 97–8).

[23] M. L. West (1966: 139–53) may well be right (following Buse 1937: 27–8 (*non vidimus*)) that 'Hesiod originally wrote the castration narrative immediately after the list of Titans and with reference to them alone'.

(1.1.5)—reasonably enough, since Cronos too needed to secure his power against possible usurpers. It was for Zeus to bring about a *second* and definitive release, in gratitude for which the Cyclopes not only gave him the three gifts mentioned by Hesiod, but also a further two, one for each of Zeus' brothers: a helmet for Hades and a trident for Poseidon (1.2.1). These latter two objects presumably required more conventional metal-working skills than those needed to fabricate thunder, lightning, and thunderbolt, whose composition and manufacture must tax even the most powerful artistic imagination (though Virgil would rise magnificently to the challenge).[24]

From the combined narratives of Hesiod and Apollodorus, a number of points emerge. The Cyclopes collaborate with the present order of the cosmos under Zeus, even if their genealogy situates them one generation earlier in primeval time. Their role is to make things for others (as do the masonic Cyclopes); specifically, for Zeus and other Olympians. Their craftsmanship involves especially the fabrication of weapons. The trident expresses Poseidon's aggressive power, while Hades' helmet is as much a superweapon as a piece of defensive armour, since the invisibility it confers, like the Tarnhelm in Wagner's *Ring*, enables the wearer to overcome a more conventionally equipped adversary.[25] Thunder, lightning, and thunderbolt are also far from being mere meteorological phenomena; they are the most formidable of weapons. There is a strong similarity with other mythological traditions that cast blacksmith deities or magicians as creators of storms.[26]

What is less evident from Hesiod and Apollodorus is where the Cyclopes are to be located. After their subterranean incarceration, they return to the world above ground to fulfil their calling as weapons manufacturers, and, by implication, as metal-workers. But *where* they work is not specified. There is no reference to a forge, much less to a forge situated in a particular place. For that we must turn to a series of passages from various post-Hesiodic Greek and Roman poets.

The *Hymn to Artemis* by Callimachus (3rd cent. BCE) records the request by the precocious young goddess to the Cyclopes to have them make her some arrows, a quiver, and a bow—not exactly superweapons, but lethal in the right hands.[27] As in Hesiod, the Cyclopes are named as Arges, Steropes, and Brontes, but in other respects the Alexandrian poet strikes out in fresh directions. Callimachus' Cyclopes have a precise location—namely, Liparē—although he learnedly notes that this Aeolian island used to be called Meligounis; and *we* can add that it is now known as Lipari, just off the north-east tip of Sicily. Here Artemis found the monstrous blacksmiths toiling 'at the anvils of Hephaestus'.

[24] Verg. *Aen.* 8.426–32. Note that the making of the trident is ascribed to the mischievous craftsmen the Telchines in Callim. *Hymn Del.* 31; see Fowler (2013: 47).

[25] Homer *Il.* 5.844–5; Apollod. *Bibl.* 2.4.2, 3; Ar. *Ach.* 390; Pl. *Resp.* 612b.

[26] Eliade (1971: 30).

[27] *Hymn Art.* 6–10; 81–6. On this hymn in general, see Bing and Uhrmeister (1994); S. A. Stephens (2015: 100–56).

Their service to this particular master (or, in his Roman guise, Vulcan) recurs countless times in the subsequent tradition, both during and after antiquity. In the *Iliad*, Hephaestus had been helped in his forge by two types of automaton: assistants made of gold in the semblance of living girls, and twenty bellows that blew of their own accord.[28] Callimachus replaces these magical beings with the altogether more robust figures of the Cyclopes, whose sweating and straining recall the portrayal given by Homer of Hephaestus himself.[29]

When Artemis interrupted them, the Callimachean Cyclopes were making an iron drinking trough for Poseidon's horses; labouring at Hephaestus' forge by no means excluded taking on commissions for other Olympians, as the present visit by Artemis confirms. The impact their work made on the senses was overwhelming. Even the local nymphs, divinities though they were, found the din terrifying—glaring giants groaning with effort, anvils echoing, bellows blasting. The whole landscape, near and far, reverberated in answer: 'For Etna cried out, and Trinacria cried out, the dwelling place of the Sicanians, and neighbouring Italy cried out, and Cyrnos too uttered a mighty shout, when [the Cyclopes] lifted their hammers above their shoulders and rhythmically struck the bronze seething from the furnace, or the iron, toiling greatly' (56–61). Cyrnos was the Greeks' name for Corsica; the resonance of Cyclopean hammering was broad indeed.

In the wake of Callimachus, several other poets locate the Cyclopes either near Etna, or in it, or under it, or on it. Virgil visits the topic twice, once tangentially and once head on. In his Fourth *Georgic*, the productive work of bees, the central focus of the poem, is compared to the alternating, cooperative labour of the Cyclopes, whose forge is situated on the volcano itself: 'Etna groans with the weight of anvils upon it' (173); the anvils are positioned above the volcanic fire, to exploit its furious power. But this is small beer compared with the terrific description of Cyclopean activity in book 8 of the *Aeneid*. Venus has wheedled her husband Vulcan into agreeing to forge weapons and armour for her son Aeneas; his acquiescence is irresistibly sealed by the pleasure she knows how to give him in bed. Waking from his delicious sleep, Vulcan sets off to do his wife's bidding. Three Cyclopes—the usual old-stagers Brontes and Steropes, along with promising newcomer Pyracmon ('Fire Anvil')—are toiling in Vulcan's forge, situated in a vast cave on the island of Volcania (422).[30] This is Virgil's variation on the Aeolian islands location: Volcania lies *near* Lipari, but is not identical with it. But a more awesome feature of the landscape looms: Etna itself. The caverns that the Cyclopes hollowed out of Volcania are '*Aetnaea*', '(like) those of Etna' (419); Vulcan addresses his workmen as '*Aetnaei Cyclopes*', 'Cyclopes of Etna' (440). As we shall

[28] *Il.* 18.417–21, 470–3. [29] *Il.* 18.372–3, 414–15.
[30] On the name Pyracmon, see Paschalis (1997: 294).

see later, the passage superbly evokes the continuity between the creative fire of the blacksmith's forge and the natural, volcanic fire that fuels it from below.[31]

The picture that emerges from Hesiod, Apollodorus, Callimachus, and Virgil is corroborated or modified by other sources. Several texts confirm that the Cyclopes made weapons, and were perhaps even the first to do so.[32] While retelling the Jupiter and Semele episode, Ovid adds the cunning touch that the Cyclopes made *two* grades of thunderbolt, the lighter, 'secondary' weapon (*tela secunda*) being the version Jupiter took with him to his lover's house when, tricked by Juno, she asked him to appear to her in all his glory. Secondary or not, it still incinerated her.[33] Other sources report that the Cyclopes taught Hephaestus and Athene how to make bronze statues, confirming that their support for the current Olympian regime went beyond the fabrication of weapons; also worth noting is the fact that the Cyclopes' role as teachers, rather than as workers contracted to fulfil a commission, lends a more positive slant to a familiar pattern.[34] As to the location (when one is mentioned at all) of the smithy, Sicily, specifically Etna, continues to predominate. The epic poet Valerius Flaccus (1st cent. CE) compares Jason, who made a beeline for a river to cool off after fighting the Sown Men, to a Cyclops who, blackened by his work at the forge, takes a dip in the Sicilian sea.[35] Back-handed confirmation of the same topography is given in Cicero's treatise *On Divination* (*c.*44 BCE) when the speaker (Cicero himself) says to his brother Quintus: 'Of course I don't think you're the sort of [credulous] person to believe that the Cyclopes fabricated the thunderbolt for Jupiter on Etna.'[36]

One other detail may be mentioned, since it bears a significance far beyond itself. The Cyclopes were reported to have been the first to fabricate weapons (*teuchea*) on the island of Euboea, in a cave called Teuchion.[37] The Cyclopes-as-smiths rarely escape from some form of confinement underground. It happened in Tartarus, where they were imprisoned. It happened on Lipari, Volcania, and Etna, where they toiled; the subterranean location of the metal ores they worked with shaped the imagined site of their forge. Even when their labour was associated with a mountain height (usually Etna), that labour was almost invariably thought of as taking place *deep within* the mountain. A connection with caverns, and subsequently with grottoes, has been a pervasive feature of the Cyclopean world during and since antiquity. As we are about to see, that connection is by no means restricted to their role as metalworkers.

[31] See p. 228.

[32] Cyclopes as weapons-makers: Sil. *Pun.* 4.433–4 (a breastplate for Mars); as *first* weapons-makers: *POxy.* 10.1241, col. iv. 12–14; Istros in *FGrH* 334 F71.

[33] Ov. *Met.* 3.305–9.

[34] *Orph. test. et frag.* 269 Bernabé; cf. Bremmer (1984: 13). Another twist on the theme of statue-making Cyclopes appears in Stat. *Silv.* 1.1.3–4: would the making of the colossal equestrian statue of Domitian in the Roman Forum have exhausted the efforts even of Steropes and Brontes?

[35] Val. Flacc. *Arg.* 7.644–8.

[36] Cic. *Div.* 2.19.

[37] See the references in n. 32, with Bremmer (2014: 194).

Pastoral Ogres in their Place

Locating the Cyclopes encountered by Odysseus and his crewmen presents a fresh set of interpretative problems, not least because, as is always the case in Greek mythology, every myth-teller has his or her own story to tell. Inevitably our point of departure is book 9 of the *Odyssey*, which offers the earliest and most influential account of the episode to survive from antiquity.

Landscapes of the *Odyssey*

According to the version of his exploits that Odysseus narrates to his Phaeacian hosts, his first landfall after leaving Troy was Ismarus, home of the Cicones, a people whom later tradition located in Thrace, to the north-west of Troy.[38] Without the slightest provocation, Odysseus and his fellow Achaeans sacked the Cicones' city, killed some of its male inhabitants and divided up the women and chattels, but were eventually beaten off and obliged to sail on. Driven by a northerly gale, they sailed, by some route or other, through the Aegean, at last reaching Cape Malea, the tip of the easternmost peninsula of the southern Peloponnese. Still the north wind blew, and still the Achaean vessels remained in 'known' waters, until they got beyond Cythera, the island lying off Malea.

But then things changed dramatically. The ships were swept along by fierce gales for nine days (82),[39] a period that in Homeric narrative is symbolic rather than literal. It is the sailing time from Aeolus' island to Ithaca; the length of Odysseus' raft-borne journey from Scylla's lair to Calypso's island; the duration of the plague launched by Apollo upon the Greek army at Troy; the number of days needed to amass the wood for Hector's funeral pyre.[40] It is simply 'a long time'.[41] And in book 9 of the *Odyssey* it marks the crucial passage whereby the Achaeans move imperceptibly into Wonderland, which is where they, or eventually just Odysseus alone, will remain, before the narrative culminates in another moment of transition, on the Phaeacians' island of Scherie: the portal back to Ithaca.

It is not that the Odyssean Wonderland is supernatural rather than real: the gods can appear anywhere, even in places as solid as Ithaca. Nor do 'strange' things happen in Wonderland but nowhere else: the metamorphosis-inhibiting plant *moly*, which preserves Odysseus' human shape and identity on Circe's island, belongs to the same amazing pharmacopoeia as the *tristesse*-removing drug that Helen slips into her guests' drinks at Sparta.[42] Nevertheless, after Malea

[38] Hdt. 7.110; cf. Pind. fr. 169.9–11 Maehler.

[39] Line references to the *Odyssey* that do not specify a book should be assumed to be from book 9.

[40] *Od.* 10.28; 12.447; *Il.* 1.53; 24.784.

[41] Similarly ('unusually long') in Heubeck and Hoekstra (1989) on *Od.* 9.82–104.

[42] *Od.* 10.286–306; 4.219–26.

nothing is quite the same. Malea is the rabbit hole, or later the looking glass, through which Alice passes; it is the wardrobe that leads to Narnia. Malea's gales equate to the tornado that whirled Dorothy towards Oz, or to the sequence of shipwreck, storm, and marooning by pirates and mutineers, which drove Lemuel Gulliver to various astonishing shores. Malea marks the beginning of Odysseus' encounters with alien life forms and living systems situated somewhere out there—a pattern familiar to every aficionado of science fiction.

Perfectly futile, then, for modern Questers to try to re-enact Odysseus' voyage of exactly nine days—not eight, not ten—in order to locate his next port of call after Malea: the country of the Lotus-Eaters.[43] For that country will be found on no real-world map, nor will the sweet but duplicitous plant that grows there appear in any botanical catalogue.[44] The land of the Lotus-Eaters is poised between dream and nightmare, for it bears a fruit that painlessly but unnaturally drains humans of all desire to return home.[45] Yet somehow Odysseus manages to get all his crew back on board, even those who have tasted lotus; and onwards they sail once more. How long the next stretch of the voyage lasts is anyone's guess. Odysseus just says it was 'further' (*Od.* 9.105). But that 'further' is far enough to bring him to a new country, a site of unprecedented danger.

It is regularly assumed, and often explicitly stated, that the Cyclopes of the *Odyssey* lived on an island.[46] They didn't; or at least, nothing in the text says they did. What *is* true is that *near* their territory (*gaia* (106)) there was indeed an island, which was where Odysseus and his men landed.[47] It was forested, uninhabited by humans, and home to the countless wild goats that roamed undisturbed by herdsmen, hunters, or farmers (whence the common modern designation 'Goat Island'). Superficially, then, the Odyssean Goat Island might seem to correspond to the pattern of numerous real-world 'goat islands' in the Aegean. As Christy Constantakopoulou has shown, these islands, usually uninhabited, were used for grazing ('micro-transhumance') by dwellers on nearby larger islands.[48] But the similarity is only partial—a refraction of the real world, not a reflection of it. The Cyclopes *cannot* exploit the island, for the purpose of micro-transhumance or anything else, for the simple reason that they have no ships on which to travel to and from it. In grammatical terms, the island exemplifies the optative mood: *if* the Cyclopes had ships and shipwrights, they *could* sail across and turn it into a strong settlement.[49] It has well-watered meadowland and

[43] Questers: see p. 15. [44] Rightly Heubeck and Hoekstra (1989) on *Od.* 9.82–104.

[45] On forgetfulness in the *Odyssey*, see Aguirre Castro (1999).

[46] e.g. Shaw (1982–3: 21); T. Gantz (1993: 703); Hartog (2001: 29).

[47] Burgess (2015: 127) rightly insists on the distinction between 'Goat Island' and the land where the Cyclopes live.

[48] Constantakopoulou (2007: 200–14).

[49] Byre (1994: 361–2) thinks the text suggests it is mankind in general, rather than the Cyclopes in particular, who 'could' have crossed over and made the settlement a strong one. In any case, the idea of unexploited potential remains at the heart of Goat Island.

rich ploughland, so it *could* bear all manner of produce, including vines (116–35). Modern critics alert to 'proto-colonial' aspects of the *Odyssey* have directed particular attention to the potentiality of Goat Island—ripe for exploitation, and so, the argument goes, likely to have caught the eye of adventurers such as Odysseus (though it must not be forgotten that Odysseus—unlike, say, Aeneas—shows no inclination to found *anything*).[50] To add to all this potential, near the harbour there was a spring of bright water beneath a cave, surrounded by poplars—an embryonic *locus amoenus*, if only there were anyone there to enjoy it (140–1).[51]

Odysseus' initial description of the Cyclopes' own territory, as opposed to the island facing it, begins with one of the many paradoxes in which book 9 abounds. The Cyclopes do, he says, have agricultural land, but they neither plough it nor plant it: the crops, including wheat, barley, and vines, just spring up untended (108–11). But from this point onwards Cyclopean ploughland barely gets a mention, being referred to only when Polyphemus tells Odysseus that the land bears both grain and vines (357–8). Another landscape feature whose presence is, perhaps more surprisingly, understated is pastureland. We hear plenty about where the sheep and goats spend the night, but less about where they graze during the day. The main exceptions are Odysseus' account of how Polyphemus, whistling loudly, used to guide his flocks up to high ground (the *oros* (315)), and a later, touching reminiscence by the now blinded ogre, addressing the leader of his flock (447–52):

> 'My dear old ram, why are you thus leaving the cave last of
> the sheep? Never in the old days were you left behind by
> the flock, but long-striding, far ahead of the rest would pasture
> on the tender bloom of the grass, be first at running rivers,
> and be eager always to lead the way first back to the sheepfold
> at evening.'[52]

Much more prominent than such references to pastureland, however, are descriptions of the places where the ogres have their dwellings. All the Cyclopes apart from Polyphemus live 'in hollow caves on the peaks of high mountains' (113–14), a phrase echoed later: '[the other Cyclopes] live around [Polyphemus] in caves on the windy heights' (399–400). The fact that Cyclopean territory includes mountains is mentioned several times (though there is no hint of a *volcanic*

[50] In his fine general account of Homer, Burgess (2015) has as many as five separate discussions of Goat Island, a mark of how this humble location has recently come to prominence.

[51] The idea put forward by Clay (1980) that Goat Island might have been Hyperia, the original habitation of the Phaeacians from which they emigrated to Scherie because of the depradations of the 'nearby' Cyclopes (*Od.* 6.4–6), is rightly rejected by Bremmer (1986) on several grounds, the most important being that nothing in the text suggests that Goat Island had ever been inhabited.

[52] There is also the briefest of references at 217, where Polyphemus is said to be pasturing his fat flocks *nomon kata*, 'in the pastureland'.

landscape—for that we shall have to wait until later myth-tellers agree on a Sicilian/Etnaean home for the Cyclopes). Yet, exceptionally, the dwelling of Polyphemus is *not* at altitude, even if he himself is likened to 'a wooded peak of high mountains, which appears separate from the rest' (191–2).[53] Rather, he lives *ep' eschatiēi*, 'at the edge' or 'at the extreme point' (182). Does this mean 'on the shore', or 'at the most outlying point of the Cyclopes' territory'?[54] Either way, there is something extreme about this particular Cyclops, who keeps himself to himself (188–9), and who has been singled out in the first book of the poem as the strongest of all the Cyclopes—another 'extreme' characteristic (1.70–1). What is certain is that Polyphemus lives by the sea—that is to say, literally 'on the margin'. Many later myth-tellers will exploit Polyphemus' ambiguous relationship with the sea—the fact of his being simultaneously drawn to and alienated from it. The seeds of this paradox are already present in the *Odyssey*. Although the Cyclopes have neither ships nor shipbuilders, Polyphemus *knows* about ships and those who sail in them ('Are you sailing on some business, or are you pirates?', he asks his unwanted guests (252–5)). Moreover he is, as we learned near the very beginning of the poem, the son of Poseidon and the sea nymph Thoosa (1.71–3), a genealogy that subsequently entitles him to pray to his marine father to visit punishment on the man who has blinded him. In that sense at least, the sea is, or ought to be, 'his' element.

Neither ploughland, nor pastureland, nor mountain, nor sea comes close to rivalling in significance another landscape feature associated with the Odyssean Cyclopes in general, and Polyphemus in particular: the cave. This connection is so pervasive and fundamental that it merits more detailed consideration.

Alongside and beyond their function as refuges offering rudimentary shelter, caves have exercised a powerful symbolic hold on the human imagination since long before recorded history, whether as privileged sites of access to altered states of consciousness, as pathways to the Underworld, as lairs of monstrous beings, as spaces associated with that which is perceived as primitive or uncivilized, or as womb-like recesses serving as conduits to and from 'mother earth'.[55] Like numerous other peoples, the ancient Greeks too invested substantial cultural capital in caves. Ritual practice, mythological narrative and imagery, and even philosophical thought were variously infused and inflected by perceptions of caves.[56]

[53] Occasionally in the folktale *comparanda* we come across Cyclops-like ogres who are *identified* with mountains. An example is Aneto, simultaneously the highest mountain in the Pyrenees and, according to a tale told by the people of the Catalan village of Graus, a one-eyed ogre who used to drag travellers to his cave to devour them. See Martín Sánchez (2002: 239).

[54] The second option is the translation in Heubeck and Hoekstra (1989), in a comment on 9.182.

[55] See e.g. S. D'Onofrio (2000); Lewis-Williams (2002).

[56] Segal (1981a: 195); Siebert (1990), focusing on art; Buxton (1994: 104–8); Ustinova (2009); Sporn (2007, 2010, and 2013). Note also Lavagne (1988) on the shift from Greek to Roman perceptions of the cave, and the parallel Hellenistic move from natural cave to grotto.

In the *Odyssey*, caves serve a variety of practical and imaginative purposes. They provide natural as opposed to constructed shelter, as when the Old Man of the Sea emerges from the deep to sleep beside the seals 'under hollow caves' (4.403), or when Odysseus and his men protectively drag their ship into a hollow sea cave on the Isle of the Sun God (12.317). Caves are places of confinement, and simultaneously sites of love-making: both functions apply to the great cavern where Calypso passionately detains Odysseus (5.57; 9.29–30). While they may be remote from the cities of men (Calypso again (5.101)), they are not necessarily rough or uncivilized. Calypso's home is sweet and fragrant, surrounded by trees, nesting birds, vines, fountains, and flowering meadows—and it also has a table, laden (for divine visitors only) with ambrosia and nectar (5.59–74, 92–4). Hardly less agreeable, although less elaborate, is the delightful, olive-shaded Cave of the Naiads on Ithaca, where the Phaeacians leave the slumbering Odysseus after conveying him home (13.102–12, 345–51, 366–71; 16.232).[57] But the poem also shows that a cave may be a place of darkness, metaphorically as well as literally. It is in a murky cave, half way up a sea cliff, 'turned towards the darkness into Erebos' (12.80–1), that the hideous, six-headed monster Scylla lurks, ready to pounce on and devour sailors who unsuspectingly come too close.

Polyphemus' dwelling plays a more prominent part in the narrative than any of the other caves we have mentioned. As we said just now, it lies beside the sea, like the enforced home of another of Odysseus' antagonists, the marooned, lame hero Philoctetes.[58] But whereas Philoctetes' cavernous isolation on deserted Lemnos reflects the fact that he was *compelled* to live in a savagely extra-societal state, Polyphemus *naturally belongs* in such a condition. Another marker of difference between the caves of Polyphemus and Philoctetes is that the latter, like the Cave of the Naiads on Ithaca, has two entrances.[59] The dwelling of the Homeric Polyphemus has only one way in and out; otherwise the motif of the boulder door would lose its impact.[60] Next, Polyphemus' cave, as befits its colossal denizen, is *big*—large enough to accommodate a substantial flock of sheep and goats, and to allow a group of men to skulk unobserved in a corner. It is high (182–3) and wide (237), and the gigantic rock that serves as its door would defeat the efforts of twenty-two four-wheeled wagons to shift it (240–3). But it does not defeat Polyphemus; like the mason Cyclopes, he too has the strength to manipulate massive rocks, as his parting shots at Odysseus will confirm. Not that he is a civic builder on the pattern of the wall-builders of Mycenae and Tiryns. But it would be a mistake to represent his environment as entirely natural: outside his cave a

[57] A nice detail: when Odysseus has stowed his treasure inside, Athene blocks the entrance with a stone *à la* Polyphemus (13.370–1).

[58] For the parallel, see McConnell (2013: 8 n. 31).

[59] Philoctetes: Soph. *Phil.* 16–19, 159–60, with J. F. Davidson (1990). Naiads: *Od.* 13.109–12.

[60] But note the contrast with the double entrance to the cave in Eur. *Cyclops*; see p. 52.

high courtyard has been built—by him, we might like to infer, though the text does not say so—out of dug-out boulders, pines, and oaks (184–6).

Three more points are worth making about Polyphemus' cave. The first both links him to and distances him from the metalworking Cyclopes. In his case, a cave is where he lives; in their case, it is where they work. But in a sense a cave is where Polyphemus too works, at least part of the time, since he needs it to house his flocks; and herding is *his* work. The overlaps between the allegedly separate types of Cyclopes are many and various; this is just one of them. Secondly, the cave is full of ordure, and presumably smells accordingly; this detail will sometimes be picked up in the later tradition.[61] Finally, the notion of a cave as a place of love-making is absent from the Homeric account of Polyphemus; his is a loveless, sexless existence. But go back one generation, and it is not so. Polyphemus' father and mother, Poseidon and Thoosa, lay together in a cave (1.73) when he was conceived. The seed is there (so to speak) for Polyphemus' later love life to be explored—but not by Homer.

After Homer: Texts from Greece and Rome

Euripides

The evocation of landscape in Euripides' satyr play *Cyclops* weaves in and out of the Odyssean account in an alternation of echo and difference. Already in the opening speech, delivered by the elderly satyr-in-chief Silenus, some markers are laid down. The play's general location is not 'somewhere out there', but very precisely 'the rock of Etna' (20), to which Silenus and the satyrs have unwillingly been driven. They were sailing in search of their master Dionysus when, at Malea—where else?—they were driven off course to the Sicilian coast, to the area where the Cyclopes dwell 'in remote caves' (21–2). After their forced landing, the satyrs fell into the clutches of Polyphemus, who made them his slaves and compelled them to tend his flocks 'at the limits' (*en eschatois*) of the cliffs (27–8). Like the other Cyclopes, Polyphemus lives in a cave (35), which the hapless Silenus has to keep clean. Here then, in relation to the *Odyssey*, is a complex play of sameness and difference. In the satyr play, as in the epic, the Cyclopes live in remote caves, while Polyphemus himself occupies an 'extreme' position. However, in contrast to the epic, a specific geographical location is spelled out: Sicilian Etna, towards which Silenus and his boys, just like Odysseus and his crew, were blown by adverse winds off the treacherous cape, which is the ultimate narrative turning point.

[61] e.g. by Synesius; see p. 219.

The play's action is sandwiched between a mountain and the sea. About the sea there is little to be said; it serves simply as a geographical frame for the plot, being the element that conveyed first Silenus and the satyrs and later the Greeks to Sicily, and that will bear them thence on their departure. But the mountain is of much more significance. Etna is named five times within the first 130 lines of the play, and several times thereafter: its presence lends shape and consistency to the landscape.[62] As soon as you move away from the shore, you get onto rocky ground (41–50, 60–2). There are rocks everywhere (82), including those thrown at the flocks if they run out of control (51). Etna's wildness does not, though, extend to an aridity inimical to life: it offers game for hunters to chase, lions and deer being among the available prey (248–9).[63] That Polyphemus should be one of those to practise this pursuit, with the aid of hunting dogs (130), is an idea not found in the *Odyssey*; it lends an incongruously pseudo-aristocratic dimension to his profile. As for Etna's volcanic aspect—the ultimate marker of wildness—this is hardly emphasized, although it is not entirely absent: the mountain is described as 'the rock which drips with fire' (298), and at one point Hephaestus is invoked as 'of Etna' (599). But mostly Etna is presented as a place not of fire but of rock, just the kind of terrain on which Polyphemus can search for a boulder to hurl at the departing Odysseus (704–7).

More than the mountain, and much more than the sea, the most significant landscape feature in *Cyclops* is, as in the *Odyssey*, the cave. All the Euripidean Cyclopes live in caves; they have no walls or city fortifications (118, 115–16). (The contrast with the mason Cyclopes looks stark, though the texts that mention *them* never bother to report what kind of dwellings they lived in.) For Euripides' Polyphemus, the cave is simultaneously a pen where he keeps his animals, a larder for his cheeses, and (as at 323–31) a refuge from bad weather. So closely does he identify with his cavernous home that he describes himself as its god (345–6). In terms of stagecraft, the procession of characters entering and leaving the cave is the hub of the entire visual action. Silenus goes in, and then brings out cheeses and lambs to exchange for Odysseus' wine. Polyphemus drives the Greeks in with the aim of cooking them. Odysseus re-emerges to report the cannibalistic goings-on within, organizes with the satyr chorus the plot to intoxicate and blind the ogre, then goes back in again. Out staggers Polyphemus, accompanied by Silenus and Odysseus. Already drunk, the ogre gets steadily more so on stage, till he drags the hapless Silenus back inside to be his reluctant Ganymede ('I prefer little boys to females' (583–4)); so the cave fulfils another of its traditional symbolic functions, as a place for sex.[64] In goes Odysseus to prepare for the blinding, then

[62] See Seaford (1984: 55) on references to Etna and/or Sicily in the play.

[63] Cf. Cusset (2011: 32–3).

[64] Cf. also *Cyc.* 515–16, where the chorus seems to fantasize about heterosexual intercourse in the cave (though the text is doubtful).

comes out again to try, but fail, to get the help of the lily-livered satyrs, then goes back in again. Finally, out stumbles the now blinded Cyclops, trying to get his hands on the Greeks, who have also crept out. But the Greeks have had enough of speleology: it is high time to set sail on the Sicilian sea (702–3). One last time Polyphemus re-enters his home, since it apparently offers alternative access to the mountain summit, which is a source of rocky projectiles with which to try to scupper his foes; evidently this cave, unlike the Homeric one, has a second entrance (706–7). The idea of blocking the cave 'door', a motif so crucial in the *Odyssey*, is absent from the satyr play, being replaced by the sense of constant movement in and out; when Polyphemus does try to effect a blockade, he does so with his brawny arms, not with a boulder (667–8).

The rest of the play's landscape is insignificant. Agricultural land seems to be non-existent, even for vines (121–4)—another difference from the *Odyssey*. Pastureland is almost as unimportant, although, when the animals they are minding wander off towards the rocky uplands, the satyrs try to coax them back down again to a nice grassy spot near the Cyclops' cave, watered by streams and cooled by gentle breezes (41–8); for this is a spot where the grass grows willy nilly, without the need for cultivation (332–3). Fundamentally, however, the world of this play is not pastoral: it is a place situated on the margins, in the no man's land between culture and savagery, rather than a self-contained environment of herds and herdsmen *parallel* to the civilized world.[65] To find such a self-contained environment, we need to look elsewhere.

Theocritus

In his sixth and eleventh *Idylls*, the Hellenistic poet Theocritus situates Cyclopean mythology firmly within the landscape of pastoral. But what kind of landscape is it? In the classic introduction to his anthology of English pastoral poetry, Frank Kermode wrote that 'the simplest kind of pastoral poetry assumes that the quiet wildness of the country is better than the cultivated and complex life of the hurrying city and court'; yet 'always at the back of this literary attitude to Nature is the shadow of its opposite, the knowledge that Nature is rough, and the natural life in fact rather an animal affair'.[66] The idea of a simple/gullible herdsman who is himself 'rather an animal' fits the Theocritean Cyclops well, though whether his wildness is all that 'quiet' may be doubted. Kermode's stress on nature is also apt, since it points a useful contrast with the cultural/constructivist mason and metalworking Cyclopes. But 'the country' is too vague a concept to help us, since the Theocritean Polyphemus inhabits a very particular landscape, whose most decisive feature is, not land, but sea.

[65] So, rightly, Voelke (1992: 18–19).

[66] Kermode (1952: 17), quoted by Halperin (1983: 56).

Like many another recluse who experiences a *coup de foudre*, the Theocritean Polyphemus finds his world view overturned by passion. His gaze is fixed on the watery deep, home of his beloved Galatea. Mountain, cave, and pastureland remain as points of reference, but it is to the sea and the shoreline that his single eye now perpetually turns. This is the space he longs to inhabit, a site of erotic enthralment. In terms of mythical chronology, the Theocritean Polyphemus lives in a time before Odysseus' fateful arrival, so his eyesight is intact. But, even when still sighted, he lacks breadth of vision, and is thus a ready stooge for any ironical spectator (or narrator).

In *Idyll* 6, two herdsmen, Daphnis and Damoetas, meet, along with their animals, at a spring, in summer, at noon: an exquisite moment of repose and equilibrium.[67] Ostensibly they indulge in a singing contest, their songs expressing two contrasting perspectives on an encounter between Polyphemus and Galatea. But the contest lacks any sense of rivalry, displaying rather 'a kind of "golden-age" equality'.[68] However, the second-order contest embodied in the idyll, that between ogre and nymph, plays itself out in a more complex space than that occupied by the herdsmen-singers, and conjures up contrasting perspectives on life and love. In the first song, Daphnis, looking on as an external observer, evokes the intersection of sea and shore, but with elements also of cultivated land. Emerging from the sea, Galatea skittishly throws apples (presumably grown on land!) at Polyphemus' flock and his sheepdog; her fickleness is compared, in a simile as unambiguously non-marine as could be, to 'dry thistledown when the fair summer parches it' (15–16). In his response, Damoetas, in the persona of Polyphemus, reports how he tries to make Galatea jealous, while she, he imagines, looks longingly at his cave and flocks. To counterbalance this assumed interest of the sea nymph in the land, Damoetas/Polyphemus recalls how he has used the sea's reflective surface to admire his own appearance. Perhaps the most learned of all Theocritean scholars gravely commented: 'There is some force in the objection, recorded by Servius against Virgil, that the sea is never still enough to provide a mirror, but a rocky pool would serve' (as it did, we might add, in the case of Narcissus).[69] At any rate, as often, and by no means only in Theocritus, Polyphemus sees what he wants to see: vision is never his strong suit.

Idyll 11 again deploys the spaces of pastureland, sea, and shore, adding in the cave for good measure. But the main burden of the poem, Polyphemus' song of yearning and attempted self-consolation, is sung from a superior vantage point (and therefore a fraction more emotional distance?): a high rock overlooking the sea (17–18).[70] Remembering how he first fell in love with Galatea when she

[67] Pastoral noon: Rosenmeyer (1969: 67, 76, 88–91).

[68] The quotation is from Hunter (1999: 245). Excellent analyses of *Idylls* 6 and 11 can be found at, respectively, pp. 243–8 and pp. 215–23 of the same book.

[69] Gow (1952: ii), on 6.35–8.

[70] Hunter (1999: ad loc.) speaks of 'a partial withdrawal from his pain'.

ventured onto land to gather flowers, Polyphemus boasts of his land-based strengths: the cheeses he makes and the animals he rears. He urges Galatea to forsake both sea and shore in order to come to his cave, which he represents as ideally provided with vines, and refreshed by cool water from Etna's snowfields. Yet all the same he is drawn seawards, regretting that he possesses neither gills nor the ability to swim, and so cannot take his beloved a bouquet of flowers. To intensify his ambivalent relationship with the sea, his own mother is a sea nymph; in fact it was in her company that Galatea came to pick flowers, when Polyphemus first sighted her. But in the end Polyphemus tells himself to snap out of it and go back to his cheese and his lambs. His cave is, in his own view, a little paradise, sandwiched between pastureland and sea—a place where he might make love with someone else, if Galatea continues to say no.

One more spatial detail is worth highlighting. In *Idyll* 6, Damoetas/Polyphemus threatens to 'shut the door' unless Galatea promises to 'spread' his bed (and presumably lie in it with him) (32–3). Scholars have rightly seen in this idea a reversal of the usual poetical motif of the *paraklausithuron*, the song sung by the excluded lover outside his beloved's door in order to gain entry.[71] In Polyphemus' view, the door in question is of course the door of his cave, over which he usually (as in the *Odyssey*) exercises domination. But in Theocritus the 'door'—the place of access to the world of the desired other—is the sea shore, a space beyond the ogre's area of control.

Scholars disagree about how *Idylls* 6 and 11 relate to one another. Some treat them as independent productions, with 11 getting the lion's share of attention; others, more persuasively, see the poems as closely connected, with a preference for the view that 6 is later than 11, and indeed presupposes it.[72] Either way, in no more than 127 lines (both poems together), Theocritus gives definitive expression to a fascinatingly asymmetrical mythological relationship, which would enjoy a rich and diverse afterlife in literary and artistic tradition. Already in antiquity the mismatched couple, separated by the Sicilian seashore, had become a familiar trope. In the *Lament for Bion*, for example, the unknown author (perhaps *c.*100 BCE) develops a conceit in which the now deceased bucolic poet Bion had once delighted Galatea with his singing:

> Galatea, too, weeps for your music—Galatea, whom you used to delight as she sat with you on the seashore; for you sang nothing like the Cyclops. The lovely Galatea would avoid him, but you were a more welcome sight to her than the

[71] Du Quesnay (1979: 46); Hunter (1999: 229); cf. Pretagostini (2006: 71–2).

[72] Independent: Deuse (1990); Manuwald (1990). *Idyll* 6 is closely related to, and presupposes, *Idyll* 11: Ott (1969: 72); Horstmann (1976: 101); Köhnken (1996).

> sea. Now she has forgotten the waves: she sits on the empty beach and still tends your cattle.[73]

Why the ogre and his beloved should have become so popular is no mystery. Theocritus' imaginative cocktail links two irresistible motifs: the torments of a man who can't live with his girl and can't live without her, and the asymmetrical relationship between Beauty and the Beast—more specifically, a huge, hairy, mis-shapen man lusting after a beautiful girl who habitually swims naked. Amid this emotional turbulence, the landscape plays a role far beyond that of mere background. The heterogeneous combination of high rocks, flowers on the hillside, green and shady pleasance, secluded cave/love nest, and gently murmuring sea sharpens into focus on the shore, where lover and beloved might mingle, but do not. All this constitutes a constellation of the imagery of place distinctive enough to rival that described by Homer himself.

Virgil

To rival it—but not to replace it. For the next major retelling of the myth of Polyphemus looks back precisely to the *Odyssey*. In some respects, in spite of its comparative brevity, the newer version not only echoes its great epic predecessor, but trumps it: the barbarity is more barbarous, the emotion more raw, the landscape richer in symbolic power.

Book 3 of the *Aeneid* continues Aeneas' narration of his voyage from Troy to his present location, the royal palace at Carthage, where, at a banquet, he has nearly finished the process of captivating Queen Dido with his tale of pathos, piety, and heroism. Having already reached Italian waters, his vessels had (he relates) just managed to escape the deadly suction of Charybdis, and were drifting, in a placid sea, towards the shore of the Cyclopes. But the landscape that confronted them was anything but tranquil (3.571–84):

> Close by Mount Etna thunders and hurls down its deadly debris. Sometimes it shoots a pitch-black cloud of swirling smoke and glowing ashes into the sky and tosses up balls of flame to lick the stars. Sometimes it belches boulders, tearing out the bowels of the mountain and throwing molten rock up into the air, seething and groaning in its very depths. The story goes that the body of Enceladus, half-consumed by the fire of the thunderbolt, is crushed under this great mass. Mighty Etna lies on top of him breathing fire from its shattered furnaces and every time he turns over from one weary flank to another the whole of Sicily trembles and murmurs and wreathes the sky with smoke. We hid in the woods

[73] Trans. Hopkinson (2015).

> and lived through a night of horror, not seeing what was making these monstrous sounds.[74]

Whereas Odysseus' first glimpse of Cyclopean territory was mediated by the loamy potential and the zoological abundance of Goat Island, Aeneas is faced with a more terrible prospect: Etna's amalgam of flame, smoke, ash, and rock.[75] In our account of the Cyclopes so far, volcanic activity has been largely confined to the world of the metalworkers, as in Callimachus, and has crept only fleetingly into the story of Polyphemus (as at Eur. *Cyc.* 297–8). But in Virgil's hands such eruptive activity sets the grim tone for the entire Polyphemus episode that follows.[76]

Emerging from the woods (another landscape feature of minimal importance in the *Odyssey*), an emaciated and filthy stranger, his ragged clothing pinned together with thorns, makes his way towards the shore, stretching out his hands in supplication. The astonished Trojans recognize him as a Greek. He gives his name as Achaemenides, and reports that he was left behind by Odysseus in Polyphemus' cave. He has had all too good an opportunity to study that hideous place in close detail: its enormous size, its darkness, its defilement by the Cyclops' gory feasts, its threshold swimming with the blood of victims as they were smashed upon the rock. Caves in the *Aeneid* serve a variety of imaginative purposes. They can be places of confinement (a prison for Aeolus' winds (1.52–4)), havens of tranquillity (a home for the Nymphs in Libya (1.166–8)), womb-like enclosures pregnant with danger and death (the Trojan Horse (2.18–20)), numinous sites of access to greater knowledge (the Sibyl (6.10–12)), locations for ominous love-making (Dido and Aeneas (4.165–6)), portals to the Underworld (6.237), places of new hope for the future (the suckling of Romulus and Remus (8.630–4)). But the closest parallel to Polyphemus' horrifying home is the blood-soaked, cavernous dwelling of monstrous, fire-belching Cacus, whose bestial savagery far outstrips that of the Homeric Polyphemus, and whom only a Hercules could overcome (8.190–267).

Achaemenides continues his tale by recalling Polyphemus' blinding, but only briefly; this is no time to drop one's guard. Polyphemus himself may have returned to his dairy routine in his cave, but there are, warns Achaemenides, a hundred other 'unspeakable' Cyclopes on the warpath, who live not only in the high mountains, as in the *Odyssey*, but also near the shore (3.643–4). To escape is the only possible strategy. Throwing himself on the Trojans' mercy, Achaemenides ends his narrative. Barely has he done so when Polyphemus appears, as if to confirm the veracity of the tale, and to prove to the Trojans that they do not have on their

[74] Trans. D. A. West (1990), here and in subsequent quotations from the *Aeneid*.
[75] On perceptions of Etna in antiquity, see Buxton (2016).
[76] Another Virgilian connection between the Cyclopes and volcanic Etna: *G.* 1.471–3.

hands another treacherous Greek, like perfidious Sinon. In the space of half a Virgilian sentence, Polyphemus drags his great bulk from the high mountain pastureland down to the shore (655–7). As in the *Odyssey*, his animals console him, but in Virgil pathos soon gives way to the macabre, almost Senecan grimness that is so strongly felt in this episode: 'As soon as he felt the waves deepening and reached the level ocean, he washed away with sea water the blood that was still trickling from his gouged-out eye, grinding his teeth and moaning, and as he strode now in mid-ocean, the waves still did not wet his towering flanks' (662–5). Still trickling after three months, we might add—the length of time Achaemenides has been desperately evading capture (645–8).

With the refugee in tow, Aeneas and the Trojans bid to make a silent escape (a total contrast with the Homeric Odysseus' boastful garrulity) but cannot elude the acute hearing of the blind Polyphemus. The passage that follows expresses the characteristically Virgilian symbolic interplay between action and landscape (672–81):

> He raised a great clamour which set the ocean and all its waves shivering. The whole land of Italy trembled with fear and the bellowing boomed in the hollow caverns of Mount Etna. The tribe of Cyclopes was roused and came rushing down from their woods and high mountains to the harbour and filled the shore. We saw the brotherhood of Etna standing there helpless, each with his one eye glaring and head held high in the sky, a fearsome gathering, standing like high-topped mountain oaks or cone-bearing cypresses in Jupiter's soaring forest or the grove of Diana.[77]

There are, it is true, rocks and a cave in Theocritus. But there are no volcanoes, and the gentle murmuring of the Theocritean sea differs *toto caelo* from the bellowing Virgilian deep. There is nothing remotely pastoral about the Cyclopes of the *Aeneid*. Sicilian they may be, but *their* Sicily is the reverse of a *locus amoenus*.

Ovid

The other great Roman poem that decisively inflects the mythology of Polyphemus is Ovid's *Metamorphoses*. Given the fundamental importance of landscape in that magnificent work, it may be helpful to step back in order to provide some context.

The poem teems with the symbolic representation of place. Often the location of mythical events goes beyond mere topographical specificity to achieve generic, iconic status. Unforgettable examples are Narcissus' motionless and shady pool (book 3); the overgrown cave, deep in an ancient forest, that harbours Mars'

[77] Symbolic interplay: Römisch (1976: 224).

serpent, slain by Cadmus (book 3); the barren, hostile, Scythian mountainscape where Hunger scrabbles frantically for food (book 8); the open, grassy hilltop where trees miraculously crowd around when Orpheus sings (book 10). Elsewhere landscape constitutes the ontological marrow of the poem, when individuals undergo transformation into features of the natural environment that are, if not exactly 'alive', then at least impregnated with mythical–narrative depth. Niobe becomes a rock that still trickles with tearlike drops in recollection of her pathetic rashness (book 6); no less tearlike is the amber generated by the trees that used to be Phaethon's grieving sisters (book 2); Atlas is now the great mountain into which Medusa's petrifying head changed him (book 4).

Polyphemus appears twice in the *Metamorphoses*, both times during the account of Aeneas' voyage from Troy to Italy. One of these passages exploits the landscape extensively and with tremendous panache, the other invokes it perfunctorily. We begin with the less exciting of the two.

In book 14 Ovid revisits the Virgilian Achaemenides episode: explicit echoes of the model alternate with elegantly contrived departures from it. Landing on the coast of Latium, Aeneas comes across Macareus, one of Ulixes' former shipmates. Macareus recognizes his compatriot Achaemenides among the Trojans. Achaemenides' humane treatment by his former enemies has calmed his desperation ('his garments no longer pinned with thorns' (166)), but the tale of Cyclopean savagery that he tells is no less chilling than its Virgilian predecessor. As in Virgil, the remembered action oscillates between rocky heights ('I saw when Cyclops tore up a huge rock from the mountain-side...' (181-2); 'he went prowling all over Etna, groping through the woods with his hands, and blindly dashing against the rocks...' (188–90)) and the sea ('then he would stretch out his bleeding arms to the sea' (190–1)). What is missing is any sense of the brooding vastness of the Cyclops' cave home, or any impression of Etna as an awesome presence resonating with the ogre's own savagery. Ovid's version also lacks the situational immediacy of the *Aeneid*, since the Ovidian Achaemenides tells his story on the central Italian mainland, comfortably distant from the Cyclopes' Sicilian home, whereas in the Virgilian account the story is told a stone's throw—literally—from Polyphemus' lair.

The passage from book 13 is quite a different matter. Ovid is at his brilliant best, and the Cyclopean landscape is at the heart of his brilliance. We are at an earlier stage of Aeneas' voyage, when the vessels first arrive at the Sicilian coast; more specifically, at the cliff face where Scylla has her den. Above the waist Scylla is a lovely maiden; below it, her thighs and legs commingle horrifically with an encircling pack of wild dogs; the hideous ambivalence rivals anything imagined by Dante.[78] But it was not always thus. Before her monstrous hybridization, Scylla

[78] On Scylla, Hopman (2012) is fundamental; see also Aguirre Castro (2002).

had spent her time with the sea nymphs, chatting about men, love, hate, and rejection. Her special friend was Galatea. One day Scylla asked her to explain why she was sad. Galatea's reply develops motifs familiar from Theocritus, but transforms and intensifies them, since a new character arrives on the scene, in the shape of the handsome teenage heartthrob Acis. As well as adding a stormy new dimension to the Polyphemus–Galatea relationship, the presence of Acis augments the natural topography. To cave, mountain, pastureland, seashore, and sea is now added a river, Acis' ultimate metamorphic destination. But, before evoking that astonishing change of shape, Ovid, through the eyes and narrating voice of Galatea, variously and ingeniously explores the theme of the landscape.

The overall setting is, as now habitually, Etna (770, etc.). Within that framework, Galatea offers a series of vignettes of Polyphemus' location. In the first of these, the ogre has forsaken his flocks (that is, pastureland) and cave (763), preferring to gaze at his own image 'in water' (767; whether the sea, as in Theocritus, or a rock pool, Galatea does not specify). Next we have a pair of alternative images: Polyphemus either trudges heavily along the shore, or returns wearily to his shady cave (776–7). But his real obsession is gazing at the sea, and for this he needs a vantage point, which Galatea presents in another vignette: 'A wedge-shaped promontory with long, sharp point juts out into the sea, both sides washed by the waves. Hither the fierce Cyclops climbed and sat down on the cliff's central point' (778–80).[79] In order to 'see' this, Galatea has to borrow the perspective of the main narrator, for she herself is, within the picture she paints, hiding far away under a rock, in the lap of her beloved Acis, and able only to *hear* Polyphemus as he sings to her (786–8).[80] Once his long and elaborate song is over, the action takes a new direction (so far as we can tell) in relation to the tradition. Polyphemus catches sight of the amorous couple, and vows to vent his wrath upon them. Galatea dives into the sea, but Acis runs away on land. Polyphemus breaks off a part of a mountain and hurls it at Acis; although only the edge of the rock reaches him, it is enough, reports Galatea, to crush him. In manipulating a rock, Polyphemus performs a classically Cyclopean action: the builders did it professionally; Homer's Polyphemus did it when he blocked his cave entrance, and later when he bombarded the ships of the escaping Greeks. But the blocking of the cave ultimately failed in its purpose, as did the bombardment; the crushing of Acis is the first time Polyphemus *successfully* handles a rock. It is an act that exemplifies a familiar mythological theme, whereby rocks are used as aggressive

[79] Trans. F. J. Miller.

[80] The scene is partly recreated in Ottin's sculpture in the Jardin du Luxembourg, though there the loving couple are immediately below Polyphemus rather than 'far away' (*Cat. 116* (Fig. 10.27)); see pp. 288–9.

weapons by primordial and/or monstrous beings. The Hundred-Handers, the Giants, Talos, the Centaurs, and the Laestrygonians all adopt the same tactic.[81]

As well as evoking the external environment and situating a sequence of actions within it, Galatea's narrative demands our attention for two other reasons, in relation first to Polyphemus' song, and then to the fusion of the human with the environmental.

The song of the ogre (still embedded in Galatea's narrative) is a *tour de force*, even by Ovid's standards. Throughout his attempted, grotesquely overblown persuasion of Galatea to become his lover, Polyphemus boasts of how he controls the landscape—or at least most of it. In part this control is a matter of simple ownership. He claims for his own domain a mountainside, caves, all manner of trees, as well as the flocks that wander in valleys and woods before returning to their cave-folds (810–22). His writ runs even on the summit of the mountain, where he found two bear cubs for Galatea to play with (834–7). Only the sea escapes his sway, which is why he urges Galatea to forsake it (838–9). More interesting than such instances of 'practical' control are repeated examples of *linguistic* control, this time including the sea. In simile after simile, trumping the rhetoric used by his Theocritean model in *Idyll* 11, Polyphemus heaps praise and then blame on Galatea by comparing her to the surrounding natural environment: 'more blooming than meadows…smoother than shells worn by the insistent sea…more beautiful than a well-watered garden…more perfidious than the waves…more immovable than these rocks, more boisterous than a river…deafer than the waves…' (791–804).[82] This is an ogre who is, he keeps telling himself, confident in his possessions, and ascendant over his surroundings.

Yet there is another aspect of Galatea's story that implies an altogether more intimate relationship between the natural world and those who inhabit it, a relationship that involves not domination and possession, but temperamental affinity, and even identity. The woods tremble at the sight of Polyphemus (759–60); the mountains and waves sense his music (785–6); the ogre burns with passion as if he carries the violent force of Etna within him (867–9); when he bellows, Etna shudders at the terrible sound (876–7). Such eco-empathy lies at the very heart of the *Metamorphoses*, which privileges flux and mingling over sharp edges and differentiation. So it is the reverse of surprising that the episode ends in a complex transformation, which changes forever the mythical topography of the setting (885–97):

[81] Hundred-Handers: Hes. *Theog*. 715–17. Giants: among numerous iconographical examples is *LIMC* 'Gigantes' no. 316. Talos: silver didrachm from Phaistos, Bibliothèque Nationale de France, Paris, Département de Monnaies, Médailles et Antiques (LUYNES.2365), illustrated in Buxton (2013b: 79). Centaurs: again iconographically frequent, e.g. *LIMC* 'Kentauroi et Kentaurides' no. 183. Laestrygonians: *Od*. 10.121–2.

[82] Our translation.

> Still, I did the one thing the fates allowed, and enabled him to assume the powers that belonged to his family of old. The crimson blood that trickled from under the massive rock began, in a brief space, to lose its redness, taking on at first the hue of a river discoloured by rain, but gradually clearing. Then the rock that Polyphemus had thrown split open and, through the gash, a tall sturdy reed pushed upwards. From the gaping crevasse roared leaping waters, and then something astonishing happened. Suddenly a young man, wearing a garland of waving rushes round his newly grown horns, rose out of the fissure, as far as his waist. Except that he was larger, and his face all a deep blue, it was Acis. Even in this form, he was Acis still, but Acis changed into a river, whose waters retain his original name.[83]

Astonishing indeed (*miraque res* (893)). A squashed, bleeding, dying teenager changes into a river, which not only displays the everyday characteristics of flowing, fresh water, but also simultaneously appears in the shape of a partially anthropomorphic river god, literally a reincarnation of its/his parents: Faunus, the horned deity of forest and field, and Simaethis, nymph eponym of another Sicilian river. The Cyclopean landscape, like Acis himself, will never be the same again.

The transformation of Acis brings Galatea's narrative to an end; the group of sea nymphs disperses, and Scylla goes on her way. Surely some sort of narrative closure ought to be implied? But in this poem there is no such thing. Scylla's fate is to be wooed by another marine hybrid, Glaucus; to reject him; to be horrendously transformed, thanks to a potion supplied by Circe (who loved Glaucus, but was rejected by him); and finally, now a monster, to take up residence in her cave, lying in wait for Ulysses, and in due course for Aeneas. Polyphemus, meanwhile, will wait in *his* cave, for the same two heroes to pass by.

Philostratus

It is surprisingly rare to find an author in classical antiquity who writes penetrating art criticism. One of the exceptions is Philostratus the Elder (*fl.* 3rd cent CE).[84] Among the writings with which he was credited is *Imagines* ('Images'), a brilliant evocation of a collection of works of art.[85] In introductory remarks the text's narrator tells us he had been staying near Naples with a friend, the owner of a fine set of *pinakes* (panel paintings). At the insistence of his friend's precocious 10-year-old son, Philostratus gave a discourse in which he described and interpreted the paintings.

[83] Trans. M. M. Innes, adapted.
[84] On Philostratus in general, see Anderson (1986); Billault (2000); Bowie and Elsner (2009).
[85] On *Imagines*, see e.g. Conan (1987); Bryson (1994); Schönberger (1995).

In many of the works delineated in *Imagines*, the landscape is dominant. The citadel and plain of Troy provide the backdrop for the contending elements of fire and water, as Hephaestus battles with the River Scamander (1.1). Cupids gather apples from trees growing in straight rows in a lovely garden; the trees are irrigated from a spring of deep blue water, beneath an overarching rock (1.6). A richly fertile marsh, encompassed by high mountains, is described in loving detail, complete with goatherds, shepherds, and all manner of plant and bird life, including swans ridden by Cupids (1.9). A representation of the fate of Pentheus contrasts the mountainous Dionysiac background of Cithaeron (ivy, fir, and grapes) with the Theban palace in the foreground (1.18). More grapes and ivy surround the pool into which the enraptured Narcissus gazes (1.23). The beautiful caves and springs of Mount Pelion provide the setting for a rare portrait of female Centaurs (2.3). The tempestuous seascape where the ship of Ajax the Locrian was wrecked is depicted in a manner reminiscent of Delacroix at his most dramatic (2.13). To cap it all, a virtuoso account of a series of 'Islands' links sumptuous visual description with accounts of the divinities associated with these sharply contrasting places (2.17).[86]

In 'Cyclops' (2.18), as with many of the other paintings, the description embraces more than one landscape feature.[87] As the narrator guides the eyes of the reader/viewer, the first focus is on a group of Cyclopes harvesting agricultural land and picking grapes; the allusion to *Od.* 9.106–11 is quite explicit, since in Homer, precisely as in Philostratus, it is said that the earth bears its fruits for them spontaneously.[88] But the narrator immediately segues from the Homeric Cyclopes to the Theocritean Polyphemus, introducing a vignette that constitutes the whole of the rest of 2.18.[89] Galatea is playing on the smooth sea, while her would-be lover watches her from the mountain. He is evidently on the mountain*side* rather than on a peak, however, since he sings to Galatea 'under a *prinos* [evergreen oak]'. But, for all he cares, he might be anywhere, since 'he doesn't know, any longer, where the earth is'—appropriately enough, since all that matters to him is the sea. For her part, Galatea drives a four-dolphin team, holding above her head a purple scarf/sail, in a gesture with an enormously influential artistic legacy.[90] Galatea's focus, like Polyphemus', is on the sea, since her look 'travels as far as the sea extends'.[91]

As Michael Squire puts it, 'Philostratus marshals together the literary and visual treatments of the myth [of the Cyclopes] in one fell iconotextual swoop'.[92] The prospect of seeing the picture with one's own eyes, as opposed to those of the narrator, is a mouth-watering one, but with no prospect of realization (even

[86] Baumann (2011: 76–87); Miles (2013: 128–32).

[87] See e.g. Kostopoulou (2009).

[88] Guiding by narrator: Beall (1993: 353); Squire (2009: 348–9).

[89] Homer and Theocritus in 2.18: Squire (2009: 344–8).

[90] See Rizzo (1939).

[91] On 'looking' in 2.18, see p. 121.

[92] Squire (2009: 348).

assuming the painting ever existed in the first place). But what we can do is to set the Philostratean and all the other textual versions of Cyclopean mythology alongside their *extant* artistic counterparts—as well, of course, as viewing those extant images within their own visual contexts.

Writers against the current

A recurring theme so far has been the relationship between the Cyclopes and the sea. Already in the *Odyssey* that relationship is fraught with ambiguity: in spite of the marine ancestry of Polyphemus (at least), *all* the Homeric Cyclopes remain landlubbers. But there existed a rival tradition according to which Polyphemus was no stranger to sailing. In spite of the lateness of our sources for this alternative storyline, it may go back much earlier—even, it has been ingeniously argued, to the time of the composition of the Homeric poems themselves.[93]

Commenting on a passage from near the beginning of the *Odyssey* in which Athene, in the form of Mentes, misleadingly tells Telemachus that his father is being detained by *andres…agrioi* ('wild men' (1.196–9)), a scholiast on Homer explains the allusion like this:

> That is to say, the Cyclops and those who were with him. For after Odysseus abducted the Cyclops' daughter, whom he loved as his own eye, the Cyclops, by his great strength of body, made ships and chased after Odysseus. And in this manner he prevented Odysseus from turning back toward his homeland.[94]

Another scholiast notes that 'the Cyclops outfitted ships, pursued [Odysseus], and killed many of his men. He forced Odysseus to wander on the sea.'[95] According to yet another ancient commentator, it was Polyphemus' sister whom Odysseus carried off (their brothers being Cyclops and Antitheus);[96] two other sources, again late, report that Polyphemus' daughter had fallen in love with one of Odysseus' crewmen.[97] What concerns us here is not the Cyclops' entirely unhomeric familial situation, but the sea. That Polyphemus is credited with the ability to build ships and to navigate could be interpreted as a deliberate rejection of the account in the *Odyssey*, especially the emphasis in that epic on the fact that Goat Island was a safe haven for the Greeks because the Cyclopes had no ships. Andrew Alwine has argued that what we have here is a deliberate Homeric polemic against a rival version, 'suggestive of the intensity of interactions among competing narrative traditions and the sophistication of both the ancient Greek

[93] Argued by Alwine (2009), a fine article from which we have borrowed extensively and gratefully.

[94] Schol. PY on *Od.* 1.198; trans. Alwine (2009: 326).

[95] Schol. Y on *Od.* 1.69; trans. Alwine (2009: 326–7).

[96] Schol. M^1 on *Od.* 1.69; cf. Alwine (2009: 327).

[97] Dict. Cret. 6.5; John Malalas, *Chron.* 5.18.75–8 Thurn; cf. Alwine (2009: 328–9).

epic singers who performed canonical and non-canonical songs and the audiences who listened to them'.[98] The case is a persuasive one; with earlier evidence for the rival tradition, it would be stronger still.

Cyclopean Spaces in Art

Few visual explorations of Cyclopean landscapes can match the richness, detail, and complexity to be found in many of the written sources. Sometimes, as in the case of individual portrait heads, there is no natural setting whatever, or at least none that we can recover (e.g. *Cat. 32* and *59* (Fig. 4.12)). On small-scale, mobile objects such as vases, the presence of a landscape is usually suggested in a perfunctory or schematic way. Only when it comes to larger-scale, fixed media such as wall paintings or mosaics is there scope for greater variety and detail. There are also fascinating cases where the very placing of the art object conjures up a Cyclopean landscape. Classic examples are two representations of the blinding: the sculptural group in the grotto at Sperlonga (*Cat. 39* (Fig. 4.3)) and the fresco located in the underground, funerary setting of the Tomb of Orcus II at Tarquinia (*Cat. 31* (Fig. 4.15)).

We begin with some general comments about the evocation of the natural environment in these various types of image, before looking in particular at two landscape features: the sea and the cave.

Natural settings

Investigating how Greek and Roman artists depict the natural environments within which mythological events take place is a complex matter.[99] We shall try to tease out some of the complications by examining relevant material on a genre-by-genre basis. Given the absence of artistic representations of the mason Cyclopes, and the exiguous evidence for the natural setting within which the metalworking Cyclopes worked, our attention will be directed overwhelmingly at the pastoral ogres, and specifically at Polyphemus, first in his encounter with Odysseus, and then in his relationship with Galatea.

Although natural landscapes are never portrayed in detail in Greek vase painting—unlike, say, what we see on Chinese or eighteenth-century Worcester porcelain—there are still countless instances in which Greek vase-painters represent

[98] Alwine (2009: 333). [99] Cf. Schnapp (2015).

elements of the natural world.[100] Sometimes such elements bear a pointed mythological significance: the apple tree of the Hesperides, or the Colchian grove in which the Golden Fleece hung. In other cases trees or plants appear as mere decorative space-fillers. Even when, as already on black-figure vases, we can detect an increasing tendency to portray natural settings, these invariably take second place to the human figure. We look in vain for mountainous landscapes; nor, usually, is there a sharp differentiation between land and sky, or between land and sea. An apparent exception is a Caeretan hydria depicting Europa on the bull.[101] The sea she is crossing is suggested by a dolphin; the land she is approaching is indicated by a rocky undulation, three trees, and a hare. But even here the land/sea opposition is symbolic rather than graphically precise: instead of swimming in tangible water, the dolphin is suspended in free space. This degree of schematism is typical of the semiotic system of painted Greek vases. To decipher the natural setting of a scene, the spectator has to know the code: fishes for the sea, rocks for a cave, vines for a Dionysiac environment, and so on.[102]

Greek vase paintings of Polyphemus' encounter with Odysseus correspond to this broader semiotic practice. Although we never find any hint that the episode was envisaged as taking place on a mountain, much less that its specific location was Sicilian Etna, we do come across various pointers to the imagined setting. In representations of the blinding, for example, a countryside environment is often suggested by the presence of an occasional branch or tree. Thus a black-figure oenochoe (*Cat. 17*) represents the scene against the background of some schematic branches with leaves. A Lucanian krater (*Cat. 27* (Fig. 4.13)) augments the overall impression of rusticity (huge tree trunk used for the blinding; satyrs present on all sides) with an upright tree branch with a wineskin hanging on it. On an Etruscan pithos (*Cat. 5* (Fig. 4.7)), the flora is more idiosyncratic: 'odd plants frame this scene: behind Polyphemos are large conical blossoms hung with fillets and to our far left a tall, narrow plant that looks like a tree bearing lollipops.'[103] In some representations of the blinding it looks as if 'purely decorative' is the best we can do to describe the presence of nature, as with the flowerlike designs on the proto-Attic amphora from Eleusis (*Cat. 1* (Fig. 2.1)). But occasionally the imagery is more thought-provoking. On a Laconian cup (*Cat. 10* (Fig. 3.1)) the body of a snake extends like a sinuous canopy above the assault party. Situated below Polyphemus, who sits on a rock, is a very sizeable fish. That the snake and the

[100] See Nelson (1976) on the multiple variations in such representations; Sena Chiesa and Pontrandolfo (2015).

[101] Rome, Museo Nazionale Etrusco di Villa Giulia inv. 50643, *c.*525 BCE = *LIMC* 'Europe I' no. 24; illustrated in Sena Chiesa and Pontrandolfo (2015: 43, 84).

[102] See Siebert (1990: 155).

[103] The description is by K. Hamma, in True and Hamma (1994: 184).

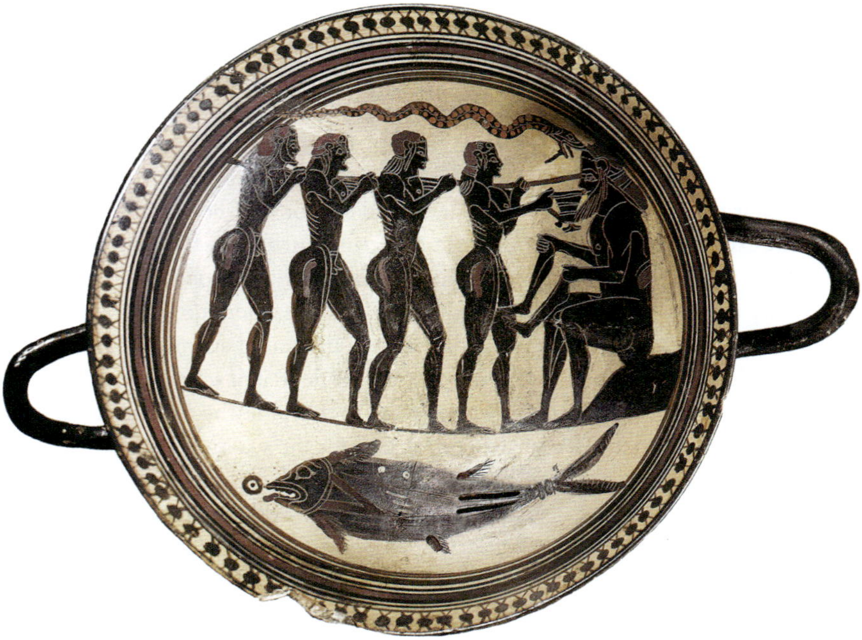

Fig. 3.1. Polyphemus as eater of men. Laconian black-figure cup, *c.*550 BCE.

rock together signify 'land'—more specifically, the cave where the ogre lived—and the fish 'sea' is plausible enough, though hardly definitive.[104]

On vases portraying the sub-ovine escape, we again typically find a rustic environment evoked by a tree or branches beside or behind the blinded Polyphemus (e.g. *Cat. 23*), or, if the ogre himself is absent, behind the rams. A seemingly incongruous feature of such images is that, although the vegetation 'should' grow *outside* the ogre's cave, the scene of the rams' exit 'should' take place *inside*—at least on a 'Homeric' reading of the action's location. But there is no need to fuss about a blending of interior and exterior, which is no more than a spatial equivalent of the synoptic presentation regularly found in Greek vase painting, whereby scenes from different moments in a narrative appear side by side.

The same general pattern—minimalist vegetation signifying a generic rural setting—recurs on three other vessels, all Hellenistic, and all dealing with the offering of wine by Odysseus. On a relief bowl from Porsuk in southern Cappadocia (*Cat. 33* (Fig. 5.5)), three trees suffice to suggest a non-urban landscape, while on two Etruscan urns (*Cat. 34* and *35*) the same purpose is served by

[104] See Buitron and Cohen (1992: 61). Other interpretations in Touchefeu-Meynier (1968: 14–15).

trees and vegetation. However in other artistic media, especially mosaics and wall paintings, there was a move during the Hellenistic and Roman periods towards the depiction of more extensive and detailed landscape backgrounds.[105] It would be misleading to describe this as a drive for photographic realism: artists still worked with recurring schemata—as artists always do—relating to both the natural and the built environment.[106] These schemata involved mountains, rocks, trees, meadows, and the sea, as well as architectural features such as temples and isolated columns. To this representative style belong several portrayals of the relationship between Polyphemus and Galatea.

One such is a remarkable painting from the House of Livia on the Palatine (*Cat. 40* (Fig. 4.6)). Polyphemus, like Galatea and some of her sister nymphs, is in the water, holding onto a big rock; in the background is a rocky coastline upon which grows a substantial tree. It is as if the painter wanted to realize visually the implications of Polyphemus' Theocritean yearnings to join his beloved in her own element.[107] Commoner in Roman representations, however—as in literary portrayals too—is a Polyphemus confined to the shore. On a mosaic from Cordoba he sits on some rocks at the shoreline; behind him extends a mountainous landscape adorned with vegetation (*Cat. 71* (Fig. 4.5)). Another littoral Polyphemus appears on a painting from Herculaneum; a cherubic Eros, mounted on a dolphin, is handing him a letter (*Cat. 53* (Fig. 8.3)). Less emotionally intriguing, but more dramatic in terms of landscape, is a painting from Boscotrecase (*Cat. 41* (Fig. 3.2)). There are rocks in the foreground and steeply wooded slopes behind, which have been interpreted as those of Mount Etna.[108] A cleaning of the work has also revealed a hitherto hidden detail: the mouth of a large cave. Goats climbing on the rocky outcrops lend, by association, a pastoral quality to the scene, even if there is little sign of grassy meadowland. In other, thematically comparable paintings, the background varies. Sometimes the impression is that of an assemblage of buildings, gardens, and vineyards reminiscent of contemporary Roman villas, converting the Cyclopean pastoral into (in Michael Squire's apt formulation) 'the sort of modern seaside resort so beloved by rich Roman city-dwellers'.[109]

[105] See Ling (1991: index s.v. 'landscape paintings').

[106] On the inevitability of the use of schemata by artists, one need only refer to the great work of Sir Ernst Gombrich—e.g. Gombrich (1960).

[107] Theoc. *Id.* 11.54–5, with Leach (1992: 70).

[108] Cf. von Blanckenhagen and Alexander (1962: 42–3).

[109] Squire (2009: 313). It has to be borne in mind, however, that some of these paintings survive only in the form of drawings made in the nineteenth century; cf. Squire (2009: 311–12 n. 31).

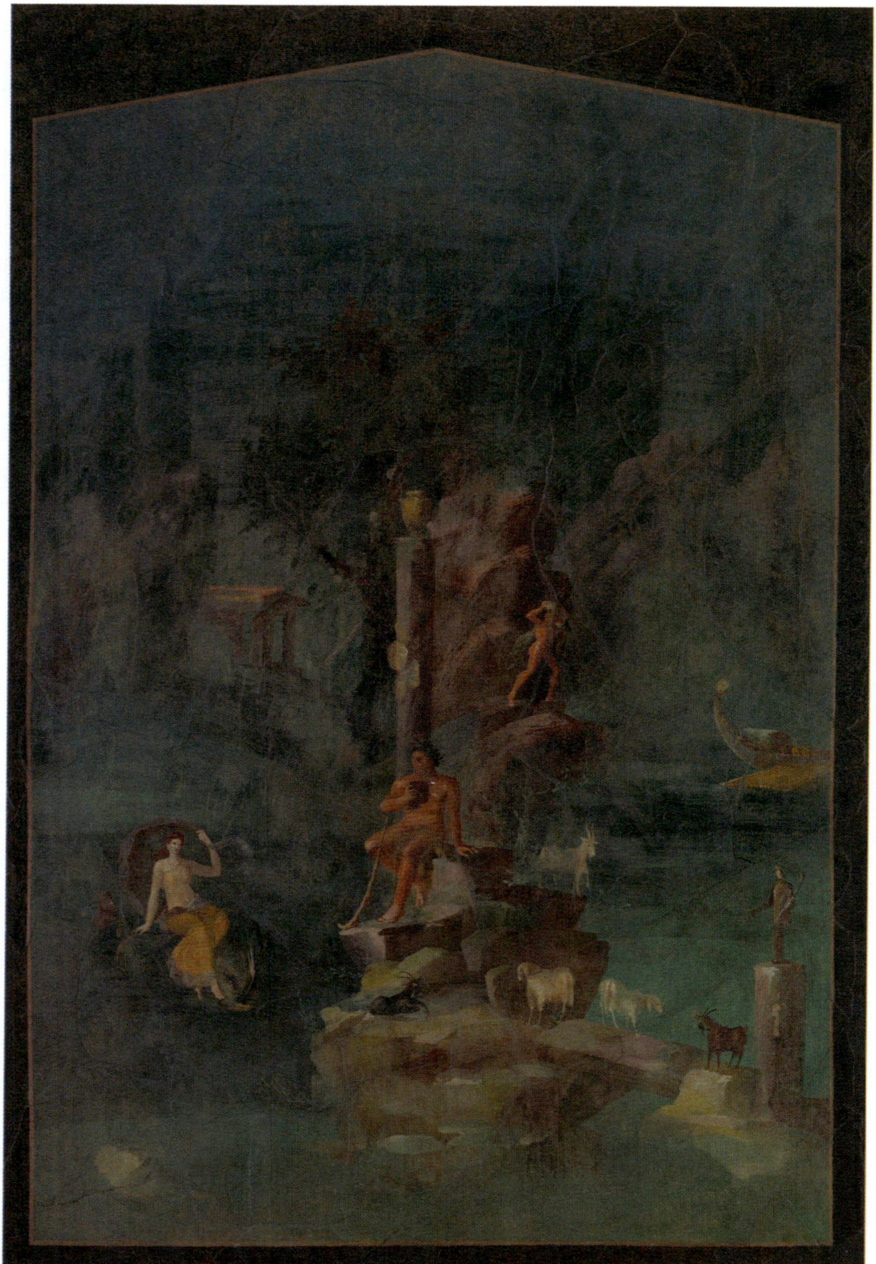

Fig. 3.2. Polyphemus in two contrasting poses. Wall painting from villa at Boscotrecase, 1st cent. BCE.

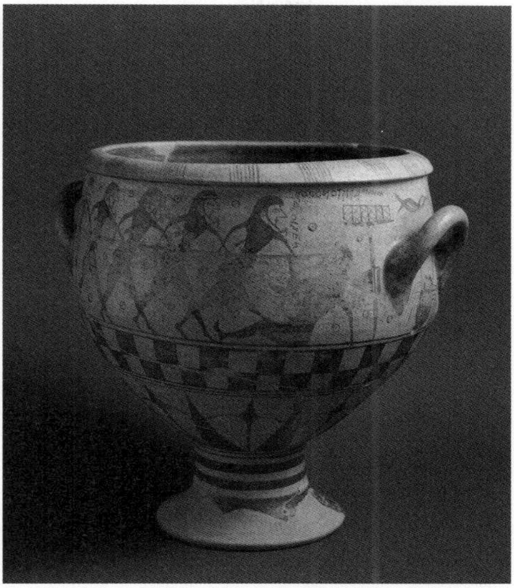

Fig. 3.3. The blinding again. One side of the Aristonothos krater, 675–650 BCE.

Sea

On Greek painted pottery, there are no certain depictions of Polyphemus threatening or attacking Odysseus' ship; the only possible exception is a fragmentary black-figure Attic *phormiskos* (a pear-shaped vase), but the interpretation is dubious.[110] The sea is also largely absent from representations of the offering of wine, the blinding, and the escape under the rams, though this time there are two possible exceptions. One is the Laconian cup (*Cat. 10* (Fig. 3.1)), if we interpret the fish as symbolizing the element that it inhabits. Far more controversial is the 'Aristonothos krater' (*Cat. 3* (Figs 3.3 and 3.4)), found in an Etruscan tomb at Cerveteri; the vase is named for the potter who signed it.[111] It bears two contrasting images. On one side is the blinding of Polyphemus, in a version that shows striking similarities to *Odyssey* book 9: a line of five men holds a long stake at waist level, driving it into the eye of the ogre seated at the far right. The other side depicts a sea battle. To the left of this latter scene is a vessel with rowers below and armed men above, carrying circular shields; the vessel itself has a large eye to bring it startlingly to life. The ship on the right also carries a contingent of warriors with circular shields, but it looks different from the other vessel, especially because of its deck supported on struts. Do the two scenes relate to each other? Much scholarly capital has been invested in the idea that both reflect a politico-military confrontation between, on the one hand, the Greeks of Sicily, and, on the

[110] Tübingen S./10 1507 = *LIMC* 'Odysseus' p. 960, section B. 4. See Mommsen (1982).

[111] Hurwit (2015: 71–3, with his pl. II and fig. 33).

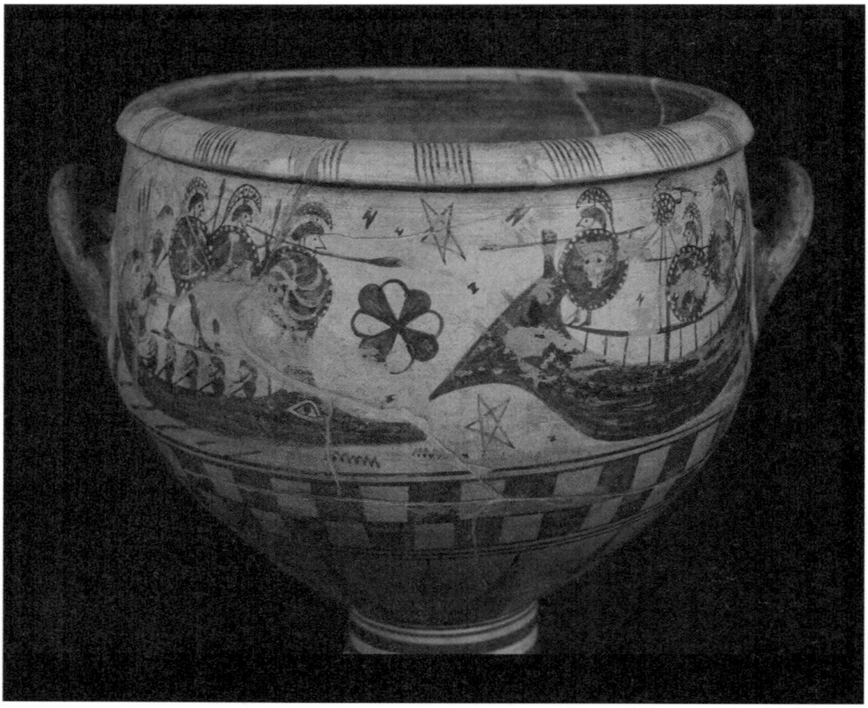

Fig. 3.4. Scene of naval battle. The other side of the Aristonothos krater, 675–650 BCE.

other, the Etruscans.[112] Mario Torelli locates the vase within the framework of an Etruscan elite attempting to identify with Greek heroes: the naval battle is then a conflict between Etruria and (Sicilian) Greeks, while the scene of the blinding confronts Odysseus (*qua* hero with whom Etruscans identify) with Cyclops (= Sicilian Greek).[113] Less contorted is the identification proposed by Marina Martelli, between Polyphemus and the Etruscans, a parallel suggested visually by the fact that both foes-of-the-Greeks are situated to the right of their respective images.[114] One may add that the left-situated ship has an eye, and that in between the Greeks who do the blinding there is a scattering of decorative eye motifs: vision is on the side of the Greeks, but lacking to their opponents.

Also belonging to an Etruscan context, but much less ambiguous in imagery, are two urns portraying maritime events. On the more poorly preserved of the two, from Volterra (*Cat. 34*), two men onboard a ship contemplate events

[112] For discussion with earlier bibliography, see Dougherty (2003: 36–7); also Izzet (2004) and Harari (2014), among many others.

[113] Torelli (1996: 568).

[114] Martelli (1987: 264).

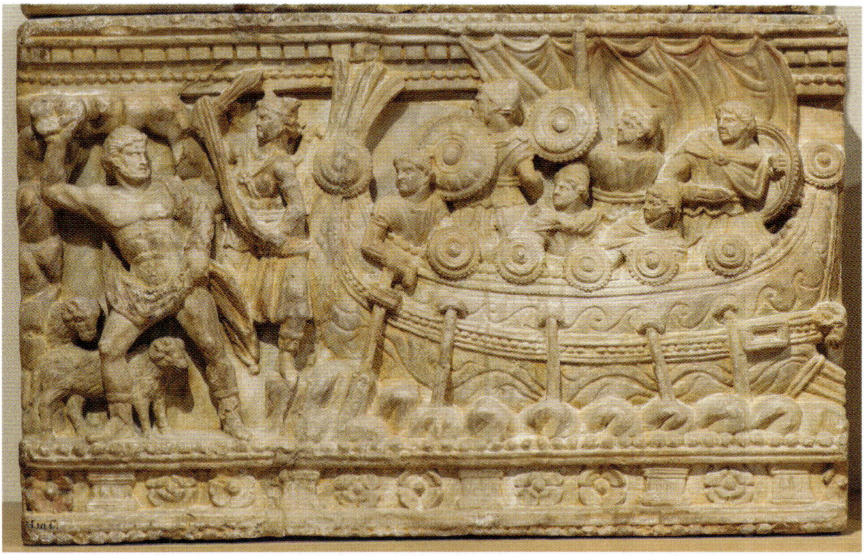

Fig. 3.5. Polyphemus the rock-thrower. Etruscan alabaster urn, *c.*150–100 BCE.

taking place before them: Odysseus and his men are preparing for the blinding in a setting that schematically suggests a cave surrounded by trees. In better condition and more interesting is a second urn, also from Volterra (*Cat. 37* (Fig. 3.5)).[115] The scene depicts the departure of Odysseus and his men from Cyclopean territory. Six grim-faced sailors on a substantial vessel are, we presume, sailing away from the shore, upon which a heroic-looking Polyphemus, boulder in hand, is poised, again following Homeric precedent, to scupper the planned escape. Between the Cyclops and his adversaries there appears a sword-wielding figure probably to be identified as a Lasa, a female Etruscan *daimōn*. Schematic waves beneath the vessel complement the picture. More fragmentary, but similar in subject, is a part of the clay mould for a piece of late-Augustan Arretine pottery (*Cat. 42*).[116] A figure we presume to be Odysseus, characteristically wearing the conical travelling hat known as a *pilos*, can be seen below a furled sail. A naked Polyphemus brandishes a massive rock, ready to launch it at the vessel.

In images of Polyphemus and Galatea, the sea becomes more than a before-and-after bracket. It lies at the very heart of the (non-)relationship between the ill-matched couple, whether as the space that divides them or, much more rarely, as the place where they come together. Symbolizing her attachment to the deep is

[115] Finely described in Andreae and Parisi Presicce (1996: 181 = 3.15 in their catalogue).

[116] See Porten Palange (1973); Andreae and Parisi Presicce (1996: 126 = 2.9 in their catalogue).

the sea nymph's association with marine animals: she is often shown riding a hippocamp or a dolphin. Polyphemus usually stays on land, except in the unusual painting in the House of Livia (*Cat. 40* (Fig. 4.6)).[117] In the scene from the villa at Boscotrecase (*Cat. 41* (Fig. 3.2)), the Cyclops sits on a rock surrounded by his flock, while to the viewer's left Galatea is seated on a dolphin: though they are physically close, the symbolic distance between them could not be clearer. Nor is this the only respect in which Polyphemus' separation from the sea is implied. Higher up on the mountain there is another, perspectivally smaller figure of Polyphemus, wielding a rock that he is about to launch at a vessel. The sea separates Polyphemus from his foes as well as from his beloved.

One other maritime image of Polyphemus is distinctive in that—at least on one possible reading—it brings him into contact with Aeneas, as Virgil and Ovid had done. On a wall painting from the House of Laocoon in Pompeii (*Cat. 52* (Fig. 3.6)) the ogre stands, as so often, on the shore, surrounded by his flock. To the viewer's right is a ship from which a number of men have presumably disembarked. At their head is the figure who might (if we allow the Latin epic tradition to fill in the gaps) be interpreted as Aeneas.[118] This time, unlike the earlier arrival of Odysseus and his men from across the sea, the vessel does not portend danger for Polyphemus. But it is still a place of suspicion, where he does not belong.

Cave

Instead of using gradations of light, colour, and perspective to suggest differentiations between the interior and exterior of a cave and within the cave itself, Greek vase-painters adopted a more schematic approach. Inside and outside are demarcated by a contour signifying the cave's rocky surrounds. The shape of the contour varies depending on whether the cave is viewed in profile or frontally; in the latter case, its usual form is that of an irregular arch. Complementing the demarcation is an iconographical schema that combines rocks with vegetation such as bushes and trees: 'the cave is a landscape of stone and greenery,' writes the most authoritative scholar on this topic.[119]

In early Greek representations, Polyphemus' dwelling appears complete only once, on a black-figure lekythos illustrating the Greeks' escape (*Cat. 26*). The cave is presented frontally, and sports the usual vegetation; Polyphemus, approached by two rams, half-reclines within.[120] Similar in this respect is a Campanian krater

[117] See p. 67.

[118] Drawing in Squire (2009: 324, fig. 5.21); *LIMC* 'Polyphemus I' no. 52 = 'Aineias' no. 208.

[119] Siebert (1990: 153); our translation.

[120] The vase appears not to be catalogued in *LIMC*. Found at Picrodafni in Attica, it was formerly in the Rhousopoulos collection in Athens (Touchefeu-Meynier 1968: 50 no. 123): 'maintenant à

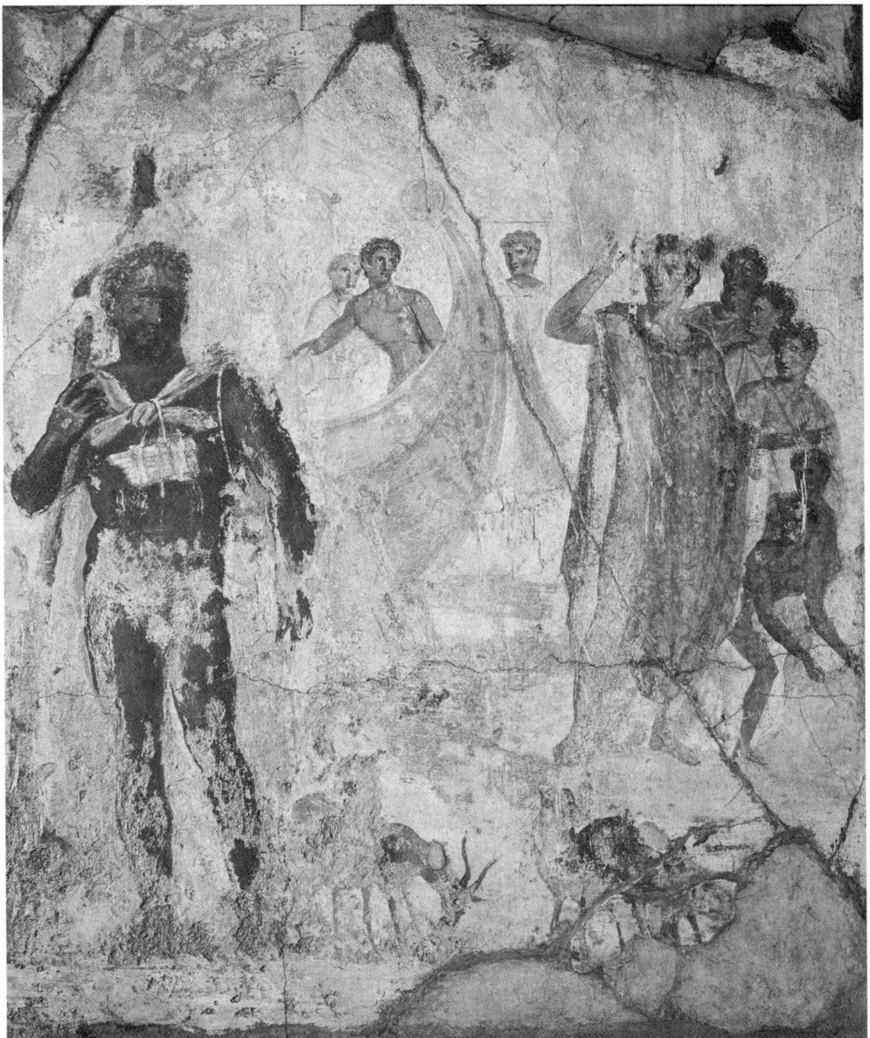

Fig. 3.6. Polyphemus with Aeneas? Wall painting from House of Laocoon at Pompeii, 1st cent. CE.

(*Cat. 28* (Fig. 4.2)), on which a kneeling Polyphemus roasts two human victims on spits: the frontally displayed cave mouth is an irregular outline, with schematic vegetation on either side. In depictions of the Greeks slung underneath the rams,

Edimbourg?'). A drawing appeared in Perdrizet (1897: figs 1 and 2), reproduced by Siebert (1990) as pl. II, fig. 2.

the most significant part of the cave is, for obvious reasons, the rock door. A red-figure stamnos represents Polyphemus apparently supporting himself against this rock, or maybe pushing it out of the way to allow the rams to go out (*Cat. 25* (Fig. 5.4)). In other cases, the cave is conventionally indicated by rocks that the ogre sits on (*Cat. 10* (Fig. 3.1)) or reclines against (*Cat. 2* and *17*).[121] But this convention is not rigid. Some vases depict him sitting or lying on the floor, without a rock in sight (*Cat. 3* (Fig. 3.3), *9*, and *27* (Fig. 4.13)).

A number of works of Etruscan art give their own, sometimes unprecedented representations of the Cyclopean cave. On three urns, its outline is displayed frontally as an archway. One image, depicting the blinding, shows Polyphemus flat on his back in front of his rocky home, which looks smaller than he is (*Cat. 34*).[122] Another, portraying Odysseus offering the wine, shows the cave as proportionally even smaller—more like a dog kennel than an ogre's residence (*Cat. 35*). On the third, Polyphemus is poised to throw a boulder at the Greeks' ship from his rocky, arch-shaped home (*Cat. 37* (Fig. 3.5)). By contrast, two more images from Etruria include items of domestic furniture that, unlike many representations of the Cyclopean cave, stress interiority. On a pithos (*Cat. 5* (Fig. 4.7)), Polyphemus, in the act of being blinded, is comfortably seated on what looks like a wooden stool with nicely carved legs, a detail that makes it more difficult to read the scene as distinguishing 'civilized' Greeks from a 'barbarous' foe. With this we may contrast the famous wall painting in the Tomb of Orcus II in Tarquinia (*Cat. 31* (Fig. 4.15)). In the scene of the blinding, the reclining ogre appears at his most grotesquely unprepossessing, yet in the background is an admirably rectangular door. Barbaric he may be, but at least his home shows evidence of serviceable workmanship. The physical context adds resonance to this aspect of the image. The Tomb of Orcus is a rock-cut underground chamber, the entrance to which was blocked by a stone that functioned as a door. As Cornelia Weber-Lehmann has persuasively suggested, it is as if the painted door echoes and complements the actual door of the tomb, thus fusing the imaginary scene with its real-world context.[123]

In perhaps the best known of all Roman representations of Polyphemus, the sculptural group at Sperlonga (*Cat. 39* (Fig. 4.3)), an analogous exploitation of natural surroundings—in this case, a natural grotto—sets off the image. The posture of the ogre harks back to some of the earliest Greek images: obliviously supine and sprawled out on rocks, he will soon be blinded by the (comparatively)

[121] Contrasting evocations of a rocky, extra-urban landscape through the image of a figure seated on a rock: Odysseus encountering Elpenor in/near/at the edge of the Underworld (red-figure pelike, Boston MFA 34.79 = *LIMC* 'Elpenor' no. 6, cf. Nelson (1976: 37–8)); Paris greeting Hermes on Mount Ida (red-figure stamnos, Antikensammlung, Staatliche Museen zu Berlin F2182 = *LIMC* 'Paridis iudicium' no. 104).

[122] Touchefeu-Meynier (1968: 40–1 no. 97).

[123] See Weber-Lehmann (1996: 160–1).

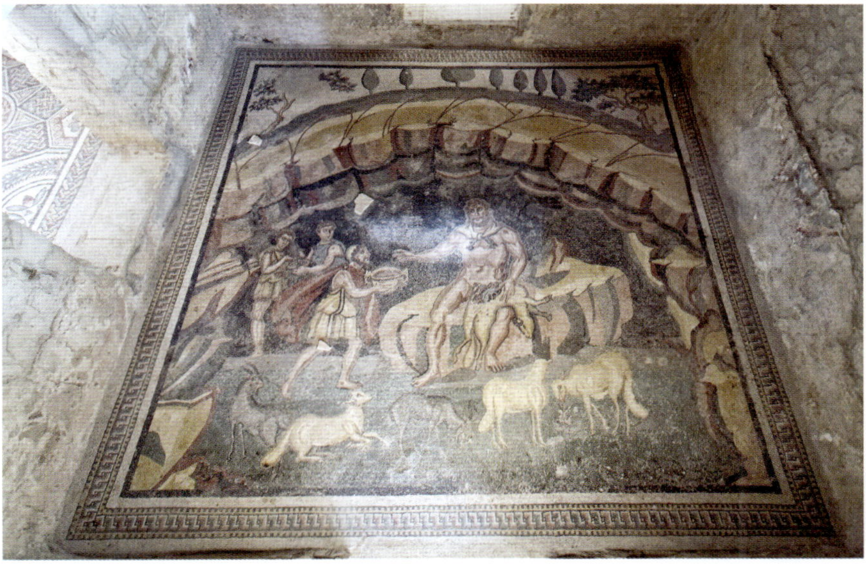

Fig. 3.7. Odysseus offers wine to Polyphemus. Floor mosaic from villa at Piazza Armerina, Sicily, 3rd–4th cent. CE

diminutive Greeks who surround him. Also drawing on traditional schemata, from the point of view of the natural setting, is the mosaic from Piazza Armerina (*Cat. 72* (Fig. 3.7)) in which Polyphemus receives Odysseus' offering of wine while seated on a rock, framed by the frontally presented arch of his cave. A unique feature is the orderly and symmetrical row of various trees shown as surmounting the arch, their dwarfish appearance plainly indicating that they are to be regarded in perspective. In contrast to these grotto-based images, the predominant strategy in Roman representations of Polyphemus and Galatea is to show the ogre in the open air, drawn out of his dwelling by the lure of his beloved. The only exception would seem to be the Boscotrecase painting (*Cat. 41* (Fig. 3.2)), where a large cave situated on a plain can be seen in the background.

We end with a brief word about the metalworkers, in representations of whom the landscape is all but absent. While the presumption may be that the action takes place in a cave, there is rarely any indication of an exterior landscape within which to localize it. An exception is a Roman sarcophagus that portrays the Cyclopes hard at work at the forge, framed by surrounding vegetation in the form of trees (*Cat. 70*). Another sarcophagus depicts a similar scene in a rocky setting (*Cat. 64* (Fig. 4.1)), while a fragmentary mosaic from Tunisia gives us the outline of a cave in the time-honoured shape of an arch (*Cat. 68*).

The Sicilian Question

We have already come across a host of conflicting modern views about the geographical location of the Cyclopes.[124] The problem was no less vigorously debated in antiquity. As we have seen, in the *Odyssey* the question remains open, but in Euripides, Theocritus, Callimachus, Virgil, and Ovid it receives specific answers, and in works by several other writers there is similar precision.[125] Almost all these texts place the Cyclopes—both the Polyphemans and those who worked at the forge of Hephaestus/Vulcan—in Sicily. Thucydides too (5th cent. BCE) opts for Sicily, though he is typically cautious, anticipating the tone later adopted by Plato's Socrates towards poetic myths (6.2.1):

> It is said that the earliest inhabitants of any part of the country were the Cyclopes and Laestrygonians. I cannot say what kind of people these were or where they came from or where they went in the end. On these points we must be content with what the poets have said and what anyone else may happen to know.[126]

'What the poets have said' was the subject of sharp dispute, particularly when it concerned the wanderings of Odysseus as described by Homer. The disagreements went beyond geography to include the very nature of myth-based fiction. Could it be that Odysseus' post-Malea travels did not reflect the real world at all, but were just fantasy? Various possibilities were touted. Some contributors to the debate located the wanderings outside the pillars of Hercules (that is, in the Atlantic Ocean); others placed them closer to home, in the region of Sicily and Italy.[127] Among the controversialists were the third-century BCE geographer and polymath Eratosthenes (largely sceptical: 'You will find the scene of the wanderings of Odysseus when you find the cobbler who sewed up the [i.e. Aeolus'] bag of winds'),[128] the second-century BCE historian and grammarian Apollodorus of Athens (critical of those who opted for a Sicilian location of Odysseus' wanderings),[129] and his contemporary the historian Polybius (in favour of Sicily).[130] Our source for the views of all three scholars is Strabo, who himself plumped for Sicily and Italy: 'Homer's narrative is founded on history [*historia*]. He tells us that king Aeolus governed the Lipari Islands, that around Mount Etna and Leontini dwelt the Cyclopes, and certain Laestrygonians inhospitable to strangers' (1.2.9).[131] The place occupied by Sicily in the Greek and Roman

[124] See pp. 14–16.

[125] e.g. Plut. *Mor.* 176a; Plin. *HN* 3.14; Stat. *Theb.* 6.716; Dict. Cret. 6.5. Cf. Oros. *Adv. Pag.* 2.14.1; Eust. 1618, 1644. See, in general, Romm (1992: 183–96).

[126] Trans. R. Warner.

[127] See Walbank (1957–79) on Polyb. 34.2.1–4.8 (= iii. 577–8).

[128] Strabo 1.2.15.

[129] Strabo 7.3.6.

[130] Strabo 1.2.15–16.

[131] Taking issue with the modern tendency (*a*) to demonize Strabo's search for the 'real geography' of Homer, and (*b*) by contrast to praise the more sceptical sophistication of Eratosthenes, Ballabriga (1998) offers a more nuanced picture of Strabo's position.

imaginaire is a topic yet to be properly explored. Clearly enough, perceptions changed over time. John Serrati wrote that 'the archaic and classical periods saw Sicily develop from a far-off land on the fringes of the Greek world to being a fully developed and powerful westward extension of Hellas'.[132] From that perspective, the fixing of the Cyclopes in such a land saw them move from being monstrous outsiders in a frontier/colonial territory, to being continuing demonstrations of the truth that wildness can exist even in a landscape relatively close to home. Pliny the Elder (1st cent. CE), after all, located the anthropophagous Cyclopes and Laestrygonians not in some remote or peripheral region, but 'in the very centre of the earth' (*HN* 7.2), Italy and Sicily being at the very focus of Roman imperial territory. But can we go further in understanding the connection between the Cyclopes and Sicily? What was there about *this* land that suggested a connection with a race of one-eyed giants?

Surprisingly, this is a question that is rarely asked.[133] When we do ask it, one possible answer is that the linking concept is herding. According to the historian Emma Dench, Greek travellers and colonists 'selected local pastoral activity as their way of conceptualizing and characterizing the difference between themselves and the native peoples they encountered in Sicily, using the story of the Cyclopes and placing the local peoples on the side of the non-human'.[134] Simon Hornblower reckons that this explanation works well for the Laestrygonians, who, like the Cyclopes, were herdsmen, and for the episode of the cattle of the Sun, as well as for the Cyclopes themselves, though it can hardly apply to the vortex Charybdis, also located post-Homerically in Sicily.[135] Kathryn Gutzwiller is another who argues for a perceived connection between real-world Sicily and herding, this time in relation to Theocritus: 'In part, as it seems,' she writes, 'Theocritus was reflecting the herding culture of his native Sicily...'.[136] However, first, there is nothing identifiably *Sicilian* about Theocritus' pastoral landscapes.[137] Secondly, how persuasive is it anyway to identify Sicilian real-world pastoralism as the missing explanatory link? One cannot help recalling the outstanding work of Franco de Angelis investigating the *agricultural* (not pastoral) pre-eminence of Sicily.[138] To that modern, etic perspective one may add the host of ancient references to the rich fertility of the Sicilian earth: the island's *kallikarpia* and *eukarpia* were proverbial.[139]

[132] In Smith and Serrati (2000: 14).

[133] An exception is Thomas (1970), which has the merit of insisting on Sicilian/south Italian aspects of the mythology of Polyphemus. Another exception is P. O'Sullivan (2012); see p. 78.

[134] Dench (1995: 37–8).

[135] Hornblower (2008) on Thuc. 6.2.1 (p. 265).

[136] In Gutzwiller (2006: 2 with n. 3).

[137] So, rightly, Rosenmeyer (1969: 232).

[138] See De Angelis (2000, 2006, 2016).

[139] Aesch. *PV* 369; Pind. *Nem.* 1.14–15; Lucr. *DRN* 1.728; Strabo 6.2.7 ('As for the fertility of the land...why should I speak of it, since it is on the lips of all men?'); Diod. Sic. 5.2.4; 69.3 (in both passages, *Od.* 9.109–11—the description of the spontaneous growing-up of crops for the Homeric Cyclopes—is cited as corroboration). More references in Kingsley (1995: 46 n. 39).

What other possibilities are there to explain the connection between the Cyclopes and Sicily? Richard Seaford rejected as fanciful some links that Leonardo Paganelli had claimed to exist between Polyphemus and Sicily ('an "almost Gorgianic rhetoric", gourmandise, despotism, and Hellenism mixed with barbarism'), but made a suggestion of his own, that, if, as Seaford thinks, Euripides' *Cyclops* was written soon after 413 BCE, the audience 'may have been reminded, as they saw the Greeks trapped in the Aitnaian cannibal's cave, of their fellow citizens imprisoned in the Syracusan quarries...'.[140] It is true that for such an audience the idea of 'cave' *might* have brought to mind the idea of 'quarry'. Equally, it might not. That's how it is with audiences.

On another tack, Patrick O'Sullivan has argued, again in relation specifically to Euripides' *Cyclops*, that the playwright has created a characteristically *satyric* Sicily, 'a location... of harshness, barbarian and cosmic monstrosity by making it a remote dystopia...'.[141] O'Sullivan sees this fictive creation of a 'barbaric, un-Greek and un-Olympian' space as suiting the generic thrust of satyric drama as a whole, with its celebration of a sense of escape 'not just from a monstrous ogre, but from a monstrous environment altogether'.[142] There is much to be said for this interpretation; yet it is avowedly genre specific. What we are looking for is something that links Sicily not just with a single late-fifth-century, satyric, Athenian dramatization of the Polyphemus tale, but with other retellings too, across the entire generic spectrum.

In his study of Greek gastronomy Andrew Dalby stressed the repeated connection made, in Athenian comic drama, between Sicily and cheese; more recently, Paul Kindstedt's fascinating account of cheese in Western culture stresses the fame of Sicilian cheese-makers.[143] But cheesiness won't get us all the way either, even though it does appear as a feature of Cyclopic culture in many genres. Of course, there is no need to come up with one single explanation for the link between Sicily and the Cyclopes; but we believe that an important consideration has been overlooked. It is not Sicily in general that we need to focus on, but Etna. But discussion of that will have to wait until we come to the crucial topic of fire.

[140] Seaford (1984: 55), citing Paganelli (1979: 121–2 n. 151).

[141] P. O'Sullivan (2012: 171).

[142] P. O'Sullivan (2012: 186–7).

[143] Dalby (1996: 108–9, 136); similarly J. N. Davidson (1997: 295); Kindstedt (2012: 76–80). (Note, though, that Kindstedt wrongly speaks (pp. 74–5) of Sicily as the location of the encounter between the *Homeric* Odysseus and the Cyclops.) On cheese in Greek and Roman culture, see Valavanis (2008).

4
Physique

Choose a dozen members of the general public and ask them which physical feature they associate with a creature called 'Cyclops'. They will all give the same answer: he has just one eye. But in the ancient sources monocularity is by no means the only aspect of a Cyclops' appearance to attract attention. Other attributes regularly mentioned are hugeness, hairiness (often associated with 'wildness'), and ugliness. We shall look at each of these characteristics in turn.

Big

What would it be like to be incredibly large or extremely small? This thought experiment underlies countless stories in myth, folklore, fantasy, and science fiction. Tale-tellers love giants: from the biblical Goliath, via the P'an Ku of Chinese creation myth, to the Gogmagog of British folklore, huge beings seize the imagination. Hardly less frequent are stories about little people, such as Irish leprechauns, Basque *mamarros,* and Germanic dwarves, not forgetting modern fictional creations such as those in Mary Norton's novel *The Borrowers* (1952). Shrinking to microscopic dimensions is a staple of science fiction (*Honey, I Shrunk the Kids* (1989)), and has a distinguished precedent in *Alice in Wonderland*, whose heroine acquires the capacity both to shrink and to grow. What matters most is *relative* size. Gulliver seemed huge in Lilliput, but minuscule in Brobdingnag. To the eyes of the 120,000-feet-tall Micromégas—visitor to Earth from a planet orbiting Sirius, as described in the eponymous short story by Voltaire—humans look no larger than atoms. Giants and dwarves are prime imaginative material because of the contrast between them and persons of more conventional dimensions.

In the ancient literary sources the Cyclopes were invariably portrayed as superhumanly strong; this applies equally to the masons, the weapons-makers, and the pastoral ogres. The masons' strength is implicit in their feats of construction. Pausanias describes the wall they built at Tiryns out of natural rocks, which were 'all so huge that a pair of mules would not even begin to shift the smallest of them' (2.25.8). The weapons-makers were no less brawny. Hesiod reports that 'strength' and 'force' (as well as 'craft') were present in their works (*Theog.* 146); the muscularity of Virgil's Etnaean smiths is similarly awe-inspiring (*Aen.* 8.452). Later in the myth-telling tradition, the epic extravaganza by Nonnus (*fl.* 5th cent. CE),

Cyclops: The Myth and its Cultural History. Mercedes Aguirre and Richard Buxton, Oxford University Press (2020).

DOI: 10.1093/oso/9780198713777.001.0001

about the war of Dionysus against the Indians, includes a long account of Cyclopean military prowess, during which Brontes, armed Thor-like with a mighty hammer, breaks off a huge crag and hurls it at the Indian king Deriades (*Dion.* 28.206–7).

But does all this power go along with vast *size*? The hugeness of the masons is never spelled out; we infer it from the massive boulders they tote. The immensity of the metalworkers is also normally a matter of inference rather than precise narrative measurement. An exception occurs in Callimachus' *Hymn to Artemis*, where the sight of colossal Cyclopes toiling in Hephaestus' forge terrifies the local nymphs, 'when they saw the grim *pelōra*, resembling the crags of Ossa...' (51–2). In Callimachus' time the word *pelōra* already had a significant literary pedigree, but its meaning is not easy to pin down. In order to tease out its implications, we need to look back to Homer.

In the *Odyssey* the size of Polyphemus' fellow ogres is never mentioned explicitly, but he himself is likened to 'a wooded peak of the high mountains, which is visible apart from the others' (9.191–2). His immensity is matched by formidable strength. Already at the beginning of the poem he is said to possess the greatest power among all the Cyclopes (1.70–1). In the encounter with Odysseus he manipulates the massive chunk of cliff that serves as his cave door, breaks off and hurls a mountain peak towards Odysseus' vessel, then throws an even bigger crag in the same direction (9.240–3, 481, 537–8). So he fully deserves the epithet repeatedly used to describe him: *pelōr(ios)* (187, 190, 257, 428). 'Monstrous' is the usual English translation, but to speak of monstrosity raises and indeed begs the tricky question of Polyphemus' relationship to humankind.[1] 'Prodigious' might be a less prejudicial alternative, since it avoids making a commitment about the boundary between what is and is not human. In any case, the word expresses the quality of going beyond the ordinary.[2] Homer applies it to a number of Greek and Trojan heroes, as well as to Hades, Ares, and a snake; in these cases 'extraordinarily formidable' might best convey the word's connotations (the same goes for the Callimachus passage). But different kinds of excess carry different implications. Most Homeric heroes are tall and strong, but there is nothing negative about their largeness; rather the reverse. Contrast this with two other characters mentioned in the *Odyssey*, the giants Otus and Ephialtes, who at the age of 9 measured around 9 cubits broad and 9 fathoms tall, and who went on to exemplify moral as well as physical excess. They threatened to pile Mount Ossa on Mount Olympus, and Mount Pelion on Mount Ossa, in order to scale heaven; Apollo killed them before they reached adolescence (11.311–20). Even bigger, and even more morally excessive, was Tityus, would-be rapist of the goddess Leto; in the Underworld he sprawled to a length of over 900 feet (11.577).[3] In the case of the Laestrygonians,

[1] See pp. 175–81. [2] See Eck (2012: 143). On *pelōr(ios)*, see also p. 176.
[3] See Hermary (2006: 121–2).

Odysseus' foes in book 10, excessive conduct again went along with immense size: their queen was as big as a mountain peak, they ate people, and their preferred form of aggression was to hurl human-sized boulders (10.112–22). Defiance of the norm, the mean, the proper measure, is a theme explored repeatedly in Greek myths, in relation both to physical size and to moral behaviour. As we shall see later, great size corresponds to behavioural excess in the case of Polyphemus too.

The hugeness of Polyphemus and his fellow Cyclopes is a given in many sources. The Spartan poet Tyrtaeus (7th cent. BCE) singles them out as paradigms of immensity as well as strength; the mythographer Apollodorus calls Polyphemus 'hyper-large'; in Nonnus, the most effective way of describing the great height of the Cyclops Brontes is to say 'he was as tall as Polyphemus'; in a vignette from a letter by the Cyrenaican bishop Synesius (4th–5th cent. CE), Odysseus refers to his captor's door-stone as 'as big as a promontory', with obvious implications about the creature capable of moving it.[4] In the *Aeneid*, Achaemenides tells of the vastness, not only of the cave, but of its owner: Polyphemus 'knocks against the stars'; his hand and his eye are huge; he is simply *immensus*; his bulk is vast; he is colossal; he can stride into mid-ocean without wetting his 'towering flanks' (3.619–65). The other Cyclopes are vast too, holding their heads in the sky like high-topped oaks or cypresses (647, 675–82).

Like any departure from the norm, colossal size can seem ludicrous in the right generic context. Gargantua needed the milk of 17,913 cows to nourish him as a baby.[5] Less extravagantly than Rabelais, the Roman satirist Lucilius (2nd cent. BCE) exemplified the precision and exaggeration in which comedy delights: 'People think that in the poetry of Homer there are many prodigies which are make-believe monstrosities [*ficta monstra*], among the chief of which is Polyphemus the Cyclops, two hundred feet tall; and furthermore he has a little walking-stick, bigger than the biggest mast of any cargo-boat.'[6] But inevitably it is Ovid who squeezes the juiciest humour out of Polyphemus' immensity. Through the eyes of Galatea we see an ogre who combs his hair with a rake, and shaves with a reaping-hook (*Met.* 13.765–6). As for Polyphemus' own perception of his qualities (still as reported by Galatea), size is one of the attributes he stresses: 'Look how big I am! Jupiter himself in the sky has no bigger body' (842–3). Everything about this assertion is incongruous; and incongruity is the very heart of comedy.

In spite of the near ubiquity of immensity in ancient literary descriptions of Polyphemus, there are exceptions. Neither of Theocritus' Cyclopean *Idylls* mentions size. Rather than embodying a physical disparity between vastness and

[4] Tyrtaeus 12.3; Apollod. *Bibl. Epit.* 7.4; Nonnus, *Dion.* 28.225; Synesius, *Letter* 121.

[5] Rabelais (1994: bk I, ch. 7).

[6] Lucil. frr. 520–3 Warmington (whose translation we have adopted).

minuteness *à la* King Kong and Fay Wray, the Theocritean Polyphemus and Galatea are juxtaposed *emotionally*: adolescent naivety versus airy coquettishness. Also worth mentioning is the relative lack of explicit attention paid to Polyphemus' hugeness in Euripides' *Cyclops*. One possible explanation is that there were inevitable physical constraints on the degree to which gigantism could be portrayed on the ancient Greek stage; after all, Polyphemus, like every other character in the drama, was played by a human actor.[7] But a contrast in stature could still be suggested by the stage action: 'We're looking right up at Zeus himself,' insists the satyr chorus-leader (212). Evoking the colossal becomes much easier, of course, when it comes to verbal narration rather than dramatic impersonation, as in Odysseus' comments about some off-stage action (382–5):

> First, after we had entered the cave,
> he lit a fire and tossed down on the huge hearth
> logs from a vast oak—you would have needed
> three wagons merely to carry the load.[8]

Whereas a textual narrative could, if the author so wished, elide the question of Cyclopean size, painters and sculptors could not avoid the issue. What matters is *relative* size: the only way to make a Cyclops look huge is to contrast him with other figures appearing alongside him. This may be tricky if the image-bearing object is itself small. The painter Timanthes of Cythnos (fifth–fourth centuries BCE) devised an ingenious solution to the problem. Even on a small painted panel he was able to suggest the vastness of the sleeping Polyphemus by showing some *comparatively* diminutive-looking satyrs in the act of measuring the ogre's thumb with a *thyrsos*.[9] By contrast, in some depictions of the metalworking Cyclopes (*Cat. 64* (Fig. 4.1) and *70*) nothing indicates how 'objectively' big they are, since they are represented next to and the same size as other figures such as Vulcan—and how big was *he*?

Vase-painters were, of course, perfectly capable of portraying *homunculi*; they did so, for instance, when representing the *psychai* (souls) of the dead. However, if they had tried to replicate the Homeric emphasis on Polyphemus' hugeness in images that included his Greek adversaries, those adversaries might have looked unheroically tiny beside him.[10] The preferred alternative was to depict Polyphemus either as only slightly larger than the Greeks, or even as the same size.[11] Doubtless

[7] Emphasized by Seaford (1984: 51).

[8] Other references to Cyclopean size are at 356 and 395. The text of the latter passage may be corrupt, but is defended by P. O'Sullivan and Collard (2013: ad loc.).

[9] Plin. *HN* 35.74. Cf. Squire (2011: 267 n. 50); S. Beta (2015: 610–11).

[10] Lowenstam (1992: 168). [11] Touchefeu-Meynier (1968: 70).

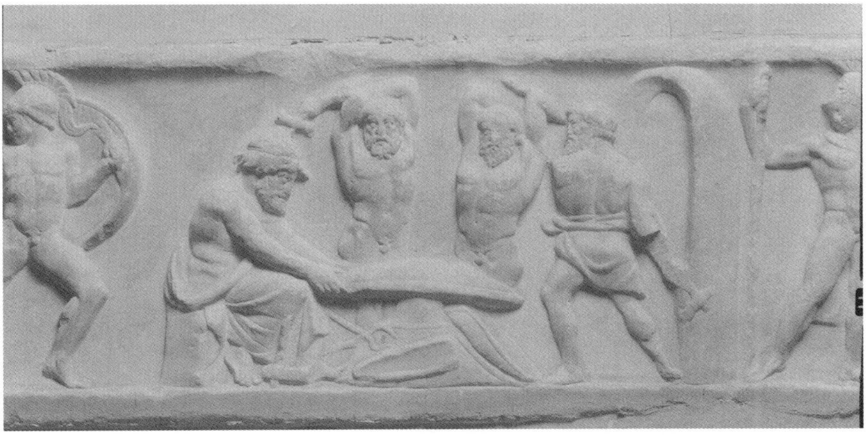

Fig. 4.1. Three Cyclopes as 'beaters'. Cover of sarcophagus, mid-2nd cent. CE.

Timanthes' thumb-measuring satyrs had less dignity to stand on than did Odysseus and his men.

Given the limited space available on a vase, a handy way of representing Polyphemus as bigger than those around him was to depict him as crouching, kneeling, sitting, or reclining. The scene of the blinding lent itself perfectly to this schema. On the Eleusis amphora (*Cat. 1* (Fig. 2.1)) he sits on the floor with knees drawn up; his aggressors attain the necessary height for their attack by simply standing up.[12] On a proto-Argive krater (*Cat. 2*) the ogre is roughly twice the size of the Greeks, but, because he is reclining as if asleep, they can shove the stake into his eye horizontally. On a black-figure cup in Berlin (*Cat. 19* (Fig. 4.14)), the size difference between blinders and blinded significantly exceeds double; given the limited size of the vessel, Polyphemus has to be shown lying down. The impact of all these images recalls the thrust of the Homeric narrative: the organized cooperation of the Greeks outwits a bigger foe. Not quite David and Goliath, though: Odysseus does not act alone.

Not all vase-painters made Polyphemus look enormous. Some made him the same height as the Greeks and gave him no other distinguishing characteristic, as on the Aristonothos krater (*Cat. 3* (Fig. 3.3)) and the Etruscan pithos (*Cat. 5* (Fig. 4.7)). An alternative was to make everyone the same height but to differentiate Polyphemus in some other way. On an Attic cup (*Cat. 11*), the image of his body is incomplete, but enough of him is intact to show his big paunch. He also looks bulkier than his assailants on the Laconian cup (*Cat. 10* (Fig. 3.1)) and the Lucanian krater (*Cat. 27* (Fig. 4.13)); on the latter he also has big ears and a snub nose. On vase paintings of the escape under the rams, Polyphemus usually looks

[12] The same applies on another amphora (*Cat. 14*) and a Corinthian alabastron (*Cat. 9*).

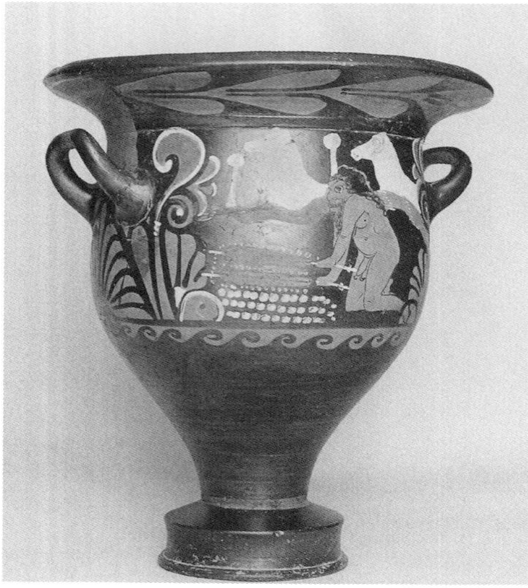

Fig. 4.2. Polyphemus the demon chef. Campanian krater from Cumae, 350–325 BCE.

larger than the escapees (e.g. *Cat. 25* (Fig. 5.4)). But it is hard to be certain how big someone is when they are half-obscured by wool.

Unique among ancient images of Polyphemus is that on an undeservedly little-known krater from Cumae, in which the ogre looks genuinely colossal in relation to the two human figures also present (*Cat. 28* (Fig. 4.2)). As we said earlier, vase-painters usually avoided juxtaposing a huge Cyclops with minuscule and, by implication, unheroic-looking Greek heroes. But the exceptional Cumae krater proves the rule. The two diminutive humans are, it would seem, deliberately portrayed as unheroic. At the very least their *situation* is unheroic: Polyphemus has stuck them onto spits and, with an idiotic expression on his face, is grilling them over a fire. The tone approaches the farcical: as well as being big and fat, the Cyclops has whopping genitals—an extreme version of the figure often cut by Silenus or the satyrs.[13]

Artists working in different media adopted different strategies for depicting the ogre's size. The physical constraints of relief bowls and funerary urns favour images in which the size differential between the figures is relatively modest (*Cat. 33* (Fig. 5.5), *35*, *36*, and *37* (Fig. 3.5)). The triangular shape of a pediment offers more scope to depict the central figure as larger than the others. To the so-called Nymphaeum of Pollio at Ephesus belongs a statue group (*Cat. 38*) in which a hefty, centrally positioned Polyphemus receives wine from a rather

[13] Buitron and Cohen (1992: 34).

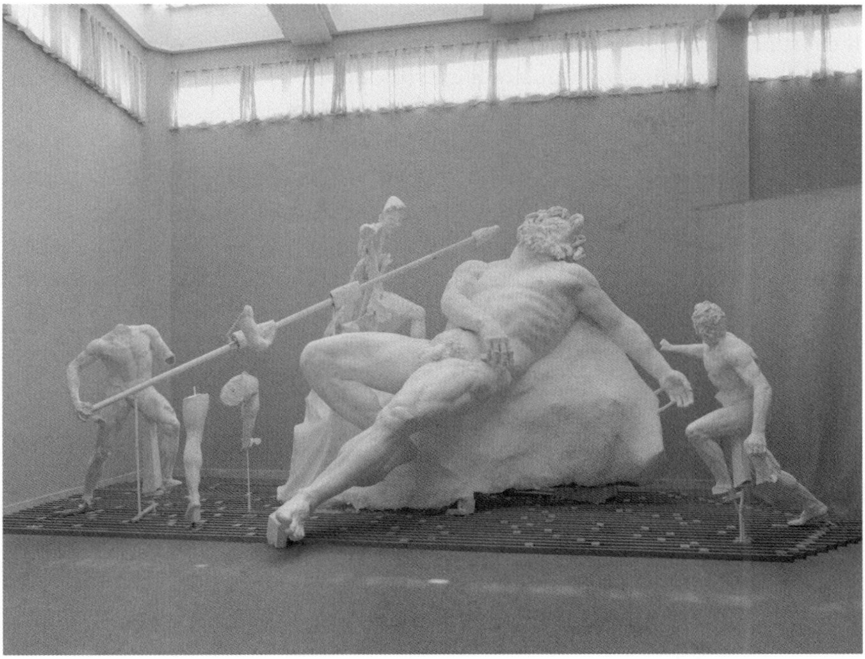

Fig. 4.3. Monumental sculptural group, Grotto of Tiberius, Sperlonga (between Rome and Naples), perhaps originally 1st cent. BCE.

smaller Odysseus to the left. But the group had been moved from another site, which was in all probability the pediment of a temple (to Dionysus?) in the forum at Ephesus, begun by Mark Antony but not completed before his defeat at Actium.[14] But it is the monumental, free-standing sculptural group at Sperlonga that stands out in its representation of a truly gigantic Polyphemus, while at the same time portraying the Greek assault party as well above normal human size (*Cat. 39* (Fig. 4.3)).

In Roman wall paintings portraying his love for Galatea, the Cyclops does not usually appear much above human size. But the medium did potentially offer artists greater freedom to play with relative dimensions than was the case in, say, vase painting.[15] The painting in the House of Livia in Rome shows the huge naked torso of Polyphemus emerging from the water (*Cat. 40* (Fig. 4.6)). Mere adolescent though he evidently is, he appears gigantic by comparison with Galatea and her sister nymphs, thanks to the artist's imaginative exploitation of perspective.

[14] Andreae and Parisi Presicce (1996: 240–3 = 4.4 in their catalogue).

[15] So, rightly, Touchefeu-Meynier in *LIMC* 'Polyphemos I', p. 1018.

As in the literary sources, so in the visual arts, the Cyclopes' size is matched by their superhuman strength. On a red-figure stamnos a muscular Polyphemus braces himself against his equally huge rock-door (*Cat. 25* (Fig. 5.4)); his tendency to throw boulders is a recurrent motif (e.g. *Cat. 33* (Fig. 5.5), *37* (Fig. 3.5), *41* (Fig. 3.2), and *42*). A more gruesome indicator of brawn is the capacity to rip apart uncooked flesh—far tougher to deal with than cooked meat. The Bacchants had this power instilled into them by Dionysus; with Polyphemus it was innate. On the Laconian cup, he grasps a couple of human legs torn from their owner's body (*Cat. 10* (Fig. 3.1)); the aftermath of a similar dismemberment is portrayed on a Campanian amphora (*Cat. 18* (Fig. 5.10)). On the Piazza Armerina mosaic, an eviscerated ram lies draped across his knee (*Cat. 72* (Fig. 3.7)).

Emblematic of Polyphemus' power is the mighty club that he often carries (e.g. *Cat. 17*, *20*, and *26*). Could this hint at a parallel with Heracles?[16] The similarities go beyond clubbing. The two characters share a susceptibility to alcohol, even if in Polyphemus' case this is a one-off rather than a habit. They also both exemplify the paradox of the astoundingly strong individual reduced to helplessness by those weaker than himself. At various points in his career Heracles was dominated by a series of feebler individuals: Eurystheus, Omphale, Deianira, and Nessus. Polyphemus too experienced episodes of subjection to those physically inferior to himself: his emotional enslavement to Galatea, and his blinding by the relatively puny Greeks. The painting in the House of Livia memorably shows him being manipulated by a little Eros, who holds the reins that pull his victim this way and that (*Cat. 40* (Fig. 4.6)). As for the blinding, in several early vase paintings Polyphemus is clearly awake, yet ineffectual in face of aggression from punier assailants, even if he raises his hand to try to avert the blow (e.g. *Cat. 1* (Fig. 2.1), *2*, *5* (Fig. 4.7), and *14*). There is a notable contrast with the Homeric narrative, in which Polyphemus is blinded while asleep, a variant that itself finds echoes in art, most vividly on the Lucanian krater in the British Museum (*Cat. 27* (Fig. 4.13); also *15* (Fig. 4.4), *17*, *39* (Fig. 4.3), and *61*).

A different kind of overlap between Polyphemus and Heracles can be found in the *Argonautica* by Apollonius of Rhodes (3rd cent. BCE). The Polyphemus in question, the son of Eilatus, and an Argonaut rather than a Cyclops, is the first to notice the absence of Heracles' beloved boy Hylas, and his grief-stricken reaction prefigures the desperation of the great hero himself (1.1240–60). On the face of it, the homonymity of the two Polyphemuses is mere accident. Yet it can happen—more often than is usually recognized—that homonyms in Greek mythology point to underlying similarities, parallels, and analogies.[17] It is not impossible that the Heraclean quality that Polyphemus-the-Cyclops sometimes embodies might play a part in this particular homonymy.

[16] Cf. Chalier (2008: 103).

[17] See Buxton (2013b).

Hairy

It would be hard to exaggerate the kaleidoscopic brilliance of Marina Warner's books about storytelling. In one of these, she reflects on the symbolic significance of hair:

> The language of the self would be stripped of one of its richest resources without hair: and like language, or the faculty of laughter, or the use of tools, the dressing of hair in itself constitutes a mark of the human. In the quest for identity, both personal and in its larger relation to society, hair can help. The body reveals to us through hair the passage of time and the fluctuating claims of gender; strangers offer us a conspicuous glossary of clues in the way they do the hair on their head, for in societies all over the world, callings are declared through hairy signs: the monk's tonsure, the ringlets of the Hassidic scholar, the GI's crewcut, the sans-culotte's freeflowing mane, the flowerchild's tangled curls, the veil.[18]

Warner here recapitulates the conclusions of many earlier scholars; for the social significance of hair is an anthropological and sociological commonplace. Numerous studies have highlighted wide cultural differences in the kinds of statements than can be made in the language of hair.[19] Even when the same 'signifier' (to borrow Saussurean linguistic terminology) is deployed—say, hair of a certain colour or length—the 'signified' may vary markedly according to different cultural contexts. Although it is hard to point to trichological semantic universals, we can identify certain cross-culturally recurrent patterns.

One such concerns the wearing of long hair by males: on the head, on the face, on the body. Warner identifies a common signification of this trait: 'Hairiness indicates animal nature: it is the distinctive sign of the wilderness and its inhabitants.'[20] The anthropologist Raymond Firth had already developed the same point: 'Man has often been differentiated from other animals by his lack of hair ("the naked ape"), so people with an unusual amount of hair may be given feral qualities. Traditional notions of man living in a state of nature have represented him as shaggy...'.[21] Hairiness can also be associated with a constellation of characteristics related to wildness: power, aggression, rebelliousness, roughness, exaggerated virility, ferality. Among the hairy possessors of these attributes—which may have a positive or a negative spin—are Enkidu in *Gilgamesh*, the biblical Esau and Samson, the medieval Wild Man of the Woods, and the Devil.

[18] Warner (1994: 371). Two splendid chapters of the same book are devoted to the whole topic of symbolic hair, at 353–86.

[19] See the classic analysis by Firth (1973: 262–98); also Hallpike (1969); Cooper (1971); Synnott (1987).

[20] Warner (1994: 358–9).

[21] Firth (1973: 264).

How does all this apply to the Cyclopes? Their shagginess recurs in written and visual media alike. In his *Hymn to Artemis*, Callimachus creates an amusing vignette of the goddess as a doughty 3-year-old, being dandled in the arms of the blacksmith Cyclops Brontes: 'You grabbed the shaggy hair of his mighty chest and pulled it out by force; and still today the middle part of his chest has no hair, as when alopecia settles on a man's temples and destroys his hair' (76–9). But, of all the Cyclopes, it is Polyphemus whose hairiness most often gets noticed. Being *lasios* (Greek for 'shaggy') or *hir(su)tus* (the Latin equivalents) is an aspect of his personal landscape. There are intimations of this already in Theocritus' *Idyll* 11, where the ogre describes his single eyebrow as *lasios* (31). Moreover, as Christophe Cusset has pointed out, the epithet that Polyphemus gives to Etna, *poludendreos* ('with many trees' (47)) is echoed three lines later by the adjective he uses of himself, *lasiōteros* ('rather shaggy' (50)); both words occur in the same metrical position in their respective lines, as if the 'hairiness' of the mountain is mirrored by that of Polyphemus' own body.[22] That might seem an over-subtle interpretation, but two later authors indisputably create an equivalence between wooded Sicilian landscape and hairy Cyclopean body. When Ovid's Galatea recalls the song Polyphemus sang to her, she makes him picturesquely observe: 'A wealth of hair overhangs my manly face, and it shades my shoulders like a grove' (*Met.* 13.844–5)—quite unlike Galatea's glamorous adolescent lover Acis, with downy hair hesitantly appearing on his soft cheeks (754). An even clearer equation between landscape and body can be found in Philostratus' evocation of a painted Polyphemus: 'He is depicted as mountainous and terrible, tossing his hair, which stands erect and as dense as the foliage of a pine tree, showing a set of jagged teeth in his voracious jaw, shaggy [*lasios*] all over—breast and belly, everything right to his finger-nails' (*Imag.* 2.18).

In visual representations from Greece, Etruria, and Rome, Cyclopes are usually depicted as hairy. But *how* hairy, on what parts of the body, and whether the hair is unkempt or neat—these are variables. Abundant Cyclopean hair on head and face is common in images of the three canonical Odyssean moments. There is a nice example on a proto-Argive krater depicting the blinding (*Cat. 2*), though Polyphemus is not the only hairy one in the picture: blinders and blinded alike sport dreadlocks and a beard. Not dissimilar are the Polyphemuses on two oinochoai, one in the Louvre (blinding) and one in the British Museum (under-ram escape) (*Cat. 17* and *23*). Altogether more unkempt is the slumped Cyclops, wine vessel in hand, on a Caeretan hydria (*Cat. 15* (Fig. 4.4)). He has a very large head, and his mane of head hair, fused with a straggly beard, contrasts with the neat coiffures of the blinding party; the same goes for a little Corinthian alabastron in New York (*Cat. 9*). Sometimes Polyphemus wears a natty little pointed beard, as

[22] Cusset (2004: 53).

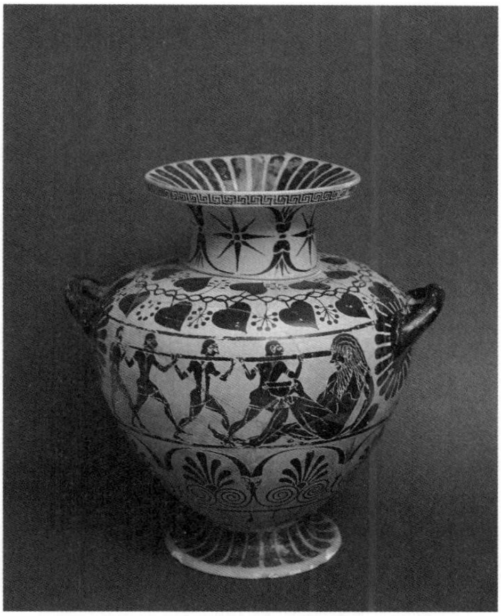

Fig. 4.4. Drunk and hairy. Caeretan hydria from Cerveteri, *c.*520 BCE.

in the frontal representation of the blinding on a vase in Berlin (*Cat. 19* (Fig. 4.14)); and in one image of the under-ram escape his distinguished beard would not disgrace an Olympian god (*Cat. 26*). But more often his facial hair is disorderly, particularly in two portrayals where his manner is decidedly feral—namely, the krater on which he is shown grilling two mini-men (*Cat. 28* (Fig. 4.2)) and the grim representation in the Tomb of Orcus at Etruscan Tarquinia (*Cat. 31* (Fig. 4.15)).

In later depictions, a mass of Cyclopean beard and head-hair is again the norm, whether on individual portrait-heads (e.g. *Cat. 32* and *59* (Fig. 4.12)), or in scenes relating to Odysseus or Galatea. The degree of (un)kemptness varies. The Polyphemus who courts Galatea on the mosaic from Cordoba (*Cat. 71* (Fig. 4.5)) badly needs a visit to the barber, as do his equivalents on the mural from Boscotrecase (*Cat. 41* (Fig. 3.2)) and the mosaic at Piazza Armerina (*Cat. 72* (Fig. 3.7)). But the pensive and near-heroic Polyphemus on a painting from Herculaneum (*Cat. 46* (Fig. 8.1)) sports a well-clipped beard. Wholly exceptional is the youthful, half-submerged, and above all clean-shaven figure depicted in the House of Livia (*Cat. 40* (Fig. 4.6)). His head-hair is neat and, by Cyclopean standards, rather short, as if this Adonian beach-boy had just had a trim in readiness for an important date.

The passages from Callimachus and Philostratus that we have just quoted describe luxuriant Cyclopean body-hair. Detecting that sort of hairiness in visual images depends on whether the body is naked or not, so we need to address the

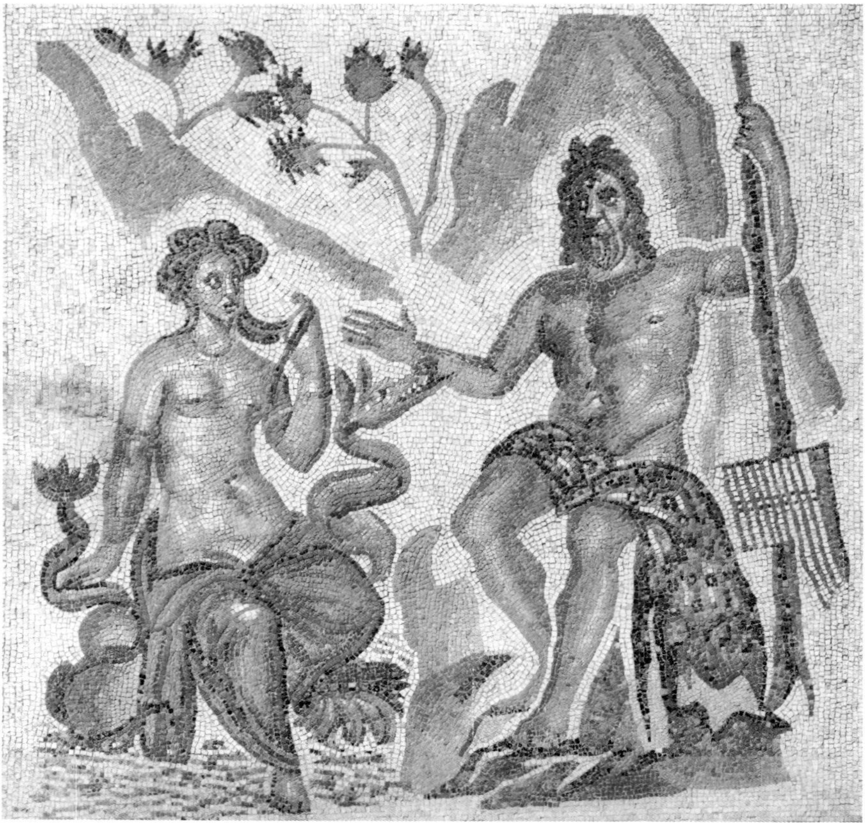

Fig. 4.5. Mosaic from Cordoba, *c.*200 CE.

prior question of clothing. In every period and virtually every medium, the Cyclopes are usually portrayed naked; but there are exceptions. On a cup from Vulci (*Cat. 13*), Polyphemus (if indeed it is he) has a cloak over one arm, but wears nothing else.[23] On the Etruscan pithos (*Cat. 5* (Fig. 4.7)), he is dressed in a snazzy mini-tunic, which differs from the garb worn by those blinding him only in its rhombus pattern and in the ornamental border that their tunics have but his does not.Closer to nature than culture is an alternative, minimalist style of dress, the animal skin knotted around the neck, as on the Lucanian krater (*Cat. 27* (Fig. 4.13)) and on a grotesque figurine from the Athenian Acropolis (*Cat. 29* (Fig. 4.9)). The same detail recurs in the Roman period—for instance, on the Piazza Armerina mosaic (*Cat. 72* (Fig. 3.7)) and on a relief from Catania depicting Odysseus' offering of wine (*Cat. 61*). In an adaptation of the motif in scenes

[23] See Touchefeu-Meynier (1968: 45).

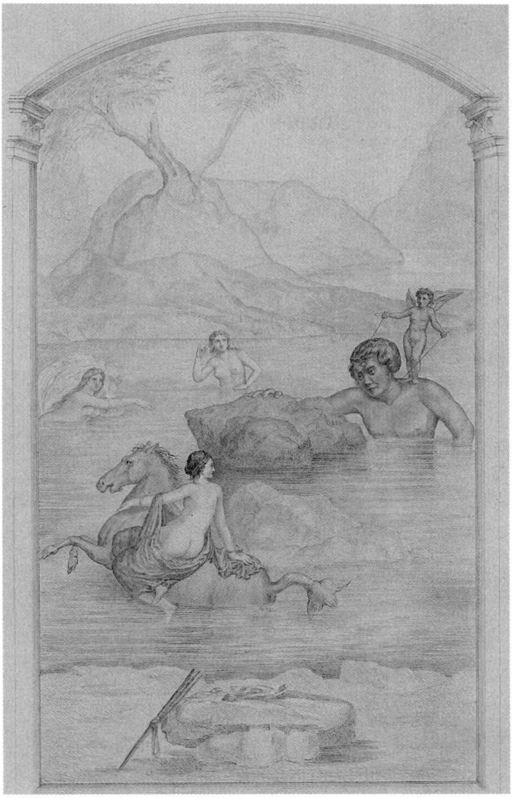

Fig. 4.6. Tugged by the reins of love. Wall painting, House of Livia, Palatine, Rome, 30–25 BCE.

representing or relating to Galatea, an otherwise naked Polyphemus sits with a cloak or animal skin draped over his thighs (*Cat. 53* (Fig. 8.3) and *71* (Fig. 4.5)).

But the norm is nudity. And when a Cyclops *is* naked, artists sometimes give him body-hair. An amphora from Vulci (*Cat. 14*) is remarkable not only for the dance-like vigour of the blinders (the leader performs an astonishing goose step) and the uncompromising physicality of the blinding, but also for the hair on Polyphemus' chest, abdomen, and thighs.[24] Even hairier is the already blinded Polyphemus on a fragmentary black-figure krater (*Cat. 8* (Fig. 4.8)) extending his hands towards a ram; it is hard to say who is fleecier, the animal or its master. Equally explicit is Polyphemus' hirsute outline on a Corinthian alabastron (*Cat. 9*) as he sits naked on the floor while being deprived of his eyesight. In Roman art,

[24] For the implausible alternative that the markings on the body might be blood not hair, see Touchefeu-Meynier in *LIMC* 'Polyphemos I', p. 1014.

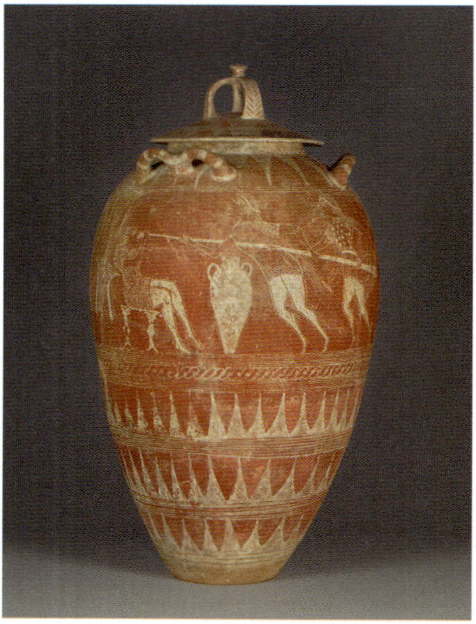

Fig. 4.7. A close resemblance between blinders and blinded. Red-clay Etruscan pithos, 650–625 BCE.

Polyphemus can have hair in the armpits, chest, and/or pubic area—and, on the sculpture in Sperlonga, on his feet and toes.[25] But this is a far cry from the representation of a feral Polyphemus in his full-body pelosity, which seems more at home in Greek than in Roman visual imagery.

To what extent can we apply the Warner–Firth 'hairiness = wildness' equation to the Cyclopes? The matter is easier to resolve for texts than for visual art, but the two types of evidence do seem to corroborate one another. Several authors explicitly use Greek *lasios* or Latin *hirsutus/hirtus*, in tandem with Greek *agrios* or Latin *ferus* ('wild'), to convey the essence of what it is to be a Cyclops.[26] The Ovidian Polyphemus uses a rake to comb his stiff hair, trims his bristly beard (*hirsutam... barbam*) with a reaping hook, and composes his wild facial expression (*feros... vultus*) by looking at its reflection in the water.[27] In one of his funniest works, *Dialogues of the Sea Gods*, Lucian records the bitchy verbal sparring between the sea nymphs Doris and Galatea.[28] Doris: 'Your lover looks hideous, sings like a donkey, and smells like a goat.' Galatea: 'He's the son of Poseidon, he's musical, *and at least I've got a lover*.' When Doris refers to Polyphemus as *lasios*

[25] Beautifully illustrated in Andreae (1999: 198).

[26] Ratcliffe (2014: 32–3) argues for an interplay of traditions about hairy Cyclopes and hairy Arimaspians.

[27] Ov. *Met.* 13.765–7. Cf. *ferus... Cyclops* (13.780).

[28] Lucian, *DMar* 1.

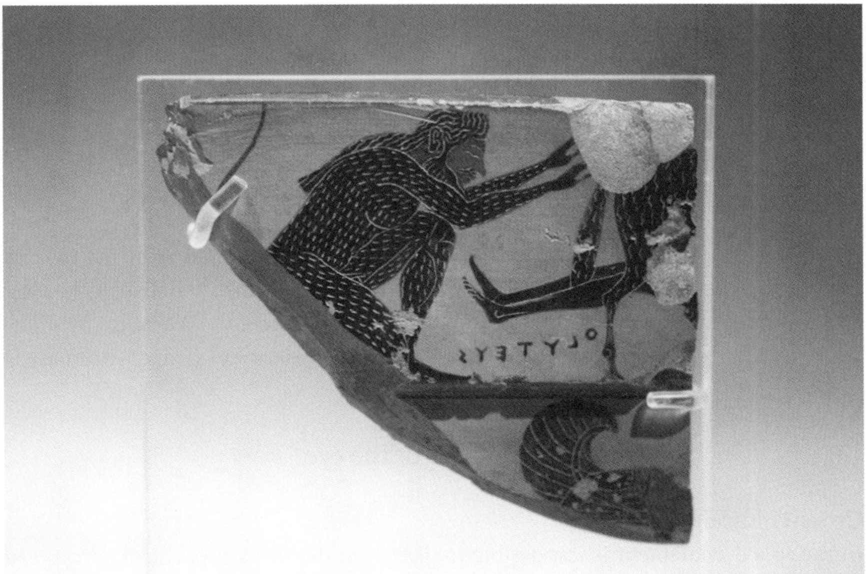

Fig. 4.8. The blinded ogre feels for his foes. Krater attributed to the painter Clitias, 600–550 BCE.

and *agrios* (adding that she saw him carrying a bear cub just as *lasios* as himself), Galatea does not disagree, but says his hairiness makes him seem manly.[29] Philostratus calls Polyphemus 'the most *agrios*' of all the Cyclopes, and caps this with a wonderful phrase that describes the ogre's gaze as '*agrios* and stealthy, like that of wild beasts subdued by necessity'. The use of *agrios* as an epithet for Polyphemus goes back to the *Odyssey* (2.19; 9.215, 494). In Homer, the word typically connotes homicidal savagery—for instance, that of furious warriors, or monstrous or otherwise excessive beings such as Scylla and the Giants; in different ways such individuals put themselves outside the norm of civilized conduct.[30] Of course 'outside' may be literal as well as metaphorical: Apollodorus relates that Polyphemus was *agrios*, having just mentioned that he lives in a cave; a fragment from the poet Philoxenus (5th–4th cent. BCE) talks of Polyphemus carrying a leather bag with *agrios* herbs in it, presumably gathered in the countryside; Horace (1st cent. BCE) compares the tormented efforts of a poet to someone 'performing the Satyr dance or the *agrestis* ('wild') Cyclops dance'.[31] *Agrios* seems less well suited to the masonic Cyclopes, with their city-oriented building projects,

[29] Cf. Ov. *Met.* 13.834–7: Polyphemus finds *two* cubs of a hairy bear for Galatea to play with.

[30] Warriors: esp. Achilles (*Il.* 21.314), cf. Mauduit (2006). Scylla: *Od.* 12.119. Giants: *Od.* 7.206. See in general Eck (2012: 137).

[31] Apollod. *Bibl. Epit.* 7.4; Philoxenus fr. 820 in D. A. Campbell (1993), with Ar. *Plut.* 296–301; Hor. *Epist.* 2.2.124–5.

nor does it seem to be used of the metalworkers, for all that they *work* in a cave. But, for a cave-dwelling pastoral ogre who gives hairy bear cubs as love tokens, it sits very well indeed.

One-Eyed

So inseparably has the notion of 'Cyclops' become intertwined with the idea of the eye that we need to pay special attention to the relationship between the two, and we make no apology for dwelling on this matter at length. We begin by offering two wider perspectives, the first cross-cultural, the second Graeco-Roman.

Symbolism of the eye

Cross-cultural

In the space available it is impossible to give even the most superficial account of the symbolism of the eye worldwide and across time.[32] We shall simply refer to a few major landmarks, especially but not exclusively from the areas of myth and religion.

Benevolence and protection

Among the most complex of all examples of ocular symbolism is one that is also among the earliest known: the elaborate set of meanings ascribed to the eye in ancient Egyptian religion. The eye is ubiquitous in Egyptian iconography, especially on amulets and mummies as a form of protection.[33] Eyes were both divine and potent: it was from the tears of the creator god that humanity was formed.[34] But the relationship of eyes to divinity was multiple. The eyes of the falcon god Horus represented the sun (right) and the moon (left); yet the right eye was also known as 'the eye of Re'.[35] Within the world of the gods, eyes could be removed and restored. In the text known as the *Contendings of Horus and Seth*, Seth gouged out Horus' eyes.[36] But the goddess Hathor bathed the sockets in gazelle's milk, and restored the eyes, which were thereafter known as *wedjat*, 'healed' or 'restored' eyes. In spite of the complexities, the primary associations of the eye in ancient Egypt are with benevolence, wholeness, creativity, and protection.

[32] General: Deonna (1965). On the vast range of folktale sources: Thompson (1955–8: vi. 263–6, s.v. 'Eye' and related entries thereafter). Good, albeit brief survey: Potts (1982). Fingesten (1959) collects useful comparative material, but presents a highly dubious general case ('when a magic world-view prevailed at a given period, eyes were exaggerated [*sc.* in their iconography]') (29).

[33] Wilkinson (1992: 43).

[34] Hornung (1982: 150); Quirke (1992: 26).

[35] Wilkinson (1992: 43).

[36] Watterson (1984: 86); Quirke (1992: 64).

Another example of the eye's symbolic benevolence belongs to a wholly different cultural context. The 'Eye of Providence in a radiant Triangle' appears on the reverse of the Great Seal of the United States, and also on the back of the one-dollar bill. The process of deciding on the design for the Great Seal was elaborate and lengthy: three separate committees deliberated between 1776 and 1782. The eye-in-a-triangle had been a persistent feature of the design since its approval by the first committee (Benjamin Franklin, John Adams, Thomas Jefferson). Rather than following European precedent for the terminology of the 'Eye of God', they opted for the less explicitly religious 'Eye of Providence'.[37] Whatever the name, the symbolism was evidently felt to involve a kind of benevolent, all-seeing surveillance, reminiscent, in respect of positive symbolism if not of design, of the eye-in-the-homestead (set into the triangular gable of a roof) watching over the residents in Chagall's *The House with the Green Eye* (1944).[38]

Destructiveness

In other cultural settings, eyes can be far from benevolent. Probably the most widespread instance concerns the 'Evil Eye', the belief that certain individuals possess the power to harm, either intentionally or unintentionally, those upon whom their glance falls.[39] From ancient Sumer onwards, there are countless examples of verbal and practical expressions of such an idea, which rests on the assumption that the eye is an active agent rather than a passive recipient. The extraordinary pervasiveness of strategies for averting such eye-generated harm through the use of apotropaic gestures, charms, and talismans demonstrates how widespread the belief has been and still is. In the authoritative words of John Elliott, 'over more than two millennia, belief in the malignant power of the Evil Eye has made its way from its circum-Mediterranean birthplace to the northernmost reaches of the Old World to virtually all the countries of the New World'.[40] Much anthropological work has been done on this phenomenon, relating it, in particular, to societies characterized both by scarcity of resources or resources stretched by competitive rivalries and envy (as between agriculturalists and pastoralists), and also by the perceived constant presence of malign human and supernatural forces. As well as offering a cognitive explanation for the occurrence of otherwise inexplicable disasters, belief in the Evil Eye has, it has been argued, the effect, among others, of reinforcing social boundaries, constraining social deviance, and enforcing the avoidance of strangers.[41] Such an etic interpretation marches well with the fact that certain groups of socially or physically

[37] Eye of God: see e.g. the image of 'Providentia Dei' in John Comenius' *Orbis Pictus*, CXLIX = Comenius (1887: 191). In general: Potts (1982: 68–78).

[38] For Chagall's Cyclops, see pp. 328–9.

[39] Comprehensive studies are now in Elliott (2015, 2016), with two further volumes promised. See also Seligmann (1910); Roberts (1976); Dundes (1992).

[40] Elliott (1994: 51).

[41] Elliott (1994: 60–2).

marginalized persons tend particularly to be regarded as possessing the Evil Eye: hunchbacks, eunuchs, epileptics, strangers, and individuals or peoples perceived as 'exotic'.[42] Not surprisingly, persons with certain kinds of ocular abnormality may arouse the same association: examples are the visually impaired or blind, and those, such as the Apostle Paul, whose bushy eyebrows allegedly joined in the middle, and who had, at the turning point of his life, been temporarily blinded.[43]

A different type of perceived ocular menace, hardly less common than the belief in the Evil Eye, is related to the idea of permanent, ubiquitous surveillance. Such an idea does not necessarily imply *malicious* surveillance: witness the Eye of Providence. Numerous religious traditions envisage the Sun as the Eye of God, which not only sees all but, on the basis of what it sees, administers justice to all.[44] But it is a short step from such a belief to a sense of oppressiveness felt by those being watched. Doubtless perceptions of the role of the official known as the 'King's Eye' in ancient Persia varied depending on whether one was the target of espionage or a beneficiary of the information that it extracted.[45] Fear of being spied on goes back a long way: Walter Burkert argued that 'the anxiety aroused by a spying eye has a biological, prehuman basis'.[46] In the modern world, the cognitive and emotional implications of mass surveillance have become pressing. George Orwell explored the theme terrifyingly in *1984*, via the notion of ubiquitous, two-way 'telescreens'; J. R. R. Tolkien did so more traditionally, through the idea of the malevolent Eye of Sauron, in *The Lord of the Rings*. Of all forms of implacable ocular monitoring, perhaps the scariest involves an eye capable of surveying everything around it in a perfect circle; the scariness derives precisely from the perfection. Jeremy Bentham's 'enlightened' concept of the Panopticon, a circular building with at its centre an observation post manned by a single watchman, allowed the inmates—prisoners, lunatics, workers, depending on the kind of institution—to be permanently observed, while remaining ignorant of whether such observation was in fact taking place.[47] The connection between the eye and circularity is one we shall meet again and again.

As well as the Evil Eye and the perceived threat posed by surveillance, a more tangible mode of ocular destructiveness is sometimes envisaged. Such a power to harm is ascribed especially to certain divinities or otherwise supernatural beings.

[42] Cf. Francis Bacon, *Of Envy*: 'Deformed persons and eunuchs and old men and bastards, are envious: for he that cannot possibly mend his own case, will do what he can to impair another's...' (in Montagu 1825: 26); cf. Freud in *The Uncanny*: 'And if anyone is too different from other people, especially because of unpleasant physical marks, he is thought to harbour unusually strong envy and the ability to translate that envy into malevolent action' (Freud 2003: 147; cited, in a different translation, by Schoeck 1992: 195).

[43] Paul: *Acts of Paul and Thecla* 2.3; see Elliott (1990: 269). For the possibility that Paul might have been the object of Evil Eye accusations, see Elliott (2011).

[44] See Durand (1992: 171–2) for examples.

[45] See e.g. Shahbazi (1988); Llewellyn-Jones (2013: 47).

[46] Burkert (1979: 157 n. 30).

[47] On Bentham and 'le panoptisme', see Foucault (1975: 201–10).

In *Cath Maige Tuired*, a key text of the mythological cycle of Irish storytelling, the tale is told of a battle between the gods of Gaelic Ireland, the Túatha Dé Danann, and the Fomoire, their gigantic/monstrous adversaries. During the battle there occurred a combat between the deity Lug and his extraordinary opponent Balor, notable above all for his maleficent eye:

> Lug and Balor of the piercing eye met in the battle. The latter had a destructive eye which was never opened except on a battlefield. Four men would raise the lid of the eye by a polished ring in its lid. The host which looked at that eye, even if they were many thousands in number, would offer no resistance to warriors. It had that poisonous power for this reason: once his father's druids were brewing magic. He came and looked over the window, and the fumes of the concoction affected the eye and the venomous power of the brew settled in it. Then he and Lug met…'Lift up my eyelid, lad,' said Balor, 'so I may see the talkative fellow who is conversing with me.' The lid was raised from Balor's eye. Then Lug cast a sling stone at him which carried the eye through his head, and it was his own host that looked at it. He fell on top of the Fomorian host so that twenty-seven of them died under his side; and the crown of his head struck against the breast of Indech mac Dé Domnann so that a gush of blood spouted over his lips.[48]

It seems to be assumed that Balor is two-eyed, but only one of the eyes has any significance.[49] What strikes the reader above all is the sheer *weight* of the eyelid, a detail that lends remarkable, even if not unique, memorability to the narrative.[50]

Three eyes, or one

Another tradition that evidences the idea of a potentially destructive eye is Hinduism, where ocular imagery is hardly less ubiquitous than in ancient Egypt, and where the notion of the Evil Eye is also pervasive.[51] But a more distinctive feature of Hinduism—albeit found with variations across the world, as in Daoism and Theosophy—is the belief in the existence of a third, invisible eye, located centrally just above the junction of the eyebrows.[52] This third eye can be thought of in highly positive, spiritual terms, as constituting a gateway to a higher consciousness; as such it is an attribute of yogi (practitioners of yoga). But in certain contexts it can also embody fearsome destructive power. When the god Śiva—an ascetic who was also a prey to lust—was distracted from his meditations by Kāma

[48] *Cath Maige Tuired* §133–5; text and trans. Gray (1982: 61). Mercedes Aguirre's modern reimagining of the tale of Balor can be found in Esteban and Aguirre (2015: 13–26).

[49] 'Although Balor is not said to be one-eyed, there is malefic power in only one of his eyes…' (Gray 1982: 107, on §133–5).

[50] Not unique: 'The savage Welsh giant Yspaddaden requires attendants to raise his eyelids by means of forks' (Gray 1982: 107, on §133).

[51] Dallapiccola (2002: 72).

[52] O'Flaherty (1973: *passim*, but esp. 247–51).

the god of desire, he opened his third eye in anger and consumed Kāma in fire, reducing him to ashes. Only on the petition of the other gods did Śiva restore him to life.[53]

If the alleged possession of a third eye features in several religious traditions, equally widespread is the notion that there might exist creatures with just one eye. In modern science fiction and computer games, one-eyed monsters are ten-a-penny, having already made their debut in the 1970s role-playing game *Dungeons and Dragons*; but the list of their ancestors is long and varied. Among these are the mischievous Japanese *hitotsume-kozō*, bald, childlike figures clad in the robes of Buddhist monks and endowed with a large, single, central eye; the Slavic bogey-figure Likho, often depicted as a black-clad old hag; the evil, red-haired, Cantabrian giant Ojáncanu; Tepegöz, the wild and hideous ogre from *The Book of Dede Korkut*; and the wholly enigmatic one-eyed figures depicted on Mesopotamian cylinder seals, the earliest dated *c.*3000 BCE—conceivably the most ancient known antecedents of Polyphemus.[54] It would be very unwise to attribute a single mythical significance to the motif of monocularity in relation to such contextually diverse creatures. But one recurring aspect of mythical monocularity does merit emphasis: the idea that a physical defect may go along with an unusual, compensating power. The best-known case is that of the Norse god Odin, who, in return for knowledge, sacrificed one of his eyes at the sacred well of the wise Mimir.[55] The balance between loss of sight and gain in insight, power, or other capacity is one that, as we shall see, finds resonance in several ancient Greek myths.

Blinding

The vindictive act of destroying the eyesight of another is by no means restricted to the world of story. In a number of societies it has been a common, indeed institutionalized practice. It was a punishment of choice inflicted on opponents of the Great King of ancient Persia; in the Norman world of medieval Europe it was an equivalent of the death penalty; under the Byzantine Empire the neutralization of rivals through facial disfigurement, especially blinding, was a standard political tactic.[56] Even in cultures where such real-world acts were relatively rare, blinding as a storytelling motif has exercised a powerful impact. Numerous folktales narrate an episode in which a giant, ogre, Devil, or other formidable adversary is blinded and thus defeated by the hero.[57] But the mythical theme of blinding

[53] *Skanda Purāṇa* 5.3.150.18.

[54] See Porada (1947: 16; 1976: 112–13, 115–16, and figs 14, 16, 18); Goff (1963: 69, 214, and fig. 283); Knox (1979).

[55] See stanzas 28–9 of *Völuspá* in the *Poetic Edda*. On Odin, see Kershaw (2000). On Odin's eye, see Dumézil (1988: 139–59, esp. 139–40). For some fascinating Irish parallels to the motif of Odin's eye, see J. Carey (1983).

[56] Persia: Llewellyn-Jones (2013: 47–8). Normans: Van Eickels (2004). Byzantium: Kazhdan (1991: i. 297–8).

[57] See our discussion of the *comparanda* at pp. 8–14.

extends far beyond such cases.[58] One dimension is cosmological: the notion that the Moon is a weaker, more 'blind' eye compared with the Sun, is found in, for example, Mayan and Burmese tales, and has analogues in Egyptian belief.[59] In the Judaeo-Christian and subsequent Western tradition, the idea of blinding is exploited in yet other ways. The biblical figure of Samson is doubtless the most memorable instance, but his story has to be seen against a rich and diverse background. The Hebrew Bible is replete with examples of blindness inflicted on those who defy God;[60] the New Testament shifts the focus, with Jesus depicted as a bringer of light in darkness and of sight to the sightless.[61]

Greece and Rome

Certain topics stand out from our brisk cross-cultural review: all-encompassing surveillance, for good or ill; the destructive gaze; the third eye; the single eye; the act of blinding. All these matters are explored in the Graeco-Roman material, being developed in often striking directions; and they are abundantly supplemented by other issues relating to vision, especially the theme of 'independent eyes'. We have already identified contexts from certain other cultures in which ocular symbolism is especially highlighted. Yet it is difficult to think of *any* cultural setting in which the visual plays such a prominent imaginative role as it does in the Graeco-Roman world.[62] Plato lent his philosophical backing to this prominence, as did Aristotle (4th cent. BCE); Cicero the rhetorician also advocated it; so did Varro (2nd–1st cent. BCE), Pliny the Elder, and, later still, Isidore of Seville (6th–7th cent. CE).[63] By no means the least powerful argument in favour of the perceived prominence of vision in classical antiquity is the large number of *myths* that explore the theme—far more than relate to any other of the senses.[64] Accordingly, myths will occupy an important place in the account that follows.

Surveillance

A recurrent feature of Greek and Roman thought is the overlap between the concepts of light and eye. In both Greek and Latin certain words can bear both meanings: Greek *phaos* and Latin *lumen*, for instance. Correspondingly there are many examples of two complementary tropes: the Sun (or Moon) seen as an eye, and

[58] See Thompson (1955–8: vi. 76–8 s.v. 'Blind' and related lemmata thereafter).

[59] See Abbott and Khin Thant Han (2000: 88–9).

[60] e.g. Exod. 4:11; Lev. 26:16; Deut. 28:65; 2 Kings 6:18.

[61] e.g. Luke 4:18; Matt. 9:27–30, 20:30–4; John 9:5–7.

[62] Antiquity in general: G. Simon (1988). Greece: Christopoulos, Karakantza, and Levaniouk (2010). Prominence of the visual in Greece: Steinhart (1995: 1). Squire (2016: 9–10) rightly challenges attempts by anti-ocularcentrists to deny or minimize the assumed priority of the visual in classical antiquity.

[63] Pl. *Phdr.* 250d, *Resp.* 507c; Arist. *Metaph.* 980a; Cic. *De or.* 2.357; Varro, *Ling.* 6.80; Plin. *HN* 11.52.139; Isid. *Etym.* 11.36, with Rizzini (1998: 9).

[64] Bader (1985: 10).

the eye seen as the Sun (or Moon).[65] Eyes, it was widely assumed, send out rays; so does the Sun (or Moon). To be sure, this assumption was not universally held. Various Presocratic philosophers took a different view, while Aristotle voiced strong objections to the idea of the eye as an organ that emitted rays.[66] Yet such views were in a minority; the emission theory would be consolidated by Galen and Claudius Ptolemy (both 2nd cent. CE).[67] In keeping with this way of thinking is the frequent association between the god Helios (to the Romans, Sol) and vision—specifically, *omni*vision. During his daily, chariot-borne progress across the sky from east to west, Helios saw—and heard—everything.[68] From his unique vantage point he was able to inform Demeter about Hades' abduction of her daughter Persephone, and to report to Hephaestus the news about his wife Aphrodite's adultery with Ares.[69] Not only was Helios a bringer of daylight and the light of knowledge: he also had other kinds of power over light. He could blind the wicked; but he could also reverse the process. When Orion raped Oinopion's daughter Merope, her outraged father put out her assailant's eyes; but eventually Helios restored his sight after befriending the blind and by now pitiable wanderer.[70]

Although Helios was positioned at the apogee (literally) of surveillance, he was not the only mythical character to possess extraordinary vision. Argus, the divinely appointed watcher/gaoler of Io, was known as Panoptes ('All-Seeing').[71] He had four eyes (evidently two in front and two behind); or a hundred; or two hundred; or a thousand; or eyes all over his body; or countless.[72] The only way to outmanoeuvre him was to lull each of his eyes to sleep, as Hermes/Mercury did before killing him. Equally multi-ocular, but more problematic for the reader/viewer to envisage, is Fama, Virgil's extraordinary personification of Rumour, with as many eyes (and tongues, mouths, and ears) as feathers on her body: perpetually on the *qui vive* for any new piece of scandal.[73] Finally we should mention a character whose sight was exceptional for sharpness rather than breadth. Like Superman, Lynceus could see over vast distances and through solid objects. He was, however—like Argus, but unlike Helios/Sol and Fama—a mortal. When he

[65] For details, see Rizzini (1998: 128–44, esp. 132–3).

[66] See Rizzini (1998: 140–1), esp. on Arist. *Sens.* 1.437–8.

[67] Rizzini (1998: 139). On ancient optics in general, see G. Simon (1988).

[68] *Il.* 3.277; *Od.* 11.109; Aesch. *TrGF* fr. 192. Other refs. in *Der Kleine Pauly* (1964–75: ii, s.v. 'Helios', col. 1000).

[69] Demeter: *Hom. Hymn Dem.* 26 and 62–89. Hephaestus: *Od.* 8.270–1.

[70] Eratosth. [*Cat.*] 32. For an overlap between Orion and the Cyclopes, see pp. 122–3 .

[71] Aesch. *Supp.* 303–5.

[72] Two plus two: Hes. fr. 294 M–W. A hundred: Ov. *Met.* 1.625, 721. Two hundred: Ov. *Am.* 3.4.19–20. A thousand: Stat. *Silv.* 5.4.11–13. All over: Apollod. *Bibl.* 2.1.2; Hyg. *Fab.* 145; and often in art, cf. Steinhart (1995: 121–3). Countless: Aesch. *PV* 568. See Pettazzoni (1956: 151); Fowler (2013: 241 with n. 14).

[73] *Aen.* 4.181–3. Dyer (1989) argues improbably that these eyes belong to the people below on earth.

and his brother Idas were in dispute with their cousins Castor and Polydeuces, Lynceus used his penetrative sight to locate the pair of them while they were hiding in a hollow oak tree. Idas killed Castor, but Polydeuces killed Lynceus; his superpowers were not enough to save him.[74]

The destructive gaze

In Graeco-Roman culture we meet several different types of ocular aggression. Foremost among these is the 'Evil Eye'.[75] The ubiquity of the idea is evidenced by the enormously widespread presence of means of averting it. Grotesque masks, amulets, and images of phalluses and testicles were all designed to distract the eye of the potentially malevolent gazer by their conspicuousness, oddness, or absurdity.[76] The phenomenon of *baskania* appears extensively in Heliodorus' novel *Aethiopica* (perhaps 3rd cent. CE), but the *locus classicus* is a dialogue by Plutarch (1st–2nd cent. CE).[77] At a dinner party hosted by the Roman proconsul Lucius Mestrius Florus, the conversation turns to the topic of those alleged to cast the Evil Eye. All the guests dismiss the idea, until Florus himself argues that the facts point in the opposite direction: people can indeed be harmed by a look. Plutarch then follows his patron's lead, suggesting that the harm is caused by emanations from the eye: just as a lover's look can powerfully affect the beloved, so the look of an envious person can enter and harm a victim.[78] In terms of the mechanics of the operation, vision is said to be 'carried by an essence that gives off a flame-like brilliance' (681a).[79] In this dialogue and elsewhere—for instance, in reports by the Elder Pliny and Philo of Alexandria (*fl.* 1st cent. CE)—there is general agreement that 'outsiders' of one kind or another are typically responsible for the casting of evil glances. Among those singled out are Egyptians, other peoples in Africa, Triballi, Illyrians, women of Scythia, and the Thibii of Pontus. Noteworthy too is the attribution of some kind of irregularity of the eyes or eyebrows to those with the power to cast the Eye. Particularly to be avoided are an eye that looks askance, eyes with double pupils, and eyebrows that are knitted together.[80]

[74] Pind. *Nem.* 10; Apollod. *Bibl.* 3.10.3.

[75] Rakoczy (1996); Rizzini (1998: 144–54); Elliott (2016).

[76] Barton (1993: 168); Elliott (1994: 56–7; 2016).

[77] On Helidodorus, see Yatromanolakis (1988); Dickie (1991); Rakoczy (1996: 205–13). Plutarch: *Quaest. conv.* 5.7 (=680c–683b), on which see Dickie (1991); Rakoczy (1996: 186–216); Elliott (2016: *passim*, but esp. 48–56).

[78] See Dickie (1991); Johnston (1999: 172, 187–8, 196–8, 215). On the emanation ('extramissionist') theory of ocular activity—as opposed to the view that posited that objects emit *eidola*, which impact on the eye—see Squire (2016: 16–17).

[79] We reserve for Chapter 9 discussion of the connection between looking and fire; see p. 228.

[80] Askance: Hor. *Epist.* 1.14.37–8. Double pupils: Plin. *HN* 7.2.16 (NB also 11.52–7 on ocular characteristics); Ov. *Am.* 1.8.15–16; see Rizzini (1998: 10–11), who tellingly speaks of 'a maleficent doubling of the power of the look' (our translation). Knitted eyebrows: Plin. *HN* 11.114. See also Elliott (2016: 123–5).

Real-world practices and beliefs are habitually refracted and intensified in mythology. In regard to the Evil Eye, two formidable female figures exemplify this truth: Medea and Medusa.

One of Medea's most chilling exploits concerns her lethal attack on the bronze Cretan giant Talos, whom the Argonauts encountered on their return from Colchis to Greece.[81] Talos was invulnerable apart from a tiny weak point in the ankle, where a thin membrane covered the vein through which his life-*ichōr* flowed. Medea's tactic for causing his downfall involved an unusual ocular assault. Holding her robe on either side of her cheeks in order to focus her gaze with absolute concentration, she invoked the spirits of death. Then, in the words of Apollonius of Rhodes (*Argon.* 4.1669–88):

> Setting her mind to evil, with her malevolent glance she bewitched the eyes of Talos, the man of bronze; and her teeth ground out bitter fury against him, and she sent forth dark phantoms in the frenzy of her rage... And as he was heaving huge rocks to stop them from reaching the haven, he grazed his ankle on a pointed crag; and the *ichōr* gushed out like melting lead; and not for much longer did he remain standing on the jutting cliff.

The subject of manifold reappropriations in modern times, not least by feminist writers such as Hélène Cixous, who have seen in her a model to be aspired to, Medusa and her sister Gorgons were depicted in antiquity as embodiments of horror: their hair consisted of writhing snakes, and to look at them turned the looker to stone.[82] Two aspects of visual representations of the Gorgons are especially relevant to an enquiry into the symbolism of the eye. First, they are typically depicted full face, with implacably staring eyes; no monocularity there.[83] Secondly, time and again we find ancient depictions with an unmistakable *circularity*, belonging not only to the Gorgons' faces, but also to the objects, large and small, that bear their images. Coins, dishes, and shields, as well as the facades, *acrōtēria,* and antefixes of temples, all display not just the head of a Gorgon, but a head with a roughly circular shape.[84] Such *gorgoneia* typically have other characteristics too, notably a grotesquely protruding tongue and rows of fangs. But it is the unblinking, full-frontal gaze, as often as not set within a near-circular face fringed by a periphery of snakes, that arrests the attention of any viewer bold enough to risk petrifaction by gazing back. Not for nothing does Homer say of Hector, fearsome in his homicidal battle rage, that 'his eyes were the eyes of a Gorgon, or of Ares the plague of mortals' (*Il.* 8.349).[85]

[81] See Buxton (2013b). [82] Cixous (1976: 885). [83] Full face: see Vernant (1991: 112).
[84] See Steinhart (1995: 63–4); Aguirre Castro (1998a); Leeming (2013: 19–29).
[85] See Eck (2012: 144–5) on the murderous *look* of the furious warrior.

The third eye

Nothing in Greece or Rome rivals the prominence of the 'third eye' in some other cultures. Some sporadic and diverse instances are, however, of considerable interest.

Describing the topography of Argos, Pausanias comes to its citadel, Larisa (2.24.3–4):

> There is also a temple of Athene worth seeing. Here are placed votive offerings, including a wooden image of Zeus, *which has two eyes in the natural place and a third on its forehead*. This Zeus, they say, was a paternal god of Priam, the son of Laomedon, set up in the uncovered part of his court, and when Troy was taken by the Greeks Priam took sanctuary at the altar of this god. When the spoils were divided, Sthenelus, the son of Capaneus, received the image, and for this reason it has been dedicated here. The reason for its three eyes one might infer to be this. That Zeus is king in heaven is a saying common to all men. As for him who is said to rule under the earth, there is a verse of Homer [*Il.* 9.457] which calls him, too, Zeus: 'Zeus of the Underworld, and the august Persephone.' The god in the sea, also, is called Zeus by Aeschylus, the son of Euphorion. So whoever made the image made it with three eyes, as signifying that this same god rules in all the three 'allotments' of the Universe, as they are called.

In Pausanias' opinion, Zeus' three eyes stand for his presumed role as overseer of the provinces, which most mythological accounts distributed between three separate deities: Zeus himself (sky), Poseidon (sea), and Hades (Underworld).[86] Whatever we make of Pausanias' interpretation, it is clear that the third eye of Zeus is intended as a positive symbol signifying an extra power, generated by an enhanced ability to see.

A very different three-eyed image has been analysed by Matthias Steinhart.[87] A Hellenistic terracotta figurine from Egypt (late 2nd–early 1st cent. BCE) represents a donkey wrapped in a cloak, standing as if in an oratorical posture.[88] Above and attached to the donkey's head is a sculpted eye, in addition to the two normally positioned eyes possessed by the humanoid donkey. Steinhart relates this to an anecdote reported by Origen (2nd–3rd cent. CE) about Plato according to which, after developing his Theory of Ideas, the philosopher 'saw himself to possess a third eye'—evidently the soul-eye, which, according to Plato himself, was drawn towards *nous* or the truth by dialectic.[89] Steinhart persuasively suggests that the donkey–orator is a caricature of Plato himself. Its third eye is looking upwards—at the Ideas.

[86] See Pettazzoni (1956: 152). [87] Steinhart (1995: 28–31).

[88] Berlin, Ägyptisches Museum X 668 = Pl. 6, 1–2 in Steinhart (1995).

[89] Riginos (1976: 147), on *Anecdote* 102; Origen, *C.Cels.* 6.8; Pl. *Resp.* 533d, cf. 527d–e.

In the world of everyday experience—a world far more real, to anyone but a Platonist, than that of Platonic Ideas—to be three-eyed qualified the individual concerned for inclusion in the Roman 'monster market'. Plutarch reports that people 'who have no calves, or who are weasel-armed, or have three eyes, or are ostrich-headed', could be found in this market, though whether to be bought and sold or merely gawped at is uncertain.[90] The condition of these three-eyed persons perhaps resembled that of Alabama-born Bill Durks ('The Man with Three Eyes and Two Noses'), whose face was genetically cleft by a deep rift from the brow downwards, and who was exploited as a circus 'freak' for several decades in the mid-twentieth century. (Apparently he painted his so-called third eye in the depression between his widely separated eye sockets.) A far cry, whether in Rome or Alabama, from the idealized third eyes of Zeus and Plato.

The single eye

In the classical world the condition of being one-eyed is a signifier with multiple meanings.

The most anomalous mythological example is that of the Graeae (Grey Ones), three women old since birth, and at once cognitively wise and facially extraordinary. They had just one eye and one tooth between them; these were removable—a condition almost, but not quite, unique in mythological narratives.[91] While the eye was being passed from one Graea to the other, it could no longer, or not yet, exercise its function of seeing. Thus Perseus could intercept its passage, extracting information from the old women in return for restoring their capacity to see.[92]

Poised on the boundary between myth and history is a quite different variant of monocularity. The Arimaspians were an 'exotic' race located by several sources in northern Scythia, at the very limit of the known world.[93] At least in the view of Strabo (1.2.10), they were 'perhaps' the model on which Homer based his Cyclopes.[94] Herodotus (5th cent. BCE) knew of them from the *Arimaspea*, a now lost poem composed by Aristeas of Proconnesus (7th cent. BCE): '[Aristeas] tells us that "inspired by Phoebus" he journeyed to the country of the Issedones, and that beyond the Issedones live the one-eyed Arimaspians, and beyond them the griffins which guard the gold, and beyond the griffins the Hyperboreans, whose

[90] *De curios.* 520c. See W. F. Hansen (1996: 150); Trentin (2013: 93).

[91] Not quite unique: the eyes of the ogress Lamia (she was not monocular) were also removable. She had been Zeus' lover, but her newborns were all vindictively killed by Hera. Lamia's perpetual grief led to unending sleeplessness, but Zeus conferred on her the ability to remove her eyes and pop them temporarily into a basket. With no eyes to remain wakeful, she could at last sleep. See Diod. Sic. 20.41.3–6, with the splendid study by Patera (2015: 1–105, esp. 34–8).

[92] Apollod. *Bibl.* 2.4.2.

[93] See Skinner (2012: 64–8), and above all the important discussion by Ratcliffe (2014), who emphasizes the overlap between the Arimaspians and the monocular, remotely dwelling beings described in Inner Asian thought.

[94] Ratcliffe (2014: 32–3); cf. Bolton (1962: 194–5 n. 20).

land comes down to the sea' (4.13.1). You can tell a person by the company they keep. Griffins, part lion, part eagle, and guardians of a priceless treasure, are marvellous hybrids at home on the very edge of civilization; their neighbours the Arimaspians belong in the same fantastic space. As Herodotus observes in another passage, after reporting that the Arimaspians are in the habit of stealing the griffins' gold: 'The most outlying lands, though, as they enclose and wholly surround all the rest of the world, are likely to have those things which we think the finest and the rarest' (3.116.1). Other sources confirm the Arimaspians' proximity to the griffins, the antagonism between the two groups, and the extreme remoteness of the location. There is also agreement about the Arimaspians' facial peculiarity: they are all born with just one eye.[95] It is not usually specified that their monocularity is a defect, nor that it is ugly or monstrous; indeed, in a fragment from Aristeas, the single eye of each Arimaspian is said to be set in a 'charming' forehead.[96] In any case, as with the hybridity of the griffins, the trait of having only one eye most certainly *is* a marker of strangeness and alterity. This is why the Arimaspians figure so often in ethnographic contexts that include other 'single-defect' races: people with their feet turned backwards; dogheads; androgynes; the one-legged, who shade themselves by lying on their backs and using their feet as parasols; people with eyes in their shoulders.[97]

A different kind of monocularity befalls humans who start out with the usual quota of eyes but lose one. According to some Greek sources, the appropriate term for such individuals was *heterophthalmoi*, as opposed to the *monophthalmoi*, who were one-eyed from birth.[98] High-profile examples include Hannibal, who lost vision in his right eye as a result of an eye infection, and the Roman military commander Sertorius, who lost an eye in battle.[99] But such misfortunes were commonplace among ordinary individuals too. The leather eye-patch found at Vindolanda (a frontier fort near Hadrian's Wall) provides one sort of physical proof.[100] Another is provided by the inscription referring to a cure at Asclepius' shrine at Epidaurus:

> Ambrosia of Athens, blind of one eye. She came as a suppliant to the god. As she walked about in the sanctuary she mocked some of the cures as incredible and impossible, that the lame and blind should be healed by merely seeing a dream.

[95] Aesch. *PV* 802–7; Hdt. 4.27.1; Paus. 1.24.6; Plin. *HN* 7.2.10; *Suda* s.v. 'Arimaspeios'.

[96] Fr. 3 in Bolton (1962: 207); cf. Bowra (1956: 9).

[97] Plin. *HN* 7.2; Aul. Gell. *NA* 9.4; August. *De civ. D.* 16.8. On postclassical ramifications of the 'monstrous races', see pp. 235–43.

[98] Poll. *Onom.* 2.61–2; Herennius Philo, *De diversis verborum significationibus* E, 62 (in Palmieri 1988); Ammonius Grammaticus, *De differentia adfinium vocabulorum* 60 Valckenaer. Cf. Samama (2013: 242).

[99] Hannibal: Polyb. 3.79; Nep. *Han.* 4; Livy 22.2.10–11. Sertorius: Sall. *Hist.* 1.88; Plut. *Sert.* 1.4; 4.2. See Africa (1970); Samama (2013: 241–3); Trentin (2013: 99 n. 37).

[100] See Birley (1992).

> In her sleep she had a vision. It seemed to her that the god stood by her and said that he would cure her, but that in payment he would ask her to dedicate to the temple a silver pig as a memorial of her ignorance. After saying this, he cut the diseased eyeball and poured in a drug. When day came she went away cured.[101]

Inevitably—given comedy's delight in exploiting the incongruous—the one-eyed were objects of mockery. The comedian Plautus (3rd–2nd cent. BCE) and the satirist Persius (1st cent. CE) confirm this, while for the poet Martial (*fl.* 1st cent. CE) the *luscus* ('one-eyed') was a regular target.[102] No less inevitably, monocular individuals might be nicknamed 'Cyclops'. The sobriquet of one of Alexander's generals, Antigonus I 'Monophthalmos', perhaps, although not certainly, resulted from a war wound.[103] When the sophist Theocritus mockingly referred to him as 'Cyclops', Antigonus had him executed.[104] An even more august Macedonian 'Cyclops' was Philip II. The historian Marsyas (4th cent. BCE) reported that, just before the king lost an eye in battle, three entries in a local dithyrambic competition had been devoted to the subject of the Cyclops. Thus, in the words of Susan Stephens, 'poetry "predicted" Philip's loss, and by recording the anecdote Marsyas guaranteed its survival in the biographical tradition'.[105]

Another one-eyed historical figure who, even more clearly than Philip of Macedon, carries a heavy load of mythological baggage, is Horatius 'Cocles', celebrated defender of the bridge over the Tiber. As Plutarch wrote in his *Life of Publicola* (16.5):

> Horatius had been given his surname of Cocles because he had lost one of his eyes in the wars.[106] Some, however, say that his nose was flat and sunken, so that there was nothing to separate his eyes, and his eyebrows ran together, and that for this reason the people wished to call him Cyclops, but by a slip of the tongue the name of Cocles became generally prevalent instead.

In a famous analysis of the episode from the perspective of Indo-European studies, Georges Dumézil noted that various sources stress the stupefying effect that Cocles had on his Etruscan enemies, who regarded him as mad.[107] Particularly startling was the savage and menacing way in which he *looked* at his foes, a detail

[101] Trans. Edelstein and Edelstein (1945: 423.4), amended; cf. Garland (2010: 137).

[102] Plaut. *Curc.* 392–6; Pers. *Sat.* 1.128. Martial: see Watson (1982). In general: Garland (2010: 78).

[103] Billows (1990: 27–9); Lascaratos (1999); Lascaratos, Lascaratos, and Kalantzis (2004); Samama (2013: 242 with n. 66).

[104] Plut. *De lib.* 11b–c.

[105] Oiniades, *PMG* 840; quotation from S. A. Stephens (2006: 105). Philip's eye injury: Lascaratos, Lascaratos, and Kalantzis (2004); Samama (2013: 236–8).

[106] For this view, see Dion. Hal. *Ant. Rom.* 5.23.2.

[107] Polyb. 6.55; Dion. Hal. *Ant. Rom.* 5.24; Dumézil (1988: 144–8).

highlighted by Livy (1st cent. BCE–1st cent. CE).[108] It is hard to resist the force of Dumézil's comparison between this passage and texts about the Irish hero Cú Chulainn and the Viking Egil, who had the terrifying tendency to open one eye to maximum size and monstrously compress the other tight shut.[109] Whether Cocles–Cyclops deliberately contrived such a berserk appearance, or had no choice in the matter because of his previous loss of an eye, the connection between battle fury and monstrous grimace could well be, as Dumézil put it, 'maintaining the memory of analogous and very ancient beliefs or practices in the Latin world'.[110]

Blindness and being blinded

Eleftheria Bernidaki-Aldous (herself blind from the age of 3) was quite right in saying that the Greeks 'were clearly fascinated by blindness, both as a topic of philosophical discussion and as a reality of human experience'.[111] A good deal of modern scholarly work has been devoted to this fascination, in regard to everyday life and especially to mythology.[112] The equivalent situation in Rome has been less well explored, though the balance is being redressed.[113]

'To see the light (of the Sun)' is, in a common ancient Greek idiom, synonymous with 'to be alive'.[114] Moreover, according to a view widely held in classical antiquity, seeing and knowing are inseparable.[115] As Aristotle succinctly put it in his *Metaphysics*: 'We prefer sight, generally speaking, to all the other senses. The reason for this is that of all the senses sight best helps us to know things, and reveals many distinctions' (980a25–7). It follows that being deprived of one's eyesight entails losing not only the first of the senses, but also the most important source of knowledge. This primacy of sight applies to Roman contexts as to Greek. When the dream interpreter Artemidorus (2nd cent. CE) cites a wide range of examples in which people dream of losing their eyesight, with very few exceptions such dreams are said to portend one or another kind of misfortune.[116] A corollary of the high value placed on sight is the fact that deliberate blinding of an enemy was an all-too-common mode of aggression; some of the grimmest episodes of Roman historical narrative turn on this theme.[117] Nor was vindictive blinding confined to warfare. If anecdotal evidence is to be believed, both Hadrian (exceptionally) and Commodus (typically) demonstrated the limitless power that

[108] Livy 2.10: *circumferens...truces minaciter oculos.*
[109] Cú Chulainn: J. Gantz (1981: 136). Egil: *Egil's Saga* 55.
[110] Dumézil (1988: 148).
[111] Bernidaki-Aldous (1990: 3).
[112] e.g. Létoublon (2010); Tatti-Gartziou (2010); Buxton (2013c).
[113] See the excellent paper by Trentin (2013); also Vlahogiannis (1998); M. L. Rose (2003).
[114] Squire (2016: 10, with n. 34), commenting on e.g. *Od.* 4.539–40.
[115] Giuman (2013: 2–4); Squire (2016: 13).
[116] Artem. 1.26.
[117] Nowhere grimmer than in Lucan, *Phars.* 2.184–5. During a single engagement in the Roman Civil War, four centurions out of one cohort reportedly lost their eyes (Caes. *B.Civ.* 3.53). See in general Nutting (1922); Trentin (2013: 100–4).

belonged to an emperor by blinding those who displeased them.[118] They were following sound Hellenistic precedent: when his lieutenant Telesphorus ridiculed the wife of King Lysimachus, the latter caged the unwise joker and dug out his eyes, as well as inflicting other dire tortures.[119] The vast majority of eye injuries were, however, more mundane. Trauma will have been one frequent cause, as with the Cnidians who suffered eye wounds while breaking stones to dig across an isthmus. (For once the Delphic oracle was unambiguous: 'If Zeus had wanted it to be an island, he would have made it one.'[120]) Even more common will have been total or partial pathological blindness, either congenital or acquired through infectious disease. Evidence includes images of eyes from healing shrines, Thucydides' account of the plague, and Hippocratic discussion of periodic outbreaks of ophthalmia.[121]

But of all the areas of ancient discourse it is mythology that explores the topic of blindness most densely. According to a recurring pattern, the blind are imagined as deprived and dependent, yet simultaneously endowed with an exceptional gift, usually that of poetic skill or prophetic insight. Homer himself, usually portrayed as blind, relies on the goodwill of others to sustain his everyday needs, yet stands close to the gods for his matchless poetic brilliance.[122] The experience of the blind Phaeacian bard Demodocus is even more explicitly paradoxical: 'The Muse loved him exceedingly, and gave him a good gift and a bad one: she deprived him of his eyes, but gave him sweet song' (*Od.* 8.63–4). The lyric poet Stesichorus (6th cent. BCE) allegedly lost his sight for slandering Helen, but regained it when he recanted (Helen here clearly figures as a goddess; local Spartan cult may have been a factor in shaping the anecdote).[123] The accomplishment that compensated for Teiresias' lack of eyesight was not song but prophetic insight. In the Odyssean Underworld, Persephone is said to have granted to him alone the capacity to retain his intelligence and understanding after death (10.490–5); in Sophocles' *Oedipus Tyrannus* (perhaps 420s BCE), the prophet's reliance on a boy to guide his steps, combined with his unique, indeed tragic, insight into the past, present, and future of the doomed House of Laius, are the visible embodiments of the paradox of the blind 'seer'. Another blind prophet was Phineus, eventually liberated by the Argonauts from being tormented by the Harpies. His insight enabled him to predict his own rescue.[124]

Given the almost infinite capacity of Greek mythology to vary and recombine motifs rather than recycling identical ones, it is no surprise that the same is true

118 Hadrian: Galen v. 17–18 Kuhn. Commodus: SHA *Comm.* 10.6.

119 Plut. *De exilio* 606b; Ath. *Deipn.* 616c, with the comments of M. L. Rose (2003: 82).

120 Hdt. 1.174.

121 Healing shrines: Aleshire (1989: 42). Plague: Thuc. 2.49. Ophthalmia: Hippoc. *De vid. acie* 9. See M. L. Rose (2003: 85–6).

122 Graziosi (2002: 125–63) is outstandingly good on Homer's blindness.

123 Or perhaps Locrian cult; see Graziosi (2002: 149, with nn. 65, 66).

124 Ap. Rhod. *Argon.* 2.194–6.

of myths of blindness. According to the *Iliad* (2.594–600), when Thamyris (a.k.a. Thamyras) boasted that he was a better singer than the Muses, they 'maimed' him (other sources specify blinding) *and also* removed his gift for singing and caused him to forget his lyre-playing: intensification of punishment replaces an equivalence between power and defect.[125] In Sophocles' definitive dramatic treatment, when Oedipus recognizes 'the truth' at the moment of ending for ever his own capacity to see the light of day, he gains insight into his own identity, but does not achieve the broader and deeper insights associated with the skill of the prophet. These and other variations are all part of the mythological web. But what recurs again and again is the narrative motif that blinding follows the act of exceeding permitted limits.[126] It happened to Orion, blinded by his victim's father for drunkenly raping the girl to whom he had been promised; thus, as with the even more drastic deeds of Oedipus, transgressive behaviour within an *oikos* can precipitate blinding. Commoner still is the idea that penetrating the space of a divinity is a motive for blinding. This was true of the Thracian king Lycurgus, hybristic opponent of Dionysiac worship. Thamyris and Teiresias are analogous cases, as is Stesichorus (to the extent that Helen is regarded as a divinity). Phineus, too, exemplifies the pattern, especially according to the version that attributes his blinding to the fact that he divulged to mortals 'the sacred mind of Zeus himself'.[127] Finally—and, from a Cyclopean perspective, most relevantly—there is the case of Polymestor, like Lycurgus a mythical ruler of Thrace. When Troy was threatened with capture by the Greeks, Priam entrusted his youngest son Polydorus (along with a quantity of gold) to his guest-friend (*xenos*) Polymestor, for safe keeping. When Troy fell, Polymestor treacherously killed the boy and pocketed the gold. In his tragedy *Hecuba*, Euripides dramatizes the dénouement. Polydorus' mother Hecuba, now a prisoner of the Greeks, conspires with her fellow captive women to take dreadful revenge on Polymestor, using their brooch pins to put out his eyes. This is another variation of the pattern according to which transgression of limits begets blinding. In this instance the boundary that is overstepped, the custom that is vilely abused, is hospitality.

While on the topic of lethal brooch pins, we can hardly pass over the most famous *self*-blinding of all time. But *why* does Oedipus do it? In a memorable passage towards the end of *Oedipus Tyrannus*, Sophocles definitively encapsulates three interrelated themes: the damage caused by looking; a frantic attempt to undo that damage through self-harm; and one possible relationship between seeing and knowing. In the face of the horror he must confront, Oedipus' reported outburst is as syntactically convoluted as it is referentially opaque (1268–74):

[125] Other sources: Eur. *Rhes.* 921–5; Paus. 10.30.8; Poll. *Onom.* 4.141. [126] Buxton (2013c).
[127] Ap. Rhod. *Argon.* 2.181–2. Blindness as punishment: Tatti-Gartziou (2010).

> For he broke off the golden pins from [Jocasta's] raiment, with which she was adorned, and lifting up his eyes struck them, uttering such words as these: that they should not see his dread sufferings or his dread actions, but in the future they should see in darkness those they never should have seen, and fail to recognise those he wished to know.[128]

Any translation of these extraordinary lines can represent at best a vague approximation towards the meaning of the original Greek. But the gist is clear: eyes are a medium of (self-) knowledge; their removal should be a way of eradicating that knowledge. And yet, even when one sees 'in darkness', one cannot stop knowing.

Independent eyes

In Greece and Rome we frequently find moulded or painted representations of independent eyes, in a variety of contexts and with a variety of functions. Sometimes it is the anatomical quality of the independent eye that comes to the fore. Among the countless moulded representations of various body parts dedicated in the sanctuaries of healer deities, those of eyes are especially numerous. The interpretation of such objects is uncontroversial: they were expressions of gratitude for eye problems already cured, or offerings in anticipation of cure.[129] Equally widespread, however, are depictions of eyes in a variety of other contexts; and here interpretation is less secure.

Singly or in pairs, eyes frequently decorate ceramic cups and pots, 'oscillating between the realms of figure and ornament'.[130] Such images have been understood as apotropaic; or as representations of masks, which turn the reveller at a symposium into a follower of Dionysus; or as vehicles for bringing the inanimate to life.[131] A recent, highly sophisticated approach interprets them as invitations to the viewer to reflect on the complex interplay between sight and reflexivity: 'When the beholder regards an eye regarding him, he is alerted to his own act of seeing.'[132] Despite the tendency of many critics to privilege one or other of these approaches, there is much to be said for stressing plurality: none of these modes of seeing need exclude the alternatives.

A favourite context for representations of the free-floating eye is a ship's bow. In the Greek world, this motif can be traced back at least as far as the second millennium BCE, on a model boat from Phylakopi on Melos.[133] A memorable later example appears on the inner surface of an Attic black-figure dish, depicting a

[128] Trans. Lloyd-Jones. [129] Squire (2016: 20–3).

[130] The quotation is from Grethlein (2016: 87). Numerous illustrations in Steinhart (1995). Discussion also in Lissarrague (1990: 140–3), especially of eye motifs on vases in a sympotic context.

[131] Apotropaic: Jahn (1855). Masks: Kunisch (1990). Life-bringing: Martens (1992: 284–363).

[132] Grethlein (2016: 88).

[133] Basch (1987); Steinhart (1995: 88–102); Carlson (2009). Model boat: Basch (1987: 142, fig. 296); Steinhart (1995: 90, fig. 8).

recumbent, ship-borne Dionysus surrounded by dolphins below and grape clusters above; the eye in the prow, as well as the sleek hull, makes the vessel itself resemble a dolphin, while the pair of staring eyes on the dish's outer surface gives the impression of animating the inert.[134] But animation is not the only way of reading ships' eyes. An alternative approach takes such images to signify aggression: Philostratus describes a painting of a pirate ship that 'seems to see with grim eyes set into its prow' (*Imag.* 1.19). But this will hardly work for every image or every type of ship. On a more broadly applicable interpretation, an eye enables a ship to find its direction. For this approach too there is emic testimony: a character in Aeschylus (*fl.* early 5th cent. BCE) refers to a ship's prow 'scanning its way forward with eyes'.[135] Even though navigation in the real world relies on a human steersman, every ship equipped with its own symbolic eyes aspires to the condition of the self-propelling Phaeacian vessels, whose conscious minds possess humanlike understanding of peoples and places (*Od.* 8.555–63).

Ostensibly differing *toto caelo* from ships' eyes are the eyes found on images of the phallus.[136] That there is a connection between the sexual act and the act of looking is an axiom of ancient thought, but the link receives idiosyncratic expression in the recurrent image of a phallus equipped with eyes. Numerous examples in Greek and Roman plastic or painted art—whether free-standing (as in phalliform ceramic vessels), or attached to a male figure (most conspicuously Priapus), or embodied in the so-called phallus bird—have generated various interpretations. 'Apotropaic' has been a buzz word.[137] But may there not be a functional analogy with ships' eyes? The idea that to be sighted enables one *to find one's proper direction* works perfectly for the phallus, whose biological role is to aim for and dock in 'harbour'.[138]

Another locus for depictions of the independent eye is the shield. For both Greece and Rome we have abundant evidence for numerous different shield devices.[139] Among these we occasionally find depictions of the eye, whether as stand-out features of the physiognomy of a *gorgoneion*, or as stand-alone emblems.[140] Though one should always hesitate before ascribing an 'obvious' meaning to any form of symbolic behaviour, it hardly seems rash to assert that the main function of the image of the Gorgon on a shield was to provoke fear in an enemy.[141] Less obvious, perhaps, is the role of a single eye as a shield device, as

134 Munich, Staatliche Antikensammlungen 2044 = *LIMC* 'Dionysos' no. 788.

135 Danaus in Aesch. *Supp.* 716.

136 Steinhart (1995: 82–7); Frontisi-Ducroux (1996).

137 Boardman (1976: 288).

138 Steinhart (1995: 83): it is one of the class of 'things that have to find their own way' (our translation).

139 Greece: still excellent is Chase (1902); also Steinhart (1995: 110–14). Rome: Travis and Travis (2014).

140 *Gorgoneion*: Steinhart (1995: 63–4); Grethlein (2016: 96–105); NB. the black-figure cup (Cambridge, Fitzwilliam Mus. GR.12.1937) illustrated as his fig. 4.11.

141 Vernant (1991: 148–9). For an elegant analysis of images of the Gorgon's head *reflected in* a shield as depicted on two Apulian red-figure vases, see Grethlein (2016: 96–100).

represented for example on two sixth-century BCE images. On an Attic black-figure amphora by the Chiusi painter, one of the combatants in an infantry battle bears a circular shield whose only device, centrally placed, is a single large eye with a white pupil.[142] More unusual is a Boeotian terracotta statuette of a long-haired cavalryman wielding spear and circular shield; the latter bears a series of simple concentric designs, culminating in a solitary central eye.[143] Nothing can disprove either the 'Evil Eye/apotropaic' reading of these and comparable images, or the reading that sees these men's armour as coming frighteningly alive. In any case, perhaps one should not seek to pin the issue down any further: in the heat of battle an adversary would be more interested in self-preservation than in hermeneutics.[144] But it is worth stressing a separate point—namely, the pervasive connection between the eye and circularity, and specifically between the single eye and the round shield. This connection will occupy us repeatedly again, as we now turn to the Cyclopes.

Eye of the Cyclops

Although by no means all our sources for the ancient Cyclopes discuss their eye(s), many of them do. In the case of the Cyclopes as a group (or groups), when ocular matters arise they often concern an anatomical deformity, or at least peculiarity. In the specific case of Polyphemus, however, to deformity/peculiarity is added another factor related to his vision: the acquired disability of blindness.

Texts

The monocularity of the Hesiodic arms-producers is unambiguous to the point of tautology, as is the related idea of circularity: 'In other respects they were like the gods, except that each had a single eye in the middle of the forehead; accordingly they were called Circle-eyes [*Kuklōpes*], since a single circular [*kukloterēs*] eye lay in the forehead [of each]' (*Theog.* 142–5). We shall come back later to the enigma of the name 'Cyclopes', and hence to the accuracy of the translation 'Circle-eyes'. For the present we are interested only in Hesiod's view of Cyclopean anatomy; and about that there can be no argument. But the significance of this monocularity within Hesiod's narrative is less evident. The central placement of the eye clearly distinguishes the Hesiodic Cyclopes from the one-eyed mythical/historical figures—Antigonus Monophthalmos, Horatius Cocles, Hannibal, and so

142 Tübingen Antikensammlung 2451 = *CVA* Tübingen (2) Pl. 38, 2 = Pl. 42,1 in Steinhart (1995: discussed at 111).

143 Formerly on the market in Basel: details at Steinhart (1995: 110 n. 987, and pl. 42, 2).

144 Chase (1902: 85) classifies the eye device on shields as inspiring terror. Wilk (2000: 156–9) suggests that eyes-on-shields may momentarily distract an enemy, whose gaze is inexorably drawn to them. Apotropaic: Ducrey (1985: 53). Steinhart (1995: 114) rejects the apotropaic view.

on—who started out with a pair but lost the left or the right. The Hesiodic Cyclopes are physiologically closer to the Arimaspians, whose single eyes were also centrally positioned.[145] But circularity, an idea with which Hesiod makes great play, is every bit as important as centrality. In other contexts, roundness has been interpreted as a perfect or ideal form.[146] Nothing in the Hesiodic text suggests such a sense of perfection. Yet neither does there seem to be anything explicitly flawed or defective about Hesiod's Cyclopes: 'Strength and force and craft were upon their works' (146).

When we turn to the eye(s) of the Homeric Cyclopes, the picture becomes thematically richer but physiognomically more enigmatic. Within the overall plot structure of the *Odyssey*, Polyphemus' blinding is of prime importance, since it motivates the wrath of the ogre's father Poseidon towards Odysseus throughout the epic (1.68–79). In the more restricted context of book 9, the blinding takes on that much more meaning thanks to the stress on seeing and looking: Odysseus and his men turn their eyes towards the land of the Cyclopes (166); Odysseus wants to *see* the giant (229). When the narrative shudders to a halt in describing, through two momentous similes, the act of blinding itself—an extraordinary amalgam of burning, sizzling, boiling, and screaming—the effect rivals for impact some of the key incidents in the poem. In relation to Polyphemus' Homeric biography, it constitutes both the climax and, in effect, the end of his story. Yet what is its relationship to the physical attribute that allegedly defines the Cyclopes?

Homer nowhere explicitly describes the Cyclopes as one-eyed.[147] This was already noted in antiquity. In one of his treatises the poet Accius (2nd–1st cent. BCE) used this absence to make a point about the relative dates of Homer and Hesiod: Homer, he maintained, would never have omitted an explicit reference to Cyclopean monocularity if it had not already been made well known by Hesiod.[148] If it is true that the *Odyssey* takes it for granted that the Cyclopes had only one eye, then it does indeed become likely that someone (though not necessarily Hesiod) had already ascribed that characteristic to them before Homer. But *is* it true? The answer has to be yes, since Polypheman monocularity is a prerequisite for the narrative logic of a *single* act of blinding: nothing suggests that Odysseus and his men blind first one eye and then its hypothetical twin. As for the ingenious ancient suggestion that Polyphemus had originally been two-eyed but had lost one of them in an accident, nothing gives this idea the slightest credibility.[149] The Homeric text consistently refers to 'the eye' of Polyphemus in the singular,

145 See pp. 104–5.

146 Roundness as perfection: see Harpham (1982: 8), citing Bachelard, Jaspers, and Van Gogh ('elle aussi, la vie, est probablement ronde' (letter to Emile Bernard, 26 June 1888)).

147 See e.g. Mondi (1983: 35); Auffarth (1991: 296–7); Warner (1998: 87).

148 Quoted in Aul. Gell. *NA* 3.11.

149 Ingenious suggestion: Philoxenus cited in schol. *Od.* 9.106 (Dindorf 415) plus Eust. on *Od.* 9.183 (1622.47); see Mondi (1983: 35 n. 62).

rather than using a dual or a plural form; even when, during the account of the blinding, there is an exceptional, plural reference to the singeing of the Cyclops' 'eyelids and eyebrows', these are said to belong to 'the burning eyeball', in the singular (389–90).[150] All in all, it seems safe to conclude that the *Odyssey* presupposes, even if it does not state outright, that Polyphemus (and presumably his fellow Cyclopes too) was congenitally rather than accidentally one-eyed. Moreover, the fact that the poem does not explicitly highlight Polyphemus' facial oddity suggests, even if it does not definitely entail, that such a characteristic had already become his attribute before the poem was composed.

If Polypheman monocularity is taken for granted by Homer rather than explored, the same cannot be said for the blinding. The act is meticulously prepared for and lavishly described. It is also richly significant, not just for Odysseus' subsequent fate and for some of the poem's major themes, but also for the later tradition about the Cyclopes. The version in *Odyssey* 9 would become, if not the only model for later representations of the act, then at least by some distance the most influential one.

The blinding is, or is made by Odysseus-as-internal-narrator to seem, inevitable. Polyphemus' habit of blocking the cave entrance with a huge rock means that killing him with a sword is not an option (299–305): if the ogre were to die, the certain outcome for the imprisoned Greeks would be a slow, dark death from starvation (perhaps preceded by intra-Greek cannibalism?). Blinding has the unique advantage of removing Polyphemus' ability to pinpoint his captives' whereabouts while leaving him enough strength to unblock the cave entrance.

Given the ogre's immensity, his eye is, presumably, proportionately large; at any rate the Greeks use an object of considerable size—a length cut from Polyphemus' own olive-wood stake—in order to blind him. It takes four of Odysseus' men to wield it, plus the hero himself as a fifth (318–35). The fateful implement passes from Polyphemus' control rhetorically as well as practically: Odysseus and his men liken it to the mast of a twenty-oared merchant ship (321–4), the kind of vessel of which the Cyclopes, unlike the Greeks, have no knowledge, ignorant as they are of shipbuilding and navigation (125–30). Nor does the significance of the stake end there. Its composition from olive wood locates it within an *Odyssey*-wide sequence of meanings: the olive as the symbol of Athene, Odysseus' loyal champion; the olive tree beneath which Odysseus slept on his arrival at Phaeacia; the immovable bed of living olive wood that Odysseus constructed for Penelope and himself in their home on Ithaca.[151] In turning the stake against its owner, Odysseus appropriates the strongly positive symbolic charge that the olive tree

[150] Singular: *Od.* 1.69; 9.333, 383, 387 (cf. 390), 394, 397, 453, 503, 525; see Létoublon (2010: 177 n. 18); Derksen (1984: 21).

[151] Bed: Dougherty (2001: 178–81). Symbolism of the olive: S. D'Onofrio (2003: 143–5).

normally possesses, and thus implicitly lays claim—in his own, self-narrated self-presentation, of course—to the values of civilization against those of barbarity.

The manner of the blinding illustrates the Greeks' craftsmanly skills and propensity for teamwork, as contrasted with Cyclopean solitariness. When Odysseus has cut a length from the stake, he hands it to his men to plane; then he sharpens it, and hardens the point in the fire. The first of the two similes used to describe the blinding highlights cooperation, drawing once again on an area of craftsmanship foreign to the Cyclopes but familiar to the Greeks (382–90):

> They seized the beam of olive, sharp at the end, and leaned on it
> into the eye, while I from above leaning my weight on it
> twirled it, like a man with a brace-and-bit who bores into
> a ship timber, and his men from underneath, grasping
> the strap on either side whirl it, and it bites resolutely deeper.
> So seizing the fire-point-hardened timber we twirled it
> in his eye, and the blood boiled around the hot point, so that
> the blast and scorch of the burning ball singed all his eyebrows
> and eyelids, and the fire made the roots of his eye crackle.[152]

The second simile, no less graphic, involves a different type of artisanship, this time individual rather than collective (391–4):

> As when a man who works as a blacksmith plunges a screaming
> great axe blade or plane into cold water, treating it
> for temper, since this is the way steel is made strong, even
> so Cyclops' eye sizzled about the beam of the olive.

The relative dating of the Hesiodic and Homeric accounts of the Cyclopes is uncertain, but, *if* the Hesiodic account is the earlier, then it may not be far-fetched to detect an intertextual effect: in behaving like 'a blacksmith', the Greeks would be implicitly turning a traditional Cyclopean skill against Polyphemus, just as they *ex*plicitly deploy his stake against him. One might even fantasize that the profession of the *other* Homeric Cyclopes is that of blacksmiths rather than herdsmen. But, of course, the text is silent on this—as we shall be also.

The sighted Polyphemus is never presented as especially keen of vision—he is no Lynceus or Helios. On the contrary, he gives a touchy-feely impression, habitually using his hands for eating his human victims, milking his flock, and shifting his rocky door. After the blinding he becomes even more reliant on touch. He feels his way around the cave, then stretches out his arms in the doorway to

[152] Trans. Lattimore (1965), here and in subsequent quotations.

capture any would-be escapees (415–18). But, as usual, Odysseus' cunning has led him to anticipate. Whereas Polyphemus feels the *backs* of the rams as they leave the cave, the Greeks outwit him by clinging to the fleece *underneath*. Touch without sight is inadequate.

Prompted by Odysseus' boastful revelation of his own identity, Polyphemus achieves retrospective understanding of what has happened to him (502–16):

> 'Cyclops, if any mortal man ever asks you who it was
> that inflicted upon your eye this shameful blinding,
> tell him that you were blinded by Odysseus, sacker of cities.
> Laertes is his father, and he makes his home in Ithaca.'
> So I spoke, and he groaned aloud and answered me, saying:
> 'Ah now, a prophecy spoken of old is come to completion.
> There used to be a man here, great and strong, and a prophet,
> Telemus, Eurymus' son, who for prophecy was pre-eminent
> and grew old as a prophet among the Cyclopes. This man told me
> how all this that has happened now must someday be accomplished,
> and how I must lose the sight of my eye at the hands of Odysseus.
> But always I was on the lookout for a man handsome
> and tall, with great endowment of strength on him, to come here;
> but now the end of it is that a little man, niddering, feeble,
> has taken away the sight of my eye, first making me helpless
> with wine.'

Does Polyphemus, then, exemplify the mythical pattern of the blind man who possesses supra-human insight—a Teiresias or a Phineus? It seems not: after all, it is Telemus, not Polyphemus, who prophesies. The pattern is closer to that exemplified by Heracles in Sophocles' *Women of Trachis*, who, in the manner of Shakespeare's Henry IV and Macbeth, recognizes too late the true meaning of enigmatic prophecies relating to his death: that he will be killed by one already dead, and that 'this present, living moment' will witness the end of his labours.[153] Heracles is no prophet: his fate illustrates the truth that extraordinary physical strength is not necessarily accompanied by penetrative inner vision. The same seems true of Polyphemus. Yet there is a moment just before the end of book 9 that casts the matter in a slightly different light: not a prediction, but a prayer. Polyphemus invokes his father Poseidon in terms that strikingly anticipate the future direction of the plot. 'If I am truly your son,' cries the ogre, 'grant that Odysseus shall never reach home; or if he *does* get home...' (534–5):

[153] Soph. *Trach.* 1159–74; *2 Henry IV*, IV.v.236–40; *Macbeth*, IV.i.79–80, 91–3; V.vi.69–71.

> let him come home later, in bad case, with the loss of all his
> companions,
> in someone else's ship, and find troubles in his household.

This second, projected future will be fulfilled in all particulars. To this limited extent, therefore, Salvatore D'Onofrio is justified in suggesting a parallel between the Cyclopes and the Phaeacians: whereas the latter have the blind singer Demodocus, the former have the 'prophesying' Polyphemus.[154]

The Euripidean Cyclopes differ from their Homeric counterparts in that the former—all of them, not just Polyphemus—are explicitly monocular. When Silenus mentions them for the first time, the distinguishing epithet he gives them—even before he gets to their name—is *monōpes* ('one-eyed' (21–2)); to the satyr chorus, their ogrish master is *monoderktēs* ('sole-seeing' (79)), and later once again *monōps* (648). This facial idiosyncrasy, confirmed repeatedly later in the play, is the anatomical equivalent of the Cyclopes' social monadism (*monades* (120)).[155] Just as in Hesiod, their single eye is placed 'in the middle' (174, 235). Occasional plurals (*koras*, 'pupils' (463, 611); *ommata*, 'eyes' (470); *blepharōn*, 'eyelids' (485)) do not invalidate the general picture: *ophthalmon*, 'eye' (475), restores the singularity. As for the satyr chorus's comparison of Polyphemus to a tender young bridegroom 'looking handsomely with his eyes' (*ommasin dedorkōs* (511)), this plural is best interpreted not as undermining Polypheman monocularity, but as corroborating it: a recent commentary rightly calls the expression 'heavily sarcastic for the one-eyed monster'.[156]

Although the preparations for the blinding, the act itself, and its aftermath echo the *Odyssey* in many respects, there is a game of differences as well as similarities. As in Homer, Odysseus sharpens the olive stake, heats it, and drives it into the Cyclops' eye, like a shipwright who bores a timber by pulling his drill this way and that with two leather thongs (454–63). As in Homer, the sighted Polyphemus is touchy-feely, as when he selects two human victims and 'weighs them with his hands' because their flesh is fattest (379–80). More crudely than in Homer, the blinded ogre's slapstick staggering and blundering emphasize the inadequacy of his other senses to compensate for loss of vision. Quite unlike in Homer, the satyrs at first offer to help with the blinding, then spinelessly excuse themselves from participating when push comes to shove (469–71, 635–48). Echoing but also greatly amplifying Homer, the heated stake is repeatedly represented as a firebrand, *dalos*, which will smoke out, singe, burn, scorch, and carbonize the ogre's eye.[157]

[154] S. D'Onofrio (2003: 142).

[155] The conjecture *monades* is a highly plausible emendation of the transmitted text *nomades* ('nomads'); see Seaford (1984: ad loc.).

[156] O'Sullivan and Collard (2013) on 511–12.

[157] *Dalos*: 484, 593, 614, 630, 647. For more on fire and the Cyclopes, see pp. 227–30.

One other implied allusion to the Cyclopean eye merits attention. As soon as Polyphemus enters, the chorus liken him to two other mythological figures (211–13):

CYC. Look up and not down!
CHO. There! I'm looking up at Zeus himself, and I can see the stars and Orion.

The comparison with Zeus is mere craven flattery; more interesting is the identification with Orion. The Euripidean Polyphemus is a gigantic, club-wielding hunter, and a son of Poseidon; Orion had the same characteristics (though in the *Odyssey* Orion is described as extraordinarily handsome—hardly a conventional trait of Polyphemus).[158] A more significant parallel is the fact that Orion too was blinded, after raping Merope; her father avenged her by getting the rapist drunk and putting out his eyes.[159] It is true that Orion's serial sexual transgressions—he also tried to rape Artemis and the Hyperborean maiden Opis[160]—are hardly matched by Polyphemus; it should not be forgotten that in Euripides the ogre is sexually obsessed, and at one point, as we have seen, takes an unwilling Silenus into his cave to be his Ganymede (582–9).[161] Of course Odysseus does not blind Polyphemus because of *that* escapade, or because of his sexual conduct more generally. Nevertheless, albeit in a weaker form than in the case of Orion (or Oedipus), the association between blindness and unbridled sexual behaviour may conceivably be hinted at for the Euripidean Polyphemus too.

In Hellenistic and post-Hellenistic texts, we meet a variety of explorations of the look, and the looking, of the Cyclopes. We begin with two Hellenistic poets who exploit these interrelated motifs in contrasting ways.

Callimachus creates a memorable vignette of the scary appearance of the blacksmith Cyclopes—scary, that is, to anyone but the tough little Artemis who has come to visit them (*Hymn to Artemis* 52–4):

> All had a single eye beneath the brow, like a shield with four
> layers of hide, glowering fiercely...

Brief though it is, this passage is full of interest. First, *ophrun*, 'eyebrow', is grammatically singular; this could be a clever Callimachean 'correction' of *Od.* 9.389, where Polyphemus is said to have 'eyebrows'. This possibility becomes the more plausible as immediately afterwards Callimachus uses the expression *phaea mounoglēna*, 'eyes with a single eyeball'—*glēnē*, 'eyeball', occurs in the same

[158] Orion as gigantic, club-wielding hunter: *Od.* 11.572–5. As son of Poseidon: Pherec. fr. 52 Fowler. As handsome: *Od.* 11.310; and see pp. 134–8 on ugliness.

[159] Apollod. *Bibl.* 1.4.3; see p. 100.

[160] Artemis: Hor. *Od.* 3.4.70–2. Opis: Apollod. *Bibl.* 1.4.5.

[161] See p. 51.

Odyssean passage. Next, *phaea*, which we have translated as 'eyes', also means more literally 'lights'.[162] Both meanings recur elsewhere in the poem (71, 182), and also lie at the heart of Callimachus' account, in his *Hymn to Athene*, of the blinding of Teiresias for having unwittingly but transgressively seen Athene naked.[163] Finally, each eye is compared to 'a shield with four layers of hide'. This might be another piece of Callimachean sophistication: the Alexandrian physician Herophilus argued that the anatomy of the human eye was characterized by four-fold layering.[164] Be that as it may, there is surely a literary and artistic dimension to the shield analogy. As we have seen, shield devices consisting of a centrally placed eye are recurrent in Greek iconography. The Callimachean Cyclopes both echo and adapt this image: they bear, centrally, their own kind of 'shield-eye'.

Theocritus' accounts of the Cyclopean eye belong to his two poems about Polyphemus and Galatea. In the 11th *Idyll* the ogre describes his single eye ('than which nothing is dearer to me' (53)) in all-too-graphic detail, as if to rectify what some sources, not least the *Odyssey*, had forgotten to mention: 'I know, fair maid, why you are fleeing. It is because a shaggy eyebrow stretches over the whole of my forehead—a single long brow from one ear to the other. Underneath it is a single eye, and a wide nostril over my lip' (30–3).[165] He assumes that Galatea regards his monocularity as a disfigurement, for which he hopes to compensate with the economic attractiveness of a large herd and a well-stocked larder. But, although the Cyclops' 'look' is in this respect a feature of the poem, nothing much is made of the idea of looking. In *Idyll* 6, by contrast, the entire poetic armature is based on a play of viewpoints. Looking at or away from another person; seeing what one wants to see when gazing at oneself or at another; contemplating reflections; avoiding the Evil Eye; swearing an oath by one's one and only eye—these are the steps in an intricate ocular ballet.[166] Even the motifs of blinding and prophetic insight feature in the choreography: although, in terms of mythical chronology, the Polyphemus who courted Galatea was still sighted, the myth-telling tradition that Theocritus inherited was well aware of Odysseus' 'future' visit and its ruinous outcome for Polyphemus. Yet, even in face of that seemingly definitive fate, the Theocritean Cyclops can defy the prophet who foretold it: 'Let Telemus, the seer, carry home the trouble he predicts, and keep it for his own children' (23–4). The trope is a clever one: it is as if Polyphemus were knowingly asserting a freedom of action parallel to that claimed for themselves by post-Homeric and post-Hesiodic narrators, simultaneously enmeshed in and independent of precedent.[167]

[162] See p. 99. [163] See S. A. Stephens (2015) on *H.Art.* 53.

[164] See Oppermann (1925), cited by S. A. Stephens (2015) on 53.

[165] 'Underneath it': adopting the emendation *hupesti* ('is under') rather than the transmitted *epesti* ('is above'); see Hunter (1999: ad loc.).

[166] See Voelke (1992: 9 n. 14): 'Sight and looking constitute without doubt the dominant isotopy in the poem' (our translation).

[167] See the subtle analysis by Hunter (1999: 247).

Virgil's account of the Cyclopean eye in *Aeneid* book 3—narrated, it will be recalled, by Achaemenides, an ex-internee in Polyphemus' cave—contains powerful echoes of Homer, but goes far beyond that debt. In the brief but densely resonant description of the blinding, the differences from the *Odyssey* are as striking as the similarities: 'With a sharp weapon we drilled the huge single eye which lurked below the grim forehead, like an Argive shield or Phoebus' lamp...' (635–7). The 'sharp weapon' presumably alludes to the Odyssean (and Euripidean) sharpened stake. 'Drilling' (reading *terebramus*, 'we drill', from *terebro*) nods to the Homeric timber-boring simile, though one should not entirely discount the alternative reading *tenebramus*, 'we darken', which suits the noun here used associatively for 'eye'—namely *lumen*, 'light'—a Latin equivalent of the Callimachean double meaning.[168] The shield-like quality of the eye also owes something to Callimachus, and perhaps more distantly to the blacksmith simile in *Odyssey* 9. Shield-*making* was certainly a *forte* of the metalworking Cyclopes, as they will demonstrate in Vulcan's forge in *Aeneid* book 8 (447). The idea that the eye of Polyphemus 'lurked below' (*latebat*) his forehead may convey a sense of its being recessive or deeply set; it is hard to find an exact equivalent in earlier literature. As for the analogy between the Cyclopean eye and 'Phoebus' lamp'—that is, the Sun—the oxymoronic image combines an impression of superhuman omnivision with its opposite: *this* 'sun' has been extinguished for ever.

Ovid's engagement with the ogrish eye joins in the intertextual fun, above all in *Metamorphoses* book 13, in a virtuoso reimagining of the look of Polyphemus (as recollected by Galatea). The notion that Polyphemus, Narcissus-like, gazed at his own reflection in the water (767, 840-1) is a development of Theocritus. The reference to Telemus' prophecy about the blinding echoes the *Odyssey* and Theocritus' *Idyll* 6, but with two twists (770–5):

> Meanwhile Telemus had come to Sicilian Aetna, Telemus, the son of Eurymus, whom no prophetic bird had ever deceived; and he said to grim Polyphemus: 'That one eye [*lumen*] which you have in the middle of your forehead, Ulysses will take from you.' He laughed and answered: 'Most stupid of seers, you are wrong: another [*altera*] has already taken it.'

The twists are these. First, Ovid/Galatea tells us that Telemus came to Cyclopean territory from outside: apparently, then, he was a non-Cyclops, who, exceptionally, was not eaten on arrival. Secondly, the 'another' who has 'taken' Polyphemus' eye is, of course, Galatea: *altera*, 'another', is feminine. Via a tiny grammatical detail, Ovid segues effortlessly from Homeric to Theocritean, from epic to erotic

[168] For *tenebramus* as the reading preferred by 'many', see Servius ad loc. *Lumen* recurs at 658 (Polyphemus has been deprived of both eye and light) and 677–8 (each of the Cyclopes has a 'grim *lumen*').

mode. Densest of all, in terms of intertextual allusions, is the passage in which Polyphemus describes his own eye: 'True, I have only one eye [*lumen*] in the middle of my forehead, but it is as big a huge shield. And what of that? Doesn't the great Sun see everything here on earth from the sky? And the Sun has only one eye' (851–3). The literary ancestry of 'middle of the forehead' and 'big as a shield' are familiar enough, but it is worth saying a word about the analogy with the Sun, which assumes added relevance in its Ovidian telling. Ovid's introduction of Galatea's lover Acis adds fresh purpose to Polyphemus' vision: what precipitates the dénouement is the moment when the ogre *spies* the loving couple (874).

Lucian and Philostratus exploit the motif of Polyphemus' eye profitably and contrastingly. In Lucian's splendid dialogue between Galatea and her sister nymph Doris, Galatea stoutly defends the appearance of her monocular (*monophthalmos*) lover: 'His eye goes very nicely with his forehead, and it sees just as well as if he had two.' From Galatea's point of view, he puts that eye to good use: 'He caught sight of us from his look-out point, as we were playing on the shore at the foot of Etna...He didn't even look at you, but thought me the prettiest of us all, and turned his eye on me and only me.' Doris counter-punches: 'Do you think people should be jealous of you because a shepherd with bad eyesight thinks you're pretty?' This is funny but superficial, and is designed to be no more than that.

Utterly different in tone is a tricolon of ascending imaginative power in Philostratus' account of a picture of the Cyclop(e)s (*Imag.* 2.18). First comes the familiar, externalized portrait: 'he has a single eyebrow extending above his single eye, and a broad nose astride his upper lip...' Nothing here to surprise a reader of Callimachus or Theocritus. But then the viewer of the painting becomes more reflective—and so, the viewer imagines, does Polyphemus also: 'He thinks, because he is in love, that his glance is gentle, but in fact it is still wild and stealthy, like that of wild beasts subdued by necessity.' His look is a mixture of ferocity and suppression, brought about by the power of desire. Lastly, the gaze of Galatea. The description is as marvellous as the wonder that it describes: 'Her eyes are wonderful, for they have a kind of distant look that travels as far as the sea extends.' Our translation is prosaic, but the imagination that it haltingly tries to capture is not.

Several textual evocations of the Cyclopean eye can be found in Nonnus' *Dionysiaca*. Among countless other Dionysiac themes, Nonnus records the exploits of a host of Cyclopes who fight on the side of Dionysus in his war against the Indians, a war whose triumphant conclusion earns Dionysus the right to enter Olympus in glory. At one point in the fighting, the Indian king Deriades instructs his troops not to try to *kill* the Cyclopes, or to wound them in the belly or the neck. Rather they should *blind* them, by piercing their 'one eye as round as a wheel' with a bronze spear (27.85–98). Deriades wants to set the (blinded) Cyclopes to work in his own forge—an innovative crossover between poetic ancestries that we might summarize as Hesiodic and Callimachean. A little later, when battle is tumultuously joined, the descriptions of two named Cyclopes focus on their single eyes. First comes Brontes: 'In the middle of this grim champion's forehead glared the light of one single round ('wheel-shaped') eye... [the Indians] thought Olympian Selene must have come down from the sky and risen in the earth-born Cyclops' face, shining with her full orb, to defend Lyaeus [i.e. Dionysus]' (28.226–32). Previous literary comparisons of the single eye alternated between solar and lunar; here the (full) moon is preferred. Brontes' name looks back, of course, to Hesiod. Another Nonnian Cyclops has a newer name, but his physiognomy is anchored in precedent: 'Another Cyclops of the same kin went scattering his foes in Bacchic frenzy, the foremost warrior Halimedes, a monster [*pelōr*] with towering limbs; protecting his face he held before him the back of a round shield with a central boss' (28.257–60).[169] Nowhere in the literary tradition is the eye/shield likeness more relevant than here, in a war of cosmic proportions.

We end this section with two mythological afterthoughts, either or both of which might preserve more widespread, but now lost, traditions. The first is mentioned by a scholiast on the *Odyssey*: Odysseus, it was related, abducted the daughter of the Cyclops and sailed away with her. The Cyclops loved this daughter 'like his own eye'.[170] The chronicler John of Antioch (6th cent. CE) reports a similar tale, embellishing it with the details that this was Polyphemus' *only* daughter, and that the canonical version of the blinding-by-burning-stake in the *Odyssey* had been allegorized by some poets as referring to Odysseus' abduction of a girl 'burning with love'.[171] That Polyphemus' daughter was (as *we* say, changing the metaphor) the apple of his eye, adds a new dimension to Cyclopean family life, as well as repositioning the implied simile from the usual 'an eye is like *x* (shield, Sun, Moon, etc.)' to '*x* is like an eye'.

The second out-of-the-way tale is more intricate. It takes us back to the myth of Orion, who, it will be recalled, raped the daughter of Oenopion, son of Dionysus, and was blinded by Oenopion in revenge.[172] According to the commentary on Virgil by Servius (4th–5th cent. CE), the blinding was achieved when, at Oenopion's request, Dionysus sent his satyrs to make Orion drunk, thus facilitating the blinding.[173] The parallel with the blinding of Polyphemus can hardly be missed—above all, the similarity to the Euripidean satyr play—even though Orion had two eyes rather than one. But the Cyclopean atmosphere goes beyond that. An oracle had predicted that Orion's sight could be restored only if he were carried eastwards across the sea towards the light of the Sun. In the version preserved by Servius, Orion was drawn towards the deafening sound of the Cyclopes' forge, as they were making Zeus' thunderbolts. Hoisting one of the Cyclopes onto

[169] On the name 'Halimedes', see p. 200.
[170] Schol. PY on *Od.* 1.198, in Pontani (2007); see Alwine (2009: 326).
[171] John of Antioch 48.2, in Roberto (2005); see Alwine (2009: 329).
[172] See p. 118.
[173] Serv. on *Aen.* 10. 763.

his broad shoulders, gigantic Orion strode across the sea towards a solar cure—and who better than a son of Neptune, Servius observes, to act as the blind man's guide?

Images

Anyone looking for ancient images of the eyes of the masonic Cyclopes will be disappointed: no artist took the slightest interest in the subject (or in any other aspect of these master builders). Similarly absent from Greek and Roman iconography are the Cyclopes who made lightning and thunderbolts, even though in literary sources as early as Hesiod these Cyclopes are the very ones attributed with a central, circular eye. Of the lightning-makers' occupational descendants, by contrast, we have plenty of visual evidence, since several images show the Cyclopes hammering away in the forge of Hephaestus/Vulcan. But what is noticeable—and surprising to anyone familiar with the blacksmiths' physiognomy in, for example, Callimachus' *Hymn to Artemis* (single, shield-like eye)—is the ocular *normality* of these strongmen (e.g. *Cat. 70)*. The only possible exception is a marble slab in Rome (*Cat. 63* (Fig. 5.13)) depicting three Cyclopes beating out a shield; preternaturally lynx-eyed scholars have claimed that the two smiths depicted frontally have two blind eyes, together with a third eye on the forehead.[174]

The masons work in concert; so do the metalworkers. But an alternative characteristic of the Cyclopes, especially the pastoral ogres, is singularity, whether behavioural or anatomical. Corresponding to this monadism are a number of individualized portrait heads and figurines of a one-eyed ogre (it is best not to identify him as 'Polyphemus', since, in the absence of context, nothing warrants that degree of specificity). The single eye is the predominant feature, though it never exhibits the circularity described by Hesiod; the preferred form is an oval. Two Greek figurines represent a grotesque figure half-reclining as if at a symposium, his forehead adorned by a massive caricature of an eye (*Cat. 29* (Fig. 4.9) and *30* (Fig. 4.10)).[175] A third statuette portrays a big-eared, one-eyed, naked, squatting ogre, whose genitals dangle between his knees (*Cat. 12* (Fig. 4.11)).[176] These images recall Marina Warner's comment about some early representations of the Cyclops: he resembles, she remarks, 'nothing more than a giant orifice, with lids for lips. He is all mouth, all appetite.'[177] A ritual function for these figurines must be a possibility, though it is difficult to be precise about its nature; in any case, it is hard to deny that the single eye is the dominating characteristic. The same can be said for a number of Hellenistic and Roman portrait heads, mostly in stone or terracotta. In each case, the focus is a single, central eye; sometimes it

[174] See Touchefeu-Meynier on *LIMC* 'Kyklops, Kyklopes' no. 37.

[175] *Cat. 29* (Fig. 4.9) = Buitron and Cohen (1992: pl. 5); Fellmann (1972: 130 V 4 fig. 20). *Cat. 30* (Fig. 4.10) = Fellmann (1972: 131 V fig. 21).

[176] Buitron and Cohen (1992: pl. 6).

[177] Warner (1998: 87).

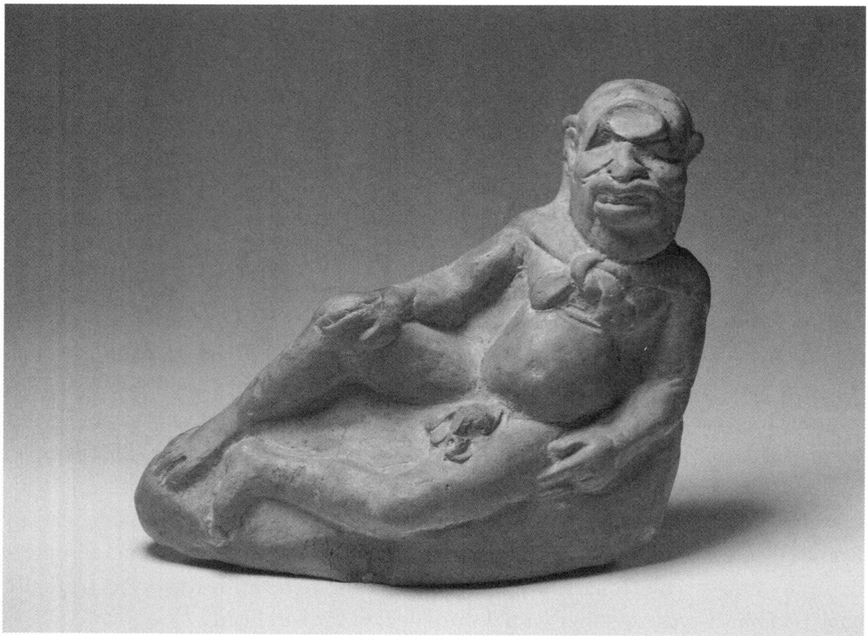

Fig. 4.9. Terracotta figurine from Athenian Acropolis, 400–350 BCE.

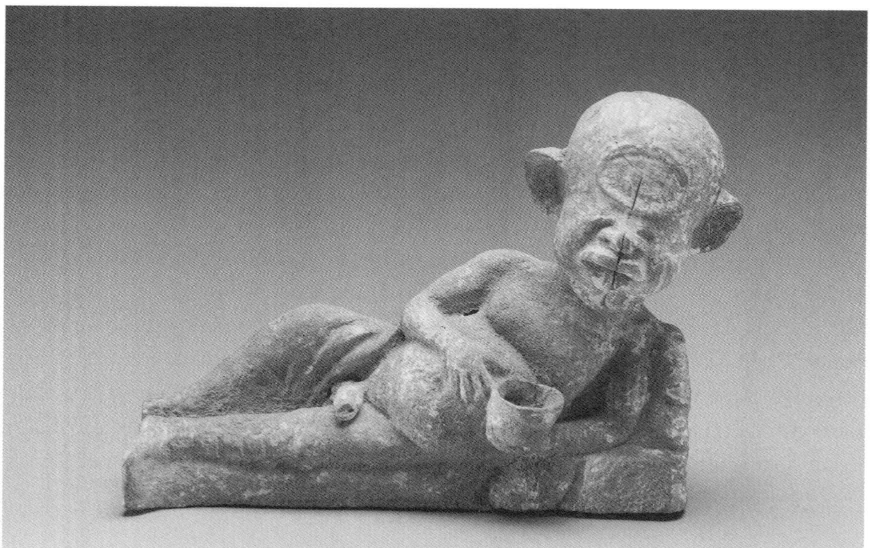

Fig. 4.10. Terracotta figurine from Sanctuary of Cabiri in Thebes, perhaps early 4th cent. BCE.

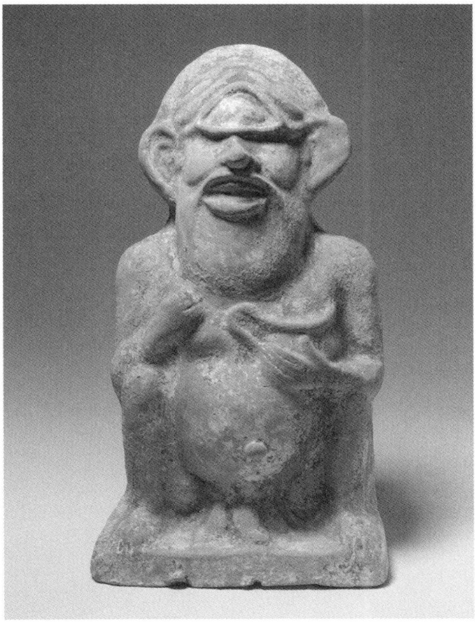

Fig. 4.11. Terracotta figurine from Boeotia, 550–500 BCE.

accompanies two other, normal eyes, which may be open, closed, or replaced by swellings in the face. On a marble head from Paros (*Cat. 32*), the third eye lies at the bridge of the nose between two normal, closed eyes. On another marble head (*Cat. 59* (Fig. 4.12)), the only working eye is the central one; the other two, beneath it, are reduced to facial swellings. A third example, found near Lyons, is a stone head that served as the decorative aperture of a fountain (*Cat. 43*); the central eye surmounts the face, from whose gaping mouth water would have spouted.

Comfortably outnumbering these solo Cyclopes are images whose implied narrative context leaves no doubt that they depict Polyphemus. Given the subtle differentiations in this material, it seems sensible, as with the texts, to proceed case by case.

On the earliest Greek and Etruscan vase paintings representing the blinding, the victim appears in profile with, on one side of his face, a complete, oval eye, identical or similar to that of the other figures present at the scene; the only difference may be in size, in proportion to the greater dimensions of the ogre.[178] However, it is unclear how the painters of these images might have envisaged the *frontal* view of their ogre: with one eye, or two, or three? The Eleusis amphora (*Cat. 1* (Fig. 2.1)) exemplifies this uncertainty. The body of the vase portrays a decapitated Medusa, along with two of her sister Gorgons in pursuit of Perseus;

[178] On the ogre's eye in these vase paintings, see Touchefeu-Meynier (1968: 73–6).

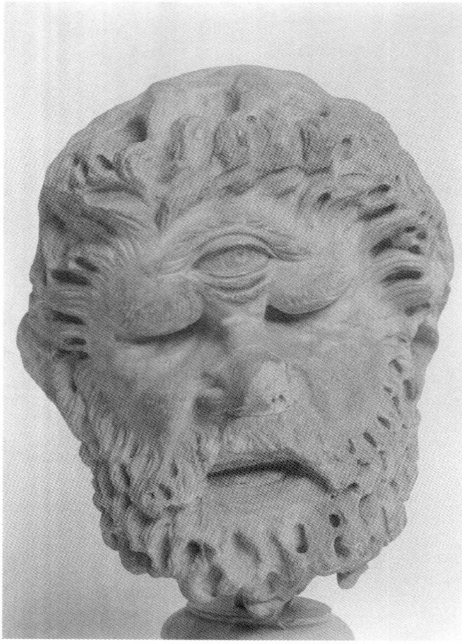

Fig. 4.12. Marble head of Cyclops, 150–200 CE.

the neck shows Polyphemus being blinded through his visible, lateral eye. One myth expresses the eye's power to harm, the other its vulnerability.[179] The krater from Argos (*Cat. 2*) follows the same schema, with the addition of spots of blood spattered over the ogre's face and neck. In other images, however, such as the Laconian cup (*Cat. 10* (Fig. 3.1)) and the Etruscan pithos (*Cat. 5* (Fig. 4.7)), the stake seems to be driven into the further, invisible side of the face, as if the target eye lay just beyond the viewer's sight. A black-figure oinochoe (*Cat. 17*) provides yet another variation: the eye visible to the viewer is almost closed—asleep? already blind?—while the stake is being thrust towards a point *above* the visible eye, perhaps towards a to-be-inferred third eye.[180] Different again, and *possibly* exceptional, is the Caeretan hydria (*Cat. 15* (Fig. 4.4)), showing, in profile, a sitting ogre without any normally positioned eyes. Arguably, but far from definitely, the artist has sought to portray the stake being driven into a centrally placed eye.[181]

[179] Grethlein (2016: 90–4) interprets the juxtaposition as a complex playing with the idea of seeing.

[180] See Touchefeu-Meynier on *LIMC* 'Kyklops, Kyklopes' no. 18.

[181] For Touchefeu-Meynier (1968: 74), the Caeretan hydria is 'un exemple sûr' of a representation in profile of a single, centrally placed eye. We do not share that confidence.

Some scholars have tried to explain this group of images by positing—on the basis of (later) folktale analogues—a variant in which, although the ogre had the normal quota of eyes, one of the two was, for some reason or another (eye disease? congenital infirmity?), *already* blind.[182] However, in Greek tradition there is no evidence of such a variant; which is, to say the least, a reason for caution. It may be better to look for the explanation elsewhere, in one or both of two factors—namely, the technical difficulty of representing a single, central eye in profile, and the general familiarity of ancient viewers with the 'blinding the Cyclops' motif, even in the absence of physiological precision in any given image.

Contrasting with these minutely differentiated depictions of Polyphemus in profile are two frontal images.[183] On the Lucanian krater (*Cat. 27* (Fig. 4.13)), the sleeping ogre faces the viewer, revealing two closed, normally positioned eyes, and a further, large, oval eye in the middle of the forehead. This third eye too seems to be closed; at any rate it lacks a pupil. More enigmatic is a black-figure wine cup in Berlin (*Cat. 19* (Fig. 4.14)). A recumbent, two-eyed Polyphemus turns towards the viewer/drinker. The stake is being driven into his right, pupilless eye; his left eye stares out at us. What makes the image unique is that *on the ogre's chest* the artist has added what looks like a third eye, larger than the other two, and fringed with a circle of markings resembling eyelashes or rays. Does this pectoral 'eye' echo and reinforce the forwards-facing, Gorgon-like stare of the ogre with a further locus of danger, similar in function and location to the aegis worn by Athene?[184] Or could it be that this is not an eye at all, but a nipple, surrounded by chest hair?[185] There are comparable images of satyrs in which *two* nipples are prominently displayed (on rather feminine breasts), but the position of Polyphemus' arm on the Berlin cup obscures the side of the chest where a second chest-eye 'might' have been. The impression given, therefore, is that of a *single* chest-eye. All in all, Polyphemus' chest-eye/nipple is a riddle for which no persuasive solution has so far been found. The other puzzle in the image derives from the fact that the ogre has two normally positioned eyes, of which only one is being blinded. Does this corroborate the hypothesis that there existed a tradition in which one of Polyphemus' eyes had already somehow become blind before Odysseus ever set foot in Cyclopia?[186] As in the case of the eye-in-profile images, we prefer an alternative explanation. Could it not be that the painter of the Berlin cup had not fully thought through the logic of his own design? Given a certain naivety in the portrayal, this does not seem unlikely. Such things do happen.

To find an image of the blinding in which Polyphemus has a single eye portrayed frontally, we must turn from Greece to Etruria. The astonishing mural on

[182] See Snodgrass (1998: 94), following Page (1955: 14–16). In Snodgrass's view: 'We cannot absolutely exclude the possibility that the painters knew of, and were portraying, some such version.'

[183] On frontal faces in Archaic Attic vase painting, see Korshak (1987).

[184] So Touchefeu-Meynier (1968: 19).

[185] Brommer (1983: 63, with pl. 14b).

[186] See previous paragraph.

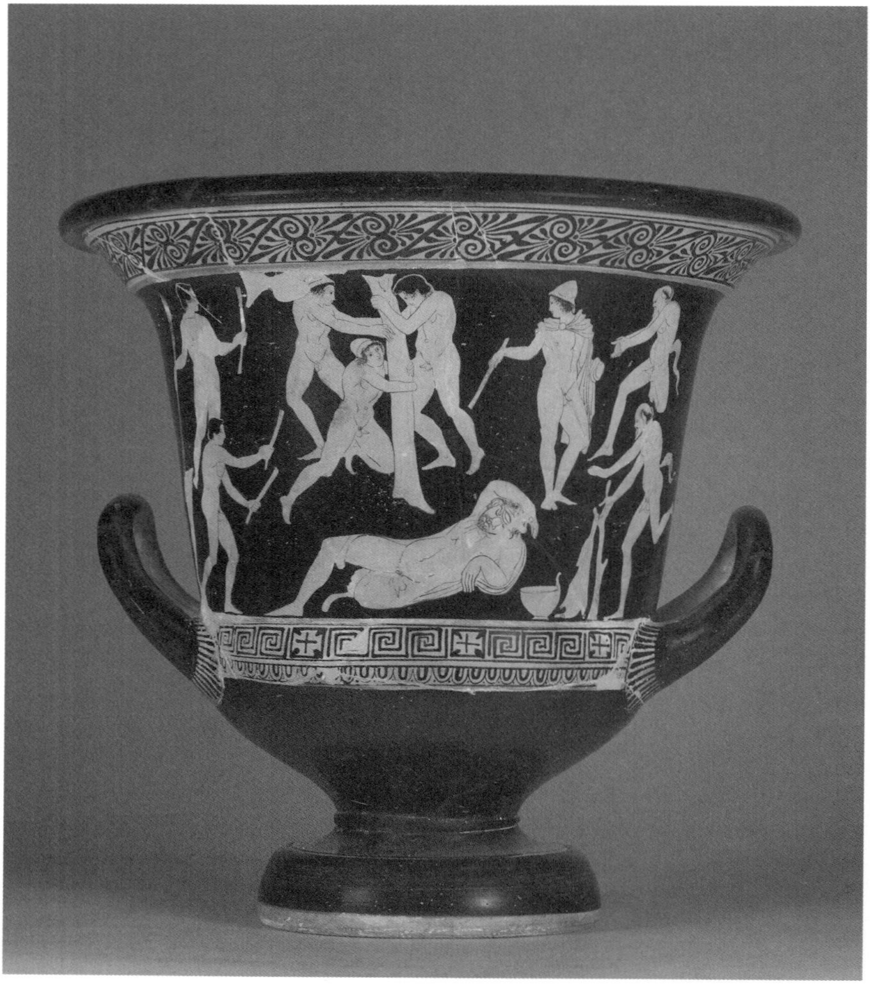

Fig. 4.13. Polyphemus asleep and about to be blinded with a tree trunk. Lucanian krater, *c*.410 BCE.

the front wall of the corridor that links the Tombs of Orcus I and II in Tarquinia (*Cat. 31* (Fig. 4.15)) shows a huge, recumbent, fearsome-looking ogre, whose enormous, circular eye occupies the whole of his forehead. The lashes or ray-like markings that surround the eye are strikingly reminiscent of the chest-eye on the Berlin wine cup. The mural is now in poor condition, but we can supplement it with watercolours done in 1908, based on the painting when it was better preserved.[187]

[187] Reproduced in Andreae (1999: 137, fig. 50). See also Moltesen and Weber-Lehmann (1991: 87, fig. 59).

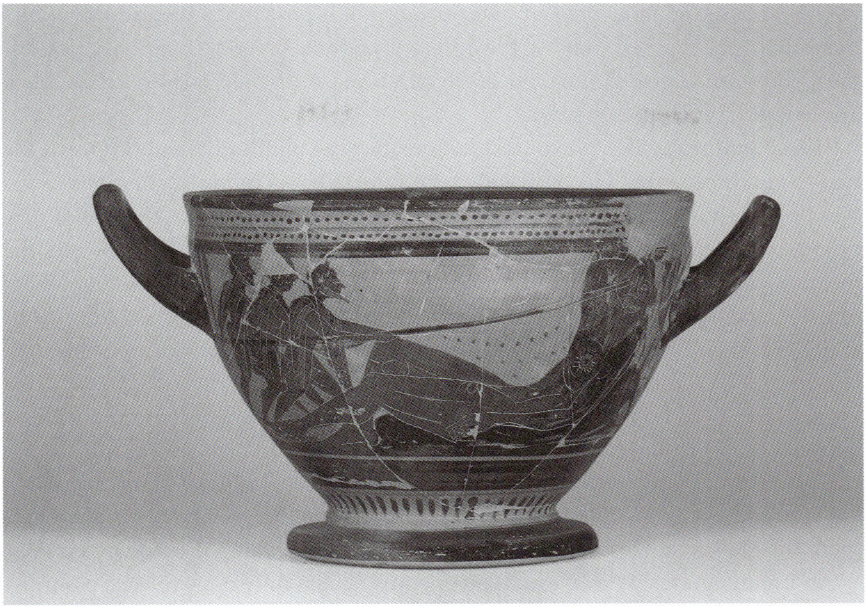

Fig. 4.14. How many eyes? Attic black-figure skyphos, *c.*500 BCE.

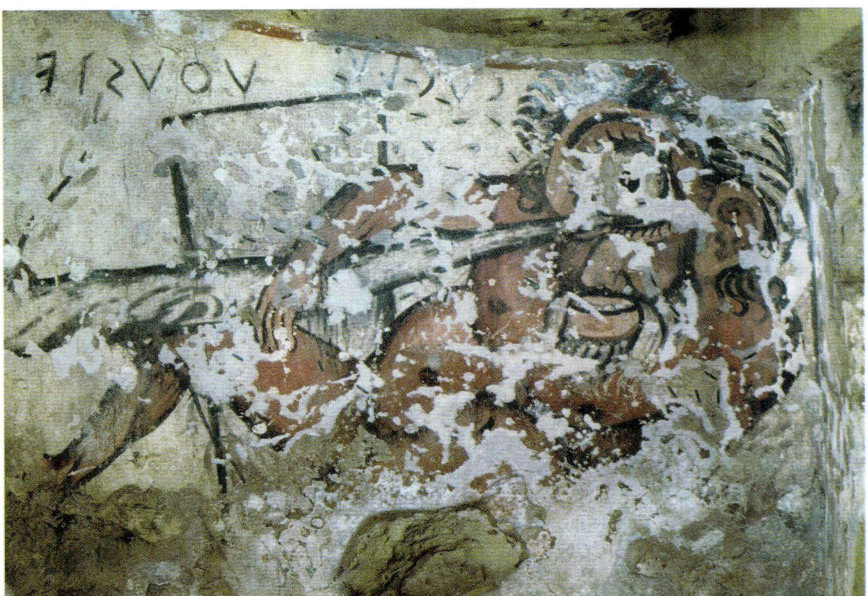

Fig. 4.15. Wall painting from Tomb of Orcus II, Tarquinia, 300–275 BCE.

Even on the mural in its present state, however, it is possible to discern the implement that is being used to blind the ogre: a long stake tapering to a sharp point—the clearest analogue of the olive stake described in the *Odyssey* to be found in any extant visual representation.

Vase paintings of Polyphemus' situation after the blinding mainly concern the under-ram escape. His face is usually seen in profile. As in representations of the blinding, an inquisitive viewer might wonder how many eyes the Cyclops is supposed to have. But this may be a question without an answer—it is simply not the focus of these paintings. An example is the vase on which Polyphemus braces himself against his rock-door (*Cat. 25* (Fig. 5.4)). Here his one visible eye, laterally presented, is closed. This has nothing to do with sleep: closure stands for blindness.[188] Whether any other eyes are to be imagined as situated beyond the viewer's ken is of no importance beside the main interest, which is the interplay between the ogre and the ram that gently nuzzles him. There are several similar examples of the ogre blindly feeling for his sheep, his blindness being expressed via a closed eye (e.g. *Cat. 21* (Fig. 5.3)). Once more the eye is in profile. Once more the question, 'How many *other* eyes?', is largely beside the point.

An unambiguously three-eyed Polyphemus occurs only once in vase painting, on the Lucanian krater (*Cat. 27* (Fig. 4.13)). But in later art it is a recurrent feature. On the mosaics from Piazza Armerina (*Cat. 72* (Fig. 3.7)) and Cordoba (*Cat. 71* (Fig. 4.5)), the ogre has three open, oval eyes: a central one on the forehead and two below it in the usual place. The effect is the reverse of unsettling: the third eye is decorative rather than menacing. The same is true of the Sperlonga statue (*Cat. 39* (Fig. 4.3)), where, for all his two-plus-one, closed eyes, the reclining, sleeping Polyphemus looks facially heroic rather than grotesque. We must say 'seems to be' rather than 'is', however, in view of the ongoing controversy over the reliability of the reconstruction, not only of this statue, but also of the entirety of the Sperlonga installation, which was smashed in antiquity into more than 7,000 marble fragments. In 2001 Mary Beard and John Henderson claimed to have detected a conspiracy of misdirected, ideologically driven 'mythologization' behind modern attempts to put together and make sense of these fragments.[189] Most scholars, however, have been less dismissive of such reconstructive efforts, examples of which can be seen in a sumptuous book by Bernard Andreae.[190]

In representations of Polyphemus with Galatea, a topic raised already by Philostratus is that of the gaze. Roman wall paintings, the bulk of them from Campania (for obvious archaeological–volcanological reasons), configure the reciprocal gazes of the two figures in various ways. Michael Squire has written a

[188] Compare the image of Teiresias appearing to Odysseus at the edge of the Underworld: Lucanian krater, *LIMC* 'Teiresias' no. 11.

[189] Beard and Henderson (2001: 74–82).

[190] Less dismissive: e.g. Squire (2009: 210 n. 21). See Andreae (1999: 188–205).

full and richly nuanced account of this phenomenon, so we can afford to be brief.[191]

Sometimes the couple look at each other. On the painting from the House of Livia (*Cat. 40* (Fig. 4.6)), an adolescent Polyphemus looks ardently at his beloved, who is separated from him by water and rocks; she meanwhile, mounted on a hippocamp, returns his gaze impassively.[192] Even closer reciprocity can be seen on a painting from Pompeii (*Cat. 47* (Fig. 5.7)): the two are locked in a tight embrace, a culmination only rarely evidenced in our literary sources. A different schema shows one of the pair looking at the other, with a gaze that is not reciprocated. This seems to be the case with the painting from Herculaneum (*Cat. 46* (Fig. 8.1)), in which Galatea looks at Polyphemus, but he, mature, handsome, and pensive, looks slightly upwards and out of the picture, rather than at her; alternatively, he might be imagined to be *beginning to turn towards her*, as if having heard her voice.[193] According to a third schema, both characters may look away from each other into the distance. In the painting from Boscotrecase, the principals—he seated on a rock, she riding a dolphin and supporting herself with her right hand—seem oblivious of one another (*Cat. 41* (Fig. 3.2)). Eleanor Winsor Leach has suggested an intriguing comparison with two of the most powerful ancient literary descriptions of an equivalent scene: 'as in Philostratus, Galatea faces the spectator, holding her arched purple veil with a distant look in her eyes. Since she is actually floating behind the Cyclops' line of vision, the spectator may question whether she is literally present as an audience or merely intended as a figure of the Cyclops' imagination, as is so clearly the case in Theocritus.'[194] As we shall see later, the spectator of some of Gustave Moreau's explorations of the Polyphemus/Galatea theme may ask her-/himself precisely the same question.

Ugly

Ugliness in antiquity

Judgements of ugliness are subject to extreme variation from one culture to another.[195] To have a hope of understanding perceptions of ugliness (and its opposite) in Graeco-Roman antiquity, we must try to recover the assumptions that underpinned those perceptions. The evidence of images alone is insufficient:

[191] Squire (2009: 300–56).

[192] There is a similar mutual gaze in a reconstructed wall painting from the House of M. Lucretius, Pompeii IX.3.5, illustrated in Squire (2009: 318, fig. 5.18).

[193] *Contra* Squire (2009: 331), and Montón Subías in *LIMC* 'Galateia' no. 20. Both scholars state that Polyphemus is looking at Galatea; but if this had been the case, he would have been represented in profile.

[194] Leach (1992: 70–1).

[195] On the cultural history of ugliness, see Eco (2007); Henderson (2015).

in order to reduce the element of subjectivity, we also need concepts, as inscribed in words.

Several Greek and Latin terms for ugliness connote a departure from due, right, or proper form. The Greek adjectives *amorphos* and *dusmorphos*, and their Latin near-equivalents *deformis* and *informis*, make this explicit, since they involve negations of, respectively, *morphē* and *forma* ('form', 'shape'). But ugliness may extend beyond physical form into morality: the meaning of the adjectives we have mentioned, especially *deformis*, can be stretched to describe 'ugly' *conduct*. Moreover, another group of words, this time unconnected with the idea of 'form', even more comprehensively spans the gap between the aesthetic and the moral. Greek *aischros* ('disgusting') and *kakos* (*to eidos*) ('evil (to look at)'), together with Latin *foedus* ('disgusting') and *turpis* ('unsightly', 'repulsive'), designate equally that which is visually repugnant and that which disgusts the moral sense.[196]

These linguistic features point to broader aspects of Greek and Roman culture: specifically, the importance of form, and the overlap between aesthetics and morality. The high artistic value placed by Greeks and Romans upon formal wholeness and due proportion is beyond dispute.[197] The 'Canon' of sculptural balance and harmony created by Polyclitus (5th cent. BCE), and the doctrine of architectural proportion established by Vitruvius (1st cent. BCE), are merely two expressions of a widely held attitude. A corollary was the negative valuation of anything that *lacked* due proportion, or that—even worse—was disfigured, misshapen, or deformed. Although the boundary between physical integrity and its opposite was particularly emphasized in the hyper-militaristic societies of Sparta and Rome, its significance was felt throughout the Graeco-Roman world. One sphere in which this applied was that of religious practice: certain priesthoods stipulated wholeness of body —or sometimes even handsomeness—as a qualification for office.[198] To be sure, the body–mind equation did not always work. Socrates was notoriously as ugly as a satyr, yet his unsightliness was compatible with what some people, if not all, considered to be a beautiful mind.[199] But far the commoner pattern was that exemplified by the Homeric character Thersites, whose 'disorderly' mind and tendency to abuse his superiors were mirrored in a cocktail of bodily defects (*Il.* 2.216–19): 'He was the basest [*aischistos*] man to come to Troy. He was bandy-legged and lame in one foot, with shoulders stooped and drawn together over his chest, and above this his skull went up to a point with the hair spare on top of it.' When this poor wretch spoke 'out of turn', Odysseus brutally smashed a sceptre between his shoulder blades, producing hilarity among the Greek army.

196 *aisch(r)os*: M. L. Rose (2003: 12–13). *kakos*: Lefkowitz (2008).

197 Garland (2010: 31).

198 Pl. *Leg.* 759c; Dion. Hal. *Ant. Rom.* 2.21.3; Aul. Gell. *NA* 1.12.3; Paus. 7.24.4; cf. Garland (2010: 64).

199 Socratic ugliness: Pl. *Tht.* 143e, and *Symp.* 215a–c, 216c–d, 221d–222a; Xen. *Symp.* 4.19, 5.5–7.

Thersites embodies an all-too-human truth: a standard response to ugliness is mockery.[200] As Cicero put it: 'In deformity and bodily disfigurement there is good material for making jokes' (although he does at least add: 'though here as elsewhere one has to know the limit').[201] Ridicule of deformity applied even to divinities: when lame Hephaestus bustled around Zeus' palace, the other Olympians laughed uncontrollably.[202] Deformity went hand in hand with exclusion: Hephaestus was physically hurled out of Olympus, either by Zeus or by his own mother Hera, who wanted to conceal him for being lame.[203] In real-world human society as in myth, any individual or social group perceived as being 'outside' was liable to be associated with ugliness, and with the derision that accompanied it. A woman who was old, or ugly, or both, was a prime target, for she was no longer an object of male sexual interest. The three 'hags' in Aristophanes' *Assemblywomen* (*c.*391 BCE) are spiritual descendants of two memorable creations of Greek lyric poetry dating from more than two centuries earlier: the 'hateful', fat-ankled woman described in a line by Archilochus, and Semonides' hideous 'monkey-woman', mocked as she walked around town.[204] Nor was the ridicule directed only at females. Lucian satirizes a misshapen (*amorphos*) male entertainer, significantly named Satyrion; he would amuse guests at dinner parties by combining contorted dancing with the singing of rude songs in a cod Egyptian accent (*Symp.* 18–19). The same prejudice affected the great as well as the humble. A letter allegedly written by Augustus to his wife Livia suggests the need to develop a policy about her grandson, the future emperor Claudius, whose bodily unsoundness might provoke public ridicule.[205] His twitching, stumbling, stuttering manner was certainly ripe for mockery. According to Seneca's satire on Claudius' supposed postmortem ascent to heaven (1st cent. CE), even Hercules was taken aback when he spotted the peculiar new arrival on Olympus.[206]

If derision was one possible reaction to ugliness, repulsion was another (the two reactions could, of course, be combined). The disgusting appearance of the old was notoriously targeted by Juvenal (1st–2nd cent. CE) in his tenth Satire: misshapen faces, skin wrinkled like a baboon's, bald heads, dribbling noses, toothless gums (191–200). Going beyond ugliness in the direction of deformity was the portrait habitually given of Aesop. According to the fictional *Life of Aesop*

200 See Beard (2014: 116), arguing that the perception of ugliness as ridiculous is guided and shaped by a 'joker'.

201 Cic. *Orat.* 2.239. See Garland (2010: 76).

202 *Il.* 1.599–600. One may doubt whether Hephaestus was acting as a *conscious* joker in order to defuse a tense intra-divinity situation on Olympus; *contra* Burkert (1985: 168).

203 *Il.* 1.590–4; 18.394–7; *Od.* 8.306–12; *Hymn. Hom. Ap.* 316–18.

204 Archil. fr. 206 West; Semon. 7.71–4 West. Cf. by contrast Hdt. 6.61.3–5, on a nurse who regularly took an ugly female child to a shrine of Helen, after which the girl gradually turned into a great beauty. See Garland (2010: 42–3).

205 Suet. *Claud.* 4.

206 Sen. *Apocol.* 5. On Claudius' disabilities, see Goodey and Rose (2013: 34–5).

(1st cent. CE), the legendary fabulist, in spite of the benefits that his stories brought to mankind, was supposed to have been 'potbellied, misshapen of head, snub-nosed, inarticulate, swarthy, dwarfish, bandy-legged, short-armed, squint-eyed, liver-lipped—a portentous monstrosity'.[207] The list of the repulsive ugly can easily be lengthened from the world of myth: prime examples are the Harpies, the Gorgons, and Scylla.

Ugly Cyclopes?

How far do these general characteristics of ancient ugliness apply to the Cyclopes? The answer is inseparable from two other questions. *Were* the Cyclopes ugly? And, if so, in what did their ugliness consist?

According to one illustrious commentator, the Cyclopes *were* ugly: what made them so was their size. In his *Philosophical Enquiry into the Origin of our Ideas of the Sublime and Beautiful* (1757), Edmund Burke was in no doubt about the incompatibility of gigantism and beauty:

> The large and gigantic, though very compatible with the sublime, is contrary to the beautiful. It is impossible to suppose a giant the object of love. When we let our imaginations loose in romance, the ideas we naturally annex to that size are those of tyranny, cruelty, injustice, and everything horrid and abominable. We paint the giant ravaging the country, plundering the innocent traveller, and afterwards gorged with his half-living flesh: such are Polyphemus, Cacus, and others, who make so great a figure in romances and heroic poems. The event we attend to with the greatest satisfaction is their defeat and death.[208]

Burke's views would not have been widely shared in antiquity. The Olympian gods were well known to be extraordinarily tall when they appeared in their 'true'—that is, unmetamorphosed—shape; and no one was more beautiful than they were.[209] Giants, too, such as Otus, Ephialtes, and Orion, could be considered not just as handsome, but as the most handsome beings imaginable (*Od.* 11.308–12). *Pace* Burke, then, the Cyclopes' hugeness would not in itself have qualified them as ugly. But the distinctiveness of their appearance was not confined to size. As we have seen, many ancient accounts portrayed them not just as enormous but also as disfigured, and it was this, rather than their vastness, that militated against their being thought handsome. But, of course, in the ancient sources descriptions

[207] Trans. L. W. Daly in W. F. Hansen (1998: 111). See Lefkowitz (2008: 59–60 and *passim*).

[208] E. Burke (1757/1958: pt IV, sect. 24, pp. 157–8).

[209] Cf. Demeter in Callim. *Hymn Dem.* 6.58: her footsteps touched the earth, but her head touched Olympus.

of Cyclopean physique vary with the context. To be sure, some artists and writers portray the ogres as hideous; but it is not always so. Best, as always, to look at individual cases.

On Greek vases depicting the blinding, even when Polyphemus has 'wild' traits such as extreme hairiness, his appearance remains essentially human. He often closely resembles the men in the same scene, apart from his greater size (as on *Cat. 1* (Fig. 2.1), *2*, and *5* (Fig. 4.7)); if *they* are not to be described as ugly, there is no reason to call him ugly either. Moreover, the tendency in such images to depict the ogre's face in profile has the effect of minimizing, or even removing altogether, any uglifying consequence of his ocular anomaly (if he has one). The same can be said of some images of a full-frontal Polyphemus: nothing about the three-eyed ogre on the Lucanian krater (*Cat. 27* (Fig. 4.13)) marks him out as less handsome than the Greeks who are preparing to blind him. Sometimes, indeed, his appearance hardly falls short of that of an Olympian god. One might certainly say this of one image of the escape under the rams (*Cat. 25* (Fig. 5.4)), and it applies even more forcefully to several later representations. Classic examples are the relief on an Etruscan urn (*Cat. 37* (Fig. 3.5)) and the Sperlonga statue (*Cat. 39* (Fig. 4.3)). On wall paintings, Polyphemus can appear as a handsome juvenile lead (*Cat. 40* (Fig. 4.6)), or as a figure both more mature and more thoughtful—but still eminently worth a part as a muscular hunk in a sword-and-sandals movie (*Cat. 46* (Fig. 8.1)). Similarly robust, and far from unsightly, are some images of the blacksmith Cyclopes (*Cat. 63* (Fig. 5.13) and *70*).

The strongest candidates for 'ugly' Cyclopes are a number of figures who resemble satyrs, or the satyrs' elderly boon companion Silenus. Two hairy Polyphemuses, depicted in profile in the scene of the blinding, fall into this category (*Cat. 9* and *15* (Fig. 4.4)). So does the Silenus-faced Polyphemus on the Berlin cup (*Cat. 19* (Fig. 4.14)). Satyrs constitute one of the major categories of characters portrayed *en face* on Greek vases, and their symbolic closeness to Polyphemus is further stressed by the ogre's frontal posture.[210] (One may compare the Silenus on a black-figure amphora from Tarquinia, though his absurdly enlarged penis trumps anything that any extant image of Polyphemus can offer.[211]) Equally Silenus-like are two terracotta figurines (*Cat. 12* (Fig. 4.11) and *29* (Fig. 4.9)) depicting pot-bellied and generally grotesque Cyclopes. One of these (*Cat. 12*) bears a striking similarity to a terracotta Silenus from Thebes, the only differences being the monocularity of the Cyclops and the erection displayed by the Silenus.[212] As a rule, Cyclopes are not ithyphallic, nor are their genitals unheroically large. An exception is the paunchy and snub-nosed Polyphemus in the act of roasting two human victims (*Cat. 28* (Fig. 4.2)); although not

[210] Frontal satyrs: Korshak (1987: 5–11).
[211] *LIMC* 'Silenoi' no. 112. [212] *LIMC* 'Silenoi' no. 35.

ithyphallic, he certainly has a sizeable member, and only his mother would describe him as anything but ugly. What these Silenus-like Cyclopes do *not* have are the horse tails and pointed ears that locate satyrs and Sileni in a condition of semi-animal hybridity. Cyclopes belong 'outside'—but they *stay* outside, and only threaten the world of 'civilization' if its representatives (like Odysseus) come to visit them. Satyrs and Sileni, by contrast, can turn up anywhere and jump about disruptively.

Turning now to literature, we begin with some texts in which Cyclopean ugliness is absent or downplayed. Hesiod tells us nothing about the attractiveness, or otherwise, of his one-eyed weapons-makers. In the *Odyssey*, Cyclopean ugliness is largely irrelevant. For all the grossness of Polyphemus' *behaviour*, only once does the narrative explicitly touch on the aesthetics of his *appearance*, in a typically self-aggrandizing remark by Odysseus: 'Cyclops, if anyone among mortal men should ask you about the hideous [*aeikeliēn*] blinding of your eye, say that the one who blinded you was Odysseus the city-sacker, son of Laertes and dweller in Ithaca' (9.501–5). *Aeikelios* certainly connotes ugliness, but this defect is a consequence of the blinding, not an innate characteristic of a Cyclops. Like Homer, Euripides concentrates on the excesses in Polyphemus' behaviour, his drunken vomiting being supplemented in the satyr play by masturbation and farting. When attention does turn to the ogre's appearance, it is paradoxically to his alleged *handsomeness* that the satyrs sarcastically allude. He resembles, they suggest, the best-looking of bridegrooms (511–12):

> Looking handsomely with his eyes [*sic*—the plural is doubtless ironical],
> Handsome he strides forth from the halls.

It is with Theocritus that the motif of Cyclopean ugliness gets into its stride. In *Idyll* 11 Polyphemus admits that his disfigurement is likely to put off a potential lover, but presents this as unimportant in the light of his economic pulling power (30–7):

> I know, pretty girl, why you're running from me: it's because a single, long, shaggy eyebrow stretches over the whole of my forehead from one ear to the other; and there's one eye underneath it, and a flat nose over my lip. But even if that's how I am, I rear a thousand cattle, and from them I draw and drink the finest milk. I'm not short of cheese in summer or autumn, or in the depth of winter; and my cheese racks are always brimful.

There is a nice parallel in the third of Karl Marx's *Economic and Philosophical Manuscripts* (1844): 'I am ugly, but I can buy for myself the most beautiful of women. Therefore I am *not* ugly, for the effect of ugliness, its deterrent power, is nullified by money.'[213] In *Idyll* 6, the Cyclops modifies the proto-Marxist stance of *Idyll* 11. This time, rather than seeing his ugliness as a defect for which his material possessions can compensate, Polyphemus goes sturdily into denial (34–40):

> Truly I don't have an ugly [*kakon*] appearance, as people say I do. A while ago I was looking into the sea—there was a calm—and my beard was handsome [*kala*], and so was my one eye/pupil—at least so it seemed to me; and [the sea] reflected the gleam of my teeth whiter than Parian marble. To avoid the Evil Eye, I spat three times into my chest; that's what the old woman Cotyttaris taught me.

Exactly *why* Polyphemus takes steps to avoid the Evil Eye is debatable.[214] Is he afraid that his own reflection might cast the Eye on him, since those (like himself) with an ocular abnormality might have that covert power? Does he fear that other people, envious of his good looks, might cast it? Does he want to avoid the risk of harm from his own self-admiration? Perhaps all three possibilities are in play. In any case, the overall impression is one of narcissism: another aspect of Cyclopean singularity. Not that he is *completely* isolated. The idea that he has received magical advice from a wise woman—Thracian, to judge by her name—is a pleasing Theocritean idiosyncrasy, which raises the unanswerable question: where did he meet *her*?[215]

Horace's satire recounting his journey from Rome to Brindisi (*Sat.* 1.5) includes a comic interchange between two mimes/actors called Sarmentus and Messius Cicirrus. The latter looks especially grotesque because of the unsightly (*foeda*) scar on the left side of his bristly brow. Sarmentus' joke is inevitable: in order to perform the Cyclops shepherd dance, Cicirrus does not need a mask (60–4). This number presumably involved ungainly contortions, since elsewhere (*Epist.* 2.2.124–5) Horace refers to a dancer who will be 'twisted' like one performing 'the Satyr' or 'the rustic Cyclops'. Elsewhere in Latin poetry, Cyclopean ugliness is a topos. Martial refers to a slave named Polyphemus who was of such size and such appearance that even the Cyclops himself would look upon him with astonishment.[216]

Two other evocations of Cyclopean ugliness take us back to the Polyphemus-and-Galatea relationship. Both passages rest on the assumption that, dispassionately observed, Polyphemus is indeed unsightly to look at. Yet both passages deflect such a reaction by mounting a defence of the way the ogre looks. First there is Polyphemus' own self-defence, in typically Ovidian virtuoso style (*Met.* 13.846–53):

[213] Marx (1975: 324) (we omit some of the italics in the translation); cited by Eco (2007: 12).
[214] See Hunter (1999: 39–40).
[215] On a possible Thracian tinge to the name, see Hunter (1999: ad loc.).
[216] Mart. 7.38; cf. Garland (2010: 46).

> And don't think it ugly [*turpe*] that my whole body is covered with thick, bristling hair. A tree is ugly without leaves, and a horse is ugly if a mane does not cover its tawny neck; feathers clothe the birds, and their own wool is an adornment to sheep; so a beard and shaggy hair on his body well become a man. True, I have only one eye in the middle of my forehead, but it is as big as a huge shield. And what of that? Doesn't the great Sun see everything here on earth from the sky? And the Sun has just one eye.

In the second passage, from the first of Lucian's *Dialogues of the Sea Gods*, Galatea cunningly resists the attempt of a sister sea-nymph to rubbish Polyphemus' appearance:

> DORIS: A good-looking [*kalos*] lover they say you have, Galatea, in this Sicilian shepherd who's so mad about you!
>
> GALATEA: None of your jokes, Doris. He's Poseidon's son, whatever he looks like.
>
> DORIS: What of it? Though it was a son of Zeus himself that had so wild and hairy an appearance and, most hideous [*amorphotaton*] thing of all, only one eye, do you think his birth would help him to be any better-looking?
>
> GALATEA: His wild and hairy appearance, as you call it, isn't ugly [*amorphos*]. It's manly. And his eye goes very nicely with his forehead, and it sees just as well as if it were two.[217]

Although in a sense the joke is on Polyphemus both times, there is wit and irony in both passages. And in neither case is the overall effect openly sarcastic: Polyphemus himself (in Ovid) and Galatea (in Lucian) give as good as they get.

The Cyclopes are by no means the only characters in Greek mythology to be known for an anatomical peculiarity. The list includes hideously bitchy Scylla, partly goatish Pan, and three-bodied Geryon, as well as the Harpies, the Centaurs, the Furies, the Sirens, and (by terrible choice) the single-breasted Amazons. In many cases these physical anomalies correspond to behavioural distinctiveness: Pan and the Centaurs share some of the diversely feral energies of the goat and the horse, while the facial repulsiveness of the Furies matches the horror of the kin-killers whom it is their duty to pursue; the Amazons occupy a no (wo)man's land between the genders. But what of the Cyclopes? As this chapter has shown, the nature of their physical peculiarity is complex and shifting. How that nature relates to their behaviour is the no less complex question to which we now turn.

[217] Trans. M. D. MacLeod.

5
Lifestyle

How did the Cyclopes live? We begin with subsistence and diet. On these matters the ancient sources are silent about the builders, and virtually silent about the metalworkers, but about Polyphemus and his kin they have much to say. After that we turn to social interaction, first among the Cyclopes themselves, and then between the Cyclopes and those with whom they came into contact. Finally, adding the evidence about lifestyle to the previous chapter's findings about physique, we examine the question of classification. What exactly *were* the Cyclopes: humans, or monsters, or neither, or both?

Subsistence

Pastoralism is a recurrent feature in the life of the Cyclopes—or at least in the life of one of them. In order to provide a context for understanding Cyclopean herding, it will be useful to review the general ideological background of this means of subsistence.

In ancient thought, herding is consistently represented as a distinct way of living.[1] An often-stressed feature of pastoralism is mobility: herdsmen have to follow wherever their animals' quest for food may take them, most conspicuously in the practice of transhumance.[2] The *bios nomadikos* is habitually contrasted with the sedentary lifestyle associated with agriculture, a conceptual distinction going back at least as far as Cain the farmer and Abel the shepherd (Gen. 4:2). For Herodotus, the pastoral/agricultural dichotomy becomes a basic tool for categorizing the vast diversity of human societies, from Persia and India to Scythia and Africa.[3] He applies the dichotomy normatively as well as descriptively, tending to associate pastoralism with 'barbarian' behavioural traits. Thus 'the Scythians blind all those prisoners whom they capture since they [*sc.* the Scythians] are not ploughmen but pastoralists (*nomades*)' (4.2.2). Less polarized is Aristotle's schema in the *Politics*: agriculture and the *bios nomadikos* are two out of five possible modes of subsistence, the others being banditry, fishing, and hunting/gathering (1256a–b). But the negative connotation of pastoralism persists: the way of life of the pastoral nomad is the most indolent of the five, since it involves leisure

[1] See e.g. Gutzwiller (2006).
[2] e.g. Arist. *Pol.* 1256a32–5.
[3] See B. D. Shaw (1982–3: 8–17).

Cyclops: The Myth and its Cultural History. Mercedes Aguirre and Richard Buxton, Oxford University Press (2020).

DOI: 10.1093/oso/9780198713777.001.0001

without hard work, while rendering the herdsman subservient to natural circumstances beyond his control—especially the movements of his flocks.[4]

A different strategy for placing pastoralism casts it as a distinct stage in human development. For the Peripatetic philosopher Dicaearchus (4th–3rd cent. BCE), first on the scene were people who enjoyed a care-free, labour-free, war-free, agriculture-free, Cronian phase of existence. Next came those who lived a pastoral existence characterized by superfluity of possessions and by warfare, as well as by the combined practices of taming some animals and hunting others. Only at a third stage did agriculture make its appearance.[5] A different developmental take on pastoralism is offered by Plato in his *Laws*, within the framework of the discussion, by the Athenian Stranger and his interlocutors, of the entire span of human communal living since the primeval Flood. In the wake of that cataclysm, speculates the Athenian, 'those who escaped . . . must have been pretty nearly all hill-shepherds—a few embers of mankind preserved, I imagine, on the tops of mountains' (677b). In spite of or because of its technological simplicity, this way of life had much to recommend it. In contrast to their Dicaearchan equivalents, the primordial herdsmen of the *Laws* inhabited a world free from warfare and unsullied by the twin evils of extreme poverty and excessive wealth: since they lacked metals in general, it follows that they specifically lacked both metallic weaponry and the gold and silver needed for the accumulation of riches. True, they were 'lawless', but only in the sense that they had no *need* for laws (678e–680a). In a word, continues the Athenian, they were just like the Homeric Cyclopes: 'These people have no assemblies to debate in, and no ancestral ordinances; they dwell in hollow caves on the peaks of high mountains, and each governs his own children and wives, without any heed for one another' (*Od.* 9.112–15). This picture chimes in with an interpretative tradition going back to Antisthenes the Cynic (5th–4th cent. BCE), for whom all the Cyclopes lived just and pious lives *except the villainous Polyphemus*.[6] What seems not to have been stressed, however, is that Plato's Athenian positions the Cyclopes at a different stage of social evolution, not just from agriculturalists per se, but specifically from those agriculturalists who 'build rings of dry stones to serve as walls to protect themselves against wild animals' (681a). But that is precisely the activity to which one of the other groups of Cyclopes devoted their professional skills. In other words, one conceivable gambit for differentiating the pastoral ogres from their masonic homonyms may have been to link them to different notional stages of human development.

How far does the idea of Cyclopes-as-herdsmen anticipate the general ideological placement of pastoralism by later historians and philosophers? The Homeric account is the *locus classicus*. Writing about three pivotal episodes in the

[4] Aristotle on pastoralism: B. D. Shaw (1982–3: 17–20).

[5] Porph. *Abst.* 4.2.

[6] See Prauscello (2017: esp. 14–15).

Odyssey—the encounters with Polyphemus, Circe, and the Cattle of the Sun—Egbert Bakker observes: 'Each of these three adventures confronts Odysseus with a different type of Master of Animals.'[7] But the wonderfully rich cake of the *Odyssey* can be cut in countless ways. Another approach situates Cyclopean herding against a background of more prosaic cases of humans who tend animals, especially on Ithaca itself.[8] The swineherd Eumaeus is matched in his loyalty to Odysseus by the oxherd Philoetius; the upright morality of the pair of them contrasts starkly with that of Melanthius, the treacherous and soon to be horribly chastised goatherd. A final and unique example of those who herd in the *Odyssey* is the shepherd boy—in external appearance the youngest of all the poem's Masters of Animals—into whose shape Athene turns herself when she greets Odysseus on his return to Ithaca in book 13. Poised on the cusp between the extraordinary and the mundane, s/he shepherds him (one might say) into devising a workable strategy to confront the challenge ahead.

In situating Cyclopean pastoralism in relation to such cases as these, we must first differentiate between the wealth of data about Polyphemus himself and the miserly information concerning his fellows. The race of Cyclopes knows nothing of agriculture. True, they benefit from the natural produce of the land—wheat, barley, vines—but they neither plough nor sow nor irrigate: Zeus' rain does the job (9.108–11). The non-cultivation of Goat Island confirms the point: it *could* be a farmer's paradise, yielding all manner of rich crops, but the Cyclopes do not exploit it (131–5). Do they, then, as a race, live by the type of subsistence that Greeks habitually contrasted with agriculture—namely, herding? We can make that assumption if we like, presuming that what Polyphemus does, they do too, but if so we shall be doing exactly that: making an assumption. It has even been suggested that their occupation *might* have been, not that of the herdsman, but that of the metalworker: the text tells us, after all, that Polyphemus had 'cut' his olive-wood staff (320)—presumably with a metal tool, which he must have got from somewhere.[9] But that is the merest speculation, however ingenious. The only thing we are told explicitly about the occupation of the Cyclopes as a whole is that they do *not* herd the abundant wild goats on Goat Island (122). In any case, if they *are* herdsmen, it remains uncertain how they go about it. As Jonathan Burgess has observed, it is unclear whether they are nomadic, transhumant, or sedentary.[10]

Polyphemus himself is no more an agriculturalist than are his fellow Cyclopes. But what he, unlike they, *explicitly* is, is a herdsman. On arriving at the ogre's dwelling, Odysseus remarks that it is a place where sheep and goats are stabled. There is no sign of the cave's owner, who is presently far away, apart from his

7 Bakker (2013: p. xi), drawing on Burkert (1979: 33 with index s.v. 'master of animals').

8 Herding in Homer: Berman (2005: 232–6).

9 S. D'Onofrio (2003: 141). 10 Burgess (2015: 127).

fellow Cyclopes, herding his fat flocks (as Odysseus-as-narrator observes, with the advantage of hindsight) (217). This leaves the Greeks free to admire the properly compartmentalized pastoral richness of the cave's interior (219–28):

> Baskets were there, heavy with cheeses, and the pens crowded
> with lambs and kids. They had all been divided into separate
> groups, the firstlings in one place, and then the middle ones,
> the babies again by themselves. And all his vessels, milk pails
> and pans, that he used for milking into, were running over
> with whey. From the start my companions spoke to me and
> begged me
> to take some of the cheeses, come back again, and the next time
> to drive the lambs and kids from their pens, and get back quickly
> to the ship again, and go sailing off across the salt water;
> but I would not listen to them...[11]

The dairy theme continues with an act of out-and-out theft committed by the intruders (231–3):

> There we built a fire and made sacrifice, and helping
> ourselves to the cheeses we ate and sat waiting for him
> inside, until he came home from his herding.

When Polyphemus eventually arrives with his sheep and goats, he keeps the males outside in the yard, while driving the females inside for milking. This is, of course, prudent herdsmanship, which depends upon appropriate segregations.[12] (The peerless Ithacan swineherd Eumaeus will do exactly the same: while the sows are kept in an enclosure, the males remain outside.[13]) Having blocked the cave entrance to prevent the females from escaping and the males from entering, Polyphemus sits down to milk the females 'all in order' (*panta kata moiran* (309)).[14] Another separative procedure follows, this time of dairy products (246–9):

> then [he] drew off half of the white milk and put it
> by in baskets made of wickerwork, stored for cheeses,

[11] Trans. Lattimore (1965), here and in subsequent quotations.

[12] See Auffarth (1991: 337 n. 4), citing Brendel (1934: 80). Separations: S. D'Onofrio (2003: 134).

[13] *Od.* 14.13–20; cf. 14.411.

[14] As Kathryn Gutzwiller has pointed out, the Greek language of herding involves a connection between the root of the verb νέμω (*nemō*), 'I distribute in an orderly fashion', and both νομός (*nomós*), 'place of pasture', and νόμος (*nómos*), 'law' or 'custom' (Gutzwiller 2006: 5). For Polyphemus' orderliness, see Austin (1975: 143) (Polyphemus as 'addicted to system') and Mastromarco (1998: 15).

> but let the other half stand in the milk pails so as to have it
> to help himself to and drink from, and it would serve for
> his supper.

In paradoxical complementarity to Polyphemus' attention to segregating his animals is his own inseparability from them. After devouring two of Odysseus' men raw, he lies on the floor of the cave 'sprawled out among his sheep' (298).

Come the dawn, the daily pastoral round begins once more. Polyphemus milks the females 'all in order', then puts a lamb or kid to each (308–9). After a second dramatic departure from routine—a savage breakfast identical to the previous night's dinner—normal service is resumed: the Cyclops drives his flocks out of the cave and up into the hills, whistling jauntily as he goes (315–16). He spends the rest of the day, as he always does, tending his flocks. However, his eventual return to the cave is marked by a startling deviation from habit (336–9):

> With the evening he came back again, herding his fleecy
> flocks, but drove all his fat flocks inside the wide cave
> at once, and did not leave any outside in the yard with the deep
> fence,
> whether he had some idea, or whether a god so urged him.

Exceptionally, Polyphemus drives *all* the animals, males as well as females, into the cave. This is, of course, convenient for the subsequent plot, since it opens the way for the Greeks' escape underneath some well-nourished and fleecy rams (425–6). But is there no other explanation for Polyphemus' flagrant divergence from normal herding procedure than mere narrative convenience? Odysseus-as-narrator offers two possibilities: either the Cyclops himself 'had some idea' (*ti oisamenos*), or it was a god who urged him to do it. The first alternative takes refuge in quirky Cyclopean psychology: Polyphemus somehow or other got an idea into his head.[15] This is so vague as, in effect, to leave Polyphemus' behaviour unmotivated. The second alternative hints that a god might have been favouring the Greeks' plans, not for the first or last time in the *Odyssey*. This alternative too is hardly clear-cut, since in Greek thought explanatory invocation of a god often amounts to an admission that this or that action is otherwise inexplicable. How much simpler if a storm had been forecast: the good herdsman Polyphemus

[15] See Heubeck and Hoekstra (1989) on 338–9. A number of commentators and translators have interpreted *oisamenos* as 'having some foreboding', or the equivalent; e.g. Merry and Riddell (1886); A. T. Murray (1919); Shewring (1980); Rieu (1991). But why, if he *had* some suspicions, would Polyphemus have adopted a procedure that would enable the eventual escape of his adversaries? Better to keep the translation neutral: 'idea' rather than 'foreboding'; so, rightly, in addition to Lattimore (1965), e.g. Bérard (1924) ('avait-il son idée?') and Pabón (2007) ('con algún pensamiento').

would then have had every reason to bring all his flocks under cover, male and female alike. As it stands, a pivotal detail in the narrative turns out to be enigmatic—by no means the only puzzle in book 9.

In spite of the presence of the male animals, the evening milking goes on as usual and, needless to say, 'all in order' (341–2). There follows a third act of double anthropophagy, which is fast establishing itself as a subsidiary mini-routine in Polyphemus' life. But all that regularity, whether long or short term, is about to be overturned. After the blinding, it is Odysseus—though no herdsman—who temporarily usurps the role of Master of Animals (425–35):

> There were some male sheep, rams, well nourished, thick and fleecy,
> handsome and large, with a dark depth of wool. Silently
> I caught these and lashed them together with pliant willow
> withes, where the monstrous Cyclops lawless of mind had used to
> sleep. I had them in threes, and the one in the middle carried
> a man, while the other two went on each side, so guarding
> my friends. Three rams carried each man, but as for myself,
> there was one ram, far the finest of all the flock. This one
> I clasped around the back, snuggled under the wool of the belly,
> and stayed there still, and with a firm twist of the hands and enduring
> spirit clung fast to the glory of this fleece, unrelenting.

The symbolism is obvious: the rams are, in their own way, as heroic as the Greeks who cling on to them. But one ram stands out above the rest, just as Odysseus is superior to his men.[16] In using the rams, Odysseus cunningly turns something possessed by the Cyclops against its owner; he had done the same with the olive-wood stake. Yet, for all his craftiness, Odysseus is obliged to adopt the least dignified of postures in order to achieve his objective. 'With enduring spirit', *tetlēoti thumōi*, is the identical phrase applied to Menelaus and his men when they adopt an equally unheroic posture by hiding themselves inside stinking sealskins, to ambush the Old Man of the Sea (4.447).

The way the flock leaves the cave re-emphasizes the collapse of pastoral routine. The females, their udders full to bursting, wait in vain to be milked. The males head for pasture, but without the guidance of their now blinded master. Their order on leaving is another reversal of the norm (444–52):

[16] Note the difference from Apollodorus' version, in which Odysseus seems (though the text is uncertain) to escape beneath the largest of *three* rams tied together (*Bibl. Epit.* 7.8).

> Last of all the flock the ram went out of the doorway,
> loaded with his own fleece, and with me, and my close counsels.
> Then, feeling him, powerful Polyphemus spoke a word to him:
> 'My dear old ram, why are you thus leaving the cave last of
> the sheep? Never in the old days were you left behind by
> the flock, but long-striding, far ahead of the rest would pasture
> on the tender bloom of the grass, be first at running rivers,
> and be eager always to lead the way first back to the sheepfold
> at evening. Now you are last of all.'

Having escaped to Goat Island, the Greeks divide up the flocks they have stolen (just as they pilfered cheese earlier), reserving the alpha male for Odysseus. The hero shows none of the affection expressed by its former master for this beast. Instead he briskly sacrifices it to Zeus—who pays no attention (550–5).

The slaughter of the ram brings the pastoral theme of *Odyssey* 9 to a close. Looking back over the narrative, we can hardly conclude that its overall effect is to portray Polyphemus' herding in a negative light. On the contrary: his pastoralism shows him to be disciplined, careful, and even sympathetic. Nor is there any explicit indication that herding is perceived as of lower or developmentally differentiated status compared with agriculture. There is negativity aplenty in the Homeric portrayal of Polyphemus, but it does not stem from his treatment of his animals.

In Euripides' satyr play, the representation of herding is transformed by the presence of Silenus and the satyrs. As Polyphemus' slaves they have been forced to take over much of the drudgery, leaving the ogre the gentlemanly leisure that he never enjoys in the *Odyssey*; he even goes hunting with dogs (130). When the play begins, Silenus is brandishing the rake he uses to clean up the dung in the cave (32–5); the scene partly echoes the excremental prologue to Aristophanes' *Peace*. Next, the goatskin-clad satyrs try in vain to control the recalcitrant flock.[17] But neither males nor females pay them any attention—not surprisingly, since the satyrs are hopelessly unpastoral. Silenus would give away all the herds in return for one cup of Odysseus' delectable wine (164–5); indeed he offers to barter his master's lambs and cheese for strong drink. For his part, the Cyclops begins by maintaining the dairy solicitude of his counterpart in the *Odyssey* (206–9):

> How are my newborn lambs in the cave?
> Are they at the teat, nuzzling their mothers?
> Are the wicker presses filled with fresh cheese?

[17] Goatish satyrs: Seaford (1984) on l. 80.

But his pastoral interests soon evaporate. The dominant fluid in the play is wine not milk, and the dramatic exigency to allow characters, including Odysseus, to enter and leave the cave removes the motif of the under-sheep escape.[18]

Given the generic context, it might reasonably be assumed that Theocritus' two *Idylls* about Polyphemus would inhabit a full-blown pastoral landscape. Yet Polyphemus' commitment to pastoralism has been overturned by obsessive infatuation: his preoccupations are poetry, song, and love, not sheep or goats.[19] In *Idyll* 6 it is his dog, rather than he himself, that looks after the flock (9–10); in *Idyll* 11 his animals make their way home unshepherded (12–13). The reason for the upheaval is Galatea. It is true that the etymologically milky nymph ought to be at home among dairy products. Such a connection was indeed occasionally asserted: according to the historian Duris of Samos (4th–3rd cent. BCE), 'Polyphemus built a shrine to Galatea near Mount Etna in return for the rich pasturage for his flocks and the abundant supply of milk'.[20] But it was far commoner to highlight a sharp antithesis between the lifestyles of the ogre–herdsman and his beloved, a strategy emphatically followed by Theocritus. In *Idyll* 6 'goatherd' is an insult directed mockingly by Galatea at her hapless suitor (7). Wasting away with love, the Polyphemus of *Idyll* 11 looks seawards rather than landwards (18); his pastoral persuasions have no effect ('Consent to herd with me, and to milk, and to set cheese with drops of acid curd' (65–6)). Only at the very end of the poem does he tell himself—with what success we do not know—to see sense and revert to type: 'Milk the ewe that's nearby' (75).

Later Greek sources return to the interwoven motifs of the Cyclops' rejection of pastoral duty, and the counterpoint between herdsman and nymph. Galatea's only point of contact with the dairy—her whiteness—is a detail waspishly exploited by Lucian's Doris: 'Anyway, what else could he see to praise in you but your white skin? And he only likes that, I imagine, because he's used to cheese and milk, and so thinks everything like them beautiful.'[21] In profounder mood, Philostratus evokes the disruptive effect of infatuation on pastoral routine as Polyphemus gazes out to sea, 'not knowing where his flocks are feeding, nor how many of them there are, nor even, any longer, where the earth is' (*Imag.* 2.18). The final, telling detail about the Cyclops' anti-terrestrial disorientation typifies Philostratus' subtle imagination. Less unusual, but still worth noting, is the fact that *all* the Philostratean Cyclopes are said to be herdsmen. Like many ancient myth-tellers, Philostratus chose to make explicit something left opaque or open-ended in the *Odyssey*.

[18] See Seaford (1984: 51 and n. on l. 441).

[19] See Cusset (2004: 55–6).

[20] Schol. Theoc. 6(f) (p. 189 Wendel) = Philoxenus fr. 817 in D. A. Campbell (1993). On Duris: Landucci Gattinoni (1997).

[21] *DMar* 1.2.

Latin authors weave in and out of the accounts of their predecessors. The Polyphemus of the *Aeneid*, as described to the Trojans by Achaemenides, lacks a Galatea to gaze at; indeed, his blindness rules out gazing altogether. But he sticks to his pastoral routines, keeping his woolly sheep penned in his hollow cave and squeezing the milk from their udders (*Aen.* 3.641–2). Virgil retains from Homer the pathetic, affective relationship between ogre and flock: 'they were the only pleasure he had left, his sole consolation in distress' (660–1). Ovid's Achaemenides, by contrast, stresses only the ogre's goriness, not his tender side (*Met.* 14). But earlier in the poem Ovid has dwelt lovingly on the Cyclops' pride in his flocks, as expressed in his vain (in both senses) persuasions of Galatea (13.821–8):

> And all this flock is mine. Many besides are wandering in the valleys, many are in the woods, still others are safe within their cavern-folds. Nor, should you chance to ask, could I tell you how many in all I have. It's a poor man's business to count his flocks. And you need not believe my praises of them; here you can see for yourself how they can hardly walk for their distended udders. And I have, coming on, lambs in my warm folds and kids, too, of equal age, in other folds...[22]

In visual representations of Polyphemus' relationship with animals, the under-ram escape outnumbers all other scenes. Two iconographical strategies may be distinguished. The first omits the Cyclops altogether—even without his presence, the mythological reference of men clinging to the underside of rams is unambiguous. The earliest example we know of is a proto-Attic oenochoe (*Cat. 4*): the large rams are shown in profile, with schematic rows of wavy lines to depict the fleece.[23] Concerning this and similar images, discussion has focused on whether an Odysseus figure can be distinguished from the others: often, it cannot. It is also worth noting the tendency to show the animals going singly rather than in threes. Presumably the divergence from the *Odyssey* version offered greater graphic clarity.[24]

Artists adopting the second strategy depict the Cyclops as well as his flock. Often he sits or lies to one side of the scene as one or more animals approach him, with a man clinging underneath each. A distinctive way of imagining the episode is illustrated on a Caeretan hydria (*Cat. 16* (Fig. 5.1)).[25] Behind a reclining, hairy, satyr-like Polyphemus grasping a wine cup can be seen two relatively small sheep. In front of the ogre are three rams, very much larger than the other two animals; beneath each ram clings the small figure of a man. All the animals have noticeably longer legs than in real life—probably an artistic convenience to make the men underneath more clearly visible. Given that the humans are dwarfed by the three

[22] Trans. F. J. Miller, amended.
[23] See Giles-Watson (2007: 567–8).
[24] So Touchefeu-Meynier (1968: 66).
[25] See detailed discusion in Hemelrijk (2000).

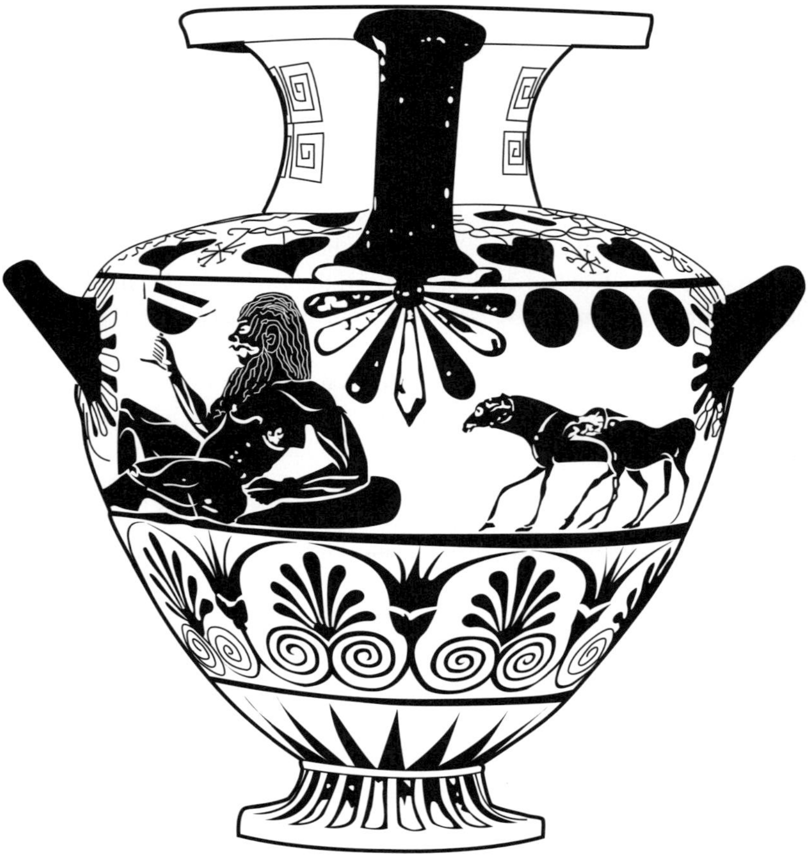

Fig. 5.1. Drawing of Caeretan hydria, *c.*520 BCE.

rams, one cannot exclude the possibility of a version of the tale in which, as in Gulliver's Brobdingnag, the animals themselves are extra large in proportion to the ogre who tends them. (In the ethnographical account of India by Ctesias of Cnidus (5th cent. BCE), the flocks and herds of the Indian Pygmies are correspondingly smaller than average size, while the reverse is true of the animals belonging to another Indian people.[26]) But it may simply be that the animals' unusual size symbolizes their importance to the action. Very large rams appear elsewhere too, as on a Cypriot sarcophagus (*Cat. 22* (Fig. 5.2)) and an Attic black-figure krater (*Cat. 21* (Fig. 5.3)), on which the ram is bigger than Polyphemus himself. Elsewhere the disproportion is less obvious (e.g. *Cat. 13* and *26*). Virtually every artist gave his own twist to this familiar scene. What is rather uncommon is

[26] Ctesias *Ind.* F45.22; F45fβ-γ; F45iα-γ.

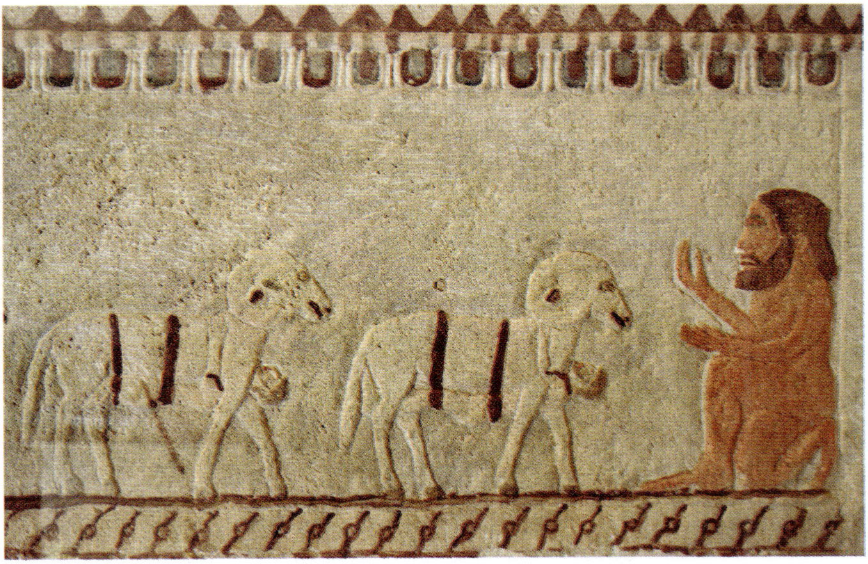

Fig. 5.2. A procession of rams with the Greeks slung underneath. Sarcophagus from Palaipaphos, Cyprus, 500–450 BCE.

any attempt to convey Polyphemus' pathetically close relationship with his animals after the trauma of the blinding. A mosaic in Rome (*Cat. 62*) hardly fits the bill, since there is little emotional subtlety in the face of this Cyclops as he stretches out his hands to feel the back of one of his rams. A more plausible example is a red-figure stamnos (*Cat. 25* (Fig. 5.4)) on which a ram seems to be affectionately nuzzling its master's beard.

Although the under-ram escape predominates in visual accounts of Polyphemus with his flocks, other episodes and motifs appear too. Given the prominence of milk and cheese in the literary accounts, it might be expected that the same theme might be replicated in art. But in fact there seem to be only two candidates. The less plausible is the Caeretan hydria (*Cat. 16* (Fig. 5.1)). Above the two smaller sheep are three round objects, which, it has been suggested, might depict cheeses stored on some sort of (invisible) shelf.[27] The more plausible candidate is the Aristonothos krater (*Cat. 3* (Fig. 3.3)). Behind the about-to-be-blinded Polyphemus stands an object decorated with cross-hatching on top of a long pole. Could this be a compartmentalized rack or draining basket, perhaps a visual echo of one of the containers heavy with cheeses noticed by Odysseus (*Od.* 9.219)?[28] Differently pastoral is the suggestion of a container for fodder.[29] Also

[27] Hemelrijk (2000: 145). [28] Dougherty (2003: 38–9); cf. Kindstedt (2012: 75).
[29] Touchefeu-Meynier (1968: 11).

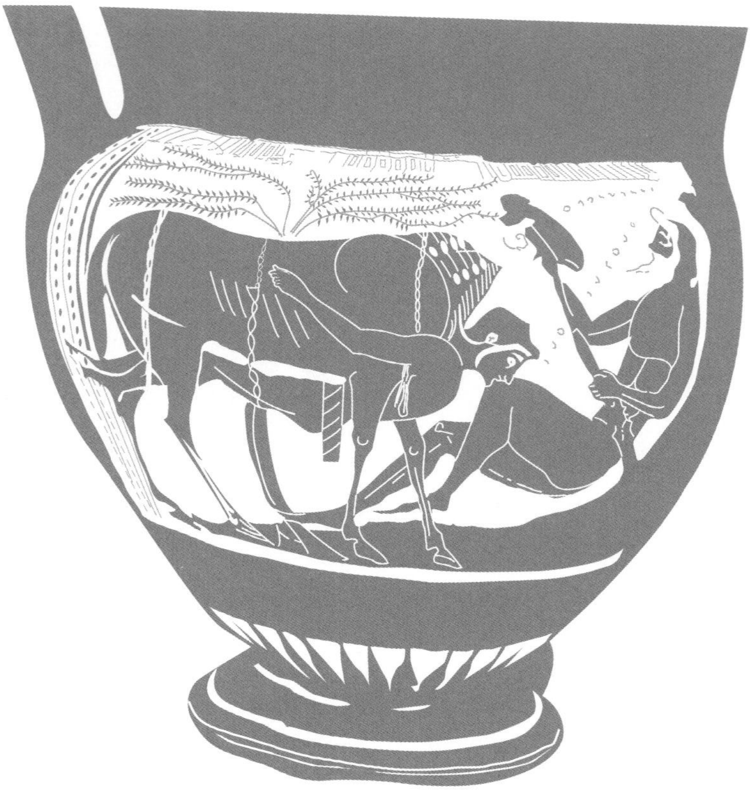

Fig. 5.3. Drawing of Attic black-figure krater, *c.*500 BCE.

possible is the idea that it is an implement used for stirring during cheese production, to remove lumps and render the end product homogeneous.[30] Whether or not the object did have a dairy function, no animals are visible (if they had been, this might have corroborated the pastoral context).

Turning from dairy products to the animals themselves, we have a range of images setting Polyphemus within a pastoral context. In some depictions of the offering of wine and the blinding, rams appear as incidental bystanders; the same goes for the less common scene of Polyphemus preparing to launch a rock towards Odysseus' ship (*Cat. 37* (Fig. 3.5)). *Sui generis* in relation to surviving Cyclops-related art is the Hellenistic bowl (*Cat. 33* (Fig. 5.5)) which came to light in 2004; found in Porsuk in Cappadocia, it apparently originated from a

[30] Cf. the *brise-caillé* used today (we are indebted here to our Swiss informant Heidi Dal Lago). For a not dissimilar implement used in modern Cyprus, see Rizopoulou-Egoumenidou (2008: 421, fig. 22); the nearly 600-page volume from which the article comes is an exhaustive study of the history of Greek dairy products.

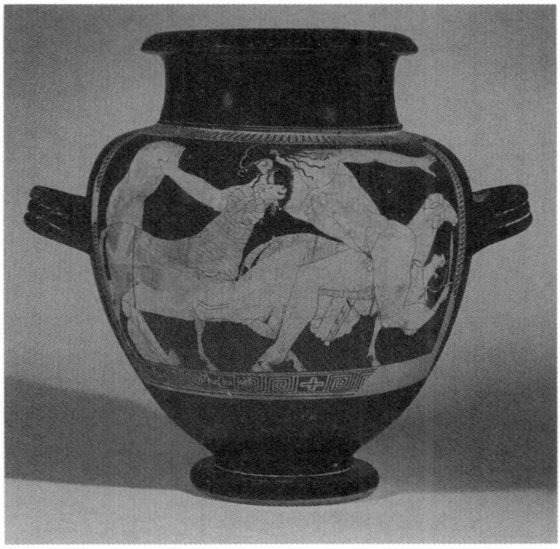

Fig. 5.4. The gentle friendship between ram and ogre. Attic red-figure stamnos, *c.*480 BCE.

workshop in Antioch.[31] What distinguishes its imagery from the Homeric version, and approximates it rather to the Euripidean, is the absence of the under-ram escape, and the depiction of a Polyphemus accompanied by dogs—presumably hunting dogs, as in the satyr play. The ogre appears several times in cartoon-like, sequential images. In one vignette Odysseus offers him a drinking cup, the classic gesture depicted also in a work that in most other respects contrasts starkly with the Porsuk bowl: the Piazza Armerina mosaic (*Cat. 72* (Fig. 3.7)). Several rams in the foreground enhance the pastoral setting, echoing the rural landscape evoked by the distant trees visible above the cave roof. But the placid relationship between master and flock is belied by the gutted ram lying across the ogre's knee, a dramatic variation on other Roman images that portray a standing or seated Polyphemus grasping the arm of a limp or lifeless man (e.g. *Cat. 65* (Fig. 5.11) and *66* (Fig. 5.12)). That the Piazza Armerina ram is about to constitute the ogre's next meal is the inevitable conclusion.

Before leaving Odysseus-related pastoral images we cannot resist returning to the Campanian krater, which depicts a frankly imbecilic ogre grilling two men on spits (*Cat. 28* (Fig. 4.2)). In the background, beyond the roof of the ogre's cave, are what are evidently intended to be large rams. Painted in a striking white, only the head, neck, and part of the back are visible. They look more equine than ovine, as if the artist wanted to caricature Polyphemus' animals as well as their master.

For images of Polyphemus more specifically as a herdsman, as opposed simply to representations of him in various types of association with animals, the place

[31] See Chalier (2008: 98–100).

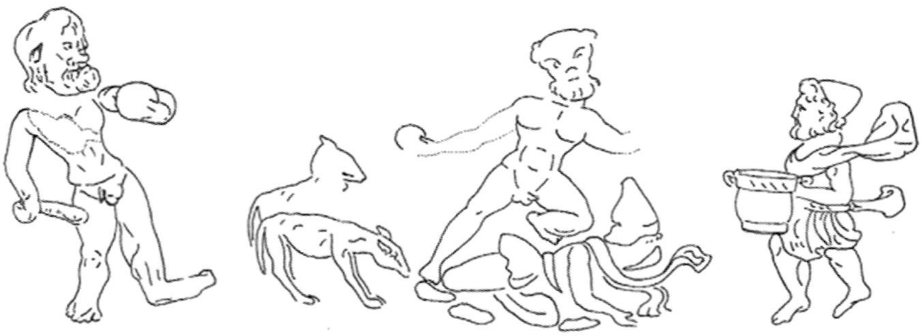

Fig. 5.5. Drawing of images on relief bowl from Porsuk, Cappadocia, 150–100 BCE.

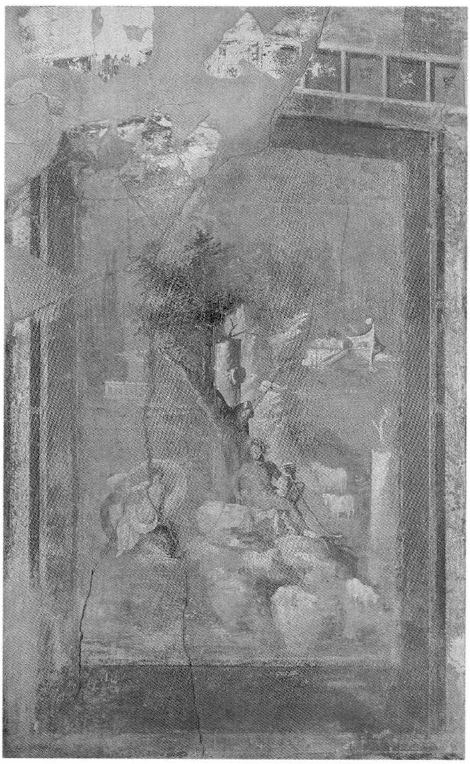

Fig. 5.6. Ogre and nymph on the rocks. Wall painting from House of the Priest Amandus at Pompeii, 1st cent. CE.

to look is a series of Roman wall paintings exploring his relationship with Galatea. The painting from Boscotrecase (*Cat. 41* (Fig. 3.2)) shows the Cyclops contemplating his beloved, but still equipped with the tools of his trade—staff and syrinx—from which she has distracted him. Roaming idly over the rocky hillside, or

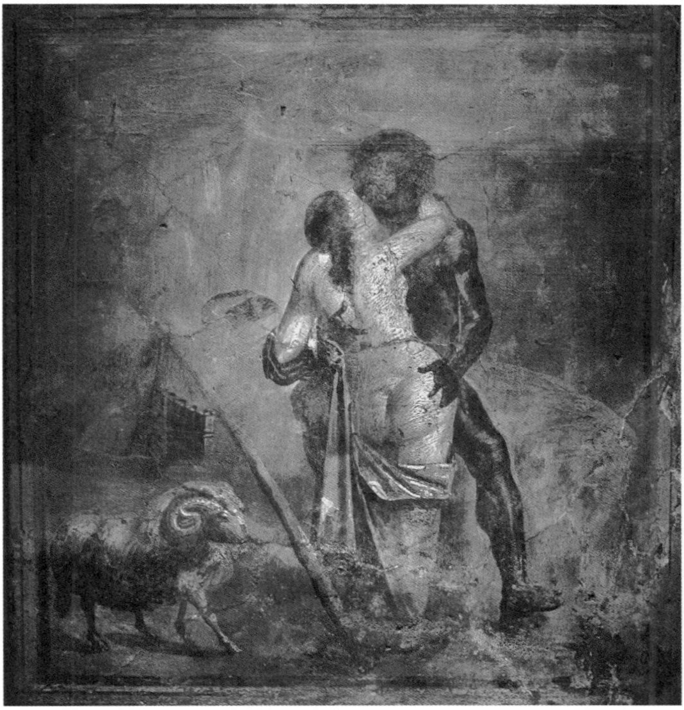

Fig. 5.7. Wall painting from House of the Ancient Hunt at Pompeii, *c.*62–79 CE.

in one case lying placidly on the stony ground, are his sheep and goats, three white and two black. Unlike the impression given by some of the vase paintings discussed earlier, there is nothing unusually large about the animals' dimensions; at least they seem in normal proportion to the figure of the presumably non-gigantic Galatea. A similar schema underlies the delightful Pompeian painting from the House of the Priest Amandus (*Cat. 45* (Fig. 5.6)). Once again the Cyclops is intent on paying court to his nymph (who offers a provocative rear view to the painting's external viewer, rather than to her would-be suitor); the animals surrounding him remind us of the occupation he is neglecting. A similar conception lies behind two wall paintings, where Polyphemus and Galatea are locked in explicitly erotic positions (*Cat. 47* (Fig. 5.7) and *48* (Fig. 5.8)). The incidental presence of ram, staff, and syrinx serve merely to frame and contextualize the main action: the last things on the mind of the fully occupied couple are bleating flocks.

A final image of Polyphemus the herdsman is at once unique and frustrating. The Pompeian wall painting from which it comes (*Cat. 54* (Fig. 5.9)) no longer survives—hence the frustration. The uniqueness relates to the composition. Polyphemus is depicted with his flock and a sheepdog; in the background is the

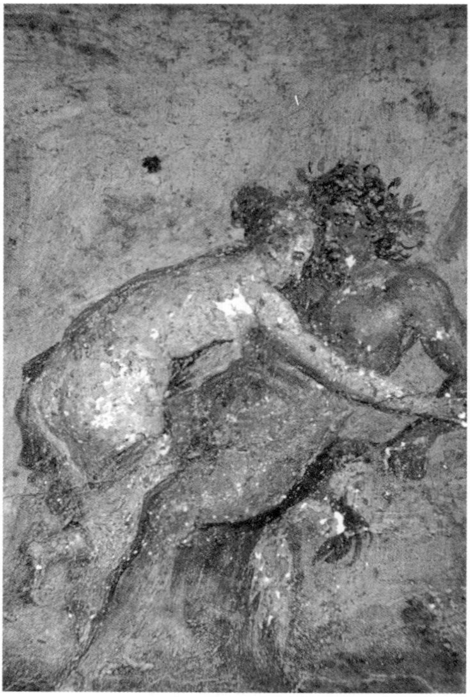

Fig. 5.8. Wall painting from House of the Red Walls at Pompeii, *c.*62–79 CE.

much smaller figure of another herdsman—presumably Acis—with *his* flock.[32] Acis is in vigorous movement, with outstretched hand; presumably the knowing viewer interprets the gesture, and the emotion that it implies, as that of one 'in flight', even though the seated Polyphemus shows no sign of being in pursuit.

Diet

That diet is an immensely powerful cultural symbol is a truism of archaeology, anthropology, sociology, and history. The bibliography is gargantuan, far beyond the capacity of any one scholar to digest.[33] Cultural studies of food items proliferate. Alongside descriptions of the alimentary habits of particular past and contemporary societies, important general questions have been addressed, including animal sacrifice, table manners, cannibalism, and the opposition between raw

[32] See von Blanckenhagen (1968: 109, with pl. 47, 1 and 2). Other bibliography at *LIMC* 'Galateia' no. 47.

[33] Four points of reference: Flandrin and Montanari (1999); Kiple and Ornelas (2000); Fernández-Armesto (2002); Toussaint-Samat (2009).

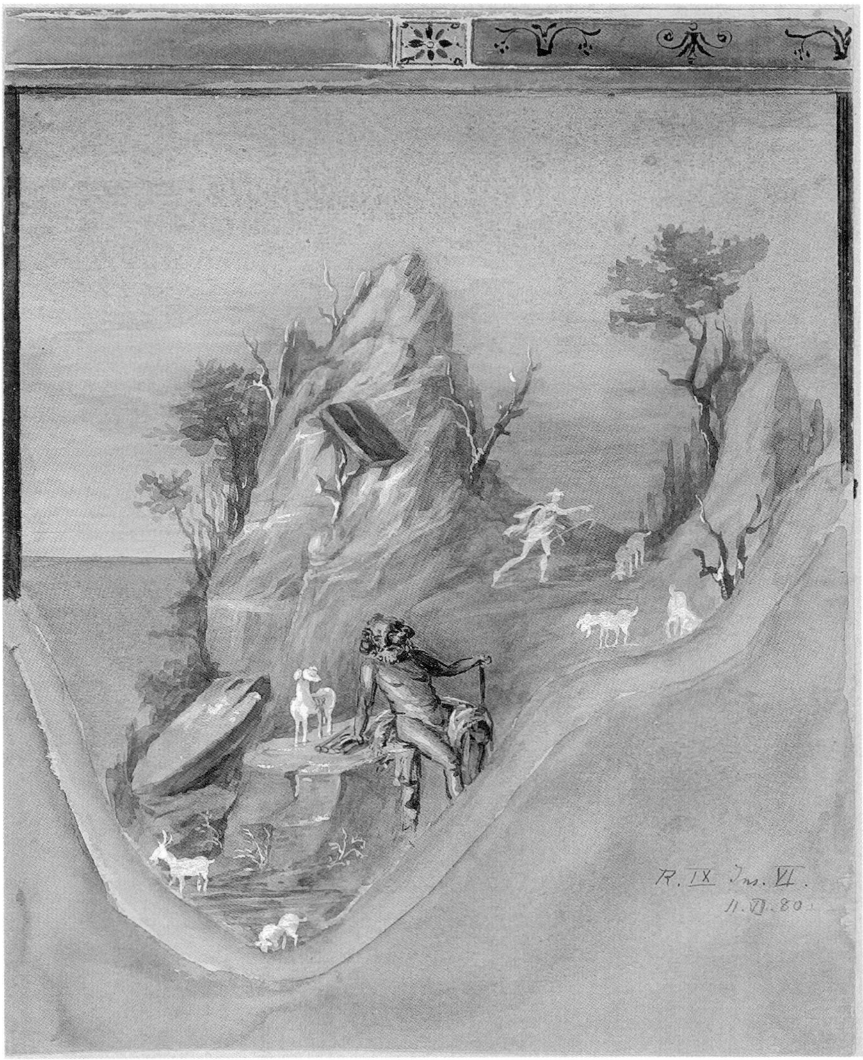

Fig. 5.9. Polyphemus and, in the background, Acis. Wall painting, now lost, from Pompeii, 1st cent. BCE/1st cent. CE.

and cooked.[34] Regarding classical antiquity in particular, there has been a wealth of academic analysis, some general, some dedicated to conceptual issues, and

[34] We mention a handful of studies *exemplorum gratia*. Sacrifice: Bremmer (2007); C. A. Murray (2016). Table manners: Lévi-Strauss (1978); Visser (1991). Cannibalism: Arens (1979); Barker, Hulme, and Iversen (1998); Goldman (1999); Pancorbo (2008); Bourke (2011: 299–325). Raw/cooked: Lévi-Strauss (1970). There is still much of value in Firth (1973: 243–61) and Goody (1982).

some product specific.[35] In classical mythology the pickings are especially rich. The violent drunkenness of the Centaurs at the wedding of Peirithous and Hippodamia; the taste for human flesh that characterizes the Laestrygonians, Thyestes, Tereus, Cronos/Saturn, and the mares of King Diomedes; the emblematic status of the olive in the *Odyssey*;[36] the innumerable episodes of appropriate or inappropriate animal sacrifice that permeate mythological narratives of every genre: all this is the staple diet of Graeco-Roman myth.

When it comes to the diet of the Cyclopes, we know nothing about the masons or the metalworkers; whether they took a packed lunch to work, and, if so, what it consisted of, are matters forever hidden. About Polyphemus and his fellow ogres we have much more information, but even this is often incomplete, allowing different interpreters to fill in the gaps as they see fit. As usual, generic discrimination is fundamental: epic is not satyr play; a Roman mosaic is not a Greek vase.

What we can glean from the *Odyssey* about the eating and drinking habits of the Cyclopean community as a whole is at best sketchy. According to Odysseus' narrative, wheat and barley grow spontaneously for them, as also do vines 'which produce wine rich in grapes' (*Od.* 9.109–11). Putting the matter beyond doubt, Polyphemus later confirms that the earth 'produces wine rich in grapes' for himself and his fellows (357–8). Yet how easy it is to assume the contrary, as if the dramatic effect of the wine offered by Odysseus to Polyphemus depended, not on the special deliciousness and potency of that particular vintage, but on the ogre's unfamiliarity with *any* kind of wine. Even the peerless Walter Burkert nodded when he stated that the Cyclopes lived in a paradise with neither agriculture *nor wine*.[37] The reason for the lapse may be that we hear nothing about Cyclopean wine-*making*. Nor is this the only textual silence. Beyond the perfunctory details we have just mentioned, we hear nothing about the dietary habits of the Cyclopes as a group—nothing, for instance, about whether *all of them* eat people.

About the diet of one particular ogre, however, the text tells us much, though even here there is incompleteness and ambiguity. Baskets of cheese, pens for kids and goats, pails containing whey: these are what the Greeks immediately notice in Polyphemus' cave. Though we are never told so explicitly, we must surely assume that he *eats* the cheese. (What else could he do with it?) But does he also eat goat and sheep? It has been argued that the answer is no, since 'everything suggests that his diet is dairy-based and strictly vegetarian'.[38] That is one way of filling in

[35] General: André (1981); Dalby (1996, 2003); Garnsey (1999); Scarpi (2005); Wilkins and Hill (2006). Concepts: Detienne and Vernant (1979) (sacrifice); O. Murray (1990) (symposium). Specific products: Foxhall (2007) (olive); Bakker (2013) (meat).

[36] On which, see Detienne (1973); Bonnafé (1985).

[37] Burkert (2003: 9). Interestingly, the same great scholar once commented elsewhere (1979: 31) that if he had to memorize the story he would forget the details of Cyclopean life described at 106–12—and he has done!

[38] Bakker (2013: 57), citing E. F. Cook (1995: 102).

the lacuna, but we have no way of telling whether it is the right one.[39] Something he does *not* eat is bread; or at any rate, 'he was not like a man that eats bread' (190–1). So: cheese, yes; bread, not as far as we know; goat and sheep, maybe. But his most memorable food preference is human flesh—presumably an occasional delicacy, and all the more enjoyable for that. In the *Odyssey* this proclivity is highlighted in several passing references (2.20; 10.200; 20.19–20; 23.313), but the iconic account is in book 9. His first dinner after discovering the Greek intruders makes short work of two of them (288–93):

> He sprang up, and stretching his hands towards my companions clutched two at once and battered them on the floor like puppies; their brains gushed out and soaked the ground. Then cutting them up limb from limb he made his supper of them. He began to eat like a mountain lion, leaving nothing, devouring flesh and entrails and bones and marrow…

A subtle simile, this, with a nice distinction between tenor and vehicle. Polyphemus first cuts his victims limb from limb, and only then devours them, the act of cutting being a 'cultural' detail to distinguish the ogre's culinary technique from that of the indiscriminate, 'natural' lion.[40] Breakfast consists of two more Greeks identically consumed (311), and the same goes for the evening meal (344)—two at a time, because he presumably grabs one with each hand, the use of hands being another humanizing characteristic in contradistinction to the lion.[41] Although this has sometimes been questioned, we are surely bound to presume that the six men are eaten *raw*.[42] True, Polyphemus does not lack the *means* of cooking: already from their initial landfall on Goat Island the Greeks looked across to the ogres' territory and noticed smoke rising from their fires (166–7). Moreover, when Polyphemus came back to his cave on the first evening, he carried a big bundle of firewood 'to accompany his supper' (233–4). But he is never shown cooking anything, whether human flesh or something else. The firewood serves to provide warmth and light in the cave.[43]

Qua anthropophage, Polyphemus belongs to a tradition with universal resonance: this, above all, is why he deserves the appellation 'ogre'. The fear of being eaten echoes through countless horror narratives. From *Hansel and Gretel* and *Jack and the Beanstalk* ('Fee-fi-fo-fum, I smell the blood of an Englishman'), to

[39] So, rightly, B. D. Shaw (1982–3: 22–3).

[40] For the lion's indiscriminate method of eating, see Arist. *Hist.an.* 594b, with the subtle analysis by S. D'Onofrio (2003: 136). On the Cyclops' diet, see also Longo (1987).

[41] Hands: 288, 311, 344, with Mastromarco (1998: 16–17).

[42] Questioned: e.g. by Burgess (2015: 127), who thinks he 'probably' cooks his victims; the adverb concedes that there is no evidence for this.

[43] So Stanford (1965) on 234. Auffarth (1991: 304 n. 42) argues that the firewood is used to *light* the cave. That is certainly one of its functions: only after Polyphemus has lit his fire does he catch sight of the Greeks, who had scuttled away into a far corner (236, 251).

the quasi-mythical trope of the European explorer simmering in a native cooking-pot, to the modern cinematic icon-of-evil Hannibal Lecter (as in *The Silence of the Lambs* (1991), and its sequels), the notion of being devoured alive by a fellow human being persists as the ultimate phobia. Like any motif, it can be diverted to humour, most memorably in *The Gold Rush* (1925), where Charlie Chaplin's Little Tramp narrowly avoids being ingested by a large, hairy, famished fellow prospector; the horror is defused because he deliriously imagines Charlie as a human-sized chicken.

So far as humour is concerned, there is little enough in book 9; but there is, arguably, at least one linguistic joke.[44] This occurs when Polyphemus washes down his first pair of victims with *akrēton gala*, 'unmixed milk' (297). Although scholarly ingenuity has suggested that this phrase might be designed to distinguish the Cyclops' practice from that of the normal Greek habit of drinking milk mixed with honey, it is far more plausible that the implied contrast is with unmixed wine, as opposed to the more usual and (from a Greek perspective) civilized custom of drinking wine mixed with water.[45] The joke, then, is that the Cyclops is doubly uncivilized: not just milk but (for heaven's sake!) *undiluted* milk.[46]

One more detail may be added about the contrast between milk and wine. Polyphemus washes down the first evening's anthropophagous dinner with unmixed milk; after the second evening's dinner, he drinks unmixed wine. After the first dinner, he simply lies down and sleeps till morning. After the second, he again lies down to sleep, but subsequently vomits up the wine with chunks of undigested human flesh. The first evening demonstrates that, evidently not lactose intolerant, he can comfortably digest both human flesh and undiluted milk. The second evening shows him incapable of combining the same flesh with undiluted wine—a drink so strong that even dilution at one cup of wine to twenty measures of water leaves a marvellous aroma (203–11). It is hard to say which of the two meals is, from the perspective of customary Greek alimentary practices and values, the more revoltingly uncivilized.

The manner and content of Polyphemus' eating and drinking contrasts sharply with those of the Greek intruders. The behaviour of the new arrivals on Goat Island lays down a number of symbolic markers, though, as usual, some matters are left implicit. The Greeks go hunting and bag nine wild goats for the crews of each of the twelve ships, with a bonus animal for Odysseus' own vessel. The slaughtered animals provide an all-day, communal feast (161–2)—as distinct

[44] We owe this suggestion to David Miller. Another possible candidate for linguistic humour is the pun on the word *mētis*; see p. 205.

[45] Milk and honey: Privitera (1993: 29–30), on Ael. *NH* 15.7, where Indian drinkers of pure milk are contrasted with Greeks who sweeten it with honey; cf. Mastromarco (1998: 17 n. 20).

[46] See Auffarth (1991: 316–18).

from the boorishly solitary eating that characterizes Polyphemus.[47] Nor was wine lacking, since the Greeks had filched many jars of it when they sacked the Ciconians' citadel soon after leaving Troy. What we are not told is that the meat was shared with the gods according to proper sacrificial procedure, or that the wine was cut with water. But such things go without saying, since no breach of these customs could have been passed over in authorial silence.

The next stage of the narrative shows Odysseus' trademark forethought: he carries with him a goatskin of super-strong wine given to him by a Thracian priest of Apollo, and a leather bag containing food—just in case they came in handy. (The wine certainly did.) What they found in the Cyclops' cave was another sign of forward planning, but this time by Polyphemus: baskets laden with cheeses, processed in anticipation of his own future needs. The inclination of Odysseus' crewmen was to replenish their own food stocks by stealing cheeses and driving some goats and sheep to their ship. But Odysseus wanted first to set eyes on the cave's owner. Instead of taking food and making off, 'we lit a fire and made offerings [*ethusamen*] and took cheeses and ate them' (231–2). The act of sacrifice constitutes an absolute distinction between the Greeks and Polyphemus: they do it, and he does not. But what actually is it that they 'sacrifice'? The verb *thuō* signifies making an offering to the gods according to due procedure, usually, but not necessarily, by burning it. In the context, not only cheeses but also sheep and goats were available. Although the language suggests that the offering was of cheese, the text is finally inconclusive—allowing room for later interpreters to fill in the gap one way or another.[48]

Having escaped from the cave, the Greeks take on board ship the animals that have been their means of salvation (464–6), and sail back to Goat Island. A second feast takes place, almost, but not quite, mirroring the first (548–57). As before, the eating is communal, and lasts all day; as before, everyone gets equal shares; as before, one feaster is more equal than the others, since he gets the alpha ram. What differentiates the second feast on Goat Island from the first (aside from the fact that the animals consumed are domesticated sheep rather than wild goats) is that the eating is situated within an explicitly sacrificial context of cooked offerings, including thigh bones set aside for Zeus (551–3). All is orderly and in accordance with custom. Does this constitute an absolute contrast with Cyclopean practice? Not entirely. There may be no sacrifice in Cyclopia, but nor is there total alimentary chaos. When Polyphemus drinks Odysseus' wine, he does so three

[47] For 'solitary eater' as an insult, cf. Ar. *Vesp*. 923; Amipsias fr. 23 *PCG*, with Bremmer (2002: 141 n. 27). See also Braund (1996).

[48] e.g. Apollod. *Bibl. Epit*. 7.5 ('they lit a fire and sacrificed some of the kids'). According to the *Suda* E 336 (ii. 211–12 Adler), Homer meant that the Greeks made a burnt offering of cheeses (text in Philoxenus fr. 823 in D. A. Campbell 1993). For a Hittite parallel for cheese as a burnt offering, see Kindstedt (2012: 46), citing Hoffner (1966).

times—just as he eats three, successive, identical meals of paired human victims.[49] There is method in his barbarism, pattern in his wildness.

Of all the differences between the Homeric and the Euripidean Cyclopes, perhaps the most striking relates to eating and drinking.[50] About the diet of the ogres as a group, the satyr play goes into much more detail than the epic. Regarding Polyphemus in particular, the play raucously explores a new world of fiendishly sophisticated culinary experience. Add to that the obsessive importance of wine-drinking in the minds of the satyrs, Silenus, and eventually Polyphemus himself, and eating and drinking may reasonably be placed at the head of the play's concerns.

The initial interchange between Odysseus and Silenus spells out the basics of Cyclopean mealtimes (121–8):

ODYSSEUS: Do they sow Demeter's grain, or on what do they live?
SILENUS: On milk and cheese and the flesh of sheep.
ODYSSEUS: Do they have the drink of Bromios, the juice of the vine?
SILENUS: Not at all. So it is a joyless land they dwell in.
ODYSSEUS: Are they hospitable and reverent towards strangers?
SILENUS: Strangers, they say, supply the daintiest meat.
ODYSSEUS: What? Do they delight in killing men and eating them?
SILENUS: No one has ever arrived here without being butchered.

So they are *all* man-eaters—a significant completion of a lacuna in the *Odyssey*. The developing dialogue reveals more about the Cyclopes' diet: though lacking bread, they do have meat, cheese, and milk, including cows' milk—another amplification of Homer (133–6). And they have no wine *at all*.

With Polyphemus' arrival the plot turns to what one particular ogre eats and drinks. Whatever the content of the meal he expects the satyrs to have prepared for him, it is clear what he will wash it down with: vast quantities of milk, whether from sheep, cows, or a mixture of the two (214–19).[51] This paradoxical sophistication in the gross Polypheman palate shows the ogre *au fait* with the 'civilized' idea of 'mixing', as opposed to the unmixed drinks associated (by Greeks, of course) with 'the Barbarian', or with 'barbarian' conduct.[52] The moment he hears about the Greeks' alleged, attempted theft of his sheep and cheese, however, the Cyclops' thoughts turn punitively from drink to food (241–9):

[49] See Aguirre Castro (1999: 13–14) for the repetition of six as the number of Odysseus' crewmen killed or eaten in various episodes.

[50] On eating and drinking in Euripides' *Cyclops*, see especially Konstan (1990) and Mastromarco (1998).

[51] Seaford (1984: ad loc.) is right to reject the idea that 'mixed' means 'mixed with honey', *contra* Ussher (1957).

[52] Mastromarco (1998: 22).

> [*To a servant*] You there, go straightaway and sharpen my carving-knives and start a big bundle of wood blazing on the hearth. They shall be slaughtered at once and fill my belly, presenting the server with a feast hot from the coals and the rest boiled and tender from the cauldron. I have had my fill of mountain fare: I have dined enough on lions and deer and have gone far too long without a meal of man's-flesh.

This is a far cry from mountain-lion-like chomping. To diversify his diet from his normal fare (which includes animals he has hunted), the Euripidean ogre enjoys human flesh meticulously prepared and differentially cooked: some grilled, some boiled.[53] On a rainy day he likes nothing better than hunkering down in his cave to eat calf or wild beast, roasted (another diversification) and washed down with the inevitable amphora of milk (323–7). But now it is time for something more special (356–60):

CHORUS OF SATYRS: Cyclops, open the gate of your yawning throat: the limbs of your guests, boiled, roasted, or hot from the coals, are ready for you to gnaw, rend, and devour as you recline dressed in a soft-fleeced goat-skin.

Echoing Homeric precedent, Polyphemus chooses two of Odysseus' men for his meal. But there the similarity ends: as Odysseus describes it, all now is prepared with grim, assiduous care, in what amounts to a parody of sacrificial procedure (382–404):[54]

> When we entered this rocky hall, he first made the fire blaze up, heaping onto the hearth thick logs from a mighty oak, enough to load three wagons, and he set the bronze kettle to boil on the fire. Then near the blaze he spread out a bed of fir branches upon the ground. After he had milked the heifers, he filled to the brim a great mixing-bowl—a ten-amphora one—with white milk, and he set next to it a cup of ivy-wood, more than four feet across and six feet deep; then spits made of thorn-wood, their ends burnt in the fire but the rest of them scraped with a scythe. There were bowls for catching blood, as big as Etna. When that god-hated and hellish cook had everything ready, he snatched up two of my companions. He cut the throat of the first over the cauldron with a sweep of the arm and drained him of blood, the second he seized by the tendon at the end of his foot, struck him against the sharp edge of a rock, and dashed out his brains. Then butchering them with a fierce blade he roasted their fleshy parts in the fire and put their arms and legs in the cauldron to boil.

[53] See Mastromarco (1998: 20–2).

[54] Parody of sacrifice: Seaford (1984) on 395; Biehl (1987); Voelke (1992: 16).

Though the text and hence the translation are at times uncertain, the gist is clear. Roasting and boiling, with spits available for human kebabs: this is one of the 'unholy meals' that Silenus darkly alluded to near the outset of the play, prepared by the Masterchef from Hades (31, 397).

David Konstan has reminded us how important it is to see the structure of *Cyclops* as ternary rather than binary: as well as Polyphemus and the Cyclopes, and Odysseus and his crewmen, there are also Silenus and the satyrs.[55] This triple perspective applies to diet: what the Cyclopes eat and drink contrasts with the practice of the other two groups. The Greeks' diet is of small importance in the play. They arrive hungry and thirsty, and Odysseus' first objective is to remedy these lacks (87–9, cf. 96–8); beyond that, their aim is not so much to eat as to avoid being eaten. The dietary position of the satyrs, however, is more interesting. About food they are indifferent: their sole interest is in wine and its god.[56] But what of the satyrs as potential objects of consumption? They fall into a special category.[57] They are not Cyclopes, whom Cyclopes do not eat; nor do they belong to the class of 'other creatures', wild and domesticated, animal and human, all of whom Cyclopes *do* eat. Apart from Polyphemus' joke that he does not eat satyrs because their incessant jumping would destroy his stomach (220–1), the main reason for excluding them from the class of the edible is that they are his slaves: to eat them would destroy his comfortable lifestyle.

A final word about beverages.[58] The first necessity Odysseus mentions is water (96–7). As for wine, he has it, but not for the purpose of carousing. He begins by using it as a means of barter, and then as a weapon to overcome Polyphemus. For Silenus and the satyrs, by contrast, wine is everything: a craving, a joy, a religious experience, a means of salvation. For Polyphemus, wine is something different again. At first he knows nothing of it: his ideal beverage is milk.[59] But as soon as he becomes acquainted with it, wine becomes a pleasure to drown in, even an accompaniment to anticipated sexual union with a fellow soak, Silenus. Not for the only time in ancient myth-telling, there is an elision of the boundary between Cyclops and satyr—'two hybrid types, who blur the boundary between man and beast'.[60]

Whatever humour may be present in a plot that depicts the easy outwitting of a self-important, self-deluding, flatulent, masturbating, tipsy ogre, the genre to which Euripides' *Cyclops* belonged was (in terms of the classification in the Athenian dramatic festivals) satyr play not comedy. But the gross appetites of the Euripidean Polyphemus recurred often in plays that *were* classified as comedies.

[55] Konstan (1990). [56] Konstan (1990: 211). [57] Konstan (1990: 209–11).

[58] Konstan (1990: 212–13).

[59] Burzacchini (1979) shows that Polyphemus' milk-based idyll is a transposition of an equivalent scene in a (wine-)drinking song by the lyric poet Alcaeus; cf. Mastromarco (1998: 27–8).

[60] Konstan (1990: 227). For another overlap, see *Cat. 24* (Fig. 5.14), a vase depicting two *satyrs* assisting Hephaestus in his forge; see pp. 168–9.

Although none of these works survives in more than fragmentary form, we still have several tasty passages. Thanks to such gourmands as Gargantua, Falstaff ('that roasted Manningtree ox with the pudding in his belly',[61]) and the Cookie Monster of *Sesame Street*, we have become familiar with the idea of an outrageous individual whose capacious gullet leads to an even more enormous stomach.[62] The figure cut by the Cyclops in Greek comedy loses little by comparison. Already in the *Cyclops* by the early Sicilian dramatist Epicharmus (6th–5th cent. BCE), the ogre displays an unnerving discrimination: 'tripe is tasty, and so is the thigh-bone' (there may be a *double entendre*—'thigh-bone' = penis).[63] Whether he ate these delicacies raw or cooked we do not know, but they certainly demonstrate a sophistication undreamed of by the Homeric ogre.[64] Even more full of panache is the threat embodied in lines that can have been spoken by no one but Polyphemus, from *Odysseuses* [*sic*], a play by a later comic dramatist, the Athenian Cratinus (5th cent. BCE): 'In return for which I shall seize all you "loyal comrades", roast you, boil you, barbecue and bake you, dip you into brine and vinegar and warm garlic sauce, and whichever of you soldiers all appears to be the best cooked, that's the one I shall munch down.'[65]

The original introduction of the Cyclops-in-love theme, anecdotically ascribed to Philoxenus, opened up fresh possibilities for comedy, including the comedy of food. To what extent this new comedic direction can be linked with Philoxenus' alleged mockery of his one-time patron, the Sicilian tyrant Dionysius I, is unknowable, and in the end unimportant.[66] What is not in doubt is that the role of Polyphemus as lover could have amusing dietary implications. The nicest example is a passage from the *Cyclops* of another comic dramatist, Antiphanes (*fl.* 4th cent. BCE), presumably listing delicacies with which Polyphemus tempts Galatea:

> These land animals shall come to you as a present from me: an ox from the herd, a forest-roving he-goat, a she-goat from heaven, a castrated ram, a castrated boar, a pig not castrated, a full-grown pig, a hare, kids...green cheese, dry cheese, chopped cheese, grated cheese, sliced cheese, cream cheese.[67]

Whether a sea nymph would in fact have relished such resolutely land-based fare may be doubted. A lavish banquet of fish, described elsewhere in the same play, might have attracted her more.[68]

[61] *1 Henry IV*, II.iv.446–7. See Fisher (2009).
[62] Warner (1998: 73).
[63] Epicharm. fr. 71 *PCG*, with Mangidis (2003: 36) and Venezia (2007: 104 n. 13).
[64] Mastromarco (1998: 34).
[65] Fr. 150 *PCG*; trans. I. C. Storey.
[66] The Dionysius link is proposed by Dörrie (1968: 21).
[67] Antiphanes fr. 131 *PCG*.
[68] Antiphanes fr. 130 *PCG*.

Other Greek and Roman texts agree that the Cyclopes' diet differed from that of civilized, bread-eating, wine-mixed-with-water-drinking human beings. But the nature of that difference varies. In the same vein as Antiphanes, Theocritus has his Polyphemus appeal to Galatea using dietary rhetoric. She is whiter than curd, softer than a lamb, more skittish than a calf, sleeker than an unripe grape; he, for his part, can draw on the milk of a thousand cattle, and never lacks for cheese (*Id.* 11.20–37). Ovid's Galatea is offered the prospect of apples, grapes (golden yellow and deep red), strawberries, cherries, plums (two varieties), chestnuts, and the fruit of the arbutus (if you like that sort of thing), not to mention lambs, kids, and the inevitable milk, some to drink and some to coagulate (*Met.* 13.812–30). More modest, but still combining spontaneously growing fruits of the earth with meat and milk, is the *Odyssey*-inspired Cyclopean diet described by Philostratus (*Imag.* 2.18). Most frugal of all are the herbs collected in a leather bag by the Cyclops of Philoxenus: this is a pre-pastoral Cyclops-as-gatherer.[69] But the anthropophage is not forgotten. Apparently unlike his fellows, the Philostratean Polyphemus *normally* eats people 'in the manner of savage lions'; but love for Galatea has made him abstain from such nasty foods 'to avoid seeming gluttonous or unpleasant'. Neither Virgil nor Ovid leaves any room for doubt that Polyphemus devours his human victims raw. The Virgilian ogre chews their still-twitching warm limbs and drinks their blood (*Aen.* 3.622–7); the Ovidian, staying closer to his Homeric predecessor, crouches over them like a lion, chomps them up bones and all, and partly vomits them up again vilely mingled with wine (*Met.* 14.207–12). From Theocritus onwards, all these passages refer to Polyphemus the pastoral ogre. There is, though, an exception that mentions the diet of the metalworkers. When Callimachus' Artemis bribes the Cyclopes to fulfil her commission, she promises to go hunting and shoot some solitary wild creature or 'monstrous [*pelōron*] wild beast' for them to eat (*H.Art.* 84–5). *Pelōron* echoes, of course, the epithet applied to Polyphemus in the *Odyssey*.[70] As well as containing an implied crossover between two of the three homonymous Cyclopean groups, this Callimachean passage shows us a unique example of the Cyclopes eating *that which resembles themselves*.

Compared with the variety in the textual examples, visual art tackles Cyclopean eating and drinking more restrictively. There is nothing about the metalworkers or the relationship with Galatea: the overwhelming emphasis is on the encounter with Odysseus.

The most striking images, unsurprisingly, are those that evoke anthropophagy. Although Polyphemus is never shown devouring a human victim (in the manner of, say, Goya's gruesome *Saturn Devouring his Son*), we do see him either preparing to do so, or having already (partially) done so. As to whether he cooked them

[69] Philoxenus fr. 820 in D. A. Campbell (1993), based on Ar. *Plut.* 296–301, with schol. ad loc.
[70] See p. 80.

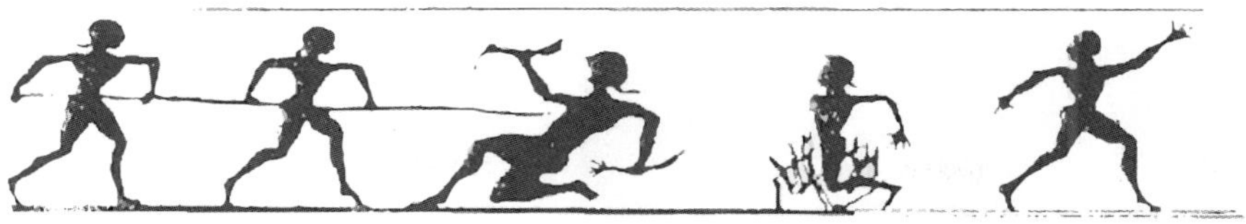

Fig. 5.10. Vignettes from a horror story. Redrawn Campanian amphora, *c.*500 BCE.

or ate them raw, artists, like writers, took different views. A unique portrayal of Cyclopean cookery can be seen on our old friend the Campanian krater (*Cat. 28* (Fig. 4.2)). The fact that the backdrop is a cave, and that there are *two* humans on Polyphemus' spit, are details that might just possibly recall Homer; but there the resemblance ends. Here is an artist who looks to have struck out in a new direction, graphically distancing himself from all those who thought the Cyclopes devoured their victims raw. Another vase from Campania (*Cat. 18* (Fig. 5.10)) ghoulishly combines the themes of cooking and dismemberment. While the Cyclops holds a human leg in one hand and an arm in the other, their former owner, a human lacking these limbs, is being roasted on a fire. An artist who, by contrast, opted for the 'raw' approach is the painter of the Laconian cup (*Cat. 10* (Fig. 3.1)), which shows the ogre placidly grasping a dismembered human leg in each hand; nothing in the picture suggests cookery.

Another approach to Cyclopean diet is envisaged in the mosaic from Piazza Armerina (*Cat. 72* (Fig. 3.7)). One way of reading this image is that we are being reminded of Polyphemus' customary diet, on the assumption that his flocks provide him with meat as well as milk. Alternatively—or additionally—the artist may be adapting representations in which the ogre grasps the wrist of a collapsed, inanimate human (as in *Cat. 36*, *65* (Fig. 5.11), and *66* (Fig. 5.12)), a schema that we *may* read as 'in preparation for eating him' (although these images lack any sense of explicit aggression). In that case the Piazza Armerina image of a gutted ram would amount to an implicit mitigation of Polyphemus' savagery: it is only an animal, not a human being.[71] In this spirit, a recent interpreter sees the Piazza Armerina mosaic as a *dilution* of the motif of anthropophagy 'to a more civilized and domesticated setting [*sc.* the setting of the mosaic], more fit to greet and welcome guests'.[72] Yet is the ram, with its guts spilling out, really such a calming, anodyne image? There is a great deal of openness about the mosaic's meaning.

When it comes to beverages, the only drink of interest to Polyphemus and his portraitists is wine. One common schema, exemplified in Greek and Roman art from the Hellenistic period onwards, depicts Odysseus offering wine in a scene preliminary to the blinding. Usually the hero holds out a cup (*Cat. 35*, *36*, *61*, and

[71] Mitigation: Touchefeu-Meynier (1968: 28); cf. Andreae and Parisi Presicce (1996: 248).
[72] Dunbabin (2015: 46).

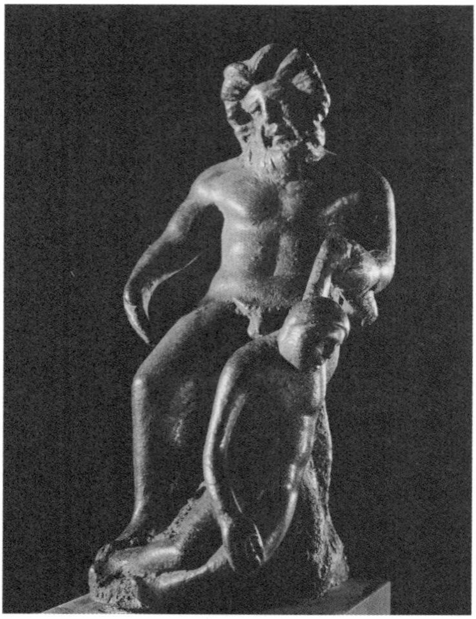

Fig. 5.11. Hairy and furious, Polyphemus is about to make a meal of one of Odysseus' companions. Bronze statuette, 2nd cent. CE.

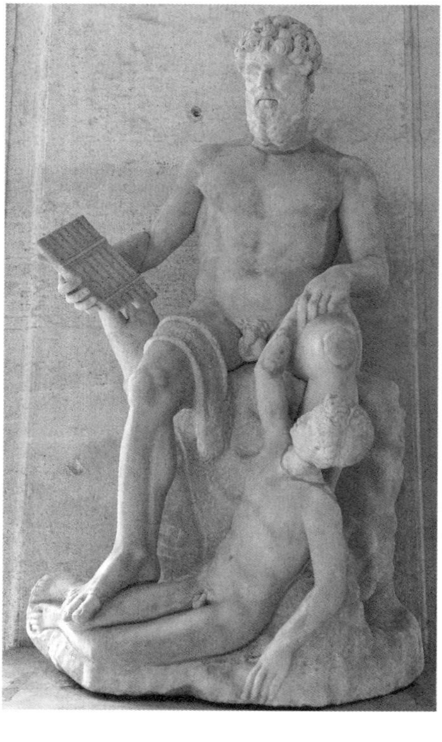

Fig. 5.12. The grim musician. Marble statue in Rome, 2nd cent. CE.

72 (Fig. 3.7)), though on the bowl from Porsuk (*Cat. 33* (Fig. 5.5)) he carries a substantial krater. An alternative approach, often exemplified on Greek vases that would themselves have contained wine and/or water, highlights the presence of wine at the moment of the blinding: without wine, the implication is, the blinding could not have taken place. Already on the Eleusis amphora (*Cat. 1* (Fig. 2.1)) the Cyclops holds a cup, even as the stake is being driven into his eye; similarly on a Caeretan hydria (*Cat. 15* (Fig. 4.4)). On the Laconian cup (*Cat. 10* (Fig. 3.1)) the man at the head of the blinding party, presumably Odysseus, simultaneously holds a wine cup. The theme is reinforced severalfold on the British Museum krater (*Cat. 27* (Fig. 4.13)): on the floor beside the Cyclops in his drunken stupor there stands a wine cup, with a wineskin hanging beside it; satyrs complete the picture. Although a cup is the commonest visual emblem of drunkenness in these scenes, it is not the only one: presumably the enormous jar depicted on the Etruscan pithos (*Cat. 5* (Fig. 4.7)) has the same symbolic function.

Two more vases offer distinctive variations on the same theme. A black-figure cup (*Cat. 11*) shows, to the left, a man carrying a wineskin; behind him are two men brandishing swords. Polyphemus is central, while to the right is a figure, presumably Odysseus, carrying an oinochoe. The absence of any exact extant parallel, in text or art, to this image is as evident as the presence of general thematic links to other versions of the Odysseus-and-Polyphemus encounter. Much the same applies to the Caeretan hydria (*Cat. 16* (Fig. 5.1)) which depicts the escape from the cave. A half-reclining, Silenus-like Polyphemus holds the stem of a wine cup, showing no sign of suffering torment after being blinded—a clear demonstration of the precedence of the synoptic over the linear.

Social Interaction

A notable difference between the three main groups of Cyclopes concerns the manner in which they interact, both among themselves and with non-Cyclopes. We shall look in turn at these two kinds of interaction, beginning with the intra-Cyclopean.

Although we hear little about interrelationships between the masons, the clear implication of the repeated use of plurals ('a work of the Cyclopes…', 'made by the Cyclopes', etc.) is that they worked cooperatively rather than as individuals.[73] The same goes for the primordial arms manufacturers and their functional descendants the metalworkers. Even if their names might be taken to indicate separate functions, such apparent separations are concentrated into joint action. The

[73] e.g. Eur. *HF* 943–6; Paus. 2.16.5; 25.8.

Hesiodic Brontes, Steropes, and Arges are engaged in a common enterprise, an expression of their shared possession of 'an overwhelmingly forceful spirit'.[74] The same community of purpose applies to the identically named trio in Callimachus' *Hymn to Artemis*. Their successors in the *Aeneid* are even more harmonious in their work practices: 'dividing their labour equally between them', 'they raised their arms...in time with one another'.[75] Texts are corroborated by art—for instance, a marble slab and the cover of a sarcophagus from the early Roman Empire, on which three Cyclopes assist Hephaestus (*Cat. 63* (Fig. 5.13) and *64* (Fig. 4.1)). More unusually, on a red-figure vase (*Cat. 24* (Fig. 5.14)) two *satyrs* are shown helping a metalworking Hephaestus—but could they be playing the role of Cyclopes? Neither texts nor images ever describe one of the primordial weapons-makers, or a blacksmith Cyclops, as labouring on his own. One detail, however, is worth mentioning, in connection, not with work, but with another kind of social relationship. The mythographer Pherecydes reported that, when Apollo took vengeance on the Cyclopes for making the thunderbolt with which Zeus slew Asclepius, it was not Brontes, Steropes, or Arges whom Apollo killed, but their

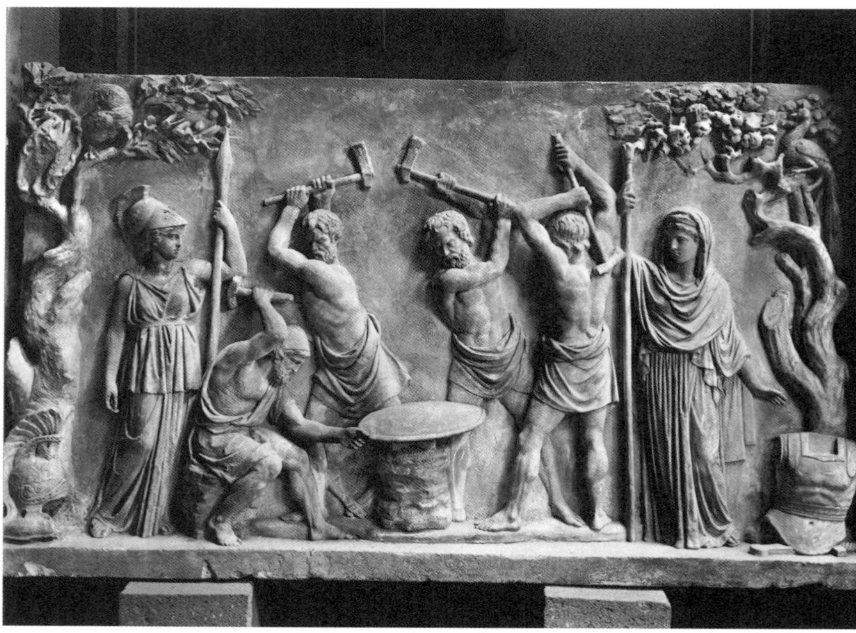

Fig. 5.13. The Cyclopes beat out a shield. Marble slab, 100–150 CE.

[74] Hes. *Theog.* 139–41. [75] *Aen.* 8.443–5, 452–3.

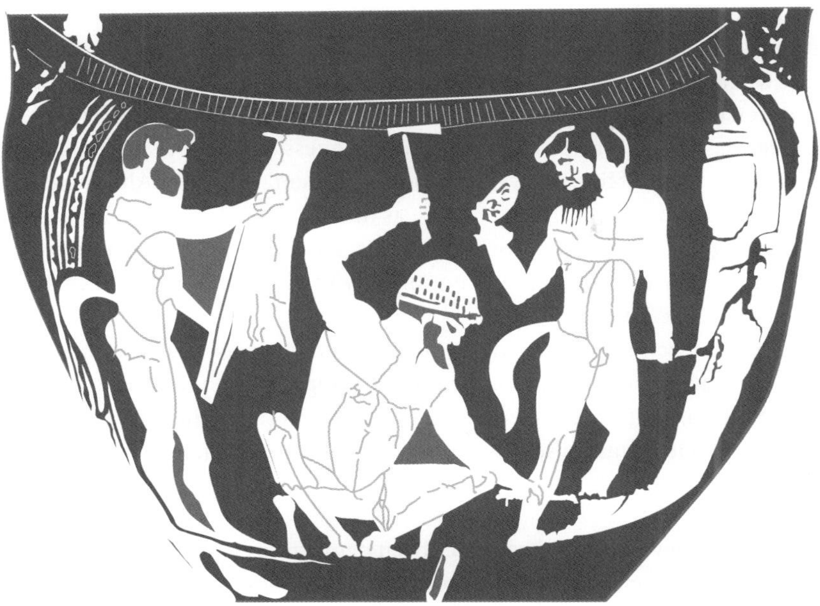

Fig. 5.14. Hephaestus flanked by satyrs-as-Cyclopes? Redrawing of Attic red-figure krater from Sabucina, 490–480 BCE.

sons.[76] Unfortunately, as soon as the curtain rises on the domestic arrangements of the arms manufacturers, it falls again; we know no more.

With the pastoral ogres, matters are, as usual, more complicated. According to Philostratus, the earth produces its fruits for *all* the Cyclopes; they are *all* shepherds; they *all* consume milk; *none* of them knows of an assembly, a council, or an *oikos* (household); they *all* inhabit the clefts of mountains. The only distinction between them is that Polyphemus is the wildest (*agriōtatos*) of the lot.[77] This is a change of tack from the *Odyssey*, where, in the authoritative words of Zeus, it is Polyphemus' power, rather than his wildness, that is 'the greatest over all the Cyclopes' (1.70–1). However, nothing in the rest of the *Odyssey* spells out the nature of this superiority. In particular, nothing suggests that the power imbalance has anything to do with politics, in the widest sense of that word. On the contrary, what comes across strongly from book 9 is the Cyclopes' autonomy: 'each governs his own children and wives [*sic*], without any heed for one another' (114–15). By implication, they live in households,

[76] Schol. Eur. *Alc.*1 = Pherec. fr. 35 Fowler. The orthodox version—that it was the Cyclopes themselves who were slain—is found at e.g. Eur. *Alc.* 3–6; Apollod. *Bibl.* 3.10.4; Hyg. *Fab.* 49.

[77] Cf. Val. Flacc. *Arg.* 4.104–7, where the *rabidi Cyclopes* round up shipwrecked mariners to become 'dire fodder and wretched feasts' for Polyphemus—who is presumably even more *rabidus* than they are.

unlike their Philostratean equivalents; but there is no sense of interdependence between those households, which are, as Aristotle noted, *sporades* ('scattered').[78] True, when the blinded Polyphemus cries out to summon his fellow Cyclopes, he addresses them as his *philoi*, his kinsmen (or 'nearest and dearest') (408). But the nature of this reciprocity is anyone's guess. Nor does it appear that Polyphemus himself lives in even the most rudimentary family. Although at one point Odysseus refers to the ogre's cave as his *oikos* (478), there is not a wife or child in sight. Polyphemus' social monadism is even more emphasized than that of the other Cyclopes: 'it was not his way to visit the others of his tribe: he kept aloof...' (188–9).

The plot structure of Euripides' *Cyclops* means that for many dramatic purposes the satyrs take the place of the other Cyclopes, who never make it into the limelight. Even so, they are mentioned from time to time. The dialogue between Silenus and Odysseus raises the question of socio-political arrangements in Cyclopia (119–20):

OD.: Who do they obey? Or has power been democratized here?
SIL.: They are solitary: no one takes notice of anyone else.

As we have already noticed, the Greek word we translate as 'solitary' is conjectural: *monades* in place of the manuscript reading *nomades*, 'nomads'.[79] The emendation is convincing: 'solitary' makes perfect sense as a corrective to the notion of public power implicit in 'democratized'. The idea that no Cyclops bothers about any of the others echoes the *Odyssey*, but thereafter the picture alters, owing, like so much else in the play, to the influence of wine. The intoxicated Polyphemus longs to share the novel beverage with his 'brother Cyclopes' in a drunken revel (445–6); later, in maudlin high spirits, he again calls them his brothers and his *philoi* (kin/friends (509, 531–4)). Such is the power of wine that it might even bridge the ultimate social fissure: that between one Cyclops and another.

So much for intra-Cyclopean relationships; but how did they interact with those who were not of their own kind? The non-Cyclopes with whom the masons came into contact were their employers. It would be fascinating to hear about the Cyclopes' reaction to non-payment of wages, as in the case of the walls of Troy built for Laomedon by Apollo and Poseidon, or the great castle of Valhalla constructed by the giants Fasolt and Fafner.[80] Unfortunately no such stories survive: presumably the commissioners of the walls of Mycenae and Tiryns settled the bills on the dot. Similarly, the arms-manufacturers and metalworkers interacted

[78] Arist. *Pol.* 1252b. [79] See p. 117.
[80] For the theme in folklore, see Fontenrose (1983). Fasolt and Fafner appear most famously in Wagner's *Ring*.

uncontroversially with those they worked for: Zeus (thunder, lightning, thunderbolt), Hades/Pluto (helmet), Poseidon (trident, horse trough), Artemis (bow, arrows, quiver), Mars (chariot), and Minerva/Pallas Athene (armour).[81]

Much more complex are the external relationships of the pastoral ogres. Most challenging of all is the account in the *Odyssey*, which already generated disagreement in antiquity. Opinions differed especially about whether the behaviour of Polyphemus should be distinguished from that of the rest of the Cyclopes—whether, that is, the group might be exculpated from the crimes of which Polyphemus was manifestly guilty. At the beginning of book 6 the Cyclopes are described as 'overbearing', a demeanour that expressed itself in their 'doing harm' to the Phaeacians, thanks to their superior force (4–7). As a result, the Phaeacians, who originally lived near the Cyclopes, migrated *en masse* to their present home on Scherie. At first sight this looks like an unequivocally negative portrayal of the treatment of their neighbours by *all* the Cyclopes, not least because the word we translate as 'overbearing', *huperēnoreontōn*, is used elsewhere of the Trojans and the Suitors. But there might just be a loophole: etymologically, at least, the word means 'exceedingly manly'.

The first adjectives applied to the Cyclopes by Odysseus-as-narrator in book 9 are *huperphialos* and *athemistos* (106), for which the respective translations 'arrogant' and 'lawless' carry prima facie conviction. The significance of the latter term is plain enough: 'lacking *themis* (proper order)'. The sense of the former, etymologically very interesting epithet ('overflowing the *phialē* (bowl)') is less obvious, though the sense of 'overweening' or 'arrogant' seems to be supported by its application to the Suitors and Trojans.[82] Nevertheless, in antiquity a major strand of interpretative opinion, as evidenced by Homeric scholia, sought to deny the negativity of both epithets. *Huperphialos* could, it was argued, refer simply to extreme *size*, while *athemistos* might mean 'lawless' only in the sense that the Cyclopes *did not need* laws because of their naturally virtuous, primitive lifestyle.[83] Although such views seem to cut across the grain of the text, the fact that they could be persistently articulated in antiquity is one more reflection of the intriguing openness, at so many points, of book 9.

In the *Odyssey*, hospitality (*xe*(*i*)*nia*) and its opposite are fundamental to an understanding of Polyphemus' behaviour towards the Greeks, and theirs towards him. A test of hospitality is what motivates Odysseus to sail across from Goat Island: 'My friends, let the rest of you stay here. I myself with my own ship's crew will go and find out what manner of men live yonder. Are they arrogant, wild, and unjust, or hospitable [*philoxeinoi*] and godfearing?' (172–6).[84] Polyphemus' first

[81] Hes. *Theog.* 139–41; Callim. *H.Art.* 50, 81–3; Apollod. *Bibl.* 1.2.1; Verg. *Aen.* 8.424–38.

[82] Parallels between Suitors and Polyphemus: Bakker (2013: 53–7).

[83] These matters are explored in the fine article by Prauscello (2017).

[84] S. West (2013: 194) shrewdly contrasts Eur. *Cyc.* 96 and 133–7, where Odysseus' much more basic motivation is to find water and food.

words to the intruders acknowledge that they belong in the category of *xeinoi* (252-5): 'Strangers [*xeinoi*], who are you? What land did you sail from, over the watery paths? Are you bound on some trading errand, or are you random adventurers, roving the seas as pirates do, hazarding life and limb and bringing havoc on men of another stock?' (252–5). Each side assumes that the social game being played is that of host/stranger/guest. Yet neither side plays fair. The Greeks enter the cave uninvited and help themselves to cheese. Odysseus may assert that he wants to find out whether the cave's owner will offer him guest gifts (*xeinia* (229)), and may later invoke Zeus Xeinios (269-71). But that initial intrusion (quite unlike the behaviour of Athene/Mentes at 1.102–4, where the goddess waits in the outer porch of Odysseus' palace until she is invited in), together with the theft of food, undermines the claim.[85] Polyphemus' rejection of *xeinia* goes much further. Dismissing the relevance of Zeus, Xeinios or otherwise (273–8), he consumes his guests instead of feeding them. Yet, in however perverted a fashion, he continues to pay lip service to hospitality. He *will* grant Odysseus a *xeinēion*—that of eating him last (369–70). Even in the wretchedness of his blindness, as his foes sail out of reach, he still, deceitfully but naively, tries to lure them back with a promise of *xeinia* (517). But between one who has savagely violated hospitality, and others who have treated it with self-interested disdain, the hope of true reciprocity is zero.

One more aspect of Cyclopean 'external relations' remains to be mentioned. On hearing the fateful name 'Odysseus', Polyphemus recalls an oracle he once heard: 'We once had a prophet here, noble and mighty, Telemus son of Eurymus, who excelled in divination and grew old prophesying to the Cyclopes. He predicted that all this would happen in the future, that I would lose my sight at the hands of Odysseus' (508–12). So Telemus grew old among the Cyclopes. But did he grow *up* amongst them? In other words, was he too a Cyclops, or did he originate outside (as Ovid, for one, maintained that he did)?[86] If he was an outsider, why was he not eaten? If he was a Cyclops, was divination the only non-traditional occupation that the Cyclopes practised? These are yet more of the unanswerable questions posed by book 9.

As we have repeatedly noted, the presence of Silenus and the satyrs in Euripides' version constitutes a decisive shift in the myth. But one theme common to the epic and the satyr play is hospitality. Throughout the play, Polyphemus interacts with two groups of non-Cyclopes: Odysseus and the Greeks, and Silenus and the satyrs. The satyrs' inferior status as slave-workers rules them out of the reciprocal demands of hospitality. But the Greeks emphatically *are* in the hospitality game: Silenus and the satyrs repeatedly identify them as *xenoi*. However, being in that category does them no more good in *Cyclops* than it does in the *Odyssey*. Indeed,

[85] See S. West (2013: 195).
[86] 'Telemus meanwhile had been brought to Sicilian Etna…' (Ov. *Met.* 13.770).

in contrast to the *Odyssey*, the attitude of *all* the Euripidean Cyclopes towards strangers is unambiguous (125–8):

OD.: Are they hospitable (*philoxenoi*) and god-fearing towards strangers (*xenoi*)?
SIL.: Most delicious, they maintain, is the flesh of strangers (*xenoi*).
OD.: What? Do they feast on the men they have killed?
SIL.: Everyone who has come here has been slaughtered.

As for Polyphemus in particular, Odysseus urges on him the claims of *xenia* (299–301, 354), but to no avail (342–4):

CYCL.: Guest-presents you shall have—you won't blame me there: fire, and this ancestral cauldron, which, when it boils, will hold your torn flesh nicely.

The Cyclops' promise to eat Odysseus last of all (550) renews the Homeric motif of the travestied guest gift, but on the whole the Euripidean version presents the moral issues surrounding *xenia* with fewer nuances than does the epic. As the chorus puts it, the Cyclops is a *xenodaitumōn* and a *xenodaitēs*: both words mean 'a feaster on guests' (610, 658).

In texts that explore Polyphemus' yearning for Galatea, the idea of a Cyclops' relationship with a non-Cyclops moves into uncharted social and emotional waters. But in one respect the affective situation remains unchanged since the *Odyssey*: what persists, in the vast majority of texts and images, is a total breakdown in reciprocity. Whether sparring with a wily hero or pursuing an elusive sea nymph, Polyphemus lacks even the rudiments of mutuality in his treatment of and by others. Whereas the *Odyssey* and Euripides' *Cyclops* witness a sequence of dishonest negotiations about gifts of hospitality, in Theocritus and Ovid the dysfunctionally proffered and hopelessly ineffective gifts are those of love. The ogre of *Idyll* 11 combines would-be seductive language (whiter than curd, softer than a lamb, my sweet honey-apple) with pledges of more practical delights, both pastoral (cattle, milk, cheese, a *locus amoenus*) and feral (fawns, bear cubs). He receives no response. In Ovid the similes, more extensive and more lavish (smoother than sea shells, softer than swan's down), are complemented by insults (tougher than willow twigs, deafer than the sea), which in turn lead to a vast range of promised natural gifts, ranging from plums and chestnuts to every sort of dairy product, not forgetting does, hares, goats, doves, and the inevitable bear cubs (*Met.* 13.789–837). Once more, Galatea will have none of it: she is lying in Acis' arms. A visual analogue can be seen on a sarcophagus (*Cat. 67* (Fig. 8.2)). While Polyphemus is in the act of offering Galatea a bear cub (?), both Galatea and, exceptionally, Acis are also depicted, she astride a dolphin, he seated on a mountainside. Polyphemus' gift is met with indifference.

In examining Greek and Roman myth, of course, one should never say 'never'. This applies to reciprocity as much as to anything else. In Theocritus' *Idyll* 6 there is at least *some* sort of responsiveness from Galatea: she pelts Polyphemus' flock and sheepdog with apples, and reciprocates his compliments with curses. But for evidence of warmer reciprocity we need to turn to art. A wall painting from Herculaneum (*Cat. 46* (Fig. 8.1)) shows a stately Polyphemus sitting on a rock, looking pensively upwards. To the left stand Galatea and another woman, perhaps her maid and/or go-between—for the scenario is quite unlike that in which Polyphemus contemplates from afar an inaccessible and coquettish nymph. Here, rather, the artist seems at least not to rule out the possibility of an eventual coming-together of the couple. There is no such ambiguity in another wall painting, this time from Pompeii (*Cat. 47* (Fig. 5.7)), in which a naked Polyphemus receives the evidently willing embrace of a semi-naked Galatea. No less explicit is another Pompeian image (*Cat. 48* (Fig. 5.8)) in which the nymph gingerly tries to balance on top of her naked lover.

These exceptions apart, the presence of reciprocity in the mythology of Polyphemus is small. The absence of social reciprocity in *Odyssey* book 9 is manifest, not just in the matter of guest gifts, but also in Polyphemus' failure to communicate with the other Cyclopes: when he calls them to his aid, they literally cannot understand him (the Outis trick). So far as concerns himself and Galatea, lack of reciprocity is not just a matter of spurned gifts, since a central feature of their (non-)relationship lies in the idea of the non-reciprocated gaze.[87] Bearing all this in mind, we are tempted to see absence of reciprocity as a key characteristic of at least *some* Cyclopean mythology. It is worth pausing to explore this.

While at work, two kinds of Cyclopes interacted cooperatively within their respective groups: the arms-manufacturers/blacksmiths and the builders. About the pastoral ogres, matters are less certain. We know virtually nothing about how they worked, only that they *lived* apart from one another; but that in itself suggests that the interaction between them was limited. Suppose, now, that storytellers took this idea of limited intra-Cyclopean interaction and developed it further. Imagine that *one* of the pastoral ogres was *even more* isolated from his fellows than was the norm for a Cyclops. Maybe he was wilder, or more powerful, than they were; at any rate, he was somehow different, and also physically separate. This idea of separation was then accentuated in depictions of his relationships with *non*-Cyclopes, relationships in which all reciprocity became dysfunctional. What, though, of those occasional depictions of physical intimacy with Galatea—the closest possible kind of reciprocity? We confess—as lovers of effective stories, rather than as academics—that we find such depictions imaginatively unsatisfying. Putting it metaphorically, we might say that, instead of merely stretching the

[87] See pp. 130–1.

highly elastic membrane that envelops the distinctive Polypheman character, they rupture it. The greatest fictional characters—Antigone, Medea, Falstaff, Don Quixote, Faust, Don Juan, Sherlock Holmes—have about them a unique behavioural and cognitive configuration that fosters their metamorphosis into 'myths' in their own right. To defy that configuration—a lean and hungry Falstaff, a pipe-and-slippers Don Juan—is, of course, an author's or artist's perfect right; but such reversals come at a price. Doubtless Polyphemus and his fellow Cyclopes have not etched themselves into the collective Western and post-Western psyche to the same extent as these other mighty cultural icons. But in their own way the Cyclopes too are powerful cultural presences. And that is due in large part to their distinctiveness.

Humans or Monsters?

After a careful analysis of Polyphemus-as-monster in the *Odyssey*, Ray Clare reaches a persuasive if not wholly original conclusion: monstrosity is in the eye of the beholder.[88] Clare's point is that different narrative perspectives shape the ways in which the Cyclopes' characteristics are presented. While thoroughly agreeing with this, we may also take Clare's epigram in a rather different direction: not towards texts, but towards images. *The beholder*—the viewer of visual images—enjoys a crucial vantage point from which to observe 'the monstrous'. Crucial, but also peculiarly subjective. Not that visual material should be set aside: on virtually *any* definition of 'monstrosity', artistic and, in the case of recent cultures, photographic images provide a compelling body of evidence.[89] But to decide whether this or that individual is 'a monster' involves the drawing of conceptual distinctions. In visual images such distinctions can only be implicit. Words, and the categories they express, offer a more fruitful starting point.

Book 9 is not the first moment in the *Odyssey* when the Cyclopes are characterized. Already in book 1, Zeus' Olympian perspective describes Polyphemus as *antitheos*, 'like a god' (1.70)—a worthy opponent for a Greek hero.[90] Less flattering is the epithet *agrios*, 'wild' (2.19), applied to the ogre in the context of an assembly at Ithaca, when the principal narrator relates that the son of one of the Ithacan elders had been killed and eaten by Polyphemus. However, neither *antitheos* nor *agrios* tells us what *class* of creature the ogre belonged to. We have to

[88] Clare (2002: 17). More recently Winkler-Horaček (2015: 6): 'What a monster is, is also—or especially—a question of point of view' (our translation).

[89] Dell (2010) consists largely of illustrations of grotesque monstrosity; fewer pictures but more analysis in Piñol Lloret (2015). For visual aspects of monstrosity in early Greek art, see Winkler-Horaček (2015). Monstrosity in general: Mittman and Dendle (2012).

[90] Clare (2002: 5). But an alternative reading preserved by a scholiast (see Stanford 1965: ad loc.) is 'opposing the gods'—yet another possible Cyclopean ambiguity?

wait till book 6 to learn that the Cyclopes were *andres* (6.5). In Homer an *anēr* is a male human being, as contrasted with, for example, a woman, or a god (throughout Homeric epic Zeus is the father of *andres* and gods), or a Centaur (*Od.* 21.303).

So far, so relatively straightforward. It is with Odysseus' own narration in book 9 that the complications set in. The description of the Cyclops' cave is coupled with an account of its owner (187–92):

> Inside
> there lodged a monster of a man [*anēr* . . . *pelōrios*], who now was herding
> the flocks at a distance away, alone, for he did not range with
> others, but stayed by himself; his mind was lawless,
> and in truth he was a monstrous wonder [*thauma* . . . *pelōrion*] made to behold, not
> like a man [*andri*], an eater of bread, but more like a wooded
> peak of the high mountains seen standing away from the others.

So the ogre both did and did not look like an *anēr*. One respect in which he did *not* resemble an *anēr* was his prodigious (*pelōrios*) size. Another was his diet: he ate no bread. As book 9 develops, we hear more about the classification of Polyphemus. His status as *anēr* and his wildness are both confirmed (214–15), as are his non-cereal diet and his hugeness. Does this package of characteristics amount to monstrosity? It is important to stress that Homer does not mention any hideous deformity in Polyphemus' appearance; as we have already noticed, the question of Cyclopean monocularity is never explicitly addressed.[91] Does Polyphemus' *size* make him monstrous? Even if it might be said (following Georges Canguilhem) that enormity *tends towards* monstrosity, the Cyclops' hugeness is evidently compatible with his being an *anēr*.[92] What of his wildness? Does *that* imply monstrosity? Hardly: even though he is *agrios*, he remains an *anēr*. What *does* put him beyond the pale of humanity, likening him to a wild animal rather than to a human being, is his outrageous diet, which involves a wholesale confusion of categories.[93] Whereas his treatment of his flocks follows every rule of orderly pastoral behaviour, his predatory consumption of humans negates every propriety.[94] Is he therefore a 'cannibal'—an eater of his own kind? A pedant might deny it, since the ogre does not devour his fellow Cyclopes. But he is still—sometimes—an *anēr*, and eats others who belong in the same category. In the end, the narrative makes nothing of this conceptual nicety; to the Greeks cowering in the cave, such a detail was the last thing on their minds.

[91] Rightly: Bremmer (2002: 141).
[92] Canguilhem (1962: 30).
[93] Seidensticker (1982: 61 n. 68).
[94] Cf. Privitera (1993: 31 n. 24).

The question, 'Exactly what kind of creature is a Cyclops?' recurs implicitly in several other texts, but the varying terms in which it is framed suggest continuing ambivalence on the part of the myth-tellers. In Euripides the classification is, as in Homer, ambiguous, but the nature of the ambiguity has changed (115–18):[95]

OD.: Where are the walls and the city towers?
SIL.: There aren't any. No men [*anthrōpoi*] inhabit the headlands.
OD.: But who does live here? A race of wild beasts [*thēres*]?
SIL.: Cyclopes. They live in caves not houses.

At least in Silenus' view, the Cyclopes are not human beings; whether they are 'wild beasts', or something different from *both* human beings *and* wild beasts, remains unclear. Apollodorus, by contrast, takes us back to Homer: Polyphemus is *agrios* and a man-eater, but also an *anēr*. However outrageous his behaviour, from the species point of view he remains within the boundary of humanity.[96]

For a portrayal of Polyphemus as out-and-out monster we may turn to *Aeneid* book 3. He is described first by Achaemenides, the comrade of Odysseus who has experienced all the horrors of the cave, and then by Aeneas, who witnesses with his own eyes the dreadful creature he has just heard about. For Achaemenides, everything about Polyphemus is inconceivably huge. His cave is vast (617–19); his head strikes against the stars (619–20); his colossal single eye is like a shield or the Sun (635–7). The other Cyclopes are no less gigantic (647). In addition to his vastness and deformity, Polyphemus is also behaviourally monstrous. Thanks to his ghastly, man-eating feasts, he is a *pestis* (620), something between a plague and a ruin; the other Cyclopes are similarly *infandi*, 'unspeakable' (644). When Aeneas and his men see the ogre and his brothers in the flesh, the impression of monstrosity is intensified. He is a *monstrum horrendum, informe, ingens*, 'horrible, hideous, huge monster' (658). The flow of epithets (*vasta, immensum, horrendum* (656, 672, 679)) is torrential.

The monstrosity of the Cyclopes seems then, in some ancient texts at least, to be undeniable. But it is worth reconsidering the question of definition. According to widespread modern usage, a monster is any person or creature who grossly transgresses the boundaries of normality, whether in behaviour, anatomy, or size. In the spirit of this broad definition, a wide range of characteristics is typically embraced, ranging from the anomalous and the disproportionate to the psychologically disturbing. Mythical and/or fictional anomalies such as Grendel, Godzilla, Kraken, or Bigfoot are habitually described as monsters. Enormously large animals get the same linguistic treatment ('the fish that got away was a monster'). As for the psychologically disturbing, some journalists (and their readers) habitually categorize serial killers or paedophiles as monsters. There is no doubt

[95] Ambiguous: Konstan (1990: 212).

[96] Apollod. *Bibl. Epit.* 7.4.

that in certain ancient accounts the Cyclopes merit the epithet 'monstrous' under any or all of these headings. Yet is is doubtful that this broadbrush phraseology gets us very far. More productive is an approach that pays closer attention to culturally specific concepts of monstrosity.

For Greece and Rome, we can draw on some fine previous scholarship.[97] A superb essay by Dominique Lenfant analyses the fundamental distinction, in Greek discourse about monstrosity, between the individual biologically malformed *teras*, 'monster', born from time to time in real-world human societies, and idiosyncratic groups of remotely situated peoples identified in ancient ethnographical accounts, and said to exhibit various types of extraordinary anatomical abnormality.[98] The vital point about the individual *teras* is made by Aristotle: 'Anyone who does not resemble his parents is in a certain way a monster [*teras*]. For nature in these cases has in a way strayed from the generic type' (*Gen.an.* 767b). Aristotle was far from unique in relating the definition of *teras* to heredity. The Athenians' oath before the battle of Plataea asserted a similar connection: 'And if I keep true to what has been written in the oath... may the women bear children like their parents, but if not, monsters [*terata*]'.[99] Individual monstrosity equates to dysfunctional heredity: the anomalous condition is *almost* never thought of as transmissible from parent to child.[100]

As for Greek views of *collective* monstrosity, matters are quite different. Among the ethnographic anomalies, as described, for example, by Herodotus and Ctesias of Cnidus (physician to Artaxerxes II of Persia), two main kinds may be distinguished.[101] On the one hand, there are animal–human hybrids, such as the goat-footed and the dog-headed peoples, the former located at the margins of Scythia, and the latter, the Cynocephali, in westernmost Libya or in India.[102] On the other hand, there are peoples—once more imagined as dwelling near the confines of the world—who were thought to possess an excess or lack of a particular physical characteristic, or to embody a reversal of a normal biological process. They are bald from birth; endowed with knee-length hair and an ankle-length penis; possess huge ears or feet; have extra digits; or big heads; or no anus; or no mouth; or no nose; or just one eye; or they start life with white hair that grows progressively darker.[103] Whatever anatomical anomalies observed in real-world individuals

[97] Atherton (2002); Chappuis Sandoz (2008); Charlier (2008); Garland (2010: 159–77); Gevaert and Laes (2013).

[98] Lenfant (1999).

[99] *GHI* 88.39–44, with Garland (2010: 60). On *terata*, see also Delcourt (1938).

[100] For exceptions mentioned by Hippocrates, Aristotle, and Pliny the Elder, see Lenfant (1999: 208 n. 72); Gevaert and Laes (2013: 221 n. 29). Inability of individual monstrous or misshapen creatures to reproduce: Lucr. *DRN* 5.837–48.

[101] On Ctesias, see Lenfant (2004); Stronk (2007).

[102] Hdt. 4.25, 191; Ctesias *Ind.* F45.37–43; Strabo 2.1.9 (thoroughly sceptical).

[103] Respectively: Hdt. 4.23; Ctesias *Ind.* F45.21; F45fα; F51a, 51b, 60; F 45.50; F.45.44; Hdt. 3.116; 4.13, 27; Ctesias *Ind.* F45.50.

might or might not have encouraged the conception that whole populations might share those same unusual features, in the case of those whole populations the anomalous feature—be it hybridity, excess, or lack—is regarded as hereditary: 'an ethnic feature'.[104]

A similar division recurs in Roman teratological texts.[105] There are numerous references to one-off cases of individual 'monstrosity', whose ominous quality receives linguistic confirmation from the word *monstrum* itself—that which 'shows' or 'points to' (*monere*) some future event. Examples range from very ugly people, to peculiar animals, to mutilated persons, to deformed babies, to the emperor Claudius himself.[106] The prime authority for *collective* monstrosity—indeed for all forms of monstrosity—is Pliny the Elder in book 7 of his *Natural History*. The kinds he identifies correlate closely with those found in the Greek texts: animal–human hybrids; races of humans with one anomalous body part; races abnormally large or small.[107] Once more, heredity is paramount. Whereas a naturally born, monstrous individual constitutes an exception to the rule 'like parent, like child', the monstrous races are evidently thought of as self-reproducing in their physical idiosyncrasy.

There are clearly overlaps between *some* of these aspects of monstrosity and *some* representations of the Cyclopes. The geographical remoteness of the monstrous races corresponds to the Cyclopes' isolation; even when the myth-tellers relocate them to Sicily, the Cyclopes' habit of dwelling in caves situates them in an *eschatia*, a boundary zone. Extreme size, and an anomalous body part, are other traits that the Cyclopes share with the monstrous races. On a broader definition of 'monster', Cyclopean anthropophagy surely qualifies as a 'psychologically disturbing' trait. One characteristic *not* shared by the Cyclopes with *some* of the monster races is hybridity: in spite of the occasional symbolic proximity of the Cyclopes to satyrs, the ogres are never credited with a partly animal, partly human anatomy.

Most intriguing of all is the question of heredity. How far does the dichotomy between monstrous individuals (who do not resemble their parents) and monstrous races (who self-perpetuate their anomaly) apply to the Cyclopes? At first sight the monstrous races constitute the closer parallel, since the Cyclopes' anatomical peculiarity is obviously a group characteristic, just as it is for the anomalous races described by Herodotus, Ctesias, and Pliny. That is to say, Cyclopean abnormality is *not* the product of a one-off teratological birth (even if Polyphemus,

[104] Lenfant (1999: 207).

[105] See Benabou (1975); Chappuis Sandoz (2008); Gevaert and Laes (2013).

[106] Mart. *Epig*. 7.38, 87; Ter. *Eun*. 696; Sen. *De ira* 3.17.4; Quint. *Inst*. 5.12.19; Firm. Mat. *Math*. 7.7.2; August. *Ench*. 23, 87; Suet. *Claud*. 3; Sen. *Apoc*. 5.3. See especially Gevaert and Laes (2013: 213).

[107] We follow Gevaert and Laes (2013: 218 n. 21) in persisting with the term 'race' (as in: 'the Plinian races'), while being aware of the potential pitfalls of anachronistic connotation; cf. Isaac (2004).

for one, could be proverbially described as a *teras*).[108] Yet the parents of the Cyclopes—whether Ouranos and Gaia or Poseidon and Thoosa—are emphatically not monocular, nor in other respects 'Cyclopean'; so such characteristics cannot have been inherited. What of the children of the Cyclopes? Do they replicate their parents? This is imponderable, since on the rare occasions when children of Cyclopes are mentioned, nothing is said about their physical appearance or behaviour.[109] Overall, then, the Cyclopes do not inhabit what one might describe as an unchanging ethnographic present; but the nature of intergenerational change amongst them is enigmatic.

We spoke earlier of the difficulty of defining monstrosity on the basis of visual evidence alone; hence the need to begin by examining the relevant classifications expressed in texts. What is clear, though, from the surviving images of the Cyclopes is that they involve a broad spectrum, extending from the indisputably grotesque to the undeniably ideal-heroic, via a number of intermediate positions. A few cases of surely indisputable monstrosity in Cyclopean anatomy centre (literally) on the exaggerated portrayal of monocularity, as on the super-ogrish figure in the Tomb of Orcus (*Cat. 31* (Fig. 4.15)), and three equally grotesque figurines (*Cat. 12* (Fig. 4.11), *29* (Fig. 4.9), and *30* (Fig. 4.10)). A less extreme but still marked form of corporeal anomaly, leading away from the human and towards the monstrous, is extreme hairiness (*Cat. 9*, *15* (Fig. 4.4), *16* (Fig. 5.1), *19* (Fig. 4.14), *54* (Fig. 5.9), and *65* (Fig. 5.11)). When it comes to monstrous behaviour, there are no ancient images of Polyphemus in the act of eating a human being (or anything else). What we do have are several depictions that come close: the grilling of the human kebabs (*Cat. 28* (Fig. 4.2)), and the holding of human body parts (*Cat. 10* (Fig. 3.1) and *18* (Fig. 5.10)). But this, of course, is not the whole story. Many images of the Cyclopes as a group—that is, the metalworkers—as well as of Polyphemus in particular, portray individuals with idealized physiques indistinguishable from those of the great heroes (*Cat. 25* (Fig. 5.4), *37* (Fig. 3.5), *39* (Fig. 4.3), *46* (Fig. 8.1), *52* (Fig. 3.6), *63* (Fig. 5.13), and *66* (Fig. 5.12)).

Is all this contradictory? Perhaps less so than it might seem. As Angelo Brelich brilliantly demonstrated in the middle of the twentieth century, many Greek heroes and heroines—Ajax, Heracles, Theseus, Medea, Antigone, Clytemnestra—exhibit a quality of *metaphorical* monstrosity, in that they transgress the boundaries of normality, often bringing catastrophe upon themselves and others as a consequence.[110] It is no coincidence that such characters furnish the staple diet of Greek tragedy, a genre that typically focuses on the 'monstrosity' *of humans* rather

[108] Zenob. 5.45 (i. 139 Leutsch-Schneidewin) = Philoxenus fr. 824 in D. A. Campbell (1993).

[109] Examples: the children of Polyphemus' fellow-ogres (*Od.* 9.115); Celtus, Illyrius, and Galas, sons of Polyphemus and Galatea (App. *Ill.*1.2); the children of Brontes, Arges, and Steropes, killed by Apollo (schol. Eur. *Alc.* 1); Deusos, Atron, and Atrene, the three children of Arges and a Phrygian nymph (Steph. Byz. s.v. Ἀτρήνη).

[110] Brelich (1958).

than the more obvious and less unsettling behavioural extravagances of Chimeras, Empusas, and Hydras. These same heroic, *metaphorically* monstrous humans frequently exemplify a pattern that the Cyclopes too embody: a combination of power with defect. One need look no further than Oedipus, Teiresias, and Philoctetes. The Cyclopes are among the most ambivalent characters in the whole of classical mythology. Of all the ambiguities that surround them, not the least remarkable is the ambiguity that they share with the heroes.

6
Gods

(Im)Mortality and Genealogy

We ended our account of Cyclopean lifestyle on a note of ambivalence. When we turn to the relationship between the Cyclopes and the gods, the same note repeats itself: the whole topic is a nest of paradoxes.

In Hesiod's *Theogony* the Cyclopes are major players in the primordial struggles of the gods, both before and after the Olympians' rise to power. Brontes, Steropes, and Arges are the proud-hearted children of Ouranos and Gaia (132–3, 139–40), and thus belong to the same generation as some of the most genealogically influential members of the cosmos, including Oceanos, Rhea (mother of Zeus), Tethys (mother, by her brother Oceanos, of the river gods), and Cronos, brutal president of a Golden Age. Thanks to the Cyclopes, Zeus will eventually possess the thunder and lightning with which he will crush the Titans and assume control of the universe.

Are the Hesiodic Cyclopes, as well as being deeply implicated in the gods' conflicts, also themselves gods? Although nothing in the text spells it out explicitly, the presumption must be that they are. Already in his prologue Hesiod refers to the song of the Muses as beginning by glorifying the 'revered race of gods [*theoi*] born to Ouranos and Gaia' and the gods (*theoi*) who were born to them (43–6). The Cyclopes fall squarely into the category of 'those born to Ouranos and Gaia'. Moreover, the Cyclopes were imprisoned by Ouranos (501–2), evidently because, as in the case of their three formidable brothers the Hundred-Handers, they threatened his power.[1] But, if they were so dangerous, why did Ouranos not remove them definitively by killing them? Presumably because that was not an option. Imprisonment and, as in the case of Cronos' subsequent aggression towards his own children, swallowing are methods used by divinities to control opponents whom they are unable to kill, for the simple reason that those opponents are immortal. Zeus' confinement of the still-living monster Typhon/Typhos/Typhoeus/Enceladus under Mount Etna exemplifies the same pattern.

One other detail might be regarded as relevant to the question of Cyclopean immortality. After relating how the Cyclopes gave Zeus the thunder and the thunderbolt, Hesiod observes that 'in other respects they were like the gods, except

[1] Fowler (2013: 53).

Cyclops: The Myth and its Cultural History. Mercedes Aguirre and Richard Buxton, Oxford University Press (2020).

DOI: 10.1093/oso/9780198713777.001.0001

that each had a single eye in the middle of the forehead' (142–3). Martin West commented that 'Hesiod does not mean that they are not themselves gods, only that in most respects their physique is like that of an ordinary god, i.e. like that of a perfect man…'.[2] However, even if this is so, for Hesiod to say that the Cyclopes were 'like the gods' is not exactly the same as to say that they were like the *other* gods. The divinity of the Hesiodic Cyclopes is a very strong likelihood, but cannot quite be called a certainty.

Of the various types of Cyclopes, it is the arms-manufacturers, and subsequently the metalworkers, who are most closely *connected* with the gods. They consistently support the Olympians, even to the extent of making for the three supreme rulers of the universe the attributes that characterize them: thunder, lightning, and thunderbolt (Zeus); helmet (Hades); trident (Poseidon).[3] According to an Orphic hymn (late 2nd–1st cent. BCE), the Cyclopes not only created the *schēmata* ('forms') of the whole cosmos, but also more specifically taught Hephaestus and Athene 'all the *daidala* [intricately crafted creations] which are under heaven'.[4] Nowhere is the mighty blacksmiths' integration into Olympian society clearer than in Callimachus' *Hymn to Artemis*. They work at Hephaestus' anvil; they make a horse trough for Poseidon; Brontes dandles Artemis on his knee. However, integrated though they may be, they are also scary. The Oceanids dare not look at the Cyclopes as they sweat at their forge. Even the grown-up daughters of the 'blessed ones' (presumably the Olympians) can be terrified into obedience when their mother invokes the Cyclopes as bogey figures. Nothing in all this suggests a yawning gap between merely mortal Cyclopes and effortlessly superior divinities. Much the same can be said of Virgil's account of Cyclopean forging in *Aeneid* book 8. Under Vulcan's supervision, the Cyclopes work on behalf of the Olympians: a thunderbolt for Jupiter, a chariot for Mars, armour for Pallas Athene, and now armour for Venus' son Aeneas. Subordinate they may be, but they are still a permanent fixture in the way Olympus operates. Their immortality is never affirmed, but nor is it denied.

However, context is all. Some other sources were in no doubt: the Cyclopes were mortal. We have already come across the tale that Apollo killed the Cyclopes (or their sons) for making the thunderbolt with which Zeus had annihilated Apollo's son Asclepius.[5] Less familiar, but eminently logical, was the idea that Zeus himself slew the Cyclopes to prevent them from making weapons with which his own power might ultimately be destroyed (the Prometheus syndrome).[6] Even more intriguingly, we know of the isolated and enigmatic detail that there existed a grave of the Cyclops Geraistos.[7] The mythographer Apollodorus relates

[2] M. L. West (1966) on *Theog.* 142. [3] Apollod. *Bibl.* 1.2.1.

[4] Fr. 269 Bernabé; see Bernabé (2004–5: fasc. 1, pp. 228–9).

[5] Eur. *Alc.* 3–6, with schol.; Apollod. *Bibl.* 3.10.4; Diod. Sic. 4.71.3; Lucian *De Sacr.* 4; Hyg. *Fab.* 49.

[6] Pind. fr. 266 Snell-Maehler. [7] Apollod. *Bibl.* 3.15.8.

that the Athenians, during their war against Minos, tried to avert famine and pestilence by sacrificing the daughters of a Spartan named Hyacinthos on Geraistos' grave. The notion of sacrificing to avert pollution is perfectly standard in an ancient Greek religious context; but why a *Cyclops'* grave?[8] Could this have been a Cyclops worshipped as a 'hero'—since a hero's grave was a regular site for dedications and offerings? If so, could there be a link with the tale that Nestor, on his way back from Troy, put in at Geraistos (a harbour on the south coast of Euboea) and sacrificed to Poseidon in order to smooth the voyage?[9] Could this location have been named after Geraistos, a mortal son of Poseidon, and a Cyclops into the bargain? One of the most frustratingly difficult questions to ask about Greek mythology is: what proportion of 'the whole' has survived in our extant sources? Doubtless the very notion of 'the whole' imposes a misleading sense of finitude upon a network of stories that more closely resembles a spider's web of untraceable complexity and extent. Nevertheless, the 'what proportion?' question is not without sense. It would be no surprise to discover one day, if more material came to light, that a Cyclops called Geraistos, a mortal son of Poseidon, had a fascinating mytho-biography of which we presently know nothing. We badly need corroboration in religious practice as opposed to myth. Unfortunately, the only evidence we have of a cult to the Cyclopes is a report by Pausanias of an altar of the Cyclopes at the Isthmus of Corinth, in an area sacred to Poseidon (2.2.1).[10] Conceivably this too could have been a case of Cyclopes in the role of heroes; but this is mere speculation.

If the Cyclopes' (im)mortality varies from source to source, the same is true of their genealogy. Hesiod's version—that their parents were Ouranos and Gaia—is echoed by other myth-tellers.[11] But an alternative view holds that either all the Cyclopes, or just Polyphemus, had Poseidon and the sea nymph Thoosa as parents.[12] The latter version introduces yet another paradox: that an ogre who had the sea 'in his blood', and who was erotically drawn towards a sea nymph, should be (at least according to most sources) unable to mate with her because his world—unalterably confined to the dry land—was the antithesis of hers. On the other hand, that one or all the Cyclopes could claim Poseidon/Neptune as father demonstrates its own logic. In the words of the miscellanist Aulus Gellius (2nd cent. CE): 'The poets have called…the sons of Neptune, the Cyclops, Cercyon, Sciron, and the Laestrygonians…most haughty and cruel, and strangers to all refinement, as being sprung from the sea.'[13] Generalization about Poseidon's

[8] The Byzantine geographer Stephanus (s.v. 'Tainaros') reports that Tainaros, founder of a temple of Poseidon, was a brother of Geraistos, and a son of Zeus. The same author (s.v. 'Geraistos') traces the name of a district of Euboea to 'Geraistos the son of Zeus'. Was this a 'different' Geraistos from the one mentioned by Apollodorus? A question without an answer.

[9] *Od.* 3.177–9. On Geraistos: Schumacher (1993); P.-J. Shaw (2001: 176–8).

[10] See M. L. West (1966) on *Theog.* 139.

[11] e.g. Apollod. *Bibl.* 1.2.

[12] All the Cyclopes: e.g. Eur. *Cyc.* 21–2. Just Polyphemus: e.g. Apollod. *Bibl. Epit.* 7.4.

[13] Aul. Gell. *NA* 15.21.1, trans. J. C. Rolfe.

offspring may not be so straightforward—Theseus hardly fits the profile reported by Gellius. But the sea god's children are no strangers to unconventional shape or size: Pegasus and Arion are both equine (conceived from unions with Medusa and Demeter respectively), while Otus and Ephialtes are simply colossal. Poseidon himself embodies raw, natural energy—sea, horse, earthquake—so that to associate him with a group of ferocious ogres makes eminent sense in the logic of myth. At the same time, exemplifying the oppositional logic that makes Apollo both an agent of healing and a sender of plague, Poseidon is not only a seismic disrupter but also a builder of walls—most famously, those of Troy (with Apollo, for Laomedon)—as well as a bringer of safety and security, as expressed in the epithet Asphal(e)ios, rooted in the idea of 'keeping safe'.[14] To *that* extent, his constructive powers sit well with those of the mason Cyclopes. The genealogical subtleties of the Greek pantheon are hardly ever random.

Homeric Gods

In the *Odyssey* as in the *Iliad*, the balance between divine and human agency is complex and shifting.[15] Odysseus' fate is partly in his own hands, thanks to his human strengths and weaknesses, but he is also caught in a divine sandwich, being positioned between his staunch helper Athene, and his inveterate foe Poseidon. Given the hero's need to negotiate a series of dangerous sea passages in order to return home, the hostility of the supreme sea god constitutes one of the most important determinants of the plot. What drives that hostility—which is unique to Poseidon among all the gods (1.19–21)—is spelled out by Zeus (1.68–75):

> But Poseidon, Holder of the Earth, ever relentless,
> nurses a grudge because of the Cyclops, whose eye he blinded—
> godlike Polyphemus, whose power is greatest
> over all the Cyclopes. Thoösa, a nymph, was his mother,
> the daughter of Phorcys, lord of the barren salt water.
> She in the hollow caves had lain with Poseidon.
> For his sake Poseidon, Shaker of the Earth, although he does not
> kill Odysseus, yet drives him back from the land of his fathers.[16]

Two points in this passage are worth noting. First, Zeus calls Polyphemus *antitheos*, 'like a god'—*like* a god, but not actually divine: one would hardly

[14] Graf (2009: 5).

[15] This twin focus is already clear from the beginning of the *Odyssey*. Divine: 1.267–9; human: 1.32–43.

[16] Trans. Lattimore (1965), and in subsequent quotations; here considerably adapted.

describe Apollo, say, as 'god*like*'. (Though we have to be careful. The preposition *anti* in Greek is capable of many senses: not just 'equivalent of', but also 'opposed to'. Is this another possible case of Cyclopean ambiguity?) Secondly, what motivates Poseidon throughout the epic, until Odysseus eventually reaches Ithaca (6.330–1), is concern for the outrage that his son has suffered. Aristotle may have found Polyphemus' descent from Poseidon surprising, but the narrative function of the motif, in binding the plot together, is clear.[17] In a poem that, as we shall see, repeatedly highlights the distance between the Cyclopes and the gods, here is a case where that distance is bridged.

Another case of proximity-as-opposed-to-distance concerns not just Polyphemus, but all the Cyclopes; and not just Poseidon, but all the gods. Addressing his fellow Phaeacians after a feast at which the as-yet anonymous Odysseus has been treated with exemplary hospitality, Alcinous reflects on how he can best serve his guest. If that guest is a mortal, his conveyance home can soon be arranged. But there is another possibility (7.199–206):

> But if he is one of the immortals come down from heaven,
> then this is a new kind of thing the gods are devising;
> for always in time past the gods have shown themselves clearly
> to us, when we render them glorious grand sacrifices,
> and they sit beside us and feast with us in the place where we do,
> or if one comes alone and encounters us, as a wayfarer,
> then they make no concealment, *as we are very close to them,*
> *as are the Cyclopes and the savage* [agria] *tribes of the Giants.*[18]

In what sense are the Cyclopes—and for that matter the Giants—'close to the gods'? Not, presumably, in the same sense that the far-off-dwelling Aethiopians are close to the gods; that is a case of *metaphorical* closeness, since the gods have to journey a great distance to share in the Aethiopians' banquets.[19] The proximity expressed by communal feasting is unheard of between gods and Cyclopes (and one might speculate about exactly which tastes in food and drink the two groups might have in common). Close geographically, then?[20] That seems implausible; in any case, where *is* 'the land of the gods'? Close genealogically? Maybe: Polyphemus' father Poseidon is Alcinous' grandfather (7.56–63). Close in status? That also is just conceivable, given the hints we have noticed, albeit in other parts of the mythological tradition, about the Cyclopes' possible immortality.

[17] Aristot. fr. 172 Rose = schol. *Od.* 9.106; see Montanari (1998: 68).

[18] Emphasis added.

[19] Poseidon (*Od.* 1.22–6); Zeus and the other gods (*Il.* 1.423–4); Iris (*Il.* 23.205–7). See M. L. West (2014: 145 n. 3).

[20] So Bremmer (1984: 16; 2002: 144).

When we reach book 9, Cyclopean relationships with the gods remain paradoxical; it is just that the paradoxes are different. Even before his tale reaches landfall on Goat Island, Odysseus tells his Phaeacian audience two things about the gods' role in Cyclopia: that the Cyclopes 'put their trust in the immortal gods', so that they neither sow nor plough (107–8); and that such crops as do (spontaneously) grow are watered by the rain of Zeus (111). The first detail implies nothing about Cyclopean piety; rather, it indicates a laissez-faire attitude.[21] The same goes for the rain: the Cyclopes leave irrigation to the gods. When Odysseus warns Polyphemus that Zeus avenges the mistreatment of strangers and suppliants, the ogre takes one stage further the idea that the Cyclopes simply do not bother about the gods (275–8):

> The Cyclopes do not concern themselves over Zeus of the aegis,
> nor any of the rest of the blessed gods, since we are far better
> than they, and for fear of the hate of Zeus I would not spare
> you or your companions either, if the fancy took me
> otherwise.

Greek mythology abounds in mortal heroes whose hybristic arrogance towards the Olympians causes their catastrophic destruction: Ajax son of Telamon, Ajax son of Oileus, Arachne, Ixion, Lycaon, Marsyas, Niobe, Pentheus, Salmoneus, Sisyphus, Tantalus... The boastfulness of Polyphemus might seem to bring him dangerously close to this category of reckless sinner. Yet no punishment is forthcoming: *something* allows the Cyclopes to continue in their state of breezy autonomy. That something is yet another aspect of Cyclopean marginality, and of the difficulty of securely classifying them.

It is not that Polyphemus in particular, or the Cyclopes in general, deny the *existence* of the gods. Polyphemus knows that Zeus sends the rain (358). When he cries out to his fellow Cyclopes that 'nobody' is killing him, they interpret this strange behaviour as a mental infirmity sent by Zeus, and recommend him to pray to his father Poseidon (411–12). Polyphemus continues to pay scant attention to Zeus, but now, in his distress, sees his father as a potential source of help (519–21):

> For I am his son, he announces himself as my father.
> He himself will heal me, if he will, but not any other
> one of the blessed gods, nor any man who is mortal.

As for being healed, Polyphemus would have a better chance if his father were Apollo. What Poseidon can do is to cause shipwrecks, and this is the burden of

[21] Stanford (1965), on 107.

Polyphemus' prayer. 'Father, grant that Odysseus never gets home; or if he does...' (534–5):

> let him come late, in bad case, with the loss of all his companions,
> in someone else's ship, and find troubles in his household.

Poseidon carries out this request to the letter. It ceases to take effect, sequentially, in two locations. The first is the harbour of Phorcys on Ithaca (13.96–112). Phorcys is an Old Man of the Sea, but not just that: being Thoosa's father, he is Polyphemus' grandfather (1.71–2). There is an element of 'ring composition', of symbolic appropriateness, here: the persecution of the man who blinded Polyphemus ends in a place linked with Polyphemus' own ancestry. The second location is Phaeacia, where Poseidon turns to stone the vessel that has conveyed his foe Odysseus home (13.159–64). Poseidon's anger ceases with an act of petrifaction, as it had begun when his son hurled mighty boulders at the departing Odysseus: a second symbolic circle closes.

Perhaps the endless richness of the *Odyssey*, its genealogies in particular, can tell us even a little more. As we know from the start of book 6, the Phaeacians once lived next to the Cyclopes, before their neighbours' harmful arrogance induced the Phaeacians to migrate. And from many points of view the Phaeacians and the Cyclopes are indeed poles apart. On the one side, hospitality, shipbuilding, proper sacrifice to the gods; on the other, none of the above. Yet Alcinous' grandmother, Periboea, who lay with Poseidon, was a daughter of Eurymedon, king of the 'over-spirited' Giants (7.56–9). Such an ancestry, from an aggressive race whose relationships with the Olympians were hardly smooth, situates the Phaeacians symbolically—and, we need hardly add, paradoxically—further from the Olympians than is the case with the ogrish, intractable, and wild Cyclopes.

Gods and Satyrs

One god, it seems, presides over Euripides' *Cyclops*: Dionysus. That the second and the penultimate words of the play should be alternative names for the god of wine confirms Dionysiac supremacy within the action. Here is a fundamental difference from the *Odyssey*, indeed from Homeric poetry in general. The transgressive and disruptive divinity who is an outsider to the epic view of the world takes centre stage at the Athenian dramatic festival, in satyr play above all. Yet he plays no part in the stage action of *Cyclops*: a present absence. The only 'god' who is present is Polyphemus. The interplay between the two figures permeates the drama.

Silenus' prologue locates the plot within the world of the Olympians, their struggles and rivalries. Hera, hostile to Dionysus (the son of Semele, her rival in Zeus' bed), urged some pirates to seize him and sell him abroad as a slave. His willing devotees Silenus and the satyrs set out in the hope of rescuing him, only to be shipwrecked and driven ashore in the land of the 'unholy' Cyclops (26). But their patron's absence only intensifies their longing for what they lack: hence the effectiveness of the wine that Odysseus barters for food. However, with the arrival of Polyphemus, the focus on divinity shifts radically. The satyr chorus looks up (literally) to the Cyclops as if to Zeus himself (212). But Polyphemus is not just *like* a god (231):

CYC.: Didn't they [the interloping strangers] know that I'm a god, and descended from gods?

Polyphemus' paternal origin, like that of all the Cyclopes, is unambiguous: he and they are all sons of Poseidon (21–2, 262, 286). Indeed, Odysseus invokes this ancestry as an argument to avoid being eaten, by reminding the Cyclops that the Greeks had preserved Poseidon's temples, at Tainaron, Sounion, and Geraistos (!) (290–5). But what of Polyphemus' mother? In a fascinating and easily overlooked line (648), the chorus of satyrs refers to the blinding of 'the one-eyed son of Earth'. Is this a one-off suggestion that Poseidon once mated with Gaia in order to produce the Cyclopes, or at any rate one of them? (In Hesiod, the primordial sea god Pontos had sired numerous offspring with Gaia, *Theog.* 238.) At the very least, the Euripidean line gives yet one more hint at an overlap between the Hesiodic and Homeric Cyclopes.

What of Polyphemus' *own* claim to divinity? The attitude of the Euripidean Cyclops towards religion, and towards his own 'divinity' in particular, radically and coarsely redefines Cyclopean autonomy as it was sketched out in the *Odyssey*. After a generalization that has been linked with the demystifying arguments of the sophists, Polyphemus pooh-poohs his father's sanctuaries, and then modulates to a rejection of Zeus' superiority more trenchant than anything in Homer (316–21):[22]

> Money is god for the wise, little man;
> the rest is hot air and fine words.
> As for my father's seaside shrines,
> I care nothing for them...
> Nor do I tremble at Zeus' thunderbolt, stranger,
> In fact I don't know that Zeus is a god any stronger than I am.

[22] Sophists: Seaford (1984) on 316.

As for Zeus' thunder, Polyphemus can rival it with one of his own farts (327–8).[23] Not content with that, he proceeds to give a dietary twist to the idea of god (334–8):

> So I sacrifice to no one but myself: not to the gods,
> but to the greatest divinity of all, My Belly.
> To drink, to eat, from day to day, to have no worries –
> *That* is Zeus for a man of good sense.

Odysseus' own conception of the gods stays firmly within the framework of the traditional Olympians: Athene (350), Zeus (354–5, 375), and Hephaestus (599–600). But Polyphemus persists in his outrageous religious solipsism. At one point, flooded with wine, he does have a vision of Zeus' throne and the gods' glory (579–80), but this acknowledgement of the divinity of others is instantly replaced by a projection of his own monstrous ego: Cyclops *is* Zeus (585). Even after the blinding, Poseidon is forgotten. All that remains is for the chorus to reaffirm their loyalty to Dionysus, the one god whose power is never tarnished throughout the play. For this is a satyr play, and, as we have said so often, it is imperative to distinguish between contexts.

A Dionysiac Epic

The Dionysiac connection distinguishes Euripides' satyr play from most of the rest of Cyclopean mythology. Apart from some visual images that portray Polyphemus either resembling Silenus or accompanied by satyrs, there is little in our other sources to associate him, or the rest of the Cyclopes, with the son of Zeus and Semele. To this there is one remarkable exception: Nonnus' forty-eight-book epic poem *Dionysiaca*, which dates, it will be recalled, from the fifth century CE.

Nonnus charts the myth-biography of Dionysus, in particular his triumphant military campaign against the Indians, an exploit that eventually qualifies him to join the gods of Olympus. Criticism of the poem used to be uniformly dismissive; the comment that 'his work is a good example of the degeneracy of Greek myth by this stage' is typical.[24] More recently, in keeping with a salutary tendency to re-evaluate the Greek literature of the Roman Imperial period, Nonnus' work has been viewed more positively. Instead of being regarded as a mishmash of 'invented' mythological lore, or at best as a hunting ground for myths otherwise forgotten, it has come to be seen as a virtuoso and innovative exercise in

[23] Less plausibly, Seaford (1984), on 327–8, interprets these lines ('I push out my blanket in rivalry with Zeus' thunder') as referring to masturbation rather than farting.

[24] Rautenbach (1984: 53).

myth-telling.[25] What makes the *Dionysiaca* relevant to our present concerns is that the Cyclopes feature prominently at certain points in the story.

As in Hesiod, they participate in the primordial conflicts between different generations of gods. But Nonnus has rewritten the Hesiodic script. This is clearest in book 2, which narrates the assault on Zeus' power by the many-armed, many-throated, metamorphic monster Typhoeus. This formidable creature threatens to enact a number of cosmic reversals: to make Zeus jealous by becoming Hera's bridegroom, to bring incarcerated Cronos back up to the light, to restore the other Titans to cosmic power—and to settle the Cyclopes in heaven (340–1). Typhoeus needs the Cyclopes on his side because he plans to forge weapons of fire, new and more explosive lightning, and thunderbolts—plenty of them, since he has two hundred hands to fight with, not just a paltry two like Zeus (342–4). (The humour of wild exaggeration is one of Nonnus' trademarks.) The clear—and clearly non-Hesiodic—implication is that hitherto the Cyclopes have been Zeus' *opponents*, which is why they have been imprisoned.[26] In Hesiod, of course, it was Zeus himself who freed the Cyclopes from imprisonment by Ouranos. Given the non-dogmatic status of Greek mythology at every period, it is pointless to accuse Nonnus of 'getting it wrong'. In any case, it is not illogical to 'remember' the Cyclopes, primordial beings that they consistently are, as belonging to a pre-Olympian stage of the cosmos *and as owing their sympathies to their coevals.*

However that may be, in the war against the Indians the Cyclopes ally themselves with Dionysus, along with other marginal groups such as Cabiri, Dactyli, Corybantes, Couretes, Telchines, and Centaurs. At three moments in particular, the Cyclopes dominate the battle: in books 14, 28, and 39.

The Cyclopes' characteristics in book 14 are profoundly novel yet at the same time a composite reflection of earlier tellings. They advance in phalanxes, yet comprise named individuals: Brontes, Steropes, Euryalos, Elatreus, Arges, Trachios, and Halimedes (59–60).[27] Their weapons consist of torn-off chunks of the landscape (recalling Homer), but these are complemented by fiery brands from the Etnaean forge (reminiscent of Callimachus and Virgil).[28] Only Polyphemus is absent, for he is pouring out his heart to Galatea—adding Theocritus and Ovid to the list of precursors.

Book 28 adds expansively to the description of the Cyclopes at war. There are seven of them, and magnificent they are. None of the fearsome exploits of Trachios, Elatreus, or Euryalos raises the question, What class of creature is a Cyclops? Halimedes is *pelōr* (258), which, as usual, leaves the matter of (im)mortality unresolved. Far more fascinating, indeed unique in the ancient tradition,

[25] See e.g. Vian et al. (1976–2006); Hopkinson (1994); Shorrock (2001, 2011); Gigli Piccardi et al. (2006–10); Accorinti (2016).

[26] Same implication at 600–1.

[27] For the names, see pp. 199–200.

[28] Cf. also Lucian, *Timon* 19.

are the accounts of the remaining three Cyclopes. Argilipos, an alias of Arges, is all fire. More particularly, he fights with an *earthly* thunderbolt, one that is *earthborn,* one *like* that of heaven, a *bastard* thunderbolt (173–86). Similarly, Steropes (187–94) is armed with *imitation* lightning, which *mimics* that of the sky, but actually derives from the Sicilian forge. Brontes too is playing the imitation game (195–9):

> Brontes also was in the battle, rattling a noisy tune with a din like rolling thunderclaps: he poured an earthborn shower of his own with strange drops falling through the air, and lasting but a moment—an unreal Zeus he was, with imitated raindrops and no clouds.[29]

If there were any doubt that Nonnus is writing tongue in cheek here, it is dispelled by Zeus' reaction (233–7):

> Father Zeus, seeing how the Cyclops imitated his own [i.e. Zeus'] noise, laughed on high in the clouds that the earth was then flooded with a strange kind of shower from earthclouds through its breast—which had never experienced this before, while the thirsty air had no downpour through its bare dry expanse.[30]

Nonnus has just mentioned Salmoneus (184), the king of Elis who hybristically imitated thunder and lightning and was smashed by a real thunderbolt as punishment for disrespecting Zeus. Yet now Zeus laughs: the Cyclopes pose no threat to his honour, since they are fighting on his side. We might add that the repeatedly stressed difference between the powers of the Cyclopes and those of the Olympians—imitation versus real—suggests a radical gap in status between the two groups, though not one that necessarily aligns with the disjunction between god and mortal.

Earlier myth-tellers had explored the love–hate relationship between the Cyclopes and the sea. In book 39, Nonnus' take on the matter is typically idiosyncratic. As the Cyclopes swing into action in a naval battle, the sea is reddened with the blood of the dead. The implication is that the Cyclopes, like other combatants, could die, though this is never spelled out; no Cyclops, named or unnamed, is explicitly said to die. At all events, the carnage is disturbing enough to bring some sea nymphs to the surface. Among them is Galatea, anxious that Polyphemus may be involved in the fighting. She implores Aphrodite, as well as Polyphemus' father Poseidon, to protect him. Why Aphrodite? Because Nonnus has opted for the minority view that Galatea reciprocated Polyphemus' affection. As for Poseidon, he reproaches Dionysus for not bringing Polyphemus to war; for

[29] Trans. W. H. D. Rouse.

[30] Trans. W. H. D. Rouse, adapted.

Polyphemus would have won it single-handed. However, the 'love-mad' Polyphemus (294) is absent, his mind being on things other than warfare. This brings shame to his mother Thoosa, whose name takes us back to Homer, but whose reaction recalls the emotional world of Theocritus. Prolix he may be, but Nonnus' myth-changing panache is as remarkable as his linguistic lushness.

One of the most distinctive features of Nonnus' treatment of the Cyclopes is the number of them whom he names individually. But the naming of the Cyclopes, and of those with whom they come into contact, adds a new dimension to their mythological profile. To this theme we now turn.

7
Names

Graeco-Roman mythology abounds in 'speaking names' that express aspects of this or that god or hero. Some names of deities are semantically transparent, being identical with a geographical or astronomical feature or with other characteristics associated with the divinity concerned: Ouranos (Heaven, Sky), Gaia (Earth), Pontos (Sea), Helios (Sun), Calliope (Beautiful Voice), Terpsichore (Delight in the Dance), Metis (Cunning Intelligence), Mnemosyne (Memory), and so forth. Equally transparent are the names of many heroes and heroines: Eteocles (True Glory), Polynices (Much Quarrelling), Neoptolemus (New War), Creon and Creusa (Ruler, male or female), and Pentheus (Grief). But many other names are opaque, or at least require intricate linguistic unpacking. The etymologies of Helen, the Titans, and Cronos—to mention only three among countless others—have been disputed since antiquity. Then there are cases of apparently 'speaking names' that speak with unclarity. Since the goddess Hera persecuted Heracles throughout his life, in what sense can he have been nominally 'the Glory of Hera'? Melampous evidently means 'Black Foot'; but *why* was he called that?[1] One complicating factor is that the connotations of mythological names are heavily context dependent: the signification of the 'same' name may lie dormant in one context but spring into active life in another, or be exploited in quite different senses in different contexts. Another complication derives from the fact that the scope and ambitions of ancient etymology are quite distinct from those of modern etymology. Ineke Sluiter puts the point superbly:

> ancient etymology is not about the reconstruction of the single, historically accurate, route from word form to word form, but about using language as a tool for thinking about contemporary reality. This intellectual framework does not require just one single and accurate etymology for each word: several explanations can co-exist, they can be true *simultaneously*, because different ones can elucidate and highlight different aspects of the same concept, and there is virtually always a certain *fluidity* to etymological discourse.[2]

[1] See Buxton (2013d: 70–1).

[2] Sluiter (2015: 902–3). More on ancient etymology: Sulzberger (1926); Lallot (1991); Wolanin (1995); Peraki-Kyriakidou (2002); Nifadopoulos (2003); Tsitsibakou-Vasalos (2007).

Cyclops: The Myth and its Cultural History. Mercedes Aguirre and Richard Buxton, Oxford University Press (2020).

DOI: 10.1093/oso/9780198713777.001.0001

It follows that, when investigating the 'etymology' of a mythological name, we must be absolutely clear about the sense in which we are using that term.

When we consider the names of characters who appear in Cyclopean myths, all these complexities come into play. The *Odyssey* will claim much of our attention because of its rich exploitation of nomenclature. But the rest of the literary tradition too makes play with the names of Cyclopes, and of those with whom they come into contact.

Cyclops

Modern discussions of the name 'Cyclops' (Greek *Kuklōps*) usually take their cue from the passage in Hesiod's *Theogony* referring to the three cosmic weapons-makers (144–5):

> *Kuklōpes d'onom' ēsan epōnumon, hounek' ara spheōn*
> *kukloterēs ophthalmos heeis enekeito metōpōi...*

> They were called Circle-eyes [*Kuklōpes*], since a single circular [*kukloterēs*] eye lay in the forehead [of each]...

In itself, the adjective *kukloterēs* is straightforward. It derives from the noun *kuklos*, meaning 'circle', 'ring', 'orbit', whence the English 'cycle' and its equivalents in other European languages. But what *is* it that is 'circular'? The suffix *-ōps* suggests the noun *ōps*, whose primary meaning seems to be, not 'eye', but 'face'. Indeed the philosopher Parmenides (6th–5th cent. BCE) applies the epithet *kuklōps* to the moon, where the translation 'round-*faced*' seems entirely apposite.[3] Yet in Hesiod 'round-faced' makes no sense: at least it corresponds to no Cyclopean feature found in texts or iconography. However, almost all the examples of *ōps* occur in contexts in which one person is looking at another 'face to face', or, as *we* say, 'eye to eye'. So the explanation 'round-*eyed*', which appears to underlie Hesiod's text, looks *in this context* rather plausible—the more so as, in similarly formed compound adjectives, the suffix *-ōps* unquestionably connotes vision (*muōps*, 'closing or contracting the eyes', hence 'myopic'; *helikōps*, 'with moving or glancing eyes').[4] To the objection that, instead of '*round*-eyed', we expect a word meaning '*one*-eyed',[5] we may reply that some of the most strikingly grotesque, indeed monstrous, ancient images of a Cyclops portray a figure with a large, central, circular

[3] Parm. B10, 4 Diels-Kranz. [4] See Mineur (1984: 2–3). [5] S. West (2013: 200).

eye—an eye 'like a [round] shield', as the often-repeated simile expresses it.[6] In short, the Hesiodic etymology looks, on its own terms, convincing.

Hesiod provides a rare example from antiquity of an explicit etymology (*onoma... epōnumon*) for *Kuklōps*. But it is crucial to recognize that what the poet is offering is—to echo Ineke Sluiter—an etymology in the ancient rather than the modern sense: instead of tracing a historical development from one word form to another based on scientific principles of linguistic change, Hesiod proposes a synchronic, semantic analysis—one among possible alternatives. Just such an alternative is put forward by Stoicizing allegorist Heraclitus (perhaps late 1st–2nd cent. CE), according to whom Cyclops was thus named for 'stealing away [*hupoklōpōn*] judgement'.[7] Also etymologically tinged are the *jeux de mots* in Euripides' satyr play—Odysseus: 'I shall *rotate* the fire-brand in the Cyclops' eye' (*kuklōsō... Kuklōpos* (462–3))—and in Nonnus—'the Cyclopes *encircled* the [enemy] fighters' (*Kuklōpes ekuklōsanto* (28.172)); both passages draw out an idea of circularity, and thus lie closer to the Hesiodic than the Heraclitean etymology. But all these explanations, including Hesiod's, are exceptional. On the whole, probing the Cyclopes' essence via their collective name seems to have aroused little interest in antiquity.

For modern investigators of Cyclopean mythology, by contrast, 'modern' etymology, informed by linguistic science, has proved a popular interpretative gambit. Hesiod's 'circle-eyed' approach has often served as a starting point, though it has been variously adapted. Some scholars have decoded the *Kuklōpes* as 'lookers-around'—that is, diviners or astrologers; or as stars, on account of their circularity; or as metalworkers who wore lamps fixed to the forehead when working underground; or as people whose ferocity was expressed in their staring eyes.[8] A differently circular approach was adopted by Georg Friedrich Schoemann, who regarded the masons as the original Cyclopes: the walls with which they fortified cities were circular.[9] Other scholars have been more sceptical, whether about circularity, or about eyes, or both. Jonathan Burgess finds Hesiod's view of the etymology as 'questionable', while Robert Mondi rejects any etymological connection with eyes.[10] In the mid-nineteenth century Karl Wilhelm Osterwald had opted for larceny (Gk. *klōps* = 'thief'), echoing Heraclitus' allegorical reading.[11] Paul Thieme modified the same idea by proposing a possible origin in Indo-European **p(e)ku-klōps*, 'cattle thief'.[12] Walter Burkert lent influential support to this view, since it sat well with his identification of Polyphemus as a 'Master of Animals'.[13] Egbert Bakker gave conditional endorsement: 'This etymology, if right, might link the Cyclops tale with the myth-type in which animals are stolen and hidden in a cave by a monstrous thief, necessitating a quest in which the animals are

[6] See Index, s.v. 'shield'.
[7] Heracl. *Alleg.* 70. 5.
[8] Schoemann (1859: 11) lists advocates of these interpretations.
[9] Schoemann (1859: 12).
[10] Burgess (2001: 98); Mondi (1983: 37).
[11] Osterwald (1853: 32–3).
[12] Thieme (1951: 177–8).
[13] Burkert (1979: 157 n. 30).

retrieved by a hero of the shaman-type who owns the cattle.'[14] There are, however, some technical linguistic grounds for scepticism about the cattle-thief approach.[15] A related Indo-European move was made by Rüdiger Schmitt, for whom Greek *Kuklōps* originated in Indo-European **kukló-klōps*, 'robber of the (sun's) wheel'—a role suited to the lightning-manufacturer Cyclopes rather than to the pastoral ogres.[16] Still within an Indo-European framework, Françoise Bader decoded *Kuklōps* as 'with shining eye'; the underlying element here is said to be **keu-k-*, a form that occurs in Indo-Iranian in contexts in which its meaning is variously 'burn', 'shine', 'clear', or 'sighted'.[17] According to yet another etymological move, the name 'Cyclops' might go back to or be associated with the Linear A of Minoan Crete, especially given the tendency in that language for 'reduplicated' names (even if we do not know what those names mean). It is worth adding that some other Greek mythological names that lack a convincing Greek etymology also involve reduplication: Titan, Sisyphos, Tartaros, Tantalos... Were a language related to Minoan once to have been spoken on the Greek mainland, then such names, perhaps including 'Cyclops', need not have originated in Crete.[18]

It is, of course, possible and legitimate to float diachronic hypotheses to cut through these etymological thickets. One of the most plausible holds that a Greek calque on a non-transparent, non-Greek name could have been interpreted *by Greek speakers* as 'round-eyed'—which *might* have led them in due course to assimilate the name with an (allegedly) pre-existing folktale about a one-eyed giant.[19] But this is just one conceivable diagonal through a notional past: no more than a 'likely story'. Just as no real-world physical object—an elephant skull, the cone of a volcano, a deformed birth—can be deemed to constitute 'the' origin of the concept of a Cyclops, so no linguistic derivation has, as yet, provided the golden key.

Polyphemus

The relationship between some homonyms in Graeco-Roman mythology looks more or less random; in other cases there are revealing overlaps.[20] In the case of the best known of the Cyclopes, we find references to an apparently quite distinct hero who shares his name. Near the beginning of the *Iliad*, Nestor recalls great

[14] Bakker (2013: 69).

[15] First, *p(e)ku* does not occur elsewhere in Greek, and the use of the form without 'e' looks unusual in Greek terms. Secondly, the type of compound word posited—'cattle thief'—is 'endocentric'—i.e. the meaning of the whole word is a subset of the meaning of the second member ('thief'); but most such compounds are post-Homeric. (We rely here on the guidance of Torsten Meissner and James Clackson.)

[16] R. Schmitt (1967: 168).

[17] Bader (1985: 11).

[18] Here again we are indebted to Torsten Meissner.

[19] Fowler (2013: 55 with n. 214).

[20] Buxton (2013b).

warriors of the past who fought against the 'wild beasts of the mountains'—that is, the Centaurs (1.262–8). Among these warriors was *antitheos Poluphēmos*, 'godlike Polyphemus'—in this context, at least, the meaning 'godlike' (as opposed to 'opposing the gods') must be uppermost.[21] Concerning, we may presume, the same character, we learn from other sources that he was one of the Argonauts—and not the least of them: he helped Heracles look for his beloved missing 'squire' Hylas, and was left behind along with Heracles when the Argo sailed away.[22] As a fighter against beasts of the mountains, this Polyphemus differs sharply from his Odyssean namesake, who in some ways resembles a beast of the mountains himself; so this seems at first sight to be a case of random homonymy. But the epithet *antitheos* should give us pause. As we have seen, in the *Odyssey* it is used of the Cyclops Polyphemus by Zeus himself (1.70):

> It is Poseidon, Holder of the Earth, who, ever relentless,
> nurses a grudge because of the Cyclops, whose eye he blinded—
> godlike [*antitheos*] Polyphemus, whose power is greatest
> over all the Cyclopes.[23]

That is one way of reading—or hearing—the passage. Walter Burkert suggested another. If *poluphēmos* is taken not as a proper name but as an adjective meaning 'much renowned', then the sense becomes 'the Cyclops...godlike, much renowned...'. In that case, Burkert argued, the naming of this particular Cyclops as 'Polyphemus' would be a secondary phenomenon ('Polyphemus evidently owes his name to the fame of the story').[24]

Even if we find Burkert's suggestion ingenious rather than compelling,[25] it alerts us to an intriguing aspect of the naming of the Cyclop(e)s in the *Odyssey*. The name 'Polyphemus' is found only four times in the whole poem (including the occurrence in book 1 just mentioned). By contrast, the name 'Cyclops' occurs more than thirty times, of which twenty-one denote the ogre usually known as 'Polyphemus'. It is not that Odysseus' adversary is merely a 'typical' Cyclops; on the contrary, he is differentiated from the rest in terms of his superior power (1.70–1) and the outlying location where he dwells (9.188–9). But he is rarely singled out by name. That makes the moments when he *is* individually named that much more significant. When he shouts for help to the other Cyclopes, they address him as 'Polyphemus' (9.403), to which he, 'powerful Polyphemus', replies (407). This is the moment when the gap in understanding between the blinded ogre and his fellows is at its most evident, and when the whole question of

21 See p. 186 for another possible meaning for the epithet *in another context*.
22 Ap. Rhod. *Argon*. 1.40–4, 1240–85; Apollod. *Bibl*. 1.9.19.
23 Trans. Lattimore (1965), adapted.
24 Burkert (1979: 153 n. 11).
25 See the comments by Bremmer (2002: 144).

naming—the Outis pun—stands in the limelight.[26] The fourth and final time that Polyphemus is named (446) is when he talks to his faithful ram, dwelling on the wrong done to him by a nobody called Outis. Once again, it is at a moment when the topic of nomenclature dominates the narrative that the poet mentions the ogre's own name.

The semantic analysis of 'Polyphemus' as 'much renowned' is by far the commonest interpretation, but it is worth looking further. Whereas the meaning of *poly-* is self-evident, *phēmos* is less straightforward. It is related to *phēmi* ('I say', 'I utter'), *phēmē* ('report', 'prophetic saying'), and *phēmis* ('speech', 'utterance').[27] But does the name denote one who says a lot, or one who is much spoken about? As an adjective, *polyphēmos* is used in the *Odyssey* both actively and passively, being applied both to a bard ('having many songs' (22.376)) and to the *agora* ('where many voices are heard' (2.150)). Although 'much spoken about' is doubtless the obvious decoding of 'Polyphemus', there is no reason why the connotation of the name should be identical in every retelling. In the *Odyssey*, Polyphemus uses different voices: his gentle manner when talking to his ram is a far cry from the tone in which he addresses Odysseus. In later tradition he employs many contrasting rhetorics, sings many different songs. Perhaps, then, it is best to allow a potential ambiguity to his name also. But, even if the sense 'saying many things' is present, one thing is sure: the ogre's capacity to say many things is vastly inferior to that of protean Odysseus. Given the hero's capacity both to tell an extraordinary range of stories suited to a series of conflicting identities (and names), and to perform exploits that ensure his undying fame, it is Odysseus, far more than his Cyclopean adversary, who truly deserves the two-faced epithet *poluphēmos*.

Other Cyclopes

The Cyclopes bear names that bespeak either their functions or other features of their mythical personae. Among the functional names, the commonest are those ascribed to the thunderbolt- and weapons-makers. Brontes (Thunder) goes back to Hesiod, as do Arges (Bright) and Steropes (Lightning); later variants of the latter two include Asteropes, Asteropoios, and Argilipos.[28] In an intriguing passage about the brilliance of the painter Apelles, Pliny the Elder praised—though without explicitly mentioning the Cyclopes—the artist's ability to paint the unpaintable—namely, Bronte (Thunder), Astrape (Lightning), and Ceraunobolia (Hurling

[26] Outis: see pp. 203–5.

[27] We find over-subtle the attempt by Bakker (2002; 2013: 121) to read major significance into the distinction between *phēmē* and *phēmis*.

[28] Asteropes (or Steropes): Pherec. fr. 35 Fowler. Asteropaios (or -oios, or -os): Euphorion *apud* schol. Nic. *Ther.* 288, on which see Van Groningen (1977: 124–5) on Euphorion 57, 11. Argilipos: Nonnus, *Dion.* 28. 174.

of Thunderbolts).[29] Pyracmon/Pyragmon (Fire Anvil) is named for one of the tools of his trade, as is Acmonides (Son of Anvil); Aortes (Sword Man) takes his name from one of the objects he forged.[30] Other Cyclopean characteristics are personified in Acama(n)s (Tireless), Trachios (Rough or Rocky), and Agriopos (Wild).[31] Whereas Polyphemus' usual relationship with the sea is antithetical or at best ambiguous, two of his brothers bear uncompromisingly maritime names: Euryalos (Broad Sea) and Halimedes (Sea Crafty), both found in Nonnus' account of the Cyclopes' prowess in a sea battle.[32] The same goes for Elatreus (Fir Man), since the wood in question was typically used for oars (Elatreus is also the name of one of Homer's Phaeacians).[33] Less transparent is the enigmatic Geraistos.[34] Presumably the root is *geras*, meaning 'honour' or 'privilege'. In that case the name would be one of non-specific praise, not unlike 'Polyphemus' in the sense of 'much renowned'.

Galatea

Polyphemus' beloved sea nymph perfectly embodies both ancient etymology's typical multivalence, and the context-dependent quality of naming. The semantic connection with *gala*, 'milk', is often stressed in the literary sources, along with the related idea of whiteness. But sometimes a different root is suggested: *galēnē*, 'calm sea'.[35] Given Galatea's dual links—with the sea, but also with an ogre who obsesses about milk and cheese—her name offers rich possibilities for the exploring of contradictions.

In Theocritus' *Idyll* 11, the operative derivation is from *gala*. Galatea's whiteness not only attracts the Cyclops erotically, but also constitutes a potential point of contact between them. She is whiter than cream cheese; he has unlimited milk and cheese with which to entice her. If only she would come out of the water, she could help him with the milking (20, 34–7, 65–6). But the sea remains a barrier: there is no hint of Galatea-as-*galēnē*. Not so, however, in *Idyll* 6. When Polyphemus recently looked into the sea to inspect his appearance, there was a calm (*galana*—the equivalent of *galēnē* in the Doric dialect (35))—a hint of future emotional reciprocity with Galatea?

The rival etymologies are implied in a pair of scholia on Hesiod's *Theogony*. Line 250, part of a catalogue of sea nymphs, ends with *eueidēs Galateia*, 'beautiful

29 Plin. *HN* 35.96.

30 Verg. *Aen.* 8.425; Val. Flacc. *Arg.* 1.583; Ov. *Fast.* 4.288; Pherec. fr. 46 Fowler.

31 Val. Flacc. *Arg.* 1.583; Nonnus, *Dion.* 14.60; 28.238; schol. T (Erbse) on Hom. *Il.* 18.483–606.

32 Nonnus, *Dion.* 14.59–60; 28.242–73; 36.289; 37.676–98, 707–11; 39.220–1, 340.

33 Nonnus, *Dion.* 14.59, cf. *Od.* 8.111. See Vian et al. (1976–2006) nn. on Nonnus, *Dion.* 14.59–60 and 28.238–41.

34 See pp. 183–4.

35 Highlighted by Dörrie (1968: 7 n. 1).

Galatea'. The parallel glosses on the epithet *eueidēs* explain it either in terms of 'the beautiful calm (*galēnē*)' or 'the whiteness of the waves, when the sea is blown by moderate breezes, and the look of them is lovely'.[36] Lucian's comic dialogue between Galatea and her sister nymph Doris (*Dialogues of the Sea Gods* 1) explicitly plays with the same two alternatives:

DORIS: Anyhow, what could he see to praise in you but your white skin? And he only likes that, I imagine, because he's used to cheese and milk [*gala*], and so thinks everything like them pretty. Apart from all that, any time you want to find out what your face really looks like, take a peep into the water from a rock when it's calm [*galēnē*] and look at yourself. You're nothing but white skin. Nobody thinks much of that, unless there's some rosy colour as well to show it off.

GALATEA: Even though I'm unmixed [*akratōs*] white, at least I've got a lover, even if it's only Polyphemus.[37]

The dermatologically applied adverb *akratōs* can hardly fail to recall the unmixed milk (*akrēton gala*) quaffed by the Homeric Polyphemus (*Od.* 9.297): this Lucianic Beauty is peculiarly well matched to her Beast. The reworking of Theocritus 6—specifically, the act of looking into the mirroring sea during a *galana/galēnē*—takes a similarly Galateocentric direction.

An even more idiosyncratic twist to the amalgam of sea and milk can be found in another work by Lucian. In the proto-science-fiction parody *True Stories*, a group of adventurers sails on an extraordinary voyage whose narrative is a cross between Herodotus, *Gulliver's Travels,* and *The Hitchhiker's Guide to the Galaxy.* At one point they approach a landscape where sea and milk literally coalesce (2.3):

> Not long afterwards we entered a sea, not of water, but of milk, and in it a white island, full of grapevines, came in sight. The island was a huge solid cheese [*turos*], as we afterwards learned by tasting it. It was twenty-five stades in circumference. The vines were full of grapes, but the liquid which we squeezed from them and drank was milk [*gala*] instead of wine. A temple had been constructed in the middle of the island in honour of Galatea the Nereid, as its inscription indicated. All the time that we stopped in the island the earth [= the cheese] was our seasoning and bread, and the milk [*gala*] from the grapes our drink. The ruler of that region was said to be Tyro ['Cheese']...

[36] Text of Hesiodic scholia: Cassanmagnago (2009).

[37] Trans. M. D. MacLeod, amended.

This is not the only source to describe Galatea as the recipient of cult in virtue of her nominally dairy associations. As we saw earlier, according to Duris of Samos, Polyphemus built a shrine to her near Mount Etna in gratitude for his abundant flocks and rich supply of milk.[38] But the Lucianic Galatea is watery as well as milky, unlike Queen Tyro, who is totally cheesy.

Another twist on the name 'Galatea' belongs to the realm of political ideology. In his account of *The Illyrian Wars* the historian Appian (2nd cent. CE) wrote this about the origin of the Illyrians (*Ill.* 2):

> They say that the country received its name from Illyrius, the son of Polyphemus; for the Cyclops Polyphemus and his wife Galatea had three sons: Celtus, Illyrius, and Galas, all of whom migrated from Sicily, and ruled over the peoples called after them Celts, Illyrians, and Galatians. Among the many myths prevailing among many peoples, this seems to me the most plausible.[39]

Plausible or not, this tale implies an understanding of Galatea's name that involves linguistic resemblance rather than semantic unpacking. It is not a *denial* of the association of the name with dairy products or with the calm sea; rather, it is a *complementary* approach from the perspective of political history, positing one link between proper names perceived as cognate (Galatea and Galas), and another between cultural groups perceived as interrelated (Sicilians and Galatians).[40] Was the Cyclopean connection designed to account genealogically for Gaulish 'wildness'?[41] An alternative version, which made Heracles the Gauls' ancestor, might suggest that it was.[42]

Another linguistic dimension of Galatea's name takes us back to the beginning of the tradition. In a gloriously melodic passage in the *Iliad*, the poet lists the Nereids, who share Thetis' pain as she weeps for her son Achilles, grief-stricken at the death of Patroclus (18.39–49):

> There were Glauce and Thaleia and Cymodoce, Nesaea and Speio and Thoe and ox-eyed Halie, and Cymothoe and Actaee and Limnoreia, and Melite and Iaera and Amphithoe and Agaue, Doto and Proto and Pherousa and Dynamene, and Dexamene and Amphinome and Callianeira, Doris and Panope *and famous Galatea*, Nemertes and Apseudes and Callianassa, and there were Clymene and Ianeira and Ianassa, Maera and Oreithyia and fair-tressed Amatheia, and other Nereids that were in the deep of the sea.

[38] See p. 146. [39] Trans. H. White, adapted.

[40] Cf. Timaios *apud Etym. Magn.* s.v. 'Galatia' (*FGrH* 566 F69): Galates as a son of Cyclops and Galatea; see Anello (1984: 50) and Coppola (1995: 92 with n. 72). Callimachus developed the same theme (frr. 378–9, with Pfeiffer (1949: ad loc.)).

[41] Rankin (1987: 81). [42] Diod. Sic. 5.24.3; Amm. Marc. 15.9.6; Parth. 30.

Only three of the nymphs are given epithets, and Galatea is one of them. Why is she called *agakleitē*, 'famous'?[43] Maybe we need look no further than the sheer beauty of assonance: *agakleitē Galateia* just *sounds* delightful. But it would be nice also to detect an anticipatory hint of a meaning that corresponds quite closely to the name of her 'future' lover: *poluphēmos*, 'much-talked-about', and therefore—he too—'famous'. Fame, after all, was one thing that the unlikely couple had in common.[44]

Acis

Acis' name encapsulates the only two features of his career that matter: his love affair and his liquefaction. In Greek *akis* means the point of a weapon; it can, specifically, be used to denote Eros' fiery arrows of desire.[45] That desire for him should strike Galatea is the beginning of his story, a beginning that already heralds the end—to become the river named for him: the Sicilian river Acis. Though various attempts have been made to link it with real-world streams to the north of Catania, its identity has effectively been buried for ever under eruptions from Etna—just one more episode in the age-old Cyclopean conflict of fire and water.

Outis

The *Odyssey* overflows with names that signify.[46] Melantho (Dark Woman) is the maid who sleeps with one of the suitors and insults Odysseus; Melanthios (Dark Man) is the arrogant goatherd who kicks Odysseus and helps the suitors in their combat; the disloyal pair are the children of Dolios (Tricky). The insolent suitor with a way with words is Antinoos (Contrary Mind), the son of Eupeithes (Persuasive). The considerate man who willingly supplies Telemachus (Far Fighter) with his ship is Noemon (Thoughtful) son of Phronios (Wise). Among the nautical Phaeacians are Nausicaa, Nausithoos, Pontonoos, and a host of others with similarly maritime names. Odysseus' grandfather Autolycus (The Wolf Himself) surpassed all men in thievery. What of Odysseus himself, so named by his grandfather? His name signifies, but not unambiguously. Autolycus says he named his grandson when he (Autolycus) came to Ithaca *polloisin . . . odussamenos*

[43] See Czapla (2006: 95).

[44] One homonymous relationship we shall not be exploring is that between Polyphemus' Galatea and the statue Pygmalion fell in love with. Pygmalion's statue had no name before the eighteenth century. It was thanks to Rousseau's melodrama *Pygmalion* (1770) that the name 'Galathée' became for ever associated with the sculptor's creation, formerly a piece of (white) marble, later a miraculously humanized woman. See Dörrie (1968: 68–70; 1974).

[45] Meleager in *Anth. Pal.* 12.76; cf. Timotheus fr. 2 *PCG*.

[46] We borrow from Buxton (2013d: 65–6).

(19.407). Does this mean 'having hated many' or 'having incurred the hatred of many'? Perhaps the distinction is more apparent than real. In any case, there is an element of trouble and restlessness in Odysseus' name, which sits well with his changeful career.[47] But what of Outis ('Nobody'), one of Odysseus' many aliases in the poem? Its main function is to enable the hero to play a linguistic trick, which would resound throughout the post-Homeric tradition, whether in its *outis* or its *nemo* formulation.[48] However, the brilliance of this trick can be fully appreciated only in its original Homeric language. It is worth examining this in detail.[49]

When they hear Polyphemus' anguished screams for help, his fellow Cyclopes come to find out what the problem is. What's all this noise? You're stopping us from sleeping! Surely someone isn't rustling your sheep? And then (406):

> Surely someone isn't killing you by a trick or by violence?

Polyphemus spells it out (408):

> My friends, Outis is killing me by a trick *oude* by violence.

The Greek word *oude* operates in two ways. Following a positive assertion it means 'and not': 'I like cricket and not [*oude*] baseball.' Following a negative assertion it means 'or': 'I do not enjoy broccoli or [*oude*] custard.' So when Polyphemus says, 'Outis is killing me by a trick *oude* by violence', this can be heard in two ways, depending on whether he is understood to be making a positive or a negative assertion. Polyphemus is *trying* to say 'My friends, [a man called] Outis is killing me by a trick'—a positive assertion—'*and not* by violence'. What the other Cyclopes *hear* is: 'My friends, nobody [*outis*] is killing me by a trick'—a negative assertion—'*or* by violence'. The ambiguity works perfectly in Greek, and is impossible to reproduce in translation.[50]

The linguistic virtuosity continues. The other Cyclopes have heard Polyphemus say (as they think), 'My friends, nobody is killing me by a trick or by violence'. Here is their response (410):

> Well, if nobody is using violence on you...

[47] See Rank (1951: 51–63); Stanford (1952); Rutherford (1992) on 19.406–9.

[48] See e.g. Ar. *Vesp.* 184–6; Cratinus fr. 145 *PCG*; Eur. *Cyc.* 548–50, 672–5; Demetr. *Eloc.* 130, 152, 262.

[49] Here we borrow from Buxton (2017b).

[50] Auffarth (1991: 302) gets this exactly right: 'Only the other Cyclopes hear it as "neither... nor..."' (our translation).

The words they use for 'if nobody...' are not *ei* ['if'] *outis*, but *ei mē tis*. There are two negative particles in Greek: *ou* and *mē*. An indicative negative assertion uses *ou*, but in certain other types of clause—for example, the protasis of a conditional sentence—the negative is *mē*. There is, then, nothing *syntactically* unusual going on when the other Cyclopes use the phrase *ei mē tis* to introduce the conditional clause 'if nobody is doing violence to you...'. But there is certainly something *semantically* unusual going on.[51] The noun *mētis*, 'cunning intelligence', is one of the key words in the *Odyssey*. Odysseus is habitually and formulaically *polumētis* ('possessing much cunning intelligence'), a quality that saves his bacon at every turn. So, while one way of hearing the Cyclopes' response to Polyphemus would be 'Well, if nobody [*mē tis*] is doing violence to you...', an alternative would be 'Well, if cunning intelligence [*mētis*] is doing violence to you...'.[52] And that is exactly what is happening: Odysseus' cunning intelligence is doing violence to Polyphemus.

These *minutiae* may seem trivial: they are not. Names, and the identities they represent, constitute the big picture in the *Odyssey*. The climax of book 9 is the moment when Odysseus finally reveals his true name (502–5); as Justine McConnell tellingly puts it: 'Odysseus cannot bear to be in the position of the [nameless] oppressed.'[53] After the revelation, Polyphemus recalls a prophecy that he would lose his sight at the hands of someone called 'Odysseus'. He had expected his adversary to be a big, fine man, not a feeble little nobody, *outidanos* (515). For much of the poem Odysseus is indeed a nobody—unrecognized, at least initially, in many of his ports of call, and then, even when back home in Ithaca, an anonymous, decrepit beggar. Under this disguise he tests out those whom he meets, and then, at a time of his own choosing, ultimately reveals himself, turning from Nobody into the greatest Somebody of all. What remains constant throughout all his metamorphoses is *mētis*, the quality that, as he himself claims (20.18–21), saved him from the Cyclops' cave.

[51] Again rightly noted by Auffarth (1991: 292–3 n. 2).

[52] De Jong (2001: 244).

[53] McConnell (2013: 29).

8
Love and Song

Sex and the Single Cyclops

Unlike his fellow Cyclopes, the Polyphemus of the *Odyssey* has no wife, nor indeed anyone else to relieve his sexual isolation (9.114–15). What a contrast with Euripides' *Cyclops*. The obsessions of the ithyphallic satyrs pervade the play and extend to other characters apart from themselves. The taste of wine induces Silenus to fantasize about the pleasures it arouses: an erection, a handful of breast, a 'meadow', dancing, oblivion (169–72). The first thing the satyr chorus wants to know from Odysseus is: 'When you recaptured Helen, did you all bang her in turn?' (179–80). For Polyphemus, the effect of a hearty meal washed down with milk is, at least on one interpretation, to produce a massive erection (327–8).[1] For the satyrs, by contrast, as for their father, the drink that stimulates sex is wine (495–502):

> Happy the man who shouts the Bacchic cry, off to the revel, the well-beloved juice of the vine putting the wind in his sails. His arm is around his trusty friend, and he has waiting for him the fresh, young body of his voluptuous mistress upon her bed, and with his locks all gleaming with myrrh he says, 'Who will open the door for me?'

They try to entice Polyphemus with the imaginary prospect of a delicate nymph waiting for him in his dewy cave (514–16), but the Cyclops' (aristocratic?) proclivities tend elsewhere (Polyphemus/Silenus = Zeus/Ganymede).[2] The hapless Silenus' parting shot is: 'Oh dear! The wine I shall drink will be bitter indeed' (589)—perhaps a hint at imminent offstage *fellatio*. If so, it is not the only time this act was imagined in a Cyclopean context on the Attic stage. At one point in Aristophanes' comedy *Wealth*, the slave Carion goes in for a song-and-dance routine with the chorus of old peasants, he taking the role of Polyphemus and they that of the ogre's goats. The repartee leaves little to the imagination: Carion suggests that the chorus/goats will be performing *fellatio* on themselves.[3]

[1] Unless the lines refer to a thunderous fart (see p. 190).
[2] Aristocratic? Cf. Seaford (1984) on 583–4; Mastromarco (1998: 32).
[3] Ar. *Plut*. 295, with note by Sommerstein (2001: ad loc.).

Cyclops: The Myth and its Cultural History. Mercedes Aguirre and Richard Buxton, Oxford University Press (2020).

DOI: 10.1093/oso/9780198713777.001.0001

Galatea, Polyphemus, Acis

Galatea's entrance into Cyclopean mythology not only refashioned the ancient tradition, but also decisively shaped post-classical artistic and textual retellings.[4] From an epic collision between Polyphemus' violence and Odysseus' guile, the emphasis shifts to a stand-off between coquettish grace and lovelorn ugliness: from the Hero and the Ogre, to Beauty and the Beast.[5] This move does not, however, constitute a total reversal of earlier tales. Indeed some myth-tellers accommodate Odysseus and Galatea simultaneously. In Letter 121 by Bishop Synesius of Ptolemais in Libya (3rd–4th cent. CE), Odysseus promises to win over Galatea for Polyphemus if only the ogre will remove the door-stone blocking the cave.[6] Even clearer is the evidence of the mural from Boscotrecase (*Cat. 41* (Fig. 3.2)) in which Polyphemus appears twice: in the foreground, juxtaposed with Galatea; in the background, hurling a rock seawards towards a vessel, presumably that of the escaping Odysseus (cf. also *Cat. 45* (Fig. 5.6)). What the emergence of the Galatea theme does is to develop rather than overturn what went before. Already in the *Odyssey* the Cyclopes' relationship to the sea is ambivalent. Polyphemus is Poseidon's son and prays to him in time of need, yet, like all the other Cyclopes, he lives in a world without ships, and his horizons stop at the sea's edge. The presence of Galatea refocuses this ambivalence, adding special poignancy to the sea-*shore*. Polyphemus is now drawn inexorably towards the sea, yet the nymph rejects him (at least in most versions). Another respect in which the Galatea theme prolongs earlier tradition is that it consolidates the contrast between Polyphemus and the other Cyclopes: he alone is a victim of *eros*. But what is absolutely new is the broadening of the range of emotions experienced by Polyphemus: not only erotic longing but, when Acis comes on the scene, homicidal jealousy.

An 'origin' in Philoxenus?

Against the background of the swirling currents of Greek myth, the relationship between Galatea and Polyphemus stands out as unusual in that its invention can apparently be located with chronological precision, in a (now fragmentary) dithyrambic composition by the late fifth–early fourth-century BCE poet Philoxenus of Cythera. Given that scholia on a passage in Aristophanes' *Wealth* (388 BCE) suggest that the comic poet was parodying Philoxenus' *Cyclops*, and that such an allusion would presumably be to a performance fresh enough in the audience's memory to make the parody effective, it seems reasonable to place Philoxenus'

4 Still fundamental is Dörrie (1968). See also Heinrich (1986); Czapla (2006).

5 For the pair of contrasts, see Dörrie (1968: 8).

6 Text available in Philoxenus fr. 818 in D. A. Campbell (1993).

version in the years immediately before the date of the play.[7] (That there might have been an older tradition connecting Polyphemus and Galatea as indigenous Sicilian deities, who were later identified with the nymph and ogre of Greek myth, is conceivable but unprovable.[8]) A number of sources agree that a key player in the genesis of the Cyclops/Galatea theme was the Syracusan despot Dionysius I, to whose court Philoxenus had travelled. Common to several sources is the idea that Philoxenus was incarcerated in the notorious Syracusan stone quarries because he mocked Dionysius. What is less clear is how Galatea and the Cyclops fit into this scenario. Phaenias, a philosopher from Lesbos (late 4th cent. BCE), reported, probably in his *On the Sicilian Tyrants*, that Philoxenus had seduced Dionysius' mistress, by the name of Galatea, for which *lèse tyrannie* he was thrown into the quarries. There he allegedly wrote a spoof allegorizing himself as Odysseus, and Dionysius as the Cyclops, with Galatea also figuring in the plot (another example, as in Synesius, of the Odysseus and Galatea motifs appearing in tandem).[9] A variant related that Philoxenus managed to escape from the quarries back to his home on Cythera, where he composed a play *Galatea*, in which Dionysius was mockingly equated with Polyphemus because both had poor eyesight.[10] Different again was a version in which Philoxenus' offence was to be uncomplimentary about the tyrant's own poetic compositions.[11]

What do we make of this farrago?[12] The alleged personal tiff with Dionysius exemplifies the sort of biographical readings of poetry to which ancient anecdotists were addicted; whether it has any basis in fact is anyone's guess. Fortunately, it hardly matters.[13] If the two men did fall out—whether because the poet got into bed with the tyrant's mistress or for some other reason—the quarrel disappears without trace in the subsequent development of the myth.

Erotic variations

Written sources give differing versions of the emotional interplay between Polyphemus and Galatea. Most accounts present the Cyclops' blandishments as unreciprocated, but there are variations that soften or complicate the polarity. In a passage (58–63) from the anonymous *Lament for Bion*, Galatea flees from

[7] Philoxenus fr. 819 in D. A. Campbell (1993). On Ar. *Plut.*, see p. 206. See also Hunter (1999: 216–17).

[8] Anello (1984) suggests such a possibility; cf. Czapla (2006: 97 n. 9).

[9] Philoxenus fr. 816 in D. A. Campbell (1993). See Dörrie (1968: 14).

[10] Philoxenus fr. 819 in D. A. Campbell (1993) (scholia on Ar. *Plut.*).

[11] Philoxenus Test. 3 in D. A. Campbell (1993).

[12] Discussions in Dörrie (1968: 12–17); Arnott (1996: 139–41); Hordern (1999); Hunter (1999: 216–17); Gutzwiller (2006: 20–1); Venezia (2007: 125–6).

[13] Luigi Venezia's no-nonsense conclusion ('But let's put anecdotes to one side' (2007: 126; our translation) is apposite.

Polyphemus, but paradoxically mimics a characteristic Polypheman pose by sitting on the shore as she grieves for the dead poet Bion, just as she sat beside Bion in life, preferring his company to the sea itself. In Theocritus' *Idyll* 11 the antithesis between Beauty and Beast is at its sharpest: Galatea shuns the ogre (19, 24, 30, 75), approaching him only while he is asleep (22). Even so, the nymph's feelings are accessible only indirectly, being interpreted through the words of the adolescent Polyphemus. Harder still to decode are her reactions in *Idyll* 6, since the behaviour of both principals is mediated through the eyes of two herdsmen. Richard Hunter aptly talks of 'the uncertainties of the game which Galatea and the Cyclops are playing'—just who is the teaser, and who is being teased?[14]

We have to wait for two later sources to hear Galatea's own voice, in dialogue with her sister sea creatures. In Lucian's first *Dialogue of the Sea Gods* she denies that she loves the ogre (*ouk erōmenon*), yet feistily praises his qualities in order to deflect the sarcasm of her interlocutrix, the nymph Doris (here apparently Galatea's sister rather than her mother): Polyphemus, Galatea points out, is a son of Poseidon; his wildness and hairiness make him manly; and he is musical. For Ovid's Galatea there is no such ambiguity: as she expresses it in conversation with Scylla, the hatred she feels for the Cyclops is as strong as her love for Acis (*Met.* 13.756–7). The presence of Acis is an emotional game-changer: with a handsome young lover on the scene, there is no possibility for a rapprochement, however qualified, between Beauty and Beast.

Amid all the variations, one erotic schema stands out from the rest: the image of Polyphemus gazing longingly out to sea towards his beloved, while her own gaze is directed elsewhere. Philostratus gives both perspectives. Whereas Polyphemus watches Galatea from his mountainous vantage point as she plays in the sea, her own eyes have a distant look directed towards the horizon: not a hint of emotional reciprocity.[15]

And yet, now and then, poets told the tale differently. What if Galatea *did* reciprocate the Cyclops' affection? That Polyphemus and his nymph were reported by some to have had children tells us nothing about the emotions involved: the ogrish Polyphemus was presumably capable of forcing himself on an unwilling partner. But a few myth-tellers explored the possibility that Beauty really did love her Beast. The Macedonian epigrammatist Posidippus (*fl.* 3rd cent. BCE) referred to 'Polyphemus the love-sick goatherd who often dived with Galatea', which seems to imply a shared playfulness.[16] Two centuries later, the Roman poet Propertius was more explicit, including Galatea among examples of the power of music and song to sway a girl's affections: she turned her horses, dripping with sea water, towards the sound of Polyphemus' songs (3.2.7–8). But top of the list of poets who saw the affection as mutual comes Nonnus, whose narrative of a ferocious

[14] Hunter (1999: 246).

[15] See p. 121.

[16] Fr. 19, 7–8 (Austin–Bastianini).

sea battle between the Indians and the Dionysians highlights the odd couple's reciprocal attraction. Surfacing from the depths, Galatea surveys the conflict and thinks she spies Polyphemus among the other Cyclopes. Fearing for his safety, she implores Poseidon, and more significantly Aphrodite, to protect him (*Dion.* 39.257–66). But Galatea's eyes, or her anxiety, have deceived her. The one Cyclops absent from the battle is lovesick (*erōmanēs*) Polyphemus, as his embarrassed mother Thoosa blushes to notice (293–4).

The most explicit representations of a mutual erotic relationship between ogre and nymph are visual. We need first to set them into the broader artistic context.

As we have seen, images of Polyphemus and Galatea appear often in Roman art, particularly in mosaics and wall paintings; the theme was especially popular in the so-called Third Style of Pompeian frescoes. A favourite schema depicts the couple confined within their characteristically separated spaces: he on land, she on water, the only link between them being—at least sometimes—the gaze. Typical in its stress on the emotional gulf between the two is the mural from Boscotrecase (*Cat. 41* (Fig. 3.2)). Galatea sits to the left, riding a dolphin and framed by her shell-like mantle, like an elegant personal sail (elsewhere a characteristic of Aphrodite/Venus). Polyphemus occupies the centre ground, seated on a rock and equally self-contained (he also appears in a separate episode in the background, aiming a boulder at a ship—it was not only texts that amalgamated the Odysseus and Galatea themes).[17] Similar in approach is the Pompeian wall painting from the House of the Priest Amandus (*Cat. 45* (Fig. 5.6)). The background again depicts a ship, presumed to be that of Odysseus. In the rocky centre-foreground Polyphemus wears a 'pastoral' crown of pine needles. To the viewer's left, Galatea perches decorously on a sea creature, but this time she has her naked back to the viewer. The Cyclops looks at her; but is she looking at him? If so, with what expression on her face? There is obviously no way of telling. Could this and the Boscotrecase painting be depicting a Polyphemus who is simply *imagining* his lover?[18] The enigmatic, isolating 'framings' of Galatea make this an intriguing possibility. The same cannot be said of the mosaic from Cordoba (*Cat. 71* (Fig. 4.5)), on which Galatea is too emotionally involved to be a figment of Polyphemus' imagination.[19] The semi-naked nymph is displayed full-frontal for the viewer to contemplate. As she turns aslant towards her hairy would-be lover, she looks alarmed; the way she plays with a tress of her hair could suggest unease, though there might be a touch of coquetry in there too. Once more she is mounted on a sea creature, while Polyphemus sits on a rock; but there is less distance between them than in either of the wall paintings just considered. Indeed, Polyphemus

[17] Von Blanckenhagen and Alexander (1962: 38–43); Ling (1991: 114–15).

[18] Cf. Leach (1992: 71).

[19] Blanco Freijeiro (1959) gives a fine account of the mosaic.

boldly invades her personal space with a rhetorical hand gesture to reinforce his attempted persuasion. No wonder she looks worried.

One more image belongs to the 'relationship at a distance' type, though it is at the same time highly idiosyncratic (or at least seems so, in view of our limited knowledge). This is the extraordinary wall painting from the House of Livia (*Cat. 40* (Fig. 4.6)), known to us now only from the sketch by the German artist A. Sikkard.[20] A handsome, young, naked Polyphemus stands chest deep in the sea, leaning on a rock and contemplating his beloved. If his infatuation were not already clear from his pose, the little winged Eros perched on his left shoulder and guiding him with reins puts the matter beyond doubt.[21] The object of the Cyclops' desire rides a hippocamp, and entices the external viewer with her naked back while simultaneously tempting Polyphemus with her front. Though the gestures of the sea nymphs in the background express alarm or admonition, Galatea's own attitude is more enigmatic—that inscrutable rear view again.

Quite different in mood and composition is a painting from Herculaneum (*Cat. 46* (Fig. 8.1)). A naked Polyphemus, exhibiting a seriously impressive torso, sits as often on a rocky seat, which is covered this time by an animal skin; he has a shepherd's crook to hand. He turns in the vague direction of a woman holding a water lily as a fan, though he looks wistfully upwards rather than directly at her.[22] The woman should probably be identified as Galatea (the aquatic plant is a hint), even though she is standing up fully clothed on land, rather than part-naked and riding a sea creature. If she really is Galatea, it is she, rather than Polyphemus, who has abandoned her own natural habitat to occupy his (the opposite scenario to that in *Cat. 40* (Fig. 4.6)). More puzzling is the identity of the woman standing next to Galatea. She seems to be indicating Polyphemus to Galatea, though with what intent it is hard to say. Is it a recommendation or a warning? Is she Polyphemus' go-between, praising the strapping herdsman to her mistress?[23] Is she one of Galatea's companions?[24] Is she Galatea's mother Thoosa?[25] Whatever this figure is telling her, Galatea looks more interested, or at any rate less disconcerted, than her equivalent on the mosaic from Cordoba.

A relief on a sarcophagus in the Palazzo Mattei di Giove in Rome (*Cat. 67* (Fig. 8.2)) gives us a not unfamiliar view of Polyphemus and Galatea, but also includes a rare image of Acis.[26] The Cyclops, partly draped in an animal skin, sits

[20] See Rizzo (1936: 35, figs 24–9, pls 2–3); Ling (1991: 113); Leach (1992: 70); Squire (2009: 306–7).

[21] Note also a mosaic from Tunisia (Sousse Museum) with images of Polyphemus (possibly) and Galatea (certainly—identified by inscription). The winged figure in the water in front of the dolphin-borne sea nymph has been very plausibly interpreted as an Eros: Montón Subías (1990: 1003, no. 26), citing Dunbabin (1978: 272, no. 1b (Themetra)), and Picard (1960: 33).

[22] See p. 131.

[23] Montón Subias (1990: 1002, no. 20).

[24] Elia (1932: 76, no. 156).

[25] So Prauscello (2007: 95–6), adducing the unidentified woman's hairstyle as indicative of someone older than Galatea (cf. Bartman 2001: 5).

[26] Guerrini (1982: 202–4, no. 52).

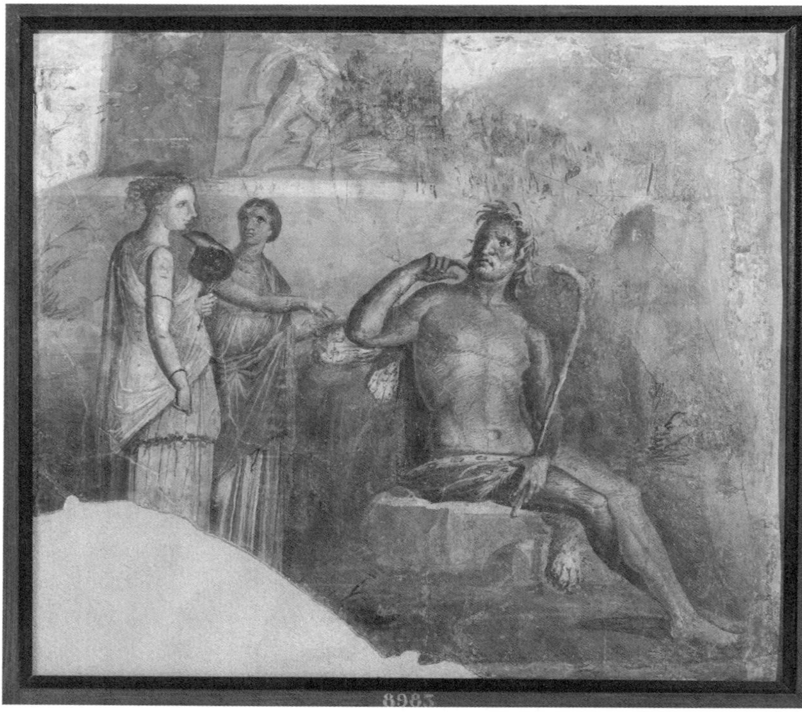

Fig. 8.1. Wall painting from Herculaneum, *c.*62–79 CE.

on a rock, while the semi-naked Galatea is in the sea on a dolphin: no surprises there. But above and to the left is a small, reclining masculine figure leaning his left arm on a jar, from which water flows. This must be Acis as river god—the 'end' (as it were) of the myth. By contrast, the Polyphemus/Galatea scene belongs to the 'middle'. He courts her by offering a young animal, maybe a bear cub or a lamb; her self-revealing posture hardly implies a definite 'no'.

On a pair of wall paintings from Pompeii, the relationship between Polyphemus and Galatea is sexually explicit. The first, from the House of the Ancient Hunt (*Cat. 47* (Fig. 5.7)), shows the standing pair in passionate embrace. The tall, dark-skinned Cyclops has his legs apart and one hand on her bottom; the undraped rear of white-skinned Galatea—the view of her that ancient artists prefer—is of course for the benefit of the painting's spectators, a taste reflected in the portrayal of Aphrodite as 'Kallipugos' ('with a beautiful arse'). The other painting goes a stage further (*Cat. 48* (Fig. 5.8)), recalling the sex scenes on many a Pompeian fresco.[27]

[27] Most famously that on the bedroom wall of the House of the Centenary (IX.8.3), though there is no shortage of other examples.

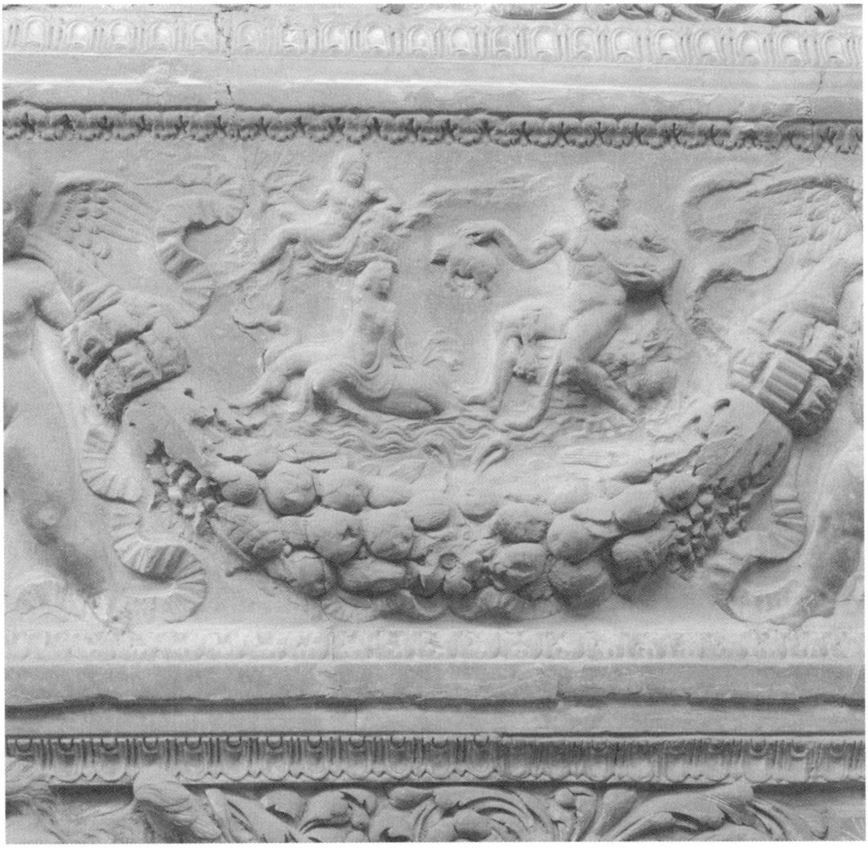

Fig. 8.2. Acis, Galatea, Polyphemus. Sarcophagus in Rome, 2nd cent. CE.

Again the opposition between dark and light skin crystallizes the polarity—perhaps a symbolic displacement of the big/small opposition?[28]

Altogether more discreet are a set of images in which Polyphemus appears without Galatea, but in a context that—even in the absence of any corroboration in our textual sources—strongly implies her offstage presence. These images show Polyphemus receiving a written message delivered by Eros. Given the identity of the postman, there can be little doubt about the sender. A fine example comes from Herculaneum (*Cat. 53* (Fig. 8.3)): an Eros riding a dolphin (suggesting that the sender has some connection with the sea) holds out a letter to Polyphemus, who reaches out to take it. The back story is lost to us, but

[28] Dark/light, big/small: Czapla (2006: 99, with n. 16).

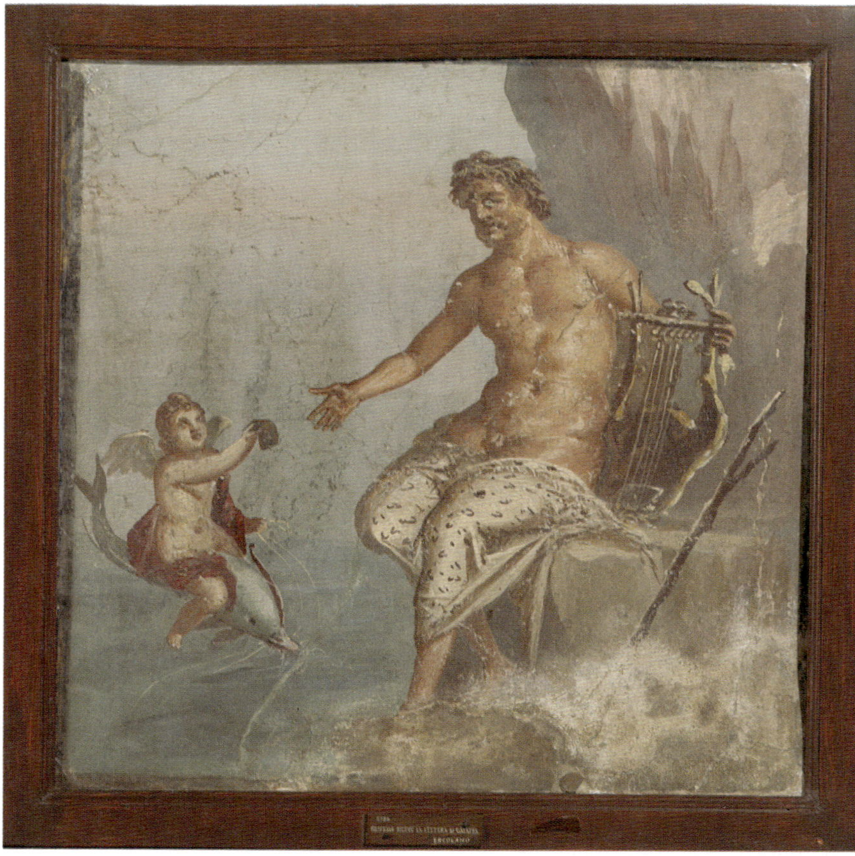

Fig. 8.3. Polyphemus receives a love letter. Wall painting from Herculaneum, *c.*62–79 CE.

everything points to a version in which Cyclops and nymph exchanged love letters. Just for once, it seems that Polyphemus found a means of communication other than song.

The songs of Polyphemus

Although the alleged rumpus between Philoxenus and Dionysius had no impact on the subsequent tradition, another aspect of Philoxenus' treatment of the myth was immeasurably more influential: that Polyphemus sang songs to his own musical accompaniment, whether addressed to himself as consolation, or to Galatea in attempted enticement. One source reported that Philoxenus portrayed the Cyclops playing the cithara;[29] another that the ogre 'tried to cure his love with the tuneful Muses';[30] a third that he poetically invoked Galatea as 'Fair-faced, golden-tressed, Grace-voiced offshoot of the Loves';[31] according to a fourth, 'Philoxenus makes the Cyclops console himself for his love of Galatea and tell the dolphins to report to her that he is healing his love with the Muses'.[32] While Philoxenus was not the first to mention Polyphemus' singing—in Euripides' *Cyclops* (425–6) Odysseus refers to the ogre's 'unmusical' (*amousa*) warbling—he did consolidate a tradition that would resonate in countless later versions, especially in comedy, pastoral, and visual art.

The Polyphemus of the *Odyssey* does not lack rhetorical power, as his pathetic address to his favourite ram makes clear (9.447–60). The Euripidean Cyclops also fancies himself as a persuasive orator, especially in the speech in which he sophistically rejects traditional concepts of divinity and law, in favour of the view that the three *really* worthwhile objects of worship are wealth, himself, and his belly (316–35). However, although the Homeric and the Euripidean speeches are both couched in verse, and although the Homeric narrator would have been performing his poems to lyre accompaniment, the connection between Cyclopean rhetoric and Cyclopean song is incidental. Only with the advent of pastoral does the link become firmly established.

The idea of the herdsman–poet dates back at least to Hesiod's encounter with the Muses while he tended his lambs on Mount Helicon, as described in the prologue to the *Theogony* (22–34). The prime intended auditors of pastoral song are, of course, the animals. The music and song of the herdsman described in Plato's *Statesman* are designed to 'encourage' and 'soothe' his flock (*Plt.* 268b). A more magical evocation of the power of pastoral music can be found in Apollonius' *Argonautica*, in a simile that describes Orpheus' Pied Piper-like conjuring-up of a fishy retinue around the *Argo* (1.575–9):

> As when a flock of sheep which have filled themselves full of grass follow to the stall in the steps of their rustic master, and he goes in front playing a lovely shepherd's tune on his shrill pipe; just so did the fish accompany the *Argo* which the strong breeze pushed ever forwards.[33]

Like many another herdsman, Polyphemus has music at his disposal. In theory, this can be directed at his flocks, but, in practice, he targets a different pair of audiences: his would-be lover and himself. The *loci classici* are the two Theocritean *Idylls* devoted to the Cyclops. *Idyll* 6, during which the herdsmen Daphnis and

[29] Philoxenus fr. 819 in D. A. Campbell (1993).
[30] Philoxenus fr. 822 in D. A. Campbell (1993).
[31] Philoxenus fr. 821 in D. A. Campbell (1993).
[32] Philoxenus fr. 822 in D. A. Campbell (1993).
[33] Trans. R. L. Hunter, adapted.

Damoetas have been singing the myth of Polyphemus and Galatea, ends as the men seal their bond of friendship by exchanging instruments: the *aulos* (similar to a recorder) and the *surinx* (pan pipes) (42–3). Polyphemus' own preference, as Daphnis tells us, is the pan pipes (8–9). In *Idyll* 11 Polyphemus also plays the pan pipes—more skilfully, he claims, than any of his fellow Cyclopes (38). But more important than his playing is his singing. The content of his song is his attempted persuasion of his beloved, and her rejection of that attempt.

By singing about Galatea, he finds—according to the poem's prologue—a 'remedy' or 'cure' for his love (1, 7). But here there is an often-noticed paradox: even after singing, Polyphemus remains in love. The key to the paradox lies in the last two lines: 'Thus did Polyphemus shepherd [*epoimainen*] his love by making music, and bore it more easily than if he had paid gold for it.' The notion of 'shepherding' has been brilliantly explained by Richard Hunter: 'His song "relieves" his love, but in "shepherding it" he keeps it alive; every song rehearses the attractions of Galatea and the course of his passion—there is no ultimate escape.'[34]

Ever since Philoxenus and Theocritus, the figure of Polyphemus has been inseparable from the songs he sings to express and to cope with his love. Indeed, song replaces herding as his main occupation.[35] An epigram by Callimachus takes a magico-medical view: through his 'Muses' the ogre finds a 'charm' for *reducing* love, as if it were a bodily swelling (*Epig.* 46). The Polyphemus of another Hellenistic poet, Bion of Smyrna (2nd–1st cent. BCE), is less sanguine about managing his emotions, conscious that he is in for the long haul, and incidentally giving us a rare glimpse of Cyclopean old age (fr. 16): 'But I will make my way down, whispering to sand and shore my supplication of cruel Galatea; for I will not give up my sweet hopes till I reach uttermost old age.'

As to the effectiveness of Polyphemus' singing, opinions differ. Propertius' Galatea *does* heed the ogre's *carmina*, 'songs' (3.2.7–8). By contrast, the Galatea in the painting evoked by Philostratus ignores the Cyclops' *poimenikon aisma*, 'pastoral song', while his *surinx* hangs under his arm unplayed. The most extravagant performance of all is that of Ovid's Polyphemus. The overture is deafening (his pipe is made of a hundred reeds (*Met.* 13.784–5)), and the song he goes on to sing is eighty sumptuous hexameters long (789–869). But he is wasting his breath. Galatea, hiding under a rock in Acis' arms, sums it up in a single word: *nequiquam*, 'in vain' (870).

The funniest account of Cyclopean music comes in Lucian's first *Dialogue of the Sea Gods*. Responding to Galatea's assertion that her lover is musical, Doris describes the impact of his 'music' on an unbiased critic:

[34] Hunter (1999: 221).

[35] Cusset (2004: 55–6); Holtsmark (1966).

> Better to keep quiet about that, Galatea; we heard him singing the other day when he serenaded you. Gracious Aphrodite! You would have thought it was a donkey braying. And his lyre! What a thing! The fleshless skull of a stag, with its horns for the uprights; he put a bar across, and fastened on the strings without any tuning-pegs! Then came the performance, all harsh and out of tune; he roared something himself, and the lyre played something else: we couldn't help laughing at that love-song. Even Echo, chatterbox that she is, would not answer his bellowing; she was ashamed to be caught mimicking such a rough and ridiculous song.

This time the Cyclops' chosen instrument is the lyre (*à la* Philoxenus) rather than the pan pipes, so that he can sing and play simultaneously.

Visual art makes occasional reference to Cyclopean music. On the mosaic from Cordoba (*Cat. 71* (Fig. 4.5)) the pan pipes are on view beside Polyphemus, confirming that this is indeed the (pastoral) Cyclops. The same clue corroborates his identity in the two *erotica* from Pompeii (*Cat. 47* and *48* (Figs 5.7 and 5.8)): he has his hands full of Galatea, so the pan pipes lie discarded to one side. On the fresco from Herculaneum depicting his receipt of a letter from postman Eros (*Cat. 53* (Fig. 8.3)), his chosen instrument is the lyre; perhaps he wants to impress his girl by playing a higher-status instrument. But it is the pan pipes that best suit a rough-and-ready cave-dweller who spends his life in the company of his flock. Nor is it only in an erotic context that he uses it. On the marble statue in Rome in which one of his soon-to-be-devoured human victims lies at his feet (*Cat. 66* (Fig. 5.12)), he grasps pan pipes in his right hand. Merely a symbolic confirmation that 'this is Polyphemus'? Or is it also a grim hint that the ogre's repertoire includes the tunes of death?

The fires of love

The Hellenistic elegiac poet Hermesianax (perhaps early 3rd cent. BCE) summarizes Polyphemus' role in the love story in a single line:

> Looking towards the wave, his single pupil burned.[36]

We owe the preservation of this verse to the grammarian Herodian (2nd cent. CE), who quotes it to illustrate a rare form of the Greek word for 'pupil' (*glēn*).[37] Although he does not specify that the subject is Polyphemus, every detail fits the Cyclopean profile: looking seawards, and blinded by love's heat in his *single* eye.

[36] Hermesianax fr. 1 in Lightfoot (2009).

[37] Cf. the description of the single Cyclopean eye in Callim. *H.Art.* 53: *phaea mounoglēna.*

Theocritus made a more explicitly proleptic allusion in *Idyll* 11: 'If it is I myself who seem too hairy to you, I have oak logs, and undying fire under the ashes; I could endure being burned by you in my soul and in my one eye, than which nothing is dearer to me' (50–3). Under the influence of such a woman, no wonder Polyphemus 'melted' (14). But it is Ovid who really turns up the heat. That Polyphemus, in Galatea's words, 'burns when seized with mighty desire' is run of the mill (*Met.* 13.762–3); but soon the ogre fleshes this out in his own words, when love has been fuelled by jealous fury: 'For I burn, and the fire, stirred to frenzy, rages more fiercely within me: I seem to carry Etna let down into my breast with all its force' (867–9). All this heat is counterpoised by Galatea's sea water, and by the cool river into which Acis will be turned, mixing his waters perpetually with hers.[38] But Polyphemus is not just hot: he is volcanic. The deep implication of Etna in Cyclopean passion raises a topic that we have already touched on several times: fire. We reserve further discussion of it for the next chapter, in which we add the final layer to our thematic investigation of the Graeco-Roman Cyclopes.

[38] Cf. Sil. *Pun.* 14. 221–6: Polyphemus' heat (*calor*) opposed to Acis' liquidity (*liquefactus*).

9
Contexts and Overlaps

The Shaping Power of Context

Like every other constellation of Greek myths, that centring on the Cyclopes was transmitted in a range of contexts, taking that tricky term to designate either the overall medium of transmission (for example, a text or a painting) or the particular literary genre or artistic subtype (for example, epic poetry or vase painting). Each of these levels of context shaped the stories, alongside, of course, the individual input of the author or artist. We have already discussed many instances of this phenomenon, but it may be useful to draw some threads together.

Medium and genre

The conflict between a man-eating ogre and the hero who encounters him is a story pattern admirably suited to epic, particularly the kind that describes a journey through here-be-dragons territory. Thus the Homeric *Odyssey*, the first, 'Odyssean', half of the *Aeneid*, and the 'Trojans en route for Italy' section of Ovid's *Metamorphoses* are ideal sites for an encounter between a hero (be it Odysseus or Aeneas) and Polyphemus. But epic was just one of many literary genres to exploit the episode. Historians and geographers, from Thucydides to Polybius, Eratosthenes, and Strabo, debated the Cyclopes' exact whereabouts within the wider travelogue of Odysseus' wanderings. From a different perspective, that the hero's ogrish adversary could be represented, not only as horrific and brutish, but also as ugly and gullible, opened the way for the counterbalancing of ghoulishness by humour. Euripides' satyr play was far from unique: many comic playwrights also capitalized on Polyphemus' appetites, especially for food and drink. This humorous take on Cyclopean grossness recurs throughout antiquity, sometimes in unexpected contexts. Bishop Synesius' *Letter* 121 includes Odysseus' memorable advice to the Cyclops to smarten up his act by cleaning and perfuming his cave—otherwise the stench might put off a delicate young nymph who takes a bath several times a day.[1]

[1] See p. 50.

Cyclops: The Myth and its Cultural History. Mercedes Aguirre and Richard Buxton, Oxford University Press (2020).

DOI: 10.1093/oso/9780198713777.001.0001

One genre that lacks a dramatization of the Polyphemus-versus-Odysseus encounter is tragedy.[2] The portrayal of 'monstrous' *behaviour* is standard tragic fare, but this tends to be the metaphorical monstrosity of a transgressive human hero or heroine—a Medea, a Thyestes, a Tereus, a Clytemnestra. Tragic references to more orthodox man-versus-monster combats—Perseus and the Gorgon, Bellerophon and the Chimera—are much thinner on the ground. When such allusions do occur, as with the catalogue of Heracles' monstrous adversaries in Euripides' *Madness of Heracles* (359–429), or Jason's boasting of his overpowering of fire-breathing bulls and a Fleece-guarding serpent in *Medea* (476–82), they serve merely as a foil for what really matters—namely, circumambient or impending familial catastrophe. So also with Odysseus. The Ithacan appears several times in tragedy, but not in combat with monsters: his typical role (*Ajax*, *Philoctetes*, *Hecuba*) is to participate in morally ambiguous and politically complex intrigues during the Trojan War and its aftermath. To find his confrontation with Polyphemus used to explore *that* kind of ambiguity and complexity, we have to wait until much later in the history of myth-telling, when the contrast between the 'civilized' but oppressive colonist and the 'bestial' and oppressed indigene climbs up the ideological agenda.

In the visual arts, an eye-catching example of the contextual shaping of the hero-versus-Cyclops conflict is the ghastly monocular giant depicted, in the act of being blinded, in the Tomb of Orcus II (*Cat. 31* (Fig. 4.15)). That such an image should appear in tandem with the underworld figure of Charun reinforces the sense of terror associated with this staging-post en route to the Etruscan Underworld.[3] This is a case where we can describe with some confidence how the context shapes the tenor of the artistic product. In many other instances, however, such assurance would be misplaced. This certainly applies to the majority of Greek vase paintings depicting the standard trio of wine-offering, blinding, and under-ram escape. Such context-related comments as we *can* make about these images tend to be pretty trivial: for example, that the reason the ogre is usually portrayed as lying down or seated is that, given his abnormal size proportionately to ordinary humans, there would be insufficient room on the vase to show him standing up. How nice it would be to suggest contextualizations of a more detailed and sophisticated kind—for instance, properly to situate, in relation to the krater which bears it (*Cat. 28* (Fig. 4.2)), the image of Polyphemus at his barbecue. Unfortunately, the evidence just is not there.

Among representations of Cyclopes are several individual portrait heads and full-body figurines displaying anatomical abnormality. In most cases it is frustratingly difficult to reconstruct a shaping context, but a partial exception is the statuette from the sanctuary of the Cabiri in Thebes (*Cat. 30* (Fig. 4.10)).[4] Recumbent,

[2] Rightly noted by Hall (2008: 38).
[3] Krauskopf (2006).
[4] On the sanctuary, see Wolters and Bruns (1940); Schachter (1986: 66–110).

big-eared, and sporting a huge circular eye in the middle of his forehead, this unprepossessing character clutches a drinking cup. What links the statuette to its context? The Cabiri were an enigmatic bunch, whose myths, together with the associated rites, are hard to make sense of because the evidence from different sites—Samothrace, Lemnos, Thebes—is rather disparate.[5] Although on Lemnos the Cabiri were associated with Hephaestus and with metalworking, the Theban cult seems to have had a more agricultural feel, as perhaps suggested by numerous finds of votive metal bulls. One distinctive feature of the Theban sanctuary is the presence of numerous wine vessels known as *kantharoi*, depicting comically distorted figures.[6] Since the Cabiri are associated in myth with orgiastic drunkenness, these caricatures could be expressing that aspect of their mythological profile.[7] This is the more plausible if the drunkenness were a feature of Cabiric cult. On one view, such drinking took place as a joyful conclusion to a puberty initiation ceremony;[8] alternatively it may have belonged to a 'carnivalesque' ritual with a more Dionysiac flavour, perhaps involving parodic theatrical performances.[9] Whether the Cyclops figurine itself had a cultic function is unknowable. The Cyclops whom it embodies certainly looks the worse for wear, and his drinking cup may well hint at the local ritualized drinking. Could there also be a connection with the blacksmith Cyclopes, given the association (at least on Lemnos) between the Cabiri and metalworking? This has to be mere speculation.

Generic differentiation applies also to stories told about Polyphemus and Galatea. For epic poets, the couple's relationship held few attractions; major exceptions are Ovid's brilliant rebranding of the genre in *Metamorphoses*, and Nonnus' Galatea-related vignettes in his *Dionysiaca*. The preferred genre is pastoral, Virgilian as well as Theocritean; its blend of wistful eroticism and ironically observed naivety offers the perfect home for Beauty and her Beast.[10] But the range of generic variation goes wider. Lucian's waspish dialogues and Philostratus' visionary readings of art create new and contrastingly distinctive tones for the relationship. We might be able to say the same for Philoxenus' dithyramb, if only more of it had survived.

As for visual treatments, a seemingly incidental but actually significant feature of many Roman wall paintings and mosaics was their considerable size. One consequence of this for portrayals of Polyphemus and Galatea was that artists could enhance the effect of that easily over-fetishized but still crucial concept of 'the gaze', by situating the gazers at an appreciable distance from one another. Another concomitant of size was to permit the framing of human figures within a complex and elaborate natural setting, which sometimes dwarfs and dominates them. Thus

[5] Bremmer (2014: 37–48); cf. also Bowden (2010) 49–67; Fowler (2013: 37–43).

[6] Mitchell (2009: 248–79).

[7] Drunkenness: e.g. frags. of Aesch. *Kabeiroi* (*TrGF* iii. 214).

[8] Bremmer (2014: 45).

[9] Wolters and Bruns (1940: 127); Schmaltz (1974: 122–3); Mitchell (2009: 279).

[10] Virgilian: cf. Moeris in *Ecl.* 9.39–43: 'Come to me, Galatea! What pleasure lives in waves?'.

landscape, which had always played a fundamental role in Cyclopean myths, achieved even greater prominence. A more general contextual aspect of these images concerns the public that viewed them. Such consumers of art evidently had a taste for overt eroticism, whose repertoire recalls the explicitness of love elegy rather than the greater discretion of pastoral. Taken together, these characteristics constituted an artistic form that made a lasting contribution to the imagining of the Polyphemus and Galatea relationship, not just by dynamically reconfiguring motifs and emphases already developed in texts, but also by striking out in new and uniquely artistic directions.

Narrative voices

If Cyclopean myths are shaped by the overarching demands of medium and genre, they are also inflected by internal narrative considerations.[11] No text exemplifies this more clearly than book 9 of the *Odyssey*, narrated by Odysseus to the Phaeacians as part of his self-glorifying presentation of his adventures. Far from providing an 'objective' account of what happened, Odysseus tailors his narrative to the interests of his hosts, and thus to his own self-interest as well. Why does he dwell so much on Polyphemus' outrageous perversion of hospitality? Because it sends out, by antithesis, a 'programmatic message' to the Phaeacians, encouraging *them* to be good hosts to their present guest.[12] Why was a story about Cyclopean aggression particularly likely to gain the favour of a Phaeacian audience? Because the Phaeacians had themselves suffered harassment at the hands of the Cyclopes, and had even been obliged to emigrate in order to escape further harm.[13] Yet the significance of book 9 is not determined exclusively by the narrative of Odysseus, but also, more broadly, by that of Homer himself (or—if uncertainty about the poem's composition induces reluctance to name the poet so specifically—the 'primary' or 'external' or 'omniscient' narrator').[14] That is to say, Odysseus' narrative has to be situated in relation to the overall thrust of the poem; and the two may not always coincide. Long after Odysseus has left Phaeacia, an intriguing parallel emerges between the return of Polyphemus to his home to discover intruders consuming his food, and the return of Odysseus to *his* home to find a comparable

[11] This clearly applies much more to texts than to art. The extent to which one can reasonably identify divergent 'narrative voices' in a work of art is debatable, though there are some very good candidates. Velázquez's astonishing *Las Meninas*, with its multi-layered figuration and its mirror, would be one; so would Magritte's image of a pipe entitled *Ceci n'est pas une pipe*. Any image that depicts another image could *potentially* fall into this category, though not all do: on an Attic red-figure cup depicting Dionysiac scenes, a maenad clutches *another* cup depicting a satyr—in this *mise en abîme*, the secondary 'voice' exactly echoes the tone of the primary one (*CVA* Berlin (2) Pl. 87, 2 = *LIMC* 'Dionysos' no. 41).

[12] 'Programmatic message': Burgess (2015: 55–6); cf. Most (1989).

[13] *Od.* 6.4–10; see S. West (2013: 193).

[14] For the terms, see De Jong (2001: 223).

crisis.[15] As Egbert Bakker puts it: 'Odysseus...has much more in common with the Cyclops than he would have liked his audience to think when he presented the Cyclopes as lawless brutes without agriculture or political culture.'[16] Many such retrospective subtleties unfold through the poem's counterpoint of narrative voices.[17]

No less narratologically intricate is Virgil's account in the *Aeneid*. The leading internal narrator in book 3 is Aeneas, who is relating to the spellbound Carthaginians (modelled on the equally spellbound Homeric Phaeacians) the tale of *his* journey from Troy—not a return *towards* home, of course, but a desperate attempt to get away from it. Instrumental in the destruction of that Trojan home was none other than the duplicitous Odysseus/Ulysses, a fact that cannot but colour Aeneas' tale. Within that tale, the secondary internal narrator of the Cyclops episode is the traumatized Achaemenides, who recollects Polyphemus' ghastliness and acknowledges Ulysses as the one who blinded him, though the epithet he applies to his former leader is *infelix*, 'unfortunate' (613) rather than anything more positively heroic (Aeneas later repeats the epithet (691)). When Achaemenides finishes speaking, Aeneas complements this account of Polyphemus' moral hideousness with his own description of the ogre's disfigurement (the Cyclops has just come into sight). Aeneas adds that the Trojans then magnanimously took the wretched Achaemenides on board ship: though a Greek, he merited their help. Is the implied subtext from Aeneas, seeing beyond the more limited perspective of Achaemenides to the Carthaginians who make up his own audience, that different peoples—Greeks and Trojans, but also Trojans and Carthaginians—can and should see the good in each other?

The interplay of narrative perspectives is no less intricate when it comes to Polyphemus and Galatea. The Theocritean Polyphemus lacks the ability to see himself as others see him; in the two Cyclops *Idylls*, contrasting voices express just this point. In *Idyll* 11, the external narrator frames the poem, beginning by describing Polyphemus' lovesickness, and ending by suggesting that the ogre's relief comes from singing about it. But it is Polyphemus' own voice that takes the lion's share, first in would-be persuasive words addressed to Galatea, then in soliloquy ('Snap out of it!'). Galatea herself is given no voice, so the irony has to emerge from Polyphemus' own self-unawareness. 'It's all my mother's fault! She can see me getting thinner by the day, but she never says anything nice to you about me. She'll be sorry: I'll tell her that I have a headache, and that both my feet are sore' (67–71).

Idyll 6 is even more narratologically complex. Again there is a framing, external narrator, who situates a song contest between herdsmen at a moment of perfect balance—in summer, at midday (not even a shadow to complicate the picture)—and concludes it with no less total poise: the contest is a draw, and the

[15] See Newton (1983: 142), for Odysseus as a 'metaphorical Cyclops' in book 17.

[16] Bakker (2013: 73).

[17] For another example, see Clare (2002) on varying presentations of Cyclopean monstrosity depending on who the narrator is.

competitors exchange musical instruments. But their two songs are not so symmetrical. This is no dialogue between Galatea and Polyphemus, for the nymph is again voiceless. The first singer, Daphnis, addresses Polyphemus, but views him and Galatea from the outside: the nymph is a coquette who gives herself airs (15). The second singer, Damoetas, impersonates the Cyclops and describes how he (Damoetas-as-Cyclops) regards Galatea: she is jealous of 'me' (27). That no one wins the contest is Theocritus' way of saying: read the Polyphemus–Galatea relationship either way, since these two songs will not resolve the dilemma for you.[18]

Most subtle of all is the account by Ovid, supreme maestro of polychoral narrative. His Polyphemus and Galatea episode is positioned within the tale, told by Ovid-as-external-narrator, of Aeneas' journey from Troy. More precisely, the narration occurs at the moment when the Trojans arrive at the rocky lair of Scylla, former maiden and now savage and semi-canine monster. The external narrator steps back from the present to evoke a time before Scylla's metamorphosis, when she used to chat with the Nereids about her rejection of male suitors. While combing Scylla's hair, Galatea relives her own comparable experiences. She remembers the beauty of her young lover Acis, cites Polyphemus' hyperbolic attempts to persuade her (a third level of narration), and finally recalls Acis' eventual metamorphosis. As Acis/river flows into Galatea/sea, so the Galateocentric narrative flows into the story of Scylla and her part-human, part-piscine suitor Glaucus. Since Scylla, like Galatea, rejects her suitor, Glaucus tries to inveigle the witchlike Circe into giving him a magic herb to inflame Scylla's passion. But Circe has herself fallen for Glaucus, and, when *she* suffers *his* rejection, maliciously supplies him with a poison that causes Scylla's horrific disfigurement. To complete the circle, Scylla, now monstrously hybrid, takes out her resentment on Circe's ex-lover Ulysses/Odysseus.[19] The whole mythical complex thus embraces Ulysses as well as Galatea, and the overarching story pattern results in the symbolic punishment of the wily hero, which stems associatively and symbolically, if not logically, from the emotional sisterhood of Galatea and Scylla. Desire reciprocated, desire spurned; repellent hybridity, seductive hybridity.[20] The blend of voices, the play of motifs: all this is orchestrated, with sublime bravura, through a kaleidoscope of narrative filters.

Cyclopean 'Types': Contrasts and Overlaps

It does occasionally happen that an ancient source explicitly highlights differences between types of Cyclopes. The most notable example is the scholion on the

[18] See Hunter (1999) for much more detail.

[19] On all this, see Hopman (2012: 233–53).

[20] Sexy, rivery Acis stands waist deep in water (*Met.* 13.893–4), both like and not like monstrous, marine Glaucus, who is anthropomorphic down to the waist but fishy below it (958–63).

Greek historian Hellanicus (*fl.* 5th cent. BCE), referring to three Cyclopean *genē*: 'the ones who built Mycenae, the ones connected to Polyphemus, and the ones who are gods.'[21] Far more often, however, the contrasts are passed over in silence, with no attempt being made to signal that there *are* contrasts. Characteristic in this respect are the two principal appearances of the Cyclopes in the *Aeneid*. In book 3 they appear as horrific, mountain-dwelling giants who lend support to their blinded fellow Cyclops, the pastoral cannibal *par excellence*. In book 8 they are busy carrying out commissions for various of the Olympians, work that they put aside when Vulcan instructs them to make glorious new armour for Aeneas. Nowhere does Virgil cross-refer from one group to the other, even though both are located near or under Etna. This is typical of most ancient accounts, which, so far from finding something contradictory in Cyclopean diversity, find it not even worth registering. Yet for the outside interpreter the problem remains: how can mythological characters exhibit such dissimilarities and still share the same name? It is time to return to the question of homonyms.[22]

It would be idle to deny the discrepancies. The Homeric, pastoral Polyphemus is a son of Poseidon (in Euripides, so are the other Cyclopes); in Hesiod the father of the weapons manufacturers is Ouranos. The Homeric ogres stand proudly aloof from the gods; their metalworking homonyms in Hesiod, Callimachus, and Virgil, and in visual art (fine examples at *Cat. 63* (Fig. 5.13) and *64* (Fig. 4.1)), cooperate willingly with the gods and with each other. In fact, the blacksmiths could be cited as perfect models of reciprocal collaboration, as in Virgil's simile from his fourth *Georgic* describing the worker bees (170–8):

> And as, when the Cyclopes in haste forge bolts from tough ore, some with oxhide bellows make the blasts come and go, others dip the hissing brass in the lake, while Aetna groans under the anvils laid upon her; they, with mighty force, now one, now another, raise their arms in measured cadence, and turn the iron with gripping tongs—even so, if we may compare small things with great, an inborn love of gain spurs on the Attic bees, each after its own office.[23]

In the same vein, the poet Statius (1st cent. CE) described the Cyclopes within Etna as being 'in peaceful agreement with each other'.[24] The mason Cyclopes too collaborate on their monumental construction projects, though our sources rarely stress the fact; presumably it was too obvious to need saying. They also work for others—namely, those (usually mortals) who commission their constructions. Nothing could be less reminiscent of the Homeric and Euripidean Cyclopes, monadic in their social isolation; whatever work *they* do (and the Euripidean Polyphemus does not do much, since he has his satyr slaves to work for him),

[21] Hellanicus Lesbius Fr. 88 Fowler. [22] See pp. 28–32. [23] Trans. H. R. Fairclough.
[24] Stat. *Theb.* 1.458–9.

there is no evidence that they do it in unison. Related to the opposition between collaboration and isolation is another behavioural divergence, which contrasts destructiveness with its opposite. Whereas the mason Cyclopes build walls by putting rocks *together*, one of Polyphemus' characteristic gestures is to hurl boulders with murderous intent, notably at Odysseus and at Acis; Nonnus' Cyclopes too are aggressive rock-hurlers.[25] Yet, even if different Cyclopes put boulders to different uses, the general habit of manipulating rocks is one that they have in common. This idea of shared characteristics points us towards something that previous analyses of Cyclopean mythology have consistently understated: the numerous and striking *overlaps* between the 'types'.

The use of the hands is one example. It obviously applies to the metalworkers and the builders, but also in several respects to Polyphemus, not least because he tears his (human) food apart with his hands, and because, when blinded, he has to feel his way around. Monocularity is another obvious common factor, being ascribed not only to the weapons-makers and the smiths (for example, in Hesiod and Callimachus) and to Polyphemus and his fellow ogres (for example, in Euripides, Theocritus, *Aeneid* 3, and Philostratus, not to mention in art), but also, albeit very rarely, to the builders (Antipater of Sidon (2nd cent. BCE) in *Anth. Pal.* 7.748). Then there is immensity. Both Polyphemus and the blacksmiths are as big as a mountain (*Od.* 9. 190–2; Callim. *H.Art.* 52), while Nonnus' Halimedes is as high as the clouds (*Dion.* 39.221). In *Aeneid* 8, there is arguably another overlap between Polyphemus and the smiths, albeit by proxy, in the person of one of Hercules' opponents. The horrible ogre Cacus, primordial denizen of the Aventine hill in Rome, has his lair in a cavern, whose doorway he blocks with a huge boulder; so far, so Polyphemus-like. But he is also a fire-breathing son of Vulcan, adding a whiff of the scorching Etnaean forge to his Homeric pedigree.

The depiction of Cacus as a cave-dweller highlights another shared characteristic of the Cyclopes. That Polyphemus lives in a cave is a fundamental aspect of his existence in the *Odyssey*, in Euripides, and in numerous other textual accounts, from Theocritus to Synesius; the same setting features in artistic representations from all periods, nowhere more impressively than on the mosaic from Piazza Armerina (*Cat.* 72 (Fig. 3.7)). But other Cyclopes have their own speleological connections. Virgil's smiths work in a vast cavern deep under Volcania (*Aen.* 8.416–25); their equivalents in Valerius Flaccus' *Argonautica* plunge into the Sicilian sea to take a cooling break from their labour in the cave furnaces (7.647–8); Strabo refers to 'Cyclopean' caves, with labyrinths constructed in them, near Nauplia (8.6.2, 11); the Cyclopes were the first to make weapons in a cave on Euboea (*POxy* 10.1241, col. iv, 12–14). In Greek and Roman perception, to be a cave-dweller, or to work in a cave, is a marker of marginality, of separateness from

[25] *Dion.* 39.340–2.

more 'central' social space.[26] But it can also be—via a structural equivalence between space and time—a marker of primordiality, the condition of belonging 'at the beginning'. This characteristic too is shared by various groups of Cyclopes. The masons build the walls that are the *pre*requisite of a civilized polity; the Hesiodic makers of thunder and lightning do their job when Zeus' supremacy *is in the process of being established*; the Cyclopes were *the first* to make weapons (Istros (perhaps mid-3rd cent. BCE) in *FGrH* 334 fr.71); they taught Hephaestus and Athene craftsmanship, implying that they were *older* than that pair of Olympians (*Orphic Hymn*, fr. 269 Bernabé). Hence in the *Laws* Plato could liken to the Cyclopes the early, immediately post-diluvian humans who lived as hill shepherds. However, this sense of anteriority needs to be clarified. In none of their roles are the Cyclopes *wholly* uncivilized. The metalworkers and the masons are in the business of *making* things, and making belongs to the cultural world. Even the Homeric Polyphemus has built a rough wall and fence to enclose the yard outside his cave (*Od.* 9.184–6).[27] There is no absolute distinction, then, between Polyphemus and the masonic Cyclopes—certainly not a distinction that can be mapped on to the nature/culture polarity.

One more overlap between the types must be mentioned. It is not the least important, but it is probably the least noticed. This is the repeated association between the Cyclopes and fire.

Associations between fire and the builder Cyclopes are thin on the ground, but they can be found. As we saw earlier, Eratosthenes related that the Cyclopes fabricated a lidded structure to conceal the fire of thunderbolts within it.[28] In *Aeneid* book 6, Virgil describes the mighty walls of Pluto's palace as 'forged in the furnaces of the Cyclopes' (630–1)—an amalgam of the roles of mason and metalworker, and a demonstration that the Cyclopes might use fire even when building walls: for *some* walls, exceptionally and extraordinarily, might be made of metal.

So far as the pastoral ogres are concerned—Polyphemus in particular—the presence of fire is pervasive. From their vantage point on Goat Island, the Greeks descry smoke rising from Cyclopean territory (*Od.* 9.166–7): evidently the inhabitants possess at least one of the rudiments of culture. Indigene and intruders alike deploy fire for their own uses: Polyphemus for light and warmth (but apparently not for cooking), the Greeks to heat the olive-wood stake. One of the similes used to describe the blinding evokes the sounds and textures of the tempering of red-hot metal, anticipating a central feature of the work of the metalworking Cyclopes, though in this case Polyphemus is the victim of fire rather than its master. In Euripides' *Cyclops* Polyphemus uses fire to keep warm, but above all to boil, roast, and grill human flesh; Odysseus employs it to heat the stake, invoking

[26] Buxton (1994: 104–8). [27] Well noted by Nieto Hernández (2000: 360 n. 41).

[28] Eratosth. [*Cat.*] 39; see Sanz Morales (2002: 70–1 with n. 142); and see p. 37 n. 5.

'Hephaestus, Lord of Etna' (599), another anticipatory connection with the 'other' Cyclopes. Contrastingly gruesome images of pre-cannibalistic cooking can be seen on the krater and the amphora from Campania (*Cat. 28* (Fig. 4.2) and *Cat. 18* (Fig. 5.10)); far less graphic, and merely *suggestive* of fire, is the image of torch-bearing satyrs bouncing around the scene of the blinding on the Lucanian krater (*Cat. 27* (Fig. 4.13)). All three images are in their way unique, and so is an oinochoe depicting two sequential scenes synchronically: the blinding itself, and the evidently prior heating of the stake in a fire, complete with logs and flames (*Cat. 17*).

If the herdsman outwitted by Odysseus suffers one sort of combustion, the lover rejected by Galatea suffers another. The Theocritean ogre says he could put up with his soul, as well as his eye, being burnt by her (11.52–3), a nicely paradoxical contrast with his description of Etna as a place of ice-cool snowfields (47–8).[29] As he looks towards the sea, the single eyeball of Hermesianax's Cyclops burns, presumably with love's passion.[30] Ovid's ogre seethes and rages with the fire, not just of love, but of jealousy: he seems to have Etna itself violently burning within him (*Met.* 13.867–9).

The overlap with the metalworking Cyclopes is clear and deliberate. The furnaces beneath Etna and the neighbouring Aeolian islands are where they toil in order to heat and temper and hammer. Greek and especially Roman authors dwell on the sweat, the noise, and above all the stifling heat of the Cyclopean forge.[31] In visual images the fire tends to be implicit; an exception is a Roman sarcophagus depicting an anvil with flames rising above it (*Cat. 70*).

Making a chariot for Mars, or a shield for Aeneas, is one thing; forging a thunderbolt is quite another. The Virgilian metalworkers include all three items in their product range, but it is what Pindar calls the 'warlike thunderbolt of ever-flowing fire' that signals the Cyclopes' importance in the divine scheme.[32] Their involvement with this supreme embodiment of aggressive, cosmic fire goes back to Hesiod's account of the establishment of Zeus' sovereignty in the *Theogony*. But a more extensive and certainly more spectacular account is provided by Nonnus, when he describes how the Cyclopes use weapons that *imitate* those of the supreme god. As with the authentic thunderbolt and lightning of Zeus, the fake versions are all about fire (28.172–94):

> Now the grim Cyclopes, allies of Zeus, surrounded the fighters. Argilipos lifted a shining torch and shed light on the throng through the dark clouds. He was armed with a fire-barbed thunderbolt from the underworld, and fought with

[29] Hunter (1999) on Theoc. 11.51; Cusset (2004: 53–4). [30] See p. 217.

[31] e.g. Callim. *H.Art.* 60; Hor. *Od.* 1.4.7–8; Verg. *Aen.* 8.416–53; Val. Flacc. *Arg.* 7.647–8; Sil. *Pun.* 4.433–4.

[32] Verg. *Aen.* 8.426–32; Pind. *Pyth.* 1.5–6.

> firebrands; the swarthy Indians trembled, amazed at that fire so like the heavenly firebursts. A champion all of fire he was, and the sparks of earthborn lightning showered upon the enemies' heads... Steropes also was armed with a mimic lightning, which he brandished like the lightningflash of the sky, but an inextinguishable brand, the child of Hesperian flame, seed of Sicilian fire and that smoky [Cyclopean] forge...[33]

In spite of Nonnus' brilliantly unconventional insistence on mimicry, his account consolidates the powerful symbolic connection between the Cyclopes and fire.

There are two ways to deal with the pervasiveness of Cyclopean fire. One option is to relate it to the *origins* of the Cyclopes, perhaps regarding it even as a key to those origins. The other is to consider it as a leitmotif in the *development* of Cyclopean myths during the period for which we have substantial evidence. We take each possibility in turn.

If fire were to count as an origin, it would presumably have to be in one of three ways. It might be that either (1) the Sun or (2) the crater of a volcano could be regarded as the underlying idea that generated the myth of the ogre with a single, round eye. Alternatively (3) one might go with the view of Samson Eitrem that 'fire demons', sometimes malevolent and sometimes benevolent, were the ultimate ancestors of the Cyclopes. The solar explanation is too reductionist: it leaves most of the rich detail of Cyclopean myths unexplained. True, the Sun looks circular (like the Cyclopean eye) and emits light (as eyes were commonly believed to do). But the time has long passed since solar gods and heroes dominated the interpretative agenda, for the very good reason that to detect the Sun lurking allegorically behind dozens, even hundreds of myths grossly reduces the capacity of those myths to mean different things. The second, volcanic approach has more to be said for it, in view of the manifest connection between Cyclopean myths and Mount Etna.[34] But *as an origin* it leaves the builders poorly accounted for, and contributes nothing to the explanation of Polyphemus as herdsman. What of the third explanation, that proposed by Samson Eitrem, in terms of 'fire demons'?[35] This has the merit of highlighting the fact that the Cyclopes can be both creators and destroyers, an ambiguity shared by fire itself. Nor is it an objection to Eitrem's view that in extant texts and images the Cyclopes are users rather than embodiments of fire. After all, Hephaestus combined both characteristics, and there is in principle no reason why the same could not be true of the Cyclopes. There are certainly enough fiery aspects of their mythology to make Eitrem's case worth taking seriously—more so than Schoemann's intriguing but ultimately less convincing view that the mason Cyclopes were the originals (apart from anything

[33] Trans. W. H. D. Rouse, adapted.
[34] See e.g. Leroux (2004: 59), detailing volcanic aspects of Polyphemus in Verg. *Aen*. 3.
[35] See p. 30.

else, the masons are totally absent from early, and indeed later art).[36] Nevertheless, there are also arguments against Eitrem's view, all of which relate to the fact that, once we set aside the Hesiodic Cyclopes, evidence for the equation of Cyclopes with fire is nugatory *in the earlier part of the surviving tradition*. For instance: in early art, fire is of little importance in representations of the Cyclopes; the Polyphemus of the *Odyssey* is a much less plausible candidate for a fire demon than is (say) Cacus; to derive the wall-builders from fire demons requires a huge leap of faith. So fire demons too, like the Sun and the volcano, ultimately fail to convince as a unitary explanation of *origins*.

What attention to the theme of fire *can* do, however, is to highlight an important feature of the *development* of Cyclopean myths in our extant textual and visual evidence, a development involving an increasingly noticeable overlap between the different Cyclopean types, and in particular a growing relevance of the location on Etna.[37] More specifically, there is a recurrent interplay between fire and liquid: in the act of blinding; in the stand-off between fired-up Polyphemus and watery Galatea; in the tempering of metal by the blacksmiths; in the fiery/fluid nature of the volcano where the post-Homeric Cyclopes live. This interplay promotes the drawing-together of different Cyclopean strands. Taken in combination with ideas of marginality, working with the hands, and primordiality, the notion of fire plays a major role, over time, in forging links between the homonyms, banishing the sense that all that the diverse Cyclopes share is a name.

Thinking with Cyclopes

As extravagant in its variety as it was formidable in its imaginative power, Greek, and later Roman, mythology developed multiple variations on the theme that physical peculiarity could be combined with behavioural abnormality. Such linkages of characteristics took various forms. One recurrent kind of physical monstrosity involves hybridity. A typical case of animal hybridity is the Chimera: lion, goat, snake, with the add-on super-weapon of being able to breathe fire. Animal–human hybridity is even more common: Harpies, Centaurs, and satyrs are examples of collectivities; the Minotaur, Pan, and Scylla stand out among the individuals. Each of these groups or individuals displays distinctive behavioural traits that accompany their physical anomaly, traits that are occasionally benign, but more often dangerous. Another sort of departure from the physical norm involves some kind of lack or absence. A classic case is that of the Amazons, who *could* be imagined as having deliberately seared one breast in order to facilitate the use of the bow and javelin. Once more, such an anomaly went along with a

[36] Schoemann (1859), and see p. 29.

[37] See Buxton (2016, 2017a).

perceived behavioural oddity: in this case, that of aggressive masculinity. What of the monstrosity of the Cyclopes? As for their physique, we have already seen ample evidence of the range of possibilities; but majority opinion was that the nature of the abnormality was a *lack*. The question of their behavioural abnormality is even more complicated. Frequently a Cyclops will demonstrate hyper-aggressive, anti-social violence and uncontrollable, transgressive appetite, especially in the matter of diet, though sometimes also in relation to sex. Yet Cyclopes can also exhibit control, order, and skill, whether collectively and cooperatively (building, metalworking) or individually (herding). This unique constellation of characteristics offered rich possibilities for later writers, artists, and others to revisit ancient traditions and redirect them for freshly innovative imaginative purposes. In the remainder of this book we shall follow some of the paths that these innovators have taken.

PART II

AFTER ANTIQUITY

New Life In Old Ogres

10
From the Medieval to the Baroque

The mentalities of the medieval and early modern worlds were home to countless monsters.[1] Not all froze the blood in the manner of Beowulf's deadly foes Grendel and his mother, but they were still a haunting feature of popular and literary storytelling, from the trolls of Norse saga and the dragons of folklore and hagiography to the werewolf in Marie de France's lay *Bisclavret*, not forgetting Shakespeare's Caliban.[2] Monsters also continued to grip the imagination within the most powerful religious traditions of the period. Behemoth and Leviathan, Satan and his Islamic near-correlate Iblis, figured as variously terrifying instantiations of the moral 'other'. Amid all these creatures, the monsters of classical antiquity never lost their resonance, at first through continuing retellings in Latin and vernacular texts and in visual media, and later through the impact of Greek scholarship on Renaissance humanism.

Within these contexts the Cyclopes enjoy several sorts of presence. The first sort situates them as one of several 'monstrous races', their distinguishing characteristic being, unsurprisingly, monocularity. The second sort involves not the Cyclopes as a group, but Polyphemus in particular, both in his dealings with Ulysses and in his frustrated love for Galatea. The third sort focuses on a variety of individual wild giants, often but not always one-eyed, who inhabit folklore, and whose confrontations with a heroic adversary have often been regarded as *comparanda* for the Odysseus–Polyphemus encounter. Next come re-presentations of the Cyclopes in their role as blacksmiths. The two remaining presences are linked by the concept of the extra-urban: the grotto in the garden; and the pastoral mode in poetry, prose, and opera. We shall review each of these presences in turn.

Monstrous Races

In the medieval period and in the Renaissance it was widely held that in certain far-flung or otherwise marginal locations you might encounter a variety of monstrous peoples, whose monstrosity reproduces itself from generation to generation rather than being the product of a series of one-off, portentous births. The strangeness of these races consists in one or another astonishing peculiarity,

[1] Bildhauer and Mills (2003).
[2] Steel (2012: 258–9). Dragons: Ogden (2013: 383–426). Caliban: Vaughan and Vaughan (1991).

Cyclops: The Myth and its Cultural History. Mercedes Aguirre and Richard Buxton, Oxford University Press (2020).

DOI: 10.1093/oso/9780198713777.001.0001

usually involving hypertrophy, hybridity, or anatomical displacement.[3] Typical examples are Giants, Pygmies, Centaurs, Cynocephali ('Dog-Heads'), Blemmyae (headless men with their faces on their chests), Sciapods or Sciopods (their huge single foot acts as a parasol as its owner lies supine), All-Ears (whose floppy appendages reach the ground and serve as blankets), and Astomi (mouthless people who live on aromas, especially those emanating from apples).[4] Besides the anatomically idiosyncratic, you might also meet those whose peculiarity was behavioural, especially dietary. Best known are the Anthropophagi, immortalized in Othello's epic tales of derring-do, which, not surprisingly, won Desdemona's heart:

> Wherein of antres vast and deserts idle,
> Rough quarries, rocks, and hills whose heads touch heaven,
> It was my hint to speak—such was the process.
> And of the Cannibals that each other eat,
> The Anthropophagi, and men whose heads
> Do grow beneath their shoulders.[5]

Amongst these strange races there dwells a group distinguished by a single, centrally positioned eye; they are often but not always named as Cyclopes. In spite of obvious differences, all the races constitute variations on the same theme, which is why they are so often listed together or pictured side by side as equivalent divergences from the norm (*Cat. 73*, *74*, *75*, *80*, and *88*). Like exhibits in a freak show, their sole function is to appear intriguingly strange to those who visit them as readers or viewers. Embedded in no narrative, they exist in a permanent ethnographic present.

Post-classical traditions about the monstrous races took their cue from Pliny the Elder, who was in his turn following Greek predecessors such as Herodotus, Ctesias, and Megasthenes (4th–3rd cent. BCE). Pliny's account, and that of his excerptor Solinus, would be drawn on by Augustine and Martianus Capella (both 4th–5th cent. CE), as well as by Isidore of Seville, who observed: 'Just as, in individual nations, there are instances of monstrous people, so in the whole of humankind there are certain monstrous races, like the Giants, the Cynocephali…the Cyclopes, and others.'[6] The same ideas were repeated by numerous subsequent tale-tellers, not least those describing the exotic peoples allegedly encountered by Alexander the Great.[7]

[3] Steel (2012: 261).

[4] See especially Friedman (2000); also Wittkower (1942); Husband (1980); Kappler (1999: 120–72); Bildhauer and Mills (2003). Dog-Heads: Bartlett (2008: 94–110).

[5] *Othello*, I.iii.140–5. Gonzalo in *The Tempest* also mentions 'men whose heads stood in their breasts' (III.iii.46–7).

[6] *Etym.* 11.3.12; trans. Barney et al. (2006).

[7] Friedman (2000: 6–7). See esp. *The Greek Alexander Romance* 2.33, trans. Stoneman (1991: 115–16).

Regarding this millennium-long tradition of monstrosity, three strands are worth highlighting. The first concerns location. From classical antiquity till the Middle Ages, preferred homes for the monstrous races were India, Africa, and 'the Orient'; the more remote, the better. Illustrative of the placement of the races are the tales told about Pres(by)ter John, whose fabulous realm was variously situated in India, Central Asia, and Ethiopia. The marvels housed in the kingdom of this legendary Christian patriarch were detailed in the spurious but hugely popular *Letter of Prester John* (*c*.1160); the extraordinary menagerie included pygmies, centaurs, and Cyclopes.[8] Later, as the world shrank in the wake of journeys of exploration from Marco Polo to Magellan, consolidated in due course with imperialistic conquest, the races withdrew to the far north and the Americas.[9] Although Marco Polo himself had little to say about the Plinian races, manuscripts of his *Travels* do illustrate them, notably a copy in Paris that places them (including a Cyclops) in Siberia (*Cat. 74*); the illustrators go well beyond Marco in emphasizing the grotesque.[10] Columbus expected to find such strange peoples on his voyage to 'the Indies', but his experience did not bear out the rumours.[11] Nevertheless, his expectations are as significant as the balanced judgement that countermanded them. When the Governor of Cuba instructed Hernán Cortés to look for the All-Ears and the Dog-Heads, his order was based on a cluster of inherited images, which, to quote Anthony Pagden, 'were thought to constitute a real world of nature in the remoter areas of the world where, precisely because they were remote, the unusual and the fantastic were thought to be the norm'.[12]

It is true that monstrous races could also be found closer to home, even in the heart of the 'known' world. According to the eighth-century *Liber monstrorum de diversis generibus*, there was a race of men in Sicily, near Etna, with one central eye as broad as a shield; they were taller than the highest trees, and anthropophagous.[13] Getting on for eight centuries later, the Leuven-based astronomer and astrologer Cornelius Gemma wrote about wild races, including Cyclopes, that 'it is not necessary to go to the New World to find beings of this sort; most of them

[8] See van Duzer (2012: 408 with nn. 86, 87); also Helleiner (1959). The text of the *Letter of Prester John* can be found in Zarncke (1879), repr. in Beckingham and Hamilton (1996: 40–102); Eng. trans. Uebel (2005: 155–60).

[9] Friedman (2000: 1). For the Americas, see Pagden (1982: esp. 10, 80–1). In modern times alien beings have migrated from the no-longer-unexplored jungle or forest to the infinitude of still-to-be-discovered planets; see C. S. Lewis (1982: 90–1).

[10] Van Duzer (2012: 409–11); also Gousset (2002) and Strickland (2008). For variability in the title of the work conventionally called the *Travels*, but also known as the *Devisement dou monde* [*sic*], see Akbari in Akbari and Iannucci (2008: 9–10). Illustrators and the grotesque: Zhang (2008: 285–6).

[11] Columbus, *First Voyage*, in Jane (1930: 14); see Greenblatt (1991: 75); Kappler (1999: 57–8); Braham (2012: 19–22). Even if no Cyclopes were found by the real Columbus, his poeticized namesake would receive this warning from a prophetic bird in Fracastoro's epic poem *Syphilis* (1530): 'Nor will Cyclopes be lacking in our world' (3.187), text in Gardner (2013); cf. H. Hofmann (1995: 35).

[12] Fernández Navarrete et al. (1842: 403), with Friedman (2000: 199, 257–8 n. 12); Pagden (1982: 10).

[13] Bologna (1977: 46).

and others still more hideous can still be found here and there among us . . .'.[14] But such cases are unusual: most medieval and early modern monsters lived 'somewhere out there', on the margins. Sometimes these margins were textual: the borders of manuscript folios were a common site for illustrations of grotesquerie (an artistic practice that had its vigorous detractors).[15] Sometimes they were geographical: mountain fastnesses, swamps, deserts, positioned as far as possible from the world's perceived centre, Jerusalem; perhaps even as far as the Antipodes, at the world's southernmost extremity, where the inhabitants are the mirror image of ourselves: heads down, feet up. On Giacomo Gastaldi's world map (*c.*1561) the southern continent was shown as containing (among other strange inhabitants) dragons, a centaur, a manticore, and a couple of Cyclopes.[16] Only at the end of time—the Apocalypse—would monsters overrun the world *here*, where *we* live.[17]

This brings us to the second strand in medieval representations of monstrosity: religion. For a Christian monotheist it was unthinkable that the monstrous races were anything other than mortal; the Cyclopes and their ilk could be neither gods nor descendants of gods. But were they *human*? Augustine's broad-minded answer had been that, although we do not *have* to accept the existence of the monstrous races, if we *do* accept it, then we have to assume that they, like all the rest of us, were descended from Adam. Just like individuals born with monstrous defects, the monstrous races were created by God in his infinite wisdom (*De civ. D.* 16.8):

> If we assume that the subjects of those remarkable accounts are in fact men, it may be suggested that God decided to create some races in this way, so that we should not suppose that the wisdom with which he fashions the physical being of men has gone astray in the case of the monsters which are bound to be born among us of human parents; for that would be to regard the works of God's wisdom as the products of an imperfectly skilled craftsman. If so, it ought not to seem incongruous that, just as there are some monstrosities within the various races of mankind, so within the whole human race there should be certain monstrous peoples.[18]

However, in many early Christian commentaries, more common than such a humane acceptance of diversity was the unequivocally negative sense that the monstrous races constituted a perverse decline from perfection. What counted

[14] Gemma (1575: 1.6 (p. 76)), cited in Daston and Park (1998: 175).

[15] Harpham (1982: 34–5); Camille (1992). Detractors: Bernard of Clairvaux in Migne, *PL* clxxxii, cols 915–16.

[16] Remote habitats: Friedman (2000: 152). Antipodes: see the important article by Flint (1988); also Kappler (1999: 39–41) and van Duzer (2012: 416–17 with n. 129). Gastaldi's map: Schilder (1987: pl. 25 on 36–7); Shirley (2001: 122–3, with pl. 92 on 124–5).

[17] Van Duzer (2012: 433).

[18] Trans. H. Bettenson in Augustine (1984).

was their descent, not from Adam as the common human parent, but from either murderous Cain or transgressive Ham; by virtue of *those* morally dubious ancestries, they possessed dispositions both uncivilized and evil.[19] The fantastical, perhaps mid-fourteenth-century bestseller *The Travels of Sir John Mandeville* related (ch. 24) that women of the line of God-defying Nimrod copulated with fiends from Hell to produce the monstrous races.[20]

The third strand of medieval monstrosity is anthropological. As well as possessing a single, defining anatomical peculiarity, the races shared characteristics that marked them out as wild and uncivilized. They were typically imagined as naked and hairy, traits sometimes mitigated—or exacerbated—by the wearing of animal skins (*Cat. 74* and *75*). To go clothed was much rarer, though the Cyclops on the Hartmann Schedel *Nuremberg Chronicle* (late fifteenth century) wears a snazzy little dressing gown (*Cat. 80*).[21] They often wielded clubs, another signifier of marginality (again, *Cat. 74* and *75*). An unconventional diet, from apple-smelling to anthropophagy via elephant-eating and dog-milking, was another recurrent feature.[22] This whole pattern of attributes recalls in several respects the constellation of characteristics associated with the pastoral ogres of antiquity.

Do the three strands—locational, religious, anthropological—amount to a positive or a negative portrayal? The answer is far from straightforward. The Wild Man, in all his variations, *could* be seen as 'the antithesis of the civilized Christian', a negatively charged symbolic role that he played regularly in medieval Europe.[23] Illustrative here is a remarkable image from an early fifteenth-century illuminated manuscript of a French translation of the *Historia de Preliis Alexandri Magni*. A platoon of very tall, barefooted, headband-wearing, one-eyed 'Saracens' (i.e. Muslims) confronts soldiers from Alexander's army, who themselves are arrayed as crusaders (*Cat. 76* (Fig. 10.1)).[24] Yet, for all their monocularity, the Saracens look imposing rather than hideous, like a troop of ferocious Odins on the warpath. More evidently unpleasant is the genus of one-eyed ogres described in *The Travels of Sir John Mandeville*, who live on an island near Dundeya (the Andaman Islands) (ch. 22): 'there is a race of great stature, like giants, foul and horrible to look at; they have one eye only, in the middle of their foreheads. They eat raw flesh and raw fish.'[25] Such a description forms part of a much wider medieval perception that strange peoples tend also to be morally repulsive, even to the extent of committing the ultimate crime of cannibalism. Already in *Mandeville* a second species of giant, residing in an isle beyond the Vale Perilous, is explicitly said to be anthropophagous (ch. 31): like the Euripidean Cyclopes, they find the flesh of

[19] Friedman (2000: 30–1, 87–107). [20] See Moseley (1983: 145).

[21] See M. B. Campbell (2002) for nude Cyclopes in sixteenth-century costume books.

[22] Friedman (2000: 26–36). [23] For the quotation and the thought, see Schama (1995: 96–7).

[24] See Strickland (2012: 378–9, with fig. 17.8 there); more generally on 'Saracens': Strickland (2013).

[25] Moseley (1983: 137).

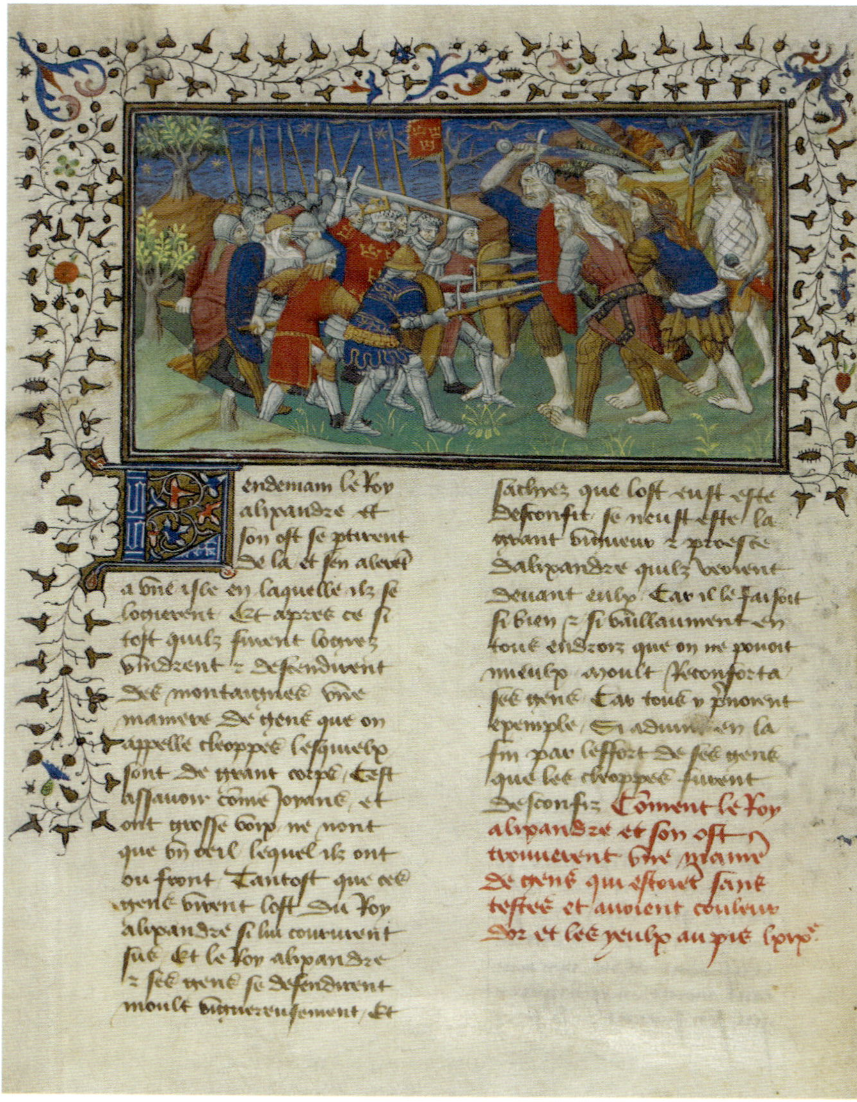

Fig. 10.1. Alexander's army fights a troop of Saracen Cyclopes. Manuscript of French trans. of *Historia de Preliis Alexandri Magni*, *c*.1420.

humans tastier than any other (they also drink milk).[26] Still more colossal, and even more barbaric, are the ogres who inhabit a yet more remote island (ch. 31):

> I had no desire to see them, for no man can go to that isle without being promptly strangled by those monsters. In these isles among these giants are sheep as big as oxen, but their wool is thick and coarse. I have often seen those sheep; and some men have often seen those giants catch people in the sea and go back to the land with two in one hand and two in the other, eating their flesh raw.[27]

The menacing image of the man-eating Tartar forms part of the same mindset.[28]

Yet such fear-driven negativity is not the whole story. In his early thirteenth-century *Historia Orientalis*, Jacques de Vitry, bishop of Acre, supplied the leaders of the Fifth Crusade with the historical and ethnographic low-down on the Holy Land and its neighbouring territories.[29] Along the way he took an intriguing step in the direction of seeing the world from a Cyclopean perspective. The monocular Cyclopes, Jacques observed, might be equally astonished at seeing two-eyed people like ourselves, as we would be at seeing people with one or even three eyes.[30] Even more positive was the fifteenth–sixteenth century theologian Giacomo Filippo Foresti, who waxed lyrical, in Augustinian fashion, about the significance of the full range of the Plinian races, including Cyclopes, within God's creation: 'There were also many kinds of monstrous men produced in various places... Indeed God himself, since He knew the proportions of likeness and diversity to employ in creating the beauty of the universe, certainly wished to produce monstrous men in the world.'[31] At all events, whether the monstrous races are viewed positively or negatively, common to all the descriptions is the focus on a single characteristic for each group. For the Cyclopes this marks a trend that recurs at several points in the reception of their myths, and that is in full swing today. What counts is their single eye: nothing else matters.

In the wake of Edward Said's path-breaking study of 'Orientalism', it became conventional wisdom to cast Western perceptions of 'the East' as indelibly stained with colonialism.[32] The portrayal of the monstrous races has been brought under the same interpretative umbrella. It is vital, then, to acknowledge the force of the case made by, for example, Longxi Zhang, that the pattern of 'othering' a foreign culture by de-civilizing it is by no means the prerogative of the colonialist West.[33]

26 Moseley (1983: 174).
27 Moseley (1983: 174–5). On Mandeville, see Akbari (2004). For giant animals, see pp. 147–8.
28 Strickland (2008: 38–44). 29 See Bird (2003). 30 *Hist. or.* ch. 92; cf. Eco (2007: 10).
31 Foresti (1538: fo. 13^r–13^v). See Friedman (2000: 184, with 254 n. 19).
32 E. W. Said (1978). 33 Zhang (2008).

It occurs throughout the world, not least in China, notably in the *Classic of Mountains and Seas*, a marvel-filled work dating from the third century BCE–second century CE. Combining myth with geography, and the ordinary with the fantastic, it charts a contrast of value between the Chinese centre and the foreign periphery. As Anne Birrell puts it: 'The sense of well-being, of order and harmony that pervaded the first five books gives way [in the remainder of the *Classic*] to the notion that beyond the sacral land of China are horrifying places and monstrous people.'[34] Among those mentioned are numerous outlandish peoples who bear an uncanny resemblance to the Western 'monstrous races', including a race with a single, centrally positioned eye.[35] Nor are the parallels restricted to China. As Jonathan Ratcliffe has brilliantly shown, the notion of a race of one-eyed giants dwelling on the remote fringes of civilization can be found in several inner-Asian locations.[36] For example, the Indian *Bṛhat Saṃhitā*, by the astronomer and astrologer Varahamihira, locates one-eyed men, as well as Amazons, to the north of India.[37] More gruesomely, Ukrainians told tales about the *edinookie*, a one-eyed race from 'somewhere far away over the seas', to whom the Mongols sold their slaves; the victims were fattened up and eaten by their merciless new owners.[38] No culture holds a monopoly of the capacity to project congenitally limited vision onto those located on or beyond the horizon of its own experience.

Not everyone regarded the stories about world's-end monsters as trustworthy. Sceptics included the thirteenth-century Flemish Franciscan missionary and traveller William of Rubruck and his Italian successors Giovanni da Montecorvino and Giovanni de' Marignolli, all of whom expressed varying degrees of disbelief about alleged monsters in the Far East.[39] The fifteenth-century cartographer Fra Mauro was similarly non-committal when it came to human or animal monsters in Africa.[40] Sometimes scepticism turned into outright ridicule. Near the beginning of book 1 of Thomas More's *Utopia* (1516), the character who describes the eponymous Noplace, Raphael Hythlodaeus ('Mr Nonsense'), had purportedly been on three of Amerigo Vespucci's voyages but opted to stay behind instead of returning home, in order to pursue his own independent travels. 'We did not', observes More, 'ask him if he had seen any monsters, for monsters have ceased to be news'.[41] Less subtle was the ridicule voiced in 1594 by Norfolk gentleman Thomas Blundeville:

[34] Birrell (1999: p. xxix). [35] Birrell (1999: 8.121; 12.145; 17.187). [36] Ratcliffe (2014).
[37] *Bṛhat Saṃhitā* XIV. 22–3; Ratcliffe (2014: 28–9).
[38] Bolton (1962: 83), citing Athanasiev (1863: 260); cf. Ratcliffe (2014: 27).
[39] See references collected in Valtrová (2010: 169–70, 172–3); van Duzer (2013: 57 with 130 n. 146).
[40] Van Duzer (2013: 57, with refs at 130 n. 145). [41] Trans. Turner (1965: 40).

> they are meere lies that are woont to be told of the Pigmeans, in that they should bee but a foote and a halfe high, and likewise that which hath bene spoken of people, that shuld haue their heads, their noses, their mouthes, and their eies in their breastes, or of those that are headed lyke a dog, or of those that haue but one eie, and that in their forehead... All these are meere lyes, inuented by vaine men to bring fooles into admiration, for monsters are as well borne in Europe, as in other partes of the world.[42]

However, neither expressions of scepticism nor open sarcasm had the effect of eradicating belief. Belief—at any rate, belief in monsters—is not that kind of flimsy thing. Such is the enduring power of the monster as a tool of thought and feeling that, at least in certain contexts, it can mount an irresistible challenge to what is taken to be everyday common sense.

Re-Imagining Polyphemus

The encounter with Ulysses: allegories and morals

Fabius Planciades Fulgentius (late 5th cent. CE) is best known as the (perhaps north African) author of *Mythologies*, a reading of classical myths that mingles etymology, allegory, and moral didacticism. Less familiar is his *Exposition of the Content of Virgil according to Moral Philosophy*, in which he summons the great poet from the dead to give an explanation of the *Aeneid*.[43] The result is a thoroughgoing allegorical reading of the poem from the Mantuan horse's mouth. When it comes to Polyphemus, the dominant feature is, as it will be in much of the allegorical tradition, the single eye (sect. 15):

> Now *acos* in Greek is grief. *Ciclos* is circle; and since *pes* is the Greek for boy, childhood, now released from respect for those who nurture it, does not know the grief of reflection and roams freely in its youthful wildness. The Cyclops is said to have one eye in its forehead because this wildness of youth takes neither a full nor a rational view of things, and the whole period of youth is roused to a pride like that of the Cyclops. So with the one eye in the head that sees and comprehends nothing but vanity. This is what the most wise Ulysses extinguishes: vainglory is blinded by the fire of the intellect. So I named him Polyphemus, as it were, *apolunta femen*, which in Latin we call 'losing reputation'. The blindness of adolescence follows youth's pride and indifference to reputation.[44]

[42] Blundeville (1594: 262).
[43] Trans. Whitbread (1971), along with Fulgentius' other works.
[44] Trans. Whitbread (1971), amended.

That the Polypheman single eye could connote the limited vision of childhood was an idea with a long history. It certainly appealed to the early-twelfth-century Neoplatonist humanist William of Conches:

> For Polyphemus, that is, childish vision, is pride, because it seems to a child that he knows and sees many things. He has only one eye, that is, only contemplation of temporal things, and this he has in his forehead, that is, an ostentatious display, because children turn their attention to ostentation and boasting. Ulysses plucks out the eye of childish pride, because the wise man Ulysses is called *olonxeon*, that is, the far-ranging wanderer... since here is (his?) pilgrimage. But our life is in heaven; he scorns the contemplation and desire for temporal things.[45]

Another approach to monocular limitation, relying on a different etymological gambit, interpreted Polyphemus' lack of vision as restricting him to *looking downwards* at earthly—and earthy—things. That, at any rate, was the opinion of the fourteenth-century Italian humanist Giovanni del Virgilio, for whom the ogre's name meant *plurima corruptio*, 'lots [*poli*] of corruption [*phemos*]'.[46]

But the symbolism of the single eye is ambivalent. So, far from always implying a limitation, it may instead/also signify exceptional prowess. Already Servius, commenting on the Virgilian Cyclops, had described the ogre as *vir prudentissimus*, because his single eye was located 'next to the brain'; he was blinded (= outsmarted) by Ulysses, who was even more *prudens* than he was.[47] The monk, theologian, and teacher Remigius of Auxerre (9th cent.) ran with the Servian baton, whereas a reviser of Remigius' text held the opposite, Fulgentian view.[48] Four centuries later the English, Paris-based grammarian John of Garland, in an allegorical explication of Ovid's *Metamorphoses* in 520 verses, was another who took Polyphemus' eye to signify rationality. In John's view, the act of blinding carried out by the Ovidian Ulysses was a sign that he was just too brainy for his adversary.[49]

Although it is Polyphemus' eye that dominates medieval and early modern reflection on his interaction with Ulysses, also prominent are his belly and the capacious maw that services it. A typical example can be found in *Mythologiae*,

[45] *Glosae in Iuvenalem*: text in B. Wilson (1980: 101); Chance (1994: 441), from whom we borrow the translation.

[46] In his *Allegories of the Books of Ovid's Metamorphoses*: text in Ghisalberti (1931: 98); see Acquaro Graziosi (1984: 26–7), also Raffa (1996: 283–4) and Black (2011: 127–8, with further bibliography at 128 n. 25).

[47] Servius on *Aen*. 3.636; the same point is made by the 2nd Vatican Mythographer, sect. 201 in Pepin (2008).

[48] Chance (1994: 233).

[49] *Integumenta Ovidii* 463–8: text in Ghisalberti (1933a). See Acquaro Graziosi (1984: 22–3); Coulson (2011: 59–65).

the huge project of myth-re-narration by the Italian scholar Natale Conti (mid-sixteenth century). His contemporary, the formidable French-born philologist Joseph Scaliger, dismissed Natale as *homo futilissimus*, but such disdain had no impact on the huge popularity of the *Mythologiae*.[50] The aim of the work was to uncover the wisdom embedded in the Graeco-Roman myths, and above all to demonstrate the ethical lessons they could teach, lessons 'that counsel proper behaviour and discourage unlawful pleasures... [and] ultimately teach us all we absolutely need to know to lead a decent human life' (1.1).[51] From the myth of Polyphemus and Ulysses, as from countless others, Natale drew a moral (9.8): 'For if a man rejects reason, is irreverent toward both gods and men, scorns justice, and puts all of his joy in his stomach, isn't he more like a beast than a man?'[52] This stress on the stomach recurs frequently in post-classical accounts. It is no coincidence that François Rabelais (*c*.1494–1553), supreme portrayer of human guzzling, integrated Polyphemus into a cosmic scheme of generations of Giants that led eventually to Gargantua and Pantagruel.[53] Pantagruel, indeed, cited the Euripidean Polyphemus *verbatim*: 'I only sacrifice to myself—to the gods never—and to this belly of mine, the greatest of all the gods.'[54]

Polyphemus, Galatea, Acis

The Polyphemus–Galatea–Acis triangle generated no less interpretative ingenuity than did the encounter with Ulysses, especially from allegorists offering an *explication de texte* of Ovid. One influential commentator was Arnulf, master of the cathedral school at Orléans. His twin-pronged, philological-cum-interpretative approach was widely read for two-and-a-half centuries after its production in *c*.1180.[55] Here is his view of the triangle:

> Galatea spurned Polyphemus and loved Acis. But Polyphemus crushed Acis, who was then changed into the river bearing his name. Galatea, which means 'white goddess', is in love with Acis, that is, 'care', from *cis*, which means 'care'. But she despises Polyphemus, who is 'of many women', from *pollonis*, which means 'plurality', and *femos*, which is a corrupt form of *femina* (?). For indeed those who have time for divine things despise a plurality of women and are

[50] Scaliger's dismissal: letter to Calvisius (19 June 1606), in Botley and van Miert (2012: vi. 441).

[51] Trans. Mulryan and Brown (2006), here and in subsequent quotations.

[52] Mulryan and Brown (2006: 849).

[53] The Giants originated as humans who consumed medlars, one of the least appealing of fruits. First on the scene was Chalbroth, who begat Sarabroth, who begat... Ten generations later came Polyphemus, who begat Cacus, who begat... Nearly fifty generations later came Gargantua, who begat Pantagruel (*Gargantua and Pantagruel* 2.1 = Rabelais 1994: 171–3).

[54] *Gargantua and Pantagruel* 4.58 = Rabelais (1994: 658); Eur. *Cyc.* 334–5.

[55] On Arnulf and his medieval reception, see Ghisalberti (1932) and Coulson (2011: 50–5).

without cares. But Polyphemus, that is, plurality of women, at last kills Acis, that is, he makes care flow away, hence Acis is said to turn into water.[56]

Lacking Arnulf's emphasis on philological exegesis, but broadly similar in its use of etymology to reveal alleged moral truth, is the approach taken by the Benedictine monk Pierre Bersuire in his *Ovidius moralizatus* (*c.*1340), a commentary on Ovid's *Metamorphoses* designed to show how the true meaning of the text is compatible with holy scripture. Galatea is again the white or milky goddess; Acis stands for chastity, Polyphemus for 'very corrupt' or 'very womanish'. What it boils down to is: corruption kills chastity, since corruption is more powerful than chastity.[57] Quite different in style and scope is the massive verse adaptation of the *Metamorphoses* into medieval French, known as *Ovide moralisé*. According to the anonymous author, Polyphemus is Satan, his flute-playing temptation, Galatea divine wisdom, and Acis human nature.[58] In spite of wide divergences in form and content, the common factor in these approaches is a thoroughly negative interpretation of Polyphemus, and a contrastingly positive interpretation of Galatea and Acis. Such characterizations suit all three figures to the overall purpose of both the *Ovide moralisé* and the *Ovidius moralizatus*—namely, to serve as storehouses of moral exempla for the use of those preaching the gospel of Christianity.[59]

Differently allegorical again is the approach of the great fourteenth-century humanist Giovanni Boccaccio, who, in the course of his *Genealogy of the Pagan Gods*, gives two alternative decodings of Polyphemus–Galatea–Acis, the first rationalising/naturalistic and the second historicizing/euhemeristic (7.17). According to the first possibility, Galatea is a goddess of the whiteness of breaking waves, so that her union with Acis simply stands for the mixing of sea and fresh water that happens when any river flows into the sea. Alternatively (according to Theodontius, a virtually unknown writer cited often by Boccaccio), the myth cloaks an everyday tale of human brutality: Polyphemus was a cruel Sicilian tyrant who raped a girl called Galatea and gave orders for her lover Acis to be eliminated by throwing him into a river.[60]

Looking back over the allegorical tradition, we might occasionally be tempted to exclaim: 'You cannot be serious!' Allegorical cashings-out of Cyclopean myths are so many and varied that any precision of significance that those myths might

[56] We are indebted to Michael Reeve for help with the interpretation of this awkward passage, the text (and therefore the translation) of which is in several places uncertain. Text in Ghisalberti (1932: 227); cf. Acquaro Graziosi (1984: 22).

[57] *Ovidius moralizatus* XV, fo. 92 = p. 170 of the Utrecht version of the text (*Reductorium morale*); see Czapla (2006: 111). On *Ovidius moralizatus* in general, see Ghisalberti (1933b); Samaran (1962); Kretschmer (2016).

[58] *Ovide moralisé* 13.4148–4294, with Blumenfeld-Kosinski (1997: 264–5 n. 83).

[59] Cf. Kretschmer (2016: 225–6).

[60] Text and trans. Solomon (2011–17: ii. 178–9); cf. Czapla (2006: 111 n. 63).

be thought to possess seems to evaporate under the heat of this or that commentator's imaginings: anything—it appears—goes. But such cynicism misreads the nature of medieval allegory. Gregory Hays hits the nail on the head when he argues, in relation to medieval commentaries on Ovid's *Metamorphoses*, that the stories 'provided a conventional arena in which scholar-grammarians…could demonstrate both their mastery of the poem and their ingenuity in drawing connections'. Hays' conclusion is even more important: that the very fact of multiplicity of allegorical interpretations places the emphasis 'not on what the myth *means*, but on what it can be *made to express*'.[61] In other words, *all* classical myths, not only Cyclopean ones, constitute a site for the display of interpretative prowess. The myths' continuing relevance, and indeed their very survival, are thereby enhanced rather than reduced: they can be understood as speaking to us about *this* matter, or about *that*, or again (if you look at it differently) about *this other* question.

Art: The Early Modern Polyphemus

In parallel and sometimes in close symbiosis with textual retellings, many visual representations of the mythology of Polyphemus were created in the early modern period. Some of these focus on Odysseus, some on Galatea and Acis, while some link the two episodes synoptically, resuming Polyphemus' whole career in a single vignette. The blinding was a perennial favourite; the main novelty, compared with representations in antiquity, lay in the range of postures ascribed to blinder and blinded. Another popular incident was the giant's launching of a mighty rock at either Ulysses or Acis; several major artists took the opportunity to envision the coiled muscularity of a huge torso poised to spring into action. Perhaps the most striking and innovative representations depict the ogre's anthropophagy, often in unmoderated goriness.

The Venice-born French poet Christine de Pizan (*c.*1365–1431) has been lauded, not without justification, as an impressive literary feminist *avant la lettre*. Her *Letter from Othea to Hector* consists of a hundred mythological 'moments': in each case a short piece of verse is glossed and then allegorized, to serve as a vehicle of moral instruction for a young knight.[62] Around thirty years after Christine's death, the author and manuscript illustrator Jean Miélot reworked and amplified the *Letter*, incorporating material from Boccaccio's *Genealogy of the Pagan Gods* and Guido delle Colonne's thirteenth-century *History of the Destruction of Troy*, and adding his own illustrations. The overall direction taken

[61] Hays (2014: 137), emphasis in original.
[62] Blumenfeld-Kosinski (1997: 172); Chance (1997); Desmond and Sheingorn (2003); H. Adams (2017).

by Miélot was, it has been convincingly argued, to reduce the moral–allegorical dimension of Christine's text and to enhance the visual–mythographical.[63] One of his images depicts the blinding of Polyphemus (*Cat. 77* (Fig. 10.2)).[64] The schema of the combat between two standing, armour-clad figures—a plucky little spear-wielding Ulysses and a cudgel-toting Polyphemus twice his size—assimilates the pair, *mutatis mutandis*, to David and Goliath.[65] Trees and rocks constitute the background; Ulysses' crewmen look on from their vessel. The ogre is no herdsman: this is a showdown between two military champions. As the spear drives remorselessly into the giant's eye, there can be only one winner.

Early printed editions and translations of Ovid's *Metamorphoses* illustrate either the encounter with Ulysses, or the Polyphemus–Galatea–Acis love triangle, or both. A recurrent feature is the synchronic juxtaposition of discrete narrative moments, with images of separate scenes appearing side by side. In Lodovico Dolce's hugely successful Italian translation/transformation of the poem, originally published in Venice in 1553, among the (unattributed) vignettes is one at the head of the '27th Canto' (*Cat. 91*). It recapitulates the Ovidian narrative in three key episodes: the blinding, Polyphemus' wielding of a colossal clod of earth, and Acis sitting on the shore next to a naked girl, presumably Galatea.[66] Like Miélot, the illustrator shows the ogre in contemporary costume. This time, instead of armour, his kit consists of a short tunic with protruding undershorts, rough footwear, and stockings tied below the knee. Similarly synoptic is the image (*Cat. 93* (Fig. 10.3)) in a Latin text of Ovid's poem dating from 1574.[67] To the left, 'Poliphemo' is holding a man upside down by the ankles; from the way the poor chap's legs are being pulled dangerously wide apart, he seems unlikely to remain in one piece for long. To the right, Ulysses is driving a spear into Polyphemus' single eye. That this particular Cyclops should be supporting the side of his head on the hand of his bent arm is one of the more unusual visual accompaniments of the gruesome act. A present-day Western observer might all too hastily interpret the posture as implying tranquillity or even boredom. But gestures have a history: they are cultural every bit as much as natural. Any reader of Jean-Claude Schmitt's ground-breaking study of medieval gesture will recognize Polyphemus' posture as signifying, in its context, a quite different mental state: extreme distress.[68]

Although Ovid was the dominant provider of the textual armature for Renaissance illustrations of Polyphemus, there were other channels of transmission too. One such was an illustrated French translation of Philostratus' *Imagines*. The translator was Blaise de Vigenère, diplomat and cryptologist (1523–96); an

[63] Brown-Grant (1994).

[64] Illustrated in Kilinski (2013: 79, fig. 38).

[65] Kilinski (2013: 73).

[66] Mangiafesta (1997: 16–17, with fig. 1).

[67] Discussed and illustrated in Mangiafesta (1997: 18, with fig. 5).

[68] J.-C. Schmitt (1990: 171, with fig. 17, 2), illustrating (from a *Livre de prière, c.*1200) two sorrowing figures in a virtually identical posture to Polyphemus. On the history of gesture more generally, see Bremmer and Roodenburg (1991).

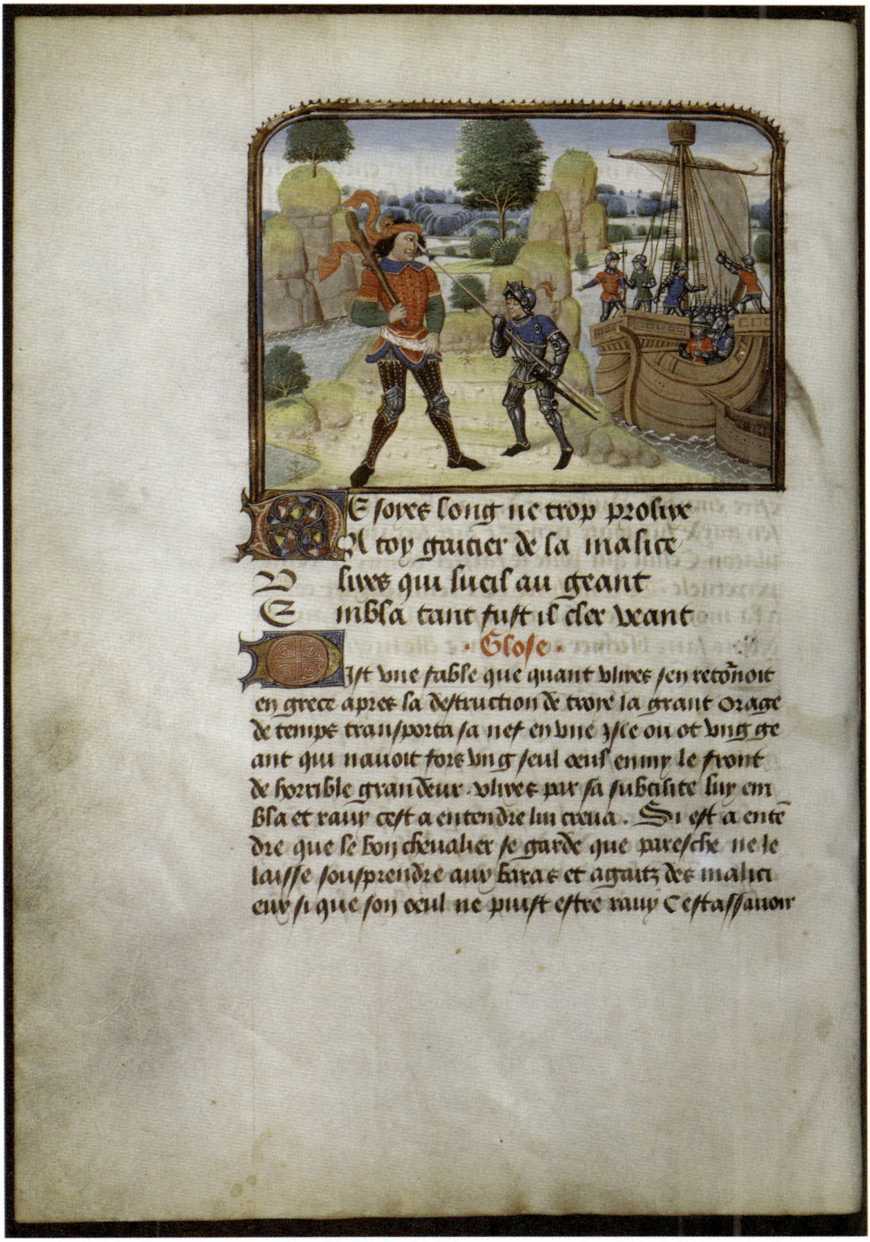
Ne soyes long ne trop prolixe
A toy gaitier de la malice
Ulixes qui loeil au geant
Embla tant fust il cler veant
· Glose ·
Dist une fable que quant ulixes sen retornoit
en grece apres la destruction de troye la grant orage
de tempes transporta sa nef en une ysle ou ot ung ge
ant qui navoit fors ung seul oeul enmy le front
de horrible grandeur. ulixes par sa subtilite luy em
bla et ravy cest a entendre luy creva. Si est a ente
dre que le bon chevalier se garde que paresche ne le
laisse sousprendre aux baras et agaitz des malici
eux si que son oeul ne puist estre ravy Cestassavoir

Fig. 10.2. Illustration by Jean Miélot in his reworking of Christine de Pizan's *Letter from Othea to Hector*, *c.*1461.

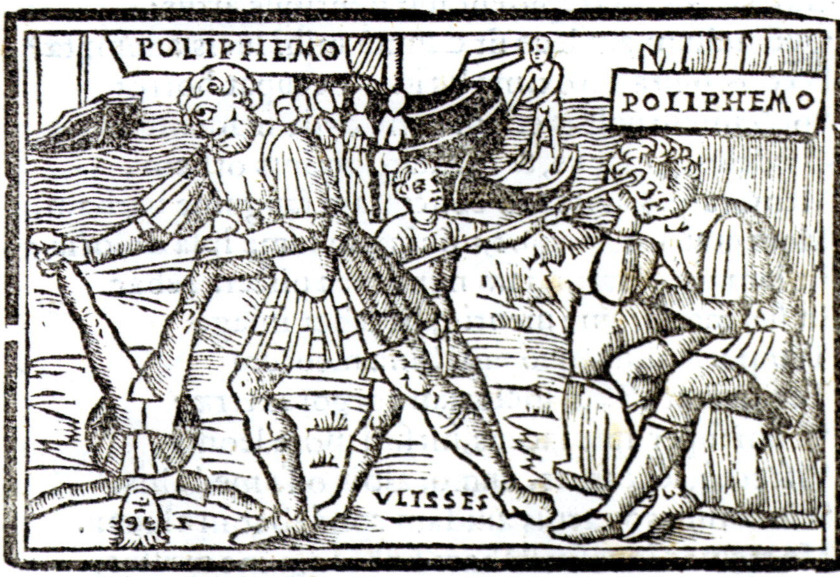

Fig. 10.3. Polyphemus in action and in agony. Woodcut from Latin text of Ovid, *Metamorphoses*, 1574.

illustrated version came out eighteen years after his death.[69] The picture of *The Cyclops* (*Cat. 101*) engraved by Jaspar Isac situates a recorder-playing Polyphemus under an oak tree, with a dog at his feet and sheep nearby. Galatea, in mid-ocean, perches on her dolphin-drawn sea carriage, guided by Tritonesque maidens. Compared with Philostratus' unforgettable textual evocation of the respective gazes of the two principals, Isac's version falls flat: nothing about his depiction of the gaze is of the slightest emotional interest, since Galatea is looking down at her dolphins while Polyphemus looks directly away from her.

That the encounter between Odysseus and Polyphemus can be reduced to a simple, one-line moral is the message of one of the publishing sensations of the sixteenth century, the *Emblemata* of Andrea Alciato (or Alciati). Though conceived as a mere recreation from its author's more sober day job as a jurist, the work eclipsed all his other writings in popularity. An 'emblem' typically combined an illustration with a motto and a brief textual summary.[70] The topics spanned the whole gamut of human concerns: love and hatred, knowledge and ignorance, life and death. The moral issues raised by the *Odyssey* lent themselves perfectly to an emblematic treatment. Along with Circe, the Sirens, and Scylla and Charybdis,

[69] Mangiafesta (1997: 18). [70] M. Bull (2005: 30).

Polyphemus was a favourite with writers of *emblemata*.[71] For it exemplified the uplifting theme of justified vengeance:

> As he sat in the mouth of his arching cave, the Cyclops sang this amid his tender sheep: 'You graze on grass; but I shall graze on the Argive companions, and last of all my innards will contain Outis.' The Ithacan heard this, and blinded the Cyclops. See how the author of misfortune reaps misfortune himself![72]

The picture is as uncomplicated as Alciato's concluding moral (*Cat. 102* (Fig. 10.4)). Odysseus acts alone, driving home the stake with the dashing bravura of a comic-book hero.

In Renaissance Italy some of the most characteristic bearers of mythological scenes were large wooden chests (*cassoni*), a type of decorative furniture typically offered as a wedding gift to a bride.[73] One example (*Cat. 81* (Fig. 10.5)) gives a synoptic version of several familiar Cyclopean scenes. Formerly ascribed to Piero di Cosimo, it has more recently been assigned to Piero's School, or to a follower of Lorenzo di Credi and Filippino Lippi (*c.*1500).[74] Front and centre stage is a huge, recumbent Polyphemus. As three tiny Greeks drive a stake into his eye, several of their comrades, no less Lilliputian, offer encouragement behind the giant's body. Elsewhere on the panel are the usual sequels. To the right, head bowed, Polyphemus feels the backs of his rams for escapees. Further to the right and in the middle distance, his alter ego prepares to throw a boulder at some distinctly early modern-looking sailing vessels. Two aspects of the painting stand out. First, the elaborate use of perspective: the only comparable precedents in extant ancient art are some of the Roman frescoes (e.g. *Cat. 40* (Fig. 4.6), *41* (Fig. 3.2), and *45* (Fig. 5.6)). Second, the implied moral context. The left side of the panel represents the fall of Troy and its aftermath. Featured deities are Athene, in the act of visiting destruction on the city, and Poseidon, trident-wielding smasher of one of the victorious Greeks—namely, the hybristic Ajax, son of Oileus. The fact that Athene and Poseidon are singled out—the very pair of divinities who plotted the downfall of the homeward-bound Greeks in the prologue to Euripides' *Trojan Women*—suggests a possible programmatic—indeed emblematic—meaning for the whole panel: provoke the anger of the gods, and you will pay the price. When the Greeks destroyed the gods' shrines in Troy, they stored up ruin for themselves. From the moment when Ajax dragged Cassandra from her refuge at Athene's altar, he was doomed. And when Odysseus blinded Poseidon's son, the god would be relentless in his vengeful wrath.

[71] Cf. Corti (1998: 203–4). [72] Alciato, *Emblema* 172. [73] M. Bull (2005: 38–9).
[74] McKnight (1924); Mangiafesta (1997: 23); Geronimus (2006: 285).

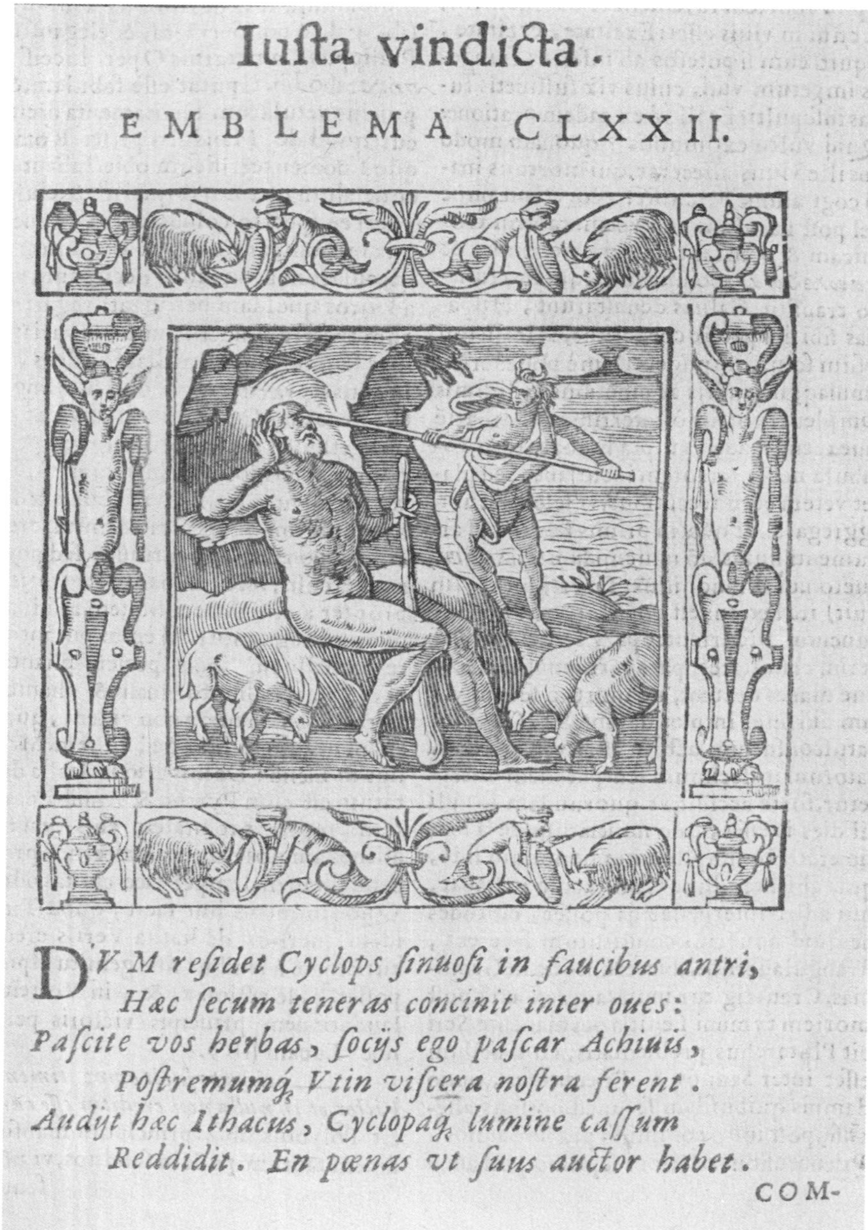

Iuſta vindicta.

EMBLEMA CLXXII.

DVM reſidet Cyclops ſinuoſi in faucibus antri,
Hæc ſecum teneras concinit inter oues:
Paſcite vos herbas, ſocijs ego paſcar Achiuis,
Poſtremumq; Vtin viſcera noſtra ferent.
Audijt hæc Ithacus, Cyclopaq; lumine caſſum
Reddidit. En pœnas vt ſuus auctor habet.

COM-

Fig. 10.4. 'Justified vengeance', fig. 172 from Andrea Alciato's *Emblemata*, 1621.

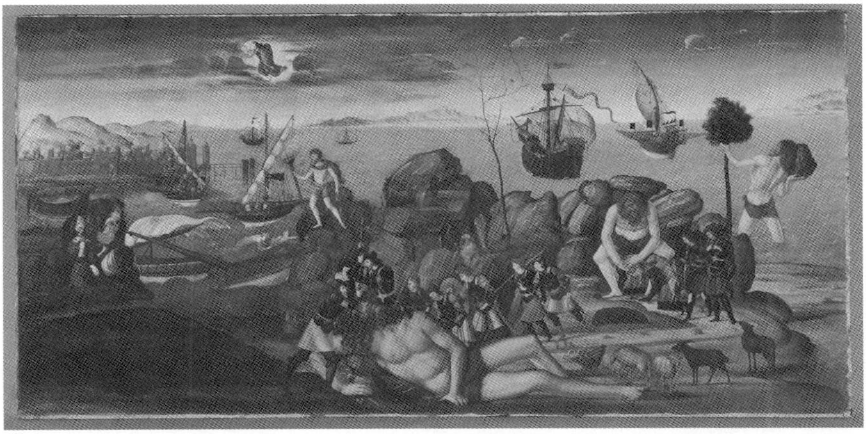

Fig. 10.5. Various episodes of the encounter between Ulysses and Polyphemus. *Cassone* panel, perhaps by Piero di Cosimo or his school, *c.*1500.

Another painted *cassone*, even more elaborate in its circumstantial detail, is attributed to the Florentine Apollonio di Giovanni (*Cat. 78* (Fig. 10.6)). Heralded as the 'Tuscan Apelles', he lived up to his billing in a remarkable evocation of the wanderings of Ulysses.[75] To the left are scenes from the encounter with the Cyclops. The landscape is rocky; the episodes of the blinding and the escape from the cave are familiar enough. But the scene in the lower-left foreground is, to say the least, eye-catching. A gorgeously dressed Ulysses offers a sumptuous wine cup to a bearded, hairy, and stark naked 'Pulifemo'. For the moment, however, the giant can drink nothing, since his mouth is crammed full: the legs of a partially swallowed *homunculus* protrude from his jaws. Evidently he is only halfway through his meal: while he extends his right hand towards Ulysses to receive the wine, his left clutches the struggling human who will soon be his dessert.

Cassoni were not the only Renaissance vehicles for the representation of Ulysses' adventures. Wall paintings and frescoes played their part too, both in the major artistic centres of central and northern Italy, and also at the sumptuous Château de Fontainebleau, to which Italian artists were summoned at royal command. A key figure in the decoration of the Château was the Bolognese artist Francesco Primaticcio, who designed the Galerie d'Ulysse there. This 150-metre-long corridor was decorated with frescoes illustrating sixty *storie* from the *Odyssey*, including five relating to the Cyclopes.[76] The frescoes no longer survive:

[75] '*Tuscus Apelles*', in Ugolino Verino's mid-Quattrocento poem *Fiammetta* (2.8.5); text in A. M. Wilson (2016: 106). On Apollonio's workshop, see Gombrich (1955).

[76] The definitive treatment is that by Béguin, Guillaume, and Roy (1985), who describe the gallery as 'the most extraordinary mythological and heroic representation ever painted in France' (105; our translation). See also Mignot (1988) and Fiorenza (2006).

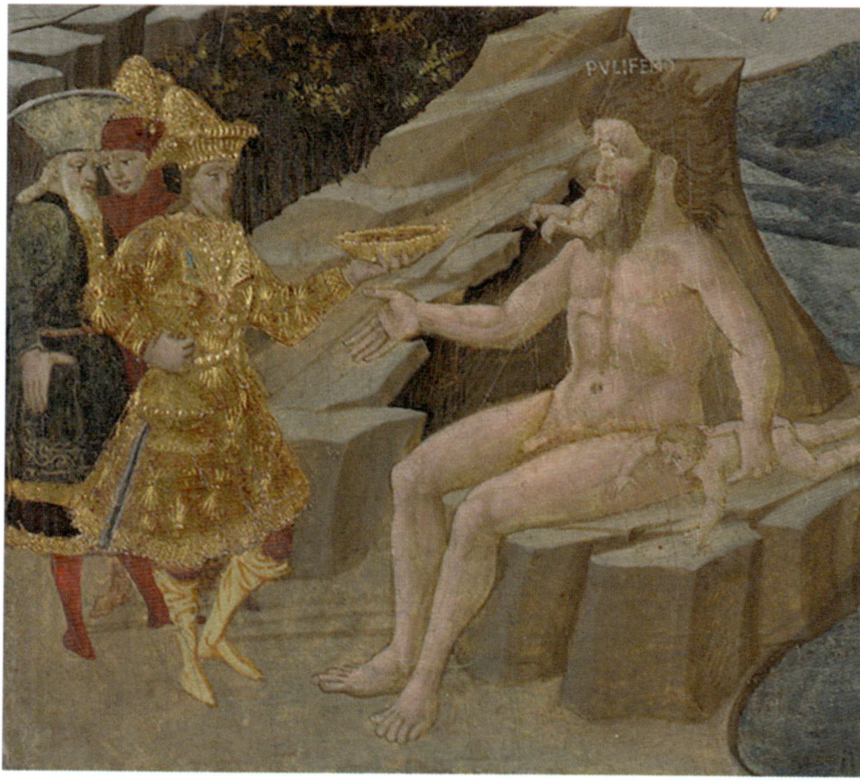

Fig. 10.6. Ulysses offers wine to his host, who is already halfway through his dinner. *Cassone* panel by Apollonio di Giovanni, 1435–45.

having fallen into decay, they disappeared for ever when the Galerie was demolished in 1739.[77] But at least we have preliminary drawings by Primaticcio himself, as well as engravings made in the 1630s by the Flemish artist Theodoor van Thulden.[78] It appears that the overall programmatic aim of the Galerie was to extol the prowess of Ulysses, heroic seeker after true wisdom in the face of countless tribulations; by implication, such an iconographical concept offered symbolic backing to the French monarchy, with whom the valiant hero could be associated.[79] To achieve this purpose, it would not do to depict the hero's adversaries as feeble nonentities. That emphatically applies to Primaticcio's Cyclops, truly formidable in his muscularity. Nothing could more clearly demonstrate that monocularity was *not* the giant's dominant characteristic than the image (*Cat. 97* (Fig. 10.7)) in which all we see of his head is a rear view. Handsome in his

[77] Fiorenza (2006: 799–800).
[78] Béguin, Guillaume, and Roy (1985: 78–80).
[79] Fiorenza (2006: 804).

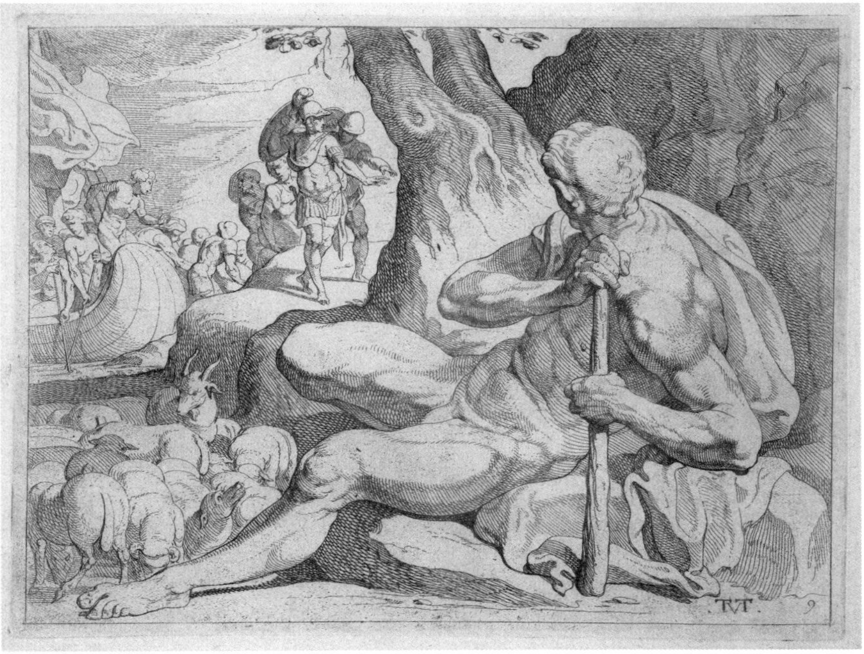

Fig. 10.7. Ulysses disembarks as Polyphemus looks on. Drawing by Theodoor van Thulden, after Primaticcio, 1633.

nakedness, and purposefully on the *qui vive*, he observes the Greeks disembarking in the distance; there is nothing grotesque about him, nothing mean, nothing uncontrolled. But another work, a representation of the blinding, presents a rather different Polyphemus (*Cat. 98* (Fig. 10.8)). Not that his *body* is any less impressive: his bulging biceps would not disgrace the Incredible Hulk. But his posture—supine, sprawling, mouth agape—reveals the effect, moral as well as physical, of too much wine. In the words of the 'morality' appended to Van Thulden's copy of the fresco, and composed by Van Thulden's editor Melchior Tavernier, 'it is useless for a man to make pretension to courage or strength, if over-indulgence in wine takes away his reason, and if he lacks the moderation necessary for the conduct of his life'.[80] Diminutive though the Greeks are, it is now *they* who are purposeful, *they* who are in control.

Bearing a resemblance to Primaticcio's version of the blinding, but raising the depiction of Polyphemus' agony several notches higher, is a fresco (*Cat. 89* (Fig. 10.9)) by an artist from the next generation: Pellegrino Tibaldi. Born in Lombardy, raised in Bologna, and trained in Rome, Tibaldi enjoyed a glittering

[80] Text in Béguin, Guillaume, and Roy (1985: 109); our translation.

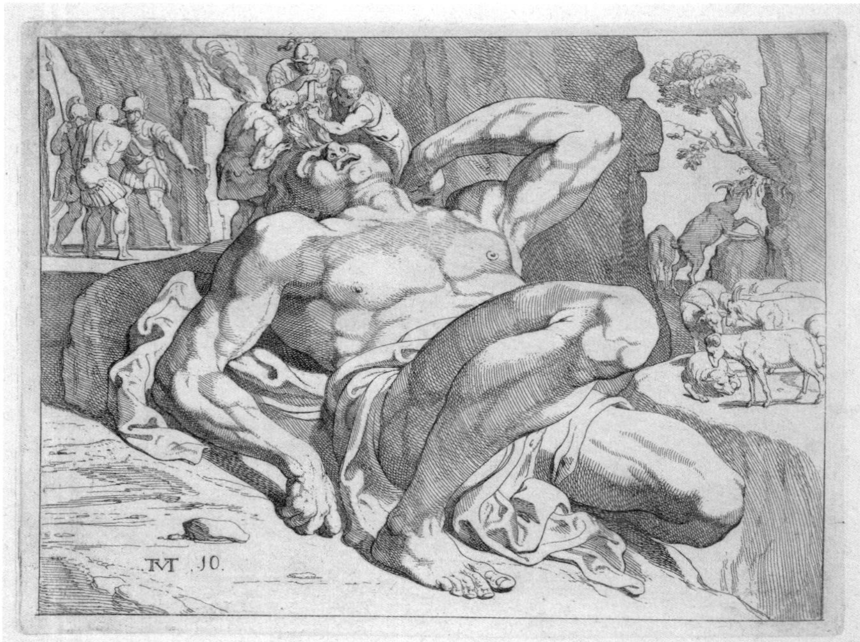

Fig. 10.8. The blinding. Drawing by Theodoor van Thulden, after Primaticcio, 1633.

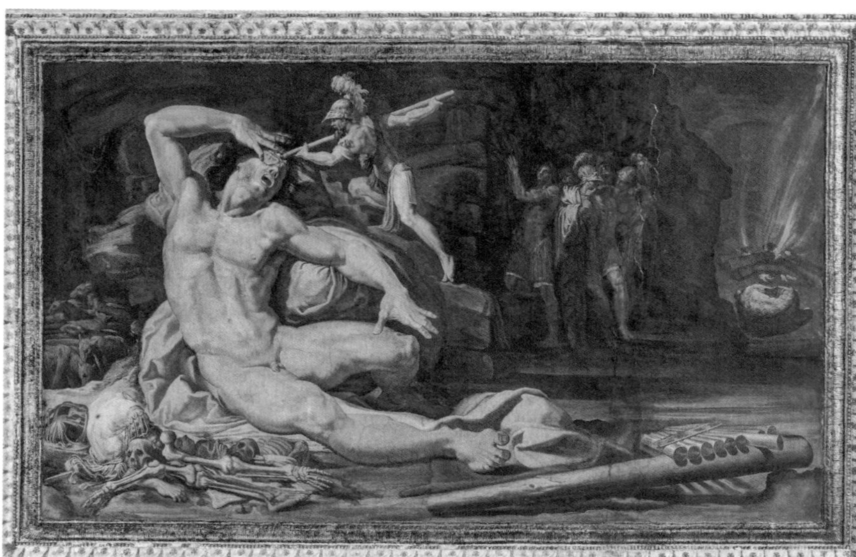

Fig. 10.9. Pellegrino Tibaldi, *Ulysses Blinding Polyphemus*, 1550–1. Fresco in Palazzo Poggi, Bologna.

career as painter and architect in many of the leading artistic centres of northern Italy, as well as at the fabulous palace of Philip II of Spain at El Escorial, where he painted the frescoes on the vaulted ceiling of the great Library. Among his works back home in Italy was a cycle of representations of Ulysses' exploits, commissioned by Cardinal Poggi for his Palazzo in Bologna. In the Sala di Polifemo, Tibaldi decorated the ceiling with episodes from the hero's adventures.[81] The scene of the blinding is placed at the very centre of the vault, perhaps symbolizing the causative importance that the act held for the unfolding of Ulysses' later troubles. Whatever the possible allegorical meanings underpinning Tibaldi's overall conception of Ulysses' progress—perhaps an escape from a (Neo)platonic/Cyclopean cave, leading to an eventually virtuous attainment of the Good—what is not in doubt is the spasm of pain that contorts the Cyclops' face and colossal naked body.[82] By comparison, his assailant looks tiny; he needs to scale some rocks to reach the height of Polyphemus' eye. But the doughty little hero, wearing armour and a plumed helmet and wielding a soldier's spear rather than a rough stake, looks resolute and balanced. He acts alone, leaving his companions huddling in the shadows. Polyphemus' trademark club and shepherd's pipes lie on the cave floor, next to a heap of human bones and skulls. For this conflict between 'civilized' aggression and raw brutishness, various influences have been proposed. Some are artistic: Adam in the Sistine Chapel, for the Cyclops' physique; the great antique sculptural group *Laocoon and his sons* (excavated in 1506), for the ogre's anguished contortion. Some are literary: Homer played a part, as of course did Ovid, and arguably even Euripides in his *Cyclops* (translated into Italian in the early sixteenth century).[83] But there is a degree of artificiality about separating out the strands. In any case, the arresting impact of the composition is Tibaldi's own.

Tibaldi had not finished with Polyphemus. In one of the side vaults of the Sala di Polifemo he gave an even more unsettling rendering of the ogre (*Cat. 90* (Fig. 10.10)). This time the theme is the Greeks' escape from the cave, not, as so often, clinging under the sheep, but concealed under sheep*skins*, a variant that has been linked with Boccaccio's version rather than Homer's.[84] Whatever literary models may lurk in the background, Tibaldi breaks new visual ground in exploring the ogre's wildness. His demonic expression would suit Stevenson's Mr Hyde, or a sinner from the lower depths of Dante's *Inferno*.[85] As for the eyes—two regular, with a third positioned centrally above them—it is hard for the earthbound viewer to be sure whether any or all of the three are closed or unseeing, even though the ogre's vacant stare, and his despairing attempt to *feel* the escapees,

[81] Also known as the 'Sala di Ulisse'; cf. Kiefer (2000: 174–5 n. 454).

[82] Allegorical meanings: see Lorandi (1996: 532); Kiefer (2000: 338–40); contrast the scepticism of M. S. Hansen (2013: 100–1).

[83] M. S. Hansen (2013: 111).

[84] M. S. Hansen (2013: 113).

[85] Lorandi (1996: 548) describes his appearance as that of a figure from beyond the grave.

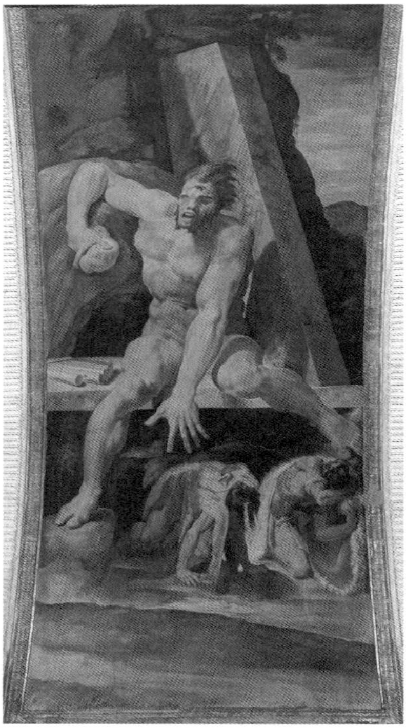

Fig. 10.10. Pellegrino Tibaldi, *Ulysses Escaping from Polyphemus*, 1550–1. Fresco in Palazzo Poggi, Bologna.

imply a total lack of vision. In any case, the painting is less about logic than about sheer visceral impact.

When it comes to Cinquecento paintings of Polyphemus as Galatea's lover, the place to begin is the Villa Farnesina, the palatial residence built by millionaire Sienese banker and art patron Agostino Chigi in the Trastevere district of Rome. The garden loggia juxtaposes two frescoes: Sebastiano del Piombo's *Polyphemus* (*Cat. 83* (Fig. 10.11)), and Raphael's *The Triumph of Galatea* (*Cat. 84* (Fig. 10.12)). Though there is some doubt about which was painted first, the pair make perfect thematic sense as a diptych.

Brought by Chigi from Venice to Rome in 1511, Sebastiano immediately set to work on some mythological scenes for the loggia lunettes. Soon afterwards he painted the *Polyphemus*.[86] Various influences have been identified: Giorgione (landscape), Michelangelo (physique), Poliziano's poetic description in his *Stanze* (details such as the sheepdog between Polyphemus' feet).[87] More intriguing is a suggested precursor in the *oeuvre* of the artist himself: a drawing in Lille that seems to be Sebastiano's own, preliminary study (*Cat. 82* (Fig. 10.13)).[88] There is a

[86] Hirst (1981: 33–4). [87] Hirst (1981: 36–7).
[88] Hirst (1981: 36–7 with n. 19 and fig. 43).

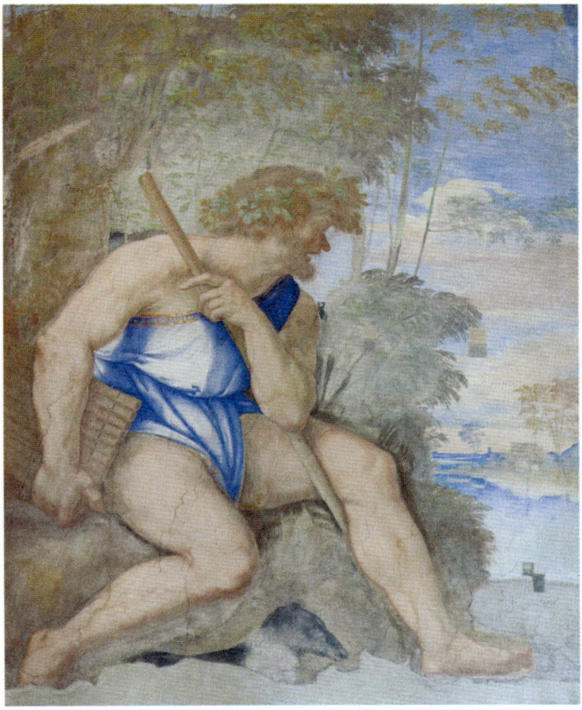

Fig. 10.11. Sebastiano del Piombo, *Polyphemus*, *c.*1512. Fresco in Villa Farnesina, Rome.

grace and wistfulness about the giant's expression in the drawing that his cruder equivalent in the fresco entirely lacks. This (the fresco) must be the only image of the Cyclops in which his most fetching feature is his ultramarine blue tunic.

Sebastiano's Polyphemus gazes in the general direction of the adjacent fresco to his right, where Galatea looks, not directly towards him, but towards the viewer's upper left. Given the traces of a painted frame surrounding the *Galatea*, it has been intriguingly suggested that Polyphemus might have been imagined as scrutinizing his adored nymph *as a work of art*.[89] However that may be, the two frescoes contrast starkly with each other. Raphael's conception is by far the more dynamic. Breeze-tossed Galatea, partly clothed in a garment of deep red, stands in a dolphin-drawn shell, inevitably recalling Botticelli's Venus of a generation earlier.[90] A squadron of three airborne cupids targets Galatea with love arrows, presumably labelled 'Acis' not 'Polyphemus'. Completing the impression of

[89] Mignosi Tantillo (1972: 35); Jones and Penny (1983: 93).

[90] Beck (1994: 96).

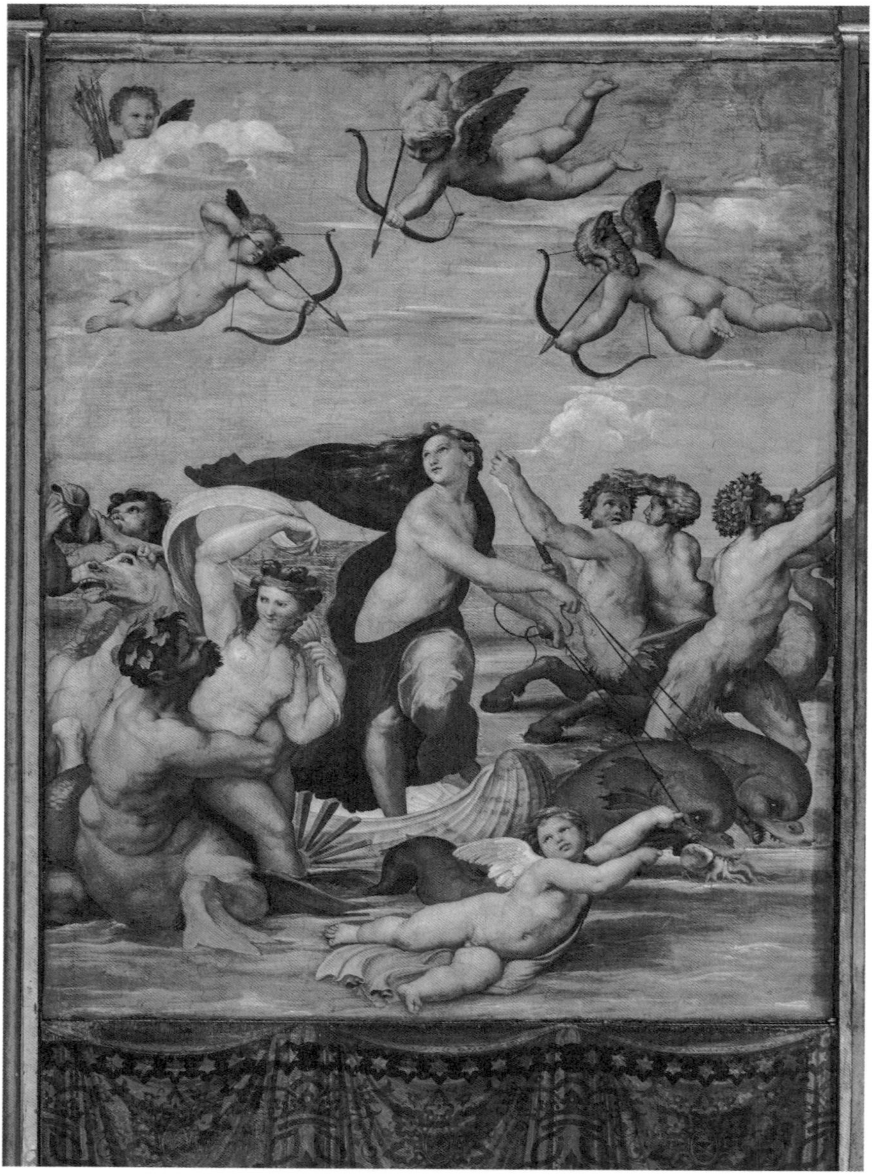

Fig. 10.12. Raphael, *The Triumph of Galatea*, *c.*1513–14. Fresco in Villa Farnesina, Rome.

hyperactive sexuality are the centaur on the right, transporting a naked Nereid, and the Triton on the left, arms firmly locked around one of her sisters.

As for a possible programmatic meaning that might link the frescoes as a pair, a clue may lurk in an unexpected detail. The nearer of the two dolphins grips an octopus in its jaws, presumably intending to devour it. Duncan Kinkead has

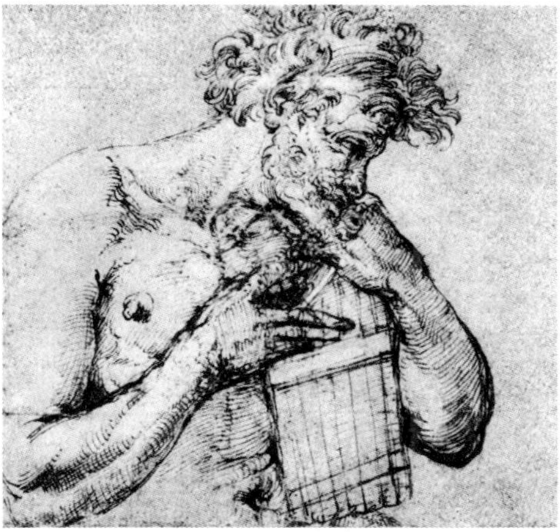

Fig. 10.13. Sebastiano del Piombo (possible attribution), preliminary study for *Polyphemus*.

ingeniously explained this detail as a symbolic opposition between the two sea creatures, citing an observation in Oppian's *Halieutica*, the (probably) late-second-century CE Greek epic on fishing, which there are independent grounds for thinking Raphael may have known.[91] For Oppian, whereas the dolphin is characterized by a morally uplifting, human-like love for its mate and its children, the octopus mates in an aggressive-bestial, self-exhausting manner, leading to its own death.[92] 'Love destroying Lust' is how Kinkead reads not only the dolphin-eats-cephalopod encounter, but also—taking the frescoes together—Galatea's implied self-distancing from Polyphemus' 'beastly' advances. To the objection that the dolphins look too ferocious to be symbols of Love, one may counter that the arrows of the Cupids are pretty aggressive too.

After Raphael's death in 1520, one of those on whom his artistic inheritance devolved was his pupil Giulio Romano. Four years later, Giulio left Rome for Mantua to work for Duke Federico II Gonzaga, enjoying total artistic superintendence over the city. His masterpiece is the Palazzo Te, Federico's amazing place of recreation-cum-pleasure on an island in a lake outside the city walls.[93] Giulio's reputation has varied. To the Third Gentleman in *The Winter's Tale* (V.ii.95) he was 'that rare Italian master'. Dickens, by contrast, found the frescoes of Giants in the Palazzo Te 'inconceivably ugly and grotesque', even if there was at the same time an element of fascination in his response.[94] Of those frescoes, the ones that concern us are found in two rooms, the Sala di Psiche and the Sala dei Giganti.

[91] Kinkead (1970). [92] Opp. *Hal.* 1.580, 732–3 (dolphin); 536–46 (octopus).
[93] Also known as the 'Palazzo del Te'. See especially Bazzotti (2013); also Verheyen (1972).
[94] Dickens (1957: 343); see Hollington (2014: 52).

The Sala di Psiche takes its name from the main subject of its lavish decorative scheme: the myth of Cupid and Psyche, inspired by Apuleius' version of the tale in his *Metamorphoses*. Amplifying these images are scenes from other myths with a blatantly erotic thrust, including one that pornographically exhibits the union of Jupiter and Olympias, and another evoking the sexual passion of Pasiphae for a bull. Quite at home in this amatory context is a fresco (*Cat. 85* (Fig. 10.14)) depicting a massive Polyphemus, as craggy as the rocks he sits on and leans against; the diminutive, embracing figures of Acis and Galatea are framed against the sea at the bottom right. Two of the Cyclops' trademark attributes appear prominently: the syrinx nestling in the crook of his right arm, and the enormous club on which his left hand rests. But look at the position of this club: between his legs. One hardly needs to be a card-carrying Freudian to detect a graphic sexual symbol here, in a room dedicated to the visual celebration of erotic enjoyment. Another nice detail is the little bear at the bottom left—doubtless one of the pair of cubs that Ovid's Polyphemus offered to Galatea as love-gifts (*Met.* 13.834–7). The whole design of the Sala presumably suited the tastes of Federico and his mistress Isabella Boschetti. As the dedicatory inscription for the villa (located in the Sala) put it: 'Federico II Gonzaga . . . commanded this

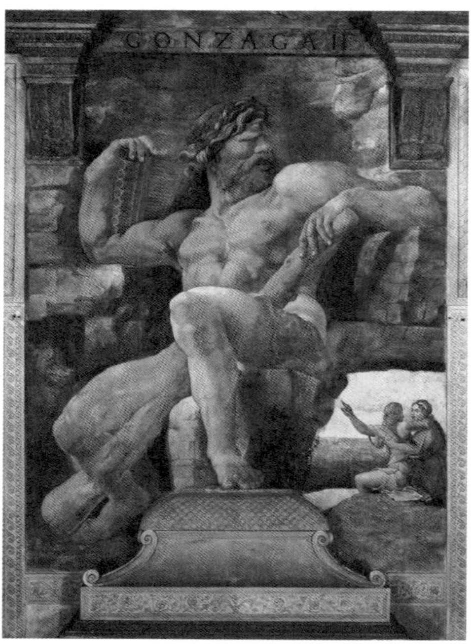

Fig. 10.14. Giulio Romano, *Polyphemus, Galatea, and Acis*, *c.*1528. Fresco in Palazzo Te, Mantua.

construction for his honest ease after his labours to restore his strength in this place of repose.'[95]

The other Cyclops in the Palazzo Te can be found in the fantastic and terrifying Sala dei Giganti. Giorgio Vasari gave an unforgettable description of the frescoes in the first and especially the second edition (1568) of his *Lives of the Most Excellent Painters, Sculptors, and Architects*: windows and walls apparently tottering, buildings and mountains crashing down, all in the context of the Olympians' overthrow of the failed insurrection of the Giants.[96] One of the Giants in process of being crushed beneath boulders consists of a figure, or, to be more precise, a distorted face, whose traits are reduced to a gaping mouth and a staring, single eye (*Cat. 86* (Fig. 10.15)). That this monocular character should be identified with one of the mythical Cyclopes is the more probable in view of the location of the image: above a fireplace.[97] Here indeed would have been a wonderful new variant on the link between the Cyclopes and fire. As the denizen of Etna is crushed between mountainous boulders, so real and imaginary fires coalesce.

For the last in the sequence of Italian depictions of Polyphemus in the early modern period, we move to the Palazzo Farnese in Rome. Familiar to opera-lovers as the location of the searing Act II confrontation between Tosca and Scarpia, the palace occupies a significant place in the myth history of the

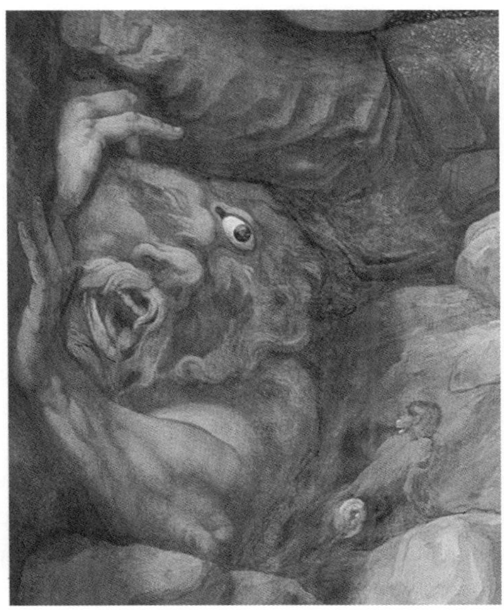

Fig. 10.15. Giulio Romano, *Head of a Giant*, *c.*1532. Fresco in Palazzo Te, Mantua.

[95] Bazzotti (2013: 161).
[96] Trans. G. Bull (1987: 224). See Carabell (1997: 87); Bazzotti (2013: 244–61).
[97] Carabell (1997: 89); Tafuri (1998).

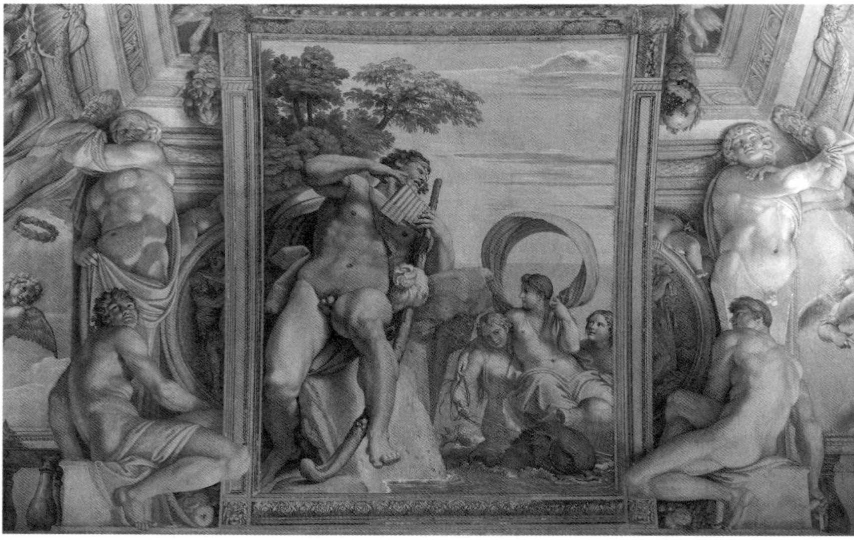

Fig. 10.16. Annibale Carracci, *Polyphemus and Galatea*, 1597–1607. Fresco in Palazzo Farnese, Rome.

Cyclopes. For it was here, on the vaulted ceiling of the Gallery, that the Bolognese artist Annibale Carracci and his assistants created a cycle of frescoes depicting *The Loves of the Gods*.[98] The centrepiece is the union of Bacchus and Ariadne on Naxos; flanking scenes portray an airborne Mercury handing the golden apple to Paris, and the temptation of Diana by Pan. Prominent too are a pair of complementary images on opposite end walls: on one, Polyphemus courts Galatea; on the other, he prepares to crush Acis with a rock.

In the representation of the wooing (*Cat. 94* (Fig. 10.16)), the naked ogre sits in an open and relaxed posture, gazing down rapturously at the nymph whom he serenades on his pan pipes. Galatea looks self-possessed, clutching the billowing red scarf that serves as her sunshade-cum-sail-cum-halo. Few Renaissance depictions of a Cyclopean scene so completely fuse the antique with the modern. The swelling, framing veil is a classic feature of ancient Roman iconography; the grouping of the Nereid with her Tritonesque servants follows Philostratus very closely.[99] Yet the influence of Cinquecento sculpture and painting is no less insistent: Giulio Romano can be felt in the Cyclops' muscles, Michelangelo's *Aurora* in the turn of Galatea's head.[100]

The other fresco of the pair shows a Polyphemus in the plenitude of his jealous fury (*Cat. 95* (Fig. 10.17)). Steadying his weight on one leg and twisting menacingly

[98] See e.g. Vitzthum (1965); M. Bull (2005: 53–4). [99] See p. 62.
[100] Michelangelo: Martin (1965: 110).

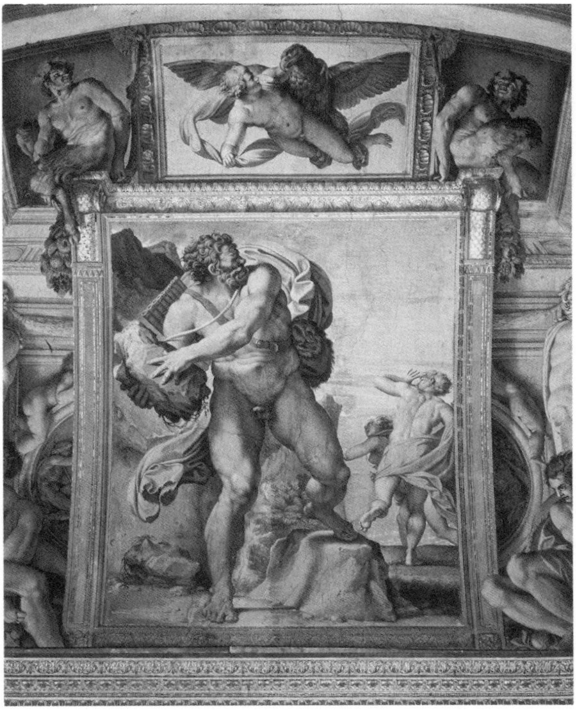

Fig. 10.17. Annibale Carracci, *Polyphemus Attacking Acis and Galatea*,1597–1607. Fresco in Palazzo Farnese, Rome.

away, he prepares to launch a huge rock at the helpless, fleeing Acis, with all the assurance of an Olympic shot-putter. Already in 1657 the biographer Giovanni Bellori (the seventeenth-century equivalent of Vasari) related this dynamic posture to the exposition given by Leonardo da Vinci in his *Treatise on Painting*: 'If someone is to throw spears or rocks, having turned his feet toward the target, he twists and bends and moves himself from there to the opposite side, where, when he gathers his strength, he returns with speed and ease to the point where he lets the weight leave his hands.'[101] As for the symbolism of the image, attempts have been made to situate it—and the other frescoes of the Galleria too—within Renaissance perceptions of love, and specifically Marsilio Ficino's threefold analysis of divine, human, and bestial love.[102] By this token, Polyphemus would certainly play the role of the beast. But we should not push this too far, since there

[101] Martin (1965: 110–11), citing ch. 182 of the *Treatise* in the translation by A. P. McMahon (1956).

[102] Vitzthum (1965: 4).

is considerable doubt about the overall iconology of the frescoes (and, in at least one case, about the subject matter being represented).[103] We prefer to dwell on a detail visible in the upper-left background: fire emerging from a mountain top—presumably the summit of Etna. The linking of the eruption to the Cyclops' 'burning fury' is the more plausible, given the precise placement of the volcanic fire: right next to the ogre's head.[104]

A Spectrum of Ogres

Alongside the medieval and early modern retellings, revisualizations, and commentaries that explicitly and unambiguously hark back to Graeco-Roman mythology, other stories from the same periods feature ogres whose characteristics partially overlap with those of the classical Cyclopes, without that ancestry being explicitly acknowledged. Such stories describe an isolated, monstrous, and sometimes one-eyed individual, who is sometimes—bringing the classical ancestry still closer—pitted against an ostensibly weaker but ultimately triumphant adversary.

Bearing no more than a passing resemblance to the Homeric Polyphemus is Fer Caille, the man-of-the-wood encountered by King Conaire in the Irish saga 'The Destruction of Da Derga's Hostel'. One-eyed, one-handed, and one-footed, he carries a squealing black pig on his back. He is also notable for his bristly hair: 'if a sackful of wild apples were emptied over it, each apple would catch on his hair, and none would fall to the ground.'[105] Also one-footed, and with a single eye in the middle of the forehead, is the giant described in *Owein or The Countess of the Fountain,* one of the tales from the Welsh *Mabinogion*. This giant is a 'great black man, no smaller than two men of this world'. He is the 'keeper of the forest': 'though ugly, he is not an unpleasant man'; a thousand wild animals graze about him.[106] Uglier still is the giant herdsman encountered by the knight Calogrenant in the twelfth-century Arthurian romance *Yvain* by Chrétien de Troyes:

> A peasant who resembled a Moor, ugly and hideous in the extreme—such an ugly creature that he cannot be described in words—was seated on a stump, with a great club in his hand. I approached the peasant and saw that his head was larger than a nag's or other beast's. His hair was unkempt and his bare forehead was more than two spans wide; his ears were as hairy and huge as an elephant's; his eyebrows heavy and his face flat. He had the eyes of an owl and the nose of a cat, jowls split like a wolf's, with the sharp reddish teeth of a boar; he had a russet beard, tangled moustache, a chin down to his breast and a long,

103 Chappell (1976).
104 Quotation from Martin (1965: 110).
105 J. Gantz (1981: 71).
106 Trans. J. Gantz (1976: 196).

> twisted spine with a hump. He was leaning on his club and wore a most unusual cloak, made neither of wool nor linen; instead, at his neck he had attached two pelts freshly skinned from two bulls or two oxen.[107]

Though not monocular, he wields a club and wears the skins of bulls or beeves. These Irish, Welsh, and French giants are far from being Cyclopes *sensu stricto*; at best they might qualify as their second cousins. Yet the resemblances are undeniable: hairiness, ugliness, great size, the connection with animals.

Considerably closer to classical, indeed Homeric, precedent is a tale from *The Book of Dede Korkut*, a collection of narratives about the heroic exploits of the Oghuz Turks.[108] The earliest written versions of the collection are variously dated to the fourteenth or fifteenth centuries.[109] Among the stories is an account of the overcoming of the monstrous one-eyed giant Tepegöz, who was persecuting the land of the Oghuz. In the end the hero Basat blinded him with a spit, escaping from the monster's cave concealed in a ram's skin.[110] Divergences from the Homeric version are obvious enough: the tale is set in inland Turkey; the famous Oghuz seer Dede Korkut persuades the monster to moderate his aggressive demands on the population; a mother who loses her son to the monster is the one who persuades Basat to take action; Tepegöz imprisons Basat in his boot; Tepegöz gives Basat a ring; Basat eventually beheads Tepegöz with the monster's own sword. Nevertheless, overlaps with the Odyssean version are evident, and are best explained through the influence, direct or indirect, of the Greek tradition, even if the precise mechanism of transmission eludes us.

A later example of proximity comes in canto 17 of Ariosto's mighty epic *Orlando furioso* (definitive, third edition in 1532). Norandin, King of Syria, and his bride Lucina, daughter of the King of Cyprus, are beset by an ogre called Orcus. Instead of eyes, he has two fungus-coloured bones protruding from his forehead; '[he is] like a mountain in motion'.[111] That is: Orcus is already facially deformed, and blind. He is also a herdsman: he stuffs some of the men he captures into a pouch 'like a shepherd's'. He lives in a cave quarried out of the rock at the edge of the sea; but he does not live alone. His wife has a face 'stamped with suffering and sadness'; with her are 'women and maidens of every age and condition, plain and fair'. Near the ogre's cave is another, where he keeps his flocks. His preferred diet is human flesh: he eats his victims raw, and swallows them whole. Having driven his flocks out of the cave, he corrals his would-be human victims into it, and closes it with (of course) a boulder. 'Then he went off with his flocks to pasture them, playing on a set of pipes which dangled from his neck.' With a nice touch of chivalry, Orcus never eats women, whom he can distinguish from men

107 See Owen (2003: 47–52). Trans. Kibler (2004: 298).
108 See pp. 8–9.
109 See e.g. Bremmer (2002: 136), citing O. Spies (1981); also Anderson (2000: 125).
110 The episode is translated in G. Lewis (1974: 140–50).
111 Trans. Waldman (1974), here and in subsequent quotations.

by their smell. He is outwitted by a trick. Norandin smears himself with ram's fat, which disguises his human smell. Then he dons a goatskin, gets down on all fours, and waits for Orcus to return. The captives in the cave similarly disguise themselves as goats. Orcus calls out his goats, feels them, and unwittingly lets out his human captives too. But he smells Lucina and thrusts her back into the cave, chaining her to a crag; she is eventually freed by a king and a mighty champion, who happen to be passing by. The presence of the classical Polyphemus is strong throughout, but the differences are no less notable. Perhaps the most remarkable is the prominence accorded to women, above all Orcus' long-suffering wife.

The five tales just considered can be dated to the medieval or early modern periods, even if precision is (except in the case of *Orlando*) impossible to achieve. Nor are they the only Cyclops-like tales that offer a chronological foothold. The oldest securely datable example is a tale preserved by Johannes de Alta Silva, a Cistercian monk from an abbey in Lorraine. In the course of his *Dolopathos, or Concerning the King and the Seven Sages* (*c.*1190), Johannes relates a story about a notorious band of robbers. Once they robbed a vastly rich giant, who lived in a remote cave.[112] In revenge, the giant dismembered, boiled, and ate all the robbers except the one who survived to tell the tale. This solitary survivor escaped in a way powerfully reminiscent of, yet also distinct from, the plot of *Odyssey* book 9. The giant complained of poor eyesight, so the robber offered to cure him in return for being spared. However, the mixture of boiling oil, lime, salt, sulphur, and arsenic that the robber poured over the ogre's face destroyed his sight for ever. The robber got away by putting on a ram's skin and horns, but the ogre's resources were not quite exhausted. He threw the robber a gold ring. No sooner did the robber put it on than he was compelled to shout 'Here I am!' Only by biting off his finger did he make his final getaway.[113]

The fact that this and the other five stories can stake claims to datability, albeit with variable degrees of certainty, constitutes them as a very small minority compared with the numerous Cyclops-like stories from every part of Europe and beyond, harvested by folklorists much later—almost all in the nineteenth century.[114] Although some, many, or all these later collections *might* preserve evidence of the content of tales already told in the medieval and early modern periods, there is no way of telling for certain. It follows that we are unable to produce a map, either geographical or chronological, of a hypothetical network of stories about Polyphemus-like figures whose deeds were being narrated during those periods. However, the existence of such a storytelling network is far from improbable; indeed, it may be the most plausible explanation for the enormously widespread *subsequent* evidence for shared tale-types throughout Europe and beyond.

[112] Gilleland (1981: 64–6); see p. 12.

[113] Appelbaum (2000: story 22); Bremmer (2002: 137).

[114] See p. 12.

At the Forge

Earlier we came across many allegorical readings of the Cyclopes *qua* pastoral ogres. But allegorical thinking could also be applied to them in their other roles.

A notable proponent of such thinking about the weapons-making Cyclopes was Francis Bacon. Given his championing of scientific method, Bacon's is perhaps not the first name that springs to mind in the context of mythography. Yet a crude myth/science polarity is here, as so often, profoundly misleading. As John Aubrey observed in his *Brief Life*, Bacon's house at St Albans, designed by the owner himself, sported figures of the pagan gods on the outside doors of the upper storey.[115] For Bacon, myths ('parables' or 'fables') fulfilled the twin purposes of simultaneously disguising and illustrating matters relating to religion, natural philosophy, and politics (but not history). As he argued in *The Advancement of Learning* (1605), such tales constituted 'allusive or parabolical poesy', 'poesy' being one of the three broad types of human learning, alongside history and philosophy.[116] The extent to which Bacon was really—as opposed to rhetorically—prepared to ascribe serious value to antique as opposed to modern (= scientific) knowledge is a matter of strenuous dispute among Baconian scholars.[117] However, it seems impossible to deny that, although he was disinclined to argue that *all* myths contained such veiled meanings, he did believe that at least some of them incorporated hidden wisdom.

In his *On the Wisdom of the Ancients* (1609), Bacon advanced a theory of myth considerably indebted (though without acknowledgement) to the often maligned Natale Conti.[118] Included as number three of his interpretations of thirty-one classical myths is an account of the weapons-making Cyclopes in their relationship with Zeus/Jupiter ('The Cyclops, or the Ministers of Terror'). Beginning in mythographical mode, Bacon narrates *his* version of the tale:

> The story is that the Cyclopes were at first on account of their fierceness and brutality driven by Jupiter into Tartarus, and condemned to perpetual imprisonment; but afterwards he was persuaded by the Earth that it would be for his interest to release them and employ them to make thunderbolts for him; which he accordingly did; and they with officious industry laboured assiduously with a terrible din in forging thunderbolts and other instruments of terror. In course of time it happened that Jupiter's wrath was kindled against Asclepius, son of Apollo, for raising a man from the dead by medicine; but because the deed was pious and famous and no just cause of displeasure, he concealed his anger and secretly set the Cyclopes upon him: who made no difficulty, but presently

115 Text in Dick (2016: 13). 116 Text in Kiernan (2000: 74–5).

117 See the fundamental article by R. Lewis (2010); book-length treatment in Lemmi (1933).

118 See Garner (1970); Briggs (2017).

> dispatched him with their thunderbolts; in revenge for which Apollo (with Jupiter's permission) slew them with his arrows.[119]

This account contains a number of innovations in relation to the ancient tradition: that it was Jupiter/Zeus, not Ouranos/Coelum, who imprisoned the Cyclopes; that it was the Cyclopes secretly, rather than Jupiter/Zeus openly, who slew Asclepius; that, instead of condemning Apollo to serve a mortal for a year, Jupiter/Zeus actually gave him licence to slay them. Thanks to these subtle twists, the myth, once ingeniously unmasked by Bacon, can be seen as narrating an episode of devious, princely *Realpolitik*:

> This fable seems to relate to the deeds of kings; by whom cruel and bloody and exacting ministers are in the first instance punished and put out of office. But afterwards by counsel of the Earth, that is by ignoble and dishonourable counsel, yielding to considerations of utility, they take them into service again, when they have need either of severity of executions or harshness in exactions. They on their part being by nature cruel and by their former fortune exasperated, and knowing well enough what they are wanted for, apply themselves to this kind of work with wonderful diligence; till for want of caution and from over eagerness to ingratiate themselves, they at one time or another (taking a nod or an ambiguous word of the prince for a warrant) perpetrate some execution that is odious and unpopular. Upon which the prince, not willing to take the envy of it upon himself, and well knowing that he can always have plenty of such instruments, throws them overboard, and leaves them to the course of law and the vengeance of the friends and relatives of their victims, and to popular hatred; and so amid much applause of the people, and great acclamations and blessings on the king, they meet at last, though late, the fate they deserve.

Perhaps for the first time in their careers, the Hesiodic weapons-makers find themselves transposed to the back-stabbing, courtly world of Shakespeare's history plays, or the shady corridors of Machiavellian power struggles.

Altogether less embroiled in political intrigue are the metalworkers (in the role of 'beaters') who hammer tirelessly in Vulcan's forge in fifteenth–seventeenth century art. A favourite context is Venus' adultery with Mars. Sometimes the Cyclopes appear in the scene where Apollo brings the awkward news to their employer. In other images they forge Aeneas' armour (typically at the request of Venus), or Cupid's arrows, or Jupiter's thunderbolts; seen against the mythical tradition stretching back to antiquity, this last motif amalgamates the Hesiodic weapons-manufacturers with the Callimachean blacksmiths. As for the physical

[119] Trans. Spedding, Ellis, and Heath (*c*.1900: 87–8), adapted, and in the subsequent quotation.

location of the representations, an apt and frequent choice is the space above a fireplace, as in Baldassare Peruzzi's fresco at the Villa Farnesina in Rome: real and imagined fires coalesce and mutually reinforce each other.

A unique Early Renaissance image of Vulcan's forge, doubtfully attributed to Ercole de' Roberti (*Cat. 79* (Fig. 10.18)), appears in the 'Sala dei Mesi' ('Hall of the Months') in the Palazzo Schifanoia ('Escape from Boredom') of Borso d'Este, Duke of Ferrara.[120] Three fresco panels adorn each of the four walls of a 24m x 12m reception hall. Each panel is divided horizontally into three parts: at the top is a procession in honour of one of the gods; in the middle, astrological material illustrates the month in question; at the bottom, Duke Borso's manifold achievements are variously celebrated. In the upper panel of 'September', the focus of attention is Vulcan.[121] At the left of the fresco, a stone-built arch frames a cave: this is where the god has his forge. A shield hung up outside, in the manner of an inn sign or a company logo, portrays the she-wolf suckling Romulus and Remus; in view of Virgil's description of the shield that Vulcan made for Aeneas (*Aen.* book 8) and that bore precisely this device, such a sign makes the perfect advertisement for the god's workshop. As for the labourers, there are four of them. To the right are two with vigorously raised hammers: the figure second from the right also holds tongs. At the far left, another blacksmith grasps the end of a long, thin implement. He and the hammer-wielders wear the same light-bluish costume, whose armour-like shape in the upper torso gives the misleading impression that they all have female breasts. Second from the left is a figure with a yellowish costume, a dark blue apron, and a single eye in the middle of his

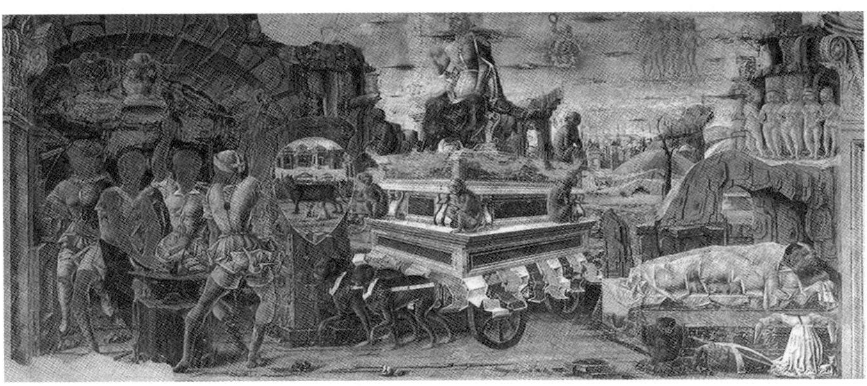

Fig. 10.18. Fresco panel 'September', *c.*1468–1470 (detail); possible attribution to Ercole de' Roberti. Hall of the Months, Palazzo Schifanoia, Ferrara.

[120] On the attribution, see Manca (1992: 169–71); he is sceptical about assigning the frescoes to Ercole.

[121] See Bertozzi (2009) for a detailed account of earlier interpretations.

forehead; if there could have been any doubt about the labourers' identity, this dispels it. To the far right, Mars and Venus lie in passionate embrace, hidden under a tightly fitting sheet; the vignette is living proof of Vulcan's humiliation, but also a reminder of his miraculous skill. But the rest of the fresco is enigmatic. Why, in particular, is Vulcan's ceremonial carriage, the centrepiece of the image, being drawn by a pair of monkeys, with several more squatting enigmatically on it for good measure? One option is to blame Boccaccio, who, citing, as so often, the now lost Theodontius, mistakenly wrote that Hephaestus/Vulcan was rescued by *simiis* (monkeys) instead of *Sintiis* (the people known as Sintians).[122] Or could there be more going on? The ape is traditionally associated with imitation and with the ridiculous.[123] Now Hephaestus/Vulcan is the god whose artistic creations imitate nature to the very life; and he also, from time to time, cuts a ridiculous figure. Maybe Boccaccio, in making his error, was writing more truly than he knew.

In 1536 the Dutch artist Maarten van Heemskerck gave a racier account of the Shield of Aeneas episode (*Cat. 87* (Fig. 10.19)), in one of several representations he painted of Vulcan's forge.[124] At the left stands Venus, with Cupid clinging to her; he is naked, she virtually so. They have obviously turned up to put in the standard order for Aeneas' armour and shield. But instead they gaze at the scene before them—in the case of little Cupid, with nervousness; in the case of the goddess of erotic desire, perhaps—who knows?—with enjoyment. For alongside her hammering husband are three ultra-macho workmen: our old friends. The one to the left, stark naked, shows off his shapely bottom to the viewer, though Venus has the opportunity to see him from the front. The other two Cyclopes are wearing rather snug briefs; it seems these were a later, censorious addition, but in fact they do nothing to diminish the Cyclopes' sexiness.[125] There is no trace of abnormality, ocular or otherwise. These are not monsters, but glamorous male models.

A nice demonstration of the truth that superficially similar visual schemata may differ *toto caelo* in their impact can be found in Titian's now lost *Cyclopes at the Forge of Vulcan*, which we know from the reproduction by the sixteenth-century Dutch engraver Cornelis Cort (*Cat. 92* (Fig. 10.20)). As in van Heemskerck's representation, the Cyclopes of Cort/Titian are vigorous and muscular, and two of them wield raised hammers; but there the resemblance ends. Carlo Ridolfi's seventeenth-century biography of Titian records that the work was commissioned by the city of Brescia.[126] Against the background of a wild and rocky landscape, six Cyclopes are forging cannons and other types of weapon; the smiths who face us are identified by a third eye in the forehead. The lion in the foreground

[122] *Gen. deor. gent.* 12.70; cf. Bertozzi (2009: 76 n. 13), citing a note by Fritz Saxl in Warburg (1932: 641).

[123] Imitation: Curtius (1953: 538–40); Vegetti (1983: 62–3). The ridiculous: Vegetti (1983: 60–1).

[124] On the artist, see Hand and Wolff (1986: 110–11).

[125] Kotková (2006: 192, citing Irr.).

[126] See Bondanella et al. (1996: 90–1).

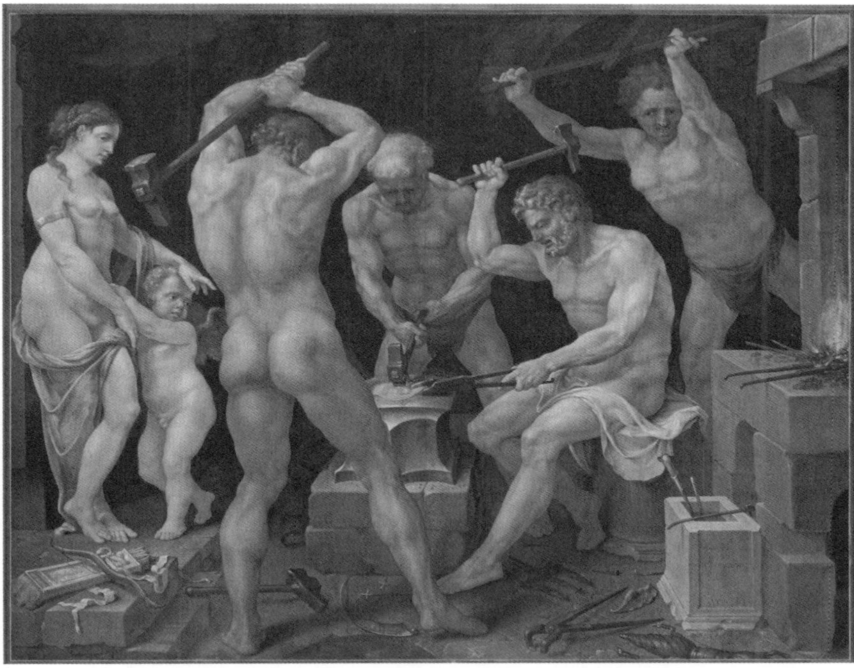

Fig. 10.19. Maarten van Heemskerck, *Venus and Cupid in Vulcan's Forge*. Oil on canvas, 1536.

symbolizes Venice, since, again according to Ridolfi, weapons were made in Brescia for the Venetian state. But by far the most impressive feature of the image is the raging fire in the background—like something from a Blake illustration of *The Divine Comedy*. Is this the controlled fire of the forge, or the erupting volcano? At all events, the imagery of fire lies at the heart not only of this image, but of Titian's vision of the world. Paul Hills has brilliantly set this vision into context:

> In Renaissance Venice, a city at the cutting edge of pharmacy and industrial processes of transmuting by distilling or by applying heat, the creative possibilities of this volatility were being explored. In this context fieriness engages the medium and subject of paint; it belongs to both tenor and substance as an energising, animating presence, embodied and loosed within the brushwork. It extends the locus of expression of fear or arousal beyond the body into the wider pictorial field.[127]

[127] Hills (2007: 190).

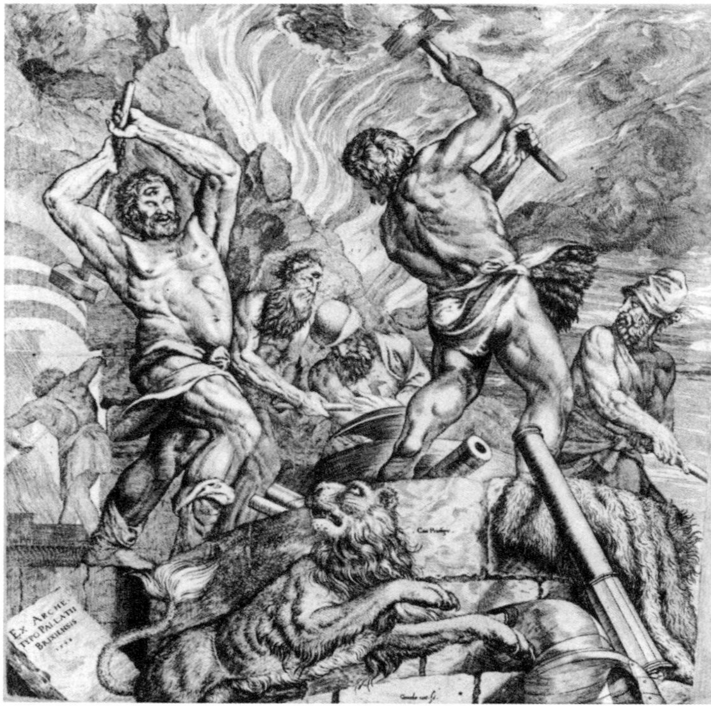

Fig. 10.20. Engraving by Cornelis Cort (*c.*1570) of Titian's lost *Cyclopes at the Forge of Vulcan.*

A city of fire in respects as diverse as artillery warfare, celebratory pyrotechnics, and destructive civic conflagrations, Venice profoundly shaped Titian's imagination. In Hills's words once more:

> Vulcan's forge is emblematic of the creative power of the artist, the site of heroic effort and fearful spectacle. As so often in Titian's art, spectacular effect becomes emotive affect. Phantasmal, irreducible to figurative narrative, the fieriness holds judgment in suspense and prolongs wonder; as an excess or efflorescence in the brushwork this fieriness renders emotive affect sensible.[128]

Titian's vision puts fire, once again, at the heart of what it is to be a Cyclops. Not without irony, Titian's original was destroyed in 1575—in a fire.

For a final image of Vulcan's forge, a world away from Titian in conception, we turn from Italy to Spain (though the work in question was in fact painted in

[128] Hills (2007: 201).

Rome). Velázquez's *Apollo in Vulcan's Forge* (1630) was bought by Philip IV for the palace of Buen Retiro in Madrid (*Cat. 105* (Fig. 10.21)). The moment chosen is that when Apollo arrives at the forge bringing Vulcan the news of Venus' adultery. The only character who has clearly stepped out of myth is Apollo, portrayed as a radiant, toga-clad, laurel-wreathed, haloed Sun God. Why Apollo? Or rather: why Apollo-as-the-Sun? Because already in Homer, and later in Ovid, it was the all-seeing eye of the Sun that detected the misbehaving pair.[129] Apollo apart, we could be in any smithy in a Spanish village. Vulcan, standing next to Apollo, has a slight but noticeable twist to his body, hinting at, rather than stressing, the lameness that affected his posture. The other four figures, interrupted in their task of forging armour, display varying degrees of astonishment. They look strong enough, but are hardly the improbably rippling Mr Universes portrayed by Titian/Cort and van Heemskerck. There is nothing anatomically unorthodox about their (two) eyes; the only striking thing about them is the look of consternation on the face of the second Cyclops from the right.

To say that art historians have disagreed about how to interpret the image would be an understatement.[130] According to some, mythology in seventeenth-century

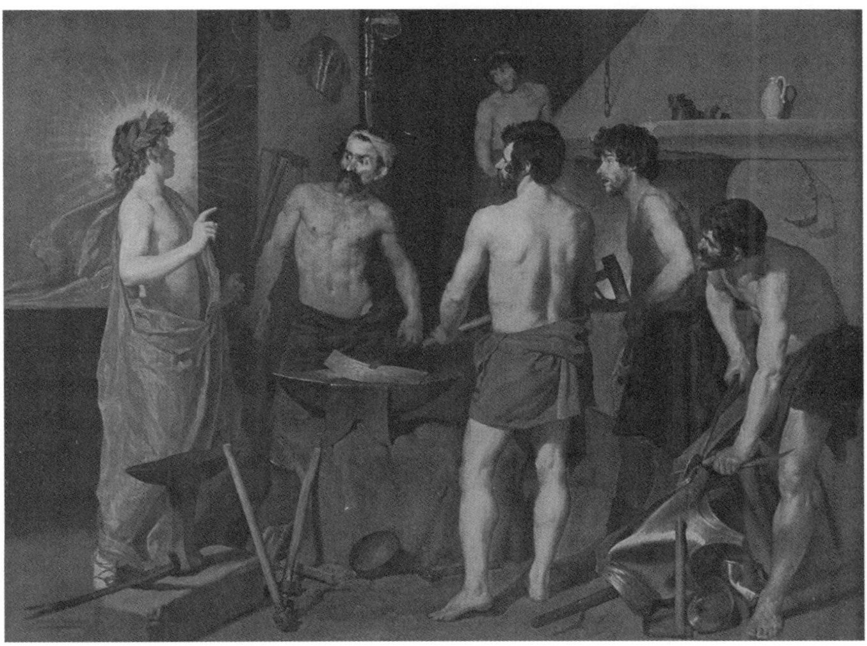

Fig. 10.21. Diego Velázquez, *Apollo in Vulcan's Forge*. Oil on canvas, 1630.

[129] Homer *Od.* 8.270–1; Ov. *Met.* 4.171–2. Helios/Sol and Apollo: cf. *LIMC* 'Helios/Sol', no. 593.
[130] For a *mise au point*, see González Estévez (2008–9).

Spain had to have a Christianizing function, the gods being transformed into moral *exempla*. On this reading, the message of the painting—predicated on the equation between Apollo–Sun and Christ—was that even the most powerful could not escape punishment, as (in the present case) the vice of adultery was overcome when it was made public.[131] Other critics have sought to equate the artisanship of Vulcan with the artistry of the painter himself.[132] From our point of view, the main thing to emphasize about the Cyclopes is their sheer ordinariness. The Cyclopean mythical tradition is a house with many mansions: Velázquez's vision is as far removed from monstrosity and ogrishness as it is possible to be.

Before leaving the weapons-makers, we cannot omit *Apollo killing the Cyclops*, an extraordinary painting by Domenichino (more properly Domenico Zampieri) (*Cat. 100* (Fig. 10.22)). Now on display as a canvas in the National Gallery in London, the work was originally part of a series of frescoes about the life of Apollo, decorating the walls of the Sala del Parnaso in the Villa Aldobrandini in

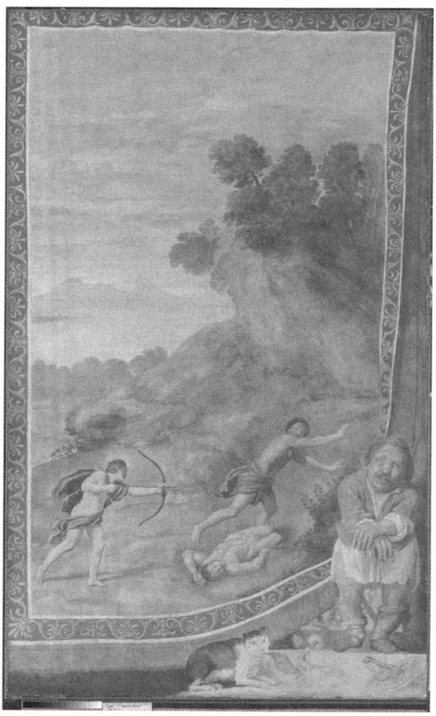

Fig. 10.22. Domenichino and assistants, *Apollo Killing the Cyclops*. Fresco, then on canvas, 1616–18.

[131] See e.g. Moffit (1983: 326); Pentecost (1986).

[132] Moffit (1983: 325).

Frascati.[133] The bulk of the now self-effacingly pallid painting represents a tapestry, drawn back at one corner: a picture within a wider pictorial frame. The tapestry portrays one of the least-often depicted episodes in the Cyclopean repertoire—namely, their slaughter at the hands of Apollo as punishment for having forged the thunderbolt with which Zeus/Jupiter had blasted Apollo's son Asclepius. One Cyclops has already been shot dead, the other soon will be, targeted by Apollo in a landscape worthy of Poussin. What makes the image remarkable is not just the rareness of the subject, but the presence of a fourth character, not *in* the scene, but outside and beside it: the dwarf in the bottom right-hand corner. Forlorn expression, humble clothing, chained hands: everything conspires to effect the starkest contrast between the world of divine myth evoked by the tapestry, and the literally and figuratively marginalized character exhibited alongside it. But, for Domenichino's public, as they gazed not just at the tapestry-within-a-painting but at the painting as a whole, the dwarf was both an artistic fiction and a living truth. Giambattista Passeri, Domenichino's pupil and biographer, relates that the dwarf was an actual member of the court (that of Cardinal Pietro Aldobrandini) for which the image was designed. At the moment when the painting was unveiled, the dwarf was—so the anecdote goes—performing a dance for the court's amusement. Apparently the sudden revelation of his painted likeness was designed to humiliate him, and doubtless also to increase the general mirth. Be that unpleasant idea as it may, the complex spatial layering in which Domenichino's doomed blacksmiths are implicated constitutes another landmark in Cyclopean history.[134]

Gardens and Grottoes

It is by now a truism that the provision of a comprehensive account of the Renaissance—if such a hybristically bold undertaking were even conceivable—demands an explanation for the presence not only of the ideal, the rational, and the harmonious, but also of the monstrous and the grotesque. The validity of such a view applies right across the aesthetic spectrum, but perhaps nowhere more powerfully than in the history of gardens. For in early modern Europe gardens constitute one of the preferred sites for the display, not only of mythological imagery in general, but of the imagery of monstrosity in particular.[135] Why should this be? In the persuasive view of Luke Morgan, author of a recent analysis of the relationship between monstrosity and early modern gardens, the reason is

[133] For an account of how the frescoes got to London, see Salerno (1963: 194). Lee (2015) discusses the implications of the transfer from fresco to canvas.

[134] Passeri (1772: 13–14); Lee (2015: 40).

[135] On gardens as the site *par excellence* for Renaissance mythological imagery, see M. Bull (2005: 82).

that the garden was a space inherently less decorum-bound, and more tolerant of contradiction and counter-normative behaviour, than alternative spaces such as the piazza or the church. 'Monsters', Morgan argues, 'can... be admitted to gardens, which... simultaneously affirm and contest norms... The garden functions as a kind of distorting or critical mirror, bringing together disparate and even opposed concepts, figures, and formations...'.[136] Among the types of monstrosity most commonly depicted in Renaissance gardens are three identified in the survey of monsters by the sixteenth-century French surgeon (and expert on battlefield disfigurements) Ambroise Paré: excess, deficiency, and hybridity.[137] Hybridity is not a Cyclopean characteristic, but excess (of size and of appetite, and sometimes—when he has three of them—of eyes) and deficiency (of both sight and insight) most definitely are. They apply particularly to Polyphemus, a repeated presence in early modern gardens, above all in grottoes.

The gardens of Roman antiquity featured two types of artificial grotto. One of these imitated a natural cave, the other was a more architecturally formal, niche-like construction known as a *nymphaeum*, semi-circular in shape and decorated with statues; the name evoked the connection with the nymphs of springs. Such landscape features, which became increasingly prevalent during the Roman Empire, were predominantly found (for obvious reasons) in gardens belonging to the wealthy elite.[138] Thus, as a constituent of the sixteenth- and seventeenth-century Italian, and then European, garden, the grotto could be said to look back to classical precedents.[139] But in truth such a debt was modest, since little relevant physical or textual evidence had survived from antiquity. Renaissance and Mannerist garden designers were establishing new rules of practice right across the board, and designers of grottoes in particular went far beyond any model distantly known from antiquity, evolving their own innovative and fantastic cavelike structures. The most spectacular example is the Grotta Grande in the Boboli Gardens in Florence, created by Bernardo Buontalenti between 1583 and 1593. To say that it 'imitates' nature is to say churlishly little: with its stalactites, its stone- and mineral-encrusted walls, its mural landscapes, and its sculpted figures of humans and animals, it reimagines and dramatically intensifies nature. It is the more precious since the majority of Italian Renaissance grottoes have not survived. However, we know that grottoes continued to feature in later sixteenth-century Italian gardens, whether in palace or villa, in city or countryside; and their model later extended to other parts of Europe.

The ideology of the Renaissance garden—and its potentially complex, allegorical significance—achieves particular resonance in the dark and secret world of

[136] Morgan (2016: 46). [137] Paré (1982); see the discussion in Morgan (2016: 82–3).

[138] Miller (1982: 17–20); Morel (1998: 7); Bowe (2004). On *nymphaea*, see Sinn (2005: 78, with pl. 6 ('Spelaion', no. 8)). On Roman gardens in general: Grimal (1984); Macdougall (1987); Macdougall and Jashemski (1981).

[139] Renaissance *nymphaea*: M. Bull (2005: 76–8).

the grotto, a space that might, when suitably decorated with human figures, be taken as illustrating two antithetical cosmic processes: the post-diluvian emergence of human life from stones and, conversely, the fossilization of living things into rock.[140] Within such an overarching concept, one element was more important than all the rest: water. Water had already been a fundamental constituent of the grotto in antiquity, but in the sixteenth-century grotto its role becomes more elaborate and more sophisticated. And with water go the *sounds* of water—and, as we shall shortly see, the sounds of Polyphemus.

Linguistically inseparable from grottoes are *grotteschi*, the term applied to the variety of fantastic ornamentation that burgeoned in sixteenth-century Italy.[141] Fundamental to the genesis of the style, and to the coining of the name, was the serendipitous rediscovery, towards the end of the fifteenth century, of Nero's Las Vegas-scale Roman palace the *Domus Aurea*, together with the hitherto undreamed-of evidence for antique painting that the edifice revealed.[142] Since the palace had long since been built over, what had originally been corridors and rooms gave the misleading appearance of subterranean caves and grottoes; hence the term *grotteschi* for the weird, hybrid, metamorphic forms that conspicuously adorned their walls and vaults.[143] The value of 'the grotesque' as an artistic style—the subject of controversy already in antiquity, as Horace and Vitruvius bear witness—soon became contentious once more, with figures as substantial as Benvenuto Cellini and Giorgio Vasari joining in the debate.[144] Particular attention was paid to the role of the grotesque in gardens.[145] And with the grotesque, the grotto: locus of mystery, strangeness, and night, a place of dreams, the atmospheric antecedent of Symbolism and Surrealism.

According to Jacques Boyceau de la Barauderie, Louis XIII's superintendent of gardens, the purpose of grottoes was to evoke the wild caves of nature.[146] Mythical cave-dwellers such as Pan, the Nymphs, and Polyphemus perfectly matched such a concept. In particular, the abnormal physique of gigantic, one-eyed Polyphemus ideally suited an environment that privileged the grotesque. More broadly, the grotto was conceived as a place where the pastoral tranquillity of the *locus amoenus* could be broken by the presence of menacing figures whose appearance or behaviour disturbed the calm. That at least is the implication of a letter written in 1551 by the poet Annibale Caro, when he recommended contrastingly appropriate subjects for depiction in a grotto: singing shepherds, dancing nymphs, as well

[140] Morel (1998: 91 and *passim*).

[141] Morel (1997, 1998); Morgan (2016: 47–81); cf. Harpham (1982). Terminology: Barasch (1971); Edwards and Graulund (2013).

[142] Dacos (1969); Chastel (1988); Miernowski (2014: 24).

[143] G. Bull (1956: 62–3), with Summers (2003: 42 n. 2); Vasari (1996: i. 924–30), with Morgan (2016: 183 n. 6).

[144] Hor. *Ars P.* 1–13; Vitr. *De arch.* 7.5; with Miernowski (2014: 24–5) and Adler (2014: 214–15); cf. M. Bull (2005: 81).

[145] Morgan (2016: 49–68).

[146] Boyceau de la Barauderie (1638: 80).

as satyrs, fauns, and sileni, but also, more unsettlingly, the Rape of Persephone, Circe's transformation of men into pigs, and Ulysses' blinding of Polyphemus.[147]

As adornments of palace gardens, grottoes were sites of a pleasure that was at once 'natural' and supremely artificial. Particularly striking was the deployment of elaborate hydraulic machinery to generate jets and fountains of water: a constantly moving theatre of automata and aquatic special effects.[148] Instrumental in these fantastic developments was the Renaissance reception of the works of Hero of Alexandria (1st cent. CE), especially his treatise *Pneumatica*, which included various descriptions of machinery that enabled human and animal figures to be moved by flows of water.[149] In the context of the Renaissance grotto, the intended impression was one of magical surprise, since the mechanisms behind the movements of both human figures and water were deftly concealed.[150]

A prime example can be found in the gardens of the villa of Pratolino near Florence, created by Buontalenti for Francesco I de' Medici. Begun in 1569, the work took fifteen years to complete. The great park was to have a complicated history. It fell into ruin during the eighteenth century, to make way for an English garden; after a century in the ownership of the Russian industrialist Prince Pavel Davidov and his descendants, it eventually became a UNESCO World Heritage Site.[151] But in its heyday it was magnificent. One of its most remarkable features, then as now, was the huge figure of the man-mountain, the 'Colosso del Appennino' by Giambologna. No less impressive was the astonishing deployment of water. As John Evelyn recorded in his *Diary*:

> The Gardens delicious and full of fountaines: In the Grove sits Pan feeding his flock, the Water making a melodius sound through his pipe, and an Hercules whose Club yeilds a Showre of Water, which falling into a huge *Concha* has a Naked Woman riding on the backs of Dolphins: In another Grotto is *Vulcan* and his family, the walls richly composd of Coralls, Shells, Coper and Marble figures; with the huntings of Severall beasts, moving by the force of Water: Here having ben well wash'd for our Curiosity, we went down a large Walk, at the sides whereof gushes out of imperceptible pipes, couched under neath, slender pissings of water, that interchangeably fall into each other's Chanells, making a lofty and perfect arch, so as a man on horseback may ride under it and not be wet with one drop, nay so high, as one may walk with a speare in ones hand under each spout, this Canopi or arch of Water, was mi thought one of the surprizings<t> magnificences I had ever seene, and exceedingly fresh during the heate of summer.[152]

147 Caro (1957–61: ii. 100), cited in Lazzaro (1990: 83 n. 31).
148 Jeanneret (2001: 136–7).
149 Strong (1979: 75–6); Laird (2017).
150 Cf. Brunon (2008: 620–1).
151 Zangheri (1987); Pozzana (2011: 82–7).
152 Evelyn (1955: ii. 418, for May 1645).

Before Evelyn, accounts by Michel de Montaigne and Fynes Moryson had similarly stressed the impact of the *jeux d'eau* and the automata.[153] A sketch by the Modenese artist Giovanni Guerra in 1598 (*Cat. 96*) shows a 'Grotto of Galatea'; the drawing bears the caption '*Suona il Tritone, Galatea vien fuori*' ('When the Triton sounds [his conch], out comes Galatea').[154] Already in 1586 the Florentine Francesco de Vieri had conjured this image into textual life:

> It is all of mother-of-pearl, with a sea of water with various reefs covered with corals and sea shells. Among the said reefs appears a Triton sounding a marine snail shell, and at this moment a reef is opened, from which issues Galatea herself on a golden shell drawn by two dolphins that spout water through their mouths; she is accompanied on the shore of the sea by two other nymphs who emerge from two other places…and throw out water from some coral branches they hold in their hands.[155]

Galatea, then, but no Polyphemus. The inspiration may have been Raphael's *Triumph of Galatea* for the Villa Farnesina in Rome, in which, as we have seen, a dolphin-powered, shell-borne Galatea steals the show, with a conch-blowing Triton in attendance.[156]

Salomon and Isaac de Caus

But Polyphemus could not be kept out of the action for long. Among those inspired by the Pratolino grotto were two hydraulic engineers, whose extraordinary imagination allowed the Cyclops not only to remain for ever in the presence of his beloved nymph, but to keep her in permanent musical thrall.

Born in Normandy, the Huguenot Salomon de Caus (1576–1626) worked for a while in England as architect and garden designer for Henry, Prince of Wales, at Richmond Palace, for Robert Cecil at Hatfield House, and for Anne of Denmark at Greenwich Palace and Somerset House.[157] Around 1595 he visited Pratolino, where, not surprisingly, he was impressed by Giambologna's mighty 'Appennino', though he misidentified it as 'a figure of a great Cyclops, in the body of which are some grottoes very artificially made'.[158] What he saw at Pratolino more generally inspired some of the designs in his treatise *Les Raisons des forces mouvantes*.[159]

[153] Montaigne (1992: 79–80); cf. W. Smith (1961: 155). On Moryson, see Willes (2011: 143).

[154] Hunt (1986: 56, fig. 37).

[155] De Vieri (1586: 35); trans. W. Smith (1961: 158).

[156] See p. 260.

[157] Strong (1979: 73–4). On Salomon, see especially Morgan (2007).

[158] S. de Caus (1615: bk II, problem 14); cf. Morgan (2007: 43). The exact date of his visit is uncertain: cf. Morgan (2007: 214 n. 42).

[159] S. de Caus (1615).

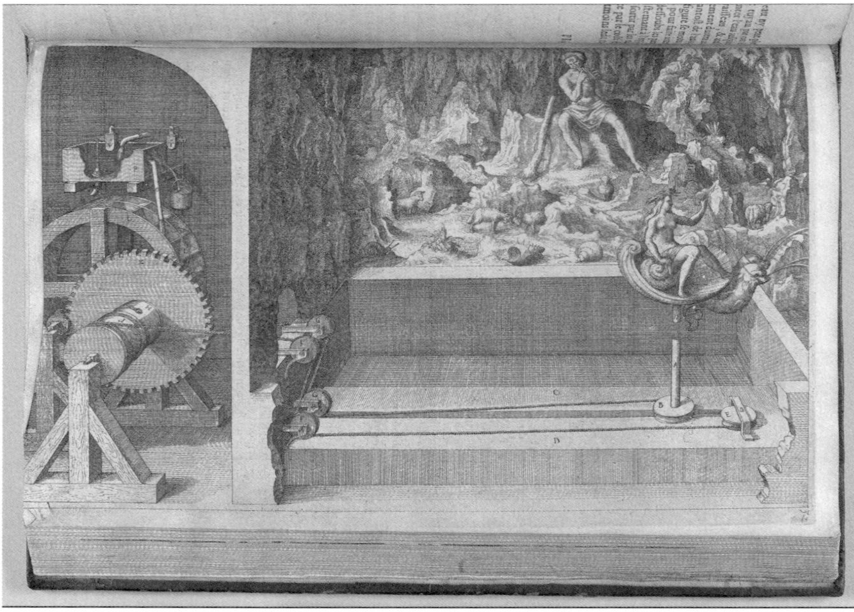

Fig. 10.23. Design for a water feature by Salomon de Caus, *Les Raisons des forces mouvantes*, 1615.

One of his most memorable drawings portrays a grotto (*Cat. 99* (Fig. 10.23)). In the foreground Galatea perches in a dolphin-drawn shell, capable of travelling laterally thanks to an intricate system of gears and pulleys. The drawing lays bare the mechanism for the guidance of anyone wanting to build it, but the engineering would have been submerged when the spectacle was in full swing, thereby arousing astonishment among spectators.[160] In the background, surrounded by his flock, sits not (as at Pratolino) Triton, but Polyphemus, playing the syrinx—winsomely pastoral, and not in the least *horridus*. The way the sounds of his piping are to be generated, and even the tune itself, are explained by de Caus with sober but delicious precision (*Problem* 25):[161]

> Here shall be represented the Engin proper to make the Flajolet Sound to the Cyclope of the precedent plate: Therefore let there be a Musical Wheel marked with A, about 4 or 5 foot in Diameter, perfect round, and divided with Teeth, as you may see in the Figure, so as a Pinion of 8 Teeth marked with B may turn the

[160] Kang (2011: 120 with n. 71), citing similar emphasis already by Aristotle and Hero on the importance of hiding the engineering workings in order to heighten wonder.

[161] We reproduce the text in I. de Caus (1659), in which Salomon's description is re-presented (*re* pl. XVI there).

> said Wheel; and to the Arber of the said Pinion there shall be a Wheel having 32 Teeth, marked with D, which another Pinion marked with C shall turn, and to the Arber of the said Pinion C there shall be a water Wheel marked with F, about 2 foot and a half or 3 foot in Diameter, which shall be turned by the water descending from the Pipe G, and so when the said water Wheel shall turn it shall cause the Musical Wheel to turn, by means of the other Wheels: afterwards there shall be put the Summer [i.e. horizontal beam or board] marked with H, the Fabrick whereof shall be shewn at large, so as the Keys of the said Summer shall be parallel at half an inch distance from the Musical Wheel: afterwards divide the said Musical Wheel in 25 or 30 equal parts, each part in turning shall be an ordinary measure of Musick: and more-over all the said parts shall be divided into 8 equal parts, to put on Crochets upon each division, if it be required, of which there are 8 for one measure; and if you will you may put on Demi Crochets, or Quavers: afterwards the pins are to be put upon the said Wheel ¾ of an inch above the Superficies of the said Musical Wheel, so as when the Wheel shall turn, the said pins may touch the Keys of the Summer and put them down and cause them to open the Valvs of the said Summer: as concerning the Pins they shall be put according to the Tune that you desire the Flajolet to play. That which is here set down begins thus [Fig. 10.24].

The instructions continue for another half-page, including the information that there needs to be a set of twelve holes in the 'Summer', one located below each key; these holes should be connected, by tubes of leather or lead, to organ pipes, in order to create the sound of Polyphemus' piping. The overall result would have been to create a sounding water ballet, in which Galatea would have moved from side to side, as if in response to the Cyclops' mesmerizing music: not so much Beauty and the Beast as Svengali and Trilby. Just for once, it would have been Polyphemus who called the emotional shots.[162]

What led Salomon to put Polyphemus in control, as opposed to taking the Raphaelesque option of accompanying a triumphant Galatea with a subsidiary

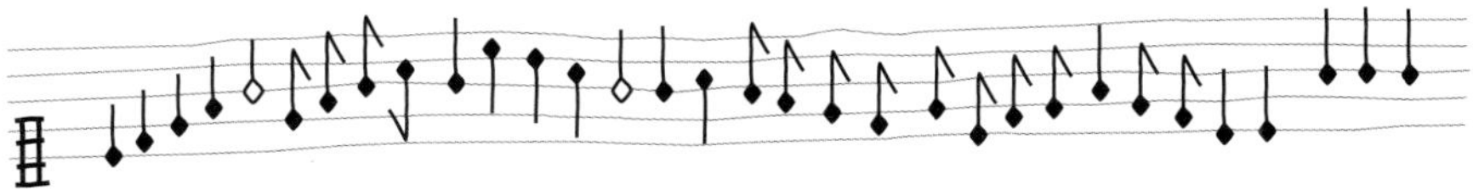

Fig. 10.24. Polyphemus' tune, as composed for De Caus's imaginary grotto. The transcription is approximate, as not every note is unambiguously clear on the printed page of De Caus's text.

[162] For the importance of the theory and practice of music in Salomon's work, see Grillner (1995: esp. ch. 3).

Triton? Ovid may have played a part, since contemporary water-driven sculptures in grottoes took their inspiration from his poetic narratives. In addition, or alternatively, Salomon may have visited the Villa Aldobrandini, where, as we shall see in a moment, a piping Polyphemus appears in the Nymphaeum (though without Galatea). Whatever the backstory, no student of Cyclopean mythology can afford to miss Salomon's enchanting and novel designs.

Isaac de Caus borrowed and adapted many of the mechanisms designed by his brother, but enjoyed his own independent career in landscape design.[163] In his (to give it its full, catchy title) *New and Rare Inventions of Water-Works, shewing the Easiest Waies to Raise Water Higher then the Spring, by which Invention the Perpetual Motion is proposed, many hard Labours performed, and Varieties of Motions and Sounds produced. A Work both Useful, Profitable and Delightful for all sorts of People*, one of the drawings depicts a grotto with Polyphemus and Galatea. There are slight differences in posture from Salomon's conception, but the focus of both schemes is the hydraulic mechanism underlying the scene.

Neither of the two de Caus designs for a Polyphemus-and-Galatea grotto made the transition to physical reality. But we know that at least some of Salomon's projects did become real, notably in the gardens of Somerset House in London, where a creation based on the Mount Parnassus fountain/grotto at Pratolino was constructed.[164] Perhaps too the de Caus influence extended to the garden of Sir Francis Carew at Beddington. In the words of the Moravian traveller Baron Waldstein, who visited it in 1600:

> The garden contains a beautiful square-shaped rock, sheltered on all sides and very cleverly contrived: the stream flows right through it and washes it all around. In the stream one can see a number of different representations: the best of these is Polyphome [*sic*] playing on his pipe, surrounded by all kinds of animals.[165]

Thanks to state-of-the-art technology, music had been promoted from the margins to the centre of Cyclopean mythology.

The Villa Aldobrandini

On a hillside above Frascati, some 20 kilometres south-east of Rome, stands a villa constructed around 1600 for the cardinal whose name it bears. The Villa

[163] Although the precise family relationship between Salomon and Isaac cannot be demonstrated with certainty, it is highly likely that they were brothers; see Morgan (2007: 33–6).

[164] Hunt (1986: 122); Morgan (2007: 115–21).

[165] In Groos (1981: 163–5); cited in Phillips and Burnett (2005: 162).

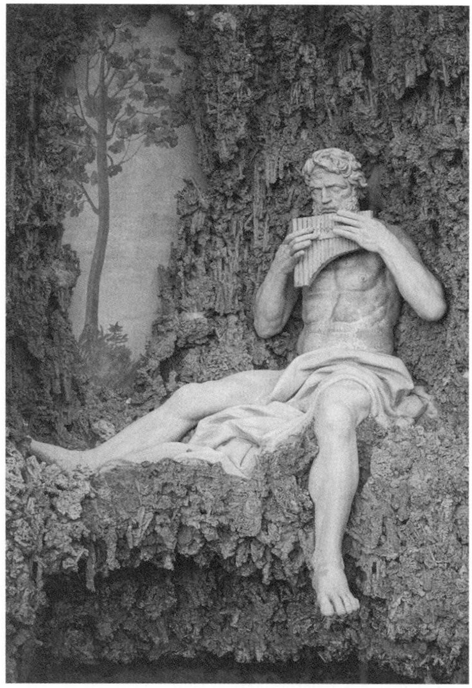

Fig. 10.25. Jacques Sarazin, statue of Polyphemus (*c.*1621) in the 'Theatre of Water', Villa Aldobrandini, Frascati.

Aldobrandini is still hugely impressive, in spite of the damage it suffered in 1943; being the base of the German High Command for the Mediterranean and of the Italian military, the town and villa were pounded by US bombing raids. One of the most spectacular features of the gardens is the so-called Theatre of Water, a semicircular construction with its walls articulated by columns and caryatids, and featuring five niches-cum-grottoes, recalling the form of the Roman *nymphaeum*.[166] Each niche contains fountains, and statues that used to emit sounds and move, powered by the kind of hydraulics evidenced at Pratolino and in the schemes of Salomon and Isaac. Though the mechanisms have not survived, the statues are in good repair. One of them, by the French sculptor Jacques Sarazin, represents Polyphemus (*c.*1621).

The presence of the Cyclops in a *nymphaeum* was not unprecedented: he figured in two ancient *nymphaea*, one at Selçuk near İzmir, and one at Baiae. But these represented Odysseus' offering of the wine.[167] The Aldobrandini Polyphemus, by contrast, blows the syrinx (*Cat. 103* (Fig. 10.25)); the implied mythical context is the courtship of Galatea.[168] Wavy-haired and rather

[166] See Steinberg (1965: 455). [167] *LIMC* 'Odysseus' nos 85 and 86.

[168] The diarist John Evelyn described a monster who made 'a terrible roaring with a horn' (Evelyn 1955: entry for 5 May 1645). *Pace* Hobhouse and Taylor (1990: 56), this was not Polyphemus

handsome, he looks more like a god of nature than a Cyclops, though his single open eye, positioned above and midway between two closed ones, leaves his identity in no doubt.[169] The prototype could have been Annibale Carracci's *Polyphemus Courting Galatea* from the Galeria Farnese in Rome,[170] though Carracci's Cyclops is a lot more muscular—and there is no Galatea in the Theatre of Water.[171] In any case, what seems to have been most notable about the Aldobrandini Polyphemus was, not his third eye, nor his size, but—once again—his music.

Orti Oricellari

Majestically solitary, an enormous plastered masonry statue of Polyphemus, a little over ten metres high, stands in the Orti Oricellari in Florence, not in a grotto but in the middle of an open meadow (*Cat. 109* (Fig. 10.26)).[172] It was sculpted around 1650 by Antonio Novelli, a pupil of Giambologna; in its restored form, it still towers over its surroundings.[173] Originally conceived as a place of recreation for literati and philosophers, the garden reinvented itself several times during the eighteenth and nineteenth centuries. But the mighty Cyclops, Herculean in physique, has remained a constant feature. What distinguishes Novelli's Polyphemus is his posture: with both hands raised, head looking upwards, and mouth open, he drinks from a wineskin. The scene has nothing of the pastoral about it, and nothing—at least at first sight—that evokes his relationship with Galatea. *This* Polyphemus is the ogre who gullibly drinks the wine offered to him by Odysseus—and he drinks it directly from the bottle, not from the iconographically traditional cup. Yet it is worth mentioning a visual similarity with several scenes in which the Cyclops raises hands above his head, not to quench his thirst, but to launch a rock, either towards the ship of the escaping Odysseus, or towards Acis. In other words, given that the wineskin is, in terms of its sculptural material, actually a rock, there *may* be a compositional hint towards the Polyphemus–Galatea–Acis triangle.

However that may be, another aspect of the scene is indisputable: the focus on Polyphemus' act of drinking. In his biography of Novelli, Filippo Baldinucci described how the statue doubled as a fountain, and that the 'wine' that flowed constantly into Polyphemus' mouth was water.[174] According to Baldinucci, the

(who blows a syrinx) but the centaur who inhabits another of the niches. The sound of the syrinx (and that of the horn) came, of course, from hydraulically generated air.

[169] Even so, the seventeenth-century British traveller Richard Lassels thought the statue was of Pan: Lassels (1670: pt II, 310); cf. Gordo Peláez (2001: 166).

[170] Schwager (1961–2: 310 n. 66).

[171] *Pace* Steinberg (1965: 460); cf. C. D'Onofrio (1963: fig. 111).

[172] Nearby, though, there was a Grotto of Polyphemus, also known as the Cave of the Winds.

[173] See Vaccari (1986) and above all Morolli et al. (1993).

[174] Baldinucci (1681–1728: 344); text quoted in Passerini (1854: 48–9), and P. Caliterna (1993: 171).

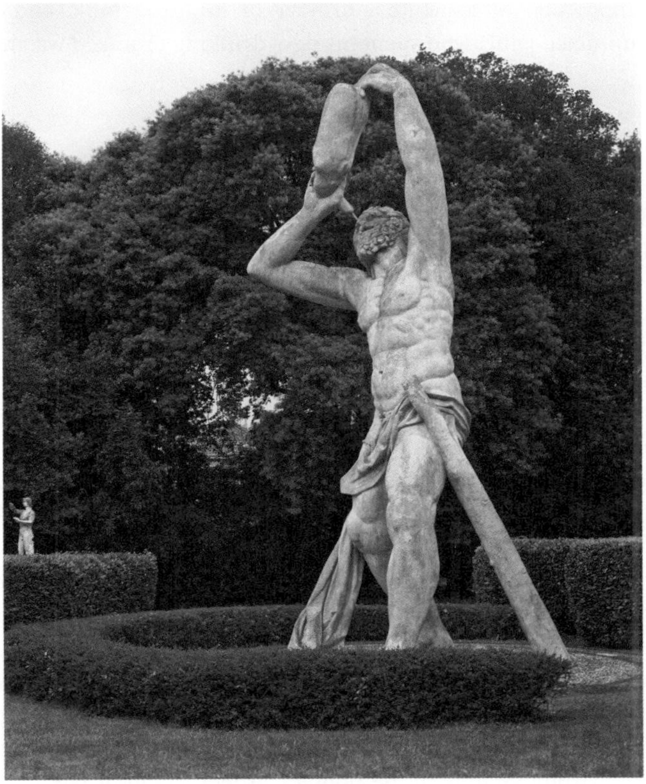

Fig. 10.26. Antonio Novelli, *Polyphemus*, *c.*1650. Orti Oricellari, Florence.

giant's torso housed a bronze container that collected the liquid the giant drank, and that then flowed down through pipes into the basin. Alas, modern geophysical analysis fails to bear out this hypothesis.[175] Moreover, Luigi Caliterna, a modern expert on the restoration of the statue, is sceptical that it was a locus of *giocchi d'acqua*, not least because the material the statue was made from would not have withstood constant moisture.[176] But Caliterna did find the remains of a glass cylinder that could have linked the mouth of the jar with the mouth of the giant, a cylinder through which a minimal quantity of water might have passed, to be conveyed by a small tube down to the basin.[177] What is lacking is evidence of a system for *raising* the water from the basin to the 'wineskin'. In the absence of this, the overall water cycle—if one ever existed—is beyond our capacity to reconstruct. A pity: such a cycle *would* have created a thoroughly innovative and

[175] P. Caliterna (1993: 176).
[176] L. Caliterna (1993: 125–6).
[177] L. Caliterna (1993: 127).

engaging impression of a habitual drinker of unmixed milk, and occasional drinker of unmixed wine, who spent his days drinking unmixed water.[178]

Le Jardin du Luxembourg

Our final grotto holds a special place in our affections since, as we said in our Preface, it was the place where we decided to write this book. The site is an elongated pool on the north-east side of the Jardin du Luxembourg in Paris, at the far end of which is an architectural niche. The fountain below it was begun in 1624 on the instructions of Marie de' Medici, widow of Henri IV of France; its designer was the hydraulics expert Tomasso Francini, whose impressive CV included work at Pratolino. The popularity of the Italian Mannerist style in France drew artists across the Alps to ply their trade, a trend that matched the inclinations of Florence-born Marie.

At the outset there was nothing Cyclopean about the Fontaine Médicis. The original sculptures showed two nymphs pouring water from jars, while a subsequent restoration carried out for Napoleon introduced a Venus in her bath.[179] Only after a further major reconstruction in the 1860s—which included shifting the position of the fountain by 30 metres—did Polyphemus make his appearance. The sculptor was Auguste Ottin. The group he made (*Cat. 116* (Fig. 10.27)) comprises a huge bronze Polyphemus kneeling on a rocky outcrop; below, in white marble, is the much smaller figure of Acis, lovingly cradling a swooning and near-naked Galatea in his arms. The niche they all inhabit is no walk-in grotto on the pattern of the Grotta Grande in the Boboli Gardens. A closer parallel, at least in respect of the artificial stalactites, is the Theatre of Water in the Villa Aldobrandini. But, whereas the Aldobrandini Cyclops is a tranquil piper, his equivalent in the Fontaine Médicis is alert, active, and menacing: the bull's hide partly draping him marks him out as a wild beast poised to pounce.

Looking back over the various grotto-esque Cyclopes, we need to distinguish their appearance from that of many of the more exaggeratedly unusual sculptures in Renaissance and Mannerist grottoes. Such Cyclopes are more notable for their Herculean physique—shades of Giulio Romano and Annibale Carracci—than for their ocular deformity, which usually takes the form of a relatively discreet, superior, third eye (which may even be hard to make out at a distance). The exception, as in the Orti Oricellari, is the Odyssean Polyphemus; far commoner is the lovesick herdsman. Most characteristic of all is Polyphemus the musician, above all in the hydraulic imaginations of the brothers de Caus.

[178] We reject the view of G. Morolli in Morolli et al. (1993: 44–5) that the giant should be interpreted as a son of Aeolus, god of the winds, and that the skin that he holds aloft is the 'bag' in which all the winds were kept. The ogre's third eye is clearly visible in an etching of *c.*1830 by Emilio Burci ('Colosso del Polifemo', V&A Museum, London, E.193–1961), and there is no reason to believe that this falsifies the original.

[179] Gaillard (1995: 71).

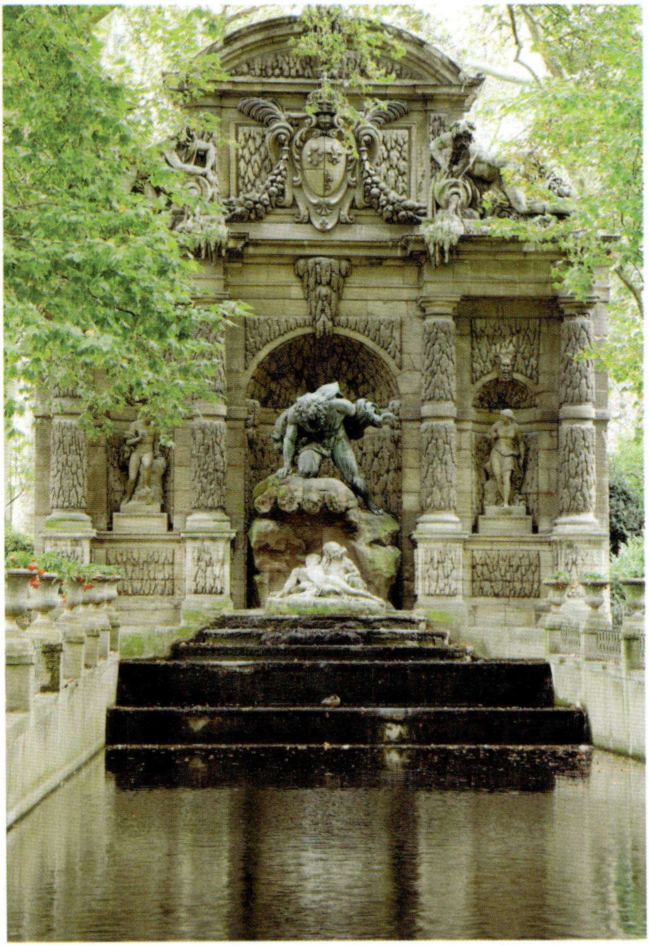

Fig. 10.27. Auguste Ottin, *Polyphemus Surprising Acis and Galatea,* 1866. Fontaine Médicis, Jardin du Luxembourg, Paris.

The Pastoral Ogre: Love and Brutality

Poetry

Parallel to and interlocking with the physical space shaped and decorated by the grotto designer is another area, no less verdant and no less artificial: the linguistic territory occupied by the writer of pastoral.[180] Like the grotto, pastoral verse created a local habitation for Polyphemus in his amorous relationship with Galatea.

[180] See still Highet (1949: 162–77).

Much more insistently than the grotto, however, it constituted a site where Cyclopean violence furiously challenged the poise and calm of reciprocal song. The Polyphemus–Galatea–Acis triangle offered wonderful material for the poetic pastoralist, providing, as it did, just the kind of rough-edged brutality needed to disrupt the otherwise Edenic lives of nymphs and shepherds.[181]

Resuming after a gap of a millennium the claims of pastoral to be regarded as a serious poetic vehicle, Dante Alighieri wrote two Latin eclogues, perhaps the least studied items in his entire output.[182] Written around 1319–20, they had to wait until the 1719 for publication.[183] Their composition was prompted by a letter sent to Dante by the humanist Giovanni del Virgilio, urging the great champion of the vernacular (witness the already published *Inferno* and *Purgatorio*, not to mention the programmatic treatise *De vulgari eloquentia*) to write instead a Latin epic on major public themes; only thus would Dante earn true fame, symbolized by the awarding of a crown of laurel, which Giovanni promised to bestow in person.[184] Dante's response was double-edged. The two poems he produced were written in Latin, but they substituted the 'humble' genre of pastoral for the requested loftiness of epic.

The second of his eclogues dramatizes a discussion between three herdsmen whose Virgilian heritage is patent in their names: Tityrus, Alphesiboeus, and Meliboeus. A fourth, Mopsus, remains offstage, but his role is pivotal to the poem's logic: he has invited Tityrus to join him at his Etnaean home. But Alphesiboeus cautions against acceptance, since Etna is where the brutal Polyphemus dwells:

> 'Who would not shudder at Polyphemus,' replies Alphesiboeus, 'accustomed as he is to dye his jaws in human blood [*rictus humano sanguine*] since the time when Galatea saw him tear the flesh of poor deserted Acis? She herself scarcely escaped. Would the force of love have kept its hold when the mad frenzy boiled up in such wrath? And what of Achaemenides, who, merely looking on him, gory with the slaughter of his comrades, could barely keep the breath within his body?'[185]

Dante both echoes and trumps another pair of classical precedents in the shape of the Ovidian narratives in *Metamorphoses* 13 (Galatea and Acis) and 14 (Achaemenides). As Guy Raffa has noted, Dante's innovation lies in the fact that the phrase used by Ovid's Achaemenides to evoke Polyphemus' anthropophagy in relation to the Polyphemus–Ulysses encounter, *illos…fluidos humano sanguine rictus* ('those jaws of his dripping with human blood' (*Met.* 14.167–8)),

[181] Helpful accounts in Acquaro Graziosi (1984), Sbacchi (2002), and Cabani (2005).
[182] Combs-Schilling (2012: 15–16).
[183] *Editio princeps* in Bottari (1719: 115–19). See Raffa (1996: with earlier biblio. at 286 n. 2); Combs-Schilling (2012: 17 n. 54).
[184] Del Virgilio: see p. 244.
[185] *Ecl.* 2.76–83; trans. Raffa (1996), adapted.

reappears virtually identically in Dante (*rictus humano sanguine* (77))—but this time with reference to the murder, and by implication the subsequent devouring, of Acis: a new and startlingly gruesome crossover between the 'Ulysses Polyphemus' and the 'Galatea Polyphemus'. And is it *just* conceivable that Dante's *Vix illa evasit* ('She herself scarcely escaped' (80)) might hint at a yet more ghastly turn of the screw: if Galatea had not escaped, might Polyphemus have devoured her too?

Dante scholars agree in detecting here the presence of a near-transparent allegorical gauze that barely veils contemporary people and places. Tityrus is a figure for Dante, Mopsus for Giovanni del Virgilio; the 'dewy pastures' currently enjoyed by Tityrus/Dante stand for Ravenna (where the poet was in exile from Florence); 'the parched rocks of the Cyclopes under Etna' evidently, though rather paradoxically, represent Bologna, the city to which Mopsus/del Virgilio has summoned the poet.[186] But who is the allegorical referent of Polyphemus? A number of Dante's bloodthirsty contemporaries have been proposed, but there is no certainty.[187] In any event, much more interesting from the viewpoint of posterity is Dante's staining of the pastoral idyll an unprecedented shade of bright crimson.

Over the next three centuries a number of Italian writers took up the theme of Polyphemus in love, whether writing (occasionally) in Latin or (usually) in the vernacular.[188] The Quattrocento humanist Giovanni Pontano offers two versions of the ogre's amorous complaint, both composed in Latin in the metre that bore the name of Sappho.[189] In the first, Polyphemus tries to arouse Galatea's jealousy by pretending he is being pursued by another would-be lover: the colossal nymph Etna (*Lyra* 13). In the second (*Lyra* 16), he decides to renounce Galatea altogether in favour of his new, volcanic beloved: 'It is Etna who will have Polyphemus, Etna, Etna the most beautiful of nymphs, Etna the mother of flowers. I greet you, you whom I have long adored. Send your fires down to your lover from your lofty summit' (71–6).[190] Here is yet one more variation on the relationship between Cyclops and volcanic fire: he is—or at least claims to be—in love with the personified source of that fire.

A later and far greater Renaissance figure, Michelangelo Buonarroti, took a more playful view of Polyphemus' song.[191] The Theocritean Cyclops had already set the topos of rustic comparisons rolling: 'whiter than curd to look upon, softer than a lamb, more frolicsome than a calf, shinier than an unripe grape' (*Id.* 11.20–1). Ovid, being Ovid, had upped the ante, inflating two lines into nineteen, both positive ('whiter than the leaf of the snowy privet . . . more welcome than winter

[186] Dante's bones still lie in Ravenna, much to the chagrin of modern Florentines.

[187] See Raffa (1996: 283).

[188] See Acquaro Graziosi (1984); Cabani (2005); Czapla (2006: 104–6); Bonilla Cerezo and Garosi (2008); Ponce Cárdenas (2010: 39–45).

[189] Ponce Cárdenas (2010: 40–1).

[190] Text in Soldati (1902: ii. 338).

[191] See Barolsky (2002).

sun or summer shade…') and negative ('more stubborn than untamed heifers… more cruel than fire…') (*Met.* 13.789–807). The motif would echo throughout Renaissance pastoral. Angelo Poliziano followed a muted Theocritean rather than a full-throated Ovidian path ('whiter than milk, prouder than a calf').[192] Lorenzo de' Medici lauded, at tremendous length, the peasant Nencia da Barberino ('Nenciozza mia') in more robust terms: among a thousand other attributes, she had two rows of teeth whiter than a horse's, and danced like a little goat.[193] But the palm for earthiness goes to the homely peasant voice created by Michelangelo:

> You have a face sweeter than grape syrup, it is as if a snail had walked across it, it shines so much, and prettier than a turnip; and teeth as white as parsnips…hair blonder than leeks…your eyebrows seem tinted from the frying pan…your breasts are like two water-melons in a bag…[194]

For all its apparent limitations, the mental world of Renaissance pastoral embraced a huge range of thought and feeling, extending to virtually everything that did not belong to the court and the courtier. It is a world in which Polyphemus—never a court figure—was perfectly in his element.

For Pontano and Michelangelo, Polyphemus was just a side show. But, for the Neapolitan Giambattista Marino (1569–1625), Cyclopean mythology carried real poetic weight. It constitutes the theme of no less than twenty-four sonnets (65–88 inclusive) of his *Rime boscherecce* ('Woodland Verses'), a collection that situates the passions of unrequited love within the idyllic, bountiful, Sicilian landscape. In the final sonnet, Polyphemus' unfulfilled desires reach their usual murderous climax, evoked in language and rhythms that would fit comfortably into the libretto of a Monteverdi opera:[195]

> 'Ah, I see you only too clearly, I see you, shameless couple, alas for me. No longer do I wish, wherever I wander, sad and disconsolate, to have my suffering renewed at the sight of your furtive pleasures.' With this cry the cruel Cyclops, drunk with pride, dislodged a great crag, and in hurling down the rocky mass, his voice was thunder and the rock lightning. Cruel stone which took the life of the handsome youth as he trembled in that sweeter death: in the midst of bliss, a most wretched lover. The beautiful nymph wept, lamenting in vain. And from

192 In Poliziano (1976), *Stanze* 1.117, 1–2.

193 'La Nencia da Barberino', in Zanato (1992: 4, 2–3; 8, 1–2).

194 Italian text in Girardi (1967: poem 20).

195 On Marino and Monteverdi, see Tomlinson (1987: 151–239); Calcagno (2012: 208–28). For Marino's quintessentially musical and performative style, see Mirollo (1963: 196–9).

> her eyes, fastened on the beloved face already dissolving in the flood, there poured a flood of tears.[196]

Marino had by no means finished with Polyphemus. He explored the ogre's character from a different angle in the *Adone*, a vast composition that uses the tale of Venus and Adonis to frame a wide range of mythological variations about love. (Nonnus' *Dionysiaca* looks puny by comparison—less than half the length of the 41,000-line *Adone*.) As well as revisiting such stalwarts as the Judgement of Paris, Hero and Leander, and Cupid and Psyche, Marino also tackles the Polyphemus, Galatea, and Acis triangle. Two emphases stand out. The first is the causal link between the murder of Acis and the blinding of Polyphemus: 'Fate's just law forbade that such a heinous deed [*sc.* the murder] should go unpunished' (canto 19, stanza 150).[197] Secondly, the Cyclops' monologue after the blinding becomes an extraordinarily complex affair, not least in respect of the succession of landscapes in which it plays out.[198] It begins with a resonant address to his now sightless eye (169):

> Go then (he said), go then, sleep, wounded eye, you to whom sleep is so dear, so sweet. And among foreign, faithless people may your sleep be deep and heavy. Go, go, sleep, but meanwhile may an ample flood of fruitless tears bathe you. Foolish eye, useless eye, burdensome eye, now is your mortal repose forever blighted.

Having moved to the summit of a mountain (183), Polyphemus continues his monologue, intuiting that his beloved Galatea is now in the company of another. His continuing restlessness soon manifests itself in a further move, this time to a precipice overlooking the sea (200), from where he launches the next stage of his lament. Bidding fond farewells to his herdsman's staff, his flocks, and his dogs, he prepares himself for a final, mortal step, unprecedented in the preceding mythical tradition: to commit suicide by throwing himself into the sea. Yet the die is not yet cast. Polyphemus appeals to Vulcan—whose function in this version (226) is to forge the thunderbolt—to blast Polyphemus before he has a chance to kill himself. In the end, Polyphemus is metamorphosed into a mountain: Etnean Mongibello, which 'still nourishes fiery burning within its breast, and, filled with furious conflagrations, never ceases to exhale horrific sighs' (232).

Two more aspects of Marino's exploration of Polyphemus-in-love deserve comment. First, his Cyclops actually *dies* of love. In fact he is the only character,

[196] Trans. Judith Bryce (personal communication), here and in the subsequent translation from stanza 169.

[197] See Acquaro Graziosi (1984: 93), echoed by Sbacchi (2002: 51).

[198] See especially Sbacchi (2002: 57–8), whom we follow closely and gratefully here.

in this vast love poem, who *does* die of love.[199] It is not completely wide of the mark to see him as a doomed Romantic hero *avant la lettre*; there is more than one analogy between Marino's ugly, forlorn Cyclops and Hugo's mighty Quasimodo (of whom much more later).[200] Secondly, the poem reimagines the link between ogre and landscape. Whereas Acis is merely transformed into one of Sicily's least conspicuous waterways, Polyphemus will for ever embody one of the most impressive landmarks in the entire Mediterranean world. And the essence of this landmark is fire. Marino carries the symbolic potential of Cyclopean fire to its ultimate conclusion.

For our final exploration of Polyphemus as distressed would-be lover, expressed in poetry like no other, we turn westwards: to the *Fábula de Polifemo y Galatea* (1612) by the Cordoban poet Luis de Góngora y Argote. Steeped in sophisticated allusions to and divergences from a wealth of predecessors, especially Greek, Latin, Italian, and Spanish, Góngora's sixty-three-stanza poem makes ferocious demands on its readers through its dazzling vocabulary and dislocated syntax; few poems stand in greater need of a learned commentary.[201] The work has not been to everyone's taste. Francisco de Quevedo, a contemporary rival whose own poetry championed pithiness and wit over ornateness and complexity, purchased the house where the ageing Góngora was living and evicted him, in order to cleanse the place of the 'pestilence' of the *Polifemo* (and the equally recherché *Soledades*).[202] Indeed, if any literary work can be said to situate a Greek-derived myth at the greatest possible distance from 'the popular', it is the *Polifemo*. And yet, for all its hyper-subtlety, the poem stands out as a landmark in Cyclopean mythology.[203]

It may be useful to begin with a narrative summary (though there are few poems whose literary effect is less easy to reduce to what it 'narrates'). The action takes place in Sicily under the pitiless midsummer sun. Adored by Polyphemus but also by local marine deities, lecherous satyrs, and a crew of infatuated farmers, herdsmen, and gardeners, Galatea seeks refuge from the heat by sleeping under a laurel. But who should accidentally penetrate her shade but Acis, son of a faun and a nymph, in search of refreshment from a nearby stream. Entranced by the sleeping beauty, he places beside her a gift of what he rustically has to hand: almonds, honey, and pats of butter rolled in green rushes. After washing his face and brow, he lies down to rest; but the momentary alteration in the sound of the tinkling stream wakens Galatea. At first Acis feigns sleep; Galatea bends over him, unaware of the cunning subtext of his 'rhetorical silence' (st. 33). Feigning no

[199] Cherchi (1996: 104). [200] See pp. 309–13.

[201] None more learned than that by D. Alonso (1985). Sources for the *Polifemo* in languages other than Spanish: Vilanova (1992).

[202] Foster and Foster (1973: 21).

[203] Ponce Cárdenas (2010) has a detailed introduction and commentary; Micó (2015: 197–302) gives a stanza-by-stanza close reading; Suárez Miramón (2002) is a convenient edition of Góngora's work as a whole; translation of the *Polifemo* in Hanak (1988).

longer, he opens his eyes and kisses the golden buckle of her shoe—which is all she seems to be wearing. They withdraw under a hollow rock curtained by ivy, taking their cue from the passionate moaning of two doves. It is not all plain sailing for Acis, though: at one point he is torn between her shining-white limbs and her 'snowy apples' (st. 41). But eventually, presided over by Cupid, matters rise to their natural climax. Yet with sunset comes the inevitable ruination of paradise. Blithely unaware of his betrayal, Polyphemus strides to a clifftop and bursts into a thunderous love song, during which he promises his own gift to his beloved—an ivory bow and quiver, previously bestowed on him by a grateful shipwrecked mariner whom he had saved. But, annoyingly, some goats decide to intrude among the ogre's carefully nurtured vines. When he slings some pebbles at them, some of the missiles pierce the ivy curtain concealing the lovers. Escape is hopeless: Polyphemus smashes Acis with the traditional boulder. But the young man's blood is transformed into river water. Clear and fresh, he will flow everlastingly into the sea.

The *Polifemo* reimagines several of this book's principal themes, notably landscape, physique, and lifestyle. First, landscape. The general location is Sicily, which, in Góngora's vision, is a land of stark contrasts and powerful symbolism. Beside the silvery marine foam is a plain strewn with ash, whose fiery genesis is associated either with Vulcan's forge or with an incinerated giant, named here as Typhoeus. Upon the plain stands a high rock 'muzzling' the mouth of the Cyclops' den, a deep, murky cave where the earth yawns; around the opening grows a 'rough garnish' of hairy foliage; above it flies a vile troop of gloomily lamenting nocturnal birds (sts 4–6). Elsewhere, however, the symbolic charge is the opposite of melancholic. The island is a cornucopia: rich in vines and fruit, copious in grain, and teeming with flocks that, Polyphemus claims, hide the mountain tops, fill the valleys, and drink the rivers dry (st. 49). So all-pervasive is the landscape that human creatures are indistinguishable from it: Polyphemus is a lofty mountain made of limbs (st. 7); terrified by the Cyclops' voice, Galatea embraces her lover/elm tree with arms that are like vine tendrils (st. 45); the blood of the metamorphosed Acis becomes liquid pearls, his bones flowing silver (st. 63). In a sense the landscape—the *animate* landscape, in all its multiplicity—is the main subject of the poem.[204]

Against that natural backdrop the three principals play out their fates. In this poem of the senses, the visual impact of their physique is palpable. All three bodies are contrastingly magnificent. That of Galatea defies the descriptive powers even of Amor (st. 14); one feature, though, singled out both by the narrating poet and by Polyphemus, is the nymph's shining pair of starlike eyes (sts 13, 46–7). Acis' appearance could not be more arousing: the sweat on the body of this 'dart

[204] Nature in the *Polifemo*: C. C. Smith (1965).

of Cupid' is like humid sparks or burning pearls (st. 24–5). As for the ogre, his own perception of his size exceeds even that of the narrator: 'What if the mountain piles clouds upon its head in vain to match me, and I, from this rock, can write my sorrows in the sky with this finger?' (st. 52). His hair is Lawrentian: unkempt, luxurious, liquid. That on his head rivals the dark waters of Lethe, that of his beard flows down like a torrent and floods his chest (st. 8). His single eye is never a token of ugliness; rather, a source of pride. The narrator calls it almost a rival of the Sun (st. 7). Polyphemus himself goes further: when once he looked into a glassy sea, 'The waters doubted if there shone on high | A heavenly Cyclops or a human sky' (st. 53).[205] Polyphemus plays Narcissus to Acis' multi-eyed Argus: the handsome youth is all eyes, as he slyly squints at Galatea (st. 37).[206]

Alongside landscape and physique: lifestyle. The lavishness of Polyphemus' day-to-day existence is far removed from the primitive. To the narrator's catalogue of the veritable orchard of fruits in the ogre's massive pouch (st. 10) there corresponds the Cyclops' own account of his limitless flocks and beehives (sts 49–50). Another aspect of his lifestyle gives a pleasing shock to anyone brought up on classical mythology. Polyphemus reminds Galatea (and us) of the 180-degree shift in his moral compass, thanks to the benign influence of his beloved (sts 54–8). Whereas in times gone by he used to decorate his cave with human heads, now he is kindness itself to visitors, especially if they are victims of shipwreck.

One more Góngoran theme merits attention. A distinctive feature of Cyclopean mythology during the two millennia through which we have so far pursued it has been the juxtaposition or amalgamation of fire and liquid. Góngora has his own take on this—not surprisingly, given his obsession with paradox and polarity. Apart from the brief reference to Vulcan's forge (st. 4), he is concerned hardly at all with volcanic Etna or with blacksmiths; *his* Polyphemus is a herdsman to the depths of his being. The heat radiating throughout the poem comes from two other sources: the burning sun and the scorching power of passion. '*Arde la juventud*', 'Youth is on fire' (st. 21)—for Galatea. In Acis the two fires combine. The spring slakes one of his thirsts, the maiden the other. Only in death and transfiguration will he attain the perennial coolness of liquid, thanks to the tears of his sea-nymph mother, and the stream he embodies.

The Singer, the Song, and the Music

Various bodily organs come to prominence in Polyphemus's myth-history—notably, eyes, mouth, and stomach. But another part of his anatomy makes its

[205] In this and other passages from Góngora, we take over or adapt the translations by Gilbert Cunningham in Parker (1977).

[206] Polyphemus as Narcissus: Barnard (2002: 77–8).

impact too, at least by implication: the lungs. He puts them to double use. He is The Voice, roaring out his passion and his fury. But he is also The Player, usually, though not always, as a deafening blower of the pan pipes.

Cyclopean musicianship flourishes mightily in the early modern and Baroque imagination. Several artistic media take up the theme. In painting and sculpture the *syrinx* regularly appears as an iconographical attribute, either to show Polyphemus in the act of piping, or, more often, to signal his identity as herdsman. In such visual images, for obvious reasons, the tune and lyrics can only be guessed at. In word- or music-based media there is no such limitation. We have already looked at examples from poetry, especially in Marino and Góngora. The latter evokes the barbarous din made by the ogre's hundred-reed pipes: forest and sea are thrown into confusion, boats on the ocean are deafened (st. 12); it is impossible not to think of the bard Assurancetourix (Eng. 'Cacofonix') from Astérix's village. Other poets take Polypheman singing in different directions. Tommaso Stigliani (1573–1651), inveterate foe of Marino, gives the ogre an unaccompanied song of lovesick anguish: 'Everything is a hell for me: I loathe my pipes, my cheese, and my milk.'[207] A century later, Giovanni Bartolomeo Casaregi imagines the voice of a quasi-Euripidean Polyphemus: overcome with strong drink, he complains of 'an infernal Vesuvius' (not Etna, for once) burning in his breast.[208] Less angst ridden is the ogre in a sonnet from the Neapolitan Emmanuele Campolongo's *La Polifemeide* (1763). Perhaps based on a traditional carnival song, the poem presents a Cyclops who serenades Galatea with the prospect of producing a brood of Polifemotti during a blissful matrimonial future.[209]

Poetic examples could be multiplied a dozenfold, but they pale beside the evidence from drama. Heinrich Dörrie counted more than 420 stage works on the Acis and Galatea theme for the sixteenth and seventeenth centuries, and its popularity continued into the eighteenth across various genres.[210] Scipione di Manzano's *Aci* (1600) was a *favola marina*, Pomponio Torelli's *La Galatea* (1603) a *tragedia*; John Eccles's early eighteenth-century *Acis and Galatea*, staged at the Theatre Royal in Drury Lane, was a masque (alongside the regular mythological characters appeared a rustic couple named Roger and Joan); Joseph Haydn's *Acide e Galatea* (1763) was a *festa teatrale*. Throughout these works, Polyphemus' dramatic voice resounds in variously modulated tones of pleading, ardour, and fury. One case may stand for all: di Manzano's incandescent 'Polifemo Ciclopo' [*sic*] assures his 'Diva', more beautiful and more fiery than the Sun, that any threats or

207 Stigliani (1600), *Polifemo*, st. 6, 7–8.

208 *Poesie*, in the last of twelve sonnets about Acis and Galatea; text in Casaregi (1782: 12, 1–2); see also Acquaro Graziosi (1984: 132–3).

209 Campolongo (1763: sonnet 69); cf. Aquaro Graziosi (1984: 144).

210 Dörrie (1968: 64, 88–92).

wild shouts of his that she might have heard were merely 'breaths of Love, lightning flashes and sparks from a heart on fire' (Act 1, scene 4).[211]

Several of these dramas were set to music, and so were numerous other sixteenth–eighteenth-century works about Acis and Galatea. To be sure, we need to get this into perspective. Baroque opera was crammed full of classical plots, whether mythological (Orpheus and Eurydice, Apollo and Daphne, Adonis, Ariadne, Helen, Alcestis, Medea, Hypermestra, Iphigenia, Circe, Procris and Cephalus, Achilles on Scyros, Semele, Pygmalion, Andromache, Dido and Aeneas…) or historical/mythological (Themistocles, Semiramis, Cato in Utica, various Alexander- and Scipio-related plots, Mithridates, Artaxerxes…). Operas based on these plots were performed as often or more often than those dramatizing the Polyphemus–Acis–Galatea triangle—not to mention the Odysseus–Polyphemus encounter, which offered too little emotional variety or dramatic scope to suit the conventions of the repertoire. Nevertheless, several of the greatest figures in Baroque opera did turn their attention to the triangle. One of these was the Florentine Giovanni Battista Lulli, who, having been talent-spotted as a teenager and brought to Paris, became the star composer at the court of Louis XIV under the name of Jean-Baptiste Lully. His last opera (or rather, *pastorale héroïque*) was *Acis et Galatée* (1686), composed for the Grand Dauphin.[212] When the young lovers elope to the Temple of Juno in order to get married, a furious Polyphemus annihilates Acis, only to see him resuscitated and turned into a river by the Cyclops' father Neptune, who has been moved by Galatea's entreaties. Galatea indeed steals the show with her lament, but Polyphemus ('*Il est mort, l'insolent!*') and Neptune ('*Je sors de mes grottes profondes…*') run her close.

Better known today, at any rate outside France, is Handel's *Acis and Galatea* (1718), an operatic reworking, after his move to England, of his earlier serenata *Aci, Galatea e Polifemo*. The opera, which has the benefit of John Gay's libretto, gives full play to Polyphemus' role as The Voice:

Recitative

I rage, I melt, I burn,
The feeble God has stab'd me to the Heart.
Thou trusty Pine, Prop of my Godlike Steps,
I lay thee by.
Bring me a hundred Reeds of decent growth,
To make a Pipe for my capacious Mouth;
In soft enchanting Accents let me breathe
Sweet Galatea's Beauty, and my Love.

[211] Libretto in di Manzano (1600).

[212] See M. Cohen (2017: 144–7).

Air

O ruddier than the Cherry!
O sweeter than the Berry!
O Nymph, more bright
Than Moonshine Night!
Like Kidlings blithe and merry.
Ripe as the melting Cluster,
No Lilly has such Lustre;
Yet hard to tame,
As raging Flame,
And fierce as Storms that bluster.
O ruddier, &c.[213]

Many of the traditional motifs are there—fire, the pan pipes, the sequence of Galatea comparisons *à la* Theocritus and Ovid—yet the combination of Gay's delicious lyrics and Handel's supreme score raises this version to new heights. In spite of the plummeting fortunes of our pastoral triangle in modern times—concomitant with the death of pastoral as a whole—this episode has not yet quite been forgotten; and the credit lies almost entirely with reperformances of Handel's masterpiece.

We cannot leave the voice and music of Polyphemus without mentioning two works from Spain, disparate in genre and tone. The first was written as an *auto sacramental*, a type of sacred morality play staged for the day of Corpus Christi. At the root of this festival was the doctrine of transubstantiation, which held that, during the Eucharist, the substance of the bread and the wine was transformed into the body and blood of Christ. Like the festival itself, the *auto sacramental* might itself dramatize, through the use of allegory, the collapsing of the gap between appearance and substance.[214] In 1628 the Madrid-born dramatist Juan Pérez de Montalbán produced just such a work, a heavily allegorical version of the Ulysses–Polyphemus–Galatea nexus of plots, a version that, in the case of some of the characters, elides the distance between their ostensible identities and what one might call their 'real substance'.[215] Among the cast are Appetite, Mirth, Judaism (figured as one of the Cyclopes), and Baby Jesus. Ulysses appears in the role of Christ, in keeping with a tendency in the Iberian *Siglo de Oro* to idealize the Ithacan hero. Galatea stands for the human soul, while Polifemo takes the role of Lucifer, having been cast by God from heaven into hell, a distance of some fifty-four million leagues. Running throughout the play—consonant, of course,

[213] Text based on Gay (1983: 271–2). [214] Labanyi (2010: 57).

[215] Text in Pérez de Montalbán (1632: fos 217^{v}–226^{v}). On Montalbán's *auto* in context, see Glaser (1960); synopsis in Leal Bonmati (2011: 38–9).

with the occasion of the dramatic performance—is the notion of extraordinary change of appearance and/or substance, within the framework of the Christian sacrament. No example is more extraordinary than Polyphemus' account of a promise made by Ulysses, that he would make wine from his own blood—the wine that would befuddle the Cyclops' wits as a prelude to the blinding. Hardly less striking is the moment when Ulysses dresses as the Lamb (*sc.* of God) when making his escape from the cave. After Galatea has been unsuccessfully tempted by Appetite to desert the (Good) Shepherd (= Ulysses = Acis), Polyphemus and the four other Cyclopes (including Judaism) come on stage playing guitars, while the female figure of Mirth sings and dances. Polyphemus elaborately contrasts his own merits with the defects of the Shepherd, but Galatea will have none of it. A long debate ensues between Galatea and the Cyclopes in which she defends, and they contest, the divinity of the Shepherd. At the climax of the action the crucified Shepherd appears with Galatea kneeling before him. Baby Jesus wraps things up by addressing Galatea as his Bride, much to the disgust of Polyphemus and Judaism. Out of this amazing cocktail of religion and myth it is hard to pick a favourite moment. But the spectacle of Polyphemus strumming along in a Cyclopean guitar ensemble is one of the more delicious byways in his musical career.

Vastly different in form and tone from the *auto* is the *zarzuela*, a lyrical–dramatic genre characterized by alternations of verse and prose, operatic and popular song. One such was put on in 1708 before Philip V in the Royal Palace in Madrid: *Acis y Galatea* (1708), with libretto by José de Cañizares and music by Antonio de Literes.[216] Little known today in Spain, and virtually unknown outside it, it is nevertheless a splendid reimagining of the myth. The tone is set by Polyphemus' costume. According to the stage directions, he wears a little leather jacket, a shoulder-length wig, and a headdress with grey and white feathers, all set off by the small tree that he carries as a staff. The locals in Trinacria (= Sicily) include the married couple Momo and Tisbe, who do nothing to raise the tone ('Your Giantship likes hunting beasts. Go over there where my husband is: he's the biggest beast of the lot' (229–32)). As for the Cyclopean voice, its power comes across in both song and speech. At one point Polyphemus is discovered hammering away in his forge; for once, herdsman and blacksmith coalesce. As he labours on a golden trident for his beloved nymph, the Cyclops sings his complaint. Her ungrateful heart is tougher than bronze: bronze he can tenderize, but not her (1195–1221). Modulating to speech, he calls on his fellow Cyclopes to bring him a mirror. After all, a fellow who wants to change his appearance from monster to smart young *beau* needs to wipe all the grimy smudges from his face after a hard day at the anvil (1275–83). To no avail: Galatea remains true to Acis, whom

[216] Stein and Leza (2009: 252); Leal Bonmati (2011).

Polyphemus inevitably squashes under a crag. But the loving couple have the last laugh: Galatea's prayer to the gods of the sea results in Acis' deification as a river. Polyphemus expresses his intention of walking off the island into the water 'like a living shipwreck' (1927). As he stomps off, Momo's choicely phrased curse rings in his ears.

Looking Back, Looking Forward

We end this chapter in the company of two mid-seventeenth-century painters whose juxtaposed visions constitute a point of transition in our story. One of these works situates Polyphemus firmly within the world of pastoral: its landscape, its animals, its rustic population, its music. The other gives us a Cyclops raw and isolated in his fury, anticipating the untamed violence that the Symbolists and the Romantics would see as characteristic of this terrifying figure.

There was something magnetic about Polyphemus: many artists returned to him again and again. Among them was Nicolas Poussin (1594–1665). On one of his canvasses (*Cat. 106*) Acis and Galatea embrace demurely, partly shielded by a pair of Cupids who gamely struggle to create a makeshift screen out of a heavy piece of symbolically appropriate red cloth. They need not have bothered: handsome young Polyphemus is 'in the zone', happily piping away and oblivious of his surroundings. Altogether more energetic are the protagonists in a drawing (*Cat. 104* (Fig. 10.28)) done by Poussin for the poet Marino, his then patron-protector

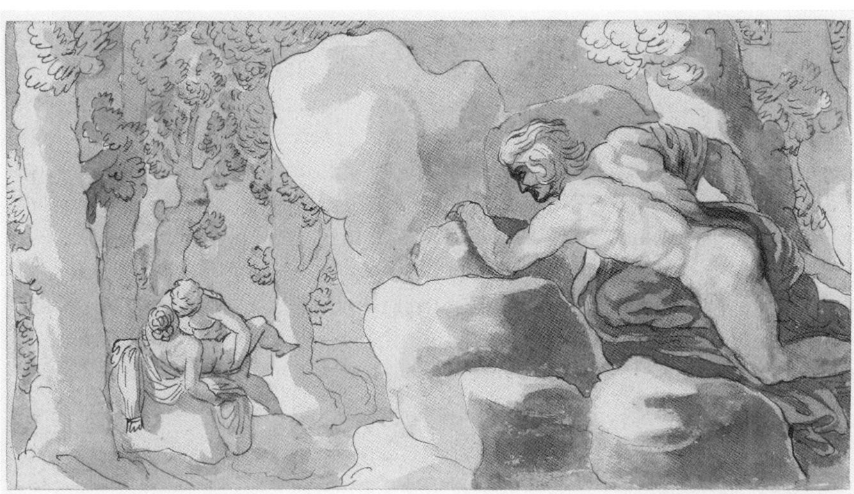

Fig. 10.28. Nicolas Poussin, *Polyphemus, Acis and Galatea*. Drawing, 1623.

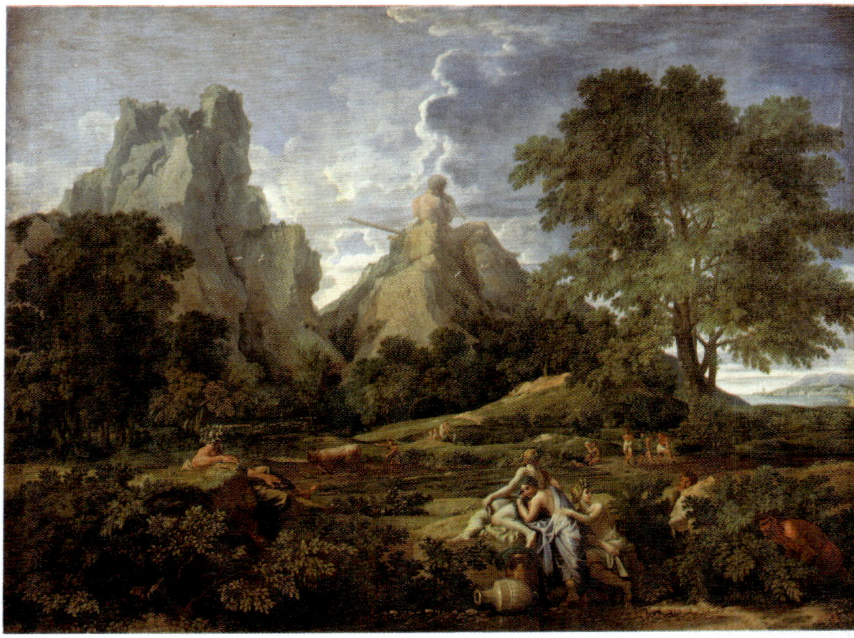

Fig. 10.29. Nicolas Poussin, *Landscape with Polyphemus*. Oil on canvas, 1649.

in Paris.[217] Acis and Galatea are at full erotic throttle, spied on from behind a rock by a dashing but clearly incandescent Polyphemus. This is quite a different Poussin from the embodiment of restrained harmony with which he was later to become synonymous.[218]

Better known than either of these works is the artist's *Landscape with Polyphemus* (1649) (*Cat. 108* (Fig. 10.29)). Two mountains rise in the background; a sea bay, fringed with buildings, can just be made out at the top right; wonderful trees grow everywhere; agricultural workers and their animals populate the middle distance; in the foreground are a river god and three nymphs, ogled by a pair of lustfully lurking satyrs. Dominating the whole scene, yet looking away from it, is Polyphemus, sitting on one of the mountaintops playing his pipes. The farm labourers in the middle distance are hard at work, but in foreground nothing is happening.[219] Whatever tune Polyphemus is playing, it has bewitched the principal actors. The sky is partially cloudy, but the 'clouds' above Polyphemus' head have a smokelike quality: this is surely Etna, an Etna in which the mountainous Cyclops seems to be organically embedded. Of Acis there is no sign. But what of

[217] Marino: see pp. 292–4.
[218] On the drawing: Costello (1955: 309). On Poussin and Marino: R. B. Simon (1978).
[219] Absence of narrative: Mérot (1990: 156).

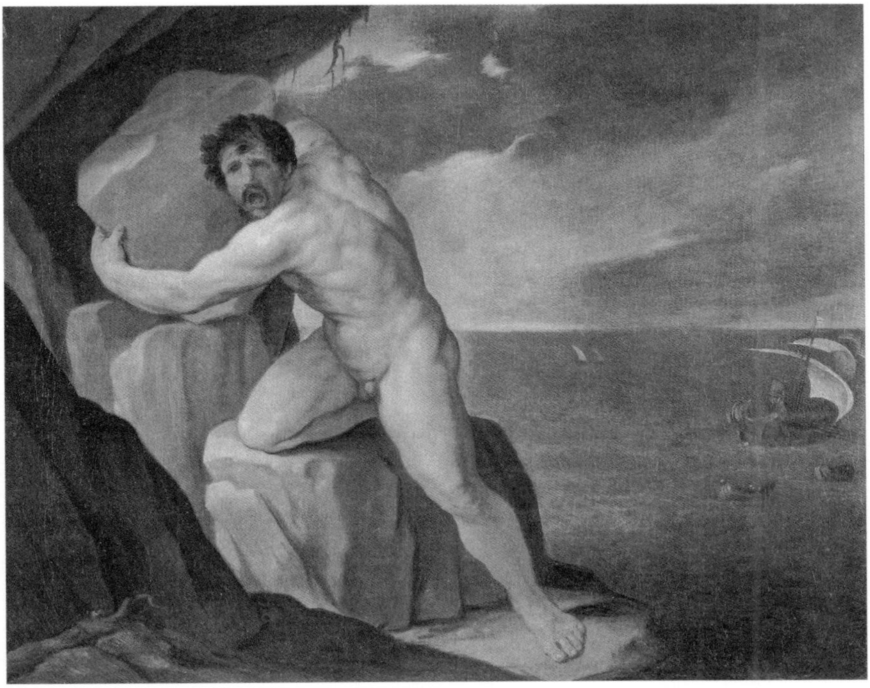

Fig. 10.30. Guido Reni, *Polyphemus*. Oil on canvas, 1639–40.

Galatea? Is she the figure in the blue robe in the foreground, facing towards us and seemingly entranced by Cyclopean music? Or could she be on the far side of the volcano, invisible to us but not to Polyphemus? That, after all, is the direction in which he is gazing, towards the sea spread out far below.[220] The world visualized in the painting is complex and multiplanar, yet the atmosphere is unified and harmonious, even if—to the knowing viewer aware of the classical narrative inhabited by the actors—the stillness is that which precedes a storm.[221] The pastoral idyll is frozen in time, but the ice can be melted at any moment by the fire smouldering within the ogre beneath the smoky clouds.

Poussin situates Polyphemus within an idealized world that never existed. Such disruption as there is is controlled and latent: no more than a suppressed hint. For Poussin's Bolognese contemporary Guido Reni (1575–1642), as central to the Italian Baroque as Poussin was to the French, there was no such holding back. His *Polyphemus* (*Cat. 107* (Fig. 10.30)) is colossal, furious, muscular, and stark naked, pink against the fifty shades of grey in the rocks, sea, and sky.[222] A single, central,

[220] The gaze here: Carrier (1990: 43). [221] Lagerlöf (1990: 103).

[222] For the suggestion that, however, such violence might have been untypical of Reni, see Spear (1997: 60).

dark eye lies above the ogre's two normal ones, but this is a mark of identity rather than monstrosity. There is no music; but there is certainly sound. The ogre's gaping mouth cries out, either in post-blinding agony (compare the screaming victim in Reni's *Apollo and Marsyas*), or with wrath against the escaping Greek fleet, whose vessels, like toy boats in a bath tub, lie far below. Those vessels, nevertheless, are crucial to the work's meaning, for they retain Polyphemus within a narrative. It will not be long, however, before the Cyclops, in at least some of his representations, sheds that narrative context altogether and becomes a solitary, solipsistic icon. But that development must wait for our final chapter.

11
The Modern Cyclops

The period from the eighteenth century until today has witnessed the most varied and most innovative explorations of Cyclopean myths since Graeco-Roman antiquity. Indeed, in visual art, reimaginings of the Cyclopes have arguably been *more* varied and *more* innovative over the past two-and-a-half centuries than at any time in the past, including antiquity. So far as literary retellings are concerned, the case for the parity of the modern with the ancient—let alone the case for the superiority of the modern—is far more difficult to sustain: the unrivalled imaginative power of the *Odyssey* speaks for itself, while several other ancient Cyclopean narratives make a forceful impact within their respective genres. Nevertheless, some major modern writers have magnificently reappropriated the figure of the Cyclops, and the sheer variety of modern literary takes on these myths is startling. Showing how all this is so will be our project in this final chapter.

Texts: From the Volcano to the City

Sir William Hamilton (1730–1803) had several strings to his bow.[1] To the gossip columnist, he was the husband of Nelson's mistress Emma. To the political historian, he was for some thirty-seven years British envoy to the court of Ferdinand IV at Naples.[2] To the historian of archaeology, he was the collector *par excellence* of Greek vases. But to the historian of science, he was the *doyen* of volcanologists. He published extensively. His *Observations on Mount Vesuvius, Mount Etna, and Other Volcanos* was followed by the sumptuous *Campi Phlegraei, Observations on the Volcanos of the Two Sicilies*.[3] These and other writings on volcanological matters were based on indefatigable fieldwork, often in conditions of extreme personal danger.[4] It is an aspect of this hands-on experience that brings Hamilton, together with the local Neapolitan guide who regularly accompanied his expeditions, into our story. That guide was Bartolomeo Pumo, with whom Hamilton climbed Vesuvius sixty-eight times.[5] Pumo was known as 'The Cyclops of

[1] See Jenkins and Sloan (1996); Constantine (2001).
[2] For Hamilton's diplomatic career, see Sloan in Jenkins and Sloan (1996: 24–39).
[3] Hamilton (1772, 1776). [4] Darley (2011: 64–95).
[5] Heringman (2013: 109–16); Darley (2011: 74).

Cyclops: The Myth and its Cultural History. Mercedes Aguirre and Richard Buxton, Oxford University Press (2020).

DOI: 10.1093/oso/9780198713777.001.0001

Vesuvius'. Although the nickname was presumably due to an ocular singularity, it also suggests some kind of identification between Pumo and the volcanic landscape he knew so intimately. The perceived assimilation of a Cyclops to a volcano evidently continued to flourish in the eighteenth century.

A more explicit, albeit whackier confirmation of the link between the Cyclopes and volcanoes comes from another remarkable figure in the history of volcanology, Rudolf Eric Raspe (*c.*1737–94). Born in Hanover, Raspe was, if anything, an even more intriguing figure than Hamilton. His scientific work included investigations into the bones and teeth of elephants, as well as a study (praised by Goethe) of the volcanic origins of basalt.[6] But he was also an ingenious con man. One of his ruses was to sell off for his own profit items from a collection of gems and coins of which he was curator. Heavily in debt, he fled to Holland and then England. He was thrown out of the Fellowship of the Royal Society 'on grounds of character', and died of typhoid in Killarney.[7] What interests *us* about Raspe, however, is his most famous, albeit anonymous, work: *The Surprising Adventures of Baron Munchausen.*[8] The eponymous character, a *miles gloriosus* from the German aristocracy, gives a first-person account of his preposterous adventures, a farrago of deliberately comic but engaging lies.

Chapter 20 takes the Baron to Etna, which has been in eruption for three weeks. Munchausen decides to jump into the crater, sustaining inconvenient bumps and burns along the way. Recovering his composure, the Baron looks about him. 'Guess, gentlemen, my astonishment when I found myself in the company of Vulcan and his Cyclops [*sic*], who had been quarrelling, for the three weeks before mentioned, about the observation of good order and due subordination...'. Vulcan thoughtfully tends Munchausen's wounds, and instructs his wife Venus to show the recuperating intruder every indulgence (details unspecified) that his situation requires. Vulcan then explains the role of the Cyclopes in Etna's eruptions. The god of fire is in the habit of chastising his servants by throwing red-hot coals at them. The servants (that is, Cyclopes) refrain from retaliating by throwing the coals back at their master, preferring to put them out of his reach by hurling them out of the volcano instead. The whole episode, we may safely infer, is quite unlike anything that Empedocles might have experienced. To be sure, Raspe's relentless humour is not everyone's cup of tea—he is no Lucian. But at least he provides a moment of whimsical relief for the student of Cyclopean myths, by situating the ogres in, for once, a situation of manifest absurdity.

The main role of the Cyclopes, however, even in the eighteenth century, is to serve as tools for thinking about altogether more serious matters. Nowhere is this

[6] Raspe and volcanology: Sigurdsson (1999: 140–7).

[7] See Linnebach (2005); Kareem (2008; 2014: 154–85).

[8] There are numerous editions, and almost as many variants of the title. We quote from Raspe (1895).

more evident than in the writings of Giambattista Vico, who spent more than forty years as professor of rhetoric in the University of Naples. Vico's treatise *New Science* (1725; third revision 1744), now recognized as a key text in the philosophy of history, is a highly speculative and brilliantly innovative investigation of the relationships between social structure, language (especially etymology), law, and mythology. One of Vico's fundamental principles is to posit a universal or 'ideal' structure for the development of humanity—the 'common nature of nations', a nature whose characteristics are revealed by an investigation of its origins. Those origins were not, however, identical for the whole of humanity, since 'the entire original human race was divided into two species: the one of giants, the other of men of normal stature: the former gentiles, the latter Hebrews' (172); the absence of gigantism among the Hebrews is ascribed to their cleanly and God-fearing lifestyle, which enabled them to perpetuate the stature in which God had created Adam and Noah (371).[9] Vico elaborates the point about a 'species' of giants, suggesting that their stature was actually a product of their enforced physical robustness as a consequence of having to survive in the wilderness (369). (Remarkably, Vico suggests that the stature of giants diminished to normality over time, since they behaved in a clean and pious manner (371).) At all events, Vico consistently ascribes a foundational role to giants, whom he etymologizes as 'sons of the earth' (13, 370). They were primordial, post-diluvial wanderers who allegedly took the crucial, inaugural step of intuiting, on the basis of their experience of the thunderbolt, the presence of a supremely powerful causal agent—namely, Zeus/Jupiter (377–9).[10] Contemporaneous with this religious intuition was the withdrawal of the giants into caves, where their thenceforth settled existence went hand in hand with the establishment of the institutions of, first, matrimony, then burial, and in due course the whole panoply of human ideas and social structures.

It is as representatives of the race of giants that the Cyclopes come into their own, being mentioned in literally dozens of separate sections of the treatise.[11] But the mere counting of citations can be misleading. In passage after passage Vico insists on the same point: that the primordial role of the Cyclopes had already been recognized by Plato—who was himself citing the *Odyssey*—in the *Laws*. For Vico, as for Plato-reading-Homer, myths embody truths about the human past: 'the fables were true and trustworthy histories of the customs of the most ancient peoples of Greece' (7). For Vico, as for Plato-reading-Homer, mountain-dwelling

[9] Trans. Bergin and Fisch (1984), here and in subsequent quotations; references are to sections within the work.

[10] Vico's speculative brio extends to geological meteorology: it took centuries after the Flood for the earth to dry out sufficiently to allow the emission of 'dry exhalations' capable of igniting in the air to generate lightning (192).

[11] See the index to Bergin and Fisch (1984: s.v. 'Cyclopes' and 'Polyphemus') (though their list is not exhaustive).

giants, exemplified by the Cyclopes, stood at the origins of post-diluvial humanity: 'In the human race first appear the huge and grotesque, like the Cyclopes' (243). Not only were these primordial figures physically extraordinary: they also displayed 'monstrous savagery and unbridled bestial freedom' (338). It was through the act of inaugurating the triad of fundamental institutions (religion, marriage, burial) that humanity's development out of bestiality began, thanks to the actions enjoined, by force of circumstance, upon the giants in general, and in particular—as already authoritatively narrated by Plato-reading-Homer—the Cyclopes.[12] Thereafter these representatives of early humanity exercised 'Cyclopean family discipline' (523), each ruling over his own wife and children from within the confines of his own cave.

One passage takes a strikingly different tack from those so far considered. The world that surfaced after the Flood was covered by forests. In order to see the sky—so as to descry the movement of thunderbolts, and hence to read the auspices—the giants/Cyclopes had to create *clearings*. With typical etymological virtuosity, Vico links the idea of a clearing in a forest with the most distinctive physical trait of the Cyclopes (564):

> Every clearing was called a *lucus*, in the sense of an eye, as even today we call eyes the openings through which light enters houses. The true heroic phrase that 'every giant had his *lucus*' was altered and corrupted when its meaning was lost, and had already been falsified when it reached Homer, for it was then taken to mean that every giant had one eye in the middle of his forehead. With these one-eyed giants came Vulcan to work in the first forges—that is, the forests to which Vulcan had set fire and where he had fashioned the first arms, which were the spears with burned tips—and, by an extension of the idea of arms, to forge bolts for Jove. For Vulcan had set fire to the forests in order to observe in the open sky the direction from which Jove sent his bolts.

Vico here effects a series of amalgamations and crossovers. The giants are, as usual in *New Science*, equated with Cyclopes; the Homeric Polyphemus is assimilated to the ogres who worked for Vulcan; the first weapons are said to be fire-hardened 'spears'—that is, tree branches, made by Vulcan—precisely the type of weapon used *against* the Homeric Cyclops; the 'eye' (that is, forest clearing) *created* by fire is misremembered by Homer as an eye *destroyed* by fire. All this is idiosyncratic, but not wholly unprecedented. The Cyclopes' primordiality, and their association with fire, are familiar features of the mythical tradition, nor would Vico's etymological panache be out of place in any number of medieval treatises claiming to uncover the meanings of myths through linguistic

[12] Sometimes Vico goes a step further, citing as his authority Strabo-reading-Plato-reading-Homer (296; the Strabo passage is 13.1.25).

investigation—according to Vico, the name *Zeus* supposedly originates from the whistling noise of the thunderbolt (447)! What distinguishes Vico, however, is his daring use of the language of mythology to uncover the rationale of the whole historical development—nothing less—of the civil society of humanity. Within that development, the Cyclopes, qua giants, are discovered to have played a uniquely transformative role. There is no clearer example, in the whole *Nachleben* of Greek mythology, of a particular mythical configuration being deliberately used to conduct a thought experiment.

Heroic deformity and doomed beauty

For all the innovativeness in Vico's *New Science*, there is also a pronounced academic formality. The constant repetitions of key or difficult points bespeak a written style developed during countless hours spent conveying information orally in the lecture room. What a contrast with our next text. A different country, a different century, a different genre, a wholly different sensibility. Its underlying narrative differs too from that highlighted by Vico: not the ogre encountered by Odysseus, but the would-be lover of a beautiful and unresponsive young woman. But of the landscape of mountain, shore, and sea—hitherto the habitual backdrop to the Polyphemus and Galatea standoff—there is no sign. In Victor Hugo's novel *Notre-Dame de Paris* (1831), the Cyclops comes to the city.

Hugo's tremendous tale narrates the fatal attraction of the hideously ugly Quasimodo, bell-ringer at the great cathedral, for the entrancing, fairy-like gipsy girl Esmeralda. Against the backdrop of a panoramic re-creation of medieval Paris, Hugo explores the themes of obsession, abandonment, heartless cruelty, and selfless adoration. From the beginning to the end of the narrative he engages profoundly and multifariously with the image of the Cyclops.

To begin with, the single eye is embedded in the cathedral itself, in all its fifteenth-century glory (before the city's—as Hugo sees it—lamentable architectural decline); not for nothing does the building lend its name to the novel. There is a moment in early spring when the sinking sun exactly faces Notre-Dame: 'the great central rose-window flames like the eye of a Cyclops ablaze with the reflection from the forge'; one single eye illuminates another.[13] Also evocative both of the Cyclopean forge and of colossal size is a description of the appearance of the cathedral towers during an assault by a mob: '[they looked] like two gigantic andirons in some Cyclopean hearth.'[14] So compulsive is this strain of imagery in Hugo's imagination that even a notable eatery specializing in roasted meats is

[13] Bk 7, ch. 1 = Hugo (2004: 245, trans. Sturrock, here and in subsequent quotations).
[14] Bk 11, ch. 1 = Hugo (2004: 456).

affectionately described as 'Cyclopean', earning fulsome praise from a passing Franciscan: '*Veramente, queste rotisserie* [sic] *sono cosa stupenda*.'[15]

But the principal referent of Cyclopean imagery is Quasimodo himself. Near the beginning of the novel the uncomprehending bell-ringer finds himself an accidental contestant for the title of 'Pope of Fools'; the winner of this lord-of-misrule competition will be the one with the ugliest grimace. Quasimodo wins without grimacing—merely by adopting his usual expression, which is, the narrator disingenuously pretends, beyond description:

> We shall not try to give the reader any idea of that tetrahedral nose, of that horseshoe mouth, of the tiny left eye, obstructed by a bushy red eyebrow, while the right eye had vanished entirely beneath an enormous wen, of those irregular teeth, notched here and there like castle battlements, of that horny lip on which a tooth encroached like an elephant's tusk, of that cleft chin, and above all of the facial expression itself, with its crowning mixture of malice, astonishment and sadness. In all, a sight for you to imagine, if you can.[16]

Soon afterwards an analogy is drawn with one Cyclops in particular:

> 'Infernal man!' said Robin Poussepain, still concussed from his fall. [He had just laughed in the face of Quasimodo, who had tossed him ten yards.] 'He appears and he's a hunchback. He walks, and he's crook-kneed. He looks at you and he's one-eyed. You talk to him and he's deaf. I don't know, what does this Polyphemus do with his tongue?'
>
> 'He talks when he feels like it,' said the old woman. 'He went deaf ringing the bells. He's not dumb.'
>
> 'It's the one thing he isn't,' remarked Jehan.
>
> 'He's got one eye too many,' added Robin Poussepain.
>
> 'No he hasn't,' said Jehan shrewdly. 'A one-eyed man is much more incomplete than a blind man. He knows what he lacks.'[17]

What was the history of this strange creature? As a 4-year-old he had been abandoned in Notre-Dame, on Quasimodo Sunday, 1467. One of the old women who gathered to gawp at the wretched foundling regarded it as 'a wild beast, an animal, fathered by a Jew on a sow; something not Christian, in fact', thus exploiting one time-honoured interpretation of a monster as a miss-conceived *monstrum*.[18] Hugo also presents us with an image almost entirely absent from our own story so far, that of a Cyclops as a child:

[15] Bk 7, ch. 4 = Hugo (2004: 269).
[16] Bk 1, ch. 5 = Hugo (2004: 70).
[17] Bk 1, ch. 5 = Hugo (2004: 72).
[18] Bk 4, ch. 1 = Hugo (2004: 156).

> 'The little monster' (we would be hard put to it ourselves to find another term for him) was indeed no new-born baby. It was a very angular, very restless small lump, imprisoned in a canvas sack...with its head protruding. This head was more than a little deformed. All you could see was a forest of red hair, one eye, a mouth and some teeth. The eye was weeping, the mouth yelling, while the teeth seemed anxious only to bite. And all of it threshing about in the sack, to the great amazement of the encircling crowd, which was growing all the time and being replenished.[19]

The 'small lump' is adopted by the Archdeacon, the cerebral and tormented Claude Frollo; to this chillingly repressed foster-father Quasimodo becomes slavishly devoted. The cathedral becomes his home, 'his hole, his envelope', like the shell of a snail; not the Cyclops' *cave*, though, since it is so evidently the work of human architects.[20] For this entirely urban, utterly un-pastoral Cyclops, stone and glass render the surroundings of the natural landscape redundant:

> The cathedral was not only society for him, but the universe too, the whole of nature. The only espaliers he could conceive were the stained-glass windows, which were always in flower, the only shade that of the stone foliage blossoming in clumps, laden with birds, on the Saxon capitals, the only mountains the colossal towers of the church, the only ocean the Paris that surged at their feet.[21]

Grown to adolescence, Quasimodo is entrusted with the responsibility that will dominate his existence: the bells. The passion he develops for them is explicitly erotic: setting them in motion brings him to the climax of excitement, accompanied by another of the traditional characteristics of Cyclopean monophthalmia: fire. As the great bell vibrated with ever greater speed, so Quasimodo's eye 'glowed like phosphorus'.[22] Yet the bells hardly reciprocate this fiery joy. In fact, as we have already learned, they cause Quasimodo one more disability to add to all the rest: deafness, a defect that distinguishes him from every one of his predecessors in Cyclopean mythology. By a cruel irony, Quasimodo's life is devoted to creating a tempestuous and glorious symphony of sound, while being himself immured in a world of almost total silence. But there is a consolation: the noise of the bells themselves. *This* ear-shattering music the poor bell-ringer can still sense.

In one episode Quasimodo's deafness precipitates a scene of heart-wrenching pathos. Charged in relation to a night affray, he is arraigned before the egregious chief magistrate of the Parisian police courts—himself deaf, though too vain to admit it. Mistaking Quasimodo's irrelevant responses for contempt of court, the

[19] Bk 4, ch. 1 = Hugo (2004: 156–7).
[20] Bk 4, ch. 3 = Hugo (2004: 164).
[21] Bk 4, ch. 3 = Hugo (2004: 166).
[22] Bk 4, ch. 3 = Hugo (2004: 167).

magistrate condemns him to a vicious and prolonged flogging at the public pillory. The torture at last completed, the narrator reverts to Cyclopean imagery:

> Then the poor devil, unable to snap the collar that tethered him like a wild animal, became still again. Only now and again did a sigh of rage swell all the cavities of his chest. On his face there was neither shame nor blushes. He was too far from the state of society and too close to that of nature to know what shame was. With that degree of deformity, moreover, can one have any sense of infamy? But anger, hatred and despair slowly descended on that hideous face in an ever more sombre cloud, full of an electricity that flashed unendingly from the eye of the Cyclops.[23]

The only redemption is the arrival of Esmeralda, who, in a scene of terrific intensity, accedes to Quasimodo's anguished request for water by lifting a gourd to his lips. The narrator calls her gesture 'sublime'; the reader can hardly dissent. One thing is certain: her act transforms Quasimodo, or rather, it transforms *his eye*. A tear wells up, 'perhaps the first tear the luckless man had ever shed'.[24] For the rest of the novel, Quasimodo gazes at Esmeralda with rapt, tender affection. Moreover, as so often in Cyclopean myth-telling, the gaze of the Cyclops forms part of a network of other gazes. In this case, the most significant looks are the malevolent, lustful voyeurism of Frollo towards Esmeralda,[25] and the all-too-trusting gaze of Esmeralda towards Phoebus de Châteaupers, the dashing but vacuously selfish Captain of the King's Archers. From the confluence of these intense gazes—more exactly, from the moment when Frollo secretly spies Phoebus about to make love to Esmeralda, then stabs his rival in a jealous frenzy—the tragedy inexorably flows.

Frollo, his precarious moral equilibrium having collapsed into depravity, escapes undetected from the scene of his attack on Phoebus, leaving Esmeralda to be falsely accused, tortured, and condemned to be hanged. Quasimodo rescues her from the scaffold with the agility of an acrobat and the strength of a lion, and installs her in the cathedral ('Sanctuary! Sanctuary! Sanctuary!'). Frollo discovers Esmeralda's refuge and attempts to rape her, only to be thwarted by Quasimodo's furious intervention. Another attempt to abduct Esmeralda, by a massed assault on the cathedral by thieves and vagabonds, is again repelled by Quasimodo, this time by hurling masonry and pouring down boiling metal, in true Cyclopean mode. But the respite is only temporary: this is no comforting, Disney remake. In the end, Esmeralda is indeed hanged. Witnessing Frollo's demented laughter at the terrible sight, Quasimodo casts him from the height of Notre-Dame, then

[23] Bk 6, ch. 4 = Hugo (2004: 241), amended. [24] Bk 6, ch. 4 = Hugo (2004: 243).

[25] Interestingly it is icy Frollo, not his heart-on-sleeve foster-son, who is compared to Etna: snow above, seething lava below (bk 7, ch. 4 = Hugo (2004: 275)).

mysteriously disappears. Some two years later, there happens to be a search of the charnel-house into which Esmeralda's corpse had been thrown. Among the countless skeletons, two are of unusual interest. One is that of a woman, the other that of a deformed man. It seems that the man had been embracing the woman: 'The man to whom the skeleton had belonged must therefore have come there and have died there. When they tried to release him from the skeleton he was embracing, he crumbled into dust.'[26]

If Hugo's Quasimodo is—as he is—a conscious and explicit reinvention of the mythical Cyclops, what of the other two apices of the classic emotional triangle? Esmeralda is heart-stoppingly beautiful; Galatea, being a sea nymph, is no less lovely. Galatea swims, Esmeralda dances; both types of movement express freedom and lightness, and both enthral the gaze of an adoring but ugly admirer. Beyond that, the differences are more evident than the similarities. Whereas Galatea has the power and confidence of a divinity, Esmeralda is a teenage ingénue whose one true friend is her little pet goat (perhaps the only hint of pastoral in the entire novel); only the eye of credulity or malice could detect in Esmeralda any trace of the superhuman (as a 'sorceress', her goat being of course the Devil). What of Phoebus de Châteaupers as Acis? In the ancient sources, Acis has little personality; the deeply unpleasant Phoebus has too much: it seems unnecessary to press the analogy very far. The crucial difference from the Cyclopean tradition resides in a fourth person. In Hugo's novel, the figure who spies 'Acis' embracing 'Galatea' is not 'Polyphemus' but a character more reminiscent of Gothic fiction than of Graeco-Roman myth: Claude Frollo. The spectral Archdeacon is Hugo's most telling, quintessentially Romantic development of the idea of a Cyclops.

Finding allusions to classical mythology in Hugo is simple enough.[27] But there is something peculiarly insistent and deeply characteristic about the pervasive role of the Cyclopes in the imagination of the mature Hugo, fascinated as he was by figures and political movements that combined, in varying degrees, the grotesque, the gigantic, and the sublime. He described the revolution of 1793 as 'days of the Cyclopean people and the Titanic spirit'.[28] A similar description in *Les Misérables* characterizes popular sovereignty in a time of social upheaval: 'That sovereignty may behave badly; it blunders, like all human action, but even in its blunderings, like the blind Cyclops, it remains great.'[29] There is something magnificent, Hugo repeatedly suggests, about gigantic, 'Cyclopean' strength, even when it is flawed or ugly, and especially when it is identified with the actions and aspirations of the people. In another of Hugo's monumental novels, *L'Homme qui rit*, the image of the Cyclops again takes on an archetypal quality, once more in relation to human deformity. The hero, Gwynplaine, was deliberately mutilated as

26 Bk 11, ch. 4 = Hugo (2004: 493), amended.
27 Comprehensive discussion in Albouy (1963).
28 Hugo, *Toute la lyre* 1.21 = Hugo (1913: i. 57); Albouy (1963: 230).
29 Hugo (1982: 733).

a child to give him a permanent *rictus* and so make him profitable to be displayed as a freak. Now, as a virile but disfigured adult, he arouses the lust of the provocative and bored Duchess Josiane, prompting her to comment: 'Olympus has two sides, one in full sun, given by Apollo, one in night, given by Polyphemus. You are a Titan. You would be Behemoth in the forest, Leviathan in the ocean, Typhon in the sewer. You are supreme. There is something of the thunderbolt in your deformity.'[30] Josiane is hardly impartial; but, for the principal narrator too, Gwynplaine is magnificent in his deformity.

This all chimes in with Hugo's wider Romantic manifesto.[31] In the words of a famous programmatic sentence from the *Préface de Cromwell*: 'It is from the fruitful union of the grotesque and the sublime that the modern genius is born.'[32] Both grotesquerie and sublimity transgress the norm, and it is the task of the Romantic writer precisely to challenge boundaries. This kind of extraordinariness is exactly what Inspector Javert detects, close to the end of *Les Misérables*, in Jean Valjean, a quality that shatters the foundation of Javert's own world view: 'A benevolent evil-doer, a man who returned good for evil, a man near to the angels—Javert was forced to admit that this monstrosity could exist.'[33] Inevitably, the notions of the titanic, the monstrous, above all the Cyclopean, were applied to Hugo himself. Charles Baudelaire described him as 'great, terrible, as immense as a mythical creation, Cyclopean so to speak'.[34] Particularly apt, especially in relation to *Notre-Dame de Paris*, was a comment by another of Hugo's contemporaries, the critic Charles Augustin Sainte-Beuve: 'Of all the Greek orders of architecture, the one he understands best is the Cyclopean.'[35]

Art: Cyclopes in Narrative Contexts

The Irish artist James Barry (1741–1806) was a pioneering and controversial advocate of the 'historical' approach to painting.[36] His approach to politics was equally uncompromising. His staunch support for the American revolutionary movement echoed the views of his compatriot Edmund Burke, who became his patron. Barry's relations with the artistic establishment were stormy: an appointment as Professor of Painting at the Royal Academy was followed later by his expulsion from the same body, not only on political grounds but also on account of his repeated scurrilous abuse of fellow Academicians. It seemed he was unable to keep his mouth shut if he felt strongly about something, whatever the consequences. He was to die poor and paranoid, though it was perhaps some

[30] Hugo (2002: 679); our translation.
[31] Falgas-Ravry (2010).
[32] Hugo (1968: 70); our translation.
[33] Hugo (1982: 1106).
[34] Baudelaire (1961: 689); our translation.
[35] Sainte-Beuve (1926: 36); our translation.
[36] See Dunne and Pressly (2010).

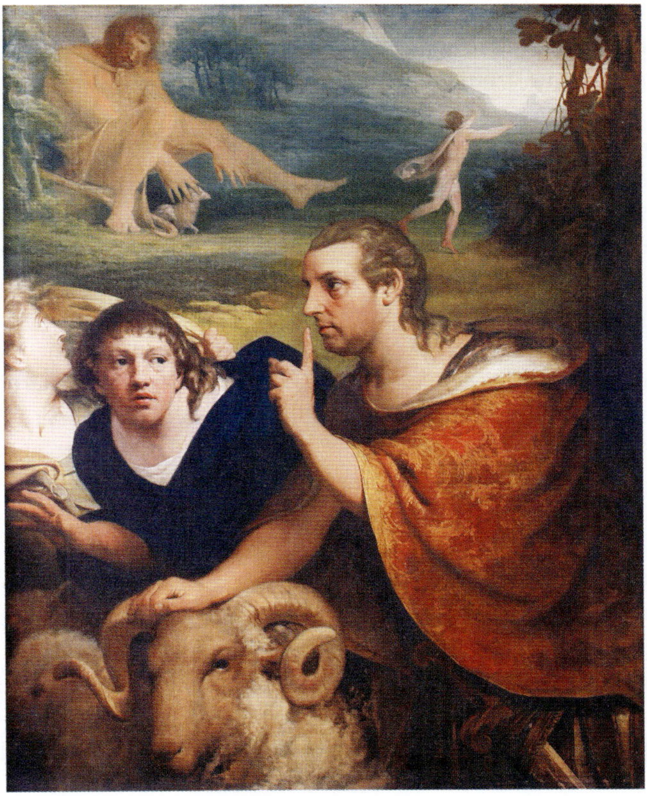

Fig. 11.1. James Barry, *Barry and Burke in the Characters of Ulysses and a Companion Fleeing from the Cave of Polyphemus.* Oil on canvas, 1776.

consolation to his posthumous reputation that his passing was crowned by burial in St Paul's Cathedral.[37]

Barry's outspokenness is remarkably visualized in his portraits of *Barry and Burke in the Characters of Ulysses and a Companion Fleeing from the Cave of Polyphemus* (*c*.1776) (*Cat. 110* (Fig. 11.1)). Like many late-eighteenth-century artists who had cut their artistic teeth in Rome, Barry privileged themes deriving from classical antiquity, and in particular those with a Homeric lineage.[38] *Barry and Burke* certainly manifests such an ancestry, but with a remarkable twist. In the foreground, leaning on a formidable ram, stand two men, each in the likeness of a real-life individual. To the left, looking very nervous, is Barry himself in the guise of the 'companion'. To his right is the impressive, alert, and gorgeously dressed figure of Burke, evidently in the role of Ulysses. At the very centre of the

[37] Solkin (2010: 12–13). [38] Facos (2011: 36).

painting is the left hand of Ulysses/Burke, with the index finger raised in a gesture of admonition: 'Be careful, and be quiet!' In the background slumps the colossal, blinded Polyphemus, from whom a tiny human figure flees in terror. If ever a painting cried out to be decoded, this one does. But the decipherment is far from straightforward. To begin with, there is an interesting reversal of the Homeric course of events. In the *Odyssey*, it was the companions of Ulysses who urged *him* to be silent after their escape from the cave, to avoid provoking the ogre further by his triumphalism; in the painting, by contrast, it is Ulysses who takes the prudent lead. More intriguing is the implied relationship between Barry and Burke. Could Burke's authoritativeness reflect Barry's wish to conciliate his patron after they had quarrelled, by acknowledging that Burke 'had a point' (literally) in urging him to mind his tongue?[39] No less enigmatic is the interpretation of Polyphemus. Is he a representative of the British establishment in general, or perhaps the Royal Academy in particular?[40] Barry had, after all, rubbed both august bodies up the wrong way during his career. It would certainly be one of the more notable post-classical reimaginings of Polyphemus to present him as a Royal Academician.

One of our principal aims in discussing artistic reworkings of Cyclopean myths has been to stress the capacity of artists to develop approaches independent of those adopted by writers: to emphasize, that is, the role of artists as self-standing innovators rather than as 'mere' illustrators. But in some cases 'illustration'—with no denigration implied—is just the right term. *Primus inter pares*, not least in terms of his Europe-wide influence, was the draughtsman and sculptor John Flaxman (1755–1826).[41] He is best known for work in three closely related areas, which together secured his reputation as a leading Neoclassicist. First, he mediated between Sir William Hamilton's pioneering publications of Greek vases and Josiah Wedgwood's revolution in industrial pottery-making: Flaxman was employed to model the reliefs from which the pottery designs were taken, and relied heavily on engravings of Hamilton's vase collection in the process. Second, Flaxman advised the British government to buy the marbles that Elgin had lifted from the Parthenon; some of his own sculptural reliefs were directly influenced by them. Finally, he was a renowned illustrator of literature: Dante, Aeschylus, Hesiod (engraved by his friend William Blake), and, above all, Homer.

His illustrations of the *Odyssey* were engraved by Tommaso Piroli in 1793, during Flaxman's artistically decisive stay in Rome.[42] One of his two drawings of the Polyphemus episode is a little-known preliminary sketch depicting the blinding

[39] So Pressly (1981: 76). For the painting in the context of the biography of Burke, see Lock (2008: 367).

[40] Myrone (2005: 92).

[41] See Essick and La Belle (1977); Bindman (1979); Irwin (1979); Symmons (1984); Wickham (2010); Aguirre Castro (2016a).

[42] Symmons (1984: 104–5).

(*Cat. 113* (Fig. 11.2)), which was omitted from the finally published collection of illustrations. The triangular and symmetrical composition depicts a supine, lolling, naked Polyphemus, with a Greek on either side of him and another group of men behind and above him manipulating the lethal stake. The design has no known precedent in antiquity; Flaxman was evidently chancing his arm. The latent raw violence, combined with the undignified posture of the ogre, make a notable contrast with the cool, restrained, clean-lined, humanely sympathetic style of the drawings in the final collection; this, it has been suggested, is precisely why it was not included.[43] No such discrepant tone belongs to the design that *was* published, *Ulysses Giving Wine to Polyphemus* (*Cat. 114* (Fig. 11.3)). The colossal Cyclops, Michelangelesque in physique, appears in profile, watchfully holding out a bowl into which Ulysses, no less meticulously, pours wine. The whole scene is decorous and elegant, even down to the protagonists' headgear: Ulysses' traveller's *pilos* is matched by the beautiful turban sported by the ogre.[44] The only

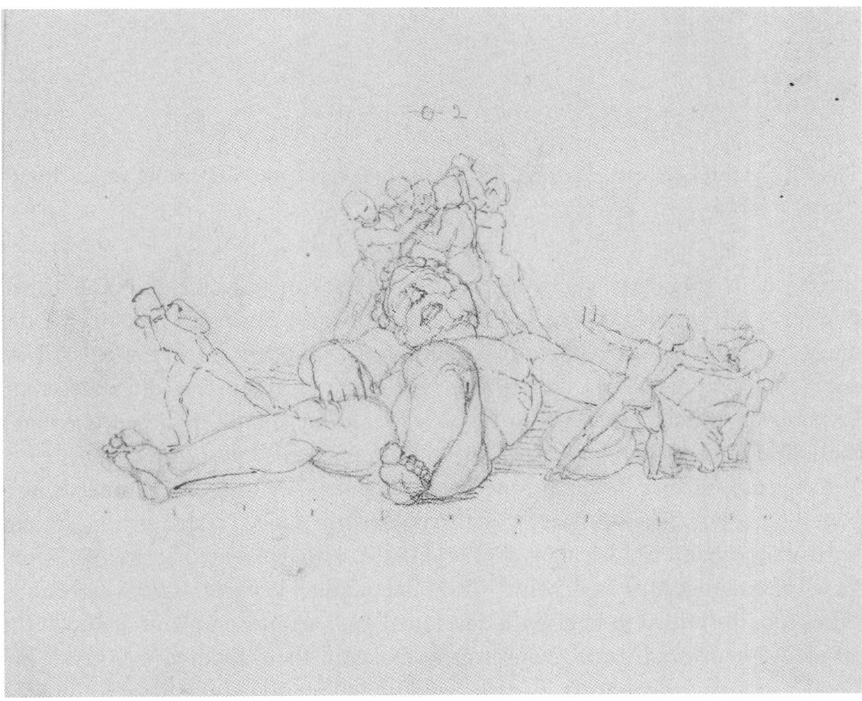

Fig. 11.2. John Flaxman, pen-and-ink sketch of the blinding of Polyphemus, perhaps 1805.

[43] Cf. Irwin (1979: 71), citing the comments of Henry Boyd, eighteenth-century translator of Dante.

[44] For a comparable turban worn by the 'Genius of Mount Olympus' in one of Flaxman's illustrations of the *Iliad*, see Essick and La Belle (1977), *Iliad*, pl. 9.

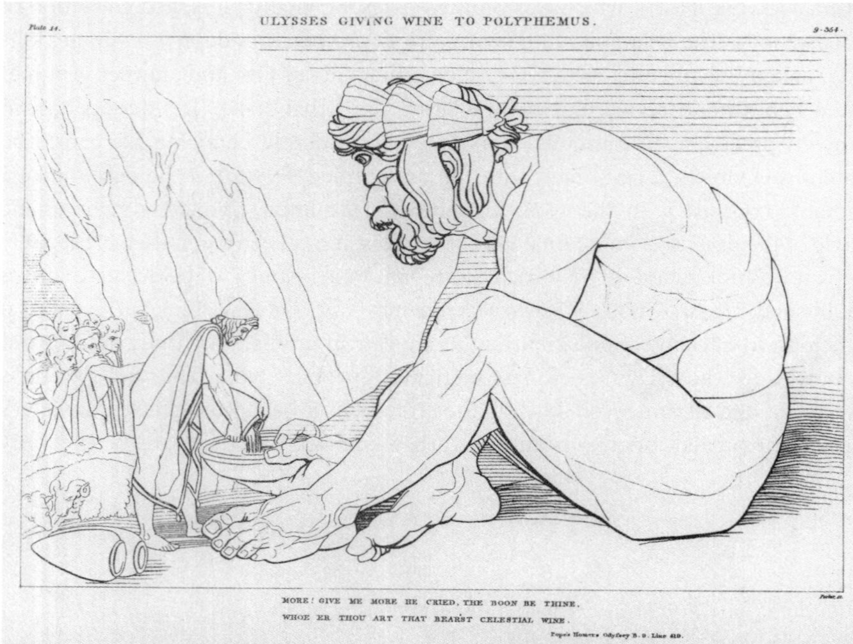

Fig. 11.3. John Flaxman, *Ulysses Giving Wine to Polyphemus*. Engraving and etching on paper, 1805.

incongruous note is struck by the group of Ulysses' men in the left-hand corner, peering out from behind a rock. Philip Otto Runge, a German Romantic painter and a contemporary of Flaxman, thought this drawing was one of the artist's least successful, singling out the little men for particular criticism: they did not seem to be *doing* anything.[45] This is a bit unfair; at least one should highlight Flaxman's incredible mastery of line, exemplified in this image as in all the others.[46]

Far removed in emotional tone from Flaxman's well-groomed, smartly turbaned ogre, but closer to Barry's, is a characteristic image created by the Zurich-born artist Johann Heinrich Füssli (1741–1825), who reinvented himself as Henry Fuseli after emigrating to Britain.[47] There are parallels between Barry's career and Fuseli's: both studied in Italy, both developed their art in Georgian London at the Royal Academy, both saw themselves as exiles in their adopted country.[48] But Fuseli's style was the more distinctive, with its exploration of the macabre and the supernatural, giving visual expression to the goals and ambitions of Gothic literature.[49]

[45] Anecdote reported by Symmons (1984: 214). [46] Cf. Wickham (2010).
[47] See e.g. Schiff (1977); Lentzsch (2005). [48] Cf. Haut (2010: 95).
[49] Myrone (2001: 43–6).

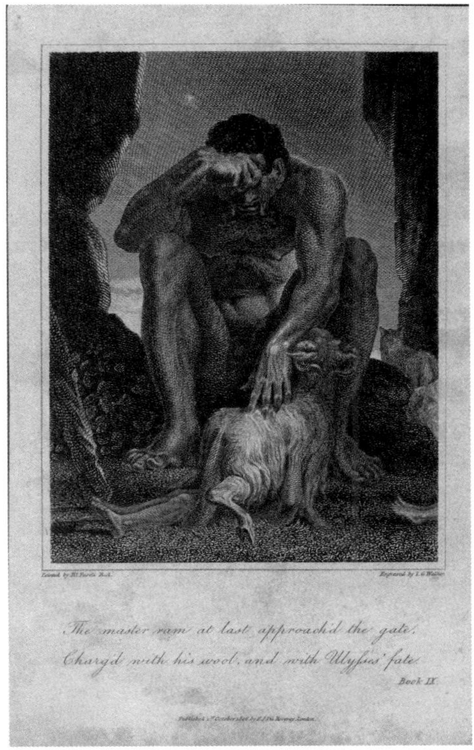

Fig. 11.4. Henry Fuseli, *Blinded Polyphemus Checks the Sheep as they Leave the Cave*. Engraving by J. G. Walker, 1806.

At the beginning of the nineteenth century, Fuseli did some sketches to illustrate a reissue of Pope's translations of Homer.[50] One of these illustrations (*Cat. 112* (Fig. 11.4)), representing the blinded Polyphemus feeling the back of a ram, has beneath it a fabulous couplet—more Pope than Homer—from the *Odyssey* translation:

> The master ram at last approach'd the gate,
> Charg'd with his wool, and with Ulysses' fate.[51]

The image reproduces Fuseli's own oil painting of *Blinded Polyphemus Checks the Sheep as they Leave the Cave* (*Cat. 111*). Both sketch and painting feature a crouching, naked Polyphemus, with head bowed and right hand covering the blinded eye. Sometimes likened to a gorilla, and sometimes to the disturbing giants whom Goya was painting around the same date, Fuseli's Cyclops has taken

[50] Cf. Pop (2015).

[51] Pope is translating *Od.* 9.444–5. A more literal though less dramatic rendering of the last four words of 445 (*kai emoi pukina phroneonti*) would be: 'and with me thinking intensely'.

its place as an iconic representation of anguish and grief.[52] The ogre's left hand is no less significant than the right, as it drops down to brush the fleece of his favourite ram, itself foregrounded by the light that falls directly on it.[53] The two human legs (presumably those of Ulysses) that protrude from beneath the ram, and the two human feet (owner unknown) at the far right, confirm the debt of sketch and painting to the familiar back-to-Homer narrative. But that it is the legs and feet—not the heads—of the humans that are visible serves to dehumanize these supposedly heroic escapees, simultaneously shifting the semantic weight onto the relationship between the ram and its master—an emphasis very unusual in the post-Homeric reception of this myth. For all the Gothic modernity of Fuseli's nightmarish vision, he really was, in one important respect, going 'back to Homer'—for whom Polyphemus' address to his ram played such an emotionally decisive role.

Sharing and even intensifying Fuseli's interest in the macabre was the work of his compatriot Arnold Böcklin, a prolific painter of mythological scenes. His *Odysseus and Calypso*, and his five versions of *The Isle of the Dead*, have shaped his reputation as a Symbolist artist through his visions of an eerily static fantasy world. But he also depicted classical and other myths in moments of furious savagery. Such is his *Odysseus and Polyphemus* (1896), representing the Greeks' shipborne escape from Cyclopia (*Cat. 123* (Fig. 11.5)). What steals the show is the landscape, a huge and stormy sea at the edge of a murderously craggy coastline, more Tintagel than Taormina. The tiny figure of Odysseus in the stern gazes towards the shore, where, balancing athletically, legs wide apart, on a huge horizontal rock, the terrifying ogre is about to launch a massive boulder. His face

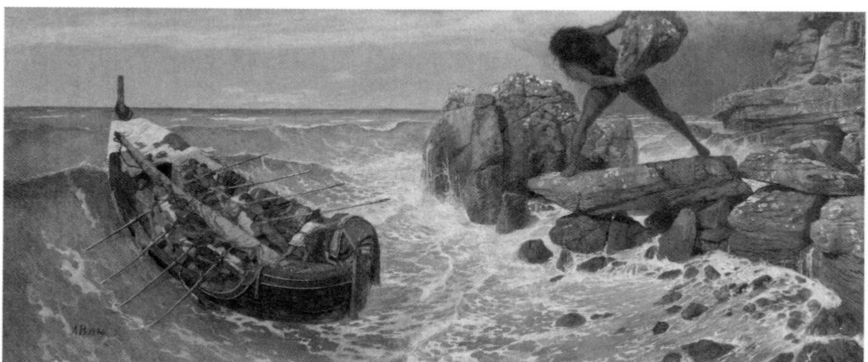

Fig. 11.5. Arnold Böcklin, *Odysseus and Polyphemus*. Oil and tempera on panel, 1896.

52 Gorilla/Goya: Mazur-Contamine (1984: 49).

53 See Pop (2015: 206–7) on the relationship between light and the sense of touch; on surface and touch, Purves (2016).

is invisible, entirely obscured by hair. In 1829, Turner had painted his own version of the Greeks' escape by ship, a typically atmospheric *Ulysses Deriding Polyphemus* (*Cat. 115*). Within the all-pervasive drama of sky, sea, and rock—not forgetting a fiery glow (molten Etnaean lava? the forge?) just above sea level—the figure of the Cyclops, his hand raised to his head in presumed agony, is difficult to differentiate from the mountainous setting ('baffled Cyclops fading in the sky', as James Elroy Flecker would put it).[54] Böcklin echoed Turner's privileging of the seascape, reducing the Greeks' ostentatious fleet to a single, unimpressive boat. He also brought the ogre from the background into the limelight. Albeit less compellingly than in Turner's vision, Polyphemus remains for Böcklin a creature whose wildness seems to flow into his body from his natural surroundings.

We turn now to a myth-teller who rivals even Victor Hugo in his importance for our story. Usually regarded as the first French Symbolist painter—he once defined painting as 'this language of symbol, myth, and sign'—Gustave Moreau (1826–98) rejected the dominant artistic trends of his time, not least Impressionism, in order to explore his own anxieties and longings by returning to the Greek myths, viewed through an idealized, fantastic lens.[55] Erudite and rich, he was, in the words of the author of a major recent study, 'an eccentric and innovative reactionary'.[56] He followed his own idiosyncratic path through the mythological tradition, privileging the portrayal of heroes in the act of magnificently succeeding or gloriously failing. Either way, they were graceful, poised, and beautiful; the Hugolean equation of sublimity with grotesquerie had no appeal for Moreau.[57] He was not—and is not—to everyone's taste. In the early and mid-twentieth century his dismissal of 'real' concerns in favour of inner feelings and fantasies was routinely laughed at as decadent and perverse.[58] Not till the advent of Surrealism did his work undergo a major revaluation—unsurprisingly, since the Surrealists claimed him as a precursor of their own anti-naturalist manifesto.[59]

Among Moreau's obsessions was the relationship between Polyphemus and Galatea. He owned a 1660 French edition of Ovid's *Metamorphoses*, but what strikes the viewer is not the proximity of Ovidian inspiration but the distance travelled from it.[60] Acis is nowhere: his presence would have aroused the irrelevantly disturbing emotion of jealousy. Ulysses is also beside the point: the epic dynamic of male–male competition has no part in Moreau's concept. Also sidelined is the polarity between Beauty and the Beast—at least if bestiality implies any hint of ugliness. Forget Quasimodo: Moreau's Cyclopes are creatures of

[54] Flecker (1907: 22); cf. Hall (2008: 11).

[55] Quotation: Moreau (2002: ii. 258). Cf. Grigorian (2009: 41–77); Allan (2016: 144). On defining 'Symbolism': Gamboni (1992), with Cooke (2014: 31).

[56] Cooke (2014: 3).

[57] Cf. Grigorian (2009: 43).

[58] Criticisms listed in Cooke (2014: 11, with 196 n. 7).

[59] e.g. Breton (1965: 363–6).

[60] Ovid edition: cf. Lacambre (1999: 42, 191).

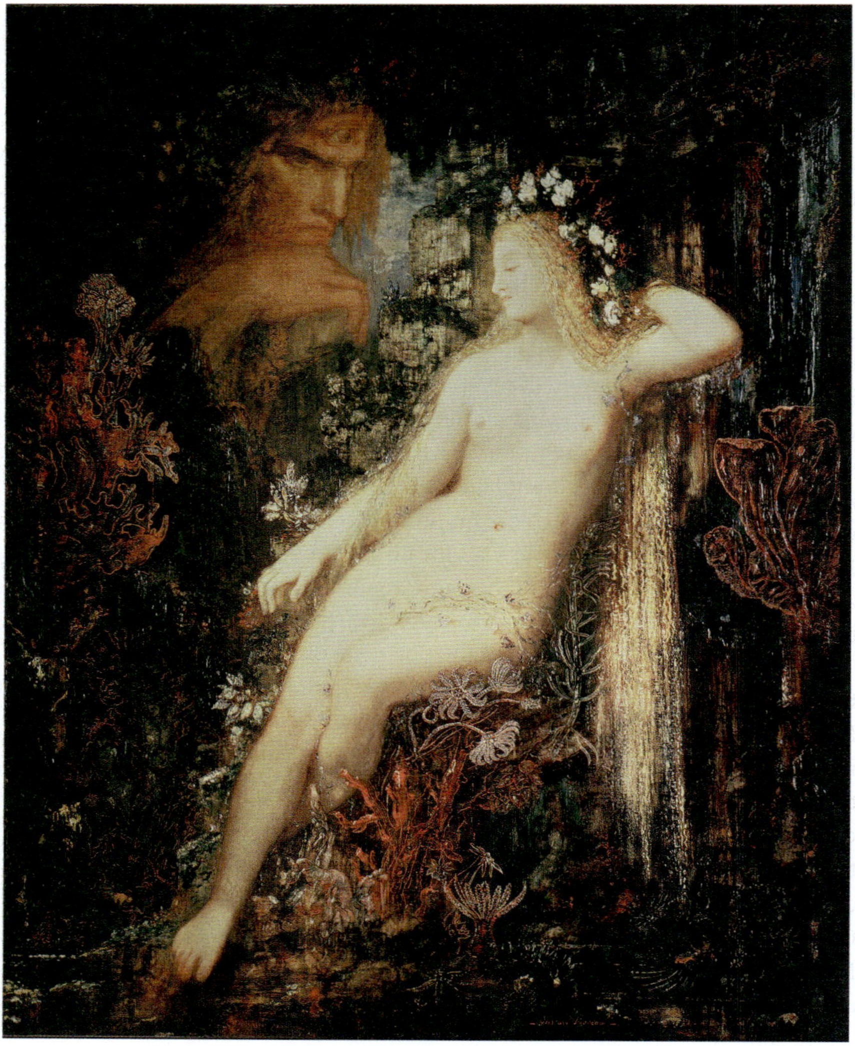

Fig. 11.6. Gustave Moreau, *Galatea*. Oil on wood, *c.*1880.

intense attractiveness, sometimes as sultrily sexy as the Galateas they contemplate. Their additional, third eye is an adornment rather than a defect, embodying Moreau's as well as Polyphemus' vision: a rapt, wistful gaze.

In his *Galatea* in the Musée d'Orsay (*Cat. 118* (Fig. 11.6), Moreau creates, as Geneviève Lacambre puts it, 'a monument to frustration and adoration'.[61] The

[61] Lacambre (1999: 191).

scene is a grotto, but it resembles nothing in earlier representations of Cyclopean landscape. The *fin-de-siècle* novelist and art critic J.-K. Huysmans, Moreau's contemporary and fan, described it as a vast jewel case full of strange animal, mineral, and vegetal creatures, suggestive of a marine environment within which Galatea somehow exists as an enchanting vision.[62] The aquatic cavern was a setting that Moreau came back to more than once, as in his *Narcissus* and *The Poet and the Siren*; but the place where Galatea sits is unique. She herself is no less extraordinary than her environment. Ivory-skinned, languid, and provocatively naked, she wears exquisite blue flowers in her hair and between her thighs. Her closed eye(s) suggest sleep, or at least tranquil relaxation. At the top left is the huge, earthily brick-red head of Polyphemus-as-voyeur, resting his chin on his hand. His beard, and his long hair mixed with leaves, might in theory suggest wildness; indeed one critic refers to him as 'a deeply menacing presence'.[63] But we should pause before seeing this image through eyes that have grown used to movie posters of evil-minded monsters looking down threateningly at helpless virgins—Lon Chaney's Wolf Man, or Bela Lugosi's Dracula.[64] Moreau's Polyphemus is neither Wolf Man nor Dracula, nor is he Caliban: there is more about him of the intense and melancholy thinker than of the malevolent would-be rapist.[65]

That Moreau found the Polyphemus–Galatea relationship irresistible is testified not only by the completed canvases but also by the numerous drawings in the Musée Gustave Moreau in Paris. A watercolour and pencil version (*Cat. 119*) more or less reproduces the composition of the Musée d'Orsay oil painting, though in the watercolour a ram's skin and pan pipes identify Polyphemus explicitly as a shepherd. In a third version, housed in the Thyssen Museum in Madrid, the Cyclops emerges a little further out of the shadows (*Cat. 124*). With his muscularity, and his very long hair entwined with greenery, he resembles a Wild or Green Man, or perhaps a Faunus or a Pan (there are similarities with the Pan in Moreau's *Jupiter and Semele*). Galatea is, as usual, naked and enticing, reclining in a cave filled with deep blue water, and surrounded by flowers, fantastic plants, and richly coloured corals. But in the distance appears a landscape beyond the cavern—a Turneresque, yellowish-orange sky, perhaps depicting a dramatic sunrise, as if Polyphemus had surprised the nymph while she was still asleep. On yet another canvas (*Cat. 122*), evidently unfinished, Galatea appears in a strange, suspended verticality, with an elaborate marine environment below her: all leaves,

[62] Huysmans (1883: 154–5); cf. Paladilhe and Pierre (1972: 153–4); Cooke (2003: 144).

[63] Cooke (2014: 109); cf. 'a monstrous... creature fixes a menacing eye...' (p. 6).

[64] Illustrations in Landis (2011: 16, 20–1).

[65] Nor, incidentally, is he like the mad Lear, whose own 'crown' was a much more disorderly affair, made as it was with (in Cordelia's words) 'rank femiter and furrow-weeds, with hardocks, hemlock, nettles, cuckoo-flow'rs, darnel, and all the idle weeds that grow in our sustaining corn' (*King Lear*, IV.iv.3–6).

seaweeds, and flowers. In the top-left corner the Cyclops gazes down into the chasm. Moreau wrote a fascinating text about this painting: 'The large eye of the astonished and troubled earth remains fixed on this pearl of limpid and pure waters. And the large eye saddens and the gaze becomes veiled with bitterness and love while contemplating this flower of the bottomless abysses.'[66] Galatea is cast as a pearl and a flower, a pure creature of water. Polyphemus, by contrast, is a creature of the earth—closer, therefore, to the Cyclopes born from Gaia than to the traditions that credited the sea god Poseidon with his parentage, or that compared the Cyclopean eye to another natural phenomenon, the Sun.

If there is one ancient myth-teller whom Moreau prompts us to reconsider above all others, it is neither Hesiod, nor Homer, nor Ovid, but Philostratus. No ancient author explores the gazes of Polyphemus and Galatea so searchingly as Philostratus; no modern artist rivals Moreau in depicting the same theme. How far do the perspectives of artist and author coincide? At first sight the differences outweigh the overlaps. Of the image of the Cyclops that *he* was viewing, Philostratus wrote this (*Imag.* 2.18): 'He thinks, because he is in love, that his glance is gentle, but in fact it is still wild and stealthy, like that of wild beasts subdued by necessity'.[67] This is not the impression we get from Moreau. Though every one of his images has its own nuance, the predominant impression is one of wistful melancholy rather than suppressed aggression. As for Galatea, Philostratus' memorable commentary runs, we recall, like this: 'Her eyes are wonderful, for they have a kind of distant look that travels as far as the sea extends.' Here the difference from Moreau is unmistakable, because in image after image he represented the nymph's eyes as tranquilly closed. However, common to both Philostratus and Moreau is the absence of overt interaction between the two figures: each is self-contained within a separate world. On one intriguing interpretation of Moreau's visions, Polyphemus is a projection—the content of Galatea's dream[68]—a dream, though, not a nightmare, since the nymph's unperturbed tranquillity—*la belle inertie*—hints that she is envisioning something agreeable rather than threatening.[69] As for Polyphemus, his posture is ambiguous. The fact that in so many images he supports his chin on his hand conveys a sense of repose, even sleepiness;[70] yet his third eye is always open. Could these scenes depict, not a dreaming Galatea, but a dreaming Polyphemus, with the content of the dream—accessed through that privileged, third eye—being the desired, naked beloved in her magical bower? There is no way—and no need—to decide which

[66] Moreau (1984: 87) trans. Lacambre (1999: 256). [67] See p. 121.

[68] Paladilhe and Pierre (1972: 154). The alternative suggestion, that Galatea might be dreaming *of Acis*, rests on the assumption that Moreau is following Ovid slavishly; cf. Cooke (2003: 142–3), citing and rightly rejecting the view expressed by Émile Bergerat in 1880.

[69] *La belle inertie*: see Allan (2016: 145–6) on Moreau's association of repose with beauty and its contemplation, as in his portrayals of Andromeda, Delilah, and Semele.

[70] For a slightly different gesture, in a quite different context, and with a wholly different meaning, see p. 248 and Fig. 10.3.

(if either) of the two figures is dreaming. To cite José Pierre: 'the two dreams cross, but the desires are incommunicable.'[71]

On the subject of reciprocal dreaming, a work by Odilon Redon (1840–1916) provides a revealing comparison. In some ways Moreau's imaginative heir, Redon pushed even further than his predecessor towards the symbolic and the visionary. His *Cyclops* (*Cat. 127* (Fig. 11.7)) shows a naked woman asleep below the brow of a hill. Above and behind her rises the gigantic figure of Polyphemus, whose head is tilted as if he were trying to gaze at the sleeping form below him. But his huge, solitary, central eye belies the angle of the head, for it gazes outwards at the viewer. The image combines the role of the eye as bearer of desire, with an expression of sexual inhibition. This is Polyphemus-as-Teletubby: tender, ingenuous, unthreatening, apparently abashed. Yet, once more, as in Moreau, one might ask the question: could this be an image of a Cyclops *dreaming*? In that case the highly sexualized content of the dream might suggest something more behind the Cyclops' gaze than childish innocence (not that Freud would have been surprised). Alternatively, could the looming Cyclops be the monstrous content of

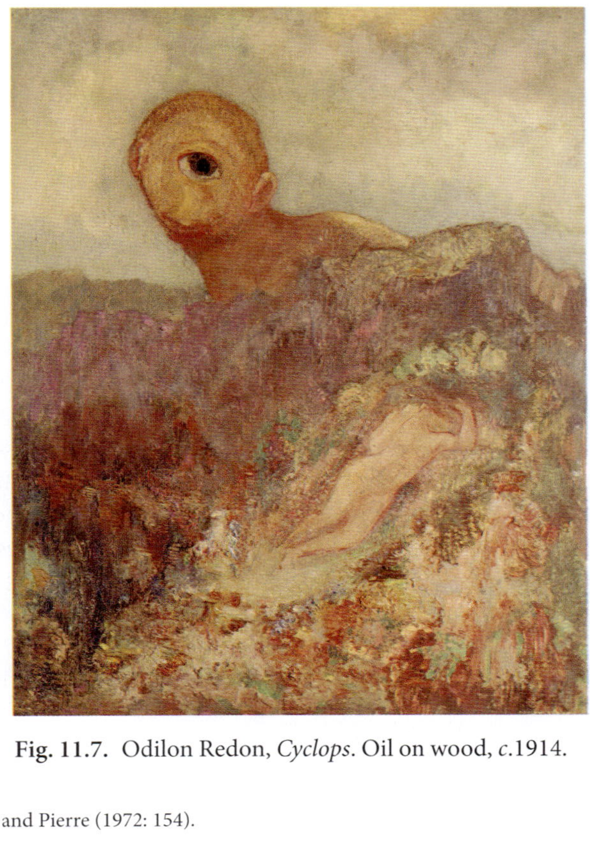

Fig. 11.7. Odilon Redon, *Cyclops*. Oil on wood, *c.*1914.

[71] Paladilhe and Pierre (1972: 154).

Galatea's dream? (Freud would not have been surprised by that, either.) *Mutatis mutandis*, the ambiguity is the same as that in several of Moreau's works. The major difference is the landscape. In Redon there is no magical, watery cavern, but rather a rocky hill slope falling away gently to a flowering meadow. Not a *pastoral* landscape, though: there are no pan pipes or flocks, nothing to mark the Cyclops out as a herdsman. Although he is evidently still part of a narrative—which is why we call him Polyphemus and her Galatea—his idiosyncratic shape probes the integument of that narrative to its very limit. As we shall see later, it is an integument through which some of Redon's other creatures burst, attaining a nightmarish existence as independent, free-floating eyes.

Returning briefly to Moreau, we cannot resist citing two more of his images of Polyphemus, both of them glamorous male pin-ups. In each case the Cyclops retains his piercing, brooding gaze, but with no Galatea in sight. The landscape is maritime but open, rather than being constrained in a watery grotto. In one case (*Cat. 125* (Fig. 11.8)) the head of a muscular, young, full-lipped Polyphemus is seen in close-up, resting his chin on his wooden staff; his third, central eye stares fixedly into the distance. In another context, the exotic thatch of greenery in his hair might raise a smile, but woe betide anyone making fun of a creature with

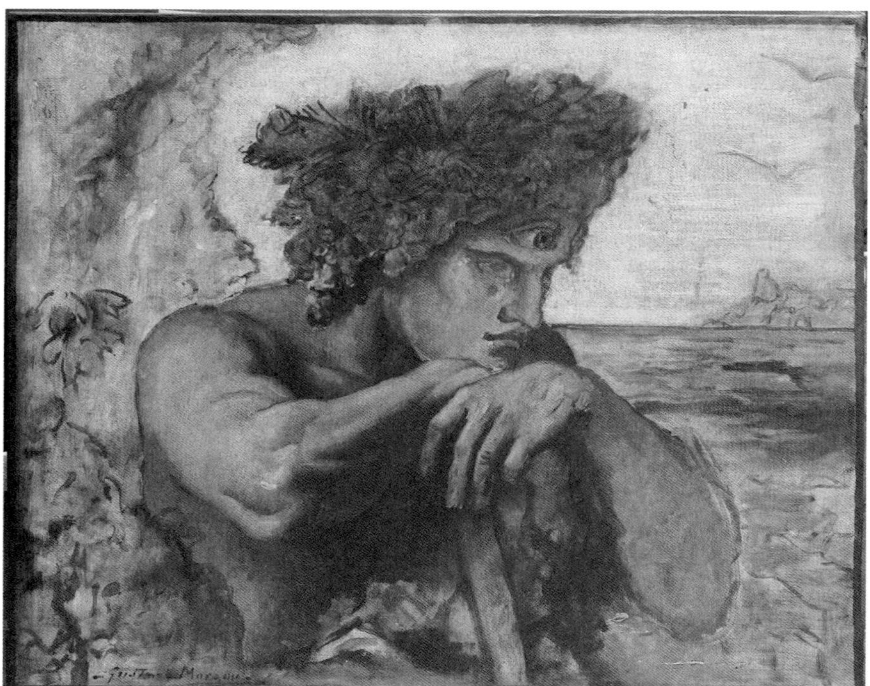

Fig. 11.8. Gustave Moreau, *Polyphemus*. Oil on wood, undated.

muscles like these. Even more provocative is a sultry, bearded, nearly nude Cyclops lying prone on a rocky outcrop, resting his chin meditatively on his crossed arms (*Cat. 126*). Since his face is in profile, his eyes attract little attention; the upper, third eye is scarcely detectable, whereas the one visible, normally positioned eye seems to be shut. Such eroto-mythological images of male beauty would not be out of place in the work of the contemporary photographers Pierre et Gilles.

There might seem little to choose between Polyphemus on the seashore—where we have seen him so often—and Polyphemus at the seaside. But the difference becomes manifest in the works of Maurice Denis (1870–1943). Born at Granville on the Normandy coast, Denis would devote his most characteristic paintings to idyllic–mythological scenes played out on beaches, inspired by the setting of the village of Perros-Guirec in Brittany, where he bought a summer villa ('Silencio'). A member of the avant-garde group self-styled as *Les Nabis* ('The Prophets'), Denis absorbed the influence of a roll call of artists and movements, from Gauguin and Cézanne to Japanism and Art Nouveau. But it is his beach scenes, investing the landscape of Brittany with the light of the Mediterranean, that express his most individual vision.[72]

The encounter between Ulysses and Nausicaa was an obvious choice, and Denis dedicated a cycle of six decorative panels to the theme. But he also repeatedly brought the Polyphemus–Galatea relationship under the same beach umbrella. In one example (*Cat. 130* (Fig. 11.9)), a naked and muscular but non-gigantic man plays on a double pipe as he faces out to sea, with his back to the viewer. Just visible in the water is a woman with hands raised, as if playing in the waves.[73] In the foreground is a group of relaxed and playful holidaymakers—naked boys and clothed or partly clothed women; the musician holds no terrors for *them*. Only the title, *Polyphemus*, leads the viewer to infer the presence of 'the mythical'; otherwise this would simply be an everyday, albeit idealized, contemporary beach scene, with the woman in the waves being anonymous instead of 'Galatea'. In another painting (*Cat. 131*), Denis shifts the emphasis, as the title (*Galatea*) implies. A woman in a thin pink dress stands at the water's edge, adjusting her hair. At her feet, emerging from the ripples in a posture of adoration, a naked youth smiles up at her. A variety of other bathers, some naked and some not, populate the background; they look like Breton cousins of the Spanish bathers in the works of Joaquín Sorolla. So far, so unmythical; it might have been called *Amitiés au bord de la mer*. But over the top of a cliff in the far background peers a naked male voyeur, presumably focusing on the couple in the foreground, who thereby 'become' Acis and Galatea. In Denis' *Polyphemus* and *Galatea* we are

[72] Cf. Groom (2001: 206).

[73] Schneider (2010: 284–7) relates this to Gauguin's *In the Waves, or Ondine*, a possible source of inspiration for Denis.

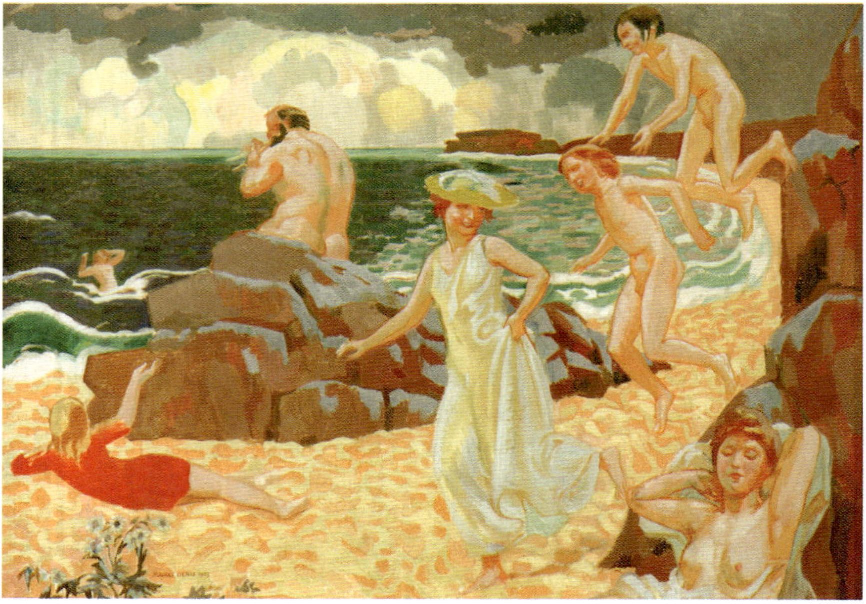

Fig. 11.9. Maurice Denis, *Polyphemus*. Oil on canvas, 1907.

back, in a sense, to pastoral: in the words of Charles Segal, what we have is 'a characteristic pastoral blurring of real and imaginary'.[74] But this is only true *mutatis mutandis*: there are no flocks, and for shepherdesses read bathing *belles*.

The narrative framework alluded to by Moreau, Redon, and Denis traces its pedigree to Ovid and ultimately Theocritus and Philoxenus, mediated by more than two millennia of artistic revisualization. But the encounter dramatized in *Odyssey* book 9, as exploited by Barry and more concertedly Flaxman, also retained its potential to stimulate major artists. The clearest twentieth-century example is Marc Chagall (1887–1985). Though Jewish–biblical themes predominate, filtered through a richly colourful and joyfully acrobatic imagination (his output might be summarized under the rubric 'everything about art that Hitler loathed'), he occasionally turned to the traditions of classical antiquity. Visits to Greece in the 1950s stimulated an interest in myth, and the result was a series of colour lithographs illustrating episodes from the *Odyssey* (run off by Fernand Mourlot in Paris in 1974–5). The representation of Polyphemus' blinding (*Cat. 144* (Fig. 11.10)) locates the event within a circle—the circus ring is one of Chagall's favourite spaces, to which he attributed a magical, other-worldly quality.[75] At the right, a man (presumably Odysseus), accompanied by two others, drives a stake

[74] Segal (1981a: 5).

[75] The circus in Chagall: Walther and Metzger (1990: 57); Foray (2013: 38–43).

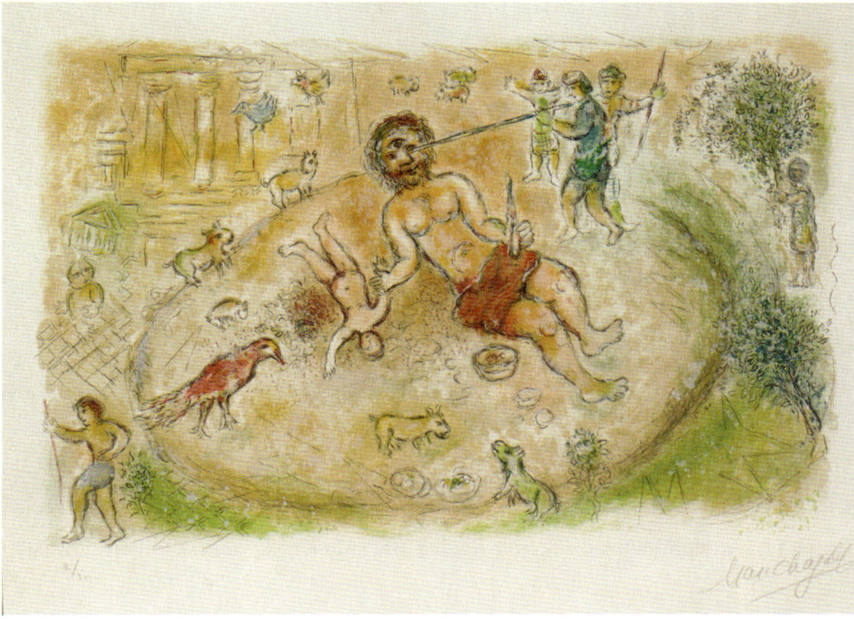

Fig. 11.10. Marc Chagall, *Polyphemus*. Colour lithograph, 1974.

as thin as a billiard cue into the left of the Cyclops' two normally positioned eyes, leaving a superior, third eye untouched. In his right hand, Polyphemus grips the arm of a naked human figure, apparently holding him over red-hot embers. A variety of typically Chagallian visual props supplements the drama, some deriving from the Homeric text, some not: goats, birds (including a big red one), a bowl, architectural columns signifying a generic 'Greece'. The goats are revealingly ambiguous: simultaneously a recurrently visualized part of Chagall's Jewish symbolic heritage and a marker of the Homeric herdsman-ogre.[76] While the portrayal of the blinding contains numerous echoes of the Homeric text, the whole image is at the same time perfectly integrated into Chagall's idiosyncratic universe. There are some hints of violence: the blinding itself, and the suggestion of imminent anthropophagy. But the savagery is muted: is there not a gentle smile on Polyphemus' face? It is hard to find any one of Chagall's pictures entirely drained of warmth, humour, or optimism.[77]

[76] Goats in Chagall: Foray (2013: 28–9).

[77] The blinding of the Cyclops also figures in Chagall's large mosaic *The Message of Ulysses* (1968) created for the Faculty of Law in the University of Nice. There are many similarities with the lithograph, but the upper part of the circus ring is predominantly red—unlike virtually the whole of the rest of the mosaic. For a painter so sensitive to the semantics of hue as Chagall, the implied meaning must surely be that the mood of the scene is one of extreme violence.

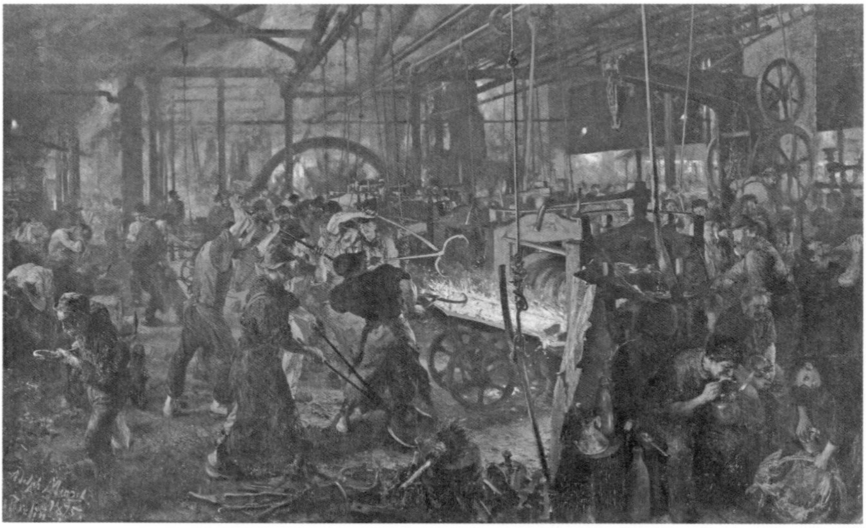

Fig. 11.11. Adolph Menzel, *The Iron-Rolling Mill* (*Modern Cyclopes*). Oil on canvas, 1875.

Modern artworks that situate the Cyclop(e)s within an implied narrative concentrate overwhelmingly on the Ulysses or Galatea motifs. But just occasionally modern artists have opted to reformulate ancient traditions about Cyclopean metalworking. The most imposing example is *The Iron-Rolling Mill* (1875) (*Cat. 117* (Fig. 11.11)) by Adolph (later 'von') Menzel, which relocates Vulcan's forge to an Upper Silesian factory making rails for railway tracks. The Etnaean cave is replaced by the searing heat of an industrial workshop; rather than working for a divine master, these modern artisans toil for the factory boss. Max Jordan, who bought the large (254 × 158 cm.) painting for the Nationalgalerie in Berlin, subtitled it *Modern Cyclopes*; maybe it helped to justify the expenditure of 30,000 thalers if the work were presented as a piece of culturally serious 'history painting'.[78] The subtitle was not, however, a whim: it echoed the artist's own trope when he spoke of having done preliminary research into 'this Cyclopean world of modern technology'.[79] In the spirit of realist painters of industrial toil such as Ignace-François Bonhommé, Menzel had dragged the Cyclopes into the tough, painful, sweat-drenched, yet (as here conceived) heroic environment of the urban factory-worker.

[78] Riemann-Reyher (1996: 384).

[79] See O. Beta (1992: 21); cf. Dufrêne (2004: 487–8). For an earlier use of Cyclopean imagery by the art critic Friedrich Eggers about work in a German factory, see Riemann-Reyher (1996: 383, 385 n. 12).

So much for the generically Cyclopean dimension of Menzel's concept. But some viewers of the painting have gone further, seeking to identify more specific mythological allusions. Thierry Dufrêne draws our attention to the huge wheel in the far distance, which both 'encloses' the workers and replicates the two cart-wheels in the foreground—a trio of 'round eyes'. Dufrêne also notes the action of the pincer-wielding operatives in the foreground, as they direct the molten iron into the 'eye' of the laminating cylinder—an echo of a quite different Cyclopean moment.[80] Bolder still is Michael Fried's reading.[81] His overall take on Menzel is that the artist's realist achievement has been systematically underappreciated by critics who privilege the work of French modernists. Fried, by contrast, stresses the uniqueness not only of Menzel's engagement with the everyday, but also of his ability to feel his way into the physicality of situations (what Fried calls 'embodiment'). In the case of *The Iron-Rolling Mill*, Fried goes for an unambiguously Freudian approach: 'the cast iron is indisputably phallic both by virtue of its form and because it is depicted being forced by the workers into the laminating cylinder as if in an industrial version of the sexual act.'[82] In the year when Menzel began the painting, Freud was only 16, so, even if Fried were to be right, Menzel must have been anticipating rather than echoing Freud. In any event, speaking for ourselves, we would put sex right at the bottom of the list of themes that Menzel might have been exploring—which is not to deny the *physicality* that Fried rightly places at the heart of Menzel's work.

Beyond Narrative: The Art of the Single Eye

In modern and contemporary art, monocularity has become *the* characteristic of the Cyclops, eclipsing every other feature. Whether he is figured as an isolated individual or just a head, the essence of the Cyclops is distilled into the form of the single eye, at once a deficiency and a trademark. However, in the absence of narrative context, identifying a given painting or sculpture *as* a Cyclops may be less than straightforward. Much may depend on the title; but the titles of modern artworks constitute an extraordinarily complex field.[83] Adolf Gottlieb painted a roundish white shape containing a black circle, on a red background; he called it *White Disk—Red Ground* (1967).[84] Paul Klee created a half-ellipse containing a single white eye with a black centre; he called it *The Eye* (pastel on jute, 1938). A lithograph by Odilon Redon depicts a strange, grinning creature with a huge single eye; he called it *The Misshapen Polyp Floated on the Shores, a Sort of Smiling and Hideous Cyclops* (1883) (*Cat. 120* (Fig. 11.13)). William Baziotes painted a schematic, flesh-coloured body-shape containing in its 'head' a central, blue circle

[80] Dufrêne (2004: 488–9). [81] Fried (2002). [82] Fried (2002: 121).

[83] Amid a large bibliography, see especially Bann (1985).

[84] For this and the following three examples, see Aguirre Castro (2016b: 99–100).

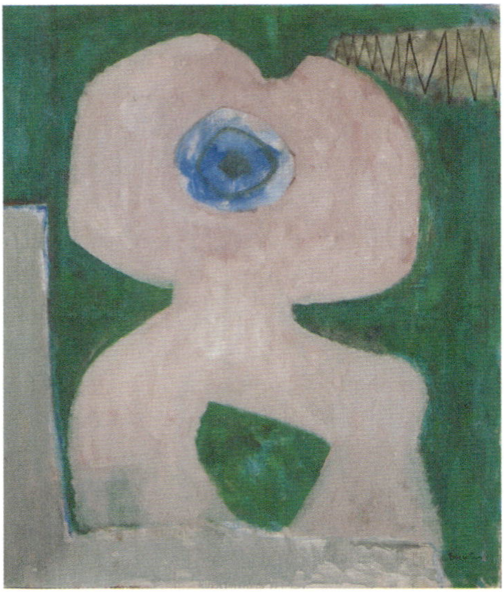

Fig. 11.12. William Baziotes, *Cyclops*. Oil on canvas, 1947.

with two more circles within that; he called it *Cyclops* (1947) (*Cat. 137* (Fig. 11.12)). In assigning a title, each of these four artists gives the potential viewer an 'instruction' (in Ernst Gombrich's formulation) to adopt an interpretative stance.[85] To entitle a work 'disk', 'eye', or 'Cyclops' is to make a choice, guiding the viewer towards or away from a series of potential precedents in the artistic tradition. The artist may even create deliberate confusion through the title, a strategy explicitly endorsed by Odilon Redon.[86] As we consider, in the next section, images that may or may not depict Cyclopes, we need to remain alert to this interpretative indeterminacy, a quality that goes to the heart of countless modern and contemporary artworks, especially to the extent that they prefer non-narrative modes of representation.

Redon's eyes

We begin by returning to Odilon Redon, an artist whose enigmatic and unsettling imagination was dominated by images of circularity, exemplified especially by isolated round heads and eyes: eyes that look, but also float and dance.[87] Among the more unusual visions depicted by Odilon Redon is *The Eye like a Strange Balloon Mounts toward Infinity* (1882). This dark image represents a spherical,

[85] Gombrich (1985: 225). Cf. also Chipp (1968: 565); Tuchman (1971); Shapiro and Shapiro (1990: 264).

[86] Cf. Gombrich (1985: 234).

[87] See Sandström (1955: 57–61); Heyd (1992); Hauptman (2005: 45–9); Noce (2011: 77–81). Lacau St-Guily (1995) is brief but excellent.

enucleated eye transformed into a hot-air balloon, the gaze of its dilated pupil directed upwards like that of the 'misshapen Polyp'; beneath the eye/balloon is slung a dish bearing a small human head.[88] As Agnès Lacau St-Guily has brilliantly argued, the eye/balloon is perfectly ambiguous: liberated and apparently heaven-regarding, yet at the same time weighed down by a macabre burden which it is unwilling to look at.[89] Other images created by Redon insist on the same theme of ocular autonomy, not only visually but also through their titles: *Everywhere Eyeballs are Ablaze* (1888), and *And Eyes without Heads were Floating like Molluscs* (1896)—titles that are fragments of poetry in their own right. For Redon, just as heads become eggs or cactuses or spiders or flowers, so eyes take on independent life, as if Empedocles' vision of primordial creation ('Here sprang up many faces without necks, arms wandered without shoulders, unattached, and eyes strayed alone, in need of foreheads') had achieved its ideal artistic realization.[90]

The titles of two of Redon's lithographs explicitly acknowledge a Greek mythological pedigree: *Cyclops* (*Cat. 121*) and *The Misshapen Polyp Floated on the Shores, a Sort of Smiling and Hideous Cyclops* (*Cat. 120* (Fig. 11.13)). The images are almost identical. Each depicts a head fringed by a semi-circle of wire-like hair; a broad nose; an improbably symmetrical row of teeth, expressing a grin situated somewhere between the frankly inane and the dreamily tender; big ears (in the case of *Cyclops* only); above all, a huge central eye, with the pupil situated at the

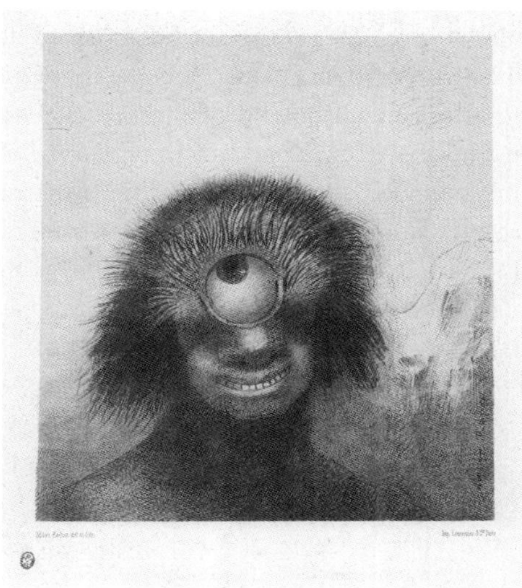

Fig. 11.13. Odilon Redon, *The Misshapen Polyp Floated on the Shores, a Sort of Smiling and Hideous Cyclops*. Lithograph, 1883.

[88] On *noirs* in Redon, see van Zuylen (2005: 66–8).
[89] Lacau St-Guily (1995: 58).
[90] Empedocles: KRS fr. 376; their translation.

top rather than in the middle. *The Misshapen Polyp* belongs to a series called 'Origins': these creatures evoke the world of the primordial. The title *The Misshapen Polyp* is doubly suggestive. 'Polyp' (in French, *polype*) is the term for an aquatic creature with a very simple structure—the lowest creature on the evolutionary scale possessing the organ of sight.[91] (Flaubert included polyps in the vision at the end of his *Temptation of St Antony*: 'polyps spread out their tentacles, jellyfish quiver like crystal balls . . .'.)[92] But there is more to Redon's imagination than the mere transcription of zoological theory.[93] 'Polyp' is also the first half of 'Polyphemus'.[94] Myth meets science in an imagery of the monstrous that simultaneously disconcerts and attracts.

It is, however, all too easy to exaggerate Redon's debt to antique images or ways of thinking, as if *that* dialogue were all he had on his mind; to do that would be to commit one of the classic errors to which the study of the reception of Greek mythology is prone. Other potential influences are more recent and more important. One possibility lies in the traditional stories told in the Médoc region of France, where Redon grew up. Might a local Gascon tale have fixed itself in Redon's imagination? After all, stories about the one-eyed cannibalistic ogre Bécut (the equivalent of the Basque Tartaro/Tartalo) were included by Jean-François Bladé in his collection of *Contes populaires de la Gascogne,* published in 1886.[95] Such a debt might indeed be present, though quantifying it is beyond speculation. That Redon had, thanks to his friend and mentor the botanist Armand Clavaud, discovered the fascinating world of life forms visible only under the microscope, and was refracting what he had seen in his art, adds another possible genesis for his repeated depictions of circular, floating, eye-like creatures.[96] No less plausible is the influence of some of Redon's literary contemporaries who narrated the fantastic.[97] Redon's interest in Edgar Allan Poe emerges in the album *To Edgar Poe*, in which the artist illustrates the author's work. His image for Poe's story *The Tell-Tale Heart* exemplifies the recurrent ocular obsession: a solitary eye views the viewer from between two planks of wood, almost as if it were itself a knot in the wood. As for the text, Poe's narrator describes an old man whose most prominent characteristic is a malevolent, dangerous eye (the narrator speaks only of one eye, not two):

> I loved the old man. He had never wronged me. He had never given me insult. For his gold I had no desire. I think it was his eye! Yes, it was this! He had the eye

[91] Sandström (1955: 80); Bindman (2009: 155, 158).

[92] Cited by Mathieu (1977: 142), in relation not to Redon but to Moreau—his *Galatea*, no less; cf. Schmidt-Burkhardt (1992: 207–8).

[93] Cf. Viola (1962–4: 45).

[94] Sandström (1955: 79–80); Schmidt-Burkhardt (1992: 50–1).

[95] Cf. Sandström (1955: 36–9), citing Bladé (1886).

[96] Schmidt-Burkhardt (1992: 208–9); Noce (2011: 20–4).

[97] See Strauss (2011) on Baudelaire, Poe, Mallarmé, and Flaubert.

> of a vulture—a pale blue eye, with a film over it. Whenever it fell upon me, my blood ran cold; and so by degrees—very gradually—I made up my mind to take the life of the old man, and thus rid myself of the eye for ever.[98]

The analogy with Redon's own *imaginaire* looks close, but the artist himself rejected the idea; or at least, in a letter written in 1898 he denied that Poe's stories were his favourite bedtime reading.[99] But Redon is a master of misdirection, refusing to acknowledge virtually any outside influence on his art. Another literary analogy approximates still more closely to the artist's work. *The Wondersmith*, a fantasy tale by the Irish–American writer Fitz-James O'Brien (1828–62), includes a remarkable episode concerning an independent, artificial eye:

> 'How does your eye get on, Kerplonne?'
>
> 'Excellently, Duke. It is finished. I have it here.'
>
> And the little Frenchman put his hand into his breeches-pocket and pulled out a large artificial human eye. Its great size was the only thing in this eye that would lead any one to suspect its artificiality. It was at least twice the size of life; but there was a fearful speculative light in its iris, which seemed to expand and contract like the eye of a living being, that rendered it a horrible staring paradox. It looked like the naked eye of the Cyclops, torn from his forehead, and still burning with wrath and the desire for vengeance.[100]

Identifying this or that influence on Redon is a complicated business, not least because it goes against the grain of his own expressions of self-determination (as in his comment about Poe): Redon too, like his creations, was, or claimed to be, an independent eye. To see him as dominated by the ancient myth-telling tradition about the Cyclopes, as opposed to merely invoking it from time to time, is to misunderstand the intricate genesis of Redon's work. But Redon still plays a significant role in the story we are telling. He draws the Cyclops into a territory beyond grotesqueness; a territory charted not by Flaubert or Zola, but by Mary Shelley and E. T. A. Hoffmann; a 'liberating space of negativity' that lies perhaps even beyond monstrosity (Paul Gauguin observed that the creatures painted by

[98] In Poe (1984: 313).

[99] Letter cited by Lacau St-Guily (1995: 63).

[100] Note also O'Brien's story *The Diamond Lens*, about a man who falls obsessively in love with an infinitesimally tiny female figure ('Animula') contained in a droplet of water, visible only through the 'perfect lens' of a microscope—to which the viewer applies *one* eye. There are affinities here not only with Redon's as-it-were 'microscopic' creatures, but also with Moreau's numerous images of Galatea—a lovely woman in a watery setting observed by a much larger male voyeur. (Both *The Wondersmith* and *The Diamond Lens* can be found in O'Brien (1977).) For the idea of independent, removable eyes (in this case, in the palm of the hand) one may compare the terrifying character of the Pale Man in Guillermo del Toro's film *Pan's Labyrinth* (2006). We take the liberty of adding that one of the authors of the present book has written a fantasy tale, inspired by Redon and entitled *Marguerite*, in which a weeping eye can be seen within a bunch of flowers (Aguirre Castro 2018: 47–63).

Redon were not monsters, just imaginary creatures), a territory in which avatars of the ancient ogre take their place alongside other creatures who are, as he is, nothing but an eye.[101]

Some twentieth-century eyes

Several major twentieth-century artists revisited the imagery of the Cyclops, usually in works that are relatively obscure or uncelebrated. Rarely does the single eye attain the thematic prominence accorded to it by Redon, but its representation often reveals something characteristic—or surprising—about the artist concerned.

Few modern artists are more difficult to pigeon-hole than Francis Picabia (1879–1953). He associated himself with a string of different styles, punctuated by episodes of 'back to the drawing board'. Having experimented with Impressionism, Abstraction, and, most provocatively and imaginatively, Dadaism, he shifted direction again towards a more figurative style, only to revert to abstract art late in life. His most impressive engagements with antiquity came at second hand as parodies of previous reworkings of myths—for instance, by Titian and Rubens. Around 1926 he painted an oil-on-cardboard that he called *Cyclops* (*Cat. 132*), part of a series of so-called monster pictures, full of misshapen lines and garish colours.[102] *Cyclops* depicts a distorted human form: no hands or feet; oval 'legs'; a circular shape at the top left, containing a single eye; a pattern of concentric circles at the top right. Without the title, it might be difficult to assign a mythological (or any other) referent. *With* the title, it becomes 'obvious' that this is indeed—could only be—a Cyclops, the concentric circles replicating the interlocking motifs of monocularity and circularity. In this case, unlike several of Picabia's better-known revisualizations of Greek myth, there is no ancient model, nor any obvious modern model either (though in the tilt of the 'head' there is perhaps a nod towards Redon's *Cyclops*). The closest stylistic affinity is with Picasso. Both Picasso and Picabia experimented with the motif of multiple eyes, eyes as independent, mobile objects separable from the face.[103] *Cyclops* inverts the theme, taking it in the direction of 'normality': at least *this* figure has the 'right' number of eyes (that is, just one), in the right place.

No artistic movement has occupied itself more obsessively with the themes of eyes and vision, sight and sightlessness, and the contrast between external perception and inner vision, than Surrealism.[104] The most notorious and shocking embodiment of these themes—the slicing through of a human eye with a razor in

[101] Gauguin: Guérin (1978: 42–3). 'Liberating space of negativity': van Zuylen (2005: 58).
[102] See Le Bot (1968); Camfield (1979: 215–28).
[103] Schmidt-Burkhardt (1992: 52–6).
[104] See e.g. Jeanne Siegel (1982); Schneede (1991); Jay (1993).

the opening sequence of the film *Un Chien Andalou* (dir. Luis Buñuel, 1929)—is only one instance among many of the Surrealists' exploration of the idea of the impairment or destruction of the outer eye in order to facilitate a more intense focus on inner vision. The Surrealists' interest in the relationship between inner and outer vision, and in the concomitant relationship between artistic creativity and the subconscious, existed in the closest symbiosis with the tenets of psychoanalysis. Also congruent with a psychoanalytical approach to vision was the notion of the sexualization of the eye, whether as the 'eye' of the penis (whence the idea that to maim the eye was to effect a symbolic castration), or as an equivalent of the female genitals.[105]

For Max Ernst, the Surrealist focus on the complexities of vision became inseparable from his affinity, both existential and artistic, with the ideas of Freud.[106] Ernst is, of course, best known for his paintings, works that typically explore, with meticulous definitional clarity, extraordinary scenes from a fantastic dreamworld populated by strange hybrid creatures inhabiting terrifyingly luxuriant landscapes. But he worked also in three dimensions, often creating sculptures composed of *objets trouvés*. His Cyclops (*c.*1934) (*Cat. 133*) is a humorous little collage made from stone, iron, and two wooden clothes pegs.[107] Standing at no more than eleven inches high, this 'giant' is an ironically reduced and simplified version of the once-mighty ogre, whose stone head is supported by spindly 'legs' and clothes-peg 'arms'. What marks him out as a Cyclops—apart, as always, from the title—is the single round protuberance to one side of the stone head. A combination of the primitive with the childish, the collage is more modest than most of Ernst's engagements with the theme of vision, not least the profoundly disturbing *Oedipus Rex* (1922). But it is one more example of the Surrealist obsession with the eye.

Far more intriguing than Ernst's manikin is a set of three near-identical works by another artist strongly influenced by Surrealism: Meret Oppenheim (1913–85), Ernst's sometime lover.[108] Her career ranged from posing for soft-porn nude photographs (most famously those taken by Man Ray at a printing press) to creating brilliant and controversial artworks in her own right. Among these are *Polyphemus in Love*, three versions of virtually the same Cyclopean image: an oil crayon on paper (1973), a pencil sketch (1974), and a coloured silkscreen on a plexiglass mirror (also 1974) (*Cat. 134* (Fig. 11.14)).[109] All three display an oval face, fringed, in the case of the work in crayon, with a mop of black hair; a single, central eye with an apparently fused double iris and pupil, beneath a single eyebrow; strongly emphasized cheeks; virtually no nose; and a mouth with a tongue

[105] Schmidt-Burckhardt (1992: 67–73). We have learned an enormous amount from Schmidt-Burckhardt's discussion of the eye in modern art.

[106] Jeanne Siegel (1982). Ernst was 'demonstrably the first artist to read Freud' (W. Spies 1991: 33).

[107] See W. Spies, S. Metken, and G. Metken (1979: 287, no. 2125).

[108] Chadwick (1985); Helfenstein (1993).

[109] All illustrated in Levy (2013: 167).

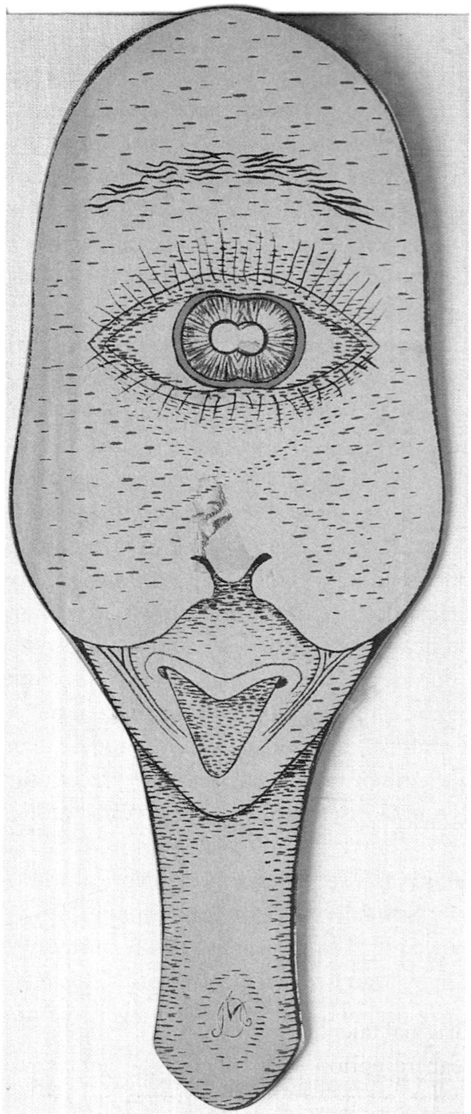

Fig. 11.14. Meret Oppenheim, *Polyphemus in Love*. Coloured silkscreen on plexiglas mirror, 1974.

stuck out rudely at the viewer. The use of the mirror for one of the images introduces the idea of reflection, destabilizing the relationship between object and viewer: just who is sticking their tongue out at whom? Another significant feature of the mirror (and of the pencil sketch) is the handle, near the end of which is another shape in the form of an eye. Given, first, the distinctly phallic shape of the handle, resembling the ancient eye–phallus or *fascinus*;[110] secondly, Oppenheim's familiarity with the ideas of Freud and, more to the point, Jung; and, thirdly, the work's title—it refers not just to any old Cyclops, nor even just to Polyphemus, but to Polyphemus *in love*—it would seem inescapable that the artist was presenting an image with a doubly sexual content, expressed through both the facial and the phallic eyes.

Nearly all the sexual content of Surrealism is filtered through the gaze of male artists, informed by the theories of Freud. Oppenheim is a hugely refreshing exception. Maybe the silly raspberry being blown by all three of her Polyphemuses—coupled, in the case of the crayon-on-paper, with the rather feminizing shock of hair—shows this figure up as being less macho than he thinks he is. If so, it would correspond to the Jungian (*not* Freudian) interest repeatedly shown by Oppenheim in the feminine side of men and the masculine side of women.[111] Nowhere is this clearer than in a remarkable ink sketch *Unicorn Witch* (1943) (*Cat. 136* (Fig. 11.15)).[112] A naked woman, legs wide apart, lies provocatively on her back. She has a woman's hair and lips, a single, central eye, and a long, narrow, pointed horn emerging from her head. This extraordinary hybrid is a cross between the Cyclops and the unicorn. The horn functions as an unambiguous sexual symbol, but also recalls the stake driven into Polyphemus' eye. The eye, the phallic horn, and the implied evocation of the Homeric ogre, conspire to tell *one* story, that of celebrated masculinity; but the hair, the lips, and the openly displayed woman's sex tell quite another, that of confident femininity. The sketch also alludes to—and radically subverts—the legend that a unicorn can only be captured by a pure virgin woman.[113] How, then, shall we describe this figure? 'Androgynous'? 'Hermaphrodite'? Neither word really does the job. 'The most striking portrait of a female Cyclops in the history of art'? That is certainly true, but it misses the nuance of the title: *Unicorn Witch*. In fact this figure is a unique/unic-... combination of Polyphemus and Circe—books 9 and 10 of the *Odyssey* rolled into one—with a nice piece of medieval lore thrown in for good measure. But the image is far more than a collection of influences: in both thought and execution, Oppenheim is a brilliantly original talent.

Within the *longue durée* of Cyclopean reception, Oppenheim is one of relatively few women to have made a major intervention. There may be several reasons. Perhaps the male-on-male jousting in Polyphemus' cave failed to generate sufficient motivation for a female (or feminist) approach. Perhaps the character of Galatea, as evoked in antiquity, was too much of an emotional cipher to engender the kind of female/feminist reaction stimulated by, say, Medea, or Penelope, or Helen, or Antigone. Be that as it may, the example of

[110] See e.g. Steinhart (1995: 82–7, with pl. 34, 4) (a particularly graphic example).
[111] See Schulz (2007: 56–9); Walda (2013). [112] Levy (2013: 123).
[113] On unicorns, see now Pastoureau and Taburet-Delahaye (2018).

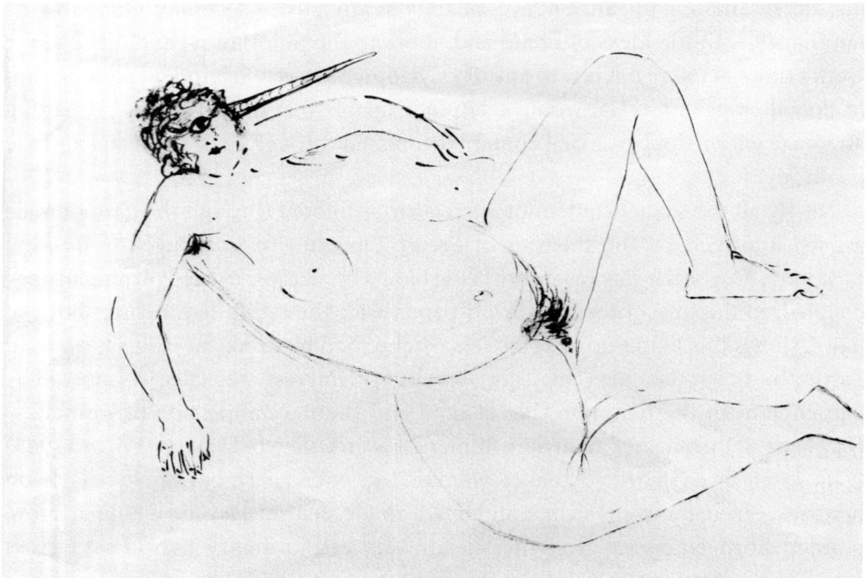

Fig. 11.15. Meret Oppenheim, *Unicorn Witch*. Ink drawing, 1943.

Oppenheim—which is, fortunately, not the only one—forcefully demonstrates the potential for a productive female/feminist take on this constellation of myths also.

Cyclops abstracted

We noticed just now the powerful role played by titles in many modern artworks. The title of William Baziotes' *Cyclops* (*Cat. 137* (Fig. 11.12)) leaves little room for doubt about the artist's general intention, but the result still leaves ample leeway for the interpreter.

Baziotes (1912–63) belonged to the movement that became known as Abstract Expressionism; along with Jackson Pollock and Mark Rothko among others, he was a member of the New York School. As well as being fired by Surrealist and Symbolist antecedents, and by contemporaries such as Picasso and Miró, he also looked back to classical mythology (his parents were of Greek origin and he attended Greek schools).[114] His overriding technique involved minimizing naturalistic figural representation and distilling a myth to its fundamental formal

[114] See Aguirre Castro (2016b), from which we borrow in this section.

essence.[115] A pervasive theme is distortion, an emphasis that he himself linked to having observed the anatomical mutilations caused by two world wars.[116] Also recurrent is a sense of the primordial, as if the worlds of Moreau and Redon had coalesced and then been visualized through a bizarrely contorted geometry. All these perspectives come together in *Cyclops*. It seems to represent a highly abstracted pink torso on a green background. The proportionately huge head has no other trait apart from a large, blue, central eye with a black pupil. The pinkness might replicate the 'baby Cyclops' of Redon's Teletubby (*Cat. 127* (Fig. 11.7)), but Baziotes himself highlighted another influence. He had seen a rhinoceros ('my favourite animal') in the Bronx zoo: 'He was playful and cute and toylike, but at the same time, he chilled me. He seemed prehistoric and his eyes were cold and deadly.'[117] At the top right is a thinnish, roughly triangular shape marked with a dark zigzag. Is this the rhinoceros's horn? Or is it, as has been suggested, the stake used for the blinding of Polyphemus?[118] Either or both would make sense, though a similar design appears elsewhere in Baziotes's work, in paintings where such meanings would be far less relevant. Maybe the recurrent triangle is more like the monolith in *2001: A Space Odyssey*: a riddle wrapped in an enigma.

The single-eye motif, a Baziotes trademark, becomes an *idée fixe* in a series of works from 1947. *Dwarf* shows a figure resembling that in *Cyclops*, but this time acid green. The 'head' has a single 'eye' consisting of concentric circles, accompanied by a zigzag that might be jagged teeth—macabre rather than innocent; another set of concentric circles appears in the torso.[119] In *Night Form* intense blues and purples replace the pink of *Cyclops*, but the concentric eye persists. *Night Mirror* is more complex, with a vertical, 'mummified' form (with zigzag) to the left of the head/torso, and an undulating, biomorphic, apparently monocular creature to the right. There are numerous formal congruences between the figure/creature in the centre and the one on the right; this is, after all, a (distorted) 'mirror', a type of object that Baziotes himself described as evocative of strangeness and otherworldliness.[120] *Water Form* transports concentricity into an environment that Baziotes loved to explore, that of an ocean deep featuring floating, jellyfish-like life forms. Dominating the scene is a Redonesque polyp; prominent as usual are the concentric eye, juxtaposed with a short zigzag.[121] Most ambitious of all is *The Flesh Eaters* (1952). The imagery again suggests the deep sea. On the left, in front of shapes that give the impression of seaweed, is an ambiguous form resembling either an armless, seated figure or a huge, single-eyed head with a gaping mouth. Above, on the right, floats another one-eyed creature, pinkish,

[115] Sandler (1965: 28–30); Tuchman (1971: 20); Hadler (1977); Polcari (1991: 213–32, esp. 213–14); Crain (2004).

[116] Polcari (1991: 220–2). [117] Cited in Polcari (1991: 218). [118] Crain (2004: 27–8).

[119] Cf. Preble (2004: 19–20, with fig. 6). [120] Baziotes (1949: 3–4); cf. Crain (2004: 7).

[121] Cf. Tuchman (1971: 12), speaking of forms that 'derive from microscope-aided vision and Redon'.

hazy, and amorphous. Below is a torso-like shape topped with what could be pointed headgear or wild hair. The title recalls the numerous zombie movies of the 1940s. In addition, even if the single eye is less dominant than in the 1947 paintings, Baziotes was surely alluding to one of his favourite motifs, the (here) anthropophagous Cyclops.

The robot and the colossus

If artistic originality implies the ability to create an imaginative world that is both distinctive and new, then the Scottish artist Eduardo Paolozzi (1924–2005) was truly original. Born in Edinburgh of Italian immigrants—they ran an ice-cream parlour—he had a less-than-easy upbringing. He and his father were interned as enemy aliens after Italy's declaration of war on Britain in 1940; his father and grandfather drowned when the ship transporting them to Canada was torpedoed. As a young artist, Paolozzi spent time in France and Germany, but produced his best-known work in Britain, being associated with the birth of British Pop Art. He never had much love for the British Establishment, though his career followed a not unfamiliar trajectory from rebelliousness to eventual recognition (CBE; Royal Academician; knighthood).

Paolozzi's signature technique was the fabrication of a new reality out of the bric-à-brac of modern popular culture, which he came across in, for instance, magazines, cinema posters, comics, and technological detritus. Not everyone appreciated his style: the *Daily Express* characteristically derided his first exhibition with the headline WOULD YOU PAY TWELVE GUINEAS FOR THIS?[122] Two recurrent emphases were science fiction and machines, which coalesced in a series of robot-like creatures spanning the worlds of space travel and classical mythology. Ancient sculptures were a particular source of inspiration because of their typically fragmentary condition, ripe for reinvention.[123] But the forms of Paolozzi's new creations, although reminiscent of the *kouroi* and *korai* statues of Archaic Greece, were reconfigured with the metallic paraphernalia of industrial mass production, morphing into life forms that anticipated those of late-twentieth- and early twenty-first-century sci-fi, such as the Borg of *Star Trek*.

Through the backstories implied by their titles, several of Paolozzi's monumental figures highlight craftsmanship: *Daedalus*, *Icarus* (two versions), *The Artist as Hephaestus*, and the 7-metres-tall *Vulcan*. The same applies to his two versions of *Cyclops* (both 1957), given the association between the ancient Cyclopes and metalworking. One of the two is a standing humanoid just over a metre tall (*Cat. 141* (Fig. 11.16)); the other is a humanoid head, well above life size (*Cat. 142*).

[122] Cited in Whitford (1971: 7). [123] Collins (2014: 26–7).

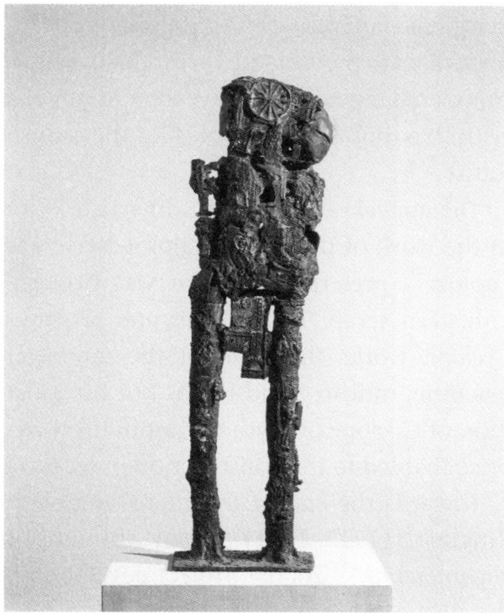

Fig. 11.16. Eduardo Paolozzi, *Cyclops*. Bronze (lost wax technique), 1957.

Both were made by the lost-wax technique, which involved finding a selection of discarded objects, natural or man-made; pressing them into a bed of clay; pouring wax into the impression; manipulating the wax sheets into a collage; putting a mould over the wax and heating it to melt the wax; pouring molten bronze into the cavity. The surface texture of the end result thus depended on the objects initially pressed into the clay. The dull-grey, standing *Cyclops*, imprinted with discarded machine parts and other assorted rubbish, displays as its focus a single, central 'eye', formed by the impression of a wheel with spokes; a smaller wheel represents the genitals.[124] The *Cyclops*-as-head has a yellowish, almost golden colour. Its front view shows two, small, irregular holes: the upper one *might* be an eye, the lower one *might* be a mouth. There is a more than passing resemblance to the 'creature' in the Hammer Films remake of *The Mummy* (1959).

Paolozzi's Cyclopes forge demonic monstrosity out of household refuse, blending 'high' with 'low' art. The fact that the artist gave the title *St Sebastian* to two sculptures similar to the standing *Cyclops* points to another shared feature of this series of works: most of them represent beings who are in some way physically damaged—aptly enough, since most of their constituent parts were already damaged before Paolozzi got his hands on them. The fact that the two Cyclopes are fabricated from what modern civilization has discarded defines them as

[124] Without for a moment suggesting that such an idea might have been present in Paolozzi's mind, we may recall that 'wheel' is one possible meaning, albeit a rare one, of the Greek word *kuklos*: Hom. *Il.* 5.722, 18.375, 23.340.

marginal—a Cyclopean trait going back millennia. But these images are not just throwbacks: they blend the archaic with the futuristic. They might have come from a galaxy far, far away; they might easily have been entitled 'Robot'; as one critic has put it, they look like the ruins uncovered by an archaeology of the future.[125]

The appeal of the Cyclops to artists working with metal continued to resonate in the work of the Swiss sculptor Bernhard Luginbühl (1929–2011).[126] Whereas Paolozzi's preferred medium was bronze, Luginbühl's was iron, welded from industrial scrap. To his *Atlas* and *Sisyphus* he added a *Big Cyclops* and a *Little Cyclops*, works that exist at the intersections of animal and human, art and machine, industry and myth. But his most significant contribution to the tradition of Cyclopean myth lay not in his own creations, but in a collaborative enterprise that led to the construction of an extraordinary work of art.

Towards the end of the 1960s Luginbühl and the Swiss kinetic sculptor Jean Tinguely (1925–1991) began thinking about an idea provisionally called *Gigantoleum*.[127] As the project developed, the number of collaborators grew, but the prime movers were Tinguely and his second wife, Niki de Saint Phalle.[128] What the group made was *The Head*, aka *Cyclops* (*Cat. 145* (Fig. 11.17)), a multi-storeyed, 22-metre-tall kinetic sculpture fabricated from 300 tons of industrial cast-offs, including pieces of metal, chunks of concrete, numerous mirrors, and a railway truck. It stands in a wooded park near the village of Milly-la-Forêt outside Paris, where visitors can gaze up at, be deafened by, and clamber about inside the colossal, alarming, funny, and altogether magnificent construction.[129]

The rural setting offers a striking contrast to the pile of metal and concrete that make up *Cyclops*. The original plan had been that the façade should be in the garish colours that characterize many of Niki's own joyous 'Nana' sculptures, but eventually she opted for a mosaic of mirrors that reflect the greens and browns of the surrounding woodland, enabling the monster to camouflage himself against prying intruders. In front, not far from ground level, a large aperture represents the giant's mouth, from which the tongue—a water slide—leads down into a pool. Far above, an enormous almond-shaped eye contains a golden, sunlike pupil. The interior of the head consists of a kind of exuberant and highly politicized museum, accessible via a network of stairways, ladders, and balconies. Among the exhibits is a 1930s railway wagon suspended high in the air, containing figures sculpted by another Swiss artist, Tinguely's first wife, Eva Aeppli; it commemorates the Jews deported during the Second World War. But the head is—at the same time as being an exhibition space—a head. Tinguely wanted it to embody

[125] Konnertz (1984: 91). More on Paolozzi in Aguirre Castro (2017).
[126] See e.g. Hesse (2008). [127] Canal (2007: 55); cf. Hultén (1996).
[128] Hultén (1995).
[129] Full description in Canal (2007); see also Hultén (1993); Müller (2015: 131–42).

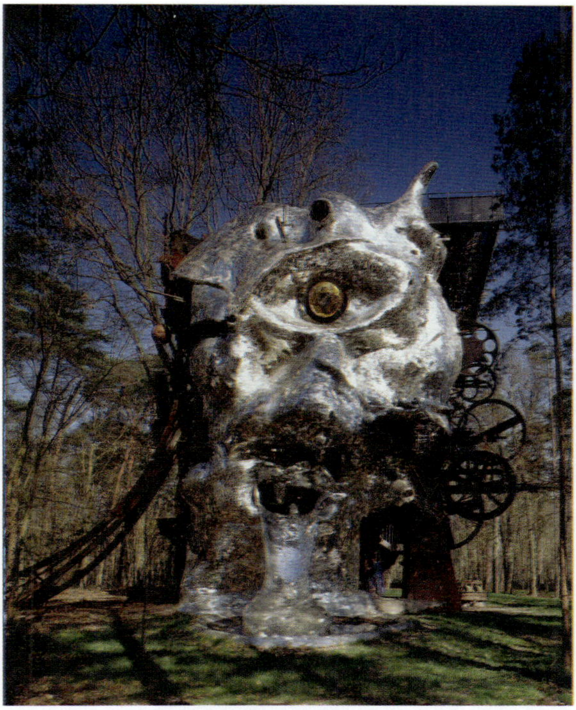

Fig. 11.17. Jean Tinguely, Niki de Saint Phalle, and others, *Cyclops*. Monumental kinetic sculpture situated at Milly-la-Forêt, France. Constructed 1969–91.

the idea of mental activity, but he expressed this in a typically graphic and sonorous way. An elaborate circuit of tubes conveys large aluminium balls in unexpected and deafening movement; while embodying the process of thinking, the din of the rolling balls also recalls nothing so much as the hammering of Cyclopes-as-blacksmiths. A partial parallel to the whole construction is Giambologna's *Appennino*, but the creation by Tinguely and friends is a one-off inspiration. So far from living *in* a cave, this Cyclops has *become* a cave. The experience of being devoured by the Cyclops turns into a masterpiece of ludic horror. In some ways, the permanence and monumentality of *Cyclops* do not typify Tinguely, some of whose works (like those of Luginbühl) were ephemeral and self-destructive. Nevertheless, his iconoclastic masterpiece is arguably the most extraordinary work of art ever dedicated to the theme of the Cyclops.

If you go to Milly-la-Forêt today, you can still climb inside Tinguely's creation (although when we went it was partly under wraps for refurbishment). But it has also enjoyed a different and even more dynamic afterlife. In the Swiss town of

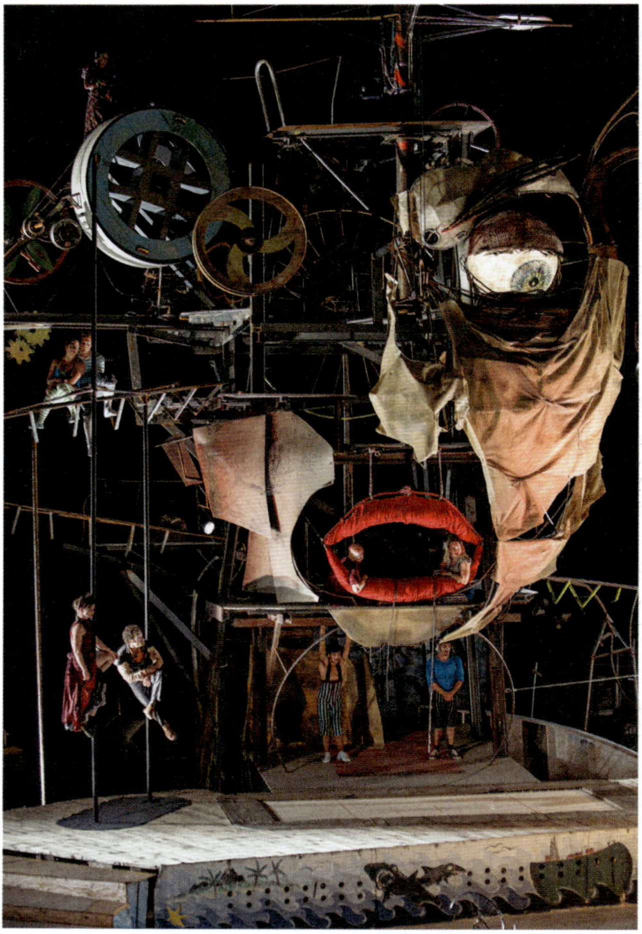

Fig. 11.18. MAAG Music and Arts AG, *Cyclops*. Still from circus-style performance in Basel, 2014.

Biel, a crazy, glorious, life-enhancing production was mounted in 2012 under the name *Cyclops*; it was later replicated at other venues in Switzerland (*Cat. 153* (Fig. 11.18)).[130] Directed by Philipp Boë and organized by MAAG Music and Arts AG, the open-air spectacle begins with a stage dominated by a gigantic, partially constructed 'head', together with assorted metal and other detritus. As the event unfolds, various circus artists, actors, gymnasts, and musicians enact a story without words, accompanying the construction of a Cyclops similar to that made

[130] The authors were privileged to see a performance in Basel in 2014. A recording of the Biel performance can be accessed at: https://www.youtube.com/watch?v=9wiBcOLAuU4.

by Tinguely: gross, poignant, fearsome, endearing, and altogether superb. At a certain moment a huge round eye is raised into position, along with a colossal ear and a pair of red lips, from which a long tongue unrolls, mimicking the water chute at Milly-la-Forêt. The extravaganza ends when a clown, mounted on a bicycle and wearing a helmet spraying out multiple jets of water, turns himself into one of Tinguely's trademark kinetic fountains, such as those on the site of the old city theatre in Basel.

We all—grown-ups no less than children—always need monsters. When they get out of place, they can destroy us. Confined within an arena, they can make us ache with laughter, shudder with terror, or weep from pity, secure in our confidence that the threat will evaporate when the show is over. Yet that is not the whole story. One of the aims of many artists, whatever their preferred medium—paint, poetry, circus—is to break down the barrier between canvas and viewer, text and reader, clown and spectator: to reach out, and draw in. Such was the effect of the Swiss circus extravaganza: crowd-pleasing in effect, sublime in achievement.

The Ogre Rewritten

Interest begets compound interest. As soon as an *Odyssey*-based novel, short story, or poem attracts more than a quantum of scholarly attention, further articles and books proliferate like bees round a honey pot. Some of these novels, stories, and poems amply repay such scrutiny; others less so. In selecting what to focus on, we have followed our own inclinations. Sometimes we throw one more pebble onto a cairn already assembled by previous scholars, and remain deeply in their debt; at other times we wander off on our own, hoping the reader will follow us.

In the course of *The Return of Ulysses*—a rich banquet of a book—Edith Hall makes a shrewd observation about post-classical restagings of the *Odyssey* as opposed to the *Iliad*:

> [The *Odyssey*] can only become sufficiently dark to make it susceptible to tragic realization as a result of radical re-topicalization or extensive surgery on the psyche, politics and motivations of its hero. Either the happiness of the reunion with child, wife and ageing father must be undermined, or the sense of tragedy imported from an extrinsic socio-political context.[131]

[131] Hall (2008: 42).

Redirecting this point towards the adversaries with whom Odysseus has to deal, we can apply it more specifically to modern literary reinventions of the encounter with Polyphemus. The closer a writer sticks to the happy-ending-oriented plot of the pre-existing story—even if s/he plays with that plot in unexpected ways—the more likely it is that the resulting work will implicitly define itself as comedic or cleverly ironic, rather than unblinkingly or even tragically serious. That is not to say that we *never* find such serious/tragic treatments; however, where we do find them, they certainly involve, in Hall's words, extensive surgery. (The same seems not to apply to visual art, since an artist can focus exclusively on the serious/tragic content of a *moment*, whereas a verbal narrator has to cope with a more broadly directional plot, which in the case of Odysseus/Polyphemus has a built-in momentum towards the hero's ultimate triumph and the ogre's definitive failure.)

Instances of the 'heroically upward' approach are alive and well. An amusing example is the micro-story *The Wrath of Polyphemus* by the contemporary Chilean writer Diego Muñoz Valenzuela.[132] Ulysses is a wine entrepreneur on the lookout for buyers; one of his prospective clients is a wealthy sot by the name of Polyphemus, rumoured to be the son of the shipping magnate Poseidon. Ulysses visits Polyphemus, gets him drunk, wheedles out of him the location of his gold and jewels, blinds him, and makes off with the loot: run-of-the-mill euhemerism. But there is a final twist. Ulysses concocts an improbable rumour about a run-in with a group of criminal cannibals, a fiction later 'taken up by an opportunistic writer and turned into a best-seller'.[133] This cheeky allusion to Homer suggests that the author of *this* example of myth-reception sees himself as principally in dialogue, not with a vast tradition of intervening myth-tellers, but with the one who started the whole thing off.

More extensive, and certainly more uproarious, is another work from 2015: Simon Armitage's stage play *The Odyssey: Missing Presumed Dead*.[134] The action alternates between a sequential narrative of the Greek hero's *nostos* and a parallel plot in which the Odysseus-equivalent, a British government minister called Smith, gets involved in a brawl in an Istanbul bar after an England–Turkey football match. In the course of the fracas, the bar-owner's daughter Briseis receives injuries from which she later dies. Smith and three companions escape arrest by diving into the sea, after which they embark on a tortuous journey home. Among a cascade of analogies with the *Odyssey* is that between the suitors besetting Penelope and a pack of tabloid journalists encamped in Smith's house, slavering to be thrown a juicy story by Smith's wife (Penelope again). The dramatizations of the original *Odyssey*-based episodes stick closely to ancient precedent, interspersed with hints of more recent retellings: the idea that Odysseus is enticed by 'the song of Penelope' echoes a scene from the Mario Camerini movie *Ulysses*

[132] Available in Serrano Cueto (2015: 49).
[133] Our translation.
[134] Armitage (2015).

(1954; *Cat. 138*) starring Kirk Douglas;[135] there may also be a nod to Wolfgang Petersen's *Troy* (2004), in which Briseis is much more prominent than she is in Homer. In Armitage's Polyphemus episode, the motifs of cheese, wine, drunkenness, blinding, and escape follow in the usual order. But one glorious innovation is the moment when Polyphemus counts his sheep, presumably using the words for numerals in the language of Cyclopia:

> Yahn,
> Than,
> Tether,
> Mether,
> Mimph,
> Hither,
> Lither,
> Danver,
> Dic...
> Yahndic,
> Tayhndic,
> Tetherdic,
> Metherdic,
> Mimphit,
> Yahn-a-mimphit
> Tayhn-a-mimphit,
> Tether-a-mimphit,
> Mether-a-mimphit...[136]

Once outwitted, the Cyclops disappears almost entirely from the narrative, only to stage a comeback just before the final curtain. Smith and Penelope have come to bed, but when Penelope goes out to the bathroom, Smith's memories begin to flood back:

> [Stage direction] *Smith reaches for a switch to turn the light on, but the light is the eyeball of the Cyclops, staring and blinking. Through the sound of wind and rain the squealing of pigs can be heard. The bed begins to pitch and roll like a boat in a storm.*

For all the impact of this monocular image, in the play as a whole Polyphemus is no more emotionally complicated than he is in Euripides' *Cyclops*, just one more in the line of traditional obstacles encountered during the hero's *nostos*.

[135] See pp. 362–4. [136] Armitage (2015: 53).

If we look back beyond Muñoz and Armitage over the preceding 'long twentieth century', several major writers had already recontextualized the Polyphemus episode within widely disparate explorations of the return of Odysseus. A poignant example can be found in *The Last Voyage* (1904), a contemplative sequence by the Italian poet Giovanni Pascoli.[137] In the wake of the restless Ulysseses of Dante (*Inferno*, canto 26) and Tennyson (*Ulysses*: 'Come, my friends, 'tis not too late to seek a newer world...'), Pascoli's ageing ex-hero retraces the stages of his original *nostos*.[138] Along the way he revisits Cyclopia, seeking revenge for the ogre's prayer to his father Poseidon that Odysseus should 'return in a bad way, and in the ships of others, and late'. If only I had my divine poet with me, exclaims Pascoli's hero:

I would have him sing the song of Odysseus
there inside the cave. When the Cyclops returned
he would remain in his blindness listening to this song,
surrounded by his flocks, his chin higher than a pine.
And I would sit in his shade on the beach![139]

But Pascoli has an ace up his sleeve. Although the sight that greets Odysseus in the cave is an ample supply of cheese and lamb, there is no ferocious ogre to boast about it: just an amiable shepherd, his wife, and their many children. 'What about the giant with a single round eye in his forehead, like a bronze shield, like the sun,' asks a puzzled Odysseus, 'the one who hurled a mountain top into the sea?' 'That must be what your father used to go on about,' says the shepherd to his wife. It seems—the shepherd vaguely recollects—that the old prophet Telemus used to describe how stones had once rained down into the sea, and how an eye had appeared on that mountain top, 'a round eye of fire'.[140] Whereas Muñoz gives us a euhemerized Cyclops, Pascoli plays a different game-of-origins, through the image of the volcano.[141] One of the serendipitous pleasures of researching Cyclopean mythology is the unearthing of unexpected cross-pollinations between academics, writers, and artists.

Tom Stoppard is not the only author to have plucked spear-carriers (Rosencrantz and Guildenstern) from a classic of earlier fiction and promoted them to stardom. Jean Giraudoux did the same in his group of four stories collectively entitled *Elpenor*, published and successively revised between 1908 and 1926.[142] Though rarely read today, it is both exceptionally funny and a literary

[137] See Pascoli (2010), though the English translation there is very unreliable.
[138] Dante, Tennyson, and Pascoli: see Sole (2003: 518–19).
[139] Pascoli (2010: 166–7); our translation. [140] Pascoli (2010: 174–6).
[141] See Citti (1997; 2003: 265–8); Sole (2003).
[142] For the complicated publication details, see Santangelo (2003: 362–3).

tour de force.[143] The eponymous character is the nonentity from the *Odyssey* who got drunk in Circe's palace and broke his neck when he fell off her roof. As reimagined by Giraudoux, Elpenor takes centre stage in the role of the clueless anti-hero (Giraudoux's Phaeacians liken him to Charlie Chaplin).[144] The first of the four stories offers a new take on *Odyssey* book 9. Trumping the ancient model, Ulysses gives his name as 'Personne', son of 'De Personne' and grandson of 'De De Personne'. The other sailors, all twenty-four of them, fabricate similarly misleading identities, each naming himself after a different part of the body as Ulysses points to it. Only Elpenor, not the sharpest knife in the drawer, misunderstands the ruse. When Ulysses indicates his own eye, the hapless Elpenor, instead of replying with the expected pseudo-name 'Monoeil', triumphantly cries out: '*Je m'appelle le Cyclope*!'

The conversation now takes a radically unHomeric turn. 'Have you ever been in love?', the ogre asks Ulysses. 'It depends what you mean by love,' replies the ever-subtle hero; at which point Polyphemus gives his own definition, in some of the most beautiful words ever given to an amorous Cyclops:

> By loving, I mean trembling with a fire that freezes, suffocating with an arid shade; I mean writing my name with an axe on the bark of oak trees, or in the sea with lumps of rock, skilfully arranged. But what a poor name! The tide covers it every day, leaving me anonymous for hours and hours![145]

Ulysses helpfully promises that he and his crewmen will jointly compose an epigram for Polyphemus that will secure the affection of Galatea. But with the promise comes a reservation. In order for the act of literary invention to be fulfilled, Ulysses will need *all* his men: eat just one of them, he warns Polyphemus, and the poem will fail. Overcome not by wine but by the Greeks' relentless eloquence, the Cyclops falls asleep: the time has come to rejoin the established *muthos*. At the moment of the blinding, Giraudoux temporarily sets humour to one side, superbly avoiding the risk of repeating what has been said a hundred times before: 'That is how the earth, had it been circular, would have overflowed and burst, if a god of steel had thrust his red finger into it. Night rose up and caught fire, like black fumes.'[146] But wit immediately reasserts itself, through a linguistic *coup* that rivals the pun on *outis* in the *Odyssey*. This time the trick depends not on Greek grammar but on French. When his fellow Cyclopes ask who has attacked him, Polyphemus replies 'C'est Personne!' Unlike their Hellenic namesakes, the Francophone Cyclopes identify the culprit as *someone called* Personne, 'since they

[143] See de Romilly (1983b); Saïd (2003: 381–91); Santangelo (2003); Duroisin (2005).

[144] Giraudoux (1990: 450); cf. Duroisin (2005: 176).

[145] Giraudoux (1990: 405); our translation. As Pierre Duroisin (2005: 181) points out, this means that, while the tide is in, Polyphemus, like Ulysses, is 'nobody'.

[146] Giraudoux (1990: 408).

saw, in the absence of negation, that Personne was a proper noun and not a pronoun'.[147] But they soon lose interest when the Cyclops lists his other attackers as twenty-four parts of the body. 'What about your navel?', they chortle, before abandoning their comrade to his delusions.

With another shift of register, there follows a gorgeous passage describing Polyphemus' prayer to be healed by his father Neptune. The god gathers into his hands various residues of the light of the dwindling day—golden in colour because they belong to the setting sun; somehow he channels them into his son's damaged eye and cures its blindness. Back then to square one for the Greeks, imprisoned by an ogre who is, once again, sighted. But the resourcefulness of Ulysses knows no limits: he has realized that, since Polyphemus' *eye* has been restored, what he needs to deprive the ogre of is his *perception*.[148] He subjects the Cyclops to a punishing week of philosophical brainwashing, covering the nature of mathematics, false syllogisms, and space–time. In the end he convinces the Cyclops that he and his men are mere 'images', like shadows in the cave in Plato's *Republic*. Urged on by Ulysses, Polyphemus tries to expel these 'images' by the traditional Cyclopean tactic of throwing rocks. During his week of sophistic hell the Cyclops has at least learned one thing: 'One should always keep one's images close by, like one's flocks. Let them escape, and they turn wild and insult you.' He returns disconsolately to his cave, but soon cheers up. As his tears drop into a bucket of curdling milk, 'he made that day the most delicious of his cheeses'.[149]

None of Giraudoux's sparkling innovations invalidates the point we made earlier: that the closer a writer sticks to what is, from the hero's perspective, the upwardly mobile plot of the *Odyssey*, the less likely we are to be in the presence of (in Edith Hall's phrase) 'tragic seriousness'. *Elpenor* is often thought-provoking, sometimes magical, and repeatedly funny, but in the end it offers us yet another Cyclops whose role is to be one of the hero's stepping stones.[150]

Can the same be said for the 'Cyclops character' in a much greater and vastly more influential book, James Joyce's *Ulysses* (1922)? This question—like virtually every other question relating to that inexhaustible work—is formidably intricate. To begin with, there is the matter of context. Academics and others regularly divide the novel into eighteen chapters bearing Homeric-sounding titles, from 'Telemachus' to 'Penelope'; 'Cyclops' comes in at number twelve. But these headings appear neither in early serializations of the work, nor in any complete edition approved during the author's lifetime; they stem, rather, from schemata offered by Joyce to friends and those working on the novel.[151] That said, most Joyceans regularly use these titles, and we follow their lead. What the titles *signify*, however, is

[147] Had a negation been implied, Polyphemus would have replied simply 'Personne'.
[148] This is acutely pointed out by Santangelo (2003: 364).
[149] Giraudoux (1990: 415).
[150] For Elpenor in modernist literature, see Savvides (1990) and Vayenas (1998).
[151] Latham (2014: 217).

quite a different matter. As one scholar phrases it: 'The Homeric parallel can be viewed as the hidden figure in the carpet that puts the seal of meaning on the novel, but it can also be seen as nothing but a temporary scaffolding that helped Joyce in his composition while being of little significance to the reader.'[152] The extent of any supposed parallel/influence/analogy between ancient and modern cannot be assumed in advance; it has to be sensed by the reader on a case-by-case, word-by-word basis.

The chapter usually known as 'Cyclops' recounts the events that unfold at 5 p.m. on 'Bloomsday' (16 June 1904) in Barney Kiernan's Dublin tavern.[153] That is to say: Joyce brings *his* Cyclops, as Hugo had brought *his*, from the wilds, the shore, the mountain, and the cave, into the heart of urban life. Joyce himself lived in several different cities—Dublin, Paris, Rome, Trieste, Zurich—but of course it is Dublin whose spirit the narrative of *Ulysses* breathes. In the eyes of the chapter's anonymous narrator, the personalities of the two protagonists could not be more starkly opposed. Leopold Bloom, the novel's sentimental, pacifist (anti-)hero, is the son of a Hungarian Jewish immigrant to Ireland; ranged against him is the Citizen, a tunnel-visioned, fervently Irish Nationalist, vitriolically anti-Semitic windbag, allegedly modelled on Michael Cusack, founder of the Gaelic Athletic Association (a wing of the Celtic Revival movement).[154] The chapter is rich in glaring stylistic contrasts, from earthy pub talk (' "Are you a strict t. t.?", says Joe. "Not taking anything between drinks," says I') to over-ripe parodies of traditional Irish epic ('In Inisfail the fair there lies a land, the land of holy Michan. There rises a watchtower beheld of men afar...').[155]

You could enjoy the chapter without the slightest awareness of any Homeric antecedents, but an alertness to potential Homeric references adds another dimension. Anyone familiar with *Odyssey* book 9 is unlikely to overlook the repeated mentions of eyes and elongated sharp objects from as early as the third sentence of the chapter: 'Lo, Joe, says I. How are you blowing? Did you see that bloody chimneysweep near shove my eye out with his brush?' From then on, Greek echoes recur sporadically—amid a seemingly limitless supply of allusions drawn from quite other sources—until the final, would-be violent moment of the drama. The Citizen's culminating, fulminating action is to pelt his adversary with a biscuit tin, the equivalent of Polyphemus' crag: 'By Jesus, says he, I'll brain that bloody jewman for using the holy name. By Jesus, I'll crucify him so I will. Give us that biscuitbox here.' It is only thanks to the Citizen's having the sun in his eyes that Bloom/Odysseus escapes a grim fate. Instead 'ben Bloom Elijah' is

[152] Kershner (2014: 175). [153] Good discussion in Rubens and Taplin (1989: 119–23).

[154] Gifford and Seidman (1988: 316); Duffy (2014: 89–90).

[155] *Ulysses* 12.52, 68. The tavern was located in the parish of St Michan: Gifford and Seidman (1988: 317).

symbolically lifted to heaven 'at an angle of fortyfive degrees over Donohoe's in Little Green Street like a shot off a shovel'.

And yet... Is it possible that the Citizen/Cyclops might have a case? After all, the internal narrator of *this* chapter, far from being a neutral observer, is himself strongly anti-Nationalist. The ruinous earthquake that is fantastically described as striking Dublin when the biscuit tin is thrown, can be seen as anticipating the dreadful consequences of the 1916 Easter uprising. Even the ancestry of the biscuit tin may not be an innocent detail, since the Jacobs' biscuit factory, where the missile was made, was a rebel bastion during the same insurrection.[156] Nor, perhaps, is a temperamentally one-eyed citizen so out of place in Joyce's fictional Dublin, where disfigured and dysfunctional bodies are so frequent.[157] Just as the idea of Bloom as Odyssean hero is undermined by his wife's 4 p.m. adultery with 'Blazes' Boynan, so there might be *some* more substance to, and justification for, the Citizen than first meets the reader's eye. Joyce is never quite what he seems.

Race, politics, colonialism: From Harlem to the Andes

Whatever else may be contestable about the Citizen episode in *Ulysses*, that it has political ramifications is not in doubt. In this respect the Joycean ogre foreshadows many twentieth- and twenty-first-century literary explorations of Cyclopean themes. But the angles of approach are extraordinarily diverse.

A fascinating, albeit mostly implicit, use of the Polyphemus-and-Odysseus encounter underlies Ralph Ellison's iconic novel *Invisible Man* (1952).[158] The narrator, who doubles as the (anti-?)-hero, is a young Southern American black man pursuing a constantly frustrated quest for identity and direction. Repeatedly disillusioned by his experiences at home and in New York, he opts for an 'invisible' mode of life in an underground room that he discovers when escaping down a manhole during a Harlem race riot: a symbolic, mythically resonant death. Avowedly influenced by both classical mythology and American folklore, Ellison attracted hostility from some fellow African Americans who saw him as selling out to a cultural discipline ('Classics'), which was, as they perceived it, indelibly Eurocentric and inseparable from the values of white oppression. Ellison's response was to affirm that he was privileging common human concerns instead of reinforcing boundaries between races.[159] That, he maintained, was why the central, narrating character of *Invisible Man* was nameless, 'out of my writer's need to project his story as an account of "Everyman"'.[160] This 'Everyman' equates to the Homeric 'Noman', the trickster whose deviousness Invisible Man learns to

[156] Jacobs' biscuits: *Ulysses* 12.495; Duffy (1994: 124).
[157] Plock (2014: esp. 192).
[158] Rankine (2006: 121–51); Hall (2008: 92); McConnell (2013: 71–105).
[159] See McConnell (2013: 74).
[160] Cited by McConnell (2013: 96).

mimic: as Noman visited the Underworld, so Invisible Man inhabits an Underground.

Among Invisible Man's adversaries are three with Cyclopean characteristics, which are embodied in, though not exhausted by, their monocularity.[161] The first two are doctors in a hospital in which Invisible Man finds himself, after an explosion in the paint factory where he had been working. Despite (or because of) the electric shock therapy that he undergoes, he refuses to reveal—or cannot remember—his name. One of the doctors has 'a bright third eye that glowed from the center of his forehead'; another has 'a circular mirror attached to his forehead'.[162] The imagery gives the game away: this seems not to be medical care but ruthless interrogation by two Polyphemuses, both of them 'bad cops'. The third Cyclops-equivalent is Brother Jack, the domineering white leader of the Brotherhood (a thin disguise for the Communist Party of the USA). Early in their relationship, Jack moulds Invisible Man according to the Brotherhood's needs; but later the two men clash angrily. During the confrontation, 'suddenly something seemed to erupt out of his face'. Jack has lost one of his eyes—a *glass* eye:

> His left eye had collapsed, a line of raw redness showing where the lid refused to close, and his gaze had lost its command...
>
> 'Brother, are you following me?' He stopped, squinting at me with Cyclopean irritation.[163]

It would be misleading to turn (mon)ocular symbolism into the magic key that unlocks a novel of nearly 600 pages. But it does occupy a significant place. Invisible Man is a magnificent street orator, and one of the tropes he uses is that he and his black brothers have each been dispossessed of one of their eyes since birth. What they need to do is to get together, helping each other, even if they stumble: 'Let's take back our pillaged eyes! Let's reclaim our sight; let's combine and spread our vision. Peep around the corner, there's a storm coming.'[164] To be one-eyed is a limitation, but not necessarily a 'Cyclopean' limitation. Instead of being an attribute of tyranny, it can also sometimes be a badge of anti-authoritarian empowerment.

Like Homer's Odysseus, Ellison's hero is a survivor; but survival comes at a psychological cost. Just before the end of the story, Invisible Man narrates a dream. He is lying as a prisoner on sharp sand beside a river of black water. Several nemeses from his past life, including glass-eyed Brother Jack, loom over him demanding that he return to them. When he refuses, they castrate him, mockingly explaining that they are freeing him from his illusions. But it is Invisible Man who, even while in terrible pain, has the last laugh:

[161] See especially Hall (2008: 92).
[162] Ellison (2014: 231, 233).
[163] Ellison (2014: 474).
[164] Ellison (2014: 344).

'Why do *you* laugh?' [Jack] said.

'Because at a price I now see that which I couldn't see,' I said.[165]

This is a new take on the Freudian/Surrealist association between blindness and castration: in Invisible Man's dream, to be castrated is to see. When he wakes, he resolves to stay, for the time being, underground, 'to think things out in peace, or, if not in peace, in quiet'. A new take, too, on the cave. For now at least, to stay in the cave is the best bet, since it offers the hero, if not an escape to freedom, at least a chance to reflect—a reversal of both the Cyclopean cave-as-prison, and the Platonic cave as a theatre of unreal shadows.

Another black voice, embodying a quite different sense of ethnicity from Ellison's, resonates through *The Odyssey: A Stage Version* (1993) by the St Lucian writer Derek Walcott. Walcott's magnificent reinvention of Homer—part Caribbean, part Greek, part epic, part lyric—shuns obvious solutions and questions stereotypes.[166] The play is centrally about identity, but, whereas the Homeric hero manipulates his own self as a defensive shield, Walcott's equivalent, conflicted character sometimes loses touch with who he is, lacking even the capacity to differentiate himself from those whom he once regarded as dangerous 'others'. On the topic of monsters, as he ends up by observing in his last words in the play: 'We make them ourselves.'[167]

The most memorable monster in the play is certainly the Cyclops. Walcott's ogre is a brutal despot, as prone to uproarious laughter as to sadistic cruelty. He is defined by his sobriquet 'the Eye'—like the ineluctable Eye of Tolkien's Dark Lord Sauron. When Odysseus and his men first encounter him, a sequence of eye-related interchanges takes place:

FIRST SAILOR: Sir, everywhere there's the sign of this giant eye!...
ODYSSEUS: Can I see the Eye?
PHILOSOPHER: No, rather the Eye sees us.
EURYLOCHUS: The Eye's their shepherd, and the nation are his sheep?...
FIRST SAILOR: The Eye has found us...
CYCLOPS: I see all. Everything. You believe I see all?
ODYSSEUS: No.
CYCLOPS: No?
ODYSSEUS: You don't see anybody.
CYCLOPS: I see you.
ODYSSEUS: I'm Nobody...
CYCLOPS: The Eye likes you...

165 Ellison (2014: 570).
166 Walcott (1993); see Tynan (2011: 145–65); McConnell (2013: 134–54).
167 Cf. McConnell (2013: 143).

In the following scene the motif is further developed, preparing the way for the blinding:

ODYSSEUS: God gave us two eyes because we're human.
CYCLOPS: I'm not.
ODYSSEUS: One is for laughter, the other one cries...
CYCLOPS: Look! Why do you need two eyes? One does just as well.
ODYSSEUS: For balance. Proportion. Contrast. Mortals need two.
CYCLOPS: I'm a demi-god.
ODYSSEUS: Left, right. Good, bad. Heaven, hell...
ODYSSEUS: I've a wife, you see. Like my eyes. We make one pair.[168]

The context for the Cyclops episode has already been set by an offstage 'martial chorus' intoning 'There is no I after the eye'.[169] As Justine McConnell has demonstrated, the implications of this expression are rich and various.[170] It projects the individualism of the Homeric Cyclopes to its logical, solipsistic conclusion: even the residual sense of Cyclopean community evidenced by Polyphemus' momentarily solicitous fellow ogres in the *Odyssey* is banished from Walcott's Cyclopia. And it is banished in a language far different from Simon Armitage's humorous Cyclops-speak. Walcott's Cyclops knows the unifying, bonding, Rastafarian dialectal expression 'I-and-I', for 'you and I' or 'me' or 'we' or 'us'—knows it and rejects it, for (as one might also hear it) 'there is no I after the I'. Polyphemus is no honest-but-exploited colonial victim, oppressed by an arrogant interloper. He is more colonel than colonial: indeed, when the character known as the Philosopher (named Socrates Aristotle Lucretius) observes: 'This is the era of the grey colonels,' it is impossible to miss an allusion to the leaders of the notorious Greek military dictatorship of 1967–74.[171] After completing the blinding and having made his escape, Odysseus shouts an unequivocally political insult: 'AND LEARN, YOU BLOODY TYRANTS, THAT MEN CAN STILL THINK!'[172] The Cyclops' response is to hurl an oil drum at the fugitive—yet another variant on the traditional boulder.

We said just now that Walcott's Odysseus sometimes loses touch with who he is. It is worth recalling, then, that the setting for the second of the two Cyclops scenes in the play is a meal shared between Odysseus and Polyphemus and presided over by the Cyclops' manservant Ram (one of the many good jokes in the play).

CYCLOPS: Know what you're eating? Your men. As good as sheep.
(*Odysseus pauses, eats.*)[173]

[168] Walcott (1993: 61–9). [169] Walcott (1993: 60). [170] McConnell (2013: 146).
[171] Walcott (1993: 62). [172] Walcott (1993: 72); capital letters in the original.
[173] Walcott (1993: 67).

One of the skewers used to grill the Cyclops' victims will later be used by Odysseus for the blinding—a knowing choice between the variants on offer in the ancient tradition. But that Odysseus himself participates in anthropophagy—even if he does so with tears in his eyes—raises the question of just how man and ogre are to be differentiated. If 'we make monsters ourselves', it may be that sometimes we make ourselves into monsters too.

In Walcott, as in Ellison, the image of the Cyclops is predominantly negative: in neither work is there any sign of the unjustly victimized Cyclops. To hear that side of the story, we need to listen to a third black voice, that of the francophone Martiniquan poet and political activist Aimé Césaire. His long poem *Cahier d'un retour au pays natal* (1939) is a lyrical articulation of anticolonialism.[174] For all his elite Parisian education in French, Greek, and Latin, courtesy of the École Normale Supérieure, Césaire distanced himself from the mindset associated with the European tradition of great canonical authors, grounded in Graeco-Roman antiquity. Yet, nor did he ignore that tradition; rather, he exploited, subverted, and reimagined it, in the service of an affirmation of the need for black people to reconnect with—and thus 'return' to—an African homeland. The *retour* of the title is thus a kind of *nostos*; somewhere in the background is Homer' *Odyssey*.[175]

At one pivotal moment the narrator encounters a fellow negro on a Paris tram: tall, gangling, smelly, weary, above all ugly. It was, the narrator observes, as if something had manipulated the man's face into a comical and hideous caricature; and that something was Poverty:

> It was quite obvious how the industrious malevolent thumb had modelled lumps into the forehead, pierced two parallel and disturbing tunnels through the nose, stretched out the oversized lower lip, and by a master-stroke of caricature had planed, polished, glossed the tiniest most lovely little ear in creation... Poverty, it couldn't be denied, had gone to great lengths to finish him off. It had pushed in the eye-socket and made it up with a cosmetic blend of dust and rheum. It had tightened the empty space between the solid connection of the jaws and the bone of an old shrivelled cheek. It had planted there the shiny little stakes of a several days' beard. It had unhinged the heart and bent the back.[176]

To his later shame, the narrator initially joins in the mocking laughter of a group of women ogling the hideous spectacle. The encounter with this Cyclops equivalent—whose repulsiveness even outdoes that of Hugo's Quasimodo—functions as a *katabasis*, an emotional lower depth through which the narrator must pass before reaching the goal of his true, affective homeland. To this extent, the

[174] Césaire (1956), with McConnell (2013: 39–69).
[175] Cf. Davis (2007).
[176] Trans. McConnell (2013: 47–8).

narrator approximates to Odysseus, though at the same time he comes to recognize what he has in common with the victim Cyclops on the tram.

Adopting an even more radical position than Césaire, the Jamaican author and academic Sylvia Wynter has argued that the figure of the Cyclops should be embraced by black writers as a powerful cultural symbol of alterity, in contradistinction to what she sees as the inevitably white-colonialist goals implicit in the career of Odysseus.[177] In the context of Cyclopean mythology as a whole, a positive evaluation of the Cyclopes' role is far from unusual. Their cooperative harnessing of their strength for the building of civic structures goes back to the earliest narratives about the masons, while their metallurgical artisanship in the service of the gods is already visible in Hesiod. What is far rarer in the ancient tradition is the mounting of a case for the defence for the behaviour of Polyphemus in particular. We have, it is true, the random detail that in the fourth century BCE one Zoilos of Amphipolis wrote an *Encomium of Polyphemus*;[178] but this work (now lost) might have been nothing more than a display of defence-lawyerly rhetorical virtuosity on behalf of a manifestly guilty client (as with Gorgias' *Encomium of Helen*). In post-classical tradition, apologists for Polyphemus and his congeners have been, until recently, similarly thin on the ground. A partial exception comes in the work of Immanuel Kant, for whom 'Cyclopean thinking' stood for a habit of thought that privileges individual experience, as opposed to the greater breadth associated with philosophical reasoning.[179] Not unrelated is the argument used in the 1940s by the social theorists Theodor Adorno and Max Horkheimer, who deployed a contrast between Odysseus and Polyphemus in the course of their critique of (what they saw as) some of the negative effects of reason, especially as contrasted with the development of human individuality. Though the Cyclops is by no means exonerated, his behaviour is presented by Adorno and Horkheimer in a comparatively positive light when set against the allegedly 'superior' rationality of his heroic adversary: 'The stupidity of the giant, an element of his barbaric crudity as long as all goes well for him, represents something better as soon as it is subverted by one who ought to know better.'[180] But it is within the framework of denunciations of colonialism that Polyphemus' situation has been viewed with the greatest sympathy. The point of reference is usually the *Homeric* Polyphemus; the gross, despotic, and *slave-owning* ogre of Euripides' satyr play tends to be quietly forgotten. Foreshadowing the Cyclops-as-victim perspective is the simile used by the great late-nineteenth-century American historian Henry Adams to describe an unprovoked attack by a British warship on an American vessel ('the *Chesapeake–Leopard* affair') in 1807: 'The brand seethed and hissed like the glowing olive-stake of Ulysses in the Cyclops' eye, until the whole American people,

[177] Wynter (2002); cf. Hall (2008: 95–6).

[178] Cf. Hall (2008: 227 n. 9), on *FGrH* 71 fr. 2.

[179] Kant (1923: sect. 903, pp. 394–5); cited in Hall (2008: 92, with 227 n. 17).

[180] Adorno and Horkheimer (1997: 67); see Hall (2008: 94–5).

like the Cyclops, roared with pain and stood frantic on the shore, hurling abuse at their enemy, who taunted them from his safe ships.'[181] However, victims can also be oppressors. The entire Columban imperialistic enterprise, of which the American colonists were themselves part, has been aligned with Odysseus' cruel subjection of a native 'savage'.[182] There is practice as well as theory behind such a view. Odysseus' strategy for overcoming Polyphemus—getting him drunk—is precisely replicated in the concerted policy of American colonists to debilitate and oppress Native Americans by plying them with alcohol.[183]

The music of Polyphemus' apologists includes many songs, some of them clamorous, some quieter. A thought-provoking example is *Revenge*, a micro-story by the contemporary Chilean writer Pedro Guillermo Jara.[184] It reports the birth of a baby Cyclops on the island of Intiqarka in the Andean Lake Titicaca. Ashamed of the anomalous infant, his parents hand him over to an old shepherd, who teaches the child what he needs to know: healthy living, good judgement, hand-to-hand combat, climbing, swimming, how to send smoke signals and set traps. His foster-father names him Juan Quispi. One night, Juan dreams of a far-off island, and of a voice that urges: 'Come and avenge me.' He sets off with his bow and arrow and other necessaries, including a bag containing the stimulating plant *coca*. Being a son of the gods, Juan flies quickly to his destination, surrounded by words from a language not his own—for Jara weaves 'rosy-fingered dawn' and other Homeric formulae into his narrative. Juan lands on a beach and makes his way to Ulysses' palace, where all is calm: Euryclea is sound asleep, while Laertes and Eumaeus are far away and hear nothing. Juan goes upstairs, finds Ulysses in bed with Penelope, and shoots him through the heart: '"For Polyphemus," murmured Juan Quispi, as his eye gleamed.' The vengeance duly accomplished, Juan flies home from Ithaca to his beloved home on Intiqarka, enveloped in a mistlike cloak of *coca*. The story is a subtle blend of the native South American with the Greek. The fact that the names Intiqarka and Titicaca resonate playfully with 'Ithaca' is no coincidence. Jara's Cyclopes are an interconnected, global race, sympathetic to each other's concerns: harm one of us, and you harm us all.

At the Movies

It can hardly be denied that few cinematic portrayals of the Cyclopes retain the depth and complexity that so often characterize these ogres in literature and visual art. Indeed, many such portrayals are totally lacking in interest by comparison

[181] H. Adams (1893: 27); cited in McConnell (2013: 9).
[182] Davies, Nandy, and Sardar (1993: 27).
[183] Coyhis and White (2006).
[184] In Serrano Cueto (2015: 50–1).

with much of the material previously discussed in this book. Nevertheless, perhaps paradoxically, if any single medium has done more than all the rest to sustain an image of the Cyclopes in the popular imagination, it is cinema.[185] People whose awareness of mythology derives mainly from watching movies far outnumber readers or gallery-goers, though obviously these publics are not mutually exclusive. Rather than simply listing movies that feature a Cyclops, we shall select a handful of landmark examples representing three distinct, although sometimes overlapping, types: reworkings of the *Odyssey*, science fiction, and mythological fantasy.

Movie *Odysseys*

One of the most remarkable talents to emerge during the early years of silent cinema was the Parisian illusionist, impresario, and director Georges Méliès. Realizing the potential of the cinematograph developed by the Lumière brothers, Méliès founded the Star Film Company in 1896. He shot hundreds of films, many based on themes from literature and popular storytelling, including classical mythology. Right from the outset of silent cinema, film-makers had reworked Homeric themes, and in 1905 Méliès created a particularly enigmatic example of the type: *The Island of Calypso: Ulysses and the Giant Polyphemus*.[186] As the title implies, it blends two episodes from Ulysses' return that the *Odyssey* had kept separate. The opening shot shows Ulysses falling exhaustedly asleep in front of the mouth of a cave. Out of the cave emerge four girls dancing and playing musical instruments; they try unsuccessfully to wake the sleeping hero. Calypso, who emerges next, does manage to wake him; after attempting to lure him inside, she disappears. From the cave there now emerges a huge hand, evidently attempting to grab Ulysses. The hand too disappears, to be replaced by a gigantic head, with two closed eyes surmounted by a third eye in the forehead. Ulysses picks up a spear/stake and blinds the ogre, causing drops of a creamy white fluid to run down his face (*Cat. 129* (Fig. 11. 19)). Calypso emerges again, trying desperately to drag Ulysses into the cave; but he stoically resists, leaving the abandoned nymph distraught.

A load of symbolism is packed into less than four minutes of running time. Pantelis Michelakis finds the key to it all in sexual anxiety. On his reading, 'the womb-like cave begins as a site of dream-like pleasures, but it soon becomes associated with the nightmarish threat of annihilation posed by Polyphemus'

[185] On the reception of the classical world in cinema, see Paul (2008); cf. Paglia (1997: 167).

[186] On Homer and silent cinema: Michelakis (2016). On *The Island of Calypso*: Michelakis (2013: 155–7). For films about the return of Ulysses, see Dumont (2009: 201–9).

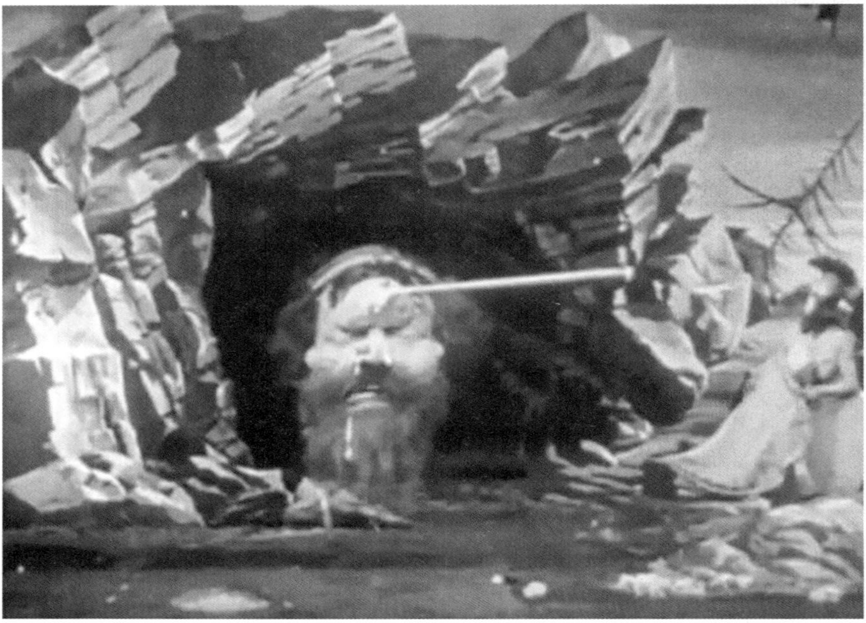

Fig. 11.19. Still from *The Island of Calypso: Ulysses and the Giant Polyphemus*. Movie, dir. Georges Méliès, 1905.

reduction to a searching hand and a monstrous face'.[187] The sexual symbolism is compounded, in Michelakis's opinion, by a phallic spear and a fluid that resembles semen. We have serious doubts about the fluid: it definitely is not blood, but it looks more like cream cheese than semen. Be that as it may, that the cave is simultaneously seductive and menacing is hardly disputable, and Méliès has certainly mixed an impressive cocktail of desire, resistance to desire, threat, and penetration. The blinding is the visual high point; and it was not the only time Méliès envisioned it. He had already done so in *A Trip to the Moon* (1902), the best known of all his films. The narrative centres on a group of doughty astronomers, headed by Professor Barbenfouillis (played by Méliès), who plan an expedition to the moon. The bullet-shaped rocket they travel in hits the Moon smack in the right eye, generating a flow of liquid that *definitely* resembles cream cheese (*Cat. 128* (Fig. 11.20)). The visual joke is a good one: this is one of the most famous images in the history of silent cinema.

Half a century later, Mario Camerini directed a full-length re-creation of the *Odyssey*. His Italian-made *Ulysses* (1954; *Cat. 138*) stars Kirk Douglas, impressive both in action and in speech. You can—it has often been done—go through the

[187] Michelakis (2013: 156–7).

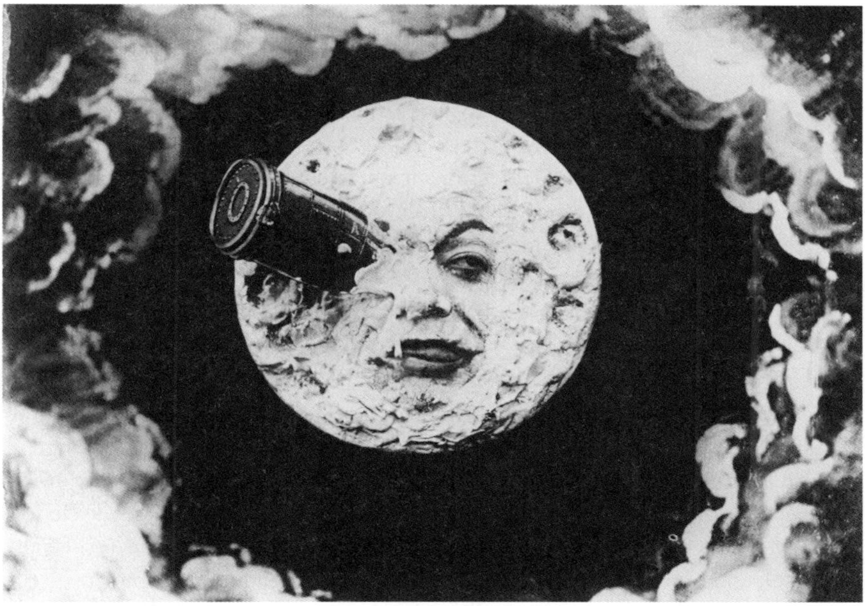

Fig. 11.20. Still from *A Trip to the Moon*. Movie, dir. Georges Méliès, 1902.

film ticking off what has been retained from the *Odyssey* and what omitted;[188] but such matters are of more interest to classical scholars than to the vast majority of cinemagoers. It is more fruitful to register the constant verve and frequent thoughtfulness on offer. In the Polyphemus episode, the two motifs with the most potential for horror—the anthropophagy and the blinding—occur off-screen, with only the lead-up and consequences being depicted; the gruesomeness was presumably ruled to be off limits for the intended category of audience. Nevertheless, the ogre's protracted pain, and his frenzied stumbling about after the blinding, make uncomfortable viewing. One surprise is the length of time devoted to the Greeks' trampling of grapes, in order to make 'wine' with which to make the ogre even more drunk. (Although one might prosaically object that fresh grape juice needs time to ferment, surely what really intoxicated Polyphemus was the hypnotic, rhythmic, manic exuberance of the satyr-like tramplers.) As well as wine there is, as so often in Cyclopean mythology, cheese; and at this point real life becomes more interesting (and comical) than fantasy. When Ulysses first enters the cave, he wolfs down a mouthful of the cheese that he finds lying around. According to Douglas's autobiography, for the first seven takes of the scene he had

[188] Roisman (2008: 320): 'For one steeped in Homer...a sense of loss is perhaps unavoidable.' Paglia (1997: 181–7) is much more enthusiastic about the film.

to eat real, strong, Italian goat's cheese. By the eighth take he felt so nauseous that he had the production assistants mix in pieces of banana instead.[189]

Another, much more indirect cinematic reworking of the plot of the *Odyssey* places comedy front and centre stage. The Coen brothers' *O Brother, Where Art Thou?* (2000) is a consistently engaging musical-cum-road-movie set in the American South during the Depression. It narrates the return of the garrulous escaped convict Ulysses Everett McGill (played by George Clooney) to his long-suffering wife, Penny, still resident in their family home in Ithaca, Mississippi. Several scholars have analysed the relationship between the film and its Homeric 'model', with each interpreting the balance between indebtedness and independence in a slightly different way.[190] The question is certainly an intriguing one: whereas the film opens with a title card showing a translation of the first lines of the *Odyssey*, the Coens themselves claimed (perhaps disingenuously) never to have read the poem.[191] What is beyond doubt is that there is more than enough in the film to satisfy two types of public (which are not, once again, mutually exclusive): on the one hand, a general, cinemagoing audience keen to see a George Clooney character parodying the actor's normally super-cool style (especially *hair*style), and to hear a soundtrack full of 1930s American popular music; on the other hand, an audience of classically trained university or school teachers and their students—in fact the film is a godsend to anyone teaching a course on the reception of classical mythology, since it keeps the feet tapping but also the mind alert. This fragmentation of potential audiences, with the consequently variable effect of 'allusions' (if that is what they are), reflects a cultural situation in which awareness of classical precedents is inconsistent, and the process of their transmission multidirectional.[192]

The Cyclops equivalent in *O Brother* is Big Dan Teague (played by John Goodman), a larger-than-life Bible salesman dedicated to making 'vast amounts of money... in the service of God Almighty' (*Cat. 146*).[193] Big Dan, who wears a patch covering his glass eye, possesses a tremendous appetite and a tendency to commit unprovoked assault. He meets Everett and his sidekick Delmar in a restaurant. Having suggested that they repair to the countryside to pursue their discussions over a picnic, he makes short work of a chicken fricassee. His meal over, he rips a branch from a tree, beats Delmar and Everett senseless, and robs them. The next time they meet, the context of Big Dan's violence is collective rather than individual: he turns out to be a high-ranking Ku Klux Klansman. Everett, Delmar, and their fellow ex-con Pete stumble across a torchlight Klan rally in which a black guitarist called Tommy, whom the trio teamed up with on

[189] Douglas (1988: 233–4); cf. Paglia (1997: 184).

[190] Flensted-Jensen (2002); Goldhill (2007); Pollio (2007); especially detailed is Janice Siegel (2007). See also now Salzman-Mitchell and Alvares (2018: 65–95).

[191] See Woods (2003: 176); Janice Siegel (2007: 213–14); Goldhill (2007: 261–2).

[192] The point is excellently made by Goldhill (2007: 267).

[193] Cf. Janice Siegel (2007: 224).

their travels, is about to be lynched. Big Dan's hood, with its single eye-hole, perfectly equips him for the role of Grand Cyclops, one of the grades in the KKK hierarchy. In order to rescue Tommy, the trio have to confront Big Dan. Having tried and failed to blind him by hurling a Confederate Flag pole, Everett dislodges a huge flaming cross, which crashes down on the 'Cyclops' and annihilates him.

There are plenty of hints for the aficionado of the *Odyssey*—for example, the single eye, the gluttony (Dan is grossly carnivorous, albeit non-anthropophagous), the (attempted) blinding with a pole, the very name of the Klan ('Ku-Klux').[194] In addition, three other motifs chime in with the traditions of Cyclopean mythology. First, blindness. At the beginning of the film the three escapees meet a blind man on a railway handcar; his predictive powers suggest a combination of Homer and Teiresias. Insightful in a different way is the blind owner of a radio station for whom the three fugitives (plus Tommy) perform a song that becomes a smash hit. Visually opaque in yet another sense is the sinister, permanently sun-glass-wearing Sheriff Cooley, who seems preternaturally to anticipate the escapees' movements. The second Cyclops-friendly motif is circularity. As Pertille Flensted-Jensen has noticed, this is a recurrent motif in Coen films, from the hula-hoop, the frisbee, and other circular objects in *The Hudsucker Proxy*, to the circular jail cell and flying saucer in *The Man Who Wasn't There*.[195] In *O Brother* it appears in the form of myriads of round tins of 'Dapper Dan', Everett's favourite pomade, which float across the screen after a providential dam burst has generated a tidal wave, thus saving Everett, Delmar, and Pete from being hanged by Cooley. The third motif is the opposition between fire and water.[196] In *O Brother* the symbolic charge of fire is predominantly negative. Cooley uses it to try to burn the fugitives out of their hiding places, while for the Klan it is associated with torchlight gatherings and flaming crosses. Opposed to these fires is the climactic tidal wave. Whereas the Poseidon of classical myth used the power of the sea to try to destroy the original Odysseus, for the Ulysses imagined by the Coens water brings redemption and salvation.

Nothing *requires* a cinemagoer to notice *any* of these recurrent images and themes, much less to attribute significance to them. On the other hand, nothing forbids it. We come back to the point about the fragmentation of audiences. To the informed student of Cyclopean mythology, *O Brother* contains a treasure trove; but to many other audiences, too, it is full of good, but perhaps different, things.

[194] Hall (2008: 92). [195] Flensted-Jensen (2002: 24). [196] See Pollio (2007).

Science fiction

Monsters are ten-a-penny in a variety of science-fiction media, whether in cinema, literature, or comics.[197] One common type, especially popular in the 1950s, consists of the 'BEM' (bug-eyed monsters) encountered and overcome by heroic space voyagers. A related category includes Creatures, often generated by atomic radiation, that threaten to trample the Earth's inhabitants into annihilation (for example, *The Beast from 20,000 Fathoms* (1953); *Them!* (1954); *The Monster that Challenged the World* (1957)). Different again are explorations of the theme of human mutation, again typically caused by scientific experiments that go horribly wrong (*The Amazing Colossal Man* (1957); *Most Dangerous Man Alive* (1961)).[198] Amid all this disfigurement and disproportion, Cyclopes put in an occasional appearance. Bert I. Gordon's *The Cyclops* (1957) is about a test pilot, lost in the Mexican jungle, who mutates into a 50-foot-tall monocular monster after exposure to radioactivity. The location echoes the age-old spatial marginalization of the Cyclopes, but the theme of radioactivity is right up to date: this is the post-Hiroshima, cold-war world of nuclear angst. The film poster (*Cat. 139* (Fig. 11.21)) trumpets the familiar definitional conundrum raised by at least one way of envisaging a Cyclops: 'Nature gone mad!... It was a monster yet it was a man!' However, nothing else about the movie merits the attention of the student of Cyclopean myths—except perhaps the title, which prompts the reflection that it would be wholly inconceivable for any work of sci-fi to portray a creature called 'Cyclops' who did *not* have an ocular peculiarity, which usually manifests itself as a single eye.

Exploring the theme of monocularity at an altogether more imaginatively impressive level is Stanley Kubrick's *2001: A Space Odyssey* (1968). Visually stunning, aurally superb, agonizingly slow, and semantically portentous, the movie has generated almost as many interpretations as it has had viewers. It features a computer called HAL 9000, which/who governs the systems on the Jupiter-bound spaceship *Discovery One*. HAL's interface with the world is a camera-lens-like 'eye', which sees everything and conveys its impressions to the computer's brain (*Cat. 143*). The motivation for some of HAL's actions is left ambiguous—malice? self-preservation?—but what is indisputable is the perfect match between the circularity of the eye and the totality of the surveillance which that eye facilitates. Nor is this the only example of circularity. From the internal architecture of the spaceship, to the surrounding planetary spacescape, to the concluding, magical image of a foetus enclosed in a deep blue orb, circularity is everywhere, providing a stark contrast with the mysterious, rectilinear monolith whose sporadic appearances articulate the plot. Any allusion to the mythical

[197] See Landis (2011); Weinstock (2012, 2014).
[198] For the various types, see Sobchack (1987: 43–55).

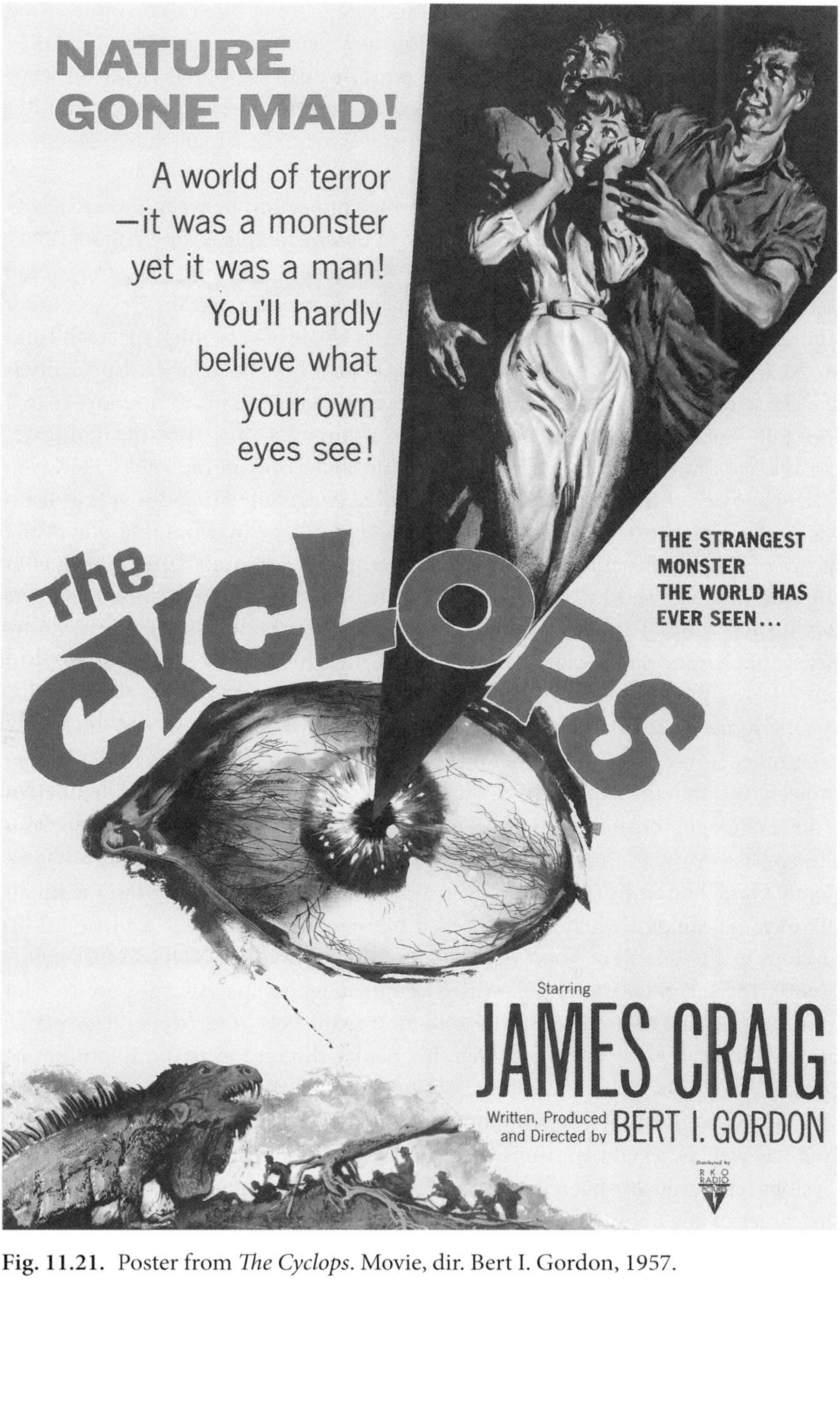

Fig. 11.21. Poster from *The Cyclops*. Movie, dir. Bert I. Gordon, 1957.

Cyclops is, at the very best, implicit—the 'odyssey' of the title can be understood in only the most general sense of 'epic journey', with no suggestion of detailed correspondences with Homer's epic. The most one can say is that HAL's unsleeping single eye parallels many earlier representations of the round-eyed ogre. But two things distinguish HAL from such predecessors. He is man-made; and he is extremely hard to fool.

Many other sci-fi/horror movies repeat the connection between monocularity and a creature explicitly called a Cyclops. An older example is *Dr Cyclops* (1940), directed by Ernest B. Schoedsack. The first American horror film to be shot in full Technicolor, it features a title character in the shape of a certain Dr Alexander Thorkel, an archetypal mad scientist who wears a pair of very thick spectacles and works in a laboratory in the Peruvian jungle (*Cat. 135*). His nefarious speciality is the abuse of natural sources of radioactivity to shrink humans to no more than a foot tall. (Such a theme is highly unusual in a film made in 1940—the nightmarish effects of radioactivity became a cinematic cliché only in the 1950s. However, horror movies of the 1920s and 1930s had already exploited the idea of the 'death ray'). Some of Thorkel's mini-victims manage to escape by smashing *one* of the lenses of his glasses while he is asleep, and eventually kill him.[199] The sobriquet in the title thus fits Thorkel in several ways. He becomes, in effect, monocular; he has turned himself into, *relatively* speaking, a giant; his power is destroyed by heroic but tiny adversaries who reduce still further his already limited capacity to see.

One more cinematic variation on the Cyclops–eye connection may be briefly mentioned, given its high profile for the contemporary cinemagoer. In the *X-Men* movies, the mutant superhero Scott Summers, alias 'Cyclops', takes his origin from a character created for Marvel Comics in 1963. He gets his nickname from the special eyewear that enables him to control and direct the energy beams ('optic blasts') he emits (*Cat. 148*); he lost the ability to control this power through his own physiology when he suffered a blow to the head after a plane crash. Cyclops is thus a kind of 'good' equivalent of the supervillain Non in *Superman II* (1980), the gigantic, mute, dull-witted criminal with supernatural powers who eventually learns to use his eyes in tandem to emit rays of terrifying destructive power. As for the Cyclops of *X-Men*, his ocular dimension is the sole point of contact with the various Cyclopes of the mythical tradition. In spite of this semantic gap, given the massive popular appeal of the *X-Men* series (2000, 2003, 2006, as well as several spin-offs; new releases in the offing), the exploits of *this* Cyclops have arguably been witnessed by more human beings than have followed the career of any of his namesakes.

[199] Landis (2011: 72).

Mythological fantasy

Among the vast number of stories in world mythology that pit man against monster, a fair proportion incorporates the subsidiary pattern: 'woman, threatened by predatory monster, awaits rescue by hero'. Countless fantasy movies, many of them advertising a mythological pedigree, make use of one or both of these motifs. Some of these movies include a one-eyed monster alongside a bunch of other, no less terrifying creatures.

A landmark in visualizations of monstrosity in twentieth-century cinema is that by Ray Harryhausen for *The 7th Voyage of Sinbad* (dir. Nathan H. Juran, 1958). Among the characters encountered by the hero are a skeleton who is expert in swordsmanship, a gigantic two-headed Roc, a fire-breathing dragon, a benevolent pre-teen djinn confined in a magic lamp, and a dastardly magician who miniaturizes a beautiful princess. Also showcased are two enormous one-eyed creatures explicitly called Cyclopes, who reside on the island of Colossa.[200] First up is a cannibal who spit-roasts his victims over an open fire. Like Homer's Polyphemus, he possesses a huge club, dwells in a cave invaded by intruders, patrols the seashore, and hurls rocks at his foes (*Cat. 140* (Fig. 11.22)).

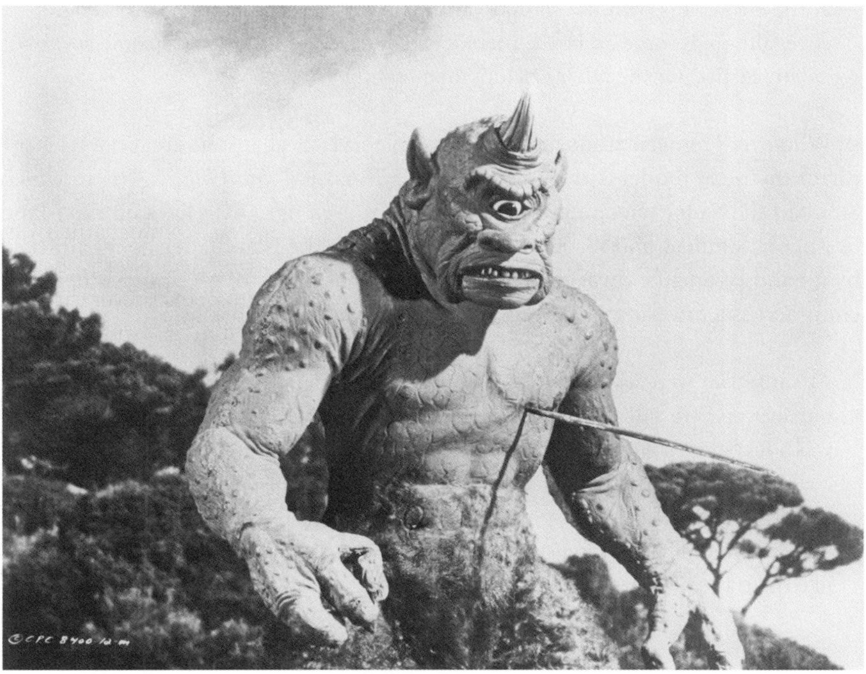

Fig. 11.22. Still from *The 7th Voyage of Sinbad*. Movie, dir. Nathan H. Juran, 1958.

[200] Excellently discussed by OKell (2013).

Also reminiscent of Homeric precedent is Sinbad's method of overcoming the ogre, by thrusting a firebrand into his eye. But Harryhausen's creature also shows distinctly unHomeric traits. He is bald and has pointed ears; his centrally placed, single eye is surmounted by a horn sticking out of the top of his head; he has just two fingers on each hand. Most unusually of all, his lower body is goatishly hairy, terminating in cloven hooves; he is thus part humanoid, part satyr, with a touch of rhino thrown in. This anatomical peculiarity arguably suggests his dubious moral standing, since his form evokes that of the horned and goatish Devil.[201]

Later in the movie Sinbad encounters a second Cyclops, physically identical with the first except for a subsidiary horn positioned behind the main one—presumably to distinguish him visually from the first, blinded ogre. The second Cyclops loses a fight to the death with the dragon, which, at the bidding of the magician, has been acting as gaoler over Sinbad and the tiny princess Parisa. The unintended consequence of the earth-shaking combat is that the dragon's attention is distracted, enabling Sinbad and the princess to escape. As Eleanor OKell has observed:

> The fight contextualises the Cyclopes within a wider world in which they are prey as well as, or instead of being, predators. That a Cyclops 'saves' the humans at the cost of his own life should gain his race some sympathy from the audience, although some audience members will perceive his death as some sort of 'poetic justice' for the other Cyclops' man-eating.[202]

Whatever Homeric traits may be detectable in Harryhausen's creation, its more direct mythical model is the episode in the *Thousand and One Nights* in which Sindbâd the Sailor encounters a fearsome, *two-eyed* ogre who lives on the island of Zugbh. Sindbâd and his men are marooned on the island after being attacked by a band of apelike dwarves. While roaming in search of food and water they come across a towering palace, in whose courtyard they fall asleep.

> At sunset we were awakened by a noise like thunder. The earth shook beneath our feet and we saw a colossal black giant approaching from the doorway. He was a fearsome sight—tall as a palm-tree, with red eyes burning in his head like coals of fire; his mouth was a dark well, with lips that drooped like a camel's loosely over his chest, whilst his ears, like a pair of large round discs, hung back over his shoulders: his fangs were as long as the tusks of a boar and his nails were like the claws of a lion.[203]

[201] See OKell (2013: 45). [202] OKell (2013: 51). [203] Dawood (1973: 130).

This ogre is, into the bargain, a cannibal, his preferred method of dining being to break his victim's neck, push a spit through his mouth down to his backside, and roast him in an oven. Sindbâd and his men escape by blinding *both* of the ogre's eyes with red-hot spits; in spite of the rocks thrown by the ogre and 'a foul hag of his own kind', the escapees manage to paddle their boat out of harm's way.

Harryhausen's concept of the Cyclops lacks the dense specificity and imaginative power of its equivalent in the *Thousand and One Nights*, not to mention the *Odyssey*. Yet that concept had a major impact on later representations of fantastic monstrosity, not only in movies (for example, the Cave Troll in Peter Jackson's *Lord of the Rings: The Fellowship of the Ring* (2001)), but also in music videos.[204] However, in spite of Harryhausen's undoubted technical virtuosity, one can hardly fail to notice the limited emotional range of his ogres. A large part of the explanation relates to language. The Cyclopes' utterances consist exclusively of roaring: the repeated engagement in ancient and later tradition with Cyclopean language and rhetoric is cancelled at a stroke of the scriptwriter's pen. Of course, language is not the only means by which a 'creature' can express emotion—witness the 1933 movie of *King Kong*. But language is certainly a major factor. Invidious though it may be to criticize apples for not being pears, we cannot resist pointing out a contrast with the half-man, half-bull in Harrison Birtwistle's opera *The Minotaur*, premiered at Covent Garden in 2008. Most of the time the Minotaur is bestially inarticulate. However, thanks to a brilliantly insightful *coup* by librettist and composer, the creature achieves *in his dreams* the capacity for human language, and the potential for reflection which that capacity enables. This is a profoundly moving dramatization of what it is to feel oneself to be unnatural, even if the Minotaur's unnaturalness derives from hybridity rather than from another (perhaps more Cyclopic) kind of monstrosity.

Some recent cinematic Cyclopes have no time to waste on such profundities. Declan O'Brien's made-for-television *Cyclops* (2008; *Cat. 149*) sets the Roman general Marcus (good) against the Emperor Tiberius (bad). The CGI-generated title character is the sole survivor of a monstrous race that waged war against the Roman Empire, the rest having been exterminated by Augustus (!). Though hornless and no more than twice human size, in other respects he resembles Harryhausen's one-eyed creatures. Marcus captures the Cyclops, who is chained and put on display in Rome *à la* King Kong. However, the ogre escapes, and proceeds to commit sundry acts of sickening violence and explicit cannibalism before being recaptured and once more incarcerated. When Marcus, too, finds himself in prison, having refused to obey the orders of Tiberius' nefarious adviser Falco, he befriends his monstrous fellow prisoner, laboriously teaching the poor, simple-minded creature to understand the words 'meat' and 'free'. In the movie's

[204] OKell (2013: 49–50).

protracted, climactic bloodbath in the arena, the Cyclops slaughters Tiberius, but then gets speared in the eye by Falco, and falls to his death. Aided by a beautiful barbarian called Barbara, Marcus duly liberates Rome from tyranny. The movie will appeal to those with a taste for extreme, gratuitous violence. Other viewers may feel they have lost ninety minutes of their lives that they will never get back.

Much classier is *Wrath of the Titans* (2012; *Cat. 151*) directed by Jonathan Liebesman. The plot, which turns on the struggle between Titans and Olympians, owes a little to Hesiod's *Theogony*, and also nods towards the Norse/Wagnerian theme of the twilight of the gods (several of the Olympians, including Zeus, crumble into nothingness as the movie proceeds). The hero, the demi-god Perseus, is tasked with rescuing his father Zeus from the clutches of Ares and Hades, who have thrown in their lot with the terrifying Kronos. To fulfil his mission, he needs to find Hephaestus, builder of Tartarus, the cosmic prison where Zeus is being held in brutal captivity. Perseus teams up with Poseidon's tricky son Agenor, whom he persuades to help by letting him use Poseidon's trident (given to Perseus by Poseidon before he disintegrated). As for the Cyclopes, they make an appearance in the form of bald, bellowing, hornless, one-eyed, forest-dwelling, tree-trunk-wielding giants who live on the mysterious island of Kail. They seem at first to threaten Perseus' mission, but later switch to the 'good' side when one of them notices Poseidon's trident, which they themselves had helped to forge. Unlike the ghoulish, gore-spattered creature of O'Brien's imagination, Liebesman's Cyclopes inhabit a more visually sophisticated world, whose monsters take shape under the influence of even higher-grossing blockbusters such as the *Star Wars*, *Lord of the Rings*, and *Harry Potter* franchises.

Another fantasy adventure featuring Cyclopes is the second movie in the *Percy Jackson* series, *Sea of Monsters* (2013; *Cat. 152*), directed by Thor Freudenthal and based on a novel by Rick Riordan. As in a thousand other movies and TV series, a world threatened with destruction is saved by a group of feisty American teenagers. In *Sea of Monsters* the group in question lives in Camp Half-Blood, the US equivalent of the Hogwarts School imagined by J. K. Rowling, in which the world is saved by a group of feisty *British* teenagers. Two of the half-blood (that is, semi-divine) inmates of the Camp are Percy and Tyson; both are sons of Poseidon, but Tyson has the added distinction of being a one-eyed Cyclops—likeable and good, though somewhat error prone. Like many adolescents, Tyson is embarrassed about his appearance, but is reassured by Percy: 'You're not a monster; don't be so hard on yourself.' Percy, Tyson, and their buddies go on a quest to find the all-healing Golden Fleece, needed to reanimate another half-blood, Thalia, who had pluckily saved her friends from an attack on the Camp by monsters, but was metamorphosed into a tree. The Fleece's guardian is none other than Polyphemus, who is as bad as Tyson is good. His cavern-like home is situated in an abandoned amusement park called Circeland—one more take on the idea of marginality. Percy succeeds in his quest: the bad Cyclops is defeated and trapped in his own lair. As in all the best pantomimes, none of the good characters dies, thanks to the restorative power of the Golden Fleece. Tyson discovers a new sense of pride: whereas he used to take refuge behind sunglasses with the conventional two lenses, he now looks forward to a bright future of self-confident monocularity.

Even the most ardent fan of on-screen mythology must admit that movie Cyclopes vary in convincingness. While some are genuinely impressive, others are trivial, sickening, or laughable, or all three. Yet *all* these creatures have the potential to arouse the viewer's curiosity in fruitful ways. Some cinemagoers, it is true, may be prompted to ask: 'What were the Cyclopes *really* like?', a question that is in the end unreal and frankly absurd. Infinitely more worthwhile is a different question: 'In what *other* ways have people imagined the Cyclopes, in the ancient world and subsequently?' *That* question has provided the rationale for this book. Even if only a small proportion of the vast cinemagoing public is tempted to ask it, they will have the chance to embark on an imaginative journey that is both exciting and rewarding.

Cyclopes for Today and Tomorrow

In the early twenty-first century, retellings of classical mythology are undergoing an extraordinary process of proliferation, cross-fertilization, and mutation, thanks not only to cinema, but also to video-gaming, comics, and fanfiction, along with the associated merchandising. The range of internet-related media involved is constantly shifting; any attempt to produce an exhaustive list would be out of date within months. The Cyclopes, along with a host of other figures from classical mythology, are part of this burgeoning development.

To the extent that *any* one-eyed creature can be identified as a Cyclops—an identification that, as this book has sought to demonstrate, is very far from being automatic—then a range of contemporary cinematic creations might be included. The most obvious examples are various mini-monsters who appear in movies aimed predominantly at a young audience. The 'Minions' of the *Despicable Me* franchise (dir. Pierre Coffin and Chris Renaud, 2010, with several sequels; *Cat. 150*) are chaotic, yellow, pill-capsule-shaped creatures who wear goggles that emphasize their one or two eyes. Mike Wazowski, from the animated film and video-game *Monsters, Inc.* (dir. Pete Docter, 2001; *Cat. 147*), is a green, one-eyed creature employed in a factory that harvests the screams of children to produce energy; later, however, he turns from a 'bad' monster into a 'good' one, when it is discovered that children's laughter makes more energy than their screams. Neither the Minions nor Mike can plausibly be said to be reworkings of the main traditions of Cyclopean mythology. The unique point of overlap is the single eye. Something similar applies to the frequent appearances of one-eyed creatures in the phenomenally successful Japanese *manga* comics.[205] They, like the Minions and Mike Wazowski, might be thought of as 'post-Cyclopes', or, better, as 'para-Cyclopes', a point that we leave to be considered by those with greater expertise in these media than ourselves.

Such developments could be situated within a yet wider context. Countless newspaper cartoons and advertisements exploit the notion of a one-eyed giant. The computer system that used to be employed in major tennis matches as an electronic line judge was known as 'Cyclops'. Even modern design gets in on the act: a cabinet created in 2013 by Italian designer Elena Salmistraro bears the name 'Polifemo' in honour of the ocular shape that is its identifying feature,[206] while Ionna Vautrin's 'Cyclope' is a golden, circular mirror that featured in *Marie Claire Maison* for September 2018. Such contemporary media have not replaced more traditional means of accessing the Cyclopes, but simply added to the existing stock, bringing the Cyclopes, like the rest of Greek mythology, to the attention of an ever wider audience, even if some of the shapes that the ogres assume are barely recognizable in relation to what went before. So much the better: we can make comparisons and contrasts with earlier Cyclopean traditions on the basis of an ever-expanding array of possible points of entry: visiting museums and galleries; watching movies; reading Homer, or Virgil, or Vico, or Walcott; experiencing a circus-themed performance in Switzerland (or at least accessing the performance retrospectively via the internet). Then again, readers of this book might begin in the very location where its authors started out: 'Tucked away in a pleasantly shady corner of the Jardin du Luxembourg in Paris, just across the road from the Café Le Rostand, the Fontaine Médicis features a grotto containing a group of figures sculpted in the 1860s by Auguste Ottin . . .'.

But it can be even better to face forwards than to look back. If only we might soon come across vibrantly fresh retellings of Cyclopean myths, retellings that would exhibit imagination, richness, and subtlety! After all, images of the Cyclopes—like those of a host of other figures from Greek mythology—retain the capacity to inspire thought and feeling about a broad range of profound issues. That beauty, disfigurement, and obsessive desire constitute a complex and deeply embedded psychological nexus is a truth well known to those who adapted Gaston Leroux's novel into the smash hit *The Phantom of the Opera*; might Polyphemus and Galatea look forward to a similar dramatization? That the process of establishing human culture may depend on habits of thinking and behavioural skills that are in some way marginal to, or even at variance with, that culture's eventual, central traits and values is a possibility that deserves consideration by palaeontologists and prehistorians; the obvious role models for such habits and skills are the 'marginal' and primordial Cyclopes. That tremendous,

[205] See e.g. M. D. Foster (2012: 142) in the context of a broader study of Japanese monsters.
[206] Salmistraro (2017).

even supernatural power may be inevitably hobbled by limits or defects is a mythical notion of great antiquity and extraordinary resilience; the Cyclopes (along with many other figures from various mythologies worldwide) exemplify such a notion. Psychology, culture, myth: how much more rewarding—one could surely argue—to explore *these* matters than to reduce a varied constellation of compelling symbolic images to a production line of uninspiring, one-eyed, CGI monsters. Yet those monsters too exercise a role in modern consciousness, by preserving and popularizing a mythical image, and hence (one may hope) stimulating interest in the investigation of that image's roots and development. Which directions future reimaginings of the Cyclopes will *actually* take is, of course, beyond our ken; only far-sighted Prometheus could tell us. Fortunately, the future is always open, never more so than when it is anchored in the past.

Catalogue of Artistic Representations Cited

[*LIMC* = *Lexicon Iconographicum Mythologiae Classicae*, Zurich and Düsseldorf, 1981–2009]

Cat. 1. Proto-Attic amphora from Eleusis, *c.*670 BCE. Eleusis Archaeological Museum (*LIMC* 'Kyklops, Kyklopes' 17 = 'Odysseus' 94 = 'Polyphemos I' 16) (Fig. 2.1)

Cat. 2. Fragmentary proto-Argive krater, mid-7th cent. BCE. Argos Museum C 149 (*LIMC* 'Odysseus' 88)

Cat. 3. Krater inscribed with name 'Aristonothos', 675–650 BCE. Rome: Pal. Cons. 172 (*LIMC* 'Odysseus/Uthuze' 56) (Figs 3.3 and 3.4)

Cat. 4. Proto-Attic oenochoe from Aegina, *c.*660 BCE. Aegina Museum 566 (*LIMC* 'Odysseus' 109)

Cat. 5. Red-clay Etruscan pithos, 650–625 BCE. Malibu: J. Paul Getty Museum 96.AE.135a (*LIMC* 'Polyphemos I' 27bis) (Fig. 4.7)

Cat. 6. Ivory Etruscan pyxis from Chiusi, end of 7th cent. BCE. Florence: Mus. Arch. 82193 (*LIMC* 'Odysseus/Uthuze' 60)

Cat. 7. Ivory Etruscan pyxis from Chiusi, end of 7th cent. BCE. Florence: Mus. Arch. 73846 (*LIMC* 'Odysseus/Uthuze' 61)

Cat. 8. Krater attributed to the painter Clitias, 600–550 BCE. Basel: Collection H.A. Cahn, HC 1418 (*LIMC* 'Kyklops, Kyklopes' 19 = 'Polyphemos I' 39) (Fig. 4.8)

Cat. 9. Corinthian alabastron, *c.*575–550 BCE. New York: Metropolitan Mus. of Art 76.12.6 (*LIMC* 'Odysseus' 89)

Cat. 10. Laconian black-figure cup, *c.*550 BCE. Paris: Cabinet des Médailles 190 (*LIMC* 'Polyphemos I' 18 = 'Odysseus' 67) (Fig. 3.1)

Cat. 11. Attic black-figure cup by the Polyphemus Painter, 550–525 BCE. Boston: MFA 99.518 (*LIMC* 'Odysseus' 68 = 'Athena' 565)

Cat. 12. Terracotta figurine from Boeotia, 550–500 BCE. Munich: Antikenslg. 5271 (*LIMC* 'Polyphemos I' 67) (Fig. 4.11)

Cat. 13. Cup from Vulci, *c.*530 BCE. Würzburg: Wagner-Mus. L 407 (*LIMC* 'Odysseus' 119)

Cat. 14. Pseudo-Chalkidian amphora from Vulci, *c.*530–510 BCE. London: British Museum 1866.8-5.3 (B 154) (*LIMC* 'Kyklops, Kyklopes' 21 = 'Odysseus' 91)

Cat. 15. Caeretan hydria from Cerveteri, *c.*520 BCE. Rome: Villa Giulia 2600 (*LIMC* 'Polyphemos I' 20 = 'Kyklops, Kyklopes' 23) (Fig. 4.4)

Cat. 16. Caeretan hydria, *c.*520 BCE. New York: Shelby White and Leon Levy Collection, inv. no. 688 (last reported location) (Fig. 5.1)

Cat. 17. Black-figure oenochoe by the Theseus Painter, *c.*500 BCE Paris: Louvre F 342 (*LIMC* 'Polyphemos I' 21 = 'Kyklops, Kyklopes' 18 = 'Odysseus' 95)

Cat. 18. Campanian black-figure amphora, *c.*500 BCE. Formerly in Berlin: Staatl. Mus. F 2123; now lost (*LIMC* 'Polyphemos I' 23 = 'Odysseus' 92) (Fig. 5.10)

Cat. 19. Attic black-figure skyphos, *c.*500 BCE. Berlin: Staatl. Mus. V.I.3283 (*LIMC* 'Kyklops, Kyklopes' 22 = 'Odysseus' 96) (Fig. 4.14)

Cat. 20. Black-figure skyphos by the Theseus Painter, *c.*500 BCE. New York: Shelby White and Leon Levy Collection 1990.1.113 (*LIMC* 'Polyphemos I' 41 = 'Odysseus' 117)

Cat. 21. Attic black-figure krater, *c.*500 BCE. London: Howard–Sneyd private collection (last reported location) (Fig. 5.3)
Cat. 22. Sarcophagus from Palaipaphos, Cyprus, 500–450 BCE. Kouklia: Mus. RRKM 485 (*LIMC* Suppl. 2009 'Polyphemos I' add. 2 = *LIMC* Suppl. 2009 'Odysseus' add. 3) (Fig. 5.2)
Cat. 23. Attic black-figure oinochoe from Camiros (Rhodes), 500–475 BCE. London: British Museum 1864.10-7.228 (*LIMC* 'Polyphemos I' 44)
Cat. 24. Attic red-figure krater from Sabucina, 490–480 BCE. Caltanissetta: Mus. Arch. CL 810 (*LIMC* 'Hephaistos' 15) (Fig. 5.14)
Cat. 25. Attic red-figure stamnos by the Siren painter, *c.*480 BCE. Malibu: Getty Mus. (*LIMC* 'Polyphemos I' 48 = 'Idomeneus' 1 = 'Odysseus' 121). (Fig. 5.4)
Cat. 26. Black-figure lekythos from Picrodafni in Attica, *c.*480 BCE. (For details and references to earlier discussions, see pp. 72–3, n. 120)
Cat. 27. Lucanian krater, *c.*410 BCE. London: British Museum 1947.7-14,18 (*LIMC* 'Kyklops, Kyklopes' 27 = 'Odysseus' 93) (Fig. 4.13)
Cat. 28. Campanian krater from Cumae, 350–325 BCE. Private collection (*LIMC Suppl. 2009* 'Polyphemos' add. 1) (Fig. 4.2)
Cat. 29. Terracotta figurine from Athenian Acropolis, 400–350 BCE. Munich: Antikenslg. 6940 (*LIMC* 'Polyphemos I' 66) (Fig. 4.9)
Cat. 30. Terracotta figurine from Sanctuary of Cabiri in Thebes; perhaps early 4th cent. BCE. Boston: MFA B 16392 (*LIMC* 'Polyphemos I' 68) (Fig. 4.10)
Cat. 31. Wall painting from Tomb of Orcus II, Tarquinia, 300–275 BCE (*LIMC* 'Kyklops, Kyklopes' 26 = 'Odysseus/Uthuze' 58) (Fig. 4.15)
Cat. 32. Marble head from Paros, *c.*150 BCE. Boston: MFA 63.120 (*LIMC* 'Kyklops, Kyklopes' 9)
Cat. 33. Relief bowl found in Porsuk, Cappadocia; now in Museum of Niğde, 150–100 BCE. Details in Chalier (2008) (Fig. 5.5)
Cat. 34. Etruscan urn, 2nd cent. BCE. Volterra: Mus. Guarnacci 268 (*LIMC* 'Polyphemos I' 28 = 'Odysseus/Uthuze' 59)
Cat. 35. Etruscan urn, mid-2nd cent. BCE. Florence: Mus. Arch. 5779 (*LIMC* 'Polyphemos I' 3 = 'Odysseus/Uthuze' 54)
Cat. 36. Etruscan urn, mid-2nd cent. BCE. Florence: Mus. Arch. 5778 (*LIMC* 'Polyphemos I' 4 = 'Odysseus/Uthuze' 55)
Cat. 37. Etruscan urn, *c.*150–100 BCE. Leiden: Rijksmuseum van Oudheden, inv. H III C (*LIMC* 'Uthuze' 63) (Fig. 3.5)
Cat. 38. Statue group from Nymphaeum at Ephesus; probably originally designed for pediment of temple of Dionysus. Statues dated 1st cent. BCE, reused in 1st cent. CE. Ephesus Museum (*LIMC* 'Odysseus' 85)
Cat. 39. Monumental sculptural group, Grotto of Tiberius, Sperlonga, perhaps originally 1st cent. BCE (*LIMC* 'Polyphemos I' 32 = 'Odysseus' 99) (Fig. 4.3)
Cat. 40. Wall painting from House of Livia, Palatine, Rome, 30–25 BCE (*LIMC* 'Polyphemos I' 54 = 'Galateia' 8 = 'Nereides' 463) (Fig. 4.6)
Cat. 41. Wall painting from villa at Boscotrecase, 1st cent. BCE. New York: Metropolitan Mus. of Art 20.192.17 (*LIMC* 'Polyphemos I' 55 = 'Galateia' 22) (Fig. 3.2)
Cat. 42. Clay mould for piece of Arretine pottery, 1st decade of 1st cent. CE. Rome: Museo Nazionale Romano inv. 364.081 (*LIMC* 'Odysseus' 138)
Cat. 43. Decorative stone fountain from Fourvière (Lyons), 1st cent. CE. Lyons: Musée Gallo-Romain (*LIMC* 'Kyklops, Kyklopes' 7)
Cat. 44. Ivory comb, 1st cent. CE. New York: Coll. Vivian Merrin (*LIMC* 'Polyphemos I' 31)

Cat. 45. Wall painting from Pompeii, House of the Priest Amandus, 1st cent. CE. Pompeii I 7,7 (*LIMC* 'Polyphemos I' 56 = 'Galateia' 13) (Fig. 5.6)

Cat. 46. Wall painting from Herculaneum, *c*.62–79 CE. Naples: Mus. Naz. 8983 (*LIMC* 'Galateia' 20 = 'Polyphemos I' 60) (Fig. 8.1)

Cat. 47. Wall painting from Pompeii, House of the Ancient Hunt, *c*.62–79 CE. Naples: Mus. Naz. 27.687 (*LIMC* 'Galateia' 37) (Fig. 5.7)

Cat. 48. Wall painting from Pompeii, House of the Red Walls, *c*.62–79 CE. Pompeii VIII 5, 37 (*LIMC* 'Polyphemos I' 59 = 'Galateia' 18) (Fig. 5.8)

Cat. 49. Marble slab from Nemi, 1st cent. CE. Rome: Mus. Naz. Rome: Palazzo Massimo alle Terme (*LIMC* 'Galateia' 27 = 'Kyklops, Kyklopes' 3)

Cat. 50. Wall painting of two heads in Roman house at Assisi, 1st cent. CE. The painting accompanies the seventh epigram on the north wall of the cryptoporticus (Squire 2009: fig. 4.14)

Cat. 51. Wall painting from Pompeii, *c*.70 CE. Naples: Mus. Naz. 9531 (*LIMC* 'Kyklops, Kyklopes' 33)

Cat. 52. Wall painting from Pompeii, House of Laocoon, 1st cent. CE. Naples: Mus. Naz. 111211 (*LIMC* 'Polyphemus I' 52 = 'Aineias' 208) (Fig. 3.6)

Cat. 53. Wall painting from Herculaneum, *c*.62–79 CE. Naples: Mus. Naz. 8984 (*LIMC* 'Polyphemos I' 64 = 'Eros/Amor, Cupido'29 = 'Galateia' 46) (Fig. 8.3)

Cat. 54. Wall painting from Pompeii IX 6, 4–5, 1st cent. BCE/1st cent. CE (*LIMC* 'Galateia' 47 = 'Polyphemos I' 65 = 'Akis' 3) (Fig. 5.9)

Cat. 55. Wall painting from House of the Coloured Capitals at Pompeii: VII 4, 51. Naples: Mus. Naz. 8886 (*LIMC* 'Galateia' 9)

Cat. 56. Wall painting from Herculaneum (*LIMC* 'Galateia' 19)

Cat. 57. Wall painting from Pompeii, House of M. Lucretius, 1st cent. CE. Pompeii IX 3, 5 (*LIMC* 'Galateia' 35)

Cat. 58. Wall painting from Pompeii, House of the Ancient Hunt. Pompeii VII 4, 48 (*LIMC* 'Galateia' 14)

Cat. 59. Marble head, 150–200 CE. Turin: Mus. Ant. 148 (*LIMC* 'Kyklops, Kyklopes' 10) (Fig. 4.12)

Cat. 60. Statue group from Papal Villa at Castel Gandolfo, 2nd cent. CE. Antiquarium 36410 (*LIMC* 'Polyphemos I' 11)

Cat. 61. Marble sarcophagus, *c*.180 CE. Catania: Mus. Civ. (*LIMC* 'Polyphemos I' 29)

Cat. 62. Mosaic, Severan period. Rome: Mus. Naz. Rome 1241 (*LIMC* 'Polyphemos I' 51 = 'Odysseus' 130)

Cat. 63. Marble slab, 100–150 CE. Rome: Pal. Cons. (*LIMC* 'Kyklops, Kyklopes' 37 = 'Athena/Minerva' 358 = 'Iuno' 352) (Fig. 5.13)

Cat. 64. Cover of sarcophagus, mid-2nd cent. CE. Rome: Mus. Cap. 1959 (*LIMC* 'Kyklops, Kyklopes' 38 = 'Antilochus I' 14 = 'Athena/Minerva' 359) (Fig. 4.1)

Cat. 65. Bronze statuette, 2nd cent. CE. Paris: Cabinet des Médailles: Inv. 812 (*LIMC* 'Polyphemos I' 13) (Fig. 5.11)

Cat. 66. Marble statue, 2nd cent. CE. Rome: Musei Capitolini, Inv. 57 (= *LIMC* 'Polyphemos I' 12) (Fig. 5.12)

Cat. 67. Sarcophagus, 2nd cent. CE. Rome: Palazzo Mattei (*LIMC* 'Galateia' 29 = 'Akis' 2) (Fig. 8.2)

Cat. 68. Mosaic from Dougga, Tunisia, 3rd cent. CE. Tunis: Bardo Mus. A 261 (*LIMC* 'Kyklops, Kyklopes' 34)

Cat. 69. Fragment of sarcophagus, *c*.300 CE. Naples: Mus. Naz. 6580 (*LIMC* 'Kyklops, Kyklopes' 30 = 'Odysseus' 71)

Cat. 70. Sarcophagus, *c*.270 CE. Rome: Musei Capitolini 329 (*LIMC* 'Kyklops, Kyklopes' 40)

Cat. 71. Mosaic from Alcázar de los Reyes Cristianos, Cordoba, *c*.200 CE (*LIMC* 'Galateia' 24) (Fig. 4.5)

Cat. 72. Floor mosaic from villa at Piazza Armerina, Sicily, 3rd–4th cent. CE (*LIMC* 'Kyklops, Kyklopes' 29 = 'Odysseus' 70) (Fig. 3.7)

Cat. 73. Manuscript of Thomas of Cantimpré, *De Naturis Rerum*, 1425. Formerly in A. Chester Beatty Collection, MS 80, fo. 9

Cat. 74. Manuscript of Marco Polo, *Livre des Merveilles*, *c*.1410–12. Paris: Bibliothèque Nationale, MS Fr. 2810, fo. 29^{v}

Cat. 75. Manuscript of *Romance of Alexander*, 1338–44. Oxford: Bodleian Library, MS 264 fo. 260

Cat. 76. Manuscript of French trans. of *Historia de Preliis Alexandri Magni* , *c*.1420. British Library, Royal MS. 20B. XX, fo. 79^{v} (Fig. 10.1)

Cat. 77. Illustration by Jean Miélot in his reworking of Christine de Pizan's *Letter from Othea to Hector*, *c*.1461. Brussels: Bibliothèque Royale de Belgique, MS Fr. 9392, fo. 22^{v} (Fig. 10.2)

Cat. 78. *Cassone* panel by Apollonio di Giovanni, 1435–45. Chicago Art Institute (Fig. 10.6)

Cat. 79. Fresco panel 'September', *c*.1468–70; possible attribution to Ercole de' Roberti. Hall of the Months, Palazzo Schifanoia, Ferrara (Fig. 10.18)

Cat. 80. Hartmann Schedel's *Nuremberg Chronicle*, 1493, fo. XII

Cat. 81. *Cassone* panel, perhaps by Piero di Cosimo or his school, *c*.1500. Vassar College, New York (Fig. 10.5)

Cat. 82. Sebastiano del Piombo (possible attribution), preliminary study for *Polyphemus*. Wicar Collection, Palais des Beaux-Arts, Lille (Fig. 10.13)

Cat. 83. Sebastiano del Piombo, *Polyphemus, c*.1512. Fresco in Villa Farnesina, Rome (Fig. 10.11)

Cat. 84. Raphael, *The Triumph of Galatea*, *c*.1513–14. Fresco in Villa Farnesina, Rome (Fig. 10.12)

Cat. 85. Giulio Romano, *Polyphemus, Galatea, and Acis*, *c*.1528. Fresco in Sala di Psiche, Palazzo Te, Mantua (Fig. 10.14)

Cat. 86. Giulio Romano, *Head of a Giant*, *c*.1532. Fresco in Sala dei Giganti, Palazzo Te, Mantua (Fig. 10.15)

Cat. 87. Maarten van Heemskerck, *Venus and Cupid in Vulcan's Forge*, 1536. Oil on canvas, in National Gallery, Prague, inv. no. DO 4290 (Fig. 10.19)

Cat. 88. Engraving by Sebastian Münster, *Cosmographia* (Basel, 1544), 628

Cat. 89. Pellegrino Tibaldi, *Ulysses Blinding Polyphemus*, 1550–1. Fresco in Sala di Ulisse, Palazzo Poggi, Bologna (Fig. 10.9)

Cat. 90. Pellegrino Tibaldi, *Ulysses Escaping from Polyphemus*, 1550–1. Fresco in Sala di Ulisse, Palazzo Poggi, Bologna (Fig. 10.10)

Cat. 91. Engraving from '27th Canto' of Lodovico Dolce's translation of Ovid, *Metamorphoses*, 1st edn (Venice, 1553)

Cat. 92. Engraving by Cornelis Cort (*c*.1570) of Titian's lost *Cyclopes at the Forge of Vulcan* (Fig. 10.20)

Cat. 93. Woodcut from Latin text of Ovid, *Metamorphoses* (Venice, 1574), 295. Biblioteca Angelica, Rome (Fig. 10.3)

Cat. 94. Annibale Carracci, *Polyphemus and Galatea*, 1597–1607. Fresco in Palazzo Farnese, Rome (Fig. 10.16)

Cat. 95. Annibale Carracci, *Polyphemus Attacking Acis and Galatea*, 1597–1607. Fresco in Palazzo Farnese, Rome (Fig. 10.17)

Cat. 96. Giovanni Guerra, *Prospettiva della Grotta della Galatea*, 1598. Architektur, Graphische Sammlung, Albertina, Vienna, no. 37216

Cat. 97. Drawing by Theodoor van Thulden, after Primaticcio, 1633 (Fig. 10.7)

Cat. 98. Drawing by Theodoor van Thulden, after Primaticcio, 1633 (Fig. 10.8)

Cat. 99. Design for a water feature by Salomon de Caus, *Les Raisons des forces mouvantes* (Frankfurt, 1615) = in Jeanneret (2001: 136, fig. 39) (Fig. 10.23)

Cat. 100. Domenichino and assistants, *Apollo Killing the Cyclops*, 1616–18. Fresco, then on canvas, in National Gallery, London, inv. no. 6290 (Fig. 10.22)

Cat. 101. Engraving by Jaspar Isac in *Les Images ou tableaux de platte peinture*, French trans. by B. de Vigenère of Philostratus' *Imagines* (Paris, 1615), 436

Cat. 102. Andrea Alciato's *Emblemata* (1621 edn), emblem 172 (Fig. 10.4)

Cat. 103. Jacques Sarazin, *Polyphemus*, *c*.1621. Statue in 'Theatre of Water', Villa Aldobrandini, Frascati (Fig. 10.25)

Cat. 104. Nicolas Poussin, *Polyphemus, Acis and Galatea*, 1623. Drawing in Royal Collection, Windsor Castle, Royal Library no. 11940 (Fig. 10.28)

Cat. 105. Diego Velázquez, *Apollo in Vulcan's Forge*, 1630. Oil on canvas, in Museo del Prado, Madrid (Fig. 10.21)

Cat. 106. Nicolas Poussin, *Acis and Galatea*, *c*.1630. Oil on canvas, in National Gallery of Ireland, Dublin

Cat. 107. Guido Reni, *Polyphemus*, 1639–40. Oil on canvas, in Musei Capitolini, Rome (Fig. 10.30)

Cat. 108. Nicolas Poussin, *Landscape with Polyphemus*, 1649. Oil on canvas, in Hermitage Museum, St Petersburg , inv. no. ГЭ-1186 (Fig. 10.29)

Cat. 109. Antonio Novelli, *Polyphemus*, *c*.1650. Statue in Orti Oricellari, Florence (Fig. 10.26)

Cat. 110. James Barry, *Barry and Burke in the Characters of Ulysses and a Companion Fleeing from the Cave of Polyphemus*, 1776. Oil on canvas, in Crawford Municipal Art Gallery, Cork (Fig. 11.1)

Cat. 111. Henry Fuseli, *Blinded Polyphemus Checks the Sheep as they Leave the Cave*, 1803. Oil painting in private collection, Switzerland

Cat. 112. Engraving (1806) by J. G. Walker of Henry Fuseli, *Blinded Polyphemus Checks the Sheep as they Leave the Cave*. London: British Museum 1863.0509.30 (Fig. 11.4)

Cat. 113. John Flaxman, pen-and-ink sketch of the blinding of Polyphemus, perhaps 1805. UCL Art Museum, University College London (Fig. 11.2)

Cat. 114. John Flaxman, *Ulysses Giving Wine to Polyphemus*, 1805. Engraving and etching on paper (Fig. 11.3)

Cat. 115. J. M. W. Turner, *Ulysses Deriding Polyphemus—Homer's Odyssey*, 1829. Oil painting in National Gallery, London

Cat. 116. Auguste Ottin, *Polyphemus Surprising Acis and Galatea*, 1866. Sculptural group. Fontaine Médicis, Jardin du Luxembourg, Paris (Fig. 10.27)

Cat. 117. Adolph Menzel, *The Iron-Rolling Mill* (*Modern Cyclopes*), 1875. Oil on canvas, in Alte Nationalgalerie, Staatliche Museen zu Berlin (Fig. 11.11)

Cat. 118. Gustave Moreau, *Galatea*, *c*.1880. Oil on wood, in Musée d'Orsay, Paris (Fig. 11.6)

Cat. 119. Gustave Moreau, *Galatea*, 1880. Watercolour and pencil, in Musée Gustave Moreau, Paris

Cat. 120. Odilon Redon, *The Misshapen Polyp Floated on the Shores, a Sort of Smiling and Hideous Cyclops*, 1883. Lithograph (Fig. 11.13)

Cat. 121. Odilon Redon, *Cyclops*, *c*.1880. Pencil. New York, private collection

Cat. 122. Gustave Moreau, *Galatea*, 1893. Oil on canvas, in Musée Gustave Moreau, Paris

Cat. 123. Arnold Böcklin, *Odysseus and Polyphemus*, 1896. Oil and tempera on panel, in Boston MFA 2012.626 (Fig. 11.5)

Cat. 124. Gustave Moreau, *Galatea*, *c*.1896. Pen and ink, gouache, and watercolour on cardboard, in Thyssen–Bornemisza Museum, Madrid, inv. no. 685 (1977.100)

Cat. 125. Gustave Moreau, *Polyphemus*, undated. Oil on wood. Musée Gustave Moreau, Paris (Fig. 11.8)

Cat. 126. Gustave Moreau, (another) *Polyphemus*, undated. Musée Gustave Moreau, Paris

Cat. 127. Odilon Redon, *Cyclops*, *c*.1914. Oil on wood, in Kröller–Müller Museum, Otterlo (Fig. 11.7)

Cat. 128. *A Trip to the Moon*, 1902. Movie, dir. Georges Méliès (Fig. 11.20)

Cat. 129. *The Island of Calypso: Ulysses and the Giant Polyphemus*, 1905. Movie, dir. Georges Méliès (Fig. 11.19)

Cat. 130. Maurice Denis, *Polyphemus*, 1907. Oil on canvas, in Pushkin Museum of Fine Arts, Moscow (Fig. 11.9)

Cat. 131. Maurice Denis, *Galatea*, 1917. Oil on canvas, in Musée de Peinture et de Sculpture, Grenoble, inv. no. 2763

Cat. 132. Francis Picabia, *Cyclops*, *c*.1924–6. Oil on cardboard, in private collection

Cat. 133. Max Ernst, *Cyclops*, *c*.1934. Collage of stone, iron, and clothes pegs, in P. J. Zahnd collection, Paris

Cat. 134. Meret Oppenheim, *Polyphemus in Love*, 1974. Coloured silkscreen on plexiglass mirror (Fig. 11.14)

Cat. 135. *Dr Cyclops*, 1940. Movie, dir. Ernest B. Schoedsack

Cat. 136. Meret Oppenheim, *Unicorn Witch*, 1943. Ink drawing, in Levy Galerie, Hamburg (Fig. 11.15)

Cat. 137. William Baziotes, *Cyclops*, 1947. Oil on canvas, in Art Institute of Chicago, Walter M. Campana Memorial Prize Fund, 1947.468 (Fig. 11.12)

Cat. 138. *Ulysses*, 1954. Movie, dir. Mario Camerini

Cat. 139. *The Cyclops*, 1957. Movie, dir. Bert I. Gordon (Fig. 11.21)

Cat. 140. Still of Cyclops from *The 7th Voyage of Sinbad*, 1958. Movie, dir. Nathan H. Juran. (Fig. 11.22)

Cat. 141. Eduardo Paolozzi, *Cyclops*, 1957. Bronze (lost wax technique), in Tate Britain, London, T00225 (Fig. 11.16)

Cat. 142. Eduardo Paolozzi, (head of) *Cyclops*, 1957. Bronze (lost wax technique), in Tate Britain, London, T06858

Cat. 143. *2001: A Space Odyssey*, 1968. Movie, dir. Stanley Kubrick

Cat. 144. Marc Chagall, *Polyphemus*, 1974. Colour lithograph (Fig. 11.10)

Cat. 145. Jean Tinguely, Niki de Saint Phalle, and others, *Cyclops*, 1969–91. Monumental kinetic sculpture, in Milly-la-Forêt, France (Fig. 11.17)

Cat. 146. *O Brother, Where Art Thou?*, 2000. Movie, dir. E. and J. Cohen

Cat. 147. *Monsters, Inc.*, 2001. Movie, dir. Pete Docter

Cat. 148. *X-Men*, 2000. Movie, dir. Bryan Singer

Cat. 149. *Cyclops*, 2008. TV movie, dir. Declan O'Brien

Cat. 150. *Despicable Me*, 2010. Movie, dir. Pierre Coffin and Chris Renaud

Cat. 151. *Wrath of the Titans*, 2012. Movie, dir. Jonathan Liebesman

Cat. 152. *Percy Jackson: Sea of Monsters*, 2013. Movie, dir. Thor Freudenthal

Cat. 153. MAAG Music and Arts AG, *Cyclops*. Basel, 2014 (Fig. 11.18) (performance at https://www.youtube.com/watch?v=UQExvyTwNhw (accessed 30 July 2019))

Bibliography

Aarne, A., and Thompson, S. (1961). *The Types of the Folktale: A Classification and Bibliography.* Helsinki (extensively revised in Uther 2011).

Abbott, G., and Khin Thant Han (2000). *The Folk-Tales of Burma: An Introduction.* Leiden.

Abel, O. L. F. A. L. (1914). *Die Tiere der Vorwelt.* Leipzig.

Accorinti, D. (2016) (ed.). *Brill's Companion to Nonnus of Panopolis.* Leiden.

Acquaro Graziosi, M. T. (1984). *Polifemo e Galatea: Mito e poesia.* Rome.

Adams, H. (1893). *History of the United States of America during the Second Administration of Thomas Jefferson*, ii. New York.

Adams, T. (2017). 'Christine de Pizan', *French Studies*, 71: 388–400.

Adler, H. (2014). 'Le Grotesque et le sublime: Deux aspects de l'impossible au XVIIIe siècle', in Miernowski (2014), 209–30.

Adorno, T. W., and Horkheimer, M. (1997). *Dialectic of Enlightenment.* London (trans. of *Dialektik der Aufklärung.* Rev. edn. Amsterdam, 1947).

Africa, T. W. (1970). 'The One-Eyed Man against Rome: An Exercise in Euhemerism', *Historia: Zeitschrift für Alte Geschichte*, 19: 528–38.

Aghion, I., Barbillon, C., and Lissarrague, F. (1996). *Gods and Heroes of Classical Antiquity.* Paris (trans. of *Héros et dieux de l'Antiquité.* Paris, 1994).

*Aguirre Castro, M. (1998a). 'Monstruos y mitos: las Gorgonas en el Mediterráneo occidental', *Revista de Arqueología*, 19: 22–31.

Aguirre Castro, M. (1998b). 'Fórmulas y expresiones genealógicas en la *Teogonía*: Las descendencias de Noche y Gea', in L. Gil, M. Martínez Pastor, and R. M. Aguilar (eds), *Corolla Complutensis in Memoriam Josephi S. Lasso de la Vega Contexta.* Madrid, 461–7.

Aguirre Castro, M. (1999). 'Los peligros del mar: Muerte y olvido en la *Odisea*', *Cuadernos de filología clásica: Estudios griegos e indoeuropeos*, 9: 9–22.

Aguirre Castro, M. (2002). 'Scylla: Hideous Monster or *Femme Fatale*? A Case of Contradiction between Literary and Artistic Evidence', *Cuadernos de filología clásica: Estudios griegos e indoeuropeos*, 12: 319–28.

Aguirre Castro, M. (2010). 'El Cíclope de Jean Tinguely y Niki de Saint Phalle: la transformación de una figura mitológica en un experimento artístico', in J. M. Losada Goya (ed.), *Mito y mundo contemporáneo.* Bari, 435–41.

Aguirre Castro, M. (2013). 'El mito del cíclope en la pintura de Odilon Redon', in J. M. Losada Goya and A. Lipscomb (eds), *Mito e interdisciplinariedad: Los mitos antiguos, medievales y modernos en la literatura y las artes contemporáneas.* Bari, 25–33.

Aguirre Castro, M. (2016a). 'La figura de Odiseo en las ilustraciones de la *Odisea* de John Flaxman', in J. A. López Férez et al. (eds), *Πολυπραγμοσύνη: Homenaje al Profesor Alfonso Martínez Díez.* Madrid, 41–9.

* Mercedes Aguirre Castro is one of the co-authors of the present book. In addition to their one or two first names (*nombres*), Spanish people usually have two surnames (*apellidos*), one deriving from the father and one from the mother. Often just the first of these surnames will be used (as in 'Mercedes Aguirre'). It may be worth adding that to cite the name as 'M. A. Castro' is to misunderstand the difference between *nombre* and *apellido*.

Aguirre Castro, M. (2016b). 'Classical Myths and American Abstract Expressionism: The Case of William Baziotes', *Collectanea Philologica*, 19: 97–104.

Aguirre Castro, M. (2017). 'Tecnología convertida en mito: La obra artística de Eduardo Paolozzi', *Icono 14*, 15: 204–30.

Aguirre Castro, M. (2018). *La pared (y otros cuentos de lo extraño y lo sobrenatural).* Fuenlabrada.

Akbari, S. C. (2004). 'The Diversity of Mankind in *The Book of John Mandeville*', in R. Allen (ed.), *Eastward Bound: Travel and Travellers, 1050–1550.* Manchester, 156–76.

Akbari, S. C., and Iannucci, A. (2008) (eds). *Marco Polo and the Encounter of East and West.* Toronto.

Albouy, P. (1963). *La Création mythologique chez Victor Hugo.* Paris.

Aleshire, S. B. (1989). *The Athenian Asklepieion: The People, their Dedications, and the Inventories.* Amsterdam.

Allan, S. C. (2016). 'Tyrannical Inopportunity: Gustave Moreau's Anti-Narrative Strategies', in P. Cooke and N. Lübbren (eds), *Painting and Narrative in France, from Poussin to Gauguin.* Abingdon, 144–59.

Alonso, D. (1985). *Góngora y el Polifemo.* 7th edn. Madrid.

Alonso, D. (1987). 'Monstruosidad y belleza en el *Polifemo* de Góngora', in D. Alonso, *Poesía española: ensayo de métodos y límites estilísticos.* Madrid, 313–92.

Alonso Miguel, A. (2002). 'La metamorfosis del Cíclope', in G. Cabello Porras and J. Campos Daroca (eds), *Poéticas de la metamorfosis.* Málaga, 273–82.

Alwine, A. T. (2009). 'The Non-Homeric Cyclops in the Homeric *Odyssey*', *GRBS* 49: 323–33.

Anderson, G. (1986). *Philostratus: Biography and Belles Lettres in the Third Century A.D.* Beckenham.

Anderson, G. (2000). *Fairytale in the Ancient World.* London.

André, J. (1981). *L'Alimentation et la cuisine à Rome.* 2nd edn. Paris.

Andreae, B. (1982). *Odysseus: Archäologie des europäischen Menschenbildes.* Frankfurt.

Andreae, B. (1999). *Odysseus: Mythos und Erinnerung.* Mainz.

Andreae, B., and Parisi Presicce, C. (1996) (eds). *Ulisse: Il mito e la memoria.* Rome.

Anello, P. (1984). 'Polifemo e Galatea', *Seia: Quaderni dell'Istituto di Storia Antica dell'Università degli Studi di Palermo*, 1: 11–51.

Anfam, D. (1990). *Abstract Expressionism.* London.

Appelbaum, S. (2000). *Medieval Tales and Stories: 108 Prose Narratives of the Middle Ages.* Mineola, NY.

Apple, D. J., and Rabb, M. F. (1991). *Ocular Pathology: Clinical Applications and Self-Assessment.* 4th edn. St Louis, MO.

Aragon, L. (1965). *Les Collages.* Paris.

Arens, W. (1979). *The Man-Eating Myth: Anthropology and Anthropophagy.* New York.

Armitage, S. (2015). *The Odyssey: Missing Presumed Dead.* London.

Arnott, W. G. (1996). *Alexis: The Fragments. A Commentary.* Cambridge.

Athanasiev, A. N. (1863). *Russian Folk Tales*, viii. Moscow.

Atherton, C. (2002) (ed.). *Monsters and Monstrosity in Greek and Roman Culture.* Bari.

Auffarth, C. (1991). *Der drohende Untergang: 'Schöpfung' in Mythos und Ritual im Alten Orient und in Griechenland am Beispiel der Odyssee und des Ezechielbuches.* Berlin.

Augustine (1984). *The City of God.* Rev. Penguin edn. London.

Austin, N. (1975). *Archery at the Dark of the Moon: Poetic Problems in Homer's Odyssey.* Berkeley, CA.

Bachelard, G. (1994). *The Poetics of Space.* New edn. Boston, MA (trans. of *La Poétique de l'espace.* Paris; 11th edn in 2012).

Bader, F. (1985). 'Introduction à l'étude des mythes i.e. de la vision: Les Cyclopes', in E. Campanile (ed.), *Studi indoeuropei*. Pisa, 9–50.

Bakhtin, M. M. (1968). *Rabelais and his World*. Cambridge, MA (trans. of *Творчество Франсуа Рабле и народная культура средневековья и Ренессанса*. Moscow, 1965).

Bakker, E. J. (2002). 'Polyphemos', *Colby Quarterly*, 38: 135–50.

Bakker, E. J. (2013). *The Meaning of Meat and the Structure of the Odyssey*. Cambridge.

Baldinucci, F. (1681–1728). *Notizie de' professori del disegno da Cimabue in qua*. Florence.

Ballabriga, A. (1986). *Le Soleil et le Tartare: L'Image mythique du monde en Grèce archaïque*. Paris.

Ballabriga, A. (1998). *Les Fictions d'Homère: L'Invention mythologique et cosmographique dans l'Odyssée*. Paris.

Bann, S. (1985). 'The Mythical Conception is the Name: Titles and Names in Modern and Post-Modern Painting', *WI* 1: 176–90.

Barandiarán, J. M. (1960). *Mitología vasca*. Madrid.

Barasch, F. K. (1971). *The Grotesque: A Study in Meanings*. The Hague.

Baridon, M. (1998). *Les Jardins: Paysagistes—jardiniers—poètes*. Paris.

Barker, F., Hulme, P., and Iversen, M. (1998) (eds). *Cannibalism and the Colonial World*. Cambridge.

Barnard, M. E. (2002). 'The Gaze and the Mirror: Vision, Desire, and Identity in Góngora's *Fábula de Polifemo y Galatea*', *Calíope*, 8: 69–85.

Barney, S. A., Lewis, W. J., Beach, J. A., and Berghof, O. (2006). *The Etymologies of Isidore of Seville*. Cambridge.

Barolsky, P. (2002). 'Michelangelo: A Version of the Pastoral', *Arion*, 10: 49–54.

Bartel, H. (2004). *Mythos in der Literatur*. Münster.

Barthouil, G. (1992). 'Le Cyclope, d'Euripide à nos jours: Permanence et variations', *Dioniso*, 62/1: 103–21.

Bartlett, R. (2008). *The Natural and the Supernatural in the Middle Ages*. Cambridge.

Bartley, A. N. (2009). *Lucian's Dialogi Marini*. Newcastle upon Tyne.

Bartman, E. (2001). 'Hair and the Artifice of Roman Female Adornment', *American Journal of Archaeology*, 105: 1–25.

Barton, C. A. (1993). *The Sorrows of the Ancient Romans: The Gladiator and the Monster*. Princeton.

Basch, L. (1987). *Le Musée imaginaire de la marine antique*. Athens.

Bataille, G. (1988). 'Gustave Moreau, "l'attardé" précurseur du surréalisme', in Georges Bataille, *Oeuvres complètes*. Paris, xii. 521–3.

Baudelaire, C. (1961). *Oeuvres complètes*. Paris.

Baumann, M. (2011). *Bilder schreiben: Virtuose Ekphrasis in Philostrats 'Eikones'*. Berlin.

Baziotes, W. (1949). 'The Artist and his Mirror', *Right Angle*, 3: 3–4.

Bazzotti, U. (2013). *Palazzo Te: Giulio Romano's Masterwork in Mantua*. London (trans. of *Palazzo Te a Mantova*. Modena, 2012).

Beagon, M. (2005). *The Elder Pliny on the Human Animal*. Translation and commentary on *Natural History* book 7. Oxford.

Beagon, M. (2007). 'Situating Nature's Wonders in Pliny's *Natural History*', *BICS* suppl. 100: 19–40.

Beall, S. M. (1993). 'Word-Painting in the *Imagines* of the Elder Philostratus', *Hermes*, 121: 350–63.

Beard, M. (2014). *Laughter in Ancient Rome: On Joking, Tickling, and Cracking Up*. Berkeley, CA.

Beard, M., and Henderson, J. (2001). *Classical Art from Greece to Rome*. Oxford.

Beck, J. H. (1994). *Raphael.* New York.

Beckett, J., and Russell, F. (2003) (eds). *Henry Moore: Critical Essays.* Aldershot.

Beckingham, C. F., and Hamilton, B. (1996) (eds). *Prester John, the Mongols, and the Ten Lost Tribes.* Aldershot.

Béguin, S., Guillaume, J., and Roy, A. (1985). *La Galerie d'Ulysse à Fontainebleau.* Paris.

Benabou, M. (1975). 'Monstres et hybrides chez Lucrèce et Pline l'Ancien', in L. Poliakov (ed.), *Hommes et bêtes: Entretiens sur le racisme.* Paris, 143–52.

Bennett, L. (2013). *The Italian Cantata in Vienna: Entertainment in the Age of Absolutism.* Bloomington, IN.

Bensimon, M. (1972). 'The Significance of Eye Imagery in the Renaissance from Bosch to Montaigne', *Yale French Studies*, 47: 266–90.

Bérard, V. (1902–3). *Les Phéniciens et l'Odyssée.* 2 vols. Paris.

Bérard, V. (1924). *L'Odyssée: 'Poésie homérique'.* 3 vols. Paris.

Bérard, V. (1927–9). *Les Navigations d'Ulysse.* 4 vols. Paris.

Bergin, T. G., and Fisch, M. H. (1984). *The New Science of Giambattista Vico,* including *Practic of the New Science.* Ithaca, NY.

Berman, D. W. (2005). 'The Hierarchy of Herdsmen, Goatherding, and Genre in Theocritean Bucolic', *Phoenix*, 59: 228–45.

Bernabé, A. (2004–5). *Poetae Epici Graeci Testimonia et Fragmenta*, pars II, fasc. 1 and 2. Munich.

Bernheimer, R. (1952). *Wild Men in the Middle Ages: A Study in Art, Sentiment, and Demonology.* Cambridge, MA.

Bernidaki-Aldous, E. A. (1990). *Blindness in a Culture of Light: Especially the Case of Oedipus at Colonus of Sophocles.* New York.

Bernstock, J. E. (1993). 'Classical Mythology in Twentieth-Century Art: An Overview of a Humanistic Approach', *Artibus et Historiae*, 14/27: 153–83.

Bertozzi, M. (2009). 'L'autunno di Schifanoia: Il mito di Vulcano nel *Mese di Settembre*', in G. Venturi and F. Cappelletti (eds), *Gli dei a corte: Letteratura e immagini nella Ferrara estense.* Florence, 71–84.

Bertrand, D. (2001) (ed.). *Figurations du volcan à la Renaissance.* Actes du Colloque international du C.E.R.H.A.C. (Centre d'Études sur les Réformes, l'Humanisme et l'Âge Classique) de l'Université Blaise Pascal, 8–9 octobre 1999. Paris.

Beta, O. (1992). 'Gespräche mit Adolph Menzel', in Lammel (1992), 5–72.

Beta, S. (2015). 'Cyclops', in R. Lauriola and K. N. Demetriou (eds), *Brill's Companion to the Reception of Euripides.* Leiden, 607–19.

Biehl, W. (1987). 'Die Funktion des Opfermotivs in Euripides' "Kyklops"', *Hermes*, 115: 283–99.

Bildhauer, B., and Mills, R. (2003) (eds). *The Monstrous Middle Ages.* Cardiff.

Billault, A. (2000). *L'Univers de Philostrate.* Collection Latomus, vol. 252. Brussels.

Billows, R. A. (1990). *Antigonos the One-Eyed and the Creation of the Hellenistic State.* Berkeley, CA.

Bindman, D. (1979) (ed.). *John Flaxman.* London.

Bindman, D. (2009). 'Mankind after Darwin and Nineteenth-century Art', in Donald and Munro (2009), 143–65.

Bing, P., and Uhrmeister, V. (1994). 'The Unity of Callimachus' *Hymn to Artemis*', *JHS* 114: 19–34.

Bird, J. L. (2003). 'The *Historia Orientalis* of Jacques de Vitry: Visual and Written Commentaries as Evidence of a Text's Audience, Reception, and Utilization', *Essays in Medieval Studies*, 20: 56–74.

Birley, A. R. (1992). 'A Case of Eye Disease (*Lippitudo*) on the Roman Frontier in Britain', *Documenta Ophthalmologica*, 81: 111–19.

Birrell, A. (1999). *The Classic of Mountains and Seas.* Translation. London.

Black, R. (2011). 'Ovid in Medieval Italy', in Clark, Coulson, and McKinley (2011), 123–42.

Bladé, J.-F. (1886). *Contes populaires de la Gascogne.* Paris.

Blakely, S. (2006). *Myth, Ritual, and Metallurgy in Ancient Greece and Recent Africa.* Cambridge.

Blanco Freijeiro, A. (1959). 'Polifemo y Galatea', *Archivo Español de Arqueología*, 32: 174–7.

Blázquez, J. M. (1981). *Mosaicos romanos de Córdoba, Jaén y Málaga.* Instituto Español de Arqueología. Madrid.

Blumenfeld-Kosinski, R. (1997). *Reading Myth: Classical Mythology and its Interpretations in Medieval French Literature.* Stanford, CA.

Blundeville, T. (1594). *M. Blundeville His Exercises...* London.

Boardman, J. (1976). 'A Curious Eye Cup', *Archäologischer Anzeiger*, 3: 281–90.

Boardman, J. (1992). 'The Phallos-Bird in Archaic and Classical Greek Art', *RA*, fasc. 2: 227–42.

Boardman, J. (2002). *The Archaeology of Nostalgia: How the Greeks Re-Created their Mythical Past.* London.

Bömer, F. (1969–86). *P. Ovidius Naso, Metamorphosen.* Commentary in 7 vols. Heidelberg.

Boitani, P. (1994). *The Shadow of Ulysses: Figures of a Myth.* Oxford (trans. of *L'ombra di Ulisse: Figure di un mito.* Bologna, 1992).

Boitani, P., and Ambrosini, R. (1998) (eds). *Ulisse: Archeologia dell'uomo moderno.* Rome.

Bologna, C. (1977) (ed.). *Liber monstrorum de diversis generibus: Libro delle mirabili difformità.* Milan.

Bolton, J. D. P. (1962). *Aristeas of Proconnesus.* Oxford.

Bondanella, J. C., et al. (1996) (eds). *The Life of Titian, by Carlo Ridolfi.* University Park, PA.

Bonilla Cerezo, R., and Garosi, L. (2008). '*Con arguta sambuca il fier sembiante*: La *Polifemeida* de Giovan Battista Marino', in R. Bonilla and G. Mazzocchi (eds), *La hidra barroca: Varia lección de Góngora.* Granada, 181–218.

Bonnafé, A. (1985). 'L'Olivier dans l'*Odyssée* et le fourré du Parnasse: Reprises de termes et reprise de thèmes', *Quaderni di storia*, 21: 101–36.

Borràs, M. L. (1985). *Picabia.* London (trans. of *Picabia.* Barcelona, 1985).

Botley, P., and van Miert, D. (2012) (eds). *The Correspondence of Joseph Justus Scaliger.* 8 vols. Geneva.

Bottari, G. G. (1719). *Carmina illustrium poetarum italorum*, i. Florence.

Bourke, J. (2011). *What it Means to Be Human: Reflections from 1791 to the Present.* Berkeley, CA.

Bowden, H. (2010). *Mystery Cults of the Ancient World.* London.

Bowe, P. (2004). *Gardens of the Roman World.* Los Angeles, CA.

Bowie, E., and Elsner, J. (2009) (eds). *Philostratus.* Cambridge.

Bowness, A. (1965) (ed.). *Henry Moore. Sculpture and Drawings*, iii. *Sculpture 1955–64.* London.

Bowra, C. M. (1956). 'A Fragment of the *Arimaspea*', *CQ* 6: 1–10.

Boyceau de la Barauderie, J. (1638). *Traité du jardinage selon les raisons de la nature et de l'art.* Paris.

Bradford, E. (1963). *Ulysses Found.* London.

Braham, P. (2012). 'The Monstrous Caribbean', in Mittman and Dendle (2012), 17–47.

Braidotti, R. (2000). 'Teratologies', in I. Buchanan and C. Colebrook (eds), *Deleuze and Feminist Theory*. Edinburgh, 156–72.

Braund, S. M. (1996). 'The Solitary Feast: A Contradiction in Terms?', *BICS* 41: 37–52.

Brelich, A. (1958). *Gli eroi greci: Un problema storico-religioso*. Rome.

Bremmer, J. N. (1984). 'Op zoek naar de Cycloop', *Hermeneus*, 56/2: 10–19.

Bremmer, J. N. (1986). 'A Homeric Goat Island (*Od.* 9.116-41)', *CQ* 36: 256–7.

Bremmer, J. N. (1999). *Greek Religion*. 2nd edn. Oxford.

Bremmer, J. N. (2002). 'Odysseus versus the Cyclops', in S. des Bouvrie (ed.), *Myth and Symbol I: Symbolic Phenomena in Ancient Greek Culture*. Bergen, 135–52.

Bremmer, J. N. (2007) (ed.). *The Strange World of Human Sacrifice*. Leuven.

Bremmer, J. N. (2014). *Initiation into the Mysteries of the Ancient World*. Berlin.

Bremmer, J. N., and Roodenburg, H. (1991) (eds). *A Cultural History of Gesture*. Ithaca, NY.

Brendel, O. (1934). *Die Schafzucht im alten Griechenland*. Diss. Giessen.

Breton, A. (1965). *Le Surréalisme et la peinture*. Paris (1st edn, 1928).

Briggs, J. C. (2017). 'Francis Bacon's *Wisdom of the Ancients*: Between Two Worlds', in V. Zajko and H. Hoyle (eds), *A Handbook to the Reception of Classical Mythology*. Hoboken, NJ, 367–77.

Brill's New Pauly: Encyclopedia of the Ancient World (2002–). Leiden.

Brommer, F. (1982–3). 'Zur Schreibweise des Namens Odysseus', *Zeitschrift für vergleichende Sprachforschung*, 96: 88–92.

Brommer, F. (1983). *Odysseus: Die Taten und Leiden des Helden in antiker Kunst und Literatur*. Darmstadt.

Brown-Grant, R. (1994). 'Illumination as Reception: Jean Miélot's Reworking of the "Epistre Othea", in M. Zimmermann and D. De Rentiis (eds), *The City of Scholars: New Approaches to Christine de Pizan*. Berlin, 260–71.

Brunon, H. (2008). 'Pratolino: Art des jardins et imaginaire de la nature dans l'Italie de la seconde moitié du XVIe siècle.' Ph.D. thesis. Paris.

Bryson, N. (1994). 'Philostratus and the Imaginary Museum', in Goldhill and Osborne (1994), 255–83.

Buitron, D., and Cohen, B., et al. (1992) (eds). *The Odyssey and Ancient Art: An Epic in Word and Image*. Annandale-on-Hudson, NY.

Bull, G. (1956). *Benvenuto Cellini: Autobiography*. Harmondsworth.

Bull, G. (1987). *Giorgio Vasari: Lives of the Artists*, ii. London.

Bull, M. (2005). *The Mirror of the Gods: Classical Mythology in Renaissance Art*. London.

Burgess, J. S. (2001). *The Tradition of the Trojan War in Homer and the Epic Cycle*. Baltimore, MD.

Burgess, J. S. (2015). *Homer*. London.

Burke, E. (1757/1958). *A Philosophical Enquiry into the Origin of our Ideas of the Sublime and the Beautiful*, ed. J. T. Boulton. London.

Burke, P. (2009). *Popular Culture in Early Modern Europe*. 3rd edn. Farnham.

Burkert, W. (1979). *Structure and History in Greek Mythology and Ritual*. Berkeley, CA.

Burkert, W. (1985). *Greek Religion: Archaic and Classical*. Oxford (trans. of *Griechische Religion der archaischen und klassischen Epoche*. Stuttgart, 1977).

Burkert, W. (2003). *Die Griechen und der Orient: Von Homer bis zu den Magiern*. Munich (trans., with revisions, of *Da Homero ai Magi. La tradizione orientale nella cultura greca*. Venice, 1999).

Burton, J. B. (1995). *Theocritus's Urban Mimes: Mobility, Gender, and Patronage*. Berkeley, CA.

Burzacchini, G. (1979). 'Eur. *Cycl.* 320-331', *Quaderni urbinati di cultura classica*, NS 3: 65–8.

Buse, H. (1937). *Quaestiones Hesiodeae et Orphicae*. Dissertation. Halle.

Butler, S. (1922). *The Authoress of the Odyssey: Where and When She Wrote, Who She Was, the Use She Made of the Iliad, and How the Poem Grew under her Hands*. 2nd edn. London (1st edn 1897).

Buxton, R. G. A. (1994). *Imaginary Greece: The Contexts of Mythology*. Cambridge.

Buxton, R. G. A. (1999) (ed.). *From Myth to Reason? Studies in the Development of Greek Thought*. Oxford.

Buxton, R. G. A. (2013a). *Myths and Tragedies in their Ancient Greek Contexts*. Oxford.

Buxton, R. G. A. (2013b). 'The Myth of Talos: Vulnerability, *ichōr*, and Boundary-Crossing', in Buxton (2013a), 73–97.

Buxton, R. G. A. (2013c). 'Blindness and Limits: Sophokles and the Logic of Myth', in Buxton (2013a), 173–200.

Buxton, R. G. A. (2013d). 'Mythological Names: The Case of *melas*', in Buxton (2013a), 53–71.

Buxton, R. G. A. (2016). 'Mount Etna in the Greco-Roman *imaginaire*: Culture and Liquid Fire', in J. McInerney and I. Sluiter (eds), *Valuing Landscape in Classical Antiquity: Natural Environment and Cultural Imagination*. Leiden, 25–45.

Buxton, R. G. A. (2017a). 'Landscapes of the Cyclopes', in G. Hawes (ed.), *Myths on the Map: The Storied Landscapes of Ancient Greece*. Oxford, 52–64.

Buxton, R. G. A. (2017b). 'My Friends, Outis is Killing me by a Trick *oude* by Violence', in P. Corcoran (ed.), *Line of Enquiry: Favourite Lines from Classical Literature*. Dublin, 34–5.

Byre, C. S. (1994). 'The Rhetoric of Description in *Odyssey* 9.116–41: Odysseus and Goat Island', *Classical Journal*, 89: 357–67.

Cabani, M. C. (2005). *L'occhio di Polifemo: Studi su Pulci, Tasso e Marino*. Pisa.

Calame, C. (1976). 'Mythe grec et structures narratives: Le Mythe des Cyclopes dans l'*Odyssée*', *Živa antika*, 26: 311–28; repr. in B. Gentili and G. Paioni (eds), *Il mito Greco*. Rome, 1977, 369–92.

Calame, C. (1977). 'La Légende du Cyclope dans le folklore européen et extra-européen: Un jeu de transformations narratives', *Études de lettres*, 3/10: 45–79.

Calame, C. (1995). *The Craft of Poetic Speech in Ancient Greece*. Ithaca, NY (trans., with revisions, of *Le Récit en Grèce ancienne: Énonciations et représentations de poètes*. Paris, 1986).

Calame, C. (2002). 'Ulysse, un héros proto-colonial? Un aspect de la question homérique', *L'Homme*, 164: 145–54.

Calcagno, M. P. (2012). *From Madrigal to Opera: Monteverdi's Staging of the Self*. Berkeley, CA.

Caliterna, L. (1993). 'Restauro di un colosso', in Morolli et al. (1993), 115–52.

Caliterna, P. (1993). 'Il consolidamento della struttura', in Morolli et al. (1993), 171–80.

Calvo Martínez, J. L. (1994). 'La figura de Ulises en la literatura española', in J. A. López Férez (ed.), *La épica griega y su influencia en la literatura española*. Madrid, 333–58.

Camassa, G. (1982). 'Il simbolismo del terzo occhio e la cecità del indovino greco', *Quaderni di storia*, 16: 249–75.

Camfield, W. A. (1979). *Francis Picabia: His Art, Life and Times*. Princeton.

Camfield, W. A. (1993). *Max Ernst: Dada and the Dawn of Surrealism*. Munich.

Camille, M. (1992). *Image on the Edge: The Margins of Medieval Art*. London.

Campbell, D. A. (1993). *Greek Lyric*, v. Edition and translation. Cambridge, MA.

Campbell, M. B. (2002). 'The Nude Cyclops in the Costume Book', in Jones and Sprunger (2002), 285–301.

Campolongo, E. (1763). *La Polifemeide*. Naples.

Canal, V. (2007). *Jean Tinguely: Le Cyclop.* Paris.
Canguilhem, G. (1962). 'La Monstruosité et le monstrueux', *Diogène*, 40: 29–43.
Carabell, P. (1997). 'Breaking the Frame: Transgression and Transformation in Giulio Romano's Sala dei Giganti', *Artibus et Historiae*, 18/36: 87–100.
Carey, J. (1983). 'Irish Parallels to the Myth of Odin's Eye', *Folklore*, 94: 214–18.
Carey, S. (2002). 'A Tradition of Adventures in the Imperial Grotto', *G&R* 49: 44–61.
Carlson, D. N. (2009). 'Seeing the Sea: Ships' Eyes in Classical Greece', *Hesperia*, 78: 347–65.
Caro, A. (1957–61). *Lettere familiari.* Edizione critica con introduzione e note di Aulo Greco. Florence.
Carpenter, R. (1958). *Folk Tale, Fiction and Saga in the Homeric Epics.* Berkeley, CA.
Carpenter, T. H. (1991). *Art and Myth in Ancient Greece: A Handbook.* London.
Carrier, D. (1990). 'Blindness and the Representation of Desire in Poussin's Paintings', *RES: Anthropology and Aesthetics*, 19: 31–52.
Casaregi, G. B. (1782). *Poesie.* Nice.
Cassanmagnago, C. (2009). *Esiodo: Tutte le opere e i frammenti: con la prima traduzione degli scolii.* Milan.
Césaire, A. (1956). *Cahier d'un retour au pays natal.* 2nd edn. Paris (1st edn 1939).
Chadwick, W. (1985). *Women Artists and the Surrealist Movement.* London.
Chalier, I. (2008). '*Le Cyclope* d'Euripide sur un bol à reliefs de Porsuk', *RA* 45: 93–105.
Chance, J. (1994). *Medieval Mythography from Roman North Africa to the School of Chartres A.D. 433–1177.* Gainsville, FL.
Chance, J. (1997). *Christine de Pizan's Letter of Othea to Hector.* Cambridge.
Chappell, M. (1976). 'An Interpretation of Agostino Carracci's "Galatea" in the Farnese Gallery', *Studies in Iconography*, 2: 41–65.
Chappuis Sandoz, L. (2008). 'La Survie des monstres: Ethnographie fantastique et handicap à Rome, la force de l'imagination', *Latomus*, 67: 21–36.
Charlier, P. (2008). *Les Monstres humains dans l'Antiquité: Analyse paléopathologique.* Paris.
Chase, G. H. (1902). 'The Shield Devices of the Greeks', *Harvard Studies in Classical Philology*, 13: 61–127.
Chastel, A. (1988). *La Grottesque.* Paris.
Cherchi, P. (1996). *La metamorfosi dell'Adone.* Ravenna.
Chipp, H. B. (1968). *Theories of Modern Art: A Source Book by Artists and Critics.* Berkeley, CA.
Christopoulos, M., Karakantza, E. D., and Levaniouk, O. (2010) (eds). *Light and Darkness in Ancient Greek Myth and Religion.* Lanham, MD.
Citti, V. (1997). 'La ricezione dell'antico nei *Poemi Conviviali*', in M. Pazzaglia (ed.), *I 'Poemi Conviviali' di Giovanni Pascoli.* Atti del Convegno di Studi di San Mauro Pascoli e Barga, 26–29 settembre 1996. Florence, 99–131.
Citti, V. (2003). 'Odisseo, metafora dell'Europa', in Nicosia (2003), 255–78.
Cixous, H. (1976). 'The Laugh of the Medusa', *Signs*, 1: 875–93.
Clair, J. (2012). *Hubris: La Fabrique du monstre dans l'art moderne: Homoncules, Géants et Acéphales.* Paris.
Clare, R. J. (2002). 'Representing Monstrosity: Polyphemus in the *Odyssey*', in Atherton (2002), 1–17.
Clark, J. G., Coulson, F. T., and McKinley, K. L. (2011) (eds). *Ovid in the Middle Ages.* Cambridge.
Clay, J. S. (1980). 'Goat Island: *Od.* 9.116-141', *CQ* 30: 261–4.
Cohen, J. J. (1996) (ed.). *Monster Theory: Reading Culture.* Minneapolis, MN.
Cohen, J. J. (1999). *Of Giants: Sex, Monsters, and the Middle Ages.* Minneapolis, MN.

Cohen, J. J. (2012). 'Postscript: The Promise of Monsters', in Mittman and Dendle (2012), 449–64.

Cohen, M. (2017). *The Politics of Opera: A History from Monteverdi to Mozart*. Princeton.

Cohen, M. M. (2010). 'Holoprosencephaly: A Mythologic and Teratologic Distillate', *American Journal of Medical Genetics Part C (Seminars in Medical Genetics)*, 154C: 8–12.

Cohen, M. M., and Sulik, K. K. (1992). 'Perspectives on Holoprosencephaly: Part II. Central Nervous System, Craniofacial Anatomy, Syndrome Commentary, Diagnostic Approach, and Experimental Studies,' *Journal of Craniofacial Genetics and Developmental Biology*, 12: 196–244.

Collins, J. (2014). *Eduardo Paolozzi*. Farnham.

Collisani, A. (2003). 'Le Molte anime dell'*Ulisse* di Dallapiccola', in Nicosia (2003), 333–46.

Combs-Schilling, J. D. (2012). 'Pastoral at the Boundaries: The Hybridization of Genre in the Fourteenth-Century Italian Eclogue Revival.' Diss. Berkeley, CA.

Comenius, J. A. (1887). *The Orbis Pictus*. Syracuse, NY.

Conan, M. (1987). 'The *Imagines* of Philostratus', *WI* 3:162–71.

Conrad, J. A. (1999). 'Polyphemus and Tepegöz Revisited: A Comparison of the Tales of the Blinding of the One-Eyed Ogre in Western and Turkish Traditions', *Fabula*, 40: 278–97.

Constantakopoulou, C. (2007). *The Dance of the Islands: Insularity, Networks, the Athenian Empire, and the Aegean World*. Oxford.

Constantine, D. (2001). *Fields of Fire: A Life of Sir William Hamilton*. London.

Conticello, B., and Andreae, B. (1974). *Die Skulpturen von Sperlonga*. Berlin.

Cook, A. B. (1925). *Zeus: A Study in Ancient Religion*, ii. Cambridge.

Cook, E. F. (1995). *The Odyssey in Athens: Myths of Cultural Origins*. Ithaca, NY.

Cooke, P. (2003). *Gustave Moreau et les arts jumeaux: Peinture et littérature au dix-neuvième siècle*. Oxford.

Cooke, P. (2014). *Gustave Moreau: History Painting, Spirituality and Symbolism*. New Haven, CT.

Cooper, W. (1971). *Hair: Sex, Society, Symbolism*. London.

Coote, C. H. and Crawford, J. L. L. (1898). *Autotype Facsimiles of Three Mappemondes*. Aberdeen.

Coppola, A. (1995). *Archaiologhía e propaganda: I Greci, Roma e l'Italia*. Rome.

Corti, C. (1998). 'Viaggiatore, governante, o cortigiano? Ulisse nel Rinascimento inglese', in Boitani and Ambrosini (1998), 201–22.

Costello, J. (1955). 'Poussin's Drawings for Marino and the New Classicism: I—Ovid's *Metamorphoses*', *JWCI* 18: 296–317.

Coulson, F. T. (2011). 'Ovid's *Metamorphoses* in the School Tradition of France, 1180–1400: Texts, Manuscript Traditions, Manuscript Settings', in Clark, Coulson, and McKinley (2011), 48–82.

Coyhis, D. L., and White, W. L. (2006). *Alcohol Problems in Native America*. Colorado Springs, CO.

Crain, S. D. (2004). 'William Baziotes' Duality: Escaping the Ordinary and Finding the Extraordinary.' MA thesis. Athens, GA.

Curtius, E. R. (1953). *European Literature and the Latin Middle Ages*. London (trans. of *Europäische Literatur und lateinisches Mittelalter*. Bern, 1948).

Cusset, C. (2004). 'Le Cyclope de Théocrite entre la force brute et le feu de la création', in Foulon (2004), 49–56.

Cusset, C. (2011). *Cyclopodie: Édition critique et commentée de l'Idylle VI de Théocrite.* Lyons.

Czapla, B. (2006). 'Die Wandlung der Nereide Galatea von einer Kokotte zur Heiligen oder die Usurpation eines griechischen Mythos durch den Petrarkismus', *Antike und Abendland*, 52: 95–125.

Dacos, N. (1969). *La Découverte de la Domus Aurea et la formation des grotesques à la Renaissance.* London.

Dalby, A. (1996). *Siren Feasts: A History of Food and Gastronomy in Greece.* London.

Dalby, A. (2003). *Food in the Ancient World from A to Z.* London.

Dalí, S. (2010). *Dalí in the Third Dimension: The Stratton Foundation Collection.* Turin.

Dallapiccola, A. L. (2002). *Dictionary of Hindu Lore and Legend.* London.

Damlé, A., and L'Hostis, A. (2010) (eds). *The Beautiful and the Monstrous: Essays in French Literature, Thought and Culture.* Oxford.

Darley, G. (2011). *Vesuvius.* London.

Dasen, V. (1993). *Dwarfs in Ancient Egypt and Greece.* Oxford.

Daston, L., and Park, K. (1998). *Wonders and the Order of Nature, 1150–1750.* New York.

Davidson, H. E. (1979–80). *Saxo Grammaticus: The History of the Danes.* 2 vols. Woodbridge.

Davidson, J. F. (1990). 'The Cave of Philoctetes', *Mnemosyne* (4th Series), 43: 307–15.

Davidson, J. N. (1997). *Courtesans and Fishcakes: The Consuming Passions of Classical Athens.* London.

Davies, M. W., Nandy, A., and Sardar, Z. (1993). *Barbaric Others: A Manifesto on Western Racism.* London.

Davies, S. (2012). 'The Unlucky, the Bad and the Ugly: Categories of Monstrosity from the Renaissance to the Enlightenment', in Mittman and Dendle (2012), 49–75.

Davis, G. (2007). '"Homecomings without Home": Representations of (Post)colonial *nostos* (Homecoming) in the Lyric of Aimé Césaire and Derek Walcott', in Graziosi and Greenwood (2007), 191–209.

Dawood, N. J. (1973). *Tales from the Thousand and One Nights.* Rev. edn. London.

De Angelis, F. (2000). 'Estimating the Agricultural Base of Greek Sicily', *Papers of the British School at Rome*, 68: 111–48.

De Angelis, F. (2006). 'Going against the Grain in Sicilian Greek Economics', *G&R* 53: 29–47.

De Angelis, F. (2016). *Archaic and Classical Greek Sicily: A Social and Economic History.* Oxford.

De Boer, C. (1954). *Ovide moralisé en prose.* Verhandelingen der Koninklijke Nederlandse Akademie van Wetenschappen, afd. Letterkunde 61, no. 2. Amsterdam.

Debus, A. A. (2010). *Prehistoric Monsters: The Real and Imagined Creatures of the Past that We Love to Fear.* Jefferson, NC.

De Caus, I. (1659). *New and Rare Inventions of Water-Works.* London.

De Caus, S. (1615). *Les Raisons des forces mouvantes avec diverses machines tant utiles que plaisantes.* Frankfurt.

De Grummond, N. T., and Ridgway, B. S. (2000) (eds). *From Pergamon to Sperlonga: Sculpture and Context.* Berkeley, CA.

Deichmann, U. (1996). *Biologists under Hitler.* Cambridge, MA (trans. of *Biologen unter Hitler: Vertreibung, Karrieren, Forschung.* Frankfurt, 1992).

De Jong, I. (2001). *A Narratological Commentary on the Odyssey.* Cambridge.

Del Corno, D. (2003). 'Ulisse in musica: *Outis* di Luciano Berio', in Nicosia (2003), 347–52.

Delcourt, M. (1938). *Stérilités mystérieuses et naissances maléfiques dans l'Antiquité classique.* Liège.

D'Elia, U. R. (2011). 'Giambologna's Giant and the Cinquecento Villa Garden as a Landscape of Suffering', *Studies in the History of Gardens and Designed Landscapes: An International Quarterly*, 31: 1–25.

Dell, C. (2010). *Monsters: A Bestiary of the Bizarre.* London.

Dench, E. (1995). *From Barbarians to New Men: Greek, Roman, and Modern Perceptions of Peoples of the Central Apennines.* Oxford.

Deonna, W. (1965). *Le Symbolisme de l'oeil.* Paris.

Der Kleine Pauly. Lexikon der Antike (1964–75). 5 vols. Stuttgart.

Derksen, J. J. V. M. (1984). 'Polyphemus in de antieke kunst', *Hermeneus*, 56/2: 20–41.

De Romilly, J. (1983a). 'À propos d'ogres', in *Mélanges Édouard Delebecque.* Aix-en-Provence, 331–40.

De Romilly, J. (1983b). 'L'Amitié de Giraudoux avec l'hellénisme: *Elpénor*', *Bulletin de l'Association Guillaume Budé*, 1: 191–7.

Desmond, M., and Sheingorn, P. (2003). *Myth, Montage, and Visuality in Late Medieval Manuscript Culture: Christine de Pizan's 'Epistre Othea'.* Ann Arbor, MI.

Detienne, M. (1973). 'L'Olivier: Un mythe politico-religieux', in M. I. Finley (ed.), *Problèmes de la terre en Grèce ancienne.* Paris, 293–306.

Detienne, M., and Vernant, J.-P. (1979) (eds). *La Cuisine du sacrifice en pays grec.* Paris.

Deuse, W. (1990). 'Dichtung als Heilmittel gegen die Liebe. Zum 11. Idyll Theokrits', in P. Steinmetz (ed.), *Beiträge zur hellenistischen Literatur und ihrer Rezeption in Rom* (Palingenesia 28). Stuttgart, 59–76.

De Vieri, F. (1586). *Discorsi delle maravigliose opere di Pratolino, e d'Amore.* Florence.

D'Huy, J. (2015). 'Polyphemus: A Palaeolithic Tale?', <https://halshs.archives-ouvertes.fr/halshs-01170837> (accessed 6 May 2017).

Dick, O. L. (2016). *John Aubrey: Aubrey's Brief Lives.* Re-edition. London.

Dickens, C. (1957). 'Pictures from Italy', in *American Notes and Pictures from Italy.* London. 1st edn. 1846.

Dickie, M. W. (1991). 'Heliodorus and Plutarch on the Evil Eye', *CP* 86: 17–29.

Diez, H. F. von (1815). *Der neuentdeckte oghuzische Cyklop verglichen mit dem Homerischen.* Halle.

Di Manzano, S. (1600). *Aci: favola marina.* Venice.

Dion, R. (1969). *Les Anthropophages de l'Odyssée: Cyclopes et Lestrygons.* Paris.

Dörrie, H. (1968). *Die schöne Galatea: Eine Gestalt am Rande des griechischen Mythos in antiker und neuzeitlicher Sicht.* Munich.

Dörrie, H. (1974). *Pygmalion: Ein Impuls Ovids und seine Wirkungen bis in die Gegenwart.* Opladen.

Donald, D., and Munro, J. (2009). *Endless Forms: Charles Darwin, Natural Science and the Visual Arts.* New Haven, CT.

D'Onofrio, C. (1963). *La Villa Aldobrandini di Frascati.* Rome.

D'Onofrio, S. (2000). 'L'antro dell'uomo selvaggio', in M. Cantelmo (ed.), *Il castello, il convento, il palazzo e altri scenari dell' ambientazione letteraria.* Florence, 17–38.

D'Onofrio, S. (2003). 'Ulisse e l'uomo selvaggio', in Nicosia (2003), 127–50.

Dougherty, C. (1999). 'The Double Vision of Euripides' *Cyclops*: An Ethnographic *Odyssey* on the Satyr Stage', *Comparative Drama*, 33/3: 313–38.

Dougherty, C. (2001). *The Raft of Odysseus: The Ethnographic Imagination of Homer's Odyssey.* Oxford.

Dougherty, C. (2003). 'The Aristonothos Krater: Competing Stories of Conflict and Collaboration', in C. Dougherty and L. Kurke (eds), *The Cultures within Ancient Greek Culture: Contact, Conflict, Collaboration.* Cambridge, 35–56.

Douglas, K. (1988). *The Ragman's Son: An Autobiography.* London.

Druick, D. W., et al. (1994). *Odilon Redon.* London.

Ducrey, P. (1985). *Guerre et guerriers dans la Grèce antique.* Fribourg.

Duffy, E. (1994). *The Subaltern Ulysses.* Minneapolis, MN.

Dufrêne, T. (2004). 'Cyclopes modernes: De Menzel à Tinguely', in H. and J. A. Schmoll genannt Eisenwerth, and R. M. Hillert (eds), *Mythen—Symbole—Metamorphosen in der Kunst seit 1800.* Berlin, 487–501.

Dumézil, G. (1988). *Mitra-Varuna: An Essay on Two Indo-European Representations of Sovereignty.* New York (trans. of *Mitra-Varuna: Essai sur deux représentations indo-européennes de la souveraineté.* Paris, 1948).

Dumont, H. (2009). *L'Antiquité au cinéma: Vérités, légendes et manipulations.* Paris.

Dunbabin, K. M. D. (1978). *The Mosaics of Roman North Africa: Studies in Iconography and Patronage.* Oxford.

Dunbabin, K. M. D. (2015). 'Image, Myth, and Epic on Mosaics of the Late Roman West', in K. M. Coleman (ed.), *Images for Classicists.* Cambridge, MA, 39–65.

Dundes, A. (1986). 'Fairy Tales from a Folkloristic Perspective', in R. B. Bottigheimer (ed.), *Fairy Tales and Society: Illusion, Allusion, and Paradigm.* Philadelphia, PA, 259–69.

Dundes, A. (1992) (ed.). *The Evil Eye: A Casebook.* Rev. edn. Madison, WI.

Dundes, A. (1997). 'The Motif-Index and the Tale Type Index: A Critique', *Journal of Folklore Research*, 34/3: 195–202.

Dunne, T., and Pressly, W. L. (2010) (eds). *James Barry, 1741–1806: History Painter.* Farnham.

Du Quesnay, I. M. Le M. (1979). 'From Polyphemus to Corydon: Virgil, *Eclogue* 2 and the Idylls of Theocritus', in D. A. West and A. J. Woodman (eds), *Creative Imitation and Latin Literature.* Cambridge, 35–69.

Durand, G. (1992). *Les Structures anthropologiques de l'imaginaire.* 11th edn. Paris.

Duroisin, P. (2005). 'Les Petites *Odyssées* de Jean Giraudoux: *Elpénor*, et de Jean Giono: *Naissance de l'Odyssée*', *Bulletin de l'Association Guillaume Budé*, 1: 172–210.

Dyer, R. R. (1989). 'Vergil's Fama: A New Interpretation of *Aeneid* 4.173ff', *G&R* 36: 28–32.

Eck, B. (2012). *La Mort rouge: Homicide, guerre et souillure en Grèce ancienne.* Paris.

Eco, U. (2007). *On Ugliness.* London (trans. of *Storia della brutezza.* Milan, 2007).

Edelstein, E. J., and Edelstein, L. (1945). *Asclepius: A Collection and Interpretation of the Testimonies.* 2 vols. Baltimore, MD.

Edmunds, L. (1990) (ed.). *Approaches to Greek Myth.* Baltimore, MD.

Edson, L. (1984). 'Confronting the Signs: Words, Images, and the Reader-Spectator', *Dada/Surrealism*, 13: 83–93.

Edwards, C. (2003). 'Incorporating the Alien: The Art of Conquest', in C. Edwards and G. Woolf (eds), *Rome the Cosmopolis.* Cambridge, 44–70.

Edwards, J. D., and Graulund, R. (2013). *Grotesque.* Abingdon.

Elia, O. (1932). *Pitture murali e mosaici nel Museo Nazionale di Napoli.* Rome.

Eliade, M. (1971). *The Forge and the Crucible.* New York (trans. of *Forgerons et alchimistes.* Paris, 1956).

Eliade, M. (1972). *Zalmoxis, the Vanishing God.* Chicago (trans. of *De Zalmoxis à Gengis-Khan.* Paris, 1970).

Elliott, J. H. (1990). 'Paul, Galatians, and the Evil Eye', *Currents in Theology and Mission*, 17: 262–73.

Elliott, J. H. (1994). 'The Evil Eye and the Sermon on the Mount', *Biblical Interpretation*, 2: 51–84.

Elliott, J. H. (2011). 'Social-Scientific Criticism: Perspective, Process and Payoff. Evil Eye Accusation at Galatia as Illustration of the Method', *HTS Teologiese Studies/Theological Studies*, 67/1, doi.10.4102/hts.v67i1.858.

Elliott, J. H. (2015). *Beware the Evil Eye: The Evil Eye in the Bible and the Ancient World*, i. *Introduction, Mesopotamia, and Egypt*. Eugene, OR.

Elliott, J. H. (2016). *Beware the Evil Eye: The Evil Eye in the Bible and the Ancient World*, ii. *Greece and Rome*. Eugene, OR.

Ellison, R. W. (2014). *Invisible Man*. New York; published as Penguin Essentials edn, London. 1st edn. 1952.

Elsner, J. (1996) (ed.). *Art and Text in Roman Culture*. Cambridge.

Essick, R., and La Belle, J. (1977). *Flaxman's Illustrations to Homer*. New York.

Esteban, A., and Aguirre, M. (2015). *Cuentos de la mitología celta*. Madrid.

Evelyn, J. (1955). *The Diary of John Evelyn*, ed. E. S. de Beer. 6 vols. Oxford.

Facos, M. (2011). *An Introduction to Nineteenth-Century Art*. New York.

Falcón Martínez, C., Fernández-Galiano, E., and López Melero, R. (1980). *Diccionario de mitología clásica*. 2 vols. Madrid.

Falgas-Ravry, C. A. (2010). 'A Dance of Angels and Monsters: Victor Hugo's Caducean Aesthetics', in Damlé and L'Hostis (2010), 55–66.

Fantuzzi, M. (1996). 'Mythological Paradigms in the Bucolic Poetry of Theocritus', *Cambridge Classical Journal*, 41: 16–35.

Fantuzzi, M., and Papanghelis, T. (2006) (eds). *Brill's Companion to Greek and Latin Pastoral*. Leiden.

Faraone, C. A. (2006). 'Magic, Medicine and Eros in the Prologue to Theocritus' *Id.* 11', in Fantuzzi and Papanghelis (2006), 75–90.

Farrell, J. (1992). 'Dialogue of Genres in Ovid's "Lovesong of Polyphemus" (*Metamorphoses* 13.719–897)', *AJP* 113: 235–68.

Fehling, D. (1977). *Amor und Psyche: Die Schöpfung des Apuleius und ihre Einwirkung auf das Märchen, eine Kritik der romantischen Märchentheorie*. Mainz.

Fellmann, B. (1972). *Die antiken Darstellungen des Polyphemabenteuers*. Munich.

Felton, D. (2012). 'Rejecting and Embracing the Monstrous in Ancient Greece and Rome', in Mittman and Dendle (2012), 103–31.

Fernández-Armesto, F. (2002). *Near a Thousand Tables: A History of Food*. New York.

Fernández Navarrete, M., et al. (1842). *Colección de documentos inéditos para la historia de España*, i. Madrid.

Fingesten, P. (1959). 'Sight and Insight: A Contribution toward an Iconography of the Eye', *Criticism*, 1: 19–31.

Finnegan, R. H. (1988). *Literacy and Orality: Studies in the Technology of Communication*. Oxford.

Finnegan, R. H. (1992). *Oral Poetry: Its Nature, Significance and Social Context*. 2nd edn. Bloomington, IN.

Finnegan, R. H. (2007). *The Oral and Beyond: Doing Things with Words in Africa*. Chicago.

Fiorenza, G. (2006). 'Penelope's Web: Francesco Primaticcio's Epic Revision at Fontainebleau', *Renaissance Quarterly*, 59: 795–827.

Firth, R. (1973). *Symbols: Public and Private*. London.

Fisher, J. B. (2009). 'Digesting Falstaff: Food and Nation in Shakespeare's *Henry IV* Plays', *Early English Studies*, 2: 1–23.

Flack, L. C. (2015). *Modernism and Homer: The Odysseys of H. D., James Joyce, Osip Mandelstam, and Ezra Pound*. Cambridge.

Flandrin, J.-L., and Montanari, M. (1999) (eds). *Food: A Culinary History from Antiquity to the Present.* New York (trans. of *Histoire de l'alimentation.* Paris, 1996).

Flecker, J. E. (1907). *The Bridge of Fire: Poems.* London.

Flensted-Jensen, P. (2002). 'Something Old, Something New, Something Borrowed: The *Odyssey* and *O Brother, Where Art Thou?*', *Classica et Mediaevalia*, 53: 13–30.

Flint, V. I. J. (1988). 'Monsters and the Antipodes in the Early Middle Ages and Enlightenment', in Flint, *Ideas in the Medieval West: Texts and their Contexts.* London, 65–80.

Fontenrose, J. (1983). 'The Building of the City Walls: Troy and Asgard', *Journal of American Folklore*, 96: 53–63.

Foray, J.-M. (2013). *Le Petit Dictionnaire Chagall en 52 symboles.* Paris.

Foresti, G. F. (1538). *Supplementum Chronicorum.* Paris.

Forsyth, D. W. (1985). 'Three Cheers for Hans Staden: The Case for Brazilian Cannibalism', *Ethnohistory*, 32/1: 17–36.

Foster, D. W., and Foster, V. R. (1973). *Luis de Góngora.* New York.

Foster, M. D. (2012). 'Early Modern Past to Postmodern Future: Changing Discourses of Japanese Monsters', in Mittman and Dendle (2012), 133–50.

Foucault, M. (1975). *Surveiller et punir: Naissance de la prison.* Paris.

Foulon, E. (2004). *Connaissance et représentations des volcans dans l'Antiquité.* Clermont-Ferrand.

Fowler, R. L. (2004) (ed.). *The Cambridge Companion to Homer.* Cambridge.

Fowler, R. L. (2013). *Early Greek Mythography*, ii. *Commentary.* Oxford.

Foxhall, L. (2007). *Olive Cultivation in Ancient Greece: Seeking the Ancient Economy.* Oxford.

Frazer, J. G. (1921). *Apollodorus: The Library.* 2 vols. Cambridge, MA.

Freed, E. K., and Sharp, E. (1957). *The Magical Worlds of Redon, Klee, Baziotes.* Houston, TX (exhibition catalogue, Houston Contemporary Arts Museum).

Freedman, L. (2011). *Classical Myths in Italian Renaissance Painting.* Cambridge.

Freud, S. (2003). *The Uncanny.* Translation. London.

Fried, M. (2002). *Menzel's Realism: Art and Embodiment in Nineteenth-Century Berlin.* New Haven, CT.

Friedman, J. B. (2000). *The Monstrous Races in Medieval Art and Thought.* Rev. edn. Syracuse, NY.

Frontisi-Ducroux, F. (1996). 'Eros, Desire, and the Gaze', in N. B. Kampen (ed.), *Sexuality in Ancient Art.* Cambridge, 81–100.

Gaillard, M. (1995). *Les Fontaines de Paris: Guide historique.* Amiens.

Gamboni, D. (1992). 'Le "Symbolisme en peinture" et la littérature', *Revue de l'art*, 96: 13–23.

Gamboni, D. (2002). *Potential Images: Ambiguity and Indeterminacy in Modern Art.* London.

Gantz, J. (1976). *The Mabinogion.* Harmondsworth.

Gantz, J. (1981). *Early Irish Myths and Sagas.* Harmondsworth.

Gantz, T. (1993). *Early Greek Myth: A Guide to Literary and Artistic Sources.* Baltimore, MD.

Gardner, J. (2013). *Girolamo Fracastoro: Latin Poetry.* Cambridge, MA.

Garland, R. (2010). *The Eye of the Beholder: Deformity and Disability in the Graeco-Roman World.* 2nd edn. London.

Garner, B. C. (1970). 'Francis Bacon, Natalis Comes and the Mythological Tradition', *JWCI* 33: 264–91.

Garnsey, P. D. A. (1999). *Food and Society in Classical Antiquity.* Cambridge.

Garzya, A., and Roques, D. (2000). *Synésios de Cyrène. Correspondance*, iii. *Lettres LXIV–CLVI.* Translation and commentary. Paris.

Gay, J. (1983). *Dramatic Works*, i, ed. J. Fuller. Oxford.

Gemma, C. (1575). *De naturae divinis characterismis*... Antwerp.

Germain, G. (1954). *Genèse de l'Odyssée: Le Fantastique et le sacré.* Paris.

Geronimus, D. (2006). *Piero di Cosimo: Visions Beautiful and Strange.* New Haven, CT.

Gevaert, B., and Laes, C. (2013). 'What's in a Monster? Pliny the Elder, Teratology and Bodily Disability', in Laes, Goodey, and Rose (2013), 211–30.

Ghisalberti, F. (1931). 'Giovanni del Virgilio, espositore delle "Metamorfosi"', *Il giornale dantesco*, 34: 1–110.

Ghisalberti, F. (1932). 'Arnolfo d'Orléans, un cultore di Ovidio nel secolo XII', *Memorie del R. Istituto lombardo di scienze e lettere*, 24, fasc. 4.

Ghisalberti, F. (1933a). *Giovanni di Garlandia: Integumenta Ovidii.* Messina.

Ghisalberti, F. (1933b). 'L'*Ovidius moralizatus* di Pierre Bersuire', *Studj romanzi*, 23: 5–136.

Gifford, D., and Seidman, R. J. (1988). *Ulysses Annotated: Notes for James Joyce's Ulysses.* 2nd edn, rev. and expanded. Berkeley, CA.

Gigli Piccardi, D., et al. (2006–10) (eds). *Nonno di Panopoli: Le dionisiache.* 2nd edn. Milan.

Giles-Watson, M. (2007). 'Odysseus and the Ram in Art and (Con)text: Arthur M. Sackler Museum 1994.8 and the Hero's Escape from Polyphemos', *Harvard Studies in Classical Philology*, 103: 555–77.

Gilleland, B. B. (1981). *Johannes de Alta Silva, Dolopathos or, the King and the Seven Wise Men.* Translation. Binghampton, NY.

Girardi, E. N. (1967). *Michelangiolo [sic] Buonarroti: Rime.* Bari.

Giraudoux, J. (1990). *Oeuvres romanesques complètes*, i. Paris.

Giuliani, L. (2013). *Image and Myth: A History of Pictorial Narration in Greek Art.* Chicago (trans. of *Bild und Mythos: Geschichte der Bilderzählung in der griechischen Kunst.* Munich, 2003).

Giuman, M. (2013). *Archeologia dello sguardo: Fascinazione e baskania nel mondo classico.* Rome.

Glaser, E. (1960). 'Quevedo versus Pérez de Montalván: The *Auto del Polifemo* and the Odyssean Tradition in Golden Age Spain', *Hispanic Review*, 28: 103–20.

Glenn, J. (1971). 'The Polyphemus Folktale and Homer's *Kyklôpeia*', *TAPA* 102: 133–81.

Glenn, J. (1972). 'Virgil's Polyphemus', *G&R* 19: 47–59.

Glenn, J. (1978). 'The Polyphemus Myth: Its Origin and Interpretation', *G&R* 25: 141–55.

Goes, F. J. (2013) (ed.). *The Eye in History.* New Delhi.

Goff, B. L. (1963). *Symbols of Prehistoric Mesopotamia.* New Haven, CT.

Goldhill, S. D. (2007). '*Naked* and *O Brother, Where Art Thou*? The Politics and Poetics of Epic Cinema', in Graziosi and Greenwood (2007), 245–67.

Goldhill, S. D., and Osborne, R. (1994) (eds). *Art and Text in Ancient Greek Culture.* Cambridge.

Goldman, L. R. (1999) (ed.). *The Anthropology of Cannibalism.* Westport, CT.

Gombrich, E. H. (1955). 'Apollonio di Giovanni: A Florentine Cassone Workshop Seen through the Eyes of a Humanist Poet', *JWCI* 18: 16–34.

Gombrich, E. H. (1960). *Art and Illusion: A Study in the Psychology of Pictorial Representation.* London (6th edn, 2002).

Gombrich, E. H. (1985). 'Image and Word in Twentieth-Century Art', *WI* 1: 213–41.

Gomez-Géraud, M.-C. (2001). '"Bocas de fuego": À la découverte des volcans du Nouveau Monde', in Bertrand (2001), 165–76.

González Estévez, E. (2008–9). 'En torno a *La fragua de Vulcano* de Velázquez: Nuevas aportaciones a la interpretación de su significado', *Laboratorio de arte*, 21: 411–26.

Goode, P., and Lancaster, M. (1986) (eds). *The Oxford Companion to Gardens*. Oxford.
Goodey, C. F., and Rose, M. L. (2013). 'Mental States, Bodily Dispositions and Table Manners: A Guide to Reading "Intellectual" Disability from Homer to Late Antiquity', in Laes, Goodey, and Rose (2013), 17–44.
Goody, J. (1982). *Cooking, Cuisine and Class: A Study in Comparative Sociology*. Cambridge.
Gordo Peláez, L. J. (2001). 'Visiones e impresiones de la Villa Belvedere de los Aldobrandini en Frascati', *Anales de Historia del Arte*, 11: 149–76.
Gousset, M.-T. (2002). *Marco Polo: Le Livre des merveilles du monde*. Paris.
Gow, A. S. F. (1952). *Theocritus*. 2nd edn. 2 vols. Cambridge.
Graf, F. (1980). 'Milch, Honig und Wein: Zum Verständnis der Libation im griechischen Ritual', in G. Piccaluga (ed.), *Perennitas: Studi in onore di Angelo Brelich*. Rome, 209–21.
Graf, F. (1999). 'Mythical Production: Aspects of Myth and Technology in Antiquity', in Buxton (1999), 317–28.
Graf, F. (2009). *Apollo*. Abingdon.
Grafton, A., Most, G. W., and Settis, S. (2010) (eds). *The Classical Tradition*. Cambridge, MA.
Graves, R. (1960). *The Greek Myths*. Rev. edn. 2 vols. London.
Gray, E. A. (1982). *Cath Maige Tuired: The Second Battle of Mag Tuired*. Naas.
Graziosi, B. (2002). *Inventing Homer: The Early Reception of Epic*. Cambridge.
Graziosi, B., and Greenwood, E. (2007) (eds). *Homer in the Twentieth Century: Between World Literature and the Western Canon*. Oxford.
Green, C., and Daehner, J. M. (2011). *Modern Antiquity: Picasso, De Chirico, Léger, Picabia*. Los Angeles, CA.
Greenblatt, S. (1991). *Marvelous Possessions: The Wonder of the New World*. Chicago.
Greenwood, E. (2005). '"Still Going On": Temporal Adverbs and the View of the Past in Walcott's Poetry', in *Callaloo*, 28/1: 132–45.
Grethlein, J. (2016). 'Sight and Reflexivity: Theorizing Vision in Greek Vase-Painting', in Squire (2016), 85–106.
Griffin, A. H. F. (1983). 'Unrequited Love: Polyphemus and Galatea in Ovid's *Metamorphoses*', *G&R* 30: 190–7.
Griffin, J. (1977). 'The Epic Cycle and the Uniqueness of Homer', *JHS* 97: 39–53.
Grigorian, N. (2009). *European Symbolism: In Search of Myth (1860–1910)*. Bern.
Grillner, K. (1995). 'Automata, Perspective and Music: Poetic Instruments in the Written Garden of Salomon de Caus.' Master of Architecture diss. Montreal.
Grimal, P. (1984). *Les Jardins romains*. 3rd edn. Paris.
Grimal, P. (1985). *The Dictionary of Classical Mythology*. Oxford (trans. of *Dictionnaire de la mythologie grecque et romaine*. Paris, 1951).
Grimm, W. (1857). 'Die Sage von Polyphem', *Abhandlungen der Königl. Akademie der Wissenschaften zu Berlin, phil.-hist. Klasse*, 1–30 = Grimm, *Kleinere Schriften*, ed. G. Hinrichs. Berlin, 1887, iv. 428–62.
Groom, G. (2001). *Beyond the Easel: Decorative Painting by Bonnard, Vuillard, Denis, and Roussel, 1890–1930*. New Haven, CT.
Groos, G. W. (1981). *The Diary of Baron Waldstein: A Traveller in Elizabethan England*. London.
Guérin, D. (1978) (ed.). *Paul Gauguin: The Writings of a Savage*. New York.
Guerrini, L. (1982) (ed.). *Palazzo Mattei di Giove: Le antichità*. Rome.
Gutzwiller, K. J. (1991). *Theocritus' Pastoral Analogies: The Formation of a Genre*. Madison, WI.
Gutzwiller, K. J. (2006). 'The Herdsman in Greek Thought', in Fantuzzi and Papanghelis (2006), 1–23.

Hackman, O. (1904). *Die Polyphemsage in der Volksüberlieferung.* Helsinki.
Hadler, M. (1977). 'William Baziotes: A Contemporary Poet-Painter', *Arts Magazine*, 51: 102–10.
Hall, E. (2008). *The Return of Ulysses: A Cultural History of Homer's Odyssey.* London.
Hallpike, C. R. (1969). 'Social Hair', *Man*, NS 4: 256–64.
Halperin, D. M. (1983). *Before Pastoral: Theocritus and the Ancient Tradition of Bucolic Poetry.* New Haven, CT.
Hamilton, W. (1772). *Observations on Mount Vesuvius, Mount Etna, and other Volcanos.* London.
Hamilton, W. (1776). *Campi Phlegraei, Observations on the Volcanos of the Two Sicilies.* Naples.
Hanak, M. J. (1988). *Luis de Góngora y Argote: The Fable of Polyphemus and Galatea.* New York.
Hand, J. O., and Wolff, M. (1986). *Early Netherlandish Painting.* Cambridge.
Hansen, M. S. (2013). *In Michelangelo's Mirror: Perino del Vaga, Daniele da Volterra, Pellegrino Tibaldi.* University Park, PA.
Hansen, W. F. (1996). *Phlegon of Tralles' Book of Marvels.* Translation and commentary. Exeter.
Hansen, W. F. (1998) (ed.). *Anthology of Ancient Greek Popular Literature.* Bloomington, IN.
Hansen, W. F. (2002). *Ariadne's Thread: A Guide to International Tales Found in Classical Literature.* Ithaca, NY.
Harari, M. (2014). 'Les Stratégies d'Aristonothos: Boire à la grecque en Étrurie: Nouvelles considérations', in L. Ambrosini and V. Jolivet (eds), *Les Potiers d' Étrurie et leur monde: Contacts, échanges, transferts. Hommages à Mario A. del Chiaro.* Paris, 35–50.
Hard, R. (2015). *Eratosthenes and Hyginus: Constellation Myths, with Aratus's Phaenomena.* Oxford.
Hardwick, L., and Stray, C. (2008) (eds). *A Companion to Classical Receptions.* Oxford.
Harpham, G. G. (1982). *On the Grotesque: Strategies of Contradiction in Art and Literature.* Princeton.
Harrison, J. E. (1882). *Myths of the Odyssey in Art and Literature.* London.
Hartog, F. (2001). *Memories of Odysseus: Frontier Tales from Ancient Greece.* Edinburgh (trans. of *Mémoire d'Ulysse: Récits sur la frontière en Grèce ancienne.* Paris, 1996).
Haspels, C. H. E. (1936). *Attic Black-Figured Lekythoi.* 2 vols. Paris.
Hauck, K. (1977). *Wielands Hort: die sozialgeschichtliche Stellung des Schmiedes in frühen Bildprogrammen und vor dem Religionswechsel.* Stockholm.
Hauptman, J. (2005). *Beyond the Visible: The Art of Odilon Redon.* New York.
Haut, A. (2010). 'Barry and Fuseli: Milton, Exile and Expulsion', in Dunne and Pressly (2010), 95–113.
Hays, G. (2014). 'The Mythographic Tradition after Ovid', in J. F. Miller and C. E. Newlands (eds), *A Handbook to the Reception of Ovid.* Chichester, 129–43.
Hedreen, G. (1996). 'Image, Text, and Story in the Recovery of Helen', *Classical Antiquity*, 15: 152–84.
Heinrich, K. (1986). 'Götter und Halbgötter der Renaissance. Eine Betrachtung am Beispiel der Galatea', in R. Faber and R. Schlesier (eds), *Die Restauration der Götter: Antike Religion und Neo-Paganismus.* Würzburg, 153–82.
Helfenstein, J. (1993). *Meret Oppenheim und der Surrealismus.* Stuttgart.
Helleiner, K. F. (1959). 'Prester John's Letter: A Mediaeval Utopia', *Phoenix*, 13: 47–57.
Hemelrijk, J. M. (2000). 'Three Caeretan Hydriai in Malibu and New York', *Greek Vases in the J. Paul Getty Museum.* Malibu, CA, vi. 87–158.
Henderson, G. E. (2015). *Ugliness: A Cultural History.* London.

Herding, K. (1990). 'Robespierre und die Magie der Zeichen: zum Augensymbol unter der Revolution', in B. Wyss (ed.), *Bildfälle: die Moderne im Zwielicht*. Zurich, 38–54.

Herding, K., and Reichardt, R. (1989). *Die Bildpublizistik der Französichen Revolution*. Frankfurt.

Heringman, N. (2013). *Sciences of Antiquity: Romantic Antiquarianism, Natural History, and Knowledge Work*. Oxford.

Hermary, A. (2006). 'Le Corps colossal et la valeur hiérarchique des tailles dans la littérature et la sculpture grecques archaïques', in F. Prost and J. Wilgaux (eds), *Penser et représenter le corps dans l'Antiquité. Actes du colloque international de Rennes, 1–4 septembre 2004*. Rennes, 115–31.

Hesse, J. (2008). *Der populäre Künstler: Das Beispiel Bernhard Luginbühl*. Bern.

Heubeck, A., and Hoekstra, A. (1989). *A Commentary on Homer's Odyssey*, ii, books IX–XVI. Oxford.

Heyd, M. (1992). 'Note sur le symbolisme d'Odilon Redon: Deux formes de fragmentation corporelle', *Revue de l'Art*, 96: 63–9.

Highet, G. (1949). *The Classical Tradition: Greek and Roman Influences on Western Literature*. Oxford.

Highmore, B. (2011). '"Image-Breaking, God-Making": Paolozzi's Brutalism', *October*, 136: 87–104.

Hills, P. (2007). 'Titian's Fire: Pyrotechnics and Representations in Sixteenth-Century Venice', *Oxford Art Journal*, 30: 187–204.

Hirst, M. (1981). *Sebastiano del Piombo*. Oxford.

Hobbs, R. (1977). *Odilon Redon*. London.

Hobhouse, P., and Taylor, P. (1990) (eds). *The Gardens of Europe*. London.

Hoffner, H. A. (1966). 'A Native Akkadian Cognate to West Semitic **GBN* "Cheese"?', *Journal of the American Oriental Society*, 86: 27–31.

Hofmann, H. (1995). 'Die Geburt Amerikas aus dem Geist der Antike', *International Journal of the Classical Tradition*, 1/4: 15–47.

Hofmann, W. (1987). *Zauber der Medusa: Europäische Manierismen*. Vienna.

Holbek, B. (1987). *Interpretation of Fairy Tales: Danish Folklore in a European Perspective*. Helsinki.

Holland, G. R. (1884). '*De Polyphemo et Galatea*', *Leipziger Studien zur classischen Philologie*, 7: 139–312. Leipzig.

Hollington, M. (2014). 'Of Giants and Grotesques: The Dickensian Grotesque and the Return from Italy', in I. Hervouet-Farrar and M. Véga-Ritter (eds), *The Grotesque in the Fiction of Charles Dickens and Other 19th-Century European Novelists*. Newcastle upon Tyne, 51–62.

Holtsmark, E. B. (1966). 'Poetry as Self-Enlightenment: Theocritus 11', *TAPA* 97: 253–9.

Hopkinson, N. (1994) (ed.). *Studies in the Dionysiaca of Nonnus*. Cambridge.

Hopkinson, N. (2015). *Theocritus, Moschus, Bion*. Edition and translation. Cambridge, MA.

Hopman, M. G. (2012). *Scylla: Myth, Metaphor, Paradox*. Cambridge.

Hordern, J. H. (1999). 'The *Cyclops* of Philoxenus', *CQ* 49: 445–55.

Hornblower, S. (2008). *A Commentary on Thucydides*, iii: books 5.25–8.109. Oxford.

Hornblower, S., Spawforth, A., and Eidinow, E. (2012) (eds). *The Oxford Classical Dictionary*. 4th edn. Oxford.

Hornung, E. (1982). *Conceptions of God in Ancient Egypt: The One and the Many*. Ithaca, NY (trans. of *Der Eine und die Vielen*. Darmstadt, 1971).

Horstmann, A. E.-A. (1976). *Ironie und Humor bei Theokrit* (Beiträge zur klassischen Philologie 67). Meisenheim am Glan.

Hugo, V. (1913). *Toute la lyre*. Paris.
Hugo, V. (1968). *Cromwell*. Text, with introduction by A. Ubersfeld. Paris.
Hugo, V. (1982). *Les Misérables*, trans. N. Denny. London.
Hugo, V. (2002). *L'Homme qui rit*, ed. M. Roman. Paris.
Hugo, V. (2004). *Notre-Dame de Paris*, trans. J. Sturrock. Repr. with additions fron 1978 edn. London.
Hultén, K. G. V. P. (1993). *Le Cyclop, Milly-la-Forêt*. Evry.
Hultén, K. G. V. P. (1995). *Niki de Saint Phalle*. 2nd edn. Bonn.
Hultén, K. G. V. P. (1996). 'The Man and his Work', in *Museum Jean Tinguely: The Collection*. Basel, 34–76.
Hunt, J. D. (1986). *Garden and Grove: The Italian Renaissance Garden in the English Imagination 1600–1750*. London.
Hunter, R. L. (1999). *Theocritus: A Selection: Idylls 1, 3, 4, 6, 7, 10, 11 and 13*. Cambridge.
Hunter, R. L. (2009). *Critical Moments in Classical Literature: Studies in the Ancient View of Literature and its Uses*. Cambridge.
Hurwit, J. M. (2015). *Artists and Signatures in Ancient Greece*. Cambridge.
Husband, T. (1980). *The Wild Man: Medieval Myth and Symbolism*. New York.
Hutchinson, G. O. (1988). *Hellenistic Poetry*. Oxford.
Huysmans, J.-K. (1883). *L'Art moderne*. Paris.
Ingram, J. E. (2001) (ed.). *John Evelyn: Elysium Britannicum, or the Royal Gardens*. Philadelphia, PA.
Irwin, D. (1979). *John Flaxman 1755–1826, Sculptor Illustrator Designer*. London.
Isaac, B. (2004). *The Invention of Racism in Classical Antiquity*. Princeton.
Izzet, V. (2004). 'Purloined Letters: The Aristonothos Inscription and Krater', in K. Lomas (ed.), *Greek Identity in the Western Mediterranean*. Leiden, 191–210.
Jachec, N. (1993). 'Myth and the Audience: The Individual, the Collective, and the Problem of Mass Communication by the Early 1950s', in D. Thistlewood (ed.), *American Abstract Expressionism*. Liverpool, 129–45.
Jahn, O. (1855). 'Über den Aberglauben des bösen Blickes bei den Alten', *Berichte über die Verhandlungen der Königlich Sächsischen Gesellschaft der Wissenschaften zu Leipzig, Philologisch-Historische Classe*, 7: 28–110.
Jane, C. (1930). *Select Documents Illustrating the Four Voyages of Columbus*. London.
Jay, M. (1993). *Downcast Eyes: The Denigration of Vision in Twentieth-Century French Thought*. Berkeley, CA.
Jeanneret, M. (2001). *Perpetual Motion: Transforming Shapes in the Renaissance from da Vinci to Montaigne*. Baltimore, MD (trans. of *Perpetuum mobile: Métamorphoses des corps et des oeuvres, de Vinci à Montaigne*. Paris, 1997; 2nd edn, Geneva, 2016).
Jenkins, I. D. (1995). Review of Goldhill and Osborne (1994), in *JHS* 115: 223–5.
Jenkins, I. D., and Sloan, K. (1996) (eds). *Vases and Volcanoes: Sir William Hamilton and his Collection*. London.
Johnston, S. I. (1999). *Restless Dead: Encounters between the Living and the Dead in Ancient Greece*. Berkeley, CA.
Jones, P. V. (1985). Review of Wolf and Wolf (1983), in *Classical Review*, 35/1: 177.
Jones, R., and Penny, N. (1983). *Raphael*. New Haven, CT.
Jones, T. S., and Sprunger, D. A. (2002) (eds). *Marvels, Monsters, and Miracles: Studies in the Medieval and Early Modern Imaginations*. Kalamazoo, MI.
Jouffroy, A., (1990). 'Max Ernst, Sculptor', in McLeod and Findlay (1990); no pagination.
Joyce, J. (1984). *Ulysses*, ed. H. W. Gabler. 3 vols. New York.
Kakridis, J. T. (1986–7) (ed.). *Ελληνική Μυθολογία*. 5 vols. Athens.

Kalantzis, G. C., Tsiamis, C. B., and Poulakou-Rebelakou, E. L. (2013). 'Cyclopia: From Greek Antiquity to Medical Genetics', *Italian Journal of Anatomy and Embryology*, 118/3: 256–62.

Kaldellis, A. (2013). *Ethnography after Antiquity: Foreign Lands and Peoples in Byzantine Literature*. Philadelphia, PA.

Kang, M. (2011). *Sublime Dreams of Living Machines: The Automaton in the European Imagination*. Cambridge, MA.

Kant, I. (1923). 'Reflexionen zur Anthropologie', in Kant, *Gesammelte Schriften*, xv. 2.1. Berlin.

Kappler, C.-C. (1999). *Monstres, démons et merveilles à la fin du Moyen Âge*. Rev. edn. Paris.

Kareem, S. T. (2008). 'Forging Figures of Invention in Eighteenth-Century Britain', in M. E. Novak (ed.), *The Age of Projects*. Toronto, 344–69.

Kareem, S. T. (2014). *Eighteenth-Century Fiction and the Reinvention of Wonder*. Oxford.

Kassel, R. (1991). 'Bemerkungen zum Kyklops des Euripides', in Kassel, *Kleine Schriften*, ed. H.-G. Nesselrath. Berlin, 191–8.

Kazhdan, A. P. (1991) (ed.). *The Oxford Dictionary of Byzantium*. 3 vols. Oxford.

Keller, J.-P. (1992). *Tinguely et le mystère de la roue manquante*. Carouge.

Kermode, J. F. (1952) (ed.). *English Pastoral Poetry: From the Beginnings to Marvell*. London.

Kershaw, K. (2000). *The One-Eyed God: Odin and the (Indo-)Germanic Männerbünde*. Washington.

Kershner, R. B. (2014). 'Intertextuality', in Latham (2014), 171–83.

Kibler, W. W. (2004). *Chrétien de Troyes: Arthurian Romances*. London.

Kiefer, M. (2000). *'Michelangelo riformato': Pellegrino Tibaldi in Bologna. Die Johanneskapelle in San Giacomo Maggiore und die Odysseus-Säle im Palazzo Poggi*. Hildesheim.

Kiernan, M. (2000) (ed.). *The Oxford Francis Bacon*, iv. *The Advancement of Learning*. Oxford.

Kilinski, K. (2013). *Greek Myth and Western Art: The Presence of the Past*. Cambridge.

Kindstedt, P. S. (2012). *Cheese and Culture: A History of Cheese and its Place in Western Civilization*. White River Junction, VT.

Kingsley, P. (1995). *Ancient Philosophy, Mystery, and Magic: Empedocles and Pythagorean Tradition*. Oxford.

Kinkead, D. T. (1970). 'An Iconographic Note on Raphael's *Galatea*', *JWCI* 33: 313–15.

Kiple, K. F., and Ornelas, K. C. (2000) (eds). *The Cambridge World History of Food*. 2 vols. Cambridge.

Kircher, A. (1664). *Mundus subterraneus, in XII libros digestus*. Amsterdam.

Kirk, G. S. (1970). *Myth: Its Meaning and Functions in Ancient and Other Cultures*. Cambridge.

Kirk, G. S. (1974). *The Nature of Greek Myths*. Harmondsworth.

Knox, M. (1979). 'Polyphemos and his Near Eastern Relations', *JHS* 99: 164–5.

Köhnken, A. (1996). 'Theokrits Polyphemgedichte', in M. A. Harder, R. F. Regtuit, and G. C. Wakker (eds), *Hellenistica Groningana 2: Theocritus*. Groningen, 171–86.

Konaris, M. D. (2016). *The Greek Gods in Modern Scholarship: Interpretation and Belief in Nineteenth and Early Twentieth Century Germany and Britain*. Oxford.

Konnertz, W. (1984). *Eduardo Paolozzi*. Cologne.

Konstan, D. (1990). 'An Anthropology of Euripides' *Kyklōps*', in J. J. Winkler and F. I. Zeitlin (eds), *Nothing to Do with Dionysos? Athenian Drama in its Social Context*. Princeton, 207–27 (rev. from earlier version in *Ramus*, 10 (1981), 87–103).

Korshak, Y. (1987). *Frontal Faces in Attic Vase Painting of the Archaic Period.* Chicago.

Kostopoulou, V. (2009). 'Philostratus' *Imagines* 2.18: Words and Images', *GRBS* 49: 81–100.

Kotková, O. (2006). 'A New Investigation of the *Venus and Cupid in Vulcan's Forge* by Maerten van Heemskerck (National Gallery, Prague)', in H. Verougstraete and J. Couvert (eds), *La Peinture ancienne et ses procédés: Copies, répliques, pastiches.* Leuven, 189–95.

Krauskopf, I. (2006). 'The Grave and Beyond in Etruscan Religion', in N. T. de Grummond and E. Simon (eds), *The Religion of the Etruscans.* Austin, TX, 66–89.

Kretschmer, M. T. (2016). 'L'*Ovidius moralizatus* de Pierre Bersuire: Essai de mise au point', *Interfaces: A Journal of Medieval European Literatures*, 3: 221–44.

Krichenbauer, A. (1877). *Die Irrfahrt des Odysseus als eine Umschiffung Afrikas.* Berlin.

Kunisch, N. (1990). 'Die Augen der Augenschalen', *Antike Kunst*, 33: 20–7.

Labanyi, J. (2010). *Spanish Literature: A Very Short Introduction.* Oxford.

Lacambre, G. (1999). *Gustave Moreau: Between Epic and Dream.* Paris and Chicago.

Lacau St-Guily, A. (1995). 'L'Oeil dans l'oeuvre d'Odilon Redon', *L'Oeil*, 468: 58–65.

Ladmiral, J.-R. (2003). 'L'*Odyssée* comme paradigme philosophique—dalla "dialettica dell'illuminismo" alla dialettica dei chiaroscuri dell'esistenza', in Nicosia (2003), 291–321.

Laes, C., Goodey, C. F., and Rose, M. L. (2013) (eds). *Disabilities in Roman Antiquity: Disparate Bodies. A Capite ad Calcem.* Leiden.

Lagerlöf, M. R. (1990). *Ideal Landscape: Annibale Carracci, Nicolas Poussin and Claude Lorrain.* New Haven, CT.

Laird, W. R. (2017). 'Hero of Alexandria and Renaissance Mechanics', in L. B. Cormack, S. A. Walton, and J. A. Shuster (eds), *Mathematical Practitioners and the Transformation of Natural Knowledge in Early Modern Europe.* Cham, 149–65.

Lallot, J. (1991). ''Ἐτυμολογία: L'Étymologie en Grèce ancienne d'Homère aux grammairiens alexandrins', in J.-P. Chambon and G. Lüdi (eds), *Discours étymologiques.* Tübingen, 135–48.

Lammel, G. (1992) (ed.). *Exzellenz lassen bitten: Erinnerungen an Adolf Menzel.* Leipzig.

Landis, J. (2011). *Monsters in the Movies: 100 Years of Cinematic Nightmares.* London.

Landucci Gattinoni, F. (1997). *Duride di Samo.* Rome.

Lane Fox, R. (2008). *Travelling Heroes: Greeks and their Myths in the Epic Age of Homer.* London.

Larson, B. J. (2005). *The Dark Side of Nature: Science, Society, and the Fantastic in the Work of Odilon Redon.* University Park, PA.

Lascaratos, J. (1999). '"Eyes" on the Thrones: Imperial Ophthalmologic Nicknames', *Survey of Ophthalmology*, 44: 73–8.

Lascaratos, J., Lascaratos, G., and Kalantzis, G. (2004). 'The Ophthalmic Wound of Philip II of Macedonia (360–336 BCE)', *Survey of Opthalmology*, 49: 256–61.

Lascault, G. (1973). *Le Monstre dans l'art occidental: Un problème esthétique.* Paris.

Lassels, R. (1670). *The Voyage of Italy, or A Compleat Journey through Italy in Two Parts.* Paris.

Latham, S. (2014) (ed.). *The Cambridge Companion to Ulysses.* Cambridge.

Lattimore, R. (1965). *The Odyssey of Homer.* Translation. New York.

Lavagne, H. (1988). *Operosa antra: Recherches sur la grotte à Rome de Sylla à Hadrien.* Rome.

Lazzaro, C. (1990). *The Italian Renaissance Garden.* New Haven, CT.

Lazzaro, C. (1991). 'The Visual Language of Gender in Sixteenth-Century Garden Sculpture', in Migiel and Schiesari (1991), 71–113.

Leach, E. W. (1992). 'Polyphemus in a Landscape: Traditions of Pastoral Courtship', in J. D. Hunt (ed.), *The Pastoral Landscape.* Washington, 63–87.

Leal Bonmati, M. del R. (2011). *José de Cañizares: Acis y Galatea*. Madrid.
Le Bot, M. (1968). *Francis Picabia et la crise des valeurs figuratives, 1900–1925*. Paris.
Lecouteux, C. (1999). *Les Monstres dans la pensée médiévale européenne*. 3rd edn. Paris.
Lee, S. (2015). 'The Disruption of Mythological Space', *Object*, 17: 33–53.
Leeming, D. (2013). *Medusa in the Mirror of Time*. London.
Lefkowitz, J. B. (2008). 'Ugliness and Value in the *Life of Aesop*', in I. Sluiter and R. M. Rosen (eds), *Kakos: Badness and Anti-Value in Classical Antiquity*. Leiden, 59–81.
Legge, E. M. (1989). *Max Ernst: The Psychoanalytic Sources*. Ann Arbor, MI.
Lehrer, M. E. (1989). *Classical Myth and the 'Polifemo' of Góngora*. Potomac, MD.
Lemmi, C. W. (1933). *The Classic Deities in Bacon: A Study in Mythological Symbolism*. Baltimore, MD.
Lenfant, D. (1999). 'Monsters in Greek Ethnography and Society in the Fifth and Fourth Centuries *BCE*', in Buxton (1999), 197–214.
Lenfant, D. (2004). *Ctésias de Cnide: La Perse, l'Inde, autres fragments*. Paris.
Lentzsch, F., et al. (2005). *Fuseli: The Wild Swiss*. Zurich.
Leroi, A. M. (2003). *Mutants: On Genetic Variety and the Human Body*. New York.
Leroux, V. (2004). 'La Représentation de l'Etna dans l'épopée latine', in Foulon (2004), 57–78.
Lesky, A. (1960). 'Homer', *Anzeiger für die Altertumswissenschaft*, 13: 1–22.
Lessing, E. (1966). *The Voyages of Ulysses*. London.
Létoublon, F. (2010). 'To See or Not to See: Blind People and Blindness in Ancient Greek Myths', in Christopoulos, Karakantza, and Levaniouk (2010), 167–80.
Lévi-Strauss, C. (1970). *Introduction to a Science of Mythology*, i. *The Raw and the Cooked*. London (trans. of *Le Cru et le cuit*. Paris, 1964).
Lévi-Strauss, C. (1978). *Introduction to a Science of Mythology*, iii. *The Origin of Table Manners*. London (trans. of *L'Origine des manières de table*. Paris, 1968).
Levy, T. (2013) (ed.). *Meret Oppenheim: Gedankenspiegel. Mirrors of the Mind*. Bielefeld.
Lewis, C. S. (1982). 'On Science Fiction', in Lewis, *Of This and Other Worlds*. London, 80–96.
Lewis, G. (1974). *The Book of Dede Korkut*. Translation. London.
Lewis, R. (2010). 'Francis Bacon, Allegory and the Uses of Myth', *Review of English Studies*, 61: 360–89.
Lewis-Williams, D. (2002). *The Mind in the Cave: Consciousness and the Origins of Art*. London.
Lexicon Iconographicum Mythologiae Classicae (1981–2009). Zurich and Düsseldorf.
Lightfoot, J. L. (2009) (ed.). *Hellenistic Collection: Philitas, Alexander of Aetolia, Hermesianax, Euphorion, Parthenius*. Cambridge, MA.
Ling, R. (1991). *Roman Painting*. Cambridge.
Linnebach, A. (2005) (ed.). *Der Münchhausen-Autor Rudolf Erich Raspe: Wissenschaft—Kunst—Abenteuer*. Kassel.
Lissarrague, F. (1990). *The Aesthetics of the Greek Banquet: Images of Wine and Ritual*. Princeton (trans. of *Un Flot d'images: Une esthétique du banquet grec*. Paris, 1987).
Livrea, E. (2004). 'Un epigramma di Posidippo e il *Cyclops* di Filosseno di Cithera', *ZPE* 146: 41–6.
Llewellyn-Jones, L. (2013). *King and Court in Ancient Persia 559 to 331 BCE*. Edinburgh.
Llinares, J. B. (1996). 'La construcción del tipo del 'salvaje' en Homero', *Ludus vitalis*, 4/6: 101–26.
Lock, F. P. (2008). *Edmund Burke*, i. *1730–1784*. Oxford.
Longo, O. (1987). 'Fra uomini e leoni: La dieta del Ciclope', in Longo, *La storia la terra gli uomini: Saggi sulla civiltà greca*. Venice, 63–77.

Lorandi, M. (1996). *Il mito di Ulisse nella pittura a fresco del Cinquecento italiano*. Milan.
Lo Schiavo, R. (2003). *La teoria dell' origine siciliana dell'Odissea: Il cieco, la giovinetta ed il malconsiglio*. Palermo.
Louden, B. (2011). *Homer's Odyssey and the Near East*. Cambridge.
Loupiac, A. (1998). *La Poétique des éléments dans la Pharsale de Lucain*. Brussels.
Lowenstam, S. (1992). 'The Uses of Vase-Depictions in Homeric Studies', *TAPA* 122: 165–98.
Lowenstam, S. (1997). 'Talking Vases: The Relationship between the Homeric Poems and Archaic Representations of Epic Myth', *TAPA* 127: 21–76.
McAvoy, L. H., and Walters, T. (2002) (eds). *Consuming Narratives: Gender and Monstrous Appetite in the Middle Ages and the Renaissance*. Cardiff.
McConnell, J. (2013). *Black Odysseys: The Homeric Odyssey in the African Diaspora since 1939*. Oxford.
McDonald, M. (2001). *Sing Sorrow: Classics, History, and Heroines in Opera*. Westport, CT.
Macdougall, E. B. (1978) (ed.). *Fons Sapientiae: Renaissance Garden Fountains*. Washington.
Macdougall, E. B. (1987) (ed.). *Ancient Roman Villa Gardens*. Washington.
Macdougall, E. B., and Jashemski, W. F. (1981) (eds). *Ancient Roman Gardens*. Washington.
McKnight, K. D. (1924). 'The Ulysses Panels by Piero di Cosimo at Vassar College', *Art Bulletin*, 6/4: 99–102.
McLeod, F., and Findlay, J. (1990) (eds). *Max Ernst: The Sculpture*. Edinburgh.
McMahon, A. P. (1956). *Leonardo da Vinci: Treatise on Painting (Codex Urbinas Latinus 1270)*. 2 vols. Princeton.
Malkin, I. (1998). *The Returns of Odysseus: Colonization and Ethnicity*. Berkeley, CA.
Malten, L. (1961). *Die Sprache des menschlichen Antlitzes im frühen Griechentum*. Berlin.
Manca, J. (1992). *The Art of Ercole de' Roberti*. Cambridge.
Mandzuka, Z. (2013). *Demystifying the Odyssey*. Bloomington, IN.
Mangiafesta, M. (1997). 'Fortuna del mito di Polifemo nelle collezioni di antichità tra XV e XVII secolo', *Bolletino d'arte*, 82/99: 13–60.
Mangidis, T. (2003). *Antiphanes' Mythentravestien*. Frankfurt.
Mannhardt, W. (1905). *Wald- und Feldkulte*, ii. *Antike Wald- und Feldkulte aus nordeuropäischer Überlieferung erläutert*. 2nd edn. Berlin.
Manuwald, B. (1990). 'Der Kyklop als Dichter. Bemerkungen zu Theokrit, *Eid.* 11', in P. Steinmetz (ed.), *Beiträge zur hellenistischen Literatur und ihrer Rezeption in Rom* (= Palingenesia 28). Stuttgart, 77–91.
March, J. (1998). *Cassell Dictionary of Classical Mythology*. London.
Margarido, A., and Germaix-Wasserman, F. (1972). 'Du mythe et de la pratique du forgeron en Afrique noire', *Diogène*, 78: 91–122.
Marold, E. (1973). 'Die Gestalt des Schmiedes in der Volkssage', in L. Röhrich (ed.), *Probleme der Sagenforschung*. Freiburg im Breisgau, 100–11.
Martelli, M. (1987) (ed.). *La ceramica degli Etruschi: La pittura vascolare*. Novara.
Martens, D. (1992). *Une esthétique de la transgression: Le Vase grec de la fin de l'époque géométrique au début de l'époque classique*. Brussels.
Martin, J. R. (1965). *The Farnese Gallery*. Princeton.
Martín Sánchez, M. (2002). *Seres míticos y personajes fantásticos españoles*. Madrid.
Marx, K. (1975). *Economic and Philosophical Manuscripts of 1844*, in K. Marx and F. Engels, *Collected Works*, iii. London.
Masson, G. (2011). *Italian Gardens*. New edn. Woodbridge.
Mastromarco, G. (1998). 'La degradazione del mostro: La maschera del Ciclope nella commedia e nel dramma satiresco del quinto secolo a.C.', in A. M. Belardinelli, O. Imperio,

G. Mastromarco, M. Pellegrino, and P. Totaro (eds), *Tessere. Frammenti della commedia greca: Studi e commenti.* Bari, 9–42.

Mastronarde, D. J. (1994). *Euripides: Phoenissae.* Cambridge.

Mathieu, P.-L. (1977). *Gustave Moreau: Complete Edition of the Finished Paintings, Watercolours and Drawings.* Oxford (trans. of *Gustave Moreau: sa vie, son oeuvre.* Fribourg, 1976).

Mathieu, P.-L. (1978). 'La Bibliothèque de Gustave Moreau', *Gazette des Beaux-Arts* 91, avril: 155–62.

Mattievich, E. (2010). *Journey to the Mythological Inferno: America's Discovery by the Ancient Greeks.* Denver, CO (trans. of *Viagem ao inferno mitológico.* Rio de Janeiro, 1992).

Matzig, R. B. (1949). *Odysseus: Studie zu antiken Stoffen in der modernen Literatur, besonders im Drama.* St Gallen.

Mauduit, C. (2006). *La Sauvagerie dans la poésie grecque d'Homère à Eschyle.* Paris.

Mayor, A. (2011). *The First Fossil Hunters: Dinosaurs, Mammoths, and Myth in Greek and Roman Times.* 2nd edn. Princeton.

Mazur-Contamine, H. E. C. (1984). 'Cyclopen in de Franse kunst: Odilon Redon en de traditie', *Hermeneus*, 56/2: 44–53.

Meeker, M. E. (1992). 'The Dede Korkut Ethic', *International Journal of Middle East Studies*, 24: 395–417.

Mérot, A. (1990). *Nicolas Poussin.* New York.

Merry, W. W., and Riddell, J. (1886). *Homer's Odyssey*, i. *Books I–XII.* 2nd edn. Oxford.

Mertz, H. (1964). *The Wine Dark Sea: Homer's Heroic Epic of the North Atlantic.* Chicago.

Metzger, H. (1988). 'Une nouvelle approche de l'image', in *Πρακτικά του XII Διεθνούς Συνεδρίου Κλασικής Ἀρχαιολογίας, Αθήνα, 4–10 Σεπτεμβρίου 1983*, ii. Athens, 146–51.

Meuli, K. (1976). *Gesammelte Schriften*, ii. Basel.

Michelakis, P. (2013). 'Homer in Silent Cinema', in P. Michelakis and M. Wyke (eds), *The Ancient World in Silent Cinema.* Cambridge, 145–65.

Michelakis, P (2016). 'The Reception of Homer in Silent Film', in A. Efstathiou and I. Karamanou (eds), *Homeric Receptions Across Generic and Cultural Contexts.* Berlin, 393–404.

Micó, J. M. (2015). *Para entender a Góngora.* Barcelona.

Miernowski, J. (2014) (ed.). *Le Sublime et le grotesque.* Geneva.

Migiel, M., and Schiesari, J. (1991) (eds). *Refiguring Woman: Perspectives on Gender and the Italian Renaissance.* Ithaca, NY.

Mignosi Tantillo, A. (1972). 'Restauri alla Farnesina', *Bolletino d'arte*, 57: 33–43.

Mignot, C. (1988). 'Fontainebleau revisité: La Galerie d'Ulysse', *Revue de l'Art*, 82: 9–18.

Miles, G. (2013). 'Genres of Painting and Genres of Text in the *Imagines* of Philostratus', in M. Borg and G. Miles (eds), *Approaches to Genre in the Ancient World.* Newcastle upon Tyne, 123–41.

Miller, N. (1982). *Heavenly Caves: Reflections on the Garden Grotto.* London.

Mineur, W. H. (1984). 'De Cyclopen in de antieke literatuur: Kleine en-cycloop-edie', *Hermeneus*, 56/2: 2–9.

Mirollo, J. V. (1963). *The Poet of the Marvelous: Giambattista Marino.* New York.

Mitchell, A. G. (2009). *Greek Vase-Painting and the Origins of Visual Humour.* Cambridge.

Mitter, P. (2013). *Much Maligned Monsters: A History of European Reactions to Indian Art.* Rev. edn. New Delhi.

Mittman, A. S., and Dendle, P. J. (2012) (eds). *The Ashgate Research Companion to Monsters and the Monstrous.* Farnham.

Moffit, J. F. (1983). 'Velázquez's "Forge of Vulcan": The Cuckold, the Poets, and the Painter', *Pantheon*, 41: 322–6.

Moltesen, M., and Weber-Lehmann, C. (1991). *Catalogue of the Copies of Etruscan Tomb Paintings in the Ny Carlsberg Glyptotek*. Copenhagen.

Mommsen, H. (1982). 'Irrfahrten des Odysseus: Zu dem Fragment Tübingen S./10 1507', in B. von Freytag, D. Mannsperger, and F. Prayon (eds), *Praestant Interna: Festschrift für Ulrich Hausmann*. Tübingen, 205–12.

Mondi, R. (1983). 'The Homeric Cyclopes: Folktale, Tradition, and Theme', *TAPA* 113: 17–38.

Montagu, B. (1825). *The Works of Francis Bacon*, i. London.

Montaigne, M. de (1992). *Journal de voyage de Michel de Montaigne*, ed. F. Rigolot. Paris.

Montanari, F. (1998). 'Lettura dell' eroe Odisseo: La guerra e il ritorno, la lotta e la riconquista', in Boitani and Ambrosini (1998), 57–76.

Montiglio, S. (2011). *From Villain to Hero: Odysseus in Ancient Thought*. Ann Arbor, MI.

Montón Subías, S. (1990). 'Galateia', *LIMC* v.1: 1000–5.

Moog-Grünewald, M. (2010) (ed.). *The Reception of Myth and Mythology* (*Brill's New Pauly Supplements*, 4). Leiden.

Moreau, G. (1984). *L'Assembleur de rêves: Écrits complets de Gustave Moreau*, ed. P.-L. Mathieu. Fontfroide.

Moreau, G. (2002). *Écrits sur l'art*, ed. P. Cooke. 2 vols. Fontfroide.

Morel, P. (1997). *Les Grotesques: Les Figures de l'imaginaire dans la peinture italienne de la fin de la Renaissance*. Paris.

Morel, P. (1998). *Les Grottes maniéristes en Italie au XVIe siècle*. Paris.

Moret, J.-M. (1975). *L'Ilioupersis dans la céramique italiote: Les Mythes et leur expression figurée au IVe siècle*. Rome.

Moret, J.-M. (1984). *Oedipe, la Sphinx et les Thébains: Essai de mythologie iconographique*. 2 vols. Rome.

Morgan, L. (2007). *Nature as Model: Salomon de Caus and Early Seventeenth-Century Landscape Design*. Philadelphia, PA.

Morgan, L. (2011). 'The Monster in the Garden: The Grotesque, the Gigantic, and the Monstrous in Renaissance Landscape Design', *Studies in the History of Gardens and Designed Landscapes: An International Quarterly*, 31: 167–80.

Morgan, L. (2016). *The Monster in the Garden: The Grotesque and the Gigantic in Renaissance Landscape Design*. Philadelphia, PA.

Mori, A. (2017). 'Archives, Innovation, and the Neomorphic Cyclops', *Aetia* (online), 7/1, https://journals.openedition.org/aitia/1696 (accessed 4 July 2018).

Morolli, G., et al. (1993). *Il gigante degli Orti Oricellari*. Rome.

Moseley, C. W. R. D. (1983). *The Travels of Sir John Mandeville*. London.

Most, G. W. (1989). 'The Structure and Function of Odysseus' *Apologoi*', *TAPA* 119: 15–30.

Müller, D. (2015). *Jean Tinguely: Motor der Kunst*. Basel.

Mulryan, J., and Brown, S. (2006). *Natale Conti's Mythologiae*. 2 vols. Tempe, AZ.

Mund-Dopchie, M. (2001). 'Les Volcans islandais dans les textes géographiques de la Renaissance: Mythes et réalités', in Bertrand (2001), 131–64.

Mundy, C. S. (1956). 'Polyphemus and Tepegöz', *Bulletin of the School of Oriental and African Studies*, 18: 279–302.

Murray, A. T. (1919). *Homer: The Odyssey*. Edition and translation. London (rev. 2nd edn, 1995).

Murray, C. A. (2016) (ed.). *Diversity of Sacrifice: Form and Function of Sacrificial Practices in the Ancient World and Beyond*. Albany, NY.

Murray, O. (1988–9). 'Omero e l'etnografia', *Kokalos*, 34/35: 1–17.

Murray, O. (1990) (ed.). *Sympotica: A Symposium on the Symposion*. Oxford.
Myrone, M. (2001). *Henry Fuseli*. London.
Myrone, M. (2005). *Bodybuilding: Reforming Masculinities in British Art 1750–1810*. New Haven, CT.
Nagle, B. R. (1988). 'A Trio of Love-Triangles in Ovid's *Metamorphoses*', *Arethusa*, 21/1: 75–98.
Naumann, H.-P. (1979). 'Das Polyphem-Abenteuer in der altnordischen Sagaliteratur', *Schweizerisches Archiv für Volkskunde*, 75: 173–89.
Nebenzahl, K. (1990). *Atlas of Columbus and the Great Discoveries*. Chicago.
Nelson, L. G. (1976). 'The Rendering of Landscape in Greek and South Italian Vase Painting'. Ph.D. thesis. New York.
Neumann, E. (1959). *The Archetypal World of Henry Moore*. London.
Newton, R. M. (1983). 'Poor Polyphemus: Emotional Ambivalence in *Odyssey* 9 and 17', *Classical World*, 76: 137–42.
Nicosia, S. (2003) (ed.). *Ulisse nel tempo: La metafora infinita*. Venice.
Niese, B. (1882). *Die Entwicklung der homerischen Poesie*. Berlin.
Nieto Hernández, P. (2000). 'Back in the Cave of the Cyclops', *American Journal of Philology*, 121: 345–66.
Nifadopoulos, C. (2003) (ed.). *Etymologia: Studies in Ancient Etymology*. Münster.
Nilsson, M. P. (1967). *Geschichte der griechischen Religion*, vol. i. 3rd edn. Munich.
Noce, V. (2011). *Odilon Redon, dans l'oeil de Darwin*. Paris.
Norris, M. (2006). 'Fact, Fiction, and Anti-Semitism in the "Cyclops" Episode of Joyce's *Ulysses*', *Journal of Narrative Theory*, 36/2: 163–89.
Nutting, H. C. (1922). '*Oculos effodere*', *CP* 17: 313–18.
Nyrop, K. (1880–2). 'Sagnet om Odysseus og Polyphem', *Nordisk Tidsskrift for Filologi*, 5: 216–55.
Obregón, M. (1971). *Ulysses Airborne*. New York.
O'Brien, F.-J. (1977). *The Fantastic Tales of Fitz-James O'Brien*, ed. M. Hayes. London.
O'Flaherty, W. D. (1973). *Asceticism and Eroticism in the Mythology of Siva*. London.
Ogden, D. (2013). *Drakōn: Dragon Myth and Serpent Cult in the Greek and Roman Worlds*. Oxford.
OKell, E. R. (2013). 'The Look of Harryhausen's Cyclops: Human vs Monster in the Eye of the Beholder', in S. Green and P. Goodman (eds), *New Voices in Classical Reception Studies Conference Proceedings*, 1: 42–63.
O'Malley, T., and Wolschke-Bulmahn, J. (1998) (eds). *John Evelyn's 'Elysium Britannicum' and European Gardening*. Washington.
O'Meally, R. G. (2007). *Romare Bearden: A Black Odyssey*. New York.
Oppermann, H. (1925). 'Herophilos bei Kallimachos', *Hermes*, 60: 14–32.
Orchard, A. (2003). *Pride and Prodigies: Studies in the Monsters of the Beowulf-manuscript*. Rev. edn. Toronto.
Osborne, R. (1998). *Archaic and Classical Greek Art*. Oxford.
Osterwald, K. W. (1853). *Homerische Forschungen*, i. Halle.
O'Sullivan, J. N. (1987). 'Observations on the *Kyklōpeia*', *Symbolae Osloenses*, 62: 5–24.
O'Sullivan, P. (2012). 'Dionysos, Polyphemos, and the Idea of Sicily in Euripides' *Cyclops*', in D. Rosenbloom and J. Davidson (eds), *Greek Drama IV: Texts, Contexts, Performance*. Oxford, 169–89.
O'Sullivan, P., and Collard, C. (2013). *Euripides: Cyclops and Major Fragments of Greek Satyric Drama*. Oxford.
Ott, U. (1969). *Die Kunst des Gegensatzes in Theokrits Hirtengedichten* (= *Spudasmata* 22). Hildesheim.

Owen, D. D. R. (2003). *The Wandering Giant in Literature: From Polyphemus to Papageno.* East Linton.
Oyler, E. (2008). 'The *Nue* and Other Monsters in *Heike monogatari*', *Harvard Journal of Asiatic Studies*, 68/2: 1–32.
Pabón, J. M. (2007). *Homero: Odisea.* Translation into Spanish. Madrid.
Paetz, B. (1970). *Kirke und Odysseus: Überlieferung und Deutung von Homer bis Calderón.* Berlin.
Paganelli, L. (1979). *Echi storico-politici nel 'Ciclope' euripideo.* Padua.
Pagden, A. (1982). *The Fall of Natural Man: The American Indian and the Origins of Comparative Ethnology.* Cambridge.
Page, D. L. (1955). *The Homeric Odyssey.* Oxford.
Paglia, C. (1997). 'Homer on Film: A Voyage through *The Odyssey, Ulysses, Helen of Troy,* and *Contempt*', *Arion*, 3rd ser., 5: 166–97.
Paladilhe, J., and Pierre, J. (1972). *Gustave Moreau.* London.
Palmieri, V. (1988) (ed.). *Herennius Philo: De diversis verborum significationibus.* Naples.
Pàmias, J. (2004). *Eratòsthenes de Cirene: Catasterismes.* Edition and commentary in Catalan. Barcelona.
Pàmias, J., and Geus, K. (2007). *Eratosthenes: Sternsagen (Catasterismi).* Oberhaid.
Pancorbo, L. (2008). *El banquete humano: Una historia cultural del canibalismo.* Madrid.
Paradis, J. G. (2007) (ed.). *Samuel Butler, Victorian against the Grain: A Critical Overview.* Toronto.
Paré, A. (1982). *On Monsters and Marvels.* Chicago (trans. of *Des monstres et prodiges*, ed. J. F. Malgaigne. Paris, 1840).
Parker, A. A. (1977). *Luis de Góngora: 'Polyphemus and Galatea': A Study in the Interpretation of a Baroque Poem.* With verse translation by Gilbert F. Cunningham. Edinburgh.
Paschalis, M. (1997). *Vergil's Aeneid: Semantic Relations and Proper Names.* Oxford.
Paschalis, M (2008). 'Tityrus and Galatea (Virgil, *Eclogue* 1): An Expected Relationship', *Dictynna*, 5, <http://dictynna.revues.org/401> (accessed 11 October 2016).
Pascoli, G. (2010). *Last Voyage: Selected Poems*, trans. D. Brown, R. Jackson, and S. Thomas. Pasadena, CA.
Passeri, G. (1772). *Vite de' pittori scultori ed architetti che anno lavorato in Roma morti dal 1641 fino al 1673.* Rome.
Passerini, L. (1854). *Degli Orti Oricellari: Memorie storiche.* Florence.
Pastoureau, M., and Taburet-Delahaye, E. (2018). *Les Secrets de la licorne.* Paris.
Patera, M. (2015). *Figures grecques de l'épouvante de l'antiquité au présent: Peurs enfantines et adultes.* Leiden.
Paul, J. (2008). 'Working with Film: Theories and Methodologies', in Hardwick and Stray (2008), 303–14.
Paulson, W. R. (1987). *Enlightenment, Romanticism, and the Blind in France.* Princeton.
Pentecost, L. A. (1986). 'Ancient Sources for Velázquez's "The Forge of Vulcan": Plutarch and Homer, with some Observations on Solar Iconography', *Pantheon*, 44: 50–2.
Pepin, R. E. (2008). *The Vatican Mythographers.* New York.
Peradotto, J. (1990). *Man in the Middle Voice: Name and Narration in the Odyssey.* Princeton.
Peraki-Kyriakidou, H. (2002). 'Aspects of Ancient Etymologizing', *CQ* 52: 478–93.
Perdrizet, P. (1897). 'Polyphème', *RA* 31: 28–37.
Pérez de Montalbán, J. (1632). *Para todos exemplos morales, humanos y divinos.* Madrid.
Perotti, P. A. (2005). 'Polifemo in Omero, Euripide, Luciano', *Minerva: Revista di filologia clasica*, 18: 39–70.

Perrault, C. (1697). *Histoires ou contes du temps passé: Avec des moralitez.* Paris.
Pettazzoni, R. (1956). *The All-Knowing God: Researches into Early Religion and Culture.* London (trans. of *L'onniscienza di Dio.* Turin, 1955).
Pfeiffer, R. (1949). *Callimachus*, i. *Fragmenta.* Oxford.
Pharand, M. (2007). 'Poetic Mythography: The Genesis, Rationale and Reception of *The Greek Myths*', *Gravesiana: The Journal of the Robert Graves Society*, 3/1: 56–73.
Phillips, J., and Burnett, N. (2005). 'The Chronology and Layout of Francis Carew's Garden at Beddington, Surrey', *Garden History*, 33/2: 155–88.
Picard, G.-Ch. (1960). 'Mosaïques africaines du IIIe S. ap. J.-C.', *RA* 2: 17–49.
Pinch, G. (2004). *Egyptian Mythology: A Guide to the Gods, Goddesses, and Traditions of Ancient Egypt.* Oxford.
Piñol Lloret, M. (2015). *Monstruos y monstruosidades: Del imaginario fantástico medieval a los X-Men.* Barcelona.
Plock, V. M. (2014). 'Bodies', in Latham (2014), 184–99.
Poe, E. A. (1984). *Tales of Mystery and Imagination*, with introduction by G. Clarke. London.
Poggi, G. (2009). *Gli occhi del pavone: Quindici studi su Góngora.* Florence.
Polcari, S. (1991). *Abstract Expressionism and the Modern Experience.* Cambridge.
Poliziano, A. (1976). *Poesie italiane*, ed. S. Orlando. Milan.
Poljakov, T. (1983). 'A Phoenician Ancestor of the Cyclops', *ZPE* 53: 95–8.
Pollio, D. M. (2007). 'Baptizing Odysseus: *O Brother, Where Art Thou?* and Homer's *Odyssey*', *Classical Outlook*, 85: 23–7.
Ponce Cárdenas, J. (2009). *Cinco ensayos polifémicos.* Málaga.
Ponce Cárdenas, J. (2010). *Luis de Góngora, Fábula de Polifemo y Galatea.* Madrid.
Pontani, F. (2007). *Scholia Graeca in Odysseam*, i. Rome.
Pop, A. (2015). *Antiquity, Theatre, and the Painting of Henry Fuseli.* Oxford.
Poppenberg, G. (2008). 'Góngora's Version Arkadiens in der *Fábula de Polifemo y Galatea*', in R. Friedlein, G. Poppenberg, and A. Volmer (eds), *Arkadien in den romanischen Literaturen.* Heidelberg, 295–321.
Porada, E. (1947). *Mesopotamian Art in Cylinder Seals of the Pierpont Morgan Library.* New York.
Porada, E. (1976). 'Sumerian Art in Miniature', in D. Schmandt-Besserat (ed.), *The Legacy of Sumer.* Malibu, CA, 107–18.
Porten Palange, F. P. (1973). 'Frammento di matrice arretina con scena dell'Odissea', *Acme*, 26: 85–90.
Potts, A. M. (1982). *The World's Eye.* Lexington, KY.
Pozzana, M. (2011). *The Gardens of Florence and Tuscany.* Florence.
Prauscello, L. (2007). 'A Homeric Echo in Theocritus' *Idyll* 11.25–7: The Cyclops, Nausicaa and the Hyacinths', *CQ* 57: 90–6.
Prauscello, L. (2017). 'Plato *Laws* 3.680b–c: Antisthenes, the Cyclopes and Homeric Exegesis', *JHS* 137: 8–23.
Preble, M. (2004). *William Baziotes: Paintings and Drawings, 1934–1962.* Milan.
Pressly, W. L. (1981). *The Life and Art of James Barry.* New Haven, CT.
Pretagostini, R. (2006). 'How Bucolic are Theocritus' Bucolic Singers?', in Fantuzzi and Papanghelis (2006), 53–73.
Price, S., and Kearns, E. (2003) (eds). *The Oxford Dictionary of Classical Myth and Religion.* Oxford.
Privitera, G. A. (1993). 'L'*aristia* di Odisseo nella terra dei Ciclopi', in R. Pretagostini (ed.), *Tradizione e innovazione nella cultura greca da Omero all'età ellenistica.* Rome, i. 19–43.

Purves, A. (2016). 'Feeling on the Surface: Touch and Emotion in Fuseli and Homer', in S. Butler (ed.), *Deep Classics: Rethinking Classical Reception*. London, 67–85.

Quint, D. (1993). 'Voices of Resistance: The Epic Curse and Camões's Adamastor', in S. Greenblatt (ed.), *New World Encounters*. Berkeley, CA, 241–71 (repr. from *Representations*, 27 (1989), 111–41).

Quirke, S. (1992). *Ancient Egyptian Religion*. London.

Raab, I. (1972). Review of Touchefeu-Meynier (1968), in *Gnomon*, 44: 709–12.

Rabelais, F. (1994). *Gargantua and Pantagruel*, trans. Sir T. Urquhart and P. Le Motteux. London.

Raby, P. (1991). *Samuel Butler: A Biography*. London.

Raffa, G. P. (1996). 'Dante's Mocking Pastoral Muse', *Dante Studies*, 114: 271–91.

Rahner, H. (1963). *Greek Myths and Christian Mystery*. London (trans. of *Griechische Mythen in christlicher Deutung*. Zurich, 1957).

Rakoczy, T. (1996). *Böser Blick, Macht des Auges und Neid der Götter: Eine Untersuchung zur Kraft des Blickes in der griechischen Literatur*. Tübingen.

Ramus, J. D. (1716). *Tractatus historico-geographicus, quo Ulyssem et Outinum unum eundemque esse ostenditur. . . Editio nova*. Copenhagen.

Rank, L. P. (1951). *Etymologiseering en verwante verschijnselen bij Homerus*. Assen.

Rankin, H. D. (1987). *Celts and the Classical World*. London.

Rankine, P. D. (2006). *Ulysses in Black: Ralph Ellison, Classicism, and African American Literature*. Madison, WI.

Raspe, E. (1895). *The Surprising Adventures of Baron Munchausen*. London.

Ratcliffe, J. (2014). 'Arimaspians and Cyclopes: The Mythos of the One-Eyed Man in Greek and Inner Asian Thought', *Sino-Platonic Papers*, 249: 1–71.

Rautenbach, S. (1984). 'Cyclopes (I)', *Acta Classica*, 27: 41–55.

Read, H. (1955). *Henry Moore, Volume Two, Sculpture and Drawings since 1948*. London.

Reckermann, A. (1991). 'Polyphem und Galatea', in Reckermann, *Amor mutuus: Annibale Carraccis Galleria-Farnese-Fresken und das Bild-Denken der Renaissance*. Cologne, 104–7.

Redfield, J. M. (1975). *Nature and Culture in the Iliad: The Tragedy of Hector*. Chicago.

Reeve, M. D. (2011). 'Da Madvig a Maas, con deviazioni', in Reeve, *Manuscripts and Methods: Essays on Editing and Transmission*. Rome, 45–54.

Reid, J. D. (1993). *The Oxford Guide to Classical Mythology in the Arts, 1300–1990s*. 2 vols. Oxford.

Reitler, R. (1913). 'Zur Augensymbolik', *Internationale Zeitschrift für Ärztliche Psychoanalyse*, 1: 159–61.

Rewald, J. (1961). 'Odilon Redon', in *Odilon Redon, Gustave Moreau, Rodolphe Bresdin* (catalogue of exhibition at Museum of Modern Art, New York), 9–93.

Richmond, H. M. (1960). 'Polyphemus in England: A Study in Comparative Literature', *Comparative Literature*, 12: 229–42.

Riemann-Reyher, M. U. (1996). 'La Forge (Cyclopes modernes)', entry in exhibition catalogue *Menzel 1815–1905: La 'Névrose du vrai'*. Paris.

Rieppel, O. (2013). 'Othenio Abel (1875–1946): The Rise and Decline of Paleobiology in German Paleontology', *Historical Biology: An International Journal of Paleobiology*, 25: 313–25.

Rieu, E. V. (1991). *Homer: The Odyssey*. Rev. translation. London.

Riginos, A. S. (1976). *Platonica: The Anecdotes Concerning the Life and Writings of Plato*. Leiden.

Rizopoulou-Egoumenidou, E. (2008). '*Τα γαλακτοκομικά προϊόντα στον ετήσιο κύκλο της παραδοσιακής ζωής στην Κύπρο*', in *Η ιστορία του ελληνικού γάλακτος και των προϊόντων του*. Athens, 401–23.

Rizzini, I. (1998). *L'occhio parlante: Per una semiotica dello sguardo nel mondo antico.* Venice.

Rizzo, G. E. (1936). *Le pitture della Casa di Livia* (Monumenti della pittura antica scoperti in Italia, Fasc. 3). Rome.

Rizzo, G. E. (1939). '*Aurae velificantes*', *Bulletino della Commissione Archeologica del Governatorato di Roma*, 67: 141–68.

Robb, G. (1997). *Victor Hugo.* London.

Roberto, U. (2005). *Ioannis Antiocheni Fragmenta ex Historia chronica.* Berlin.

Roberts, J. M. (1976). 'Belief in the Evil Eye in World Perspective', in C. Maloney (ed.), *The Evil Eye.* New York, 223–78.

Roche, I. (2007). *Character and Meaning in the Novels of Victor Hugo.* West Lafayette, IN.

Röhrich, L. (1976). 'Die mittelalterlichen Redaktionen des Polyphem-Märchens und ihr Verhältnis zur ausserhomerischen Tradition', in Röhrich, *Sage und Märchen.* Freiburg, 234–52, 326–8.

Römisch, E. (1976). 'Die Achaemenides-Episode in Vergils Aeneis', in H. Görgemanns and E. A. Schmidt (eds), *Studien zum antiken Epos.* Meisenheim am Glan, 208–27.

Roisman, H. M. (2008). 'The *Odyssey* from Homer to NBC: The Cyclops and the Gods', in Hardwick and Stray (2008), 315–26.

Romm, J. S. (1992). *The Edges of the Earth in Ancient Thought: Geography, Exploration, and Fiction.* Princeton.

Roscher, W. H. (1884–1937). *Ausführliches Lexikon der griechischen und römischen Mythologie.* Leipzig.

Rose, H. J. (1958). *A Handbook of Greek Mythology.* 6th edn. London.

Rose, M. L. (2003). *The Staff of Oedipus: Transforming Disability in Ancient Greece.* Ann Arbor, MI.

Rosenmeyer, T. G. (1969). *The Green Cabinet: Theocritus and the European Pastoral Lyric.* Berkeley, CA.

Rubens, B., and Taplin, O. (1989). *An Odyssey round Odysseus.* London.

Rutherford, R. B. (1992). *Homer: Odyssey Books XIX and XX.* Cambridge.

Said, E. W. (1978). *Orientalism.* London.

Saïd, S. (2003). 'Ulysse en France au début du XXe siècle: De Giraudoux à Giono', in Nicosia (2003), 379–403.

Saint-Hilaire, I. G. (1837). *Histoire générale et particulière des anomalies de l'organisation chez l'homme et les animaux.* Paris.

Sainte-Beuve, C. A. (1926). *Mes poisons*, ed. V. Giraud. Paris.

Salerno, L. (1963). 'A Domenichino Series at the National Gallery: The Frescoes from the Villa Aldobrandini', *Burlington Magazine*, 105: 186, 194–201, 203–4.

Salmistraro, E. (2017). https://www.elenasalmistraro.com/polifemo (accessed 9 February 2018).

Salzman-Mitchell, P., and Alvares, J. (2018). *Classical Myth and Film in the New Millennium.* Oxford.

Samama, E. (2013). 'A King Walking with Pain? On the Textual and Iconographical Images of Philip II and Other Wounded Kings', in Laes, Goodey, and Rose (2013), 231–48.

Samaran, C. (1962). 'Pierre Bersuire, prieur de Saint-Éloi de Paris', *Histoire littéraire de la France*, 39: 259–450.

Sandler, I. (1965). 'Baziotes: Modern Mythologist', *Art News*, 63/10: 28–30, 65–6.

Sandler, I. (1970). *Abstract Expressionism: The Triumph of American Painting*. London.
Sandström, S. (1955). *Le Monde imaginaire d'Odilon Redon: Étude iconologique*. Lund.
Santangelo, G. S. (2003). '*Elpénor* di Jean Giraudoux: un Ulisside nostro contemporaneo', in Nicosia (2003), 353–78.
Sanz Morales, M. (2002). *Mitógrafos griegos*. Madrid.
Savvides, G. P. (1990). *Μεταμορφώσεις του Ελπήνορα*. 2nd edn. Athens.
Sbacchi, D. (2002). 'Polifemo: Varianti del mito da Omero a Marino', *Quaderni d'italianistica*, 23: 49–64.
Scarpi, P. (2005). *Il senso del cibo: Mondo antico e riflessi contemporanei*. Palermo.
Schachter, A. (1986). *Cults of Boeotia*, ii. *Herakles to Poseidon*. London.
Schachter, A. (2003). 'Evolutions of a Mystery Cult: the Theban Kabiroi', in M. B. Cosmopoulos (ed.), *Greek Mysteries: The Archaeology and Ritual of Ancient Greek Secret Cults*, London, 112–42.
Schama, S. (1995). *Landscape and Memory*. London.
Schauenburg, K. (2002). *Studien zur unteritalischen Vasenmalerei*, iv–v. Kiel.
Schefold, K. (1984). 'Texte et image à l'époque archaïque grecque', in *Texte et image: Actes du colloque international de Chantilly (13 au 15 octobre 1982)*. Paris, 41–52.
Schein, S. L. (1970). 'Odysseus and Polyphemus in the *Odyssey*', *GRBS* 11: 73–83.
Schiff, G. (1977). *L'opera completa di Füssli*. Milan.
Schilder, G., (1987). *Monumenta cartographica Neerlandica*, ii. Alphen aan den Rijn.
Schmaltz, B. (1974). *Terrakotten aus dem Kabirenheiligtum bei Theben* = vol. v of *Das Kabirenheiligtum bei Theben*. Berlin.
Schmidt-Burkhardt, A. (1992). *Sehende Bilder: Die Geschichte des Augenmotivs seit dem 19. Jahrhunderts*. Berlin.
Schmitt, J.-C. (1990). *La Raison des gestes dans l'Occident médiéval*. Paris.
Schmitt, R. (1967). *Dichtung und Dichtersprache in indogermanischer Zeit*. Wiesbaden.
Schnapp, A. (2015). 'La rappresentazione della natura nell'arte greca', in Sena Chiesa and Pontrandolfo (2015), 24–35.
Schneede, U. M. (1991). 'Sightless Vision: Notes on the Iconography of Surrealism', in W. Spies (1991), 351–6.
Schneidau, H. (1978–9). 'One Eye and Two Levels: On Joyce's "Cyclops"', *James Joyce Quarterly*, 16/1–2: 95–103.
Schneider, E. (2010). 'Against the Tide: Paul Gauguin's Women in the Water and their Symbolist Legacy', in R. Neginsky (ed.), *Symbolism, its Origins and its Consequences*. Newcastle upon Tyne, 272–90.
Schoeck, H. (1992). 'The Evil Eye: Forms and Dynamics of a Universal Superstition', in Dundes (1992), 192–200.
Schoemann, G. F. (1859). 'Schediasma de Cyclopibus', *Opuscula academica*, iv. 325–35. Berlin.
Schönberger, O. (1995). 'Die "Bilder" des Philostratos', in G. Boehm and H. Pfotenhauer (eds), *Beschreibungskunst—Kunstbeschreibung: Ekphrasis von der Antike bis zur Gegenwart*. Munich, 157–73.
Schreiner, J. (1901). *Homers Odyssee—ein mysteriöses Epos*. Braunschweig.
Schulz, I. (2007). 'The "Omnipotence of Dream"—Dream and the Unconscious in the Oeuvre of Meret Oppenheim', in T. Bhattacharya-Stettler and M. Frehner (eds), *Meret Oppenheim: Retrospective*. Bern, 51–2.
Schumacher, R. W. M. (1993). 'Three Related Sanctuaries of Poseidon: Geraistos, Kalaureia and Tainaron', in N. Marinatos and R. Hägg (eds), *Greek Sanctuaries: New Approaches*. London, 62–87.

Schütrumpf, E. (2001). 'Dikaiarchs *Βίος Ἑλλάδος* und die Philosophie des vierten Jahrhunderts', in W. W. Fortenbaugh and E. Schütrumpf (eds), *Dicaearchus of Messana: Text, Translation, and Discussion*. New Brunswick, NJ, 255–77.
Schwager, K. (1961–2). 'Kardinal Pietro Aldobrandinis Villa di Belvedere in Frascati', *Römisches Jahrbuch für Kunstgeschichte*, 9–10: 291–382.
Scott, S. C. (1995). 'Man, Mind, and Monster: Polyphemus from Homer through Joyce', *Classical and Modern Literature*, 16: 19–75.
Seaford, R. A. S. (1984). *Euripides: Cyclops*. Oxford.
Séchan, L. (1926). *Études sur la tragédie grecque dans ses rapports avec la céramique*. Paris.
Segal, C. (1981a). *Poetry and Myth in Ancient Pastoral: Essays on Theocritus and Virgil*. Princeton.
Segal, C. (1981b). *Tragedy and Civilization: An Interpretation of Sophocles*. Cambridge, MA.
Seidensticker, B. (1982). *Palintonos Harmonia: Studien zu komischen Elementen in der griechischen Tragödie*. Göttingen.
Seligmann, S. (1910). *Der böse Blick und Verwandtes: Ein Beitrag zur Geschichte des Aberglaubens aller Zeiten und Völker*. 2 vols. Berlin.
Sena Chiesa, G., and Pontrandolfo, A. (2015) (eds). *Mito e natura: Dalla Grecia a Pompei*. Milan.
Serrano Cueto, A. (2015). *Después de Troya: Microrrelatos hispánicos de tradición clásica*. Palencia.
Severin, T. (1987). *The Ulysses Voyage: Sea Search for the Odyssey*. London.
Shahbazi, A. S. (1988). 'The "King's Eyes" in Classical and Iranian Literature', *American Journal of Ancient History*, 13: 170–89.
Shapiro, D., and Shapiro, C. (1990) (eds). *Abstract Expressionism: A Critical Record*. Cambridge.
Shaw, B. D. (1982–3). '"Eaters of Flesh, Drinkers of Milk": The Ancient Mediterranean Ideology of the Pastoral Nomad', *Ancient Society*, 13/14: 5–31 (= ch. VI in Shaw, *Rulers, Nomads, and Christians in Roman North Africa*. Aldershot, 1995).
Shaw, P.-J. (2001). 'Lords of Hellas, Old Men of the Sea: The Occasion of Simonides' Elegy on Plataea', in D. Boedeker and D. Sider (eds), *The New Simonides: Contexts of Praise and Desire*. Oxford, 14–81.
Shewring, W. (1980). *Homer: The Odyssey*. Translation. Oxford.
Shirley, R. W. (2001). *The Mapping of the World: Early Printed World Maps 1472–1700*. 4th edn. Riverside, CT.
Shorrock, R. (2001). *The Challenge of Epic: Allusive Engagement in the Dionysiaca of Nonnus*. Leiden.
Shorrock, R. (2011). *The Myth of Paganism: Nonnus, Dionysus and the World of Late Antiquity*. London.
Siebert, G. (1990). 'Imaginaire et images de la grotte dans la Grèce archaïque et classique', *Ktèma*, 15: 151–61.
Siegel, Janice (2007). 'The Coens' *O Brother, Where Art Thou?* and Homer's *Odyssey*', *Mouseion*, ser. III, 7: 213–45.
Siegel, Jeanne (1982). 'The Image of the Eye in Surrealist Art and its Psychoanalytic Sources, Part One: The Mythic Eye', *Arts Magazine*, 56: 102–6.
Sigurdsson, H. (1999). *Melting the Earth: The History of Ideas on Volcanic Eruptions*. Oxford.
Simon, G. (1988). *Le Regard, l'être et l'apparence dans l'optique de l'Antiquité*. Paris.
Simon, R. B. (1978). 'Poussin, Marino, and the Interpretation of Mythology', *Art Bulletin*, 60: 56–68.

Sinn, U. (2005). 'Spelaion', in *ThesCRA*, iv. 75–8.
Skinner, J. E. (2012). *The Invention of Greek Ethnography: From Homer to Herodotus*. Oxford.
Sluiter, I. (2015). 'Ancient Etymology: A Tool for Thinking', in F. Montanari, S. Matthaios, and A. Rengakos (eds), *Brill's Companion to Ancient Greek Scholarship*. Leiden, ii. 896–922.
Small, J. P. (2003). *The Parallel Worlds of Classical Art and Text*. Cambridge.
Smith, C., and Serrati, J. (2000). *Sicily from Aeneas to Augustus*. Edinburgh.
Smith, C. C. (1961). 'La musicalidad del *Polifemo*', *Revista de Filología Española* 44: 139–66.
Smith, C. C. (1965). 'An Approach to Góngora's *Polifemo*', *Bulletin of Hispanic Studies*, 42: 217–38.
Smith, W. (1961). 'Pratolino', *Journal of the Society of Architectural Historians*, 20/4: 155–68.
Snodgrass, A. M. (1979). 'Poet and Painter in Eighth-Century Greece', *Proceedings of the Cambridge Philological Society*, 205: 118–30.
Snodgrass, A. M. (1998). *Homer and the Artists: Text and Picture in Early Greek Art*. Cambridge.
Sobchack, V. (1987). *Screening Space: The American Science Fiction Film*. 2nd edn. New York.
Soldati, B. (1902). *Ioannis Ioviani Pontani Carmina*. 2 vols. Paris.
Sole, A. (2003). 'Il momento pascoliano dell'*Odissea*', in Nicosia (2003), 517–43.
Solkin, D. H. (2010). 'From Oddity to Odd Man Out: Contesting James Barry's Critical Legacy, 1806–66', in Dunne and Pressly (2010), 11–22.
Solomon, J. (2011–17). *Giovanni Boccaccio: Genealogy of the Pagan Gods*, i (books 1–5) and ii (books 6–10). Cambridge, MA.
Sommerstein, A. H. (2001). *The Comedies of Aristophanes*, xi. *Wealth*. Warminster.
Spear, R. E. (1997). *The 'Divine' Guido: Religion, Sex, Money and Art in the World of Guido Reni*. New Haven, CT.
Spedding, J., Ellis, R. L., and Heath, D. D. (*c*.1900). *The Works of Francis Bacon*, xiii (= vol. iii of the Literary and Professional Works). Boston, MA.
Spies, O. (1981). 'Dede Korkut Kitabi', in K. Ranke (ed.), *Enzyklopädie des Märchens*. Berlin, iii, cols 371–5.
Spies, W. (1991) (ed.). *Max Ernst: A Retrospective*. Munich.
Spies, W., Metken, S., and Metken, G. (1979). *Max Ernst, Oeuvre-Katalog: Werke 1929–1938*. Houston, TX.
Sporn, K. (2007). 'Höhlenheiligtümer in Griechenland', in C. Frevel and H. von Hesberg (eds), *Kult und Kommunikation: Medien in Heiligtümern der Antike*. Wiesbaden, 39–62.
Sporn, K. (2010). 'Espace naturel et paysages religieux: Les Grottes dans le monde grec', *Revue de l'histoire des religions*, 227/4: 553–71.
Sporn, K. (2013). 'Mapping Greek Sacred Caves: Sources, Features, Cults', in F. Mavridis and J. T. Jensen (eds), *Stable Places and Changing Perceptions: Cave Archaeology in Greece*. Oxford, 202–16.
Squire, M. (2009). *Image and Text in Graeco-Roman Antiquity*. Cambridge.
Squire, M. (2011). *The Iliad in a Nutshell: Visualizing Epic on the Tabulae Iliacae*. Cambridge.
Squire, M. (2016) (ed.). *Sight and the Ancient Senses*. Abingdon.
Stahl, A., and Tourame, P. (2010). 'De la tératologie aux monstres de la mythologie et des légendes antiques', *Archives de pédiatrie*, 17: 1716–24.
Stanford, W. B. (1952). 'The Homeric Etymology of the Name Odysseus', *CP* 47: 209–13.

Stanford, W. B. (1965). *The Odyssey of Homer*, i. *Commentary on Books I–XII*. 2nd edn. London.

Stanford, W. B. (1968). *The Ulysses Theme: A Study in the Adaptability of a Traditional Hero*. 2nd edn. Oxford (repr. with foreword by C. Boer, Dallas, TX, 1992).

Steel, K. (2012). 'Centaurs, Satyrs, and Cynocephali: Medieval Scholarly Teratology and the Question of the Human', in Mittman and Dendle (2012), 257–74.

Stein, L. K., and Leza, J. M. (2009). 'Opera, Genre, and Context in Spain and its American Colonies', in A. R. DelDonna and P. Polzonetti (eds), *The Cambridge Companion to Eighteenth-Century Opera*. Cambridge, 244–69.

Steinberg, R. M. (1965). 'The Iconography of the Teatro dell' Acqua at the Villa Aldobrandini', *Art Bulletin*, 47: 453–63.

Steinhart, M. (1995). *Das Motiv des Auges in der griechischen Bildkunst*. Mainz.

Stephens, C. (2010) (ed.) *Henry Moore*. London.

Stephens, S. A. (2006). 'Ptolemaic Pastoral', in Fantuzzi and Papanghelis (2006), 91–117.

Stephens, S. A. (2015). *Callimachus: The Hymns*, ed. with introduction, translation, and commentary. Oxford.

Stewart, A. F. (1987). 'Narrative, Genre, and Realism in the Work of the Amasis Painter', in *Papers on the Amasis Painter and his World*. J. Paul Getty Museum. Malibu, CA, 29–42.

Stigliani, T. (1600). *Il Polifemo: Stanze pastorali*. Milan.

Stonard, J.-P. (2011). 'Used Future: The Early Sculptures of Eduardo Paolozzi', in *Eduardo Paolozzi Archaeology of a Used Future: Sculpture 1946–1959*. Texts by P. Selz and J.-P. Stonard, photography by D. Farrell. London, 17–37.

Stoneman, R. (1991). *The Greek Alexander Romance*. London.

Strauss, A. (2011). *Baudelaire, Poe, Mallarmé, Flaubert: Interprétations par Odilon Redon*. Paris.

Strickland, D. H. (2008). 'Text, Image, and Contradiction in the *Devisement dou monde*', in Akbari and Iannucci (2008), 23–59.

Strickland, D. H. (2012). 'Monstrosity and Race in the Late Middle Ages', in Mittman and Dendle (2012), 365–86.

Strickland, D. H. (2013). 'Saracens, Eschatological Prophecy, and Later Medieval Art', in V. Wieser et al. (eds), *Abendländische Apokalyptik: Kompendium zur Genealogie der Endzeit*. Berlin, 505–20.

Strong, R. (1979). *The Renaissance Garden in England*. London.

Stronk, J. P. (2007). 'Ctesias of Cnidus, A Reappraisal', *Mnemosyne*, 60: 25–58.

Suárez Miramón, A. (2002). *Luis de Góngora: Poesía*. Barcelona.

Sulzberger, M. (1926). '*ΟΝΟΜΑ ΕΠΩΝΥΜΟΝ*: Les Noms propres chez Homère et dans la mythologie grecque', *Revue des études grecques*, 39: 381–447.

Summers, D. (2003). 'The Archaeology of the Modern Grotesque', in F. S. Connelly (ed.), *Modern Art and the Grotesque*. Cambridge, 20–46.

Sutton, D. F. (1983). 'Dithyramb as Δρᾶμα: Philoxenus of Cythera's *Cyclops or Galatea*', *Quaderni Urbinati di Cultura Classica*, 13: 37–43.

Symmons, S. (1984). *Flaxman and Europe: The Outline Illustrations and their Influence*. New York.

Synnott, A. (1987). 'Shame and Glory: A Sociology of Hair', *British Journal of Sociology*, 38: 381–413.

Tafuri, M. (1998). 'Giulio Romano: Language, Mentality, Patrons', in Tafuri (ed.), *Giulio Romano*. Cambridge, 11–55.

Taplin, O. (1993). *Comic Angels and Other Approaches to Greek Drama through Vase-Paintings*. Oxford.

Tatti-Gartziou, A. (2010). 'Blindness as Punishment', in Christopoulos, Karakantza, and Levaniouk (2010), 181–90.

Tchikine, A. (2010). '*Giochi d'acqua*: water effects in Renaissance and Baroque Italy', *Studies in the History of Gardens and Designed Landscapes: An International Quarterly*, 30: 57–82.

Thieme, P. (1951). 'Etymologische Vexierbilder', *Zeitschrift für vergleichende Sprachforschung*, 69: 172–8.

Thomas, R. S. (1970). 'Polyphemus in Art and Literature.' Tufts University Ph.D. diss.

Thompson, S. (1955–8). *Motif-Index of Folk-Literature*. 6 vols. Rev. edn. Bloomington, IN.

Tomlinson, G. (1987). *Monteverdi and the End of the Renaissance*. Oxford.

Torelli, M. (1996). 'The Encounter with the Etruscans', in G. P. Carratelli (ed.), *The Western Greeks: Classical Civilization in the Western Mediterranean*. London, 567–76.

Touchefeu-Meynier, O. (1968). *Thèmes odysséens dans l'art antique*. Paris.

Toussaint-Samat, M. (2009). *A History of Food*. 2nd edn. Chichester (trans. of *Histoire naturelle et morale de la nourriture*. Paris, 1987).

Travis, H., and Travis, J. (2014). *Roman Shields*. Stroud.

Trentin, L. (2013). 'Exploring Visual Impairment in Ancient Rome', in Laes, Goodey, and Rose (2013), 89–114.

True, M., and Hamma, K. (1994) (eds). *A Passion for Antiquities: Ancient Art from the Collection of Barbara and Lawrence Fleischman*. Malibu, CA.

Tsitsibakou-Vasalos, E. (2007). *Ancient Poetic Etymology: The Pelopids: Fathers and Sons*. Stuttgart.

Tuchman, M. (1971). *The New York School: Abstract Expressionism in the 40s and 50s*. London.

Turner, P. (1965). *Thomas More: Utopia*. Translation. Harmondsworth.

Tusiani, J. (1960). *The Complete Poems of Michelangelo*. New York.

Tynan, M. (2011). *Postcolonial Odysseys: Derek Walcott's Voyages of Homecoming*. Newcastle upon Tyne.

Uebel, M. (2005). *Ecstatic Transformation: On the Uses of Alterity in the Middle Ages*. New York.

Ussher, R. G. (1957). 'A Comment on Unmixed Milk', *Hermathena*, 89: 59–64.

Ustinova, Y. (2009). *Caves and the Ancient Greek Mind: Descending Underground in the Search for Ultimate Truth*. Oxford.

Uther, H.-J. (2011). *The Types of International Folktales: A Classification and Bibliography*. 3 vols. Helsinki.

Vaccari, M. G. (1986). 'Il giardino della Gherardesca e gli Orti Oricellari a Firenze', *Quaderni di Palazzo Te*, 5: 67–74.

Valavanis, P. (2008). '*Το γάλα και τα προϊόντα του στον αρχαίο ελληνικό και ρωμαϊκό κόσμο*', in Aa.Vv., *Η ιστορία του ελληνικού γάλακτος και των προϊόντων του*. Athens, 89–96.

Valtrová, J. (2010). 'Beyond the Horizons of Legends: Traditional Imagery and Direct Experience in Medieval Accounts of Asia', *Numen*, 57: 154–85.

Van Aken, A. R. A. (1965). *The Encyclopedia of Classical Mythology*. Englewood Cliffs, NJ (trans. of *Elseviers mythologische encyclopedie*. Amsterdam, 1961).

Van Duzer, C. (2012). '*Hic sunt dracones*: The Geography and Cartography of Monsters', in Mittman and Dendle (2012), 387–435.

Van Duzer, C. (2013). *Sea Monsters on Medieval and Renaissance Maps*. London.

Van Eickels, K. (2004). 'Gendered Violence: Castration and Blinding as Punishment for Treason in Normandy and Anglo-Norman England', *Gender and History*, 16: 588–602.

Van Gennep, A. (1908). 'La Légende de Polyphème', in Van Gennep, *Religions, moeurs, et légendes: Essais d'ethnographie et de linguistique, 1ère partie*. Paris, 155–64.
Van Groningen, B. A. (1977). *Euphorion*. Amsterdam.
Van Zuylen, M. (2005). 'The Secret Life of Monsters', in Hauptman (2005), 57–73.
Vasari, G. (1996). *Lives of the Painters, Sculptors and Artists*, trans. G. du C. de Vere. 2 vols. London.
Vaughan, A. T., and Vaughan, V. M. (1991). *Shakespeare's Caliban: A Cultural History*. Cambridge.
Vayenas, N. (1998). 'Elpenore: L'anti-Ulisse nella letteratura moderna', in Boitani and Ambrosini (1998), 243–55.
Vegetti, M. (1983). *Tra Edipo e Euclide: Forme del sapere antico*. Milan.
Venezia, L. (2007). 'La figura di Polifemo nel teatro greco: Trasformazioni di un mostro', *Stratagemmi*, 1: 95–135.
Vento Canosa, E. (2005). 'Antropofagia en aborígenes de Cuba', *Revista Médica Electrónica*, 27/3, <www.revmedicaelectronica.sld.cu/index.php/rme/article/view/214/html> (accessed 20 April 2019).
Verheyen, E. (1972). 'Studien zur Baugeschichte des Palazzo del Te zu Mantua', *Mitteilungen des Kunsthistorischen Institutes in Florenz*, 16: 73–114.
Verheyen, E. (1977). *The Palazzo del Te in Mantua: Images of Love and Politics*. Baltimore, MD.
Vernant, J.-P. (1991). *Mortals and Immortals: Collected Essays*, ed. F. I. Zeitlin. Princeton.
Verner, L. (2005). *The Epistemology of the Monstrous in the Middle Ages*. New York.
Vian, F., et al. (1976–2006). *Nonnos de Panopolis: Les Dionysiaques*. 19 vols. Paris.
Vidal-Naquet, P. (1981). 'Land and Sacrifice in the *Odyssey*: A Study of Religious and Mythical Meanings', in R. L. Gordon (ed.), *Myth, Religion and Society*. Cambridge, 80–94 (trans. of 'Valeurs religieuses et mythiques de la terre et du sacrifice dans l'*Odyssée*', *Annales E S C*, 25 (1970), 1278–97).
Vilanova, A. (1992). *Las fuentes y los temas del Polifemo de Góngora*. 2nd edn. 2 vols. Barcelona.
Vinci, F. (2006). *The Baltic Origins of Homer's Epic Tales: The Iliad, the Odyssey, and the Migration of Myth*. Rochester, VT (trans. of *Omero nel Baltico*. Rome, 1995).
Viola, J. (1962–4). 'Redon, Darwin and the Ascent of Man', *Marsyas: Studies in the History of Art*, 11: 42–57.
Visser, M. (1991). *The Rituals of Dinner: The Origins, Evolution, Eccentricities, and Meaning of Table Manners*. New York.
Vitzthum, W. (1965). *La Galleria di Palazzo Farnese a Roma*. Milan.
Vlahogiannis, N. (1998). 'Disabling Bodies', in D. Montserrat (ed.), *Changing Bodies, Changing Meanings: Studies on the Human Body in Antiquity*. London, 13–36.
Voelke, P. (1992). 'Monde pastoral et monde urbain: Du *Cyclope* d'Euripide au *Boucoliastes* de Théocrite', *Études de Lettres*, janvier–mars: 5–22.
Von Blanckenhagen, P. H. (1968). 'Daedalus and Icarus on Pompeian Walls', *RM* 75: 106–43.
Von Blanckenhagen, P. H., and Alexander, C. (1962). 'The Paintings from Boscotrecase', *RM Ergänzungsheft* 6. Heidelberg.
Von Geisau, H. (1969). 'Kyklopen', in *Der Kleine Pauly: Lexikon der Antike*, iii. 393–4.
Vrolik, W. (1849). *Tabulae ad illustrandam embryogenesin hominis et mammalium tam naturalem quam abnormem*. Amsterdam.
Wachter, R. (2001). *Non-Attic Greek Vase Inscriptions*. Oxford.
Walbank, F. W. (1957–79). *A Historical Commentary on Polybius*. 3 vols. Oxford.
Walcott, D. (1993). *The Odyssey: A Stage Version*. London.

Walda, C. (2013). 'Die Utopie des Androgyn/The Utopia of the Androgyne', in Levy (2013), 47–61.

Walde, C. (2003). 'Cyclopes', entry in *Brill's New Pauly. Antiquity*, iii. 1042–3.

Waldman, G. (1974). *Ludovico Ariosto: Orlando Furioso.* Translation. Oxford.

Walther, I. F., and Metzger, R. (1990). *Marc Chagall 1887–1985: Painting as Poetry.* Cologne.

Warburg, A. (1932). 'Italienische Kunst und internationale Astrologie im Palazzo Schifanoja zu Ferrara', in Warburg, *Gesammelte Schriften*, ii. Leipzig, 459–81, 627–44.

Warner, M. (1994). *From the Beast to the Blonde: On Fairy Tales and their Tellers.* London.

Warner, M. (1998). *No Go the Bogeyman: Scaring, Lulling, and Making Mock.* London.

Watson, P. A. (1982). 'Martial's Fascination with *Lusci*', *G&R* 29: 71–6.

Watterson, B. (1984). *Gods of Ancient Egypt.* London.

Weber-Lehmann, C. (1996). 'Ulisse nella Tomba dell'Orco II a Tarquinia', in Andreae and Parisi Presicce (1996), 160–73.

Webster, T. B. L. (1967). *Monuments Illustrating Tragedy and Satyr Play.* 2nd edn. *BICS* suppl. 20. London.

Webster, T. B. L. (1970). *Studies in Later Greek Comedy.* 2nd edn. New York.

Weinstock, J. A. (2012). 'Invisible Monsters: Vision, Horror, and Contemporary Culture', in Mittman and Dendle (2012), 275–89.

Weinstock, J. A. (2014). *The Ashgate Encyclopedia of Literary and Cinematic Monsters.* Farnham.

West, D. A. (1990). *Virgil: The Aeneid.* Translation. Harmondsworth.

West, M. L. (1966). *Hesiod: Theogony*, ed. with Prolegomena and Commentary. Oxford.

West, M. L. (1987). *Euripides: Orestes.* Warminster.

West, M. L. (1988). *Hesiod: Theogony, and Works and Days.* Translated with Introduction and Notes. Oxford.

West, M. L. (2014). *The Making of the Odyssey.* Oxford.

West, S. (2013). 'Odysseus' Most Memorable Exploit', *Classica Cracoviensia*, 16: 189–206.

Whitbread, L. G. (1971). *Fulgentius the Mythographer.* Columbus, OH.

Whitford, F. (1971). 'Eduardo Paolozzi', in *Eduardo Paolozzi: The Tate Gallery, 22 September–31 October 1971.* London.

Wickham, A. (2010). *The Language of Line: John Flaxman's Illustrations to the Works of Homer and Aeschylus.* London.

Wilamowitz-Moellendorff, U. von (1931–2). *Der Glaube der Hellenen.* 2 vols. Berlin.

Wilk, S. R. (2000). *Medusa: Solving the Mystery of the Gorgon.* Oxford.

Wilkins, J. M., and Hill, S. (2006). *Food in the Ancient World.* Oxford.

Wilkinson, R. H. (1992). *Reading Egyptian Art: A Hieroglyphic Guide to Ancient Egyptian Painting and Sculpture.* London.

Willes, M. (2011). *The Making of the English Gardener.* New Haven, CT.

Williams, D. (1996). *Deformed Discourse: The Function of the Monster in Mediaeval Thought and Literature.* Exeter.

Wilson, A. M. (2016). *Ugolino Verino: 'Fiammetta', 'Paradise'.* Edition and translation. Cambridge, MA.

Wilson, B. (1980) (ed.). *Guillaume de Conches: Glosae in Iuvenalem.* Paris.

Wilson de Borland, M. (1982). 'La música de Polifemo: Orfeo y lo pastoril en el poema de Góngora', in G. Bellini (ed.), *Actas del Séptimo Congreso de la Asociación Internacional de Hispanistas.* Rome, 1053–9.

Winkler-Horaček, L. (2015). *Monster in der frühgriechischen Kunst: Die Überwindung des Unfassbaren.* Berlin.

Wissowa, G., et al. (1894–1980) (eds). *Paulys Real-Encyclopädie der classischen Altertumswissenschaft.* Stuttgart. (= *RE*).

Wittkower, R. (1942). 'Marvels of the East: A Study in the History of Monsters', *JWCI* 5: 159–97.

Wolanin, H. (1995). 'Plato and the Position of Etymology in Greek Intellectual Culture', in W. Smoczyński (ed.), *Analecta Indoeuropaea Cracoviensia*. Cracow, 513–35.

Wolf, A., and Wolf, H.-H. (1983). *Die wirkliche Reise des Odysseus: Zur Rekonstruktion des homerischen Weltbildes*. Munich.

Wolters, P., and Bruns, G. (1940). *Das Kabirenheiligtum bei Theben*. Berlin.

Woods, P. A. (2003) (ed.). *Joel and Ethan Coen: Blood Siblings*. 2nd edn. London.

Woolf, G. (2014). *Tales of the Barbarians: Ethnography and Empire in the Roman West*. Chichester.

Wynter, S. (2002). ' "A Different Kind of Creature": Caribbean Literature, the Cyclops Factor and the Second Poetics of the Propter Nos', in T. J. Reiss (ed.), *Sisyphus and Eldorado: Magical and Other Realisms in Caribbean Literature*. 2nd edn. Trenton, NJ, 143–67.

Yatromanolakis, Y. (1988). '*Baskanos Eros*: Love and the Evil-Eye in Heliodorus' *Aethiopica*', in R. Beaton (ed.), *The Greek Novel* AD *1–1985*. London, 194–204.

Zaho, M. A. (2004). *Imago Triumphalis: The Function and Significance of Triumphal Imagery for Italian Renaissance Rulers*. New York.

Zajko, V. (2004). 'Homer and *Ulysses*', in Fowler (2004), 311–23.

Zanato, T. (1992). *Lorenzo de' Medici: Opere*. Turin.

Zangheri, L. (1987). *Pratolino: Il giardino delle meraviglie*. 2nd edn. Florence.

Zarncke, F. (1879). 'Der Brief des Priesters Johannes an den byzantinischen Kaiser Emanuel', *Abhandlungen der königlich sächsischen Gesellschaft der Wissenschaften, phil.-hist. Klasse*, 7. 873–934.

Zhang, L. (2008). 'Marco Polo, Chinese Cultural Identity, and an Alternative Model of East-West Encounter', in Akbari and Iannucci (2008), 280–96.

Ziolkowski, T. (2008). *Minos and the Moderns: Cretan Myth in Twentieth-Century Literature and Art*. Oxford.

Index

In a book such as this, which involves a dense network of thematic cross-reference, it would have been theoretically possible to index every such case, thus making the index as long as the rest of the book. Instead we have sometimes confined ourselves, in relation to themes, to indexing only the more important or distinctive references.

Numbers in italics indicate pages with illustrations.